D0949933

THE GM

ALSO BY TOM CALLAHAN

Johnny U

The Bases Were Loaded (And So Was I)

In Search of Tiger

Around the World in 18 Holes
(co-author: Dave Kindred)

T H E
GM

THE INSIDE STORY OF A DREAM JOB AND
THE NIGHTMARES THAT GO WITH IT

TOM CALLAHAN

Crown Publishers | New York

Copyright © 2007 by Tom Callahan

All rights reserved.
Published in the United States by Crown Publishers, an imprint
of the Crown Publishing Group, a division of
Random House, Inc., New York.
www.crownpublishing.com

Crown is a trademark and the Crown colophon is a registered
trademark of Random House, Inc.

Library of Congress Cataloging-in-Publication Data
Callahan, Tom.
The GM : the inside story of a dream job and the nightmares
that go with it / Tom Callahan.—1st ed.
p.   cm.
1. National Football League. 2. Football—United States.
3. Accorsi, Ernie.   4. New York Giants (Football team)—Biography.
I. Title. II. Title: General manager.
GV955.5.N35C35 2007
796.33206'9—dc22   2007024069

ISBN 978-0-307-39413-2

Printed in the United States of America

Design by Leonard Henderson

10   9   8   7   6   5   4   3   2   1

First Edition

For Ernie Accorsi

Setting no conditions,
asking nothing in return,
he let me in

The acknowledgment is also singular.
Thank you, John Mara, president of the
New York Football Giants, for tolerating such
a conspicuous fly on the front office wall.

CONTENTS

THE GM

PREFACE:

THE ESSENCE OF SPORTS

TEN OR TWELVE GAMES into the New York Giants' 2006 season, I turned to head coach Tom Coughlin during a players' lunch and said, "You probably haven't heard this for a while, but I like your team. It's a nice-watching football team."

"You're right," Coughlin said with a smile. "I haven't heard that for a while."

Ernie Accorsi, the Giants' general manager, had invited me inside for his farewell season. Accorsi and I go back more than forty years, to August 13, 1964, when we spent five hours in each other's company but didn't know it at the time. He was a twenty-two-year-old sportswriter for the Baltimore *Evening Sun,* tramping after Joe Louis in a local golf tournament. I was an eighteen-year-old college student on the brink of sophomore year, caddying for the former heavyweight champion. Ernie and I formally met in the late 1960s—or was it the early '70s?—by which time *I* was at the *Sun* and he had moved into the football business. In 1987, when I was working for *Time* magazine and Ernie was serving the Browns, I went to Cleveland to write a piece on Accorsi, the fans' "Dog Pound," and quarterback Bernie Kosar. At old Municipal Stadium, Ernie and I talked and laughed away a long afternoon in his office overlooking the field. "I've known Ernie Accorsi forever," I used to say, and that was true enough. But now I really know him.

We had Johnny Unitas in common. "You bull-crappers in the media" was Unitas' usual salutation to me, especially on the telephone, but he loved Accorsi and Ernie loved him. In 2005, reporting my book *Johnny U,*

I spent a bit of time in the Giants' front office talking with Ernie. Luckily, I met Wellington Mara there. He didn't hold 1958 and 1959 against Unitas. The Giants' owner didn't hold very much against very many.

"You should think of writing a book yourself," I told Accorsi in parting, and that was the beginning of this project. Months later, in a badminton game of e-mails, I said, "If you want to write a book by Ernie Accorsi as told to somebody, I can find you somebody. But it can't be me. I can only write in my own voice." He responded, "I'd rather you do it your way."

"First, we have to get John Mara's permission," Ernie said, and Mara gave it cheerfully. "Are you up to the seventies yet?" he'd kid me when we'd bump in the hallways. "Are you up to the sixties at least?" I asked Ernie, "Don't we need Coughlin's blessing, too?" "Coughlin," he said, "works for me. I'll tell him about it." Tom was gracious to me throughout. In fact, when it comes to graciousness, Coughlin is the most underrated football coach I've ever been around.

I moved to Belmar, New Jersey, for the fall and winter to be nearer the ocean than the Meadowlands. I bought an E-ZPass and commuted to Giants Stadium on the Garden State Parkway and New Jersey Turnpike three or four days a week. Pat Hanlon, the Giants' communications czar, found me a working space in the front office and made a place for me in the press box at all of the games, home and away. Curiously, my affiliation on the media badge and out-of-town seating charts read "Random House." Thanks to the Giants' director of public relations, Peter John-Baptiste, I was able to get one-on-one time with the ten or so players I wanted to know better than the others. None of them was exactly sure who I was, but they all knew I had some connection to Accorsi. "Are you the guy who owns Callahan Auto Parts?" Jeremy Shockey asked. I'll leave it to the reader to judge if Eli Manning, Plaxico Burress, LaVar Arrington, and others were more open with me on the side than they would have been with someone trawling the locker room for the *Washington Post* or *Time*.

I think of this as Ernie's book more than mine. I tried to get out of the way as much as possible and let him talk. The 2006 Giants season is really just a scaffolding for the life in sports Ernie has led at a post that is suddenly in vogue. Today's magazine stands are crowded with titles like *World Championship of Fantasy Football, Winning in Fantasy Football, Fantasy Football Draft Book, Fantasy Football Guide, Fantasy Football Cheat Sheet, Fantasy Sports, Fantasy Analysis, Fantasy Forecast* . . . In this era of make-believe football, not only fans but players and even sportswriters are thinking and acting like general managers, like Ernie Accorsi.

The GM isn't a biography of Ernie. If it were, it might contain a lot of embarrassing personal information, like the fact that he plays the accordion. ("Lady of Spain," what else?) It's closer to a biography of a job, or maybe just a long look at an inner sanctum behind the door of the front office.

Three days after the Giants' last regular-season game, Accorsi went to the Orange Bowl in Miami on his own hook, not as a scout, as an alumnus of Wake Forest University, as a fan. He didn't sit in the press box. He bought a ticket for a normal seat in the grandstand, where he fell in with Wake Forest's famous stable of golfers: Curtis Strange, Lanny Wadkins, Jay Haas, Billy Andrade. They were all there, including Arnold Palmer. Palmer from Wake Forest and Muhammad Ali—sort of from the University of Louisville—were the honorary captains, decked out in game jerseys. Ali wore Unitas' number, 19, which pleased Ernie, although he knew that John's Louisville number was 16. Arnie wore 66, six under par. "I don't think that's for the 1966 U.S. Open," Ernie said, "when he blew a seven-shot lead to Billy Casper in the last nine holes."

Though Wake lost the game in a downpour, 24–13, its supporters couldn't stop smiling. Tens of thousands of them, half a stadium full, in gold! Where did they all come from? At one point Strange turned to Andrade and said excitedly, "Billy, Billy, did you ever believe we'd be here?" "That's a two-time U.S. Open champion talking," Ernie said of Strange, "standing like a student in the rain, so thrilled to be at a football game that he could hardly stay still. There, right there. Isn't that the essence of why we love sports?"

I hope some of that essence is in here, too.

1

THE MEADOWS GAME

I F IT'S TRUE THAT THE olfactory is the keenest of the senses, the most evocative, the best one at recalling the past, then it is little wonder that a man born and raised in Chocolate Town—Hershey, Pennsylvania—can reach back for his childhood whenever he wants. Just a few days ago, on an unofficial and unremarkable playing field called the Meadows, retiring New York Giants general manager Ernie Accorsi returned to November 13, 1954, when he was thirteen. "Smell that air," he said, breathing in. It smelled like fudge bubbling on a stove.

Standing just five foot eight, Accorsi might be described as unremarkable, too, except for one thing: he is the only man in the history of sports who ever set out to be a general manager. Even Branch Rickey, the ultimate GM, didn't set out to be one. He set out to be a major league catcher, as Ernie first read in the *Sporting News* and later confirmed at the Hershey library. George Weiss of the New York Yankees represented another Accorsi study, but Rickey of the Brooklyn Dodgers was his ideal. When Ernie grew old enough to smoke cigars, he smoked only Rickey's brand, and still does. From college age on, he wielded the cigar like a baton, using it to conduct conversations.

Naturally, Accorsi set out to be a baseball general manager—football GMs were never mentioned in the *Sporting News*—but circumstances and an old college quarterback, George Welsh, redirected Ernie first to the Baltimore Colts, then to the Cleveland Browns, and finally to the Giants for the last decade of a thirty-five-year National Football League career. Now that he had time to look around a little, Accorsi wrote out a list of places he wanted to go and things he wanted to see, like the "Field of Dreams" in Dyersville, Iowa; the Negro Leagues Baseball Museum in Kansas City, Missouri; maybe a small college football game or two along the way, perhaps at Wabash or DePauw. Then there was the leaning tin barn in Commerce, Oklahoma, where father Mutt, a righty, and grandfather Charlie, a lefty, made a switch-hitter out of Mickey Mantle. But at the top of Ernie's list, a way of going back to the very beginning, was Rickey's grave in Rushtown, Ohio.

A whip-armed catcher with just an average glove and bat, Branch slipped through the systems of the Cincinnati Reds and the Chicago White Sox before reaching the big leagues with the St. Louis Browns in a June game versus Philadelphia with its managing owner, Connie Mack, squinting out from under his skimmer into the bright sun of old Athletic Park. Though Rickey should have been giving spitball pitcher Cy Morgan his full attention, he couldn't resist shooting an occasional glance Mack's way. Management fascinated Branch. Not just management of the game, management of the sport. Later, on barnstorming excursions, when both teams often rode the same train, he sought out Mack in his private Pullman car, just to sit quietly by as the "Tall Tactician," a former catcher himself, held forth on general managing.

Nearly every lesson began "Now, lookit . . ." and ended with an aphorism like "Don't ever get rid of a player until you're as sure as lightning that you have somebody just as good or better to take his place." On the other hand, "Now, lookit. Anesthetic players will absolutely ruin your team." An "anesthetic player" was defined as a subtly declining veteran whose past is so storied that it has lulled the organization into thinking at least one position is safely taken care of. Rickey converted this into his own aphorism: "Better to trade a man a year too soon than a year too late."

During off-seasons, Branch returned to his college, Ohio Wesleyan, and later to the University of Michigan, to help with football and the other sports, to see to all of the duties in the athletic department that didn't have titles then but do now. Scheduling, scouting, sports information directing, merchandising, marketing, ticketing, recruiting, and of course romancing—players and newspapermen alike. Along the way, Rickey, who enjoyed putting words together, collected a few bylines of his own. Not so long ago a sportswriter, Ford Frick for instance, could actually end up the commissioner of baseball. These were all roads to where Rickey was going, the same ones Accorsi would take as well.

More than playing, more than managing, Branch loved finding, gauging, and championing talent. Rickey could spot athletic ability, people said, from the window of a moving train. Though he specialized in beating the bushes for material, among Branch's most memorable discoveries was an eighteen-year-old freshman engineering student "with dark brown hair, serious gray eyes, and good posture" who just walked up to him one day in Ann Arbor. His name was George Sisler. Though freshmen weren't usually considered for the varsity, something in Sisler's bearing persuaded Rickey to ignore his own order and pitch the kid for seven innings in an intrasquad game. George struck out twenty men. On top of that, Sisler hit so well that in subsequent games when he wasn't pitching, he played first base and batted cleanup. Years later, while Rickey was running the St. Louis Cardinals, he sensed the same quality in a skinny twenty-year-old pitcher who had permanently wrecked his throwing shoulder in a fall. When the Cardinals' Springfield farm club was about to put the wounded boy on its drop-dead list, Branch said, "No, let's hold on to him awhile. Try him in the outfield. See if he can hit his way to Rochester." That was Stanley Musial. Of course Rickey had his misses, too. They all did.

Walter Wellesley "Red" Smith, the prince of the press box, rattled off Rickey's final record like an official scorer closing a pitching line: "Player, manager, executive, lawyer, preacher, horse-trader, innovator, husband and father and grandfather, farmer, logician, obscurantist, reformer, financier, sociologist, crusader, sharper, father confessor, checker shark, friend, fighter." General manager. "And, Judas Priest, what a character!"

The Brooklyn Dodgers today purchased the contract of
Jackie Roosevelt Robinson from the Montreal Royals.
He will report immediately.
Branch Rickey

That defining transaction in 1947 may have been grounded less in sociology than in just a simple, lifelong reverence for talent. But as far as young Accorsi was concerned, breaking the color barrier pushed Rickey over the top. Not that Ernie knew so much about black people. In 1960, the year after Accorsi left Hershey for college, a federal census taker counted six African Americans in all of Derry Township. The Italians were Hershey's minority, most of them Catholics to boot. Vowel-ending names dominate the headstones at the bottom of the town cemetery, far below the Methodists and Mennonites at the top of the hill, where the grandest marker is for Milton Snavely Hershey.

Both Ernie's grandfather, Joe Nardi, and his father, also Ernie, knew Mr. Hershey personally. Just about everyone in town had at least the illusion of being acquainted with the founder, who in this luxuriant valley, surrounded by bush-league mountains and Pennsylvania Dutchmen, built a milk chocolate factory with all of the trimmings. Including, at astonishingly affordable prices and mortgage rates, most of the homes of his employees, as well as a hospital, a stadium, an arena, an amusement park, a theater as acoustically well fitted as any on Broadway, an ornate and splendid movie house, a school, a pool, a library, a life.

Milton turned over the first floor of his mansion to serve as a clubhouse for the Hershey Country Club golf course, a handsome layout sporty enough to attract resident professionals the likes of Ben Hogan, the country's ultimate playing pro, and Masters and PGA champion Henry Picard. The ablest teaching assistant during Picard's tenure was a courtly Oklahoman, Jack Grout, who moved on to a head job in Ohio to show a precocious ten-year-old how to hit the ball left to right. Barbara and Jack Nicklaus honeymooned in Hershey.

Joe Nardi, who spoke only broken English (his grandson spoke sprained Italian), worked at a conveyor belt in the factory, molding chocolate with a mallet. He shipped over, twice, from Pitigliano in Tuscany, first to find a job and a grubstake, then to return with his family. Living on pasta and bread—meat maybe twice a week, often from rabbits he hunted himself—Joe meticulously grew a savings account to $5,000, enough to purchase a modest home in the 1920s. Carrying a note from a son-in-law spelling out the transaction in English, Nardi went to withdraw the five grand from his bank. But the teller handed him six. Several times Joe tried to point out the error, but the counterman was impatient. "Get out of here, you dumb Wop," he said.

In those days, Mr. Hershey knew his longest-serving employees by name, and by more than just their names. That afternoon, as the boss made his regular tour of the plant, Nardi approached him with a worried look. "What's the matter, Joe?" he asked. Together, in a chauffeur-driven limousine, Hershey and Nardi returned to the bank. When the smoke had cleared, the teller was fired and Nardi was told to keep the thousand, a fortune. Joe continued to be a world-class scrimper, but thereafter put his pennies into Hershey stock. Though Nardi's high salary was $21 a week, when he died he left each of his four children $11,000 in cash and a little Hershey house, fully paid for.

Ernie's father quit school in the eighth grade to begin a life of work. He also started at the chocolate factory, but after about a dozen years he went out on his own, opening a beer distributorship in a backyard shed. The first customer to drive up was Mr. Hershey. "I like my beer, Ernie," he said. "Run a clean business, and I'll be here every week to purchase a case. I'll make a big show of it, too, which won't hurt your bottom line. But become a hangout for rummies, and I promise you, I'll run you out of town." Because there weren't many beer distributorships in the area, Accorsi and son now and then loaded a small delivery truck and made a run through the Dutch country, testing their German on beer-loving customers. They knew how to say three things: "hello," "how are you doing," and "goodbye."

Like so many immigrants, Ernie's dad drew a particular joy from sports, maybe for the slight relief it seemed to offer from hard work and prejudice. He made an early pilgrimage to the Baker Bowl in Philadelphia, where a night game was never played, to see the Dean brothers, Dizzy and Paul, and the rest of St. Louis' Gashouse Gang. But he preferred the New York Yankees. They had Lazzari and Crosetti, later DiMaggio, Berra, and Rizzuto. Young Ernie saw his first major league baseball game at Philadelphia's Shibe Park in 1950. Jackie Robinson stole home, but the Phillies beat the Dodgers, 6–4. That year, every Philadelphia victory was critical, especially against the Dodgers. On the final day of the regular season, Dick Sisler, George's son, hit a tenth-inning home run to beat Brooklyn and win the pennant.

The Accorsis didn't have to go looking for pro football; it came to them in 1949 in the form of an exhibition game featuring quarterback Bobby Layne and the New York Bulldogs. In 1951, the Philadelphia Eagles established a regular training ground at the Hershey stadium, and that first summer, the New York Giants won a game there, 21–6, wearing striking red jerseys that stuck with Ernie. Someday he would retrieve those red jerseys from antiquity and dress the Giants in them once a year. In 1952, Ernie saw the Eagles and Steelers play to a scoreless tie that was memorable in its own way, and by 1956 Ernie was firmly on the side of whoever opposed the Eagles. That year the Hershey public address man mispronounced the name of a visiting quarterback making his professional debut, "Johnny YOU-knee-TASS." Come the finish of Unitas' career in Baltimore, he would present his last Colts jersey not to the National Football League Hall of Fame but to Accorsi. Ernie would feel entitled then to pass the number 19 on to a fledgling quarterback in Cleveland.

Two years before Unitas came to Chocolate Town, on a Saturday afternoon in November, the eighth-grade boys of Hershey staged a game of tackle football, without equipment, that turned out to be the game of the century. In the days ahead, players on both sides of that field, including Accorsi, would team up to miss qualifying for the Little League World Series in Williamsport by about a millimeter. Some would make all-city or all-state in baseball, football, basketball, or golf. A few would excel athletically at college. One would participate in two Super Bowls, a victory and a defeat. But of all the games of their lives, the Meadows Game is the one they still talk about when any two of them get together today.

It isn't precisely true that the sons of the town's workers took on the sons of the men they worked for, but it was pretty close to that. Maybe surprisingly, then, the game wasn't a desperate or bitter showdown. It was just sports. No class or religious wars were brought into it. No hatreds were played out. All of the players were schoolmates and, within reason, pals. But while it may have been just sports, it was serious. Especially after Paul Hummer of the other side "stole" Ernie's cousin, Gary Ponzoli, a year younger than everyone else but an all-around athlete bound eventually for West Point. "All bets are off," Accorsi told Hummer, proclaiming the dawn of free agency. In his first job of general managing, Ernie reached out to the farm areas and a couple of other distant neighborhoods for additional players. Hummer couldn't keep up, but he wasn't worried. His side already had the unstoppable Billy Myers, star of the town.

Accorsi's best recruit was a quarterback named Jimmy Warfield (Ernie would always be quarterback-oriented; all of the milestones in this story are quarterbacks) who lived over by the stadium and went on to play second base to Accorsi's shortstop all through high school and American Legion ball, and to have an honored life in baseball as a beloved trainer for the Cleveland Indians. "He was as well thought of as anyone in the game," said third baseman Travis Fryman on the day Jimmy died of a cerebral hemorrhage. "Where are we going to find a church big enough to hold everybody who loved him?" Ernie would deliver the eulogy at Jimmy's funeral. ("Somehow today, I have the feeling that my childhood is slipping through my fingers . . .")

The Saturday morning of the Meadows Game, there was a funeral as well. Joe Nardi had died of a heart attack. Because a cousin had to make his way home from the Navy, the services fell on game day, and Ernie's father was adamant: Italian mourning traditions did not allow for after-burial football games. For a loud while, a Puccini opera was sung through the house. Until, during a pause for breath, the cousin, Ron Gramigni—who knew that nobody was more brokenhearted than Ernie, and that nobody loved Joe more—pointedly informed his uncle, "If you don't let Ernie play in this game, you might as well sell the business and move to Iowa. Because he won't be able to live here anymore."

Ernie played. On a ten-yard run by halfback Bill Rollins, crossing the two goal line trees on the factory end of the field, the sons of the workers scored first. For hours then, they held on. Accorsi didn't do much on offense, but he intercepted three Gary Hinebaugh passes on defense. Hinebaugh wore a Brown University sweatshirt. (His big brother went to Brown.) Ernie wore one of those blank blue football jerseys, so popular at the time, with golden shoulders that described shoulder pads although there were no shoulder pads. No helmets, either. The days of wine and bloody noses.

They had agreed to play from the stroke of noon until the whistle signaling the ten-of-four shift change at the chocolate factory, and it was pretty late in the game when the great Billy Myers ran a sweep to the right, took off down the sideline, and sped the full length of the drainage ditch to tie the score, 6–6. By the way, a parent or two were in attendance that afternoon but none of them was a part of it. At one point, Terry Garman's father, Francis (of the bosses' team), charged the edge of the field to double-check an out-of-bounds call or to weigh in on a late hit. "Dad, stay out of this," Terry said. "We're fine." Those were the days.

With the whistle about to blow, Accorsi's team was at the five-yard line, looking sure to score the winning touchdown, when quarterback Warfield scrambled toward an opening and was bumped into and knocked down by his own halfback, Rollins. "Bill, you tackled me," he said. And the whistle blew. By that time, Chocolate Avenue had filled up with townspeople applauding. Shaking hands, Hummer and Accorsi said almost simultaneously, "We shouldn't play again." As it was, it was perfect.

That night, like the Sharks and Jets with a happier ending, they went to the dance at the "juvenile golf course" with its little log cabin clubhouse that Mr. Hershey had built. But they were too sore to dance and too excited to sit down.

Golf became Accorsi's game for a time. This was one of the elements that attracted him to Wake Forest University, Arnold Palmer's school, in Winston-Salem, North Carolina. But Ernie didn't require all eighteen holes of a practice round with another young aspirant, Jay Sigel, to realize that he wasn't nearly good enough for Wake Forest. Though Accorsi's first impulse was to run home, his father talked him out of quitting, not just Wake Forest, but anything else he started. Ernie and Hinebaugh, the bosses' quarterback in the Meadows Game, became fraternity brothers.

By Ernie's count, Wake Forest had a Roman Catholic population of "about five," one of them a freshman football player, Brian Piccolo. Together Ernie and Pic regularly hitchhiked to Sunday Mass. It seemed that the same family stopped for them every week. A tough runner, adept at lowering a shoulder just before he crashed into the line, Piccolo wasn't anything like the wisecracker actor James Caan would portray him to be in the weeper *Brian's Song*. "In that movie, Caan wasn't like Piccolo in any way, shape, or form," Accorsi said. "Brian had this wit, but it came across with Caan as a smart-ass wit. With Piccolo, you'd hear these great lines, but he always delivered them dropping his head looking into his shirt. Most of the time he was quiet. He was always humble. Hell, he was saintly." A couple of days after Piccolo sprained an ankle in a Friday frosh game at Chapel Hill, Accorsi dropped into Pic's room to see how he was mending. "Ernie," he said, "it's my own fault. In the pregame meal, I ate meat on Friday for the first time in my life. That's why I got hurt. I took one look at those fish sticks and I just couldn't bear to touch them."

Years later, at the Americana Hotel in New York, the pro football writers held a gala dinner honoring Piccolo's Chicago backfield mate Gale Sayers for an inspired comeback from injury. Ernie was in the audience. "Sayers asked all of us," he said, "when we hit our knees that night, to please pray for Brian Piccolo, who was sick. Gale said he was going to take the award he received at the banquet and hand it over to Pic in his hospital room the next day. I had no idea how bad it was until I heard the words 'Sloan-Kettering.' Gale said, 'I love Brian Piccolo. I want you to love him, too.' "

Ernie started to walk up to Sayers as the crowd was milling out, but Vince Lombardi got there first. Accorsi heard Lombardi say, "Gale, you're a great American," and decided not to follow that. He wasn't sure he could manage any words anyway.

2

MANNING VS. MANNING

FOR THE FIRST TIME in sixteen years, the New York Giants were perfect in the preseason, beating the Ravens, Chiefs, Jets, and Patriots.

By contrast, the New Orleans Saints and their rookie head coach, Giants castoff Sean Payton, were 1 and 3. Obviously these were two teams going in opposite directions in the National Football Conference. "I have no idea where we're going," Giants head coach Tom Coughlin said. "I'm not the great philosopher."

New York opened the regular season on a Sunday night at home in a game against Indianapolis that was inevitably dubbed the "Manning Bowl." For the first time in NFL history, brothers were starting at quarterback against each other in a real game. Hours before the kickoff, on different patches of the field, Peyton and Eli Manning were loosening up with their respective teammates, tossing the ball around lightheartedly. Everybody wore comically baggy shorts that went way past today's basketball bloomers almost all the way back to the boxer Archie Moore. Archie Manning, once a very good quarterback for very bad New Orleans teams, looked down from the press level high above. He was the picture of crossed signals and mixed emotions. "This feeling of dread may be a Saints hangover thing," he said, "but I know how, if it gets going bad, how really bad it can get—for the quarterback." Archie and his wife, Olivia, had accepted invitations to watch their sons from the Reebok box upstairs. "Peyton says I like to get to the games in time to see the cheerleaders stretch," Archie said, "but the truth is, I just like watching warm-ups. I'm completely nuts."

This night, more than ever. "Inside of me, I'm not sure what I'm supposed to be hoping for," he said. "Usually you can relax a little bit during the parts of the game when your boy is off the field, but what am I going to do tonight? Olivia and I didn't mean to raise quarterbacks, I swear to God. Like all parents, we just wanted them to be well rounded, go to school, grow up to be good people, do the right things. Believe me, I never tortured them on practice fields. Heck, I didn't mold them or anything. I just watched them have a dream that I understood, that I remembered having myself. I watched them work their rear ends off to attain it. Olivia was always a good sport and only pretended to get mad about spending her whole life cleaning up after football players. 'And another thing,' she'd shout, 'I'm sick and tired of washing jock straps!' Both Olivia and I mostly stood off to the side and smiled, or moved a little further away and cried."

Earlier that Sunday, Archie had told each of his sons the same thing, what he always told them before games: "I love you. Play hard. Have fun."

The New York GM, Ernie Accorsi, also stood off to the side, in one of the end zone tunnels at Giants Stadium, the one nearest both the home and the visitors' locker room, the position he had long since staked out as his game-day headquarters and bunker. Ernie was too nervous to watch from the press box and too appalled by the modern press box in any case. Those gentlemen sportswriters of sentimental memory, most of them decked out in suits, neckties, and fine felt fedoras, have all died off. They have been replaced by a convention of class clowns, some of them dressed like sharecroppers. After every play, three or five or ten or twenty of them yell out strained witticisms, the first things that pop into their heads—absolutely everything that pops into their heads—as though they were auditioning for sports talk radio, which perhaps they are. Though press box wags have existed since the Roman Colosseum, they used to have a drier style. At an early Super Bowl, when streaking was in fashion, a naked woman who ran onto the field was trundled off by four policemen. "And they took her away," someone in the press box said with a sigh, "two abreast."

"Ron Sellers was this big, tall receiver from Florida State," Ernie said, "who was constantly on injured reserve. He typified the futility of the early-seventies Patriots, who couldn't get anything right. He was always hurt. So now he's coming back again, this big bastard with all that talent. Jim Plunkett drops back to pass, and here comes Sellers over the middle. He leaps into the air—the ball is this far from his hands, left safety Jerry Logan is this far from his shoulders, right safety Rick Volk is this far from his legs—and, a split second before the crash, Will McDonough of the *Boston Globe* yells out, 'Eight to twelve weeks!' You had to laugh."

One of the Giants exercising in shorts was twenty-three-year-old Mathias Kiwanuka, New York's first pick in the most recent college draft, a six-five, 262-pound defensive end from Boston College. His grandfather, Benedicto Kiwanuka, became Uganda's first elected prime minister in 1961 and was assassinated by Idi Amin eleven years later. Only once, when he was a grade-school student, was Kiwanuka ever in Uganda. He was really from Indianapolis. With three and a half preseason sacks, Kiwanuka had made a more than promising start. In the final exhibition game against New England, he shrugged off 320-pound tackle Wesley Britt to bring about a tip and force an interception.

In the draft room, Accorsi had been the last one to come aboard for Kiwanuka, which was unusual. "I was thinking of maneuvering to get the University of Miami corner Kelly Jennings, who ended up going to Seattle. But Jerry [player personnel director Jerry Reese] and Tom both wanted another pass rusher, and I liked Kiwanuka, too. I decided to let them have their way. A GM shouldn't always be heavy-handed. The front office is a team, too. This was good for the team. And, obviously, it wasn't a franchise-changing decision. If it had been a franchise-changing decision, I'd have ignored everybody and insisted on having my own way. If it's a quarterback, absolutely, I'm making the call."

Just then, the franchise-changing decision Eli Manning passed

Accorsi in the tunnel on his way back to the locker room to get suited up for the game. "Hi, boss," Eli said.

Ernie first saw Eli in person at an Auburn game Manning's junior year at Mississippi, November 2, 2002. The word then was that Eli might come out of school early. He did not. But the scouting report Accorsi typed out in bold capital letters didn't change the next year and, to Ernie's way of thinking (although to almost no one else's), it hadn't changed in the years since.

WEARS LEFT KNEE BRACE . . . DURING PREGAME WARMUP, DIDN'T LOOK LIKE HE HAD A ROCKET ARM . . . AS GAME PRO-GRESSED, I SAW EXCELLENT ARM STRENGTH UNDER PRES-SURE AND THE ABILITY TO GET VELOCITY ON THE BALL ON MOST THROWS. GOOD DEEP BALL RANGE. GOOD TOUCH. GOOD VISION AND POISE.

SEES THE FIELD . . . IN A SHOTGUN ON MOST PLAYS AND HIS ONLY RUNNING OPTION IS A DRAW . . . HIS OFFENSIVE LINE IS POOR. RED-SHIRT FRESHMAN LEFT TACKLE. ELI DOESN'T TRUST HIS PROTECTION. CAN'T. NO WAY CAN HE TAKE ANY FORM OF DEEP DROP AND LOOK DOWNFIELD. WITH NO RUN-NING GAME (10 YARDS RUSHING THE FIRST HALF) AND NO REAL TOP RECEIVERS, HE'S STUCK WITH THREE-STEP DROPS AND WAITING TIL THE LAST SECOND TO SEE IF A RECEIVER CAN GET FREE. NO TIGHT END EITHER. NO FLARING BACK. SO HE'S TAKING SOME BIG HITS. TAKING THEM WELL. CARRIED AN OVERMATCHED TEAM ENTIRELY ON HIS SHOULDERS. I IMAG-INE, EXCEPT FOR VANDERBILT, HIS TEAM IS OVERMATCHED IN EVERY SEC [SOUTHEAST CONFERENCE] GAME . . . HE'S BIG, NEVER GETS RATTLED. RALLIED HIS TEAM FROM A 14–3 HALF-TIME DEFICIT BASICALLY ALL BY HIMSELF. LED THEM ON TWO SUCCESSIVE THIRD QUARTER DRIVES TO GO AHEAD, 17–16. THE FIRST TOUCHDOWN, ON A 40-YARD STREAK DOWN THE LEFT SIDELINE, HE DROPPED THE BALL OVER THE RECEIVER'S

RIGHT SHOULDER. CALLED THE NEXT TOUCHDOWN PASS HIM-SELF, CHECKING OFF TO A 12-YARD SLANT . . . MAKES A LOT OF DECISIONS ON PLAY CALLS AT THE LINE OF SCRIMMAGE, BUT THEY ASK TOO MUCH OF HIM. THEY DON'T LET HIM JUST PLAY. THIS IS A GUY YOU SHOULD JUST LET PLAY . . . WHEN HE'S INACCURATE, HE'S USUALLY HIGH, BUT RARELY OFF TARGET TO EITHER SIDE . . . PLAYS SMART AND WITH COMPLETE CON-FIDENCE. DOESN'T SCOLD HIS TEAMMATES [DID ACCORSI WISH HE DID?], BUT LETS THEM KNOW WHEN THEY LINE UP WRONG OR RUN THE WRONG PATTERN [AT LEAST] . . . THREW THREE INTERCEPTIONS. TWO WERE HIS FAULT. TRYING TO FORCE SOMETHING BOTH TIMES. HE COULD HAVE RUN ON ONE OF THEM, A FOURTH DOWN PLAY. HE HAS A LOT TO LEARN.

SUMMARY: I THINK HE'S THE COMPLETE PACKAGE. HE'S NOT GOING TO BE A FAST RUNNER, BUT A LITTLE LIKE JOE MON-TANA, HE HAS ENOUGH ATHLETIC ABILITY TO GET OUT OF TROUBLE. REMEMBER HOW ARCHIE RAN? IN THAT DEPART-MENT, ELI DOESN'T HAVE THE BEST GENES, ALTHOUGH I NEVER TIMED MOM OLIVIA IN THE 40. BUT HE HAS A FEEL FOR THE POCKET. FEELS THE RUSH.

THROWS THE BALL, TAKES THE HIT, GETS RIGHT BACK UP . . . HAS COURAGE AND POISE. IN MY OPINION, MOST OF ALL, HE HAS THAT QUALITY YOU CAN'T DEFINE. CALL IT MAGIC. AS [FORMER BALTIMORE COLTS DEFENSIVE BACK] BOBBY BOYD TOLD ME ONCE ABOUT UNITAS, "TWO THINGS SET HIM APART: HIS LEFT TESTICLE AND HIS RIGHT TES-TICLE." . . . PEYTON HAD MUCH BETTER TALENT AROUND HIM AT TENNESSEE. BUT I HONESTLY GIVE THIS GUY A CHANCE TO BE BETTER THAN HIS BROTHER. ELI DOESN'T GET MUCH HELP FROM THE COACHING STAFF. IF HE COMES OUT EARLY, WE SHOULD MOVE UP TO TAKE HIM. THESE GUYS ARE RARE, YOU KNOW.

ERNIE ACCORSI

"I remember everything about that day," Eli said. "It was a heart-breaker. I threw an interception on the last play to lose the game, actually. It was fourth down. I tried to scramble—maybe I could have run it in. I probably should have tried. The receiver was crossing, but he turned away just as I threw it. The ball went flying right by him. That one hurt for a long while. Still does."

Following Eli up the tunnel, Jim Finn, almost the rarest animal in the league—a fullback from the University of Pennsylvania—offered his own scouting report on the Mannings, and on the night. "Peyton always shows his excitement and always shows his disappointment," Finn said. "He walks off the field with his head shaking one way or the other. Eli doesn't show anything. A touchdown and an interception look the same. That's who Eli is. He keeps it inside."

"Yeah," quarterback coach Kevin Gilbride said, "but I think there's something in there that would like to show his big brother a thing or two."

"Any little brother has to be tough," offensive left tackle Luke Petit-gout said, "but Eli is Peyton Manning's little brother. He has to be tougher."

At school—Tennessee and Ole Miss—Peyton was the antisocial one, the football geek tethered to a film projector. Eli was the one who liked the night, music, and beer. Who wouldn't have guessed the opposite? Peyton at thirty, the omnipresent pitchman from Madison Avenue, was the oil-painted portrait of a commander in chief who, up close, appeared taller even than six-five. Eli at twenty-five, with permanently tousled hair, stood only an inch shorter, but somehow it seemed a foot. No NFL quarterback was in more extreme need of black stubble on his chin, a jagged scar across one cheek, or at least a misspelled tattoo.

"I've been playing nine years," Peyton said. "Eli's beginning his second season as a starter. Let him breathe, will you?"

He said this after the game. Before it, the Colts' quarterback reappeared in Ernie's tunnel ahead of any of his Indianapolis teammates, helmet on but with the chin strap unsnapped, standing completely still. Not ten feet separated them, but Peyton didn't seem to see Accorsi or anyone else. "Look at him," Ernie said, not bothering to whisper because Peyton couldn't hear him, either. "He isn't moving a muscle. He isn't bouncing from one foot to the other the way they do. He's come to a stop. He's calm. *Now* does he remind you of Unitas? The best ones all have this same moment of serenity just before the storm. There he is. Tiger Woods on the first tee."

Adam Vinatieri, the most dependable placekicker in the NFL, opened the scoring with a couple of field goals that Peyton stretched to a 13–0 lead in the second quarter with a short touchdown pass to tight end Dallas Clark. Near the end of the first half, beginning at his own fourteen-yard line, Eli finally replied.

GIANTS

1-10-G14 (out of the shotgun) Eli passes to Tiki Barber
　for 17
Two-minute warning
1-10-G31 (shotgun) Barber runs for 11
1-10-G42 (shotgun, no huddle) Eli passes incomplete
2-10-G42 (shotgun) Barber runs for 11
1-10-C47 (shotgun) Eli passes to Amani Toomer for 6
2-4-C41　(shotgun, no huddle) Eli passes to Barber for 7
1-10-C34 (shotgun) Eli passes to Plaxico Burress for 34
　yards and the touchdown; Jay Feely kicks the extra point
Indianapolis 13, New York 7

But twenty-eight seconds remained for rebuttal, enough time after a nice kickoff return for Peyton to push the Colts back inside Vinatieri's range.

COLTS

1-10-C38 Peyton passes to Marvin Harrison for 16
1-10-G46 (shotgun) Peyton passes to Harrison for 5
Time-out (:15)

2-5-G41   (shotgun) Peyton passes to Harrison for 9
Time-out (:10)
1-10-G32 Dominic Rhodes runs for 1
Timeout (:05)
2-9-G31   Vinatieri kicks a 48-yard field goal
Indianapolis 16, New York 7

Up in the Reebok box, Archie Manning said, "They aren't football players out there. They're my little boys."

Receiving the third-quarter kickoff, New York spent nearly eight minutes moving sixty-nine yards on eleven plays to close within two, 16–14, on Eli's fifteen-yard touchdown pass to tight end Jeremy Shockey. "Shockey reminds me of Ted Kwalick," Ernie said, recalling a Penn State tight end from the 1960s. Of course, nearly everything reminds Ernie of Penn State. "Looking at Kwalick once, Joe Paterno said, 'What God had in mind here was a football player.'"

Two points were still the difference, 23–21, with about five minutes to go in the game, when everything was resolved on a four-play Giants possession. "The reason I've always preferred baseball," Ernie muttered in his tunnel, "is that their umpires can't just blow a whistle and take away a three-run home run."

GIANTS
1-10-G10 Eli passes to Toomer for 6
2-4-G16   Barber runs for 2
3-2-G18   Eli passes to Tim Carter for 17
But Carter is called for interfering with defensive back
    Nick Harper, a venial sin all but invisible in the replay
3-11-G9   Eli's pass to Toomer is intercepted by Harper

Vinatieri made another field goal, and the final score was 26–21, Colts. "Good game," Eli told Peyton at the center of the field. "I love you," Peyton said. "I'm proud of the way you competed."

To the media in the Giants' locker room, Eli admitted forthrightly, "I think I was throwing to the right guy on the interception, but it was definitely the wrong kind of pass. You can't float that one. It has to be a line drive." Some days later, alone in a small classroom just off the clubhouse, Eli said, "Peyton is one of the best quarterbacks in the NFL, if not *the* best. In my opinion he is the best. He's the benchmark not just for me, but especially for me. He always has been.

"I'm five years younger than Peyton, seven years younger than our older brother, Cooper. When they were growing up, my dad was still playing. Cooper and Peyton hung around the locker rooms, got to know all of the players. They went along to Hawaii when Dad made the Pro Bowl. They were around it. They saw it. I just heard about it. On family car trips, Cooper and Peyton were always playing this numbers game. They would pick out a uniform number at random—eighty-four. Then, back and forth, they'd name all of the players in the NFL who wore eighty-four—sometimes college players, too. Sometimes high school players! They knew everybody. They knew everything. I was more than a little bit behind."

After Peyton elected Tennessee over Archie's alma mater, Ole Miss, "our whole family was harassed," Eli said, "especially my dad. There were death threats and everything. People expected him to force Peyton to go to Ole Miss, because he had starred there. But they didn't know Dad. 'I'm not doing that,' he said. 'It's not my job. He's a grown man. It's his decision.' Those fathers you hear about who force their kids to play sports, who hang over them at school and try to be their coaches, my dad was never that. Never. He had lived his own athletic life. He'd already had his high school days, his college days, his pro days. He didn't have to live it through us. He said, 'You know what? I went my way, you go yours. If you love football, heck, go ahead. I did. But if you don't love it, don't worry about it. It's not that important.'" It's just sports.

In 2004, when overall number one draft choice Eli maneuvered his way out of San Diego and into New York, Chargers fans considered Archie the puppet master. "The heat he took in San Diego wasn't deserved," Eli said. "It was my call, it was always my call. I did what I thought was right for me. He actually got involved only to take the pressure off me, because I asked him to. I wanted him to kind of speak for me at one point, but I told him what to say. 'No problem,' he said, 'I'll draw the fire.' He did it to protect me, as always. It's like, it was entirely my decision to go to Ole Miss. I could have gone to Texas. There were other places where I might have had a shot at a national championship. But I had to do what I thought was best. And, whatever I decided, Dad was going to back me. I can't tell you what it's meant to me to have his support, and Peyton's."

When Eli signed with Ole Miss, Peyton presented him a thick notebook he had been filling out all season on airplanes to and from Colts games. "Full of protections, plays, and reads," Eli said, "pages and pages and pages. He sat down with me and tried to teach me all of these things. I didn't ask him to do it. At the time I hardly knew what was going on. Everything in that book was new to me, and it all came into play. Now Peyton and I talk every week, a couple of times. Right after the game, I might call him just for a minute. Often I'll catch him on the team bus. Then, on Monday or Tuesday, we'll talk a bit longer. We'll actually talk some football. If we didn't see each other's games, we'll go over them a little, you know, a series here and there. I may have seen a highlight of a pass to Marvin [Harrison]. 'Hey, what was that? Take me through that, will you?' You can't have conversations like these with everyone. Not even with your closest friends. 'Yeah, yeah, they were playing a cover two, so we ran, you know, the end thing, and got a great look until they shifted the strong safety, and we had to slide the protection, and . . .' Only another quarterback really understands. I'll tell you, it's lucky to have somebody to talk to who knows exactly what you're saying, exactly what you're feeling, exactly what you're going through, without having to spell everything out."

Statistically their final passing marks were twenty-five of forty-one for Peyton, twenty of thirty-four for Eli, 276 and 247 yards. Peyton threw one touchdown pass, Eli two. They both had a solitary interception, though Peyton bounced a few incompletions off Giants defenders' chests. A two-time NFL Most Valuable Player, the only man ever to throw forty-nine touchdown passes in a season, Peyton likely wasn't halfway through his career, but he was more than halfway to Dan Marino's all-time passing record of 61,361 yards. Of course, the Indianapolis quarterback was also married to Marino at the top of the list of statistically accomplished quarterbacks who had never won a Super Bowl. In Peyton's case, he had yet even to play in the ultimate championship game.

Eli, meanwhile, was still pretty fresh out of the egg. The year before, his first as a full-time starter, he led the Giants to an 11–5 record and a division title before showing his age in a 23–0 play-off loss to Carolina at home. Bart Starr was in his fourth pro season before he got out from behind Lamar McHan and Joe Francis in Green Bay. At Eli's stage, Jim Plunkett hadn't yet been run out of New England, let alone San Francisco, on his long way to Super Bowl titles with the Raiders. At that juncture, coaches Dan Reeves and Chuck Noll were losing patience with John Elway and Terry Bradshaw. Noll was about ready to take a harder look at "Jefferson Street Joe" Gilliam.

Obviously New York isn't the kind of town that wants to hear any of that when its twenty-five-year-old quarterback throws an interception on what was supposed to be the winning drive. At the same time, wide receiver Plaxico Burress, known for a mastery of jump balls and an economy of language, made a quiet suggestion: "Shouldn't four hundred and thirty-three yards of total offense have been enough?"

Coach Coughlin was steely in the locker room. "We have to stop talking about being good," he said, "and get good." When Coughlin was hired two years earlier, Accorsi presumed Tom was going to run his own offense. "I'm not saying you're going to call every play," Ernie told him, "but it's going to be you, right? That's what we're buying, right?" Instead, hardworking, well-traveled offensive coordinator John Hufnagel was at the wheel. "He's a former Canadian League quarterback," Ernie said coolly, "and he thinks like a Canadian League quarterback. Only three downs in Canadian football, you know." At the close of the 2005 season, Accorsi tried to talk Tom into calling Hufnagel a cab and taking over the play calling himself. But Coughlin resisted. "'Okay,' I told him, 'have it your way. You won the division. But I warn you, it's at your peril.'"

Accorsi expected Tom and Eli to be much closer by now. To Ernie's way of thinking, the coach and the quarterback have to be connected tighter than everyone else. "[Pittsburgh Steelers patriarch] Art Rooney told me that years ago," Ernie said, puffing on his cigar, Rooney-like. "He said, 'The most significant relationship in all of sports is the one between the head coach and the quarterback.' How one goes, so goes the other. Come the end of this season, we won't be saying Tom had a good year and Eli a bad one, or vice versa. They're going up or down together."

Sitting in his office, Coughlin said, "Eli's such a good person, such a good kid, so dedicated. When we went to Baltimore and Washington his rookie year and we lost both of those games pretty big, he came up here and sat down in that chair right there. 'I played awful, Coach,' he said, 'but I'd like you to know something. I want to be the quarterback of the New York Giants. I want to be as good a quarterback for this team as I can possibly be.'"

Now, with the Giants standing 0 and 1, a daunting schedule looked even worse. Next up were the Eagles in Philadelphia, followed by the Seahawks in Seattle. From beneath the blackened cloud that follows most GMs everywhere, Ernie murmured, "We could be oh and three. Then we get the Redskins here, Atlanta on the road, and Dallas on the road. Somehow, someway, we've got to get to three and three."

Running back Tiki Barber, defensive end Michael Strahan, and linebacker Antonio Pierce—the Giants most corporate players, the leaders among the ones who walked around the clubhouse like stockholders instead of employees—had already declared for the Super Bowl. "I didn't like that," Accorsi said. "Tom's right about that. Say it to yourselves, but don't say it out loud."

The Monday after losing to Indianapolis, Ernie wrote what he knew was a pointless letter to Mike Pereira, the NFL's head of officials, invoking the name of Wellington Mara, the Giants owner and NFL pioneer who died in the middle of the 2005 season. It began, "Mike: Wellington Mara had a great saying. 'I say this more in sorrow than anger . . .' "

3

RED LICORICE

A FTER HE WAS graduated from Wake Forest, before he had a cup of coffee with the Air Force, Ernie rolled out Branch Rickey's blueprint and began plotting his way to the front office. Looking up newspaper addresses in *Editor and Publisher* magazine, he papered the East with writing samples. "Only two responses came back," he said. "One was from Jerry Isenberg in Newark, who took a red pen to my copy and butchered me, killed me, shattered me, demoralized me. Can you believe it? He cared enough to do that. It was the first time I ever heard of a split infinitive. 'What in the hell is a split infinitive?'" The second response was a job offer from the *Charlotte News*.

Like other sports executives who started out this way—like Frank Cashen, like Harry Dalton, like Pete Rozelle—Accorsi dabbled in sportswriting for a few years at the *Charlotte News,* the Baltimore *Evening Sun,* and the *Philadelphia Inquirer,* enjoying the experience hugely, but never intending to make a life in dangling participles. Others in the sports department had stronger syntax, but few of Ernie's colleagues could touch him for instinct or luck, that mysterious reporter's knack for regularly pulling up and parking in the vicinity of news. He just happened to be in attendance at the Polo Grounds in 1963 on the day the New York Mets (né Boston Red Sox) iconoclast Jimmy Piersall hit his one hundredth home run and ran the bases backward.

That same year, when the minor league Charlotte Hornets baseball team was on a thirteen-game losing streak, Ernie came across an eighty-two-year-old retired physician who in the middle of his medical studies had helped the Hornets win twenty-five straight games in 1902. "The NCAA was not around then to play traffic cop," Accorsi wrote in the *Charlotte News*, "and whistle down every violation. 'They didn't care in those days,' the grand little gentleman related. 'Why, to show how lax rules were, while studying medicine at the University of Maryland I played halfback for the Terps in the fall and professional baseball in the summer. Today you can't even accept a free Lifesaver while you're playing college athletics.'"

The old doc hit what Accorsi termed "a lusty .323" in Charlotte and then moved up from the North Carolina League to the Eastern League to win a batting championship in Scranton. "That's when I got my shot at the New York Giants," he said, referring to the 1905 baseball team that delivered manager John McGraw to his first World Series title, "but I didn't get any breaks there." Unless you count, as Ernie reported, a broken leg. After two innings in right field and just one unofficial trip to a major league plate, he cracked a bone and was finished. His lifetime record in the big leagues stands forever as a lonely 1 under "games played," followed by a desperate string of zeroes.

So, more than a quarter of a century before Burt Lancaster, Kevin Costner, and millions of moviegoers across America and around the world, Accorsi discovered Dr. Archibald "Moonlight" Graham, the spectral figure from *Field of Dreams*. "During our win streak," Graham told Accorsi, "we used to march around the flagpole before games, which really burned the other ball clubs. That Eddie Ashenback was a fine manager, and poor old Dan McGann, our first baseman, he committed suicide, and . . ." The *Charlotte News* declared Dr. Graham to be just the syringe the Hornets had their sleeves rolled up and waiting for, and of course the losing streak was snapped—as Ernie concluded his story— "in front of 588 howling fans last night."

In Baltimore, Accorsi was assigned to write an advance on an all-black golf tournament formally called the Three-Ring Charity Open (after the logo of its sponsor, Ballantine beer) but meanly referred to around town as the "Three-Ring Circus." For an afternoon Ernie watched the old champ Joe Louis, about a five handicapper, being skinned in a practice round by markedly better playing partners. Louis' wife rode along in a cart, guarding a black medical bag stuffed with cash. After every hole, Joe dipped into it with that great fist, pulled out a bird's nest of bills, and held it out to the hustlers. As soon as everyone had plucked what he was owed, they moved on to the next tee.

"I interviewed Jackie Robinson later," Ernie said. Cash was a melancholy part of that story, too. "At the end of the interview he indicated a slight bitterness about money. There was just this tone in his voice that, I don't know, disappointed me. I think I left that out of my piece, I can't remember. But I remember feeling a little let down." ("If I had it to do all over again," Robinson said, "I would never have played a game of football." He starred at halfback for UCLA. "I loved the game in college but the money is in baseball, and don't forget that counts. Everybody plays sports for money. If the door had been open in baseball when I was very young I would have concentrated on it alone. As soon as the game got a little tough for me and I could see there was money elsewhere, I got the heck out.")

Everybody plays sports for money.

At the *Philadelphia Inquirer,* pro basketball was Accorsi's beat. Working the night desk, he took a call from a diner at a downtown restaurant who overheard a 76ers executive talking about trading Wilt Chamberlain to Los Angeles. Ernie contacted the team's GM and its public relations director. Both laughed off the possibility, but they stammered a little first. Ernie put it to Frank Dolson, the paper's star columnist. Turning away from his column, Frank picked up the phone and began sounding out his sources. Accorsi and Dolson worked the tip together right up to the hour of the deadline, and when they couldn't knock it down, they believed it. Lakers center Darrall Imhoff would have to be a part of the deal, they reasoned—correctly. "You better be right," the managing editor told Ernie, copywriting the story and putting it on page one, "or you're going to be covering softball games the rest of your life." Accorsi knew he was right even before the bulldog edition hit the streets. The PR man called back to whisper, "I'm sorry I lied to you, but please, please, don't quote me." The straightforward copy that Ernie had batted out and handed in was headed "By Ernie Accorsi and Frank Dolson of the *Inquirer* Staff." But when the page proofs came upstairs from the composing room, Ernie saw that Frank had scratched out his own name. Accorsi threw a puzzled glance at Dolson, who couldn't have looked more uncomfortable. Generosity has always made hard-bitten newspapermen uncomfortable. "You take this one," Frank muttered.

And yet, even the exhilaration of a front-page scoop, a narcotic for most young reporters, didn't alter Accorsi's ambition. Words and public relations might seem wishful paths to front office careers now, but they were the established routes then, even for those who took that turn accidentally. In the early 1970s, when the NBA was about a hundred times smaller than it is today, commissioner Walter Kennedy sat in his boxer shorts in a Los Angeles hotel room to deliver the state-of-the-league message to ten or twelve reporters at the All-Star Game, including me. "You know something, Leonard?" the commissioner said to Leonard Lewin or Leonard Koppett or one of the other New York basketball writers, all of whom were named Leonard. "I started out to be a sportswriter. What the hell happened?"

As Rickey had Ohio Wesleyan and Michigan, Ernie would have St. Joe's in Philly and Penn State, especially Penn State. His salary as St. Joe's sports information director amounted to a Jesuitic vow of poverty, but there were intangible compensations. The basketball seasons were glorious. For watching a college basketball game, there really has never been a building quite like Philadelphia's Palestra. "I grew up loving St. Joe's for all of the craziest reasons," Ernie said, "because my grandfather, Joe Nardi, was Joseph; because Joseph was my confirmation name; and because when I was thirteen I saw a Big Five doubleheader, and St. Joe's came from way behind to win its game. I couldn't believe that I was actually working there. And Jack Ramsay was the basketball coach, the first great coach of any kind that I was ever around. When Ramsay was on one knee in front of the team, I just knew we had an edge. I was mesmerized by him."

Though he was far from a natural publicist, Accorsi's old luck remained in force. Humoring a dotty priest who came up with the dreary idea of publishing a Latin-to-English, English-to-Latin dictionary, Accorsi dashed off a press release to Frank Brookhouser of the *Bulletin*. And the next thing Ernie knew, it was a best-seller. Forty-one years later, he would stumble across a copy in Barnes and Noble.

Because Penn State had football and, as Ernie said, "was bigger and more in line with my front office quest," he accepted a job as sports information director Jim Tarman's assistant. "Penn State is where everything changed. That's when I stopped being a baseball guy and started being a football guy. Because that's when I met George Welsh."

Welsh isn't remembered as a college football player, but he ought to be. He was a rollout quarterback, about the size of a dollar and a quarter's worth of liver, who played for the United States Naval Academy when the Midshipmen could really play. At the end of George's junior season, Mississippi wasn't just upset by Navy in the 1955 Sugar Bowl, it was swamped and capsized, 21–0. "I don't think I was that good," Welsh said, typically, "but we had a pretty good team." The following year, he led the nation both in passing and in total offense and finished third in the Heisman election behind Howard "Hopalong" Cassady of Ohio State and "Swanky Jim" Swink of Texas Christian. Michigan State quarterback Earl Morrall and Notre Dame junior Paul Hornung followed Welsh, who barely noticed where he placed.

"Nah, I didn't even think about it, I'm serious," he said. "It wasn't like it is today. I suppose I would have had a chance if we'd beaten Notre Dame and Army. We were six and oh at one point, throwing the ball all over the lot, especially for that era." Sonny Jurgensen was averaging about eight passes a game for Duke when Welsh completed sixteen of twenty versus

Penn State and twenty of twenty-nine against Army. But fumbling six times against the Cadets didn't help. The Midshipmen fell, 14–6. "Football is a simple game," Welsh always said, "but it ain't easy."

For a decade as an assistant coach at Penn State, George worked first for Rip Engle and then for Paterno. Accomplishing one of the rarest feats in sports, Paterno replaced a legend and became a bigger legend. Basketball coach Dean Smith brought this off after Frank McGuire at the University of North Carolina, and football coach Tom Osborne stood pretty close to Bob Devaney at the end in Nebraska, but usually there's at least one Phil Bengston somewhere in between. Before Welsh moved up to his own commands at Navy and the University of Virginia, he learned much from Rip—"that old winged T, boy, that stuff was good, still is"—and even more from Joe. "Joe knew what he was doing, and he worked his ass off. There's a certain culture at Penn State that's different from ninety-nine percent of the colleges. A certain way of doing things. A pride. It preceded Joe, but he embellished it. I tried to install it at Virginia. I'm not sure I succeeded. I was tough, too, but not like Joe. He was a mean sucker, boy, on the field. That's why some kids couldn't appreciate him until after they left. From Joe I learned how to motivate players, how to practice. Many things."

As far as Paterno was concerned, Ernie's most vital function wasn't keeping the media informed, it was keeping a bowl in the coaches' office filled with red licorice. But Ernie managed to bootleg a number of life lessons and football lessons from Joe. Tarman schooled Accorsi on the rudiments of organization and started him on the road to being an executive. Jack Ham, Franco Harris, Lydell Mitchell, and Mike Reid showed him what football players looked like. But the game of football itself, and the love of the game, he learned from Welsh. Without knowing he was doing it, George nudged Ernie off the base paths onto a gridiron. Now Accorsi was bound to be an NFL GM.

"It seemed we were always sitting next to each other, everywhere," Welsh said. "We'd talk football coming and going, into the night. Ernie soaked up everything. He was a great confidant, a great friend. I didn't know I was having any particular influence on him, though. I was just answering his questions, telling him what I thought."

"I peppered George," Ernie said, "with millions of questions. 'What did Joe mean by this, that, or the other?' George translated everything for me. He interpreted this new language I was trying to learn. He'd laugh and say, 'Pay very close attention to this,' or 'Completely, utterly ignore that.' In 1969 we opened the season at Navy and killed them, then beat a pretty damned good Colorado team, twenty to nothing. I was really into it. But we had to go to Kansas State next. They had Mack Herron and Lynn Dickey, and speed all over the field. We had never played on Astroturf before, and we certainly didn't have anything like that kind of speed. They had just blown out Oklahoma, scoring over forty points. Paterno didn't have a particularly good feeling—at least he didn't seem to. 'Holy cow!' he kept saying, studying film. 'Holy cow! Holy cow! This is the quickest college football team we've ever faced!' Naturally, by the time I got on the plane to Manhattan, Kansas, I was sure we had no chance. I said that to George, who of course was sitting beside me. He just smiled.

" 'Ernie,' he said, 'they can't beat us. First of all, watch them when we come out on the field. They'll stop what they're doing and look at us. I guarantee you. They might move the ball early. They probably will, while we're adjusting to their quickness. But they'll get anxious and turn the ball over, you'll see. Then we'll make a big play and that will be that. Their balloon will burst.' "

Like in a movie script, the home team did stop and gawk at the visitors. Twice Kansas State drove deep into Penn State territory only to fumble. "The third time," Ernie said, "linebacker Jack Ham made the greatest interception, to this day, that I've ever seen. Coming on a blitz, he caught a Dickey fastball—Dickey had a rifle for an arm—at pointblank range. The next play, Lydell Mitchell ran a sweep, the first time we ever used that particular sweep."

Before the season, at Vince Lombardi's Redskins camp in Carlisle, Pennsylvania, Paterno told Welsh, "While I talk to Coach, you find out everything you can about that sweep." "You know," Accorsi said, "Joe and Vince were great friends. The only game Paterno's high school, Brooklyn Prep, lost his senior year was at St. Cecilia's, coached by Lombardi." Well, Mitchell swept seventy yards for a Penn State touchdown. "We built a seventeen-nothing lead," Ernie said, "before they scored late, too late. Then, following an onside kick, they got a meaningless second touchdown as time ran out. We won, seventeen-fourteen."

Those seven points weren't entirely meaningless. As a matter of fact, they may have meant everything. That same day, Texas routed Navy, jumped the Nittany Lions in the rankings, and stayed just ahead of them the rest of the year to win the national championship. For the second straight season, Penn State was unbeaten and not number one. Football is a simple game, but it ain't easy. "It's intelligent," Welsh said. "It's scientific. It's mathematical. It's artistic. It's musical. It's everything."

It's like a bowl in the coaches' office overflowing with red licorice.

"The funny thing is," Ernie said, "Paterno wasn't going to be a lifetime football coach. He promised his father he'd only coach the one year and then he'd go on to law school, Boston University. For years Joe's dad had worked during the day and gone to law school at night. He didn't take the bar exam until he was forty-four. Joe intended to stay with the team just long enough to help Rip put in the T formation. So, he's single—he's probably had about two dates his whole life—and he moves in with the O'Horas. Jim O'Hora was the equivalent of the defensive coordinator. Fifteen years later, Joe's still in the upstairs bedroom. The O'Horas have raised their entire family, all of the kids are gone, and Joe's still up there. Finally, they called him down into the living room and said, 'Joe, it's time.'" Eventually Joe met Sue, and they had five children, but their marriage constituted a kind of bigamy, because Paterno was already wed to Penn State. In 2006, fifty-six years later, the O'Horas were long gone, and eighty-year-old Joe was still the head coach, and still unable to understand why anyone would ever leave Happy Valley of his own volition.

When the Baltimore Colts summoned Accorsi in 1970, Ernie knew it wasn't just a PR job. NFL front offices were so sparse in those days that everyone—even the equipment men—scouted. And the Colts were the thinnest of all at the top because their original GM, Don Kellett, famously believed that "if there are too many workers in a front office, nothing gets done." After hearing all that, Paterno still refused to accept Ernie's resignation, at least for a day. "Go back to your roots," Joe said. "Have your wife make you a plate of spaghetti. She's Irish, I know, but can she do that?" "Yes, she has my mother's recipe." "And go get yourself a bottle of Bolla Valpolicella."

"You know Pennsylvania," Ernie said, "I had to go looking for a state store, halfway to frickin' Pittsburgh. When I got back home, my son Mike, who was just starting to walk, came toddling outside and I dropped the wine. It smashed on the sidewalk. Was this an omen? Figuring I better do it right, I drove all the way back for more Bolla Valpolicella. 'Did you already drink that first bottle?' the salesman said."

Though full of spaghetti, Ernie nonetheless had an empty feeling, the same one everyone has when leaving a place like Penn State. Don Klosterman, the Colts' GM, could hear the blues in Ernie's voice on the telephone, and upped the offer from $13,000 to $14,000. "He went to his grave thinking he bought me for a thousand dollars," Accorsi said, "but money had nothing to do with it. I loved Penn State, but I had to go." In years to come, he would wash down many hard decisions with Bolla Valpolicella. "It's good stuff," he said, "imported from Italy."

4

PLAXICO

YOU CAN'T SEE or know anybody in this league at a glance," said Eli Manning, off to the side. He was talking about the wide receiver Plaxico Burress, who came over to the Giants from Pittsburgh before the 2005 season. Plax had a sleepy manner and a penitentiary face. Noting how balletic he was in a basketball sense and how physical he wasn't in the football way of speaking, many of the New York writers considered Burress to be an NBA type out of water. The reporters who were there every day, though, liked him. That is, they appreciated the fact that, in contrast to some other stars, Burress always made himself available at his locker for a few words. A very few words. He didn't give them much. He didn't seem to have that much to give. But they could count on Plaxico not to join the crowd soaking and sulking in the training room.

"Plax is smarter than what you think, or what he shows you," Manning said. "In meetings, he doesn't say a lot. When he does say something, the coaches kind of look at him and wonder if he's taking it in or not. 'Is he half asleep?' 'Is he daydreaming?' But one time I couldn't find—this will sound bad—my playbook. So I grabbed Plax's book off the stool in front of his locker—our lockers are close by—to look up a formation or something. And when I opened it, I couldn't believe my eyes. He had written all of these little notes in the margins—in beautiful handwriting. 'I'm the hot receiver here.' 'I go here.' 'I go there.' 'I do this or that.' 'Somebody else does whatever.' All in perfect penmanship. You know, it shouldn't have shocked me. If no one else knew Plaxico was in tune with

the offense, I did. I knew how hard he worked. But I guess I didn't realize how committed he was to understanding exactly what he has to do
on each play. It's almost like he doesn't want anybody to know he knows,
but he does. As I say, you just can't see a player at a glance."

Catching balls over the middle, the six-foot-five Burress was good at
diving under the wave at the very last instant, so that most of the force
would crash over him instead of into him. But when necessary, he was
willing to go up for balls in traffic and be hit with sledgehammers. He
had courage. "He's a terrific big receiver," Ernie said. "When he became
an unrestricted free agent, we heard that Philadelphia was trying to sign
him. I told Tom Coughlin, 'If we have to defense Terrell Owens *and*
Plaxico Burress twice a year, how much are we going to enjoy that?' Tom
has had trouble with him. Tom keeps trying to change him. I said, 'Tom,
Holy Cross was not one of the schools Plax was considering when he
went to Michigan State, okay? If you don't want to coach these kinds
of kids, then go to Holy Cross.'"

Burress wasn't the renegade he appeared to be, but he had idiosyn-
crasies. "For instance," Ernie said, "he doesn't like being touched. Don't
touch him. Tom made the mistake of patting him once. 'Get your hands
off me!'" Incidentally, Accorsi tended to agree that Plax cut a pro basketball player's sort of figure. "A lot of the stylish athletes in our league,
what you might call the artists, find their role models in the highlight
films of the NBA," Ernie said. "That's just the modern circumstance of
sports. The 'performers,' the Allen Iversons, are their idols. Obviously in
pro football now, pass receivers have become the 'look at me' guys, too.
Terrell Owens. Randy Moss. Chad Johnson. Keyshawn Johnson. [The
humble Art Monks and Paul Warfields and Raymond Berrys and Del
Shofners were all long retired.] But the Steelers didn't get rid of Plaxico
for any reason. They would have loved to have kept him."

If Pittsburgh was going to keep Hines Ward, club president Dan
Rooney didn't want to put all of the team's money into receivers. "When
Plax's contract was almost up," Accorsi said, "I started doing homework
on him. People I trusted there told me he was a good kid, which is

exactly what he is. A little eccentric, a little moody, a little mercurial, but a good kid. We scouted him, watched him, observed him. We knew the thing he was most of all: a dynamic big-play receiver who probably had been underused a little bit in five years with the Steelers. And he had an agent that none of us had ever heard of. So we brought him in here, took him to dinner, hauled Tiki up to my office to help sell him on what a great place this was, blah, blah, blah. [Ironic, having Barber vouch for Coughlin's Giants.] But the agent was an amateur and shooting for a record. Minnesota was their next stop. In free agency, if you have them in your office and let them out, you're going to lose them. But after I'd thrown in the kitchen sink, and the agent still wanted to price others in the market, I decided to put out a statement. I'd never done that before. It wasn't meant as a tactic. I was actually being sincere. But it turned out to be a hell of a tactic. I announced we were no longer interested in Plaxico Burress at any price and he couldn't use our offer as a lever with the Vikings or anybody else. We were out of it."

All general managers say that the only misery worse than a famous agent is an unestablished one who is trying to use a single client to make his name. But, it turned out, Burress had wanted to say yes to New York all along. He fired his man and hired Drew Rosenhaus. "Now there," Accorsi said, "is the definition of mixed emotions. No, Drew's okay. He is what he is. We had to wait out the seventy-two-hour grace period between agents, but then we signed Plax in one hour." That was March 17, 2005, St. Patrick's Day. "Considering all of the big plays he made for us last year," Ernie said, "at just the right times to win games, I wonder if we wouldn't have been eight and eight without him, instead of eleven-five with him."

"Do you know why I wear the number seventeen?" Burress asked, lingering in a film room after everyone else had gone. Seventeen *is* rather an odd number for a receiver.

"No," I replied, "all I know about you is that you don't like to be touched. Ernie said, 'Don't touch him.'"

He laughed uproariously. "I wore eighty in Pittsburgh," Plaxico said, "but I wanted seventeen here because I signed on the seventeenth. That's how much it meant to me to be a New York Giant."

Was it true, as linebacker LaVar Arrington had whispered aside, that Plax had named a son after Eli Manning?

Burress laughed again, this time gently. "No, it's not true," he said. "My son is Elijah for my high school coach."

"My name is Elisha also," Manning said, "but it's spelled differently than Plax's boy. When he told me he just had a son, I asked, 'What's his name?' 'Elijah,' he said, and I puffed my chest out for just a moment. Elijah wasn't named for me, though."

"But he could have been," Plaxico said. Told that a number of 1950s and '60s Giants had christened their children Kyle after the revered receiver Kyle Rote, Burress said, "Someday there could be a lot of little Elis running around here, too. In five years at Pittsburgh, I had four different quarterbacks. This is the first one I'm really coming to know, and who's really coming to know me. We have a long, long way to go, but I think we're going to get there eventually. When Eli reaches his full potential, he's going to be much better than good. He's going to be absolutely great."

Was Plaxico an artist, a performer, a "look at me" guy whose role models could be found in the highlight films of the NBA?

"No, but I have a gift," he said. "The reason I know it's a gift is that I don't always understand it. Sometimes I'll reach out to touch a ball that really isn't catchable, and all of a sudden I've got it in my hands. I don't know how. I wasn't trying to catch it. I couldn't catch it. But I've got it all the same. It's amazing to me sometimes."

Though a little vain about this gift, he still sounded more blessed than boastful. While his skills mystified Plaxico, Plax was the mystery to the Giants fans. Not wanting anyone to know you know is cool, but not wanting anyone to know you care is cold. In professional sports—maybe in every other line of work, too—openly caring about what you do goes a long way with the customers. Especially in sports, it's the all-purpose antidote to venality, cynicism, even money. Fans who had no idea why

Plaxico wore number 17 sized him up as a player who simply didn't care as much about the Giants as they did. If he had opened the book to them and showed them how committed he was to understanding exactly what he has to do on each play, in perfect penmanship, he would have had a better chance to be liked. You just can't see a player at a glance.

Taking their 0–1 record to Philadelphia for a Sunday afternoon game at Lincoln Financial Field, the Giants had the general manager worried. "This is the earliest must-win situation I can ever remember," Accorsi whispered. Coming off an easy victory over Houston, meanwhile, the Eagles were on the muscle and in a bright mood during the pregame warm-ups, grateful to be rid of Terrell Owens and anxious for the subject to change. Philadelphia quarterback Donovan McNabb and New York sack king Michael Strahan wouldn't figure to be buddies. On Michael's long list of celebrity sackees, including Brett Favre, Troy Aikman, Tom Brady, Steve Young, Randall Cunningham, John Elway, Doug Flutie, Dan Marino, and Jim Kelly, Donovan was a clear number one. He had bit the dirt a dozen times, more than anyone else by at least four. But Strahan and McNabb nodded and smiled at each other like the best of friends. "T.O.! T.O.! T.O.!" Strahan sang across the field. "Oh, no! Oh, no! Oh, no!" McNabb sang back.

After kickoff returner Chad Morton got them started on the thirty-three-yard line, the Giants went directly down the field to score.

GIANTS

1-10-G33 Manning passes to Amani Toomer for 9

2-1-G42   Barber runs for –2

3-3-G40   Barber runs for 5

1-10-G45 Manning passes incomplete

2-10-G45 Barber runs for 2

3-8-G47   (shotgun) Manning passes to Burress for 16

1-10-E37 Manning passes to Toomer for 37 and the
    touchdown; Jay Feely's extra point is good

Giants 7, Eagles 0

But, from a much worse starting point, courtesy of that seemingly unavoidable illegal-block-above-the-waist penalty, Philadelphia did the same.

EAGLES

1-10-E8   Brian Westbrook runs for 3

2-7-E11   McNabb passes to L. J. Smith for 30

1-10-E41   Westbrook runs for 0

2-10-E41   McNabb passes incomplete

3-10-E41   (shotgun) McNabb passes to Smith for 24

1-10-G35 McNabb passes to Westbrook for 11

1-10-G24 McNabb passes to Westbrook for 8

2-2-G16   McNabb passes incomplete

3-2-G16   Correll Buckhalter runs for 4

1-10-G12 (shotgun) McNabb passes incomplete

2-10-G12 Westbrook runs for 12 and the touchdown;
    David Akers' extra point is good

Giants 7, Eagles 7

After which the game turned into a romp and a sackfest for the Eagles, who tackled Manning behind the line of scrimmage no fewer than eight times. With less than four minutes to go in the third quarter, New York was losing emphatically, 24–7. "All these sacks," said the right guard, Chris Snee. "I mean, that's embarrassing. I had this talk with myself when we were down by seventeen points. 'We just can't go oh and two. We can't. We can't. We just can't do it.' Maybe, at that exact moment, everybody on the team was having that same talk, you know?"

GIANTS

1-10-G12 (shotgun) Manning passes to Sinorice Moss
    for 5; offside Philadelphia, negating the play

1-5-G17   Barber runs for 4

2-1-G21   Barber runs for 2

1-10-G23 Manning passes to Barber for 10

1-10-G33 Manning sacked for −9

2-19-G24 (shotgun) delay of game, Giants

2-24-G19 (shotgun) Brandon Jacobs runs for 6

3-18-G25 (shotgun) Manning passes to Burress for 20

Third quarter ends

1-10-G45 (shotgun) Barber runs for 5

2-5-G50   Manning passes to Jim Finn for 11 yards

1-10-E39 (shotgun) Manning passes for 23 yards to
   Burress, whose fumble is recovered by Tim Carter in
   the end zone; Jay Feely kicks the extra point

Eagles 24, Giants 14

Afterward, most of the Giants would say this was the play of the game. "Lobster or steak?" Plaxico said with gratitude to Carter, figuring Tim was owed an expensive dinner at the very least. "Don't mention it," Carter replied, grinning. But there were other big plays to come. For instance, with 4:11 on the clock, Eagle running back Westbrook fumbled the ball away to Giants free safety Will Demps.

GIANTS

1-10-E33 (shotgun) Manning passes incomplete

2-10-E33 (shotgun) Manning passes to Toomer for 11 yards

1-10-E22 (shotgun) Manning passes incomplete

2-10-E22 (shotgun) Manning passes to Toomer for 22 and
   the touchdown; Feely kicks the extra point

Eagles 24, Giants 21

When next the Giants had the ball, they had fifty-eight seconds and no time-outs.

GIANTS

1-10-G20 (shotgun) Manning passes to Barber for 8 (:51)

2-2-G28   (shotgun) Manning passes to Toomer for 10 (:35)

1-10-G38 Manning passes to Carter for 22 (:16)

1-10-E40 Manning spikes the ball to stop the clock (:15)

2-10-E40 Manning passes to Jeremy Shockey for 8,
plus a 15-yard personal foul called on Eagles defensive
end Trent Cole (:10)

Maybe those penalty yards were the biggest in the game. Offensive right tackle Kareem McKenzie thought so. "I was actually helping Cole up," he said, "when he tried to kick me somewhere. He missed what he was aiming for. You can tell he doesn't play darts."

1-10-E17 Feely kicks 35-yard field goal
Eagles 24, Giants 24

On the Giants' second possession in overtime, they began the game's final drive on their own fifteen.

GIANTS

1-10-G15 Barber runs for 9

2-1-G24   (shotgun) Barber runs for 7

1-10-G31 (shotgun) Manning passes to Toomer for 10

2-1-G40   (shotgun) Manning passes to Toomer for 5

1-10-G45 Barber runs for 0

2-10-G45 (shotgun) Manning passes to Visanthe
Shiancoe for 9

3-1-E46   Barber runs for 4

1-10-E42 Barber runs for 5

2-5-E37   Manning passes to Toomer for 7

1-10-E30 Jacobs runs for 9

2-1-E21   Jacobs runs for 6

Holding penalty on Carter

2-5-E25   Barber runs for −1

3-6-E26   False start, center Shaun O'Hara
3-11-E31 (shotgun) Manning passes to Burress for 31
    and the winning touchdown
Giants 30, Eagles 24

Going for the ninth sack with a sellout blitz, the Eagles left Plaxico in the solitary custody of cornerback Sheldon Brown, seven inches shorter. Manning had just enough time and touch to throw a rainbow into the left corner of the end zone. Toomer, the regal presence on the team, who caught twelve passes for 137 yards and two touchdowns, didn't see Plaxico's winning catch. "Cutting across the middle on that last play," Amani said, "I thought, 'I'm open! I'm open! I'm open!' Then my legs told me, 'No, you're not,' and I just keeled over. As the celebration was going on, I looked at our sideline and said, 'Could somebody please come get me?'" Four bags of fluid were emptied into Toomer's veins before he was even bendable enough to take off his uniform. In fact, he couldn't remove it. That was done for him.

Barber held his left arm as if it were broken; it wasn't. Between Shockey and Snee, they totaled two working limbs, finding it convenient, therefore, to use each other for crutches. "I never felt better," Shockey said. Everybody in the room was bruised, exhausted, and rejuvenated. "That one was fun," Coughlin said, "but the most important game is the next game."

In the first game, against the Colts, the Giants played well enough to win, and didn't; in the second game, against the Eagles, they played poorly enough to lose, and didn't. Against Philadelphia, Manning passed for 371 yards and three touchdowns; McNabb threw for 350 yards and two touchdowns. Both Philly and New York were now 1 and 1.

"Are you shocked that you won?" a Philadelphia writer asked left offensive tackle Luke Petitgout. "Am I shocked?" Luke said, balancing his chin on his fist like Rodin's *Thinker*. "You're in the wrong locker room, buddy. If you're looking for shock, you'll find it next door."

"Not in a million years," veteran middle linebacker Jeremiah Trotter was muttering next door. "Not in a million years." "We let them hang around," McNabb said with a shrug. "That's on us. It's our own fault."

When the field was otherwise empty, Accorsi walked out on it alone to take a last sentimental tour of the battlefield and bid what he hoped was a final competitive farewell to Philadelphia, where he had been a sportswriter once, where Hershey's old team (but never his) resided. "I always hated the Eagles, I don't know why, since I was ten," Ernie said. "Maybe I tended to root against teams that everyone around me was rooting for. I rooted against Notre Dame that way."

Accorsi was a Rams fan first. "I liked their helmets," he said. When the Rams dropped by Hershey in 1952, Ernie and his cousin Gary Ponzoli trailed the holy-rolling fullback "Deacon" Dan Towler all over town. Towler promised them each a team picture but couldn't talk the PR director (Pete Rozelle) out of more than one. So they had to share it. "We passed it back and forth, month to month," Ernie said, "until we discovered girls." Next he became a Colts fan, "and I sort of liked the Giants, too," he said. "But I had a reason to dislike the Eagles in Hershey. They were so raucous, in that little town. They just took it over, [lineman] Bucko Kilroy and that crowd. I have nothing against [owner Jeffrey] Lurie and [president Joe] Banner—they're nice people. And Andy Reid is a hell of a coach. Before the game, I shook his hand and said, 'If this is the last one in Philly, it's been great competing against you.' He says, 'Are you going back to Hershey? You can come to our games all the time.' 'No,' I say, 'I'll be going to Giants games, thank you.' I hope this is my last trip here. I hope they miss the play-offs. I hope we make them."

It didn't occur to him that they both might make the play-offs and meet again at this same spot in January.

5

THE BALTIMORE COLTS:

DRAFTING JOHN ELWAY

THE BALTIMORE COLTS belonged to a charming rogue named Carroll Rosenbloom, who inherited a dungarees factory from his father and turned it into a hot moneymaking property—by torching the place, his sister alleged. In the late 1950s, with the help of Johnny Unitas, Rosenbloom led the National Football League into the new age. Around that time, with the help of Meyer Lansky, he bet on Fulgencio Batista against Fidel Castro and gave the points. In the early 1970s, with the help of Robert Irsay, he swapped the Colts straight up for the Los Angeles Rams, avoiding those nettlesome capital gains taxes that normally applied when property acquired for $25,000 was unloaded for many millions. In the late 1970s, Rosenbloom either was murdered off Golden Beach near Miami or became the best swimmer in the history of the NFL ever to drown accidentally.

Rosenbloom's general manager in 1970 was another colorful scoundrel, Don Klosterman, a dashing former quarterback at Loyola University in Los Angeles, and a debonair man about many towns across California, Texas, and New York. Though Klosterman was drafted in the third round by the Cleveland Browns, he had a good deal more fun playing for the Calgary Stampeders of the Canadian Football League, after which a nearly fatal skiing accident left him with a pronounced limp. As Accorsi finally touched down in his first front office, Klosterman had just taken over the GM post from Harry Hulmes, an old shoe who probably had the finest won-lost record (32–7–3) of anyone ever pushed out of the job. But, unlike Klosterman, Harry never had an actress on his arm, and Rosenbloom decided, "I want a GM who dazzles people." Klosterman went by "Duke," the "Duke of Marina Del Rey," or the "Duke of Dining Out." In addition, he was a hell of a football scout.

"I was scared of Duke, he was jazzy and slick," Ernie said. "I'd never seen anything like him. As I was pulling away from Penn State, Paterno gave me a pep talk. Here I am, moving out of this tower of morality into this den of thieves, and Joe tells me, 'You're swimming with the real sharks now, Ernie. If you try to play their game, you'll be eaten alive. Just be the way you are. Vince Lombardi and Art Rooney prove that you don't have to join 'em to beat 'em. And don't ever forget, these people are just as afraid of us as we are of them'—isn't that a great line? 'They can't handle honesty and integrity, either. That's not the game they play. Play your own game, Ernie. You can be successful playing your own game.'"

The first new colleague who walked up to Accorsi in the Colts' office, sticking out his hand, was player personnel director Upton Bell, son of the 1950s NFL commissioner Bert Bell. "He looked harried, he was a bit disheveled," Ernie said. He was wearing Columbo's raincoat. "His left arm was wrapped around a stack of newspapers. 'I'm Upton Bell,' he says. 'Welcome to the Colts. Nobody in this league has any balls.' And then he walks out."

The second time Accorsi bumped into Uppie, Ernie had his son Mike with him. "That little boy there," Bell said without smiling, "either has a quick release right now or he doesn't. He can either hit major league pitching right now or he never will. His feet have to be quick enough to pass-block. Right now! Okay? Or it's too late for him." And he raced off again.

Another member of the staff, a fellow $14,000 employee, was a large and bespectacled ex-lineman from Bucknell (he looked like a snowman), George Young. Young's eyesight was so feeble that, in the era of night games played under dim lights with white footballs, he was known for once pouncing on and "recovering" a white helmet that had flown off someone's head. George made the equally unusual jump to the NFL from high school football coach and history teacher after Baltimore head coach Don Shula hired him on a temp basis to grade an overflow of college films. More than impressed, Shula was astounded by the quality both of George's draft book and of his penmanship—Palmer method. That year, Ernie's first, Young would make another uncommon leap, from Bell's assistant to offensive line coach for the Colts in Super Bowl V. But, like Accorsi, George was really a GM-in-waiting. Both of them in turn would come to hold that title with the New York Giants.

"Did you go to readin' and writin' school?" George asked Ernie slyly when they met.

"'I went to Wake Forest,' I told him, 'okay?'"

But it didn't take even a full day for the ice to melt. That night, they bumped into each other at a diner and talked for several hours.

"More than anybody," Accorsi said, "he picked up where George Welsh left off. Young taught me. My office was in the back of that wooden firetrap, and his office was on the third floor—the attic. At the close of each day, I could hear his two hundred and ninety pounds shuffling down the stairs. He'd drop into a chair in front of my desk and just start lecturing. That was my graduate school." "Do we always have to throw long and run short?" Young would say in his high-pitched, exasperated-sounding voice. "Is there something wrong with throwing short and running long?" Football was a simple game to both Georges, Welsh and Young. "Young made me read an Alonzo Stagg book," Ernie said, "*Stagg's University*, about the University of Chicago. Knute Rockne once said, 'Stagg has tried everything that's ever been tried and ever will be tried in a football game, and the rest of us just keep recycling it.'" Out of the blue, Young might shout down from the attic, "Stagg put in the shotgun formation, for crying out loud!"

Ernie had his public relations work cut out for him, trying to make Rosenbloom and Klosterman seem like just folks to Baltimoreans. "These fuckin' people, they hate me," Klosterman told him. "Why do they hate me?" "Because you're a silk suit," Ernie answered in a perfectly concise sentence. Bell said, "What I loved most of all about Ernie, from the very first moment I saw him, was the fact that he always gave you his opinion with the bark on, whether you liked it or not. He wasn't afraid of Rosenbloom, either. Ernie figured out right away that the trick with Carroll was to try to absorb from him a little bit at a time—his brilliance—and then get the fuck away from him as fast as you can. Carroll was kind of a genius, but he trafficked in weaknesses instead of strengths. Once he knew somebody's weakness, he knew exactly how to deal with them. How to control them. Rosenbloom was always sizing up your weaknesses. Ernie was always sizing up your strengths."

To Accorsi, the football part was the authentic pleasure of the job, and his information had been correct. Though his title said public relations, he was included in the football. Just five people scouted for the Colts: Bell, Young, Accorsi, Dick Szymanski, and Fred Schubach. Szymanski—Sizzy—had been the second in a long gray line of centers for Johnny U, who, though his knees practically bent both ways, was still trudging along for Baltimore in his fifteenth NFL season; Schubach was a second-generation equipment manager. "Uppie and I went together to a West Virginia game," Accorsi said. "'Okay,' he tells me, 'I'm here to look at Dale Farley, a linebacker. I'm not going to say a word. You watch him, too, and anyone else who catches your eye, and write out a report when we get back. We'll go over it together.'" Bell looked at football as "a game of explosions" in which the basic skill was "the ability to make a quick decision." Through the eyes of Uppie and the others, Ernie started to see. "The Duke told me early on, 'Do not evaluate a quarterback the way you evaluate the other twenty-one positions. They're playing a different sport. With a quarterback, it's the things you can't put down on paper that make all the difference.'"

After history's second *Monday Night Football* game, ABC broadcasters Howard Cosell, Don Meredith, and Keith Jackson attended an elegant cocktail party at Klosterman's apartment, and Ernie was thrilled to be included. "Even though the Duke did kind of turn me into a waiter," he said. As Bell recalled, "I don't think Ernie ever said to the Duke, or to me, or to anyone, that he wanted to be a general manager. He didn't advertise himself that way. Do you know the book *What Makes Sammy Run?*, Budd Schulberg's book? Ernie wasn't Sammy Glick. Ernie was his own completely original character, like nobody else. He just *was* a GM. Later, when I became the GM for New England, I asked permission to talk to Ernie about being my assistant—twice. Rosenbloom said no both times. I'm going to say I was probably the first personnel guy to mount little nameplates of rosters and prospects all over the walls—not just my office walls, all of the walls upstairs. And it seemed that every time I came to work, there was Ernie looking up and down those charts."

"Hello, I'm John Unitas," the Colts quarterback said to Accorsi, as if an introduction were required. "I don't need a program to know who you are," Ernie thought. They became lifelong friends, fellow conspirators. Two years later, as Unitas stood at a Colts locker for the final time, Accorsi came around to collect John's last game jersey for the Pro Football Hall of Fame. Pulling the number 19 over his head, Unitas handed it to Ernie and said, "Here, I don't want you to give it to them." "What?" "I'll get them another one. One that I wore. They won't know the difference. I want you to have this one."

"My first year with the Colts," Accorsi said, "Klosterman made two important trades, both with Pittsburgh. First he traded running back Preston Pearson and defensive back Ocie Austin for linebacker Ray May. I always thought this deal cost Mike Curtis the Hall of Fame, because Curtis was moved to middle linebacker from left linebacker, where he had been making Pro Bowls. We had the Stork [Ted Hendricks] on the other side. Then, in an exchange of receivers, Klosterman gave up Willie Richardson for Roy Jefferson. I'll tell you what, we wouldn't have won the Super Bowl that year without Jefferson. Duke was great at the big picture. He just stood up in the office one day and said, 'We don't have a big-time receiver here. Let's go get Jefferson.'"

Coming off a spitting incident with the Pittsburgh writers, the unsanitary Jefferson had a reputation for belligerence that wasn't helped by the fact that he showed up in Baltimore wearing a German

World War II helmet. Like most African Americans, Roy was not deeply or philosophically attached to the Third Reich. He just liked the way the hat rode on his head. That first morning, as assistant coach Dick Bielski sought to time Jefferson in the forty-yard dash, Roy told Bielski to go fuck himself. This was a dangerous thing to say to Bielski, an old Philadelphia Eagle still in the NFL record book for catching a half-yard touchdown pass from a half-pint quarterback, Eddie LeBaron. But Colts tight end John Mackey interceded before any bones were broken. "Room Jefferson with me," Mackey whispered to Ernie. "I'll show him how we do things around here." Thereafter, through the years, Accorsi would deliver many a problematic newcomer into the care of an old pro.

"Roy was great for us," Ernie said, "but he never stopped being a little peculiar. In the clubhouse one day, he was war-dancing around the lockers naked, patting his hand to his mouth and chanting like an Apache Indian. Unitas just sat there with a wry smile on his face. John actually liked him. 'What do you see in this guy?' I whispered. 'He blocks,' Unitas answered [typically]. 'I don't care how he dresses, I don't care what he sings, as long as the son of a bitch blocks.'" Jefferson also caught three passes, including an acrobatic twenty-three-yarder, that were necessary to the Colts' 16–13 victory over Dallas in the Super Bowl.

In 1972, Rosenbloom arranged for Robert Irsay to buy the Rams, then traded him straight up for the Colts. Klosterman accompanied Carroll to L.A., as Irsay replaced the Duke with Joe Thomas, an early-day Colts assistant coach who had brokered the curious Rosenbloom-Irsay shell game that led inexorably to the franchise being moved from Baltimore to Indianapolis. Joe was another evil genius. Being the only bachelor on the Baltimore coaching staff in 1954, Thomas had been asked to stay over on the West Coast at the season's conclusion to scout college prospects through Christmas and New Year's. Come the first round of the draft, he talked the team out of Auburn quarterback Bobby Freeman or Georgia Tech linebacker Larry Morris and into Wisconsin fullback Alan "the Horse" Ameche. In the matter of a quarterback, Thomas pushed for George Shaw of Oregon or Ralph Guglielmi of Notre Dame. It was on Ameche and Shaw that the Colts' foundation was built.

Later, employed by the expansion team about to be born in Minnesota, Thomas asked Paul Brown for permission to hang around the Cleveland Browns just to see how the mundane details of a football franchise could be handled with grace. A sucker for anybody who genuflected in front of him this way, Brown let the fox inside the henhouse, and Joe absconded with placekicker Fred Cox—Lou "the Toe" Groza's secret understudy—and every other buried body on the premises. Wherever Thomas went, he was uncannily prescient and universally despised. While scouting for the Dolphins in Miami, he engaged in a high-decibel screaming match with owner Joe Robbie, who was infatuated with the Heisman Trophy–winning quarterback from the University of Florida, Steve Spurrier. Thomas preferred Purdue's Bob Griese. In the first round, Spurrier went third to San Francisco, Griese fourth to the Dolphins. "Joe picked Bert Jones for us, too," Ernie said, but as instructive as it was to be around this gifted judge of livestock, Thomas represented a challenge to a PR man. Though Charlie Finley and Alvin Dark were pretty good on the baseball side, Irsay and Thomas might have been the all-time headline waiting to happen.

In an especially drunken moment, Irsay fired head coach Howard Schnellenberger and, without consulting Thomas, named Joe his successor. "The players went crazy," Ernie said. "Joe told them, 'Hold it! Hold it! Hold it! Everybody calm down. I never wanted this to happen!' 'The hell you didn't,' Curtis said, 'you've been fueling this fire all season long.' 'You shut up!' Thomas said. 'Fuck you, I'm not shutting up,' Curtis said." A more erudite player, center Bill Curry, told Thomas flatly, "You're no football coach, Joe."

Thomas went on to prove that in the last eleven games of the season, nine of them losses. The signature moment came when halfback Don McCauley was dispatched from the bench into the huddle to tell quarterback Jones, "Thomas says to run that thing we run where we pitch the ball." As Ernie said with a sigh, "Joe didn't even know the names of the plays. But then Ted Marchibroda came in as head coach and the ship was pretty quickly righted."

For young executives in the NFL, a common path to advancement was to serve a kind of fellowship in the league's New York office. Commissioner Pete Rozelle brought them in for polishing, and then usually sent them straight back. "There were six of us when I was there," Ernie said. "Only one stayed." But all the while he was at finishing school, Accorsi never got off the phone with Thomas. "Joe would call me up to say, 'Goddamn it, we're winning the division and I'm not receiving any credit. Teddy's getting all of the credit.' I said, 'Joe, Casey Stengel got all of the credit with the New York Yankees, but George Weiss is right there in the Hall of Fame with him. Relax. You're going to be named executive of the year.' 'Yeah, but that little son of a bitch . . . and when's the last time anybody wrote anything nice about me?' I said, 'Do you know what your problem is, Joe? You've got Harry Truman's balls and Lyndon Johnson's skin.' "

Disliking the neutrality of the league office ("I'd be at the game of the week—Redskins-Cowboys—and it didn't mean a thing to me"), Accorsi was glad to return to the competitive life in Baltimore, where in 1982, after a term as assistant GM behind the well-meaning but overmatched Szymanski, Ernie ascended to the job of his dreams. "I started learning the money side," he said. "We had a linebacker named Stan White, undersized but smart, pretty good—he could see the ball and intercept it—but he was just six foot even. Stan had been offered twenty thousand and was holding out for twenty-five. That's how long ago this was. I'm having a conversation with his wife, Patty, who tells me, 'You don't know what it's like trying to raise two kids on twenty thousand dollars a year.' I say, 'You're a hundred percent right, Patty, but I do know what it's like trying to raise three kids on fifteen thousand dollars a year.' "

The money in sports would multiply like sorcerer's brooms, but the insular life of the pro athlete never changed. Years later, Giants defensive end Michael Strahan would look Accorsi hard in the eye and say without laughing, "Ernie, I don't mean to be disrespectful to the organization, but your offer of an eleven-million-dollar signing bonus doesn't really excite me." When Accorsi passed that tidbit on to Wellington Mara, the Giants' owner said, "If he had to *pay* the eleven million dollars, I'll bet it would excite him." "And just think," Ernie said, "after Mickey Mantle won the Triple Crown in fifty-six, George Weiss mailed him a contract with no raise."

Joe Thomas ended up in San Francisco, where, losing his touch, he gave away a deplorable slice of the 49ers' future for the broken-down remains of O. J. Simpson. "When Eddie DeBartolo called me at Stanford," Bill Walsh said, "and asked if I wanted to coach the 49ers, the first thing I had to know was, 'Will Joe Thomas be the GM?' I guess I asked it in such a way that he got what I was saying. 'No, not if you don't want him to be,' he said. 'Do you have somebody else in mind?'" As a matter of fact, Bill did—Accorsi.

"Bill and I talked for about four hours," Ernie said, "and when I came out of that room, my head was spinning. This guy was amazingly smart. It only began with football. But I had three kids—ten, nine, and five—and I didn't want to bring them up in California. Not that I thought the Bay Area was going to contaminate them or anything. I just figured they might wind up going to school out there and eventually living on the West Coast. I didn't want to spend my old age on an airplane, because I knew I'd end up in the East. Ironically enough, one of my sons now lives in San Jose."

Walsh said, "I think the truth was just that Ernie had started out to be a general manager in Baltimore, and he happens to be a guy who finishes what he starts." When Walsh was unable to attract any of the comers on his list—"I couldn't sell George Young, either"—Bill became his own GM in San Francisco. "A GM has to look to next month and next year and five years from now when everybody else is looking to Sunday," he said. "Everybody else is focused on one thing. The GM has to see everything. There probably are as many different kinds of general managers as there are owners, but all of the good GMs have a panoramic vision. When I went to San Francisco, I was confident about the on-the-field part. The other stuff scared the hell out of me." Not so long ago, Accorsi told him, "You were one of the best GMs of all time, Bill. Of course, you had one of the best coaches working for you—yourself."

Ernie inherited his first head coach, Frank Kush, who had hammered out a reputation for physical toughness ("when Kush comes to shove") at Arizona State, where a Sun Devils punter once sued the university for $1 million, alleging Kush socked him. In the coaching fraternity, Frank was not what you would call beloved, and one of the leaders among those who had no use for him was Jack Elway of San Jose State, whose son John played quarterback for Stanford.

"Kush wasn't nearly the maniac he was made out to be," Ernie said. "He was a better guy than he seemed. And he wasn't really all that tough, I didn't think. We draft this kid Holden Smith, a receiver from Cal, in the eleventh round. But he doesn't sign. He goes and plays baseball. A year later, he calls us back, and this time he signs with us, even though he doesn't have to. He's a free agent. Well, it turns out, Holden's a lot better than we thought—in fact, he has all of the talent in the world. Right away, he catches a couple of touchdown passes in the first exhibition game against the Vikings and I'm thinking we may have caught lightning in a bottle. But he's an independent thinker, typical Berkeley guy, and the first time Kush and he clash, Frank cuts him. In the dining hall, Smith loads up a tray of food, walks over to Kush's table, and drops it on his head. Now Frank and I are walking outside, and the food is still dripping down his face, and into his ears, and he asks me if I wouldn't mind switching rooms with him that night. He was afraid Holden might come get him in his sleep. I thought, 'This is the tough guy?' 'No trade,' I said."

Ernie and the Colts owned the top pick in the 1983 draft, and the obvious choice was John Elway. "I went to scout the East-West game," Accorsi said. "Elway was the quarterback of the West team, and his father was the coach. I had pretty much been sold on one pass John completed against Ohio State, where he threw across the field for a touchdown—

unbelievable. Now, Freddie Schubach and I are watching him at practice. Kush is supposed to be there, too, but we don't know where he is. Elway takes the snap, rolls to his right. The receiver is running down the sideline until he looks to be out of range. Elway goes, whoosh, flat-footed. Throws this missile seventy-five yards diagonally across the field. I said to Schubach, 'I have to get back to Baltimore, but if Frank shows, tell him we're picking this guy, no arguments. I've never seen a throw like that in my life.'"

Elway publicly swore he would never play for Baltimore (just as Jack Elway privately swore that his son would never play for Kush). Threatening to jilt football for baseball, John made a flourish out of signing a minor league contract with George Steinbrenner and the New York Yankees. "Do you remember Bob Nieman?" Accorsi asked. Sure, he was a left fielder with the Orioles in the fifties, number 4. "Nieman was the Yankees bird dog who scouted Elway. Bob's dead now, but if Steinbrenner finds out he slipped me his report, George will probably dig him up and fire him. I just wanted to know how serious this baseball threat was. Truth be told, Nieman didn't believe there was any way in the world that Elway would ever hit Triple-A pitching, let alone major leaguers. But that wasn't the worst of it. The line in Nieman's report that really jumped out at you was 'Elway has just an average arm.' Baseball and football arms are two different things, evidently. Anyway, that told me the baseball threat was baloney. I knew what I faced now."

With one exception, Baltimore's sportswriters were urging the team not to risk throwing away its number one pick on Elway. Only Al Goldstein of the morning *Sun* pushed for the Stanford quarterback, under the headline "Dare to Be Great." "So I come into work," Ernie said, "it's dark, and the first thing I see is 'Dare to Be Great.' That did it. Goldie screwed up my life. Nah, I was going to pick Elway, no matter what anybody said." When Accorsi reached his office, he found Irsay at the general manager's desk, working the phones personally. "He's taken over the entire situation, wheelin' and dealin', and I'm sitting on the couch in my own office. All I can think of is how Pittsburgh let Unitas get away forever. The funny thing is, Unitas thought I should take Dan Marino. There were a lot of whispers around Marino at the time, all of which turned out to be nothing. 'You're just saying Marino because he's a western Pennsylvanian,' I told Unitas. 'I'm just saying Marino,' John said, 'because he's the best passer of the lot.' It's not that I didn't love Marino, too, but I thought Elway was that much better. Well, look at the record. He was."

Patriots GM Chuckie Sullivan was on the phone with Irsay. "'Just a second, Chuckie,' Irsay says, putting his hand over the phone and turning to me. 'How about [All-Pro tackle] John Hannah?' 'And what?' I said. 'Hang up on him!'

"Irsay tells me, 'Go get the coach.' So I leave him babbling away with Sullivan and I go to Kush's office. 'Frank, he's talking about trading the pick for John Hannah. We have to stick together now. I may have to quit. We both may have to quit.' 'I'm with you, boss,' he says.

"But as we're walking into my office, Irsay calls out, 'Coach! How would you like to have John Hannah?' 'Love to, boss!' Frank says. That's how long it took for him to throw in his jock strap. I look at Kush like, if my eyes were machine gun bullets, he'd have thirty-seven holes in his body. So I say to Irsay, 'Would you please tell Sullivan you'll get back to him.' I didn't want anyone listening in as I quit.

"'If you trade him,' I say to Irsay, 'there are going to be two press conferences. You're going to announce the trade, and I'm going to announce my resignation.' The only thing I had going for me was he knew that people in the city and the media liked me. I had some capital in the bank. And he was already being lambasted as it was. Anyway, I didn't know why, but he blinked. After one more call, I took back my office. The last caller was [San Diego owner] Gene Klein, God rest his soul, the son of a bitch. 'Tell him to go to hell!' I told Irsay, and Bob finally surrendered. 'All right, do what you want to do,' he said. Exactly one second after seven A.M., the start of the draft, I pick Elway. Someone in the room screams, 'It's Jay Berwanger all over again!'"

Berwanger of the University of Chicago, the first Heisman Trophy winner, was chosen number one by Philadelphia in the inaugural NFL draft of 1936. The Eagles promptly traded his rights to Chicago. Unable to coax enough money out of George Halas, Berwanger accepted a job as a foam rubber salesman instead and never played in the pros. "In the next instant," Ernie said, "Elway has that famous press conference with his mop hair, demoralized all to pieces by being the number one pick— like we were all supposed to do everything to make him happy and to hell with the Baltimore Colts. Who's looking out for the Baltimore Colts? That night, Howard Cosell and Unitas went on *Nightline* to debate the pick. John never mentioned Marino. He just wondered who is this kid who is too good to play quarterback for the Baltimore Colts?"

Returning from the press conference to his office, Accorsi was stopped in the hallway by a secretary with an index finger pressed to her lips. "Irsay and his moneyman, Michael Chernoff, are talking," Ernie said. "Chernoff is saying, 'He doesn't have the right, you should have stopped him. Elway is going to cost us five million dollars. We can't afford five million dollars.' 'Mike, Mike,' Irsay says, 'let Ernie have his moment. We can do what we want later.'"

Accorsi said, "Here's where I made my big mistake. That Friday night, Elway called me up. 'Look,' he says, 'I'd rather play football. Let's wait until everything calms down, and then we'll talk about it.' He wouldn't have had any choice but to play for us. But, stupidly, I tell Irsay about the call, and that same night he deals Elway to Denver for quarterback Mark Herrmann, tackle Chris Hinton, a number one in the next draft, and a pair of freakin' preseason games. Because we weren't drawing in the preseason, he traded Elway for two $250,000 paydays! I found out about the deal while watching a basketball game on TV. A streamer came across the screen. So I called Kush. 'Are you watching the NBA?' 'I never watch the NBA,' he said. 'Well maybe you ought to put it on, Frank, because they've just traded your quarterback.'"

The moment for quitting had passed. The moment for insurrection was near. "The final week of the eighty-three season," Ernie said, "I called Pete Rozelle and asked if I could come to New York and see him the Monday after the game. Sitting in his office, I told him the franchise was in deep trouble, that Irsay was going to try to move the team, that I had studied the constitution and bylaws, and that there were provisions that covered suspending him for his actions and saving this franchise for Baltimore. This was much more than a general manager trying to do what was right for his franchise. This was a man fighting for his boyhood dream, the Baltimore Colts. But there wasn't much Pete could do, and I knew it. I just had to play that hand."

Accorsi went back to Baltimore and resigned. "Can we talk about this?" Irsay asked. "Are you serious?" Accorsi replied. "You have to give me a reason," the owner said. Two words were enough for that: John Elway. But, just to be perverse, Ernie said, "Michael Chernoff." Two months later, Accorsi was in Cleveland serving Art Modell first as assistant to the president and then as executive vice president for football operations. Both job titles were synonyms for general manager. The duties were the same, but Art liked to think of himself as his own GM.

About ten o'clock on a lonely March night at a Cleveland Marriott, the phone rang. It was an old video cameraman for the Colts, Art Eich. "They're moving the club," he told Accorsi. "I'm standing guard on my equipment . . . they're not stealing this equipment, it's mine. But they're taking everything else." Ernie telephoned a friend whose apartment overlooked the training facility in Owings Mills, Maryland. " 'Do me a favor,' I said. 'Take a look out your window.' " Blinking through the fog and the snow was a convoy of tractor-trailers. "From having done that stint in the league office," Accorsi said, "I had Rozelle's private home number that he answered no matter what. The phone rings. I say, 'Pete, this is Ernie, I'm really sorry to call you so late.' 'That's okay, Ernie, what's up?' 'Have you heard anything about Baltimore?' 'No.' 'They're moving tonight.' 'They are?' 'Right now.' Pete was stunned and silent. He didn't know. He absolutely didn't know. I thought to myself, 'Well, I told you all this three months ago.' But I didn't say it."

An eminent domain bill had been proposed in the state senate that afternoon, and Irsay and Chernoff were fleeing to Indianapolis while the fleeing was good. "Instead of Route 70," Accorsi said, "the normal way to drive to Indy, they took 81, the quickest way to a state line. They used Virginia instead of Maryland movers, too. They didn't miss a trick."

To this day, Accorsi remains convinced that "if Elway had been signed, everything would have been different. There would have been an excitement around the city of Baltimore. It would have translated into season ticket sales. It might even have changed the political climate around a new stadium." If Accorsi and Elway had spoken a second time on the telephone, Ernie would have told John that someone else had hired Kush, that Ernie certainly wasn't married to Frank.

"The Baltimore Colts," Accorsi said, "didn't have to die."

6

THE CLEVELAND BROWNS:

STEALING BERNIE KOSAR

THINKING QUARTERBACK AND coach—"I'm always thinking quarterback and coach"—Ernie began his new life in Cleveland convinced that with head coach Sam Rutigliano and quarterback Paul McDonald, the Browns were 0 for 2. "I'd seen plenty of McDonald in college. Southern Cal. They won a national championship. He was a soft, nice, methodical player—great guy. But he had a big windup. A left-hander with a big windup. That's okay if you're Warren Spahn, but NFL defensive backs are way too fast for that. So, we're in the preseason. We're going terrible, but it's only preseason—we're at Anaheim, playing the Rams. The game is over, and as Art would do, he held a committee meeting. He'd go around the room. When he gets to me, I say simply, 'We got no chance with this quarterback.'

"'Don't tell me that!' Art yells.

"Rutigliano had just talked him out of Brian Sipe and into McDonald. They gave McDonald all of the money and let Sipe go to the USFL. Brian had put together some good years in Cleveland. He was kind of a folk hero there. 'Okay, I won't say it,' I said, 'but we'll never win with this quarterback.' Well, we start one and seven, McDonald is terrible, and the seventh loss is to Cincinnati—Paul Brown, Modell's nemesis—and, on an impulse, Art fires Sam. 'You couldn't wait until the end of the season?' I said. Rutigliano blames me, of course. Art says, 'I want you to go to Penn State and see if Paterno is interested in the job.' 'Art, he's married to Penn State. Even if the NFL could dynamite him out of that place, which it can't, he'd never choose Cleveland. Green Bay, maybe, because of Lombardi and history, or the New York Giants. Can we be reasonable here? Let's talk about Marty Schottenheimer.' "

"I was the defensive coordinator," Schottenheimer said. "When I got the call from Art to come to his home, my first thought was that he was going to fire me. But he mentioned that Ernie was there with him, and I knew Ernie believed I could be a head coach in this league. He had told me so. And I sort of had an inkling about what was coming." When Modell informed Schottenheimer that Sam was out and offered him the head job on an interim basis, Marty was ready.

" 'I appreciate it,' I said, 'but I have no interest in taking the job on an interim basis. An interim coach has no clout, no authority. The players will say to themselves, 'I don't have to be accountable to this guy.' Art and Ernie excused themselves. They left me sitting there alone for quite a while, and I guessed that Ernie was trying to talk him into me. 'Okay,' Art said when they returned, 'we'll give you a contract for the rest of this year and two years more.' That's how my head coaching career began." Ernie said, "All I kept telling Art was, 'He ain't bluffin'.' By the end of that season, Marty and I had started to mesh."

The Browns won four more games, raising their record to 5–11. "It's around Thanksgiving," Accorsi said, "and here comes another committee meeting. I just repeat, 'We'd better get a quarterback around here.' I'm starting to convince Art, who turns to Marty and asks, 'What do you think?' 'Well,' he says, 'I think we can win with Paul if we surround him with the proper supporting cast.' I say, 'Who, for example? The AFC Pro Bowl team?' "

In the next instant, Doug Flutie of Boston College completed the all-time Hail Mary pass to beat the University of Miami, and Ernie's telephone rang. Of course it was Modell. "I want that kid!" he shouted. It's funny, but Ernie wanted the younger kid on the other side of the field, who passed for 447 yards in the loss. Earlier, on his way to a Browns game in Buffalo, Accorsi had stopped off at Penn State to have a firsthand look at Flutie, the five-foot-nine wonder. As a sophomore and junior, Doug had passed for 520 and 380 yards against the Nittany Lions. Now he added his own 447-yard day to total 1,347—more than three-quarters of a mile against Paterno alone. "After the game," Ernie said, "it took me about fifteen minutes to go down the press box elevator, because there was such a long line, and the public address announcer needed just about that long to recite all of the records Flutie had broken. But BC lost. Every time the game was on the line, he got blitzed up the middle. As incredible a college player as Flutie was, he wasn't my kind of pro quarterback. I told Art, 'Bernie Kosar is the guy. He's just a sophomore but he might be worth waiting for. Maybe we could make a stopgap trade in the meantime.' Of course, I didn't know yet that there was a way to get Kosar sooner."

"Look," Kosar said, "I realize that there are more important things in life than football. But when I played, nothing was more important to me. If a big game was coming up, nothing—not my father, who I love, not my family, not curing cancer, not world peace—meant more to me than that game. I'm sorry."

He relished being the quarterback of the Hurricanes, who by stopping a two-point conversion when a kick would have meant a tie pulled off a grand upset against Nebraska in 1983 to bag a national championship. Eligible to play two more years of college football, Kosar hoped to collect another trophy, from the favorite's position this time. But his dad wanted him to hurry up and turn pro. "If you knew my father," he said, "he's the type of guy who always has to have his own way—with me. I'm never right, and he's never wrong."

The Kosars lived near Youngstown, Ohio, where, Bernie said, "I was the first guy in my family not to work for U.S. Steel." The mills were closing, the industry was dying, unemployment was out of control, "and my dad," he said, "didn't have a very good work situation. I kept hearing 'You need to go pro, you need to go pro.' That drumbeat didn't leave me a lot of choices. I said, 'Dad, I really, really love playing football at Miami. We could win another championship.' But he used the old father guilt on me, and I was finished. The team we had coming back was absolutely loaded. It turned out they lost to Penn State in the Fiesta Bowl, with Vinny Testaverde at quarterback."

Against all percentages, Kosar's father found a loophole completely unknown to the ribbon clerks of the NFL. Provided he had already earned his degree, a sophomore could be eligible to play in the league. How often had that situation come up? And there was a second section to the Kosar puzzle. This was the part assembled by Accorsi. "I had always taken extra credits," Bernie said, "even in the summer. And instead of electing scuba diving, like a lot of football players at Miami, I took real courses—finance and economics. I was so far ahead that, if I wanted to, I could graduate in July."

Buffalo held the first pick in the draft and, because the USFL was still in competition, the Bills were already in the process of signing defensive end Bruce Smith. Houston owned the second choice. As Ernie said, "The word was going around that Bernie, his father, and his agent, a Youngstown dentist named John Geletka, had found a way for him to come out early. And, believe it or not, his preference would be to play for the team he had always rooted for, the Browns. So I'm poring over the NFL constitution and the bylaws, and I get a call from the dentist. We started talking regularly. I shouldn't have spoken to him at all. Modell said, 'If the league ever subpoenas our phone records, you're going to have to have all of your teeth pulled.' I called Joel Bussert, my old colleague in the league office—I'll never forget this conversation—and I said, 'Let me paint you a scenario . . .' 'Drop this entire thing!' he said. 'You're going to cause a hell of a lot of trouble!' I said, 'I don't have a quarterback! I don't care how much trouble I cause!' That year the combine [centralized workouts for auditioning draft choices] was in Arizona, the last time it was outside, the most un-Arizona weather you ever saw. Damp and rainy and Paul Brown gets that respiratory thing that he never fully recovered from. I go up to the Buffalo GM, Terry Bledsoe, to confirm that the Bills are really after Bruce Smith. 'If you can't sign Smith,' I said, 'what would you take for your pick?' 'We're going to sign him,' he told me. 'Who is it you're angling for?' 'Doug Flutie.' 'Come on, you're up to something.' 'No, my owner likes Flutie.'"

Because of hatred (Paul Brown), Modell would never deal with Cincinnati. Because of love (Art Rooney), he would never deal with Pittsburgh. In the division, that left only the Oilers. "Buffalo is definitely taking Smith," Ernie informed Houston GM Ladd Herzeg. "Would you trade your second pick?" "Sure," Herzeg said, "for the right price." "So," Ernie said, "we had eight million conversations. I'd say, 'Tell me who you want,' and he'd say Chip Banks or Hanford Dixon. He'd keep bringing up players and I'd keep saying yes. But the price went up and up and up until eventually he wanted a couple of Pro Bowlers, the Vatican, the Kremlin, and the Library of Congress. By the time the league meetings rolled around, he and everybody else had figured out that I wanted Kosar. Herzeg and Mike Lynn, the Minnesota GM, were walking around the headquarters hotel arm in arm, laughing at me. The Oilers already had a quarterback, Warren Moon, so Herzeg was trying to find someone who'd give him more for Kosar than I would, and he ended up trading his pick to the Vikings. In the meantime, Kosar and Geletka showed their research to the league and it was now accepted that Bernie could come out. But here was the thing—he had to write a letter within eight days of the draft applying to be included. After that, it was buyer beware, because he couldn't graduate by draft day in April—he needed summer school. Therefore, if he graduated later, the draft choice would take effect. If he didn't, it was wasted."

From scouring the bylaws, Accorsi figured out another wrinkle, which was communicated to Kosar through the dentist. If Bernie *didn't* send in that letter before the draft, he wouldn't be eligible. If he sent it in *after* the draft and then graduated, mightn't he be fair game for the supplemental draft? Buffalo topped that list as well. "When I called Bussert," Ernie said, "he double-checked what I was proposing now and came to the conclusion that I was right. I called Bledsoe and offered Buffalo our number one the following year, plus a player, for their first pick in the supplemental draft. Terry didn't want any of our players. He ended up making the deal for the number one in 1986, a third-rounder in 1985, and a sixth-rounder in 1986."

When the various mathematical possibilities were whispered to Kosar, Bernie got it immediately. He was not a scuba-diving major. "Of course I still had the pressure of graduating," he said. "Hell, I'm only twenty years old. I would be the youngest quarterback ever to start in the NFL, the youngest one ever to start a play-off game, too. There was another hitch then. The Minnesota Vikings."

On April 8, opening day of the baseball season—"it was snowing like hell," Ernie said—Terry Bledsoe felt chest pains. "They take him to the hospital and find out he needs open-heart surgery right away. I call him in his room and say, 'I hope you feel better, but have you sent in the twix yet?' In those days you had to finalize trades on the TWX wire. 'Terry, I love you like a brother, and I hope you don't die, but could you please call your office before the surgery and make sure they've sent this deal in?' He did. The trade went through. No more than twenty minutes later, Herzeg calls from Houston. 'Ernie, I thought I owed you the courtesy and the respect to tell you that I just traded Bernie Kosar to the Minnesota Vikings.' I said, 'No, you didn't. You just traded the second pick in the regular draft to the Minnesota Vikings. I think that out of all the respect due to you, I should inform you that I just traded with Buffalo for their first pick in the supplemental draft. Bernie Kosar won't be in the regular draft. He'll be in the supplemental.' That's when all hell broke loose."

Commissioner Pete Rozelle froze the many Kosar transactions and summoned representatives of the Browns, Vikings, Bills, and Oilers to New York City. Tampering charges were flying around what everyone called "the old conference room." Lawsuits were being filed and counterfiled. "And on top of a hundred lawyers," Ernie said, "Herzeg had retained the agent Howard Slusher. He was Agent Orange in those days. He was like Scott Boras is today, only worse. Slusher's the guy who held out most of the Steeler line. But I thought from the moment I saw him— after deciding not to have my own heart attack—that Herzeg had miscalculated badly by bringing Slusher into this. Rozelle probably didn't want Slusher to win anything either.

" 'What do you think?' Art whispers. 'Either we just lost it,' I say, 'or we just won it.' Bussert was there, too, but his larynx had been removed. Poor Joel was afraid to say anything. By this time, he was only talking to me from pay phones. 'This guy Bussert and Accorsi are best friends,' Slusher says to the assembly, 'and a secret road map for this nefarious transaction was passed from Bussert to Accorsi. It was a tampering plot all along. They were sending signals in the night.' I finally stood up and said, 'Here's the bottom line of this whole situation. We knew the rules and you didn't. That's *your* problem.' And a little balding attorney for Buffalo says, 'If there was a road map, and you're walking down that road, it isn't going to be a very pleasant journey for you, because there are land mines all along the way.' Rozelle doesn't say a word until he issues his finding in a press release."

> National Football League Commissioner Pete Rozelle today approved both trades involving University of Miami quarterback Bernie Kosar.
>
> Rozelle said that under current NFL rules Kosar, through academic achievement, has an option to be selected in the regular draft next Tuesday or in the supplemental draft this summer, should he choose to play in the League this year.
>
> In ruling on a dispute that included four clubs, Rozelle said that the trade will stand in which the Minnesota Vikings obtained the second spot in the April 30 draft from the Houston Oilers, as well as a separate trade in which the Cleveland Browns obtained the first choice from the Buffalo Bills in any supplemental draft involving Kosar in 1985. Buffalo has already committed the first spot in the regular draft by signing Virginia Tech defensive end Bruce Smith. The Bills also held the first choice

in any supplemental draft under the same priority order as the regular draft, a procedure followed in the League since 1977. One or more supplemental drafts have been held every year since 1969.

Rozelle said that Kosar, who played the past two seasons at Miami, must notify the League in writing by midnight, April 25, of his intent to graduate in order to be included in the 1985 regular draft. If he fails to give such notification and subsequently graduates before September 1, Kosar will be eligible for the supplemental draft. In either case he must actually have graduated before he can sign an NFL contract. If Kosar opts to do neither, his eligibility to play again for Miami is in the hands of the NCAA and the university.

"After weighing all facts in this matter, including a hearing attended by the four clubs and a thorough discussion with the Kosar interests, I have determined to apply the rule as written, and as applied in the past," Rozelle said.

"In the circumstances of this case, I did not feel it was appropriate for the NFL Commissioner to make a definitive determination of Kosar's collegiate eligibility status, as Minnesota and Houston had requested. The NCAA has informed us that it has not declared Kosar ineligible and would not further consider his status unless Kosar attempts to resume college football participation. We received no clear evidence that would justify a determination that Kosar has lost his eligibility."

In an attachment to Rozelle's decree, the Browns and Vikings were granted three days apiece to be alone with Kosar, to recruit him like a high school star. This was unprecedented in the NFL. "Our recruiting trip," Ernie said, "consisted of Art and I going to Youngstown and having dinner with him and his dad. That's all we did. Minnesota staged an extravaganza, complete with 'Kosar the Viking' campaign buttons. I still have one." Legendary coach Bud Grant, with one of those buttons pinned to his chest, was dispatched to Youngstown in a private jet. "I liked Bud Grant," Bernie said. "I was a little awed by him, to tell you the truth. And Mark Tressman, my mentor at Miami—the quarterback coach—now had a job with the Vikings. That didn't hurt their cause, either. Plus— and you may not believe this, but—I've never been a guy who likes to ruffle feathers. I don't get off on being different. Part of me wanted to conform and just go to Minnesota."

But the other part loved the Browns, and even loved Cleveland. "I signed a five-year, $6 million contract with Ernie," Kosar said, "one of the biggest at the time. The best thing he did was set it up so that a hundred thousand dollars a year would go directly to my father. It wasn't just business to Ernie. It wasn't just football. He saw the human side. This way, Dad wouldn't have to get the money from me, though of course ultimately that's where it was coming from. Ernie could see the closeness of my family, and he could see the tensions, too. He understood."

He also seemed to know exactly what Kosar could give the Browns on the field. "I'd like to tell you I was the greatest athlete in the world," Bernie said, "but I wasn't. I was tall, skinny. I certainly wasn't the fastest dude around. Minnesota kept talking about things like running, jumping, bench-pressing, getting bigger, getting stronger, and all that. But Ernie just said, 'When you're as slow as you are, Bernie, you better have something else going for you, and you do.' He saw this thing that couldn't be measured today on a computer screen. Among all these guys, I knew he was the true believer. Ernie could see what I had, and what's more, he helped me see it."

Schottenheimer said, "The whole strategy, all of that maneuvering, Ernie had discussed with me—but, hell, I didn't understand it." When the kid came in, and he could really play, Marty understood that. The coach said, "As a community, Cleveland had been taking a pounding. The town was the butt of national jokes. 'The mistake on the lake,' people called it. To have a young person like this who didn't *have* to

come to Cleveland but sincerely *wanted* to come to Cleveland, who had
no ulterior business motives—well, it did something wonderful for the
town. I'm not contending it did everything, but it helped—a lot. And
when we started to have a little success, you could actually feel Cleveland's sense of self getting stronger."

"The Browns had won just one division championship in fifteen
years," Kosar said, "the 'cardiac kids' of Brian Sipe. The city was bankrupt.
The Cuyahoga River was on fire." And with a twenty-year-old rookie quarterback who had a funny, sideways kind of style, the Browns won the division championship at 8–8 and went on to post marks of 12–4, 10–5,
10–6, and 9–6–1 as the 1980s ran out. "Bernie wanted to wear number
seventeen," Accorsi said, "for Sipe. I said, 'No way, you're wearing number
nineteen. Johnny Unitas gave it to me and I'm giving it to you.'"

In Kosar's sophomore season, the Browns were losing a divisional
play-off to the New York Jets, 20–10, with 4:14 to go in the fourth quarter. To his teammates in the huddle, Kosar said, "If every one of you does
his job from here on in, I'm going to win this game." Ozzie Newsome,
the veteran tight end and future Hall of Famer—not to mention future
GM with the Baltimore Ravens—said, "I got chills up and down my
spine when he said that." With Kosar setting postseason records for pass
attempts (sixty-four) and yards (489), Cleveland won in double overtime,
23–20. For that Jets game—for all of their play-off games—the Browns
practiced in a drier, warmer climate at Vero Beach in Florida, Dodger
Town. "Men, hold up your room keys," Schottenheimer had said after
the final workout there. They all did. "Keep them, men. Don't turn them
in. We're coming right back." In the Cleveland locker room after the
great victory, the players shook those keys like bells.

The Browns highlights and lowlights in the Kosar era were, of
course, the same. In January 1987 and 1988, Cleveland made it to the
AFC Championship Game twice, and to within a breath of the Super
Bowl both times. "The toughest one was the first one," Schottenheimer
said, "at home." A forty-eight-yard touchdown pass from Kosar to Brian
Brennan gave Cleveland a 20–13 lead over the Denver Broncos with

5:34 left in the fourth quarter. Muffing the kickoff—all but losing the ball and the game right there—the Broncos started first and ten at their own two-yard line. Ninety-eight yards to go, just to tie. The Denver quarterback was Accorsi's ghost of Christmas past, John Elway. In the Broncos' huddle, guard Keith Bishop, a Texan, started the drive off with just the note that the situation called for. "We got these guys right where we want 'em," he drawled. Elway, who afterward said he might have felt tighter at the twenty than at the two, told the boys, "We have a long way to go, so let's get going. Do whatever it takes, and something good will happen."

BRONCOS

1-10-D2   Elway passes to Sammy Winder for 5
2-5-D7   Winder runs for 3
Denver takes its first time-out
3-2-D10   Winder runs for 2
1-10-D12 Winder runs for 3
2-7-D15   Elway runs for 11
1-10-D26 Elway passes to Steve Sewell for 22 yards
1-10-D48 Elway passes to Steve Watson for 12
1-10-C40 Elway passes incomplete
2-10-C40 Elway sacked for −8
Denver takes its second time-out

"Let's try for half of it on third and half of it on fourth," Coach Dan Reeves told Elway, who wasn't listening.

3-18-C48 Elway passes to Mark Jackson for 20

"Dave Puzzuoli has just sacked Elway," Schottenheimer said, "and now it's third and eighteen. Elway's in a shotgun at about his own forty-five. He puts Steve Watson in motion, and as Watson is coming across, the center snaps the ball early and it nicks Watson on the hip. Now this, to me, is the classic difference between winning and losing a football game. Here's that serendipity we all sign up for and leave ourselves open to. A split inch farther back and that ball hits Watson flush on the hip and is rolling around on the ground. Third and eighteen." But Elway makes this terrific little athletic move to catch the carom off Watson's hip and, maintaining his poise and purpose, he moves around with the ball until he finds Jackson open. "There it is," Marty said. "There's the play. That's the play."

1-10-C28 Elway passes incomplete
2-10-C28 Elway passes to Sewell for 14
1-10-C14 Elway passes incomplete
2-10-C14 Elway runs for 9
3-1-C5   Elway passes to Jackson for 5 and the
     touchdown (:31); Rich Karlis kicks the extra point
                    Broncos 20, Browns 20 (:31)

In overtime, Karlis kicks a thirty-three-yard field goal to win for the Broncos, 23–20.

"If anyone could do it, it was us," Karlis said. "When you have Elway," Bishop said, "anything is possible." "Anytime you have John Elway," Reeves said, "you have a chance." That had been Accorsi's exact position four years earlier.

"We used to sit around Modell's office after the games," Schottenheimer said, "Ernie and I and all of our families. My son Brian was about eleven or twelve. It was a bit uncomfortable, but Art always wanted to know instantly what happened." Kosar passed for 258 yards, Elway for 244, but 120 of Elway's yards had come on Denver's final two drives, when he scrambled for twenty more. John Elway was what happened.

"All of a sudden," Ernie said, "I thought, 'Oh, my God, my mother! Did she survive this?' A ninety-eight-yard drive and a seventy-seven-year-old woman! This may be worse than crossing on the *Saturnia*—in steerage! I ran to my office to call her." All these many football seasons later, Mary Nardi Accorsi had begun to understand the sport that enchanted her son. When the Browns were on TV, she'd sit in front of the set, praying. Mary was three years old in 1913 when the *Saturnia* docked in America. She was carried off the boat in the arms of a man named Galiano Marani, whose grandson, Ed Ionni, is Ernie's best friend today. Hershey must really be Brigadoon. "Mom, are you okay?" her son asked when he finally got her on the phone. "I'm fine, Ernie," she said, "but you're going to have to do something about that coach."

Returning to the inquest, Accorsi told Schottenheimer, "You just got second-guessed." "I expected that." "By my mother!"

At the second AFC championship game, this time in Denver, the other terrible shoe fell. Rather, it was dropped by one of Accorsi's all-time proudest draft choices, an eleventh selection (the second Browns pick in the tenth round) from East Carolina, running back Earnest Byner. Perfectly turning the tables, the Browns were the ones driving to the tying touchdown with 3:51 left in the fourth quarter. Kosar, who was outgunning Elway, 356 yards to 281, took possession at the Cleveland twenty-five, first and ten.

BROWNS

1-10-C25 Byner runs for 16

1-10-C41 Byner runs for 2

2-8-C43 Kosar passes to Brennan for 14

1-10-D43 Kosar passes to Brennan for 19

1-10-D24 Encroachment, Denver

1-5-D19 Byner runs for 6

1-10-D13 Kosar passes incomplete

2-10-D13 Offside, Denver

2-5-D8   Byner runs for 5—he is officially credited for the full 5 yards, but is actually hit near the goal line by Jeremiah Castille and fumbles backward to Castille at the 3, and the Broncos conclude the scoring by surrendering a strategic safety

Denver 38, Cleveland 33

"Jeremiah Castille," Ernie said. "His son is playing for Alabama now. I hear his name and I get chills. Our wide receiver, Webster Slaughter, failed to clear Castille out. Earnest looked like he was getting ready to spike the ball in the end zone and I think Castille may have swatted it out of his hand at the goal line. I couldn't even see. It was so far away and dark. Paper was flying all over the place. All I could make out were the Broncos players jumping up and down." In a curiously grumpy mood afterward, the cornerback Castille refused to discuss the play with the Denver media. "I'll tell you about it at the Super Bowl," he said, and left.

Byner, who scored two second-half touchdowns on a thirty-two-yard pass from Kosar and a four-yard run, was actually asked in the locker room why he wasn't crying. "I played my heart out today," he said. "I don't really have any emotions left for crying. Maybe later. Twice now Bernie has brought us to the doorstep of the Super Bowl, and we just can't seem to walk in. I wasn't getting ready to spike the ball. Castille didn't hit it, either. I was splitting two defenders and it just . . . popped out. I don't know why. I gave everything I had today, and all year. I hope that helps when people start coming down on me. I mean, I know it's not going to help them. But I hope it helps me—get through it." Ernie didn't blame Byner, but ultimately traded him to Washington. "I thought he was Ralph Branca," he said, meaning the Dodgers pitcher who gave up Giant Bobby Thomson's pennant-winning home run. "I was wrong about that. Looking back, I think trading Byner away was the worst deal I ever made. He was a good player, and a good guy."

Accorsi's and Schottenheimer's working relationship and close friendship survived these most bitter disappointments, which was unusual. Coaches and GMs—coaches and personnel men generally— are normally in a triangular death dance with the owners. "There isn't enough talent here," the coach will complain. "He won't play my young players," the personnel man will reply. Or, in the alternative, "He hurried my young players." "I'm going to tell you something about Ernie Accorsi," Schottenheimer said. "The greatest thing about him is that he never gives a damn who gets the credit for success. They could put that on his tombstone. He just doesn't care. It was never about Ernie in Cleveland. And you could trust him. That quality alone almost made him unique in the business."

In between the two killer losses, Schottenheimer and Accorsi went together to St. Andrews in Scotland to play the Old Course. "Talk about bonding," Schottenheimer said. Ernie birdied the first hole—"You're leading the British Open," Marty told him. "No one's ever been better!"— and Schottenheimer birdied the last. "You know how the townspeople all stand around the fence there at eighteen?" Marty said. "The birthplace of golf. The coach and the GM are walking together through the Valley of Sin to the last green. The wind is blowing like a son of a bitch. Does it get any better than that?"

No. As Modell's and Schottenheimer's tolerance for each other ran out, Marty was gone by the end of 1988. Accorsi replaced him momentarily with a crusty old defensive genius named Bud Carson, on the theory that Carson might know how to win that last game against Elway. "I thought I was hiring Earl Weaver," Ernie said, "but I was really hiring Eddie Stanky." In 1977, Stanky managed the Texas Rangers to a victory in the season's opening game and then resigned. "Bud was ready to quit even before we started," Ernie said. Accorsi and Modell had already settled on Carson when Ernie sat down with a leftover candidate, young Bill Belichick.

"The interview took place in the Hilton lobby restaurant," Ernie said, "and I missed practice that day, he was so good. I didn't want to leave. It was like listening to John F. Kennedy when he was running for president. You said to yourself, 'This guy has been preparing to be president since he was ten years old.' That's the feeling I got with Belichick. 'Let me tell you something,' I said when we were through, 'you were down by thirty points in the last quarter and you cut it to one as time ran out. And you had the ball.' Two years later, Ernie replaced Carson with Belichick. "First I had to unhire Mike White," he said, "who won a Rose Bowl at Illinois." Acting like his own GM again, Modell had phoned Accorsi to say brightly, "Well, we got a coach! Mike White! He's at my house now! I'm sending him over to you!" But Ernie talked Art out of White and into Belichick.

"People now say Belichick failed in Cleveland before he succeeded in New England," Ernie said, "but he didn't fail in Cleveland. He went to the play-offs in ninety-four, beat the Patriots and Bill Parcells." The Browns lost to Pittsburgh then, but they were outmanned by the Steelers. "Halfway through the following season," Ernie said, "the fans were rooting against Bill in his own stadium because Art had announced he was moving the team to Baltimore." Accorsi had already departed, in 1992, Belichick's second season, "just because it was time," Ernie said. "I believe in runs, and I'd had my run there. I wanted to get back east." In 2000, during a phone conversation with Accorsi, Belichick all of a sudden blurted out, "I really screwed up that thing up in Cleveland, Ernie." " 'You didn't screw up anything,' I told him. 'You took over a head coaching job for the first time in your life, and the next thing you knew, your general manager was saying goodbye. I'm proud of the job you did there.' " Thinking back on their phone conversation, Ernie said, "Almost nothing in life touches me more than humility. People who say Belichick doesn't have it don't know him. I love Bill Belichick."

Because of a series of injuries, Bernie Kosar didn't make ten years in the league. "After that elbow in eighty-eight," Ernie said, "he hurt his hand in eighty-nine and played with a splint. He got beat up pretty bad in ninety and ninety-one—we just weren't a very good team around him. Smoky Burgess could hit a line-drive double today, if he's still alive [Burgess, the great pinch-hitting catcher, died in 1991 at sixty-four] but guys who *aren't* naturals don't last as long. Bernie put us in the Super Bowl twice. He got us the lead twice. The defense couldn't hold it. I've heard people say that Kosar didn't have a great arm—the hell he didn't! He could throw long with anybody, and he had a hair-trigger release." Bernie also had that thing no one could measure on a computer screen, that thing Accorsi saw and helped him see.

"Didn't he wear the number nineteen well?" said Ernie, who now had both John's and Bernie's jerseys framed in his home.

7

THE NEW YORK GIANTS:
SIGNING KERRY COLLINS

ACCORSI WENT TO WORK as a special advisor to Maryland governor William Donald Schaefer, trying to replace the Colts with an NFL expansion team. In six weeks, they sold out a hundred skyboxes in an imaginary new stadium. In eight weeks, all of the seventy-five hundred club seats were gone. But the league anointed Charlotte and Jacksonville instead.

"Leaving the Browns that way," Ernie said, "violated one of my theories: it's okay to be down five–nothing in the third inning, but don't take risks in the seventh inning of your career. It might be too late to recover." In any case, he felt obligated to come home, to be near his eighty-two-year-old mother in Hershey. "And if Baltimore was going to be awarded a new franchise, I wanted to position myself at least to have a shot at becoming its GM." The instant that hope fell through, Orioles owner Peter Angelos called. Ernie's luck was still pretty good.

Just as Accorsi had once imagined, he was momentarily in the baseball business. His title was "executive director of business affairs." His pleasure was to sit between Orioles GM Rollie Hemond and Hall of Famer Frank Robinson at the games. "Frank Robby would call out the pitches one after the other," Ernie said. "'Are you stealing the signs?' I asked him. 'No,' he said. 'I'm reading the outfielders.'"

But Accorsi wasn't wandering in the wilderness very long when Joel

Bussert called from the league office to feel him out about returning to pro football. The conversation was as nebulous as Ernie's baseball duties, but he could read between the lines. "Before you go any further, Joe," Ernie said, "did George Young put you up to calling me?"

"Um, yes," said Bussert, proving again that he was not cut out to be a secret agent. By now, Young had been the Giants' GM for fifteen years. "He'd like to hire you as his assistant," Joel said, "but if you don't want the job, he doesn't want to put you in the embarrassing position of turning him down." "I said, 'Tell George to call me.'

"So, the phone rings two seconds later and here's typical George: 'I don't want to ruin your life.' Those are his first words, even before hello. He starts filling me in on the entire situation. 'Look, I can't put you in this chair. I can't promise you the general managership after me. They may not like you. But I think they will.' " A dollar figure was mentioned. "Is that okay?" George said. "Yeah, that's good, George," Ernie replied, "but ask your secretary to send me the real estate section of the *Bronx Home News*—not the nice part, the part where they have the abandoned warehouses. I'll go get a sleeping bag and . . ." They fell right back into their old rhythms. When the deal was done, Young sighed and said, "Good. Maybe I'll live a little longer now." He would live seven more years. "One final condition," Ernie said. "Harry stays."

Harry Hulmes, the old shoe who was euchred out of the Baltimore GM job by Don Klosterman, had landed in Young's anteroom in his seventies. Harry was a good scout in every sense of the phrase; too good, Young would say only half kiddingly. Hulmes' reports maximized players' virtues and minimized their drawbacks. He was that way about everything in life. "Harry is such a nice guy," Ernie said, "that he even sees the good in the agents. He actually sides with the agents! Harry would come into George's office and say softly, 'George, I think Drew Rosenhaus has a point here.' Through my office wall, I could hear George bellowing, 'Harry! Harry! Harry! Call him back and tell him to go to hell!' 'I can't do that,' Harry said. 'Harry, I'm dialing the number and you're going to tell Rosenhaus to go to hell!' " But Harry stayed.

The four years that Ernie assisted George felt like a partnership to both of them. Young made most of the personnel decisions. Accorsi negotiated most of the contracts. When Young stepped down after the 1997 season, to become vice president of football operations in the NFL office, Ernie was named the new Giants' GM. "This is the right man," Young said at the press conference, "for the right job at the right time."

They still saw each other. They still talked football. "When George started working in the league office," Ernie said, "he moved to Sixty-sixth and Third in Manhattan—I got him the apartment. Mine was on Sixty-ninth. Labor Day weekend of 2000, we go to see Penn State and USC at the Meadowlands, and he's fine. We're talking strategy on the car ride home. The FDR is packed. 'Shouldn't we get off here?' he says. He was absolutely fine. We park the car, we're walking up to his apartment, and he says, 'Ernie, can I just say . . . where am I?' 'You're home, George.' As soon as he went inside, right on the spot, I called [Giants trainer] Ronnie Barnes. 'Something is wrong with George,' I said." The diagnosis was Creutzfeldt-Jakob disease, a rare U.S. relative of the UK's mad cow disease. Rapid, progressive dementia. Always fatal. Young died in a hospice that December 8, not knowing where he was.

Just about the only thing Ernie liked about Giants quarterback Dave Brown was the fact that George had liked him. But this wasn't nearly enough. "He'd look pretty for a while," Ernie said. "There've been all kinds of those guys. They look beautiful. But when you're playing against them, you don't fear them when the game's on the line." Taking over for Phil Simms in 1994, Brown was the New York starter for three and a half seasons. Accorsi said, "Mike Ditka had ripped him just before Ditka took the head coaching job in New Orleans. So, after we beat the Saints in ninety-seven, fourteen to nine—it felt like two to one, and Brown was awful—Dave ran across the field and shook his fist in Ditka's direction. 'Take that!' 'He didn't do shit,' Mike told me later. 'He was the only reason we were in the game!' I cut Brown in my first twenty-four hours as GM. So our quarterback was Danny Kanell, who had gone in after a Brown injury in ninety-seven and kind of *managed* the team to a division title. Danny didn't do badly, but he didn't have a strong arm. I liked him, but he wasn't going to get us to a championship. I signed Kent Graham, whom I wasn't in love with, either, but Kent was good enough to back up Kanell."

Then along came the troubled former Penn Stater Kerry Collins.

At college, Collins won the Davey O'Brien and Maxwell awards, signifying not only the top quarterback but also the most outstanding player. He set Penn State records for completions, completion percentage, passing yardage, and total offense. After leading the Nittany Lions to an undefeated, Rose Bowl–winning season in 1994, Collins was the fifth player taken in the first round of the NFL draft, by the Carolina Panthers. But it went bad for him there.

A drunk-driving arrest led to a stay in a rehab clinic in Topeka, Kansas, but the more defining incident occurred at a team party when—under the influence, Collins acknowledged—he aimed racial epithets at African American and Hispanic teammates Muhsin Muhammad and Norberto Davidds-Garrido. Kerry later swore this wasn't racism. Rather, it was a misguided attempt at team bonding that only made sense in a haze of alcohol. Davidds-Garrido, an offensive lineman, knocked Collins right on his ass. The quarterback was eventually waived.

"From there he went to New Orleans," Ernie said. "That was a mess. No discipline. No coaching." Finally, he was a free agent, looking for a job. "I've always believed," Accorsi said, "that if a kid was ever a good kid, he can be a good kid again. If he was never a good kid, don't waste your time." Paterno and everybody else at Penn State vouched for Collins, although they knew he drank there, too. "Kerry was a Lebanon, Pennsylvania, guy," Ernie said, "twelve miles from Hershey, so I had a certain bead on him. I went all of the way back to his junior high, checking on him." Over a disagreement with the coach, Kerry's father had pulled him out of one high school. "Then I studied tape after tape after tape. He threw a lot of interceptions. He was sloppy. But he played hard. He played his heart out. I looked at our old reports on him. All of our scouts had high grades on Kerry. *I* had high grades on him. So, on a Saturday morning in the wintertime, he and I went to breakfast at the Sheraton Meadowlands Hotel. I looked him straight in the eye. He looked me straight in the eye. 'If you didn't come from Lebanon,' I said, 'if you didn't go to Penn State, if you hadn't played for Paterno, we wouldn't be having this conversation.'

"He said, 'Ernie, I dreamed about playing in the National Football League all my life. The Eagles, the Giants, the Redskins, the Bears. But I found myself playing for the Carolina Panthers, wearing this funny-looking uniform, and I didn't even feel like I was in the NFL. That started my problems.' 'If we take a chance on you,' I told him, 'you're going to have to sign up for counseling immediately. Miss an appointment and you're gone. One slip-up and you're gone.' 'I won't let you down,' he said."

When Collins walked into the Giants' clubhouse for the first time and began emptying his duffel into a locker, a black cornerback silently got up and moved out of the locker next to him. But in a moment or two, still without a word being spoken, black fullback Charlie Way left his own station and moved into the abandoned digs. Accorsi said, "You know how, at the end of their careers, players will come back to their old team, to be a 'Giant for a day' so they can retire a Giant? The cornerback asked to do that. We told him no."

Collins had a live arm but a high release that had always bothered Ernie. "I'm not talking about beauty and esthetics here—I don't care about that," he said. "What it does—this hitch—is it gives the defensive backs a chance to react. [Coach Jim] Fassel did a great job with Collins, trying to iron that out. They never got rid of it completely, but it was a lot better." However, Kerry's biggest drawback wasn't mechanical.

"Physically he was as tough as they came," Ernie said, "but emotionally there was a fragility there. I wonder if that doesn't follow from rehab. Rehab can put a player's pieces back together, but can it make him whole again? I don't think so. He hasn't been rebuilt; he's just been repaired. And a lot of his new strength is artificial. It's words. For the rest of his life, he has to walk around on eggshells. If Kerry felt he was going to have the time back there to throw, he'd cut your heart out. But if he felt that he wasn't going to get the protection—whether he got it or not—he was skittish. It wasn't that he was gutless—he had plenty of guts. It's just that he was . . . well, *fragile*'s the only word I can think of. I figured him for moments of absolute splendor and then for four interceptions."

In the eleventh game of the 1999 season, Collins went in for Graham. With Kerry at the controls, the Giants mostly lost down that home stretch, including the last three games in a row. But the moment of absolute splendor was just ahead. Throwing twenty-two touchdown passes in 2000, recording personal bests in every category, Collins led New York to a 12–4 regular season record and a division title. When Philadelphia was beaten in the first play-off game, 20–10, only the Minnesota Vikings blocked the Giants' way to the Super Bowl.

"I'm thinking," Accorsi said, "we're going to have to score forty points to have a chance. All week long, in my dreams, the Vikings scored eight thousand points. All I dreamt of were Randy Moss, Chris Carter, and Robert Smith running up and down the field. The day before the game, John Fox, who was our defensive coordinator then, said, 'Why have you been avoiding me all week? Every time I look at you, you look the other way.' 'I don't like to think about our defense right now,' I told him. 'We're going to be fine,' he said. 'We may shut them out.' And we did. Our corner, Jason Sehorn, took Moss out of the game early, demoralizing their entire team. Moss quit and the whole team quit. It was amazing."

No more amazing, though, than Collins. "I don't think anyone will ever have a better game at Giants Stadium than Kerry had that day," Ernie said, "January fourteenth, 2001." Just four plays into the game, Collins threw a forty-six-yard touchdown pass to Ike Hilliard, ultimately completing twenty-eight of thirty-nine passes for 381 yards and five touchdowns. The Vikings were destroyed, 41–0. New York was in Super Bowl XXXV, against the Baltimore Ravens.

Ernie said, "You know how sometimes you say to yourself, 'I just wish my father could have been here tonight to see this?'" That's what the

GM was thinking when he got home from the game and saw the message light blinking on his machine. "Do you know who it was?" he said. "Beano." Carroll "Beano" Cook was a sports gadfly and football oracle from Pittsburgh, an occasional columnist, sometime broadcaster, Monongahelan Winston Churchill, and the number one advocate of Mary Tyler Moore, chocolate chip cookies, and the University of Notre Dame. Beano was the best friend of almost everyone he knew in sports, which was almost everyone. Hardly needing to identify himself—he had the voice of a plumbing fixture gargling Drano—Beano left Ernie a seven-word message that showed once again how intuitive he was: "If the Gipper knew, your dad knows." *Click.*

"In the days leading up to the Super Bowl," Ernie said, "I became more and more worried about Kerry. You could see that he wasn't taking the bit in his mouth. I knew what was coming." "That Super Bowl was over in a series," according to Tony Siragusa, the Ravens' hugest defensive tackle. "I watched Collins standing at the line, getting ready to call out the signals, and he wasn't looking up the field or at his receivers or at the defensive backs covering his receivers. He was looking at us, the guys who were coming to get him. I thought, 'Man, this game is over.'" The Ravens were better anyway—many times better defensively. They won going away, 34–7. Collins threw four interceptions.

With occasional brilliance, followed by inevitable disappointment, Collins saw the Giants through to the quarterback-rich draft of 2004, when in the fourth pick of the first round Ernie took Philip Rivers of North Carolina State and traded him to San Diego along with three draft choices (including the Giants' number one in 2005) for top selection Eli Manning. It was the Elway power play all over again, in reverse. Because this time Accorsi was on the other side. "There was no question," Ernie said, "we knew we were going to pick a quarterback. We were coming off a four-and-twelve season—Fassel had fired himself—and we told every coach whom we interviewed, 'Don't even think you're going to come in and change our mind.' When it comes to young quarterbacks, coaches have a natural tendency to think, 'By the time this guy

gets good, I might be fired. We can get by with so-and-so.' Nope. This
was going to be a franchise pick, and if everything fell into place, it was
going to be Manning." Ben Roethlisberger of Miami of Ohio was a Li'l
Abner who made plays. Rivers of North Carolina State was a brilliant
kid—that's how he got by. But Manning was the guy.

Almost the only thing Ernie knew about A. J. Smith, the Chargers'
GM, was that Smith and head coach Marty Schottenheimer barely
spoke. "I called A.J. in March," Accorsi said, "to get the ball rolling. We
touched base again in April. Finally, on the Thursday before the draft,
we really started to talk. Eli wasn't nearly as adamant about San Diego, I
didn't feel, as Elway had been about Baltimore. But historically the
Chargers hadn't been the biggest winners, and the fact that Archie had
languished his entire career for a down team in New Orleans had to be
foremost in Eli's mind. Friday, I thought the deal was dead. But I was
tipped by a writer that A.J. was going to pick Eli and call me. So, San
Diego takes Eli, Oakland takes tackle Robert Gallery, Arizona takes
receiver Larry Fitzgerald, and we're on the clock. Fifteen minutes. I'm
waiting, I'm waiting. At the seven minute mark, A.J. finally calls."

Just before that, the Browns called. Cleveland owned the sixth selection. "They offered me a second to change places," Ernie said, "and I
almost did it. But I stopped and thought, 'You know what? If I drop
down to pick up a second, and now Cleveland makes the Manning trade,
I'll kill myself.' That's when A.J. called. I knew I'd have to give up the
next year's number one, but they wanted [defensive end] Osi Umenyiora,
too. 'Deal-killer,' I said, and he knew I wasn't bluffing. We were on the
clock. So we made a package of draft choices and I picked Rivers for
them in exchange for Eli. The Browns were really mad. I reneged, they
said. But there's no such thing as reneging until the computer thing is
in. I never really said yes, I just almost said yes. So now the deal went
through and I was exhilarated. We had a quarterback. I knew what that
meant. I'd had them—the best—and I'd not had them. And I'd played
against the great ones, so I knew. I realized that I could turn out to be
wrong on this kid, there was no question about it—maybe I'm going to

be wrong. And I knew we might not know for sure until years after I leave. But I could live with it. We had a quarterback."

The following morning, Collins barged into Accorsi's office, demanding, "I want to go, I want to leave, I want out of here! I want to know what you're going to do with me!"

"I said, 'Well, you're under contract, Kerry, you're the quarterback—for the moment.'

"'I want out of here!'

"'Okay, I'll think about it.'

"'No, I want out of here *today*.'

"'Kerry, I'm sitting on this side of the desk, you're sitting on that side. I'll do this when I decide to do it.'"

A couple of days later, Accorsi released Collins, acquiring veteran Kurt Warner to squire Manning for half a season. Kerry went off to Oakland, the NFL's traditional late career stop.

The list of potential Fassel replacements was pared down to four finalists, whom Accorsi and Giants president John Mara interviewed at length: Tom Coughlin, a former Giants assistant to Bill Parcells who could have had the job after Parcells left in 1990 but didn't want it then; Lovey Smith; Romeo Crennel; and Charlie Weis. "Lovey was really sharp, impressive," Ernie said, "but we had less history with him than the others." Coughlin, Crennel, and Weis had all been Giants assistants, and now Crennel and Weis were serving Belichick. "For about two hours before a Patriots game," Ernie said, "I talked to Bill about Romeo and Charlie, and then I scouted the game and watched everything they did. I was trying to figure out how much of the defense was really run by Romeo. I knew Charlie was running the offense. Weis started out fourth on the list but finished second. Similar to that first time I interviewed Belichick, I told Charlie, 'You were down thirty-five points and you closed it to two with the ball.' I also told him, 'You know, the best thing that ever happened to Jack Kennedy was losing the vice presidential nomination to Estes Kefauver in fifty-six.' I'm not sure he got that."

A backfield mate of Larry Csonka's and Floyd Little's at Syracuse,

Coughlin played for legendary coach Ben Schwartzwalder and set records both as a pass receiver and as a student. He was the quarterback coach at Boston College, where one of his charges was Doug Flutie, and later the head coach at BC for three seasons. "I saw his second game, against Michigan," Ernie said. "They played the Wolverines tough for a long while. Near the end of his time there, Coughlin beat George Welsh's Virginia team in a bowl game. Virginia had four or five top choices; he didn't have that much, Glenn Foley at quarterback. But Welsh told me the week before, 'We can't figure out their passing game. There's a timing mechanism to it. We've studied it for three weeks, but I'm not sure we can stop it.' Well, BC completed every friggin' pass and killed them, 31–13."

A year and a half before the Jacksonville Jaguars played their inaugural NFL game in 1995, Coughlin signed on as the new franchise's charter head coach. After just one losing year, the Jaguars made it to postseason play four straight times, the only expansion team ever to do that. Twice Jacksonville reached the AFC Championship Game. "A number of coaches," Accorsi said, "including Schottenheimer, told me Coughlin was a bear to coach against. Marty said, 'You're probing all the time, you're changing all the time. You can't set a game plan for him. If something doesn't work, he's quick to try something else.' So when John Mara and I sat down with Coughlin at the Newark airport, he was the favorite."

They had streams of questions to put to him, but, pulling out a legal yellow pad, Coughlin asked if he could make an opening statement. Twenty-five minutes later, he was still filibustering. "It annoyed me, turned me off," Ernie said. "'When is this misery going to end?' I thought. I was just about ready to scream 'Enough already!' when he finally stopped. Answering our questions, though, he was good. He fit the part: Jesuit-trained, smart, devout, winner, integrity, clean. I told John Mara later, 'He double-bogeyed the first hole but he still shot sixty-eight.' Tom had done an incredible job with no players at BC. He had made Jacksonville competitive right away. All that said, you're bothered by the three losing seasons [7–9, 6–10, 6–10] at the end in Florida. But the more we studied it, the more we thought it was mostly a personnel problem, and he wasn't going to be in charge of our personnel. He had screwed up the salary cap, too, not signing the right guys, giving too much money to the wrong ones. But he wasn't going to have control of that here, either."

Wellington Mara had been a naval officer, and the Giants' organization was run by chain of command. The Maras didn't fire coaches, or anyone else, blithely. At the same time, Wellington used to say, "Though I'm loyal to you, I'm more loyal to the structure. You'll get yourself fired if you're not." Leaving the Coughlin interview, Accorsi told Mara, "If we can't win with this guy, I'm taking up tennis."

In the midst of the 11–5 2005 season, with Coughlin and Manning settling into place, Ernie was coming up on sixty-five and planning to call it a career. As a matter of fact, he threw himself a farewell party in Baltimore and started to look for a town house in Hershey to serve with his New York apartment as co-headquarters for his retirement. But Wellington's death in October, followed twenty-one days later by the death of Preston Robert Tisch, patriarch of the family that owned the other half of the Giants, made leaving then unseemly. Ernie especially didn't want to abandon John Mara. So there would be one final season for Accorsi, a sentimental last journey through all of the years.

By the way, on the final day of 2005 in Oakland, the Giants had to beat the Raiders, quarterbacked by Kerry Collins, to win the NFC East Division Championship. "I kept telling defensive coordinator Tim Lewis," Ernie said, "'You better blitz him,' 'You better blitz him,' 'You better blitz him.' It almost cost us the game, my big mouth. We blitzed the hell out of him, but the Raiders picked it up, and Kerry was great. He really wanted this one. We survived, thirty to twenty-one, but he was absolutely great. He threw for, like, three hundred thirty yards [331] and three touchdowns." Ernie sounded proud of him. "I was," he said. "I was glad we survived, but I was also glad for Kerry, that he had that moment."

Of splendor.

8

SHOCK

SEATTLE'S QWEST FIELD, known for its din as the land of false starts, had been the Giants' saddest stop in 2005, when they dominated in yardage, first downs, and takeaways but lost in overtime to the eventual NFC champions, 24–21. Near the end of the fourth quarter and twice in sudden death, Jay Feely missed field goal attempts of forty, fifty-four, and forty-five yards. "I love Jay," Accorsi said, "but I'm still pretty wounded by that." The loss reordered all of the home field advantages at the close of the season. In other words, it changed everything.

Tight end Jeremy Shockey had been particularly busy that day, catching ten Eli Manning passes for 127 yards, including a clutch two-point conversion to tie the game near the end of regulation. So it's possible that Shockey had come back to the great Northwest more bent on revenge than anyone else. But not only was there no revenge, there was hardly any football game. On five touchdown passes by Matt Hasselbeck, older brother of Giants backup quarterback Tim Hasselbeck (both of them sons of former Giant tight end Don Hasselbeck), the Seahawks built a 35–0 and then a 42–3 lead, coasting from there to a misleading 42–30 victory. Shockey caught four passes for fifty-eight yards, only one of those before halftime, when the score was 35–3. This year, he was the star of the postgame show.

Not in response to a query, but rather by way of a declaration, Shockey waited until almost everyone had showered before he suddenly announced, "We got outplayed and outcoached," accent on the latter. "Write that one down."

"We played hard," he said, but in case he wasn't heard the first time, he reiterated with fresh emphasis, "We got outplayed and *outcoached*. There are no excuses, no 'twelfth man' or crowd noise to blame. We just lost. Why do I say outcoached? You watched the game. They used defenses we weren't expecting. They did things we haven't seen. The job of the coaches is to put us in the best possible position to succeed."

Apprised of Shockey's outburst, Seattle's Hasselbeck felt unfairly shorted. "How *could* they prepare?" the Seahawks quarterback wondered. "That was the first time we used some of those formations in a game. We ran routes we've never shown before." Other Giants offered blurbs on the team's performance, but "outcoached" was the one that led the review.

"They had fourteen points before we were even lathered up," Tom Coughlin said with unusual flair.

"It's embarrassing," said Tiki Barber. "That's the easiest word."

"Right now," Antonio Pierce said, "we're a horrible team."

"Too much bad football," Manning said, in the simplest expression of all.

The last two players to leave the New York locker room were Shockey and Luke Petitgout. When Petitgout was asked if it mattered that the Giants had scored those twenty-seven late points, he responded with a ringing "No!" "I think it does," said Shockey, contrary to the end, sounding ready to reopen fire. But Luke said, "Shock, come on. The bus is leaving."

Tight ends are in a tough position. They are expected to be as fleet as wide receivers, who are much lighter, at the same time that they are required to block defensive ends, who are much larger. Tight ends get called for holding quite often, but what choice do they have? They are always a little injured, more than a little frustrated. And in Shockey, a regular at the Pro Bowl, every quality was exaggerated. Mike Pope, the Giants' assistant coach in charge of tight ends, told the *New York Times,* "Impulse can be a hard thing to control. This is a very spirited racehorse." Center Shaun O'Hara said, "He's our emotional leader, sometimes for good, sometimes for bad. But you know you're going to get the same thing from him every time, and I love him for it. I wouldn't want anyone else out there."

Ernie saw Shockey for the first time in 2001, when Miami opened its season at Penn State. "I hated him and I loved him," Accorsi said. "They killed Penn State that day [33–7], and Jeremy pranced all over the end zone after scoring touchdowns. I thought, 'I hate this guy.' But what a player."

Did he have his tattoos yet?

"I couldn't tell. I was in the stands."

Come on, Shockey's radiating tattoos were visible from at least the upper deck, if not the blimp.

"We had a psychologist here then," Ernie said. "We don't anymore. He told us flat out, 'You can't draft Shockey.' He had all of these theories about why not. He even came up with some kind of legal thing that I didn't think was true. It became personal for some reason. 'I'm not going to let you draft him,' he said. 'What?' So I went to John Mara. 'Do you mind if I ask the Tisch family [holders of the other 50 percent of the Giants] to borrow their airplane? I need to go to Ada, Oklahoma, to find out the truth about Jeremy Shockey.' Right about that same time, I get a call from the agent Drew Rosenhaus. He and I had a big fight over his constant demands to renegotiate the contract of Jessie Armstead, a linebacker from Miami. Now, Shockey was choosing an agent and Rosenhaus was taking a hell of a chance. He had Jeremy on the line. 'Other agents,' he said, 'are telling Jeremy you won't draft him if I represent him. Will you please tell him that's a crock?' I said, 'Jeremy, Drew and I had problems over one player, but that has nothing to do with you. If we decide to draft you, we'll draft you, whoever your representative is.'"

As usual that year, the University of Miami players snubbed the NFL combine in favor of their own private preview before a mass assembly of GMs and coaches. A half dozen potential first-rounders were on display: offensive tackle Bryant McKinnie, cornerback Phillip Buchanon, safety Ed Reed, cornerback Mike Rumph, running back Clinton Portis, and

Shockey. "Mike Pope was having an orgasm over Shockey's workout," Ernie said. "I told him, 'Mike, come over here. All of the other teams are watching. If you don't quit French-kissing this guy, we're not going to have any shot at him at all. Back off, will you?'"

"Of course I knew who Ernie was," Shockey said. "Everybody in the business knew Ernie Accorsi. I noticed he was the only one who didn't have a team cap on. He was wearing a black golf sweater. When it came my turn to run the forty, he ran, too, to get himself in the best position to see. That was pretty funny, but all of the other GMs moved out of his way. I thought, 'Uh-oh, I better be good now.' It was raining slightly. I was sprinting in a mist. Man, was I moving!" He must have looked like a revolving lawn sprinkler.

When Accorsi reached the Teterboro airport, bound for Oklahoma, the beautiful Tisch airliner was not there. Instead, a trade-out had been arranged. His ride was a rumpled little plane with a young pilot and a trainee for a co-pilot. But they made it to Ada all right. "Landing there," Ernie said, "was like a scene out of a Western movie. A tiny brick building. A pole with one of those wind sleeves on top. A guy with a baseball cap on backwards sitting on the fender of his pickup truck. That was Jeremy. Walking up to him, all I could think of was Mickey Mantle, Commerce, Oklahoma, 1949. Shockey asked, 'What do you want to see first?' I said, 'The police station.'"

They sat in an interrogation room with two cops. "It was a crusty old building," Ernie said. "There was everything except one of those lantern bubble lights on the desk. I began, 'There's a rumor that Jeremy was arrested the night of his high school prom or graduation, gun in the trunk, marijuana in the car, blah, blah, blah.' 'Nope,' one of the cops said deliberately, after rustling through a stack of records, 'nothin' like that, nothin' at all.' 'I ain't never done nothin' wrong!' Jeremy exclaimed [still two shy of the local record for multiple negatives]. I told him, 'Well, there's a lot of money involved here. I'm just checking you out. You want to be a multimillionaire, don't you?' 'Yeah,' he said, and smiled. We hit it off right away."

Straddling a bench in the Giants' training room, Shockey chuckled at the memory and said, 'The truth is, we did get pulled over but I wasn't the one driving. Of course, we were all drinking. And they did find a gun, but it was a paintball gun. I don't know what all they found in that car, a bunch of stuff. We were held for firearm possession and for being under the influence, but we were never charged. We went to jail, but they didn't keep us overnight. It was a place where all the drunks were taken. Concrete floors. We had a good time messing with all the drunk people there for a while. We fit right in. Everything eventually got dropped, though. I ultimately had to pay two hundred dollars to have the arrest expunged. I really didn't do anything wrong."

Their next stop was Ada High School, where as a senior Shockey returned four punts for touchdowns. A transcript was pulled for single mother Lucinda Shockey's famous son, Jeremy Charles Shockey, whose address of record was Rural Route 4, Box 388. The document showed that in his freshman year, Shockey made five C's, in English, algebra, science, history, and Introduction to Composition. The next year, he had three D's, in English, algebra, and French. But something must have happened then. In his third year Shockey posted A's and B's across the board, and in the second semester of his senior year, he received just one B, in English, otherwise all A's. The ACT testing scores were another story, but by Accorsi's reckoning, Jeremy didn't just pass, he passed with distinction.

"I picked our next stop," Shockey said, "Bob's Barbecue. I'll tell you something for a fact, I desperately wanted to be a New York Giant. To me it was the marquee franchise in the NFL. The red, white, and blue. I even more desperately didn't want to be a Cincinnati Bengal. That's where I was hearing I might go. While we were eating the barbecue, Ernie and I talked about everything, and he just seemed so honest that I finally told him the truth about the paintball gun. We talked about sports, all sports. As much as anybody I've ever met, Ernie has an amazing love of sports."

"He tells me," Ernie said, "'You're never going to eat barbecue as good as this the rest of your life.' Jeremy ate a double portion, I had a single—and I couldn't eat again for three days! It was phenomenal!

Oklahoma Sooner memorabilia was plastered all over the joint. 'Why didn't you go to OU?' I asked him. 'When I got out of high school,' he said, 'they didn't want me. Nobody wanted me. I weighed about a buck seventy-five. I hoped to go to Arizona, but I ended up playing junior college ball instead, putting on a few pounds. Then everybody wanted me. But there weren't many schools in the country—there still aren't—that threw to the tight end. Miami did, so I became a Hurricane.'

"We had just a great day," Ernie said. "He drove me everywhere around town. I didn't meet his mom. She was in Dallas. But we talked about her. I liked the way he talked about her. I liked him." Shockey mentioned that former Jet Mark Gastineau was from Ardmore, just fifty miles away, but said, "We've produced more country singers than football players." "Jerry Walker, the old Orioles bonus baby, was from Ada," Ernie told Shockey. "Did you ever hear of him?" Walker threw his arm out in the 1950s when manager Paul Richards let an eighteen-year-old kid pitch a sixteen-inning shutout. "He was the youngest pitcher ever to start the All-Star Game," Accorsi told Shockey, "the youngest one ever to win it, too." Leaning back in the training room, Jeremy said, "I always enjoy hearing someone who loves something go on and on about it. I wonder if there's anything in sports that Ernie doesn't know."

The first man drafted in Shockey's year was Fresno State quarterback David Carr, who went to Houston. Tennessee was picking fourteenth, the Giants fifteenth. As the auction moved along, Rosenhaus called Accorsi to tip him that the Titans might be trading their choice to someone who coveted Shockey. "I figured it was to Oakland," Ernie said. "Big, redheaded tight end, you know. Hadn't Al Davis been searching for another Dave Casper for about twenty-five years? I was criticized for this later, but I gave Tennessee a fourth-round pick to move up just that one rung. You know, to be sure of Jeremy. I don't have any idea who that fourth pick ended up being, and I don't want to know."

"It meant a lot to me that Ernie traded up," Shockey said. "When we were sitting around at Bob's Barbecue, just talking, he told me that a football team is a jigsaw puzzle with a lot of oddly shaped pieces. 'We need a tight end,' he said, 'and I think you just might be the perfect fit. You know, this game is all about mismatches. You're too fast for a linebacker to guard. You're too big for a safety to guard. Who are they going to put on you?' I thought of nothing else but that all through the morning of the draft."

McKinnie ended up going fifth to the Vikings, Shockey fourteenth to the Giants, Buchanon seventeenth to the Raiders, Reed twenty-fourth to the Ravens, Rumph twenty-seventh to the 49ers, and Portis in the second round to the Broncos. "Pretty good Hurricane class, huh?" Jeremy said, "but I felt like the big winner. After I ran for Ernie that time in Miami, we talked a little bit about the five other guys. He agreed with me about four of them, but about the fifth one, he wasn't so sure. And you know what? He was right."

"Jeremy says things I wish he wouldn't," Ernie said, like the word *out-coached,* "and he does things I wish he wouldn't," like throwing his arms up in dismay when Manning missed him with passes. Eli didn't respond in kind when Shockey dropped them. Perhaps he should have. Unitas would have bounced the next pass off the back of his helmet, and the one after that off the front. "But he's just a good-hearted kid from Ada, Oklahoma," Ernie said, and both Shockey and Accorsi agreed that New York City was a challenging place for a good-hearted kid from Ada.

"Yeah," Jeremy said, "I come from a town so small that you could pick up the newspaper, read it, and actually believe what's in it. It's not like I'd never been out of Oklahoma before I came to New York, but I just never dreamed of the media being like this." "Miami," Ernie said, "is a pro town primarily. Almost anything that came out of Jeremy's mouth wouldn't be the biggest story that day. But here, he's perfect for the social and rumor pages, and 'Page Six' of the *New York Post*. In the beginning, I think he got caught up a little, not realizing where he was. But all of the Shockey mannerisms, all of the things that nobody's crazy about, stem from the tremendous pride he has. Jeremy wants to dominate every game he plays in. When he doesn't, he goes almost crazy with frustration. Starting with the fact that he plays the game of football so unbelievably hard, even in practice, he's just a naturally self-destructive character, and of course he's going to clash with Coughlin."

They'd had a lot of small, stupid arguments, like the time Jeremy was fined $100 for being two minutes late to a meeting. He told Ernie, "I wasn't late; Coughlin messed with the clock." " 'Jeremy,' I said, 'pay the hundred dollars.' 'I shouldn't have to pay it. See if you can get me out of it.' 'There'll be times, if it's really important, when I'll intervene on your behalf. But this ain't one of them.' 'Well, goddamn it, I wasn't late!' 'I know what you're making, okay? Do you want me to lend you the hundred bucks?' 'No, I'll pay his fine. But I'm not happy with him.' "

Coughlin's object had never been to make Shockey or any of the other players happy with him. "I came into the league as a head coach in ninety-four, okay?" Tom said, sitting in his office. "In Jacksonville I had the most motley group of people you ever saw in your life. Now, how am I going to mold these players together? Well, one way. Be hard on them. Be tough. Nine-on-seven drills every morning. Make them go to training camp four or five days early. The union's bitching: 'That son of a bitch!' But I'll tell you something, I only had maybe one guy who didn't come the day I asked, and he was still early.

"They're coming off the field every day, every day, they're screaming, 'Aaagh!' So they hated one guy, me. But you know what? They were the toughest bunch of football players you ever saw. The next year we go to the AFC Championship Game with this bunch of guys . . . I don't even know how to describe them."

The French Foreign Legion?

"That's pretty good. The French Foreign Legion. That's it. Unbelievable. That's who you get in expansion. Mercenaries. So I got cast in a certain way. But the simple fact of the matter is, my thing—and people never look at it this way—is that I have a hard time with myself if I treat one person one way and I'm different with someone else. There are certain fundamentals that I believe in, and that's just the way it is. Coaching is making players do what they don't want to do so that they can become what they want to become."

Team leader Michael Strahan, the Giants' fourteen-year defensive end, the only NFL pass rusher ever to record a twenty-two-and-a-half-sack season, said, "The thing is, Tom doesn't make it very easy for you to like him. The first meeting I ever had with him, I walked out of there saying to myself, 'You know what? I'm playing one year with this guy and then I'm leaving.' I hated him. He kind of went at me in that first meeting, and I didn't know him from Adam. 'Why is he coming at me like this?' "

But Strahan didn't leave after a year. In fact, now he was into a third. "Because," he said, "the more I sat down with Tom one-on-one, the more I came to realize that he's a better guy than he gets credit for. He wants to win. I respect that. He really wants to win. He'll do whatever it takes. At the same time, more than almost anybody I've ever been around, he misses the human element. I think a coach has to show a human side, and that's what Coughlin doesn't do. He doesn't do it enough, anyway. Even professional players need to feel their coach cares about them. Talking to Tiki, that's Tiki's whole thing. Tiki said, 'It's like, Coach couldn't give a shit about me,' and I think that led to Tiki saying, 'Screw me? No, screw you. I'm outta here.' "

About a month before it broke in the news, Ernie mentioned that Barber's tenth pro year would almost certainly be his last. Yet Tiki was playing better than ever. "It's amazing, isn't it?" Accorsi said. "Tiki's amazing." Coughlin had long since cured Barber of his well-known case of fumble-itis. Maybe Tiki resented Tom for that, too.

It's a negotiating ploy, right? Threatening to retire at the top of his game?

"I don't think so," Ernie said. "I'm not even going to try to talk him out of it. Maybe my successor will. But, to tell you the truth, I don't believe it has anything to do with Coughlin or with anyone except Tiki. This has been the plan all along. He wants to be a television journalist, the next Matt Lauer. Tiki won't be reading the baseball scores at eleven o'clock at night, I can promise you that. He'll be interviewing kings and prime ministers in the morning."

Tiki and his identical twin, Ronde, a defensive back for Tampa Bay, played their college ball together at the University of Virginia, for George Welsh. "When Coughlin took over as the Giants' head coach," Welsh said, "I asked Tiki, 'What's he like?' 'He's like you,' he said. I took that to mean tough, maybe even too tough."

Strahan said, "Tom doesn't know it, but his main philosophy—'Treat everybody the same'—is wrong. He's scared to death someone will say, 'Look, that guy over there is getting special treatment.' Hell, special treatment is what makes a football team work. I've had conversations with Tom about this, trying to tell him that each player is not the same. You can't treat Tiki the same way you treat Brandon Jacobs. You can't treat me the same way you're going to treat a rookie, Kiwanuka. I told him, 'Coach, you just can't treat everybody the same. You don't treat your kids the same. You shouldn't treat your players the same. Hell, we're all special.'

"Listen to this. Tom once said this to me: 'I tell somebody to do something and they hate me. You tell them to do the same thing, and they go off and do it.' I said, 'Of course, Coach. You've got to know the guys. You've got to care about them, try to understand their different personalities.' But he looked at me like I was speaking a foreign language."

Interestingly, the tension between Coughlin and the New York media flowed from the same source. "I don't do any of that sidebar stuff," Tom said. "I don't have special writers or broadcasters who call me on the side for additional information, and you know, they hate me for that. Some of the media stars expect you to play this 'if you do things for me, I'll do things for you' game. The first year I was here, one of them wanted to do a family story. My family. I did it. They killed me. Another thing: we've got this little practice area, and there's a box for the media. I've always had that. Part of it's for safety. Part of it is just so I'll know where they are, so we can do our work without everybody being underfoot. Well, they hate me for that, too, because they had total free rein under Jim Fassel."

On the rare occasions when Yankees manager Joe Torre came under media fire, Tom thought he could detect a self-interested restraint on the part of the beat men and an unspoken threat from Torre. "Just reading between the lines," Coughlin said, "it sounded to me like if the writers happened to go too far, Joe just might stop playing ball with them. With me, on the other hand, they know there's no possible repercussions because I don't play ball anyway. 'Coughlin doesn't give you anything,' they tell each other, 'so there's nothing to take back.'" Out of left field, Torre telephoned Coughlin once just because Tom looked so miserable to Joe on television. Torre didn't even know Coughlin, but seeing him on the sideline, he was worried about him.

Football coaches have always been stereotyped by their sideline demeanors. Tethered to his frozen headset in Minnesota, Bud Grant used to be the "iceman." Standing as erect as a Scoutmaster at the Dallas bench, Tom Landry was the "plastic man." Tearing up yardage markers and coldcocking opposing brigands who intercepted passes off clean-cut Buckeyes like Art Schlister, Woody Hayes was the madman of Columbus, Ohio. In fact, all three could be terrifically charming people away from the field. "They've done that to me here, too," Coughlin said. "I'm that crazy person running up and down the sidelines. But I'm not going to apologize for being passionate. If they stamp you, you're stamped. But if they think I'm going to stand there like a statue, I can't do that. I'm not Tom Landry. And I don't look that good in a fedora." Finally, Coughlin allowed himself a small joke.

"Football's a complicated game," he continued in a slower meter. "The media try to make it a soap opera because they understand soap operas better than they do football. Most of them don't study the game. They don't really see it. I don't think most of them even really like it. They listen to other people who don't know, either, and formulate their opinions based on that. There's no depth to it. They latch on to everything that doesn't matter and forget about the game. That's not the game. *The game. The game.*"

Pat Hanlon, the Giants' PR man, who may be the most thoughtful one in the industry, probably knew Coughlin the best, as it usually fell to Hanlon to steer Tom through the media shoals. "This is a business," Pat said, "where the head coaches are always telling you how hard they work, how many hours they put in at the projector, how many nights they sleep in their offices. I've been with several head coaches who wore that on their sleeves as a badge of honor. How awfully, awfully hard they work. How terribly, terribly tough it is. They just can't stop reminding you.

"Well, this guy has never once even hinted that the hours are difficult, or that the work is impossible. *Woe is me. I have to be here at five in the morning and I don't leave until eleven at night, if I leave at all.* None of that. Never. And I'll tell you something, Coughlin works twice as hard as any of the others I've known. And on an intellectual level he's miles ahead of all of them. He's the brightest person, by far. I just wish he could—or *we* could—communicate to the public how much Tom loves the game of football, how much it really matters to him. That might help. He told me, 'The day I retire will probably be two days before I kick. If I didn't have football, I don't know how I'd keep living.'"

In every football town, a few of the players and a few of the reporters whisper to each other about the head coach. That's traditional. "Right, they're kindred spirits," Hanlon said. "They both feel he doesn't give them the attention they deserve, at least not in the way they want it to be given. Griping players and their media soul mates are an institution. But wouldn't it be nice if everybody would shut up for just a minute and take a closer look at this guy?"

"By the way," Ernie said, "on my return trip from Ada to Teterboro, the trainee is flying the little plane and the young pilot is talking her through it. They have all the manuals open and spread out across the dash. We're not on instruments, it's clear. I'm nervous as hell. This is no joke. We're zooming and sliding, and all of a sudden we blow right past the Meadowlands and Teterboro. I say, 'Uh, excuse me a second, but wasn't that the airport back there? Far be it for me to interfere, but we're not going to England, are we?' 'Hey, you're right!' They were from Buffalo, both of them. We made it down okay."

Accorsi didn't kiss the ground, but he thought about it. Anyway, he had his tight end.

9

THE DRAFT

ON HIS WAY TO winning the Heisman Trophy in 1972, a gas station robbery turned up in Johnny Rodgers' past. This slight embarrassment, combined with his five-nine, 165-pound dimensions, dropped the sensational Nebraska running back to the bottom of the first round of the NFL draft. In a famous colloquy repeated in draft rooms every April, Lloyd Wells, head scout of the Kansas City Chiefs, still argued for selecting Rodgers. "If we pick this guy," coach Hank Stram argued back, "we'll have to build a jail cell." "Build it in the end zone," Wells said.

"After going to ten straight championship games with Otto Graham at quarterback," said Accorsi, "the Cleveland Browns had their first losing season in 1956 with George Ratterman and Babe Parilli sharing Otto's old job. At the next draft, Paul Brown was desperate for a quarterback and the Browns were picking sixth. The guy they wanted was Len Dawson. As the first few picks were rattled off, Mike Brown told me, 'My dad was, like, he couldn't breathe.' Now came the fourth choice. Now came the fifth. The Pittsburgh Steelers took Dawson. With a thud Brown dropped his head on the table. He was despondent. 'Dad, what are we going to do now?' Mike whispered. The clock was ticking. In a resigned voice, without lifting his head, Paul said, 'I guess we're stuck with Jim Brown.'"

Looking at the board in the Giants' draft room, Accorsi said, "We start to get ready for a draft by gathering all of the scouts together—the heroes of the whole process—and talking about every player in the country who's even remotely a prospect. We grade them, both overall and by position, and stagger the names all over these walls. We'll get together often during the year, finally in a marathon meeting that lasts two or three weeks. By the time April rolls around, every top player has had five, six, seven looks. We start plugging them in by rounds, our own lists of thirty-two." Nodding toward a small photograph of Wellington Mara, Ernie said, "We put Well here because he always sat right here. From the first meeting in February, he'd have all of his materials out. He would take notes. Just take notes.

"On draft day itself, the feeling is incredibly tense. I sit here, Tom Coughlin sits here, [player personnel director] Jerry Reese sits here, scouts fan out around the room, assistant coaches huddle in the back. Reese presides. He's incredibly well organized. We'll talk about Jerry some more. You have to listen to each other. There have been too many incidents in my career where the only guy in the room who likes or dislikes a player is right, so you better hear them all. Take Tom Brady, for instance [a sixth-round pick from Michigan, the second man selected by the Patriots in that round, the 199th player chosen overall]. After Brady started winning Super Bowls with New England, I went back and looked at all of our Brady reports. Everybody killed him except one guy, Whitey Walsh. If you read Whitey's report on Brady, it's a prediction of exactly how it turned out. He was the only guy who saw it. Sometimes you have to listen to the one guy."

There were banks of phones. "But I've learned to leave the room to field trade offers on draft day," Ernie said. "You get a thousand pitches for last-minute deals, because everybody is trying to screw you. 'I've got five extra sixth-round picks. Do you want two of them for your third-rounder?' I say no to almost everything. I'm not going to sell my scouts down the river. But I stopped using this phone when Jim Fassel was still coaching here, because he would kibitz. 'What's the offer?' 'The Jets want to give us so-and-so and a fifth for our second.' 'Take it! Take it!' he'd yell. Half the time he didn't even know what kind of players those picks represented."

One of the most memorable moments in the annals of Giants drafting occurred in 2004, as the first round was bleeding into the second. "Reading the board and sort of doing the math," Ernie said, "it looked to me like we might land on Chris Snee." He was a 314-pound guard from Boston College, but there was an interesting complication. Snee was already the father of Coughlin's grandson Dylan but not yet the husband of Tom's daughter, Katie. Tennessee took Antwan Odom, defensive end from Alabama; San Francisco took Shawntae Spencer, cornerback from Pitt; Cleveland took Sean Jones, safety from Georgia. "Tom," Ernie told Coughlin, "it's looking like Snee. It's your call. I'm giving you the whole say. We can bypass him if you want." "Let's wait until we get there," Coughlin said. New Orleans took Courtney Watson, linebacker from Notre Dame; Kansas City took Kris Wilson, tight end from Pitt; Carolina took Keary Colbert, wide receiver from USC. "Tom, it's Snee. I think it's Snee. Make a decision." New England took Marquise Hill, defensive end from LSU . . .

"Finally," Ernie said, "Tom called home and spelled it out for his wife, Judy. 'We can take him or leave him,' he said," something husbands often wish they could say to wives about men who are only prospective sons-in-law. "Tom hung up," Ernie said, "and told me, 'Okay, let's take him.'" So, in the second choice of the second round, on the recommendation of the coach's wife, the Giants took Chris Snee of Boston College, who became an immediate starter. As it turned out, the ending was happy all around. Chris and Katie married, and they quickly gave Dylan a baby brother, Cooper Christopher.

Though Ernie knew he wouldn't be participating in any more college drafts, which was almost his favorite part of the job, he made a few final scouting trips anyway, sentimental Saturday journeys, starting in the Giants' post-Seattle bye week. Over Accorsi's three and a half decades as a bird dog, the only major football campuses he hadn't scoured for talent were Baylor, Oregon, Oregon State, and Purdue. "Purdue's a total mystery," he said, "I don't know how I ever missed Purdue."

His habit and pleasure was to stroll university grounds on crisp Friday afternoons searching for "the original heart of the campus before billionaire alumni and high-rise architects turned these beautiful little gardens into industrial parks." As long as he was there, he would satisfy his addiction for collegiate sweatshirts ("I can't live long enough to wear all of the ones I already have"), and he usually attended the pep rally.

The first stop, as always, was Penn State, for a game against Northwestern at Beaver Stadium. Ernie stayed in an economy hotel in the center of University Park, where the drapes could have been the same ones he remembered from the 1960s. Before meeting his old boss, Jim Tarman, for dinner, Ernie milled with the students through the streets of the college town and remembered everything. He joined the Tarmans—Louise had Beano Cook's vote for best wife in the history of collegiate athletics—at Centre Hills Country Club, hard by a golf course and in sight of Mount Nittany. Joe Paterno was too busy to join them, plotting the game and shaking off a practice-field collision that broke three ribs, though he didn't know it yet. "I can't even blow my nose," Joe said the next day, "my chest hurts so bad." A bigger collision was ahead, but nothing ever stopped Paterno. "Why would Ernie Accorsi retire?" he asked me. Why would anyone retire, he meant.

Saturday was a dingy day—gray thunderclouds sat on the stadium. But the flapping white towels and the other school cheers worked as brighteners. "The NFL doesn't have this," Ernie said, setting up his pens and notebooks in the front row of the press box. "It has a lot of great things, but it doesn't have this." A gigantic offensive tackle, Levi Brown, seemed to interest Accorsi most. Ernie also scribbled a few notes on defensive tackle Jay Alford, who wore a strange number for a lineman, 13. As usual, the Nittany Lions employed a linebacker worth evaluating, an Aliquippa, Pennsylvania, honor roll student with the football-sounding name Paul Posluszny. He must have been pretty good because Accorsi's look at him was the Giants' seventh. "Posluszny had a little problem with his right knee," Ernie said, "and I think it may have cost him some outside speed. But he's got instinctive quickness in the box. He's got nice footwork, doesn't he?"

Notre Dame was another mandatory port of call.

"I flew into South Bend on a commuter plane," Ernie said when he arrived. "Flying over the Golden Dome, all of a sudden the pilot actually dipped the wing to give us the full effect. A woman across the aisle from me was almost overcome with emotion. Not for herself, I figured. I doubt she was a football fan. I bet it was for a husband or a father. But she told us that this was her first look at Notre Dame, and it was some moment. Like landing in Lourdes." As a matter of fact, Ernie wanted to stop first at the grotto, to kneel where Paul Hornung had knelt in a classic *Life* magazine photograph, and to light a candle. All of the vigil stands were ablaze, so a couple of candles had to be discreetly blown out and relit. Then he went looking for the Irish coach, Charlie Weis, runner-up for the Giants job.

"Didn't you tell Mr. Mara I went to Mass every day?" Weis said, still a little sore. "No, I didn't tell him that," Ernie said, "because you don't. He thinks you're Jewish, Charlie." Like most football coaches, Weis was the hero of all his stories. His old boss, Bill Parcells, took Charlie's most brilliant ideas and passed them off as his own. (All former assistants tell these same exact stories.) Good-naturedly, Weis needled Accorsi for spurning him in favor of Coughlin. "You're rooting your heart out against Tom, aren't you?" Ernie said. "What d'ya mean?" Charlie said. "I'm a Giants fan!" "Save that back-door slider you throw for somebody else," Ernie said. But, in a becoming moment, Weis murmured, "Just because you want a job doesn't mean you're ready for it."

The Irish opponent the next day was North Carolina, whose coach had already been fired. So this amounted to a bye week for Notre Dame, too. At the players' final run-through in the field house, Charlie had to dig unusually deep to find something about which to sound pissed. Calling quarterback Brady Quinn and the rest of his charges together at midfield, Weis said, "If NBC homes in on any of you after the game and you're not mouthing the words to the alma mater—and they better be the right words, too—you and I are going to have a big, big problem." But after dismissing the team, Charlie giggled at Accorsi and brought him in on the evening's plot to spring "Happy Birthday" on Charlie's wife at the pep rally. "I'm going to get everyone to sing to her," he said. "She's going to kill me, but it's going to be great." Taking his cue from a profanity-laden profile of Weis on *60 Minutes*, the leprechaun mascot introduced Charlie to the assembly as "the best bleeping coach in America."

For memory collecting, Accorsi rated only two colleges ahead of Penn State and Notre Dame: the Naval Academy and West Point. Though Phil McConkeys, never mind Roger Staubachs, were becoming rarer and rarer at Navy, Ernie still liked to walk the cobblestones of Annapolis, to throw pennies like a plebe at Tecumseh, and to answer the questions in the midshipmen's Reef Points booklet: How's the cow? "She walks, she talks, she's full of chalk. The lacteal fluid extracted from the female of the bovine species is highly prolific to the nth degree." Even more, he loved West Point. Of all the side benefits that have flowed from being the GM of the Giants, by several touchdowns the most wonderful was an invitation Ernie received, as if he were MacArthur, to address the senior class of cadets.

"I have walked the streets of Saint-Lô, through the trees of the Ardennes, been to the Remagan bridge, the beaches of Anzio, stood on Monte Cassino, and been to the grave of George Patton in Luxembourg," Accorsi said in the middle of his talk. "If I have one unfulfilled dream in football, it is that I never had the chance to hire Patton as my head coach. Do you think he might have won the Super Bowl?

"When we select players, we are selecting people. In the final analysis, it's not the biggest and fastest player that prevails. It's the best competitor. The best man . . . [An old Marine] once told me, 'I learned two things from the Marine Corps. Officers eat last, and the troops fight for each other.' They don't fight for their commanders. They don't fight for their division. They fight for their buddies. When I select a football player for the Giants, I can't help thinking of that. 'Will this guy be a good teammate? Will this be the kind of man that my players will fight for?' Because that's how you win . . .

"Every fall, usually when the leaves are at the peak of their splendor, I scout an Army game at Michie Stadium. I don't expect to find Dan

Marino out there, but I don't come here for that. I come here because I want to hear the corps sing 'On Brave Old Army Team,' the grandest of all college fight songs. I don't sit in the press box. I sit in the lower stands across from the home side because I am only here for one reason—the corps. It is always my favorite trip of the season. It is my honor to be with you at this sacred place . . .

"Beat Navy!"

When the Giants' bye week ended, it seemed that a lot more than fourteen days had passed since the Seattle debacle, especially for Accorsi, refreshed from scouting. But the players hadn't exactly been on vacation, and extra time to think was, historically, never a benefit to the Giants. A lifetime supply of seventeen post-bye-week games yielded a grand total of three victories, none in the last five years. And journalistically it had been a restless fortnight in New York, where the phonograph needle was stuck on the word *outcoached*.

The Washington Redskins were in town, encouraged by two straight victories built on five-hundred-yard offensive explosions detonated by Coughlin's old Jacksonville quarterback, lefty Mark Brunell. "Our game plan was not to think too much, just go," Michael Strahan said. "Our game plan was to stop depending on our individual talent," Tiki Barber said, "and become a team." "Our game plan," said center Shaun O'Hara, "was to stop playing with a sense of entitlement and start playing with a sense of urgency." Also, O'Hara said, "to stuff the ball down their throats."

Tiki took his lead from, of all people, Coughlin, paraphrasing one of Tom's midweek addresses. "I was going to ask you for a players-only meeting," he told the coach, "but you did it for me." Stop depending on individual talent. Become a team. Coughlin also instructed John Hufnagel to instruct Eli Manning to hand the ball to Barber, which he did twenty-three times, and Tiki logged 123 yards rushing.

Washington gained only 164 total. In a defensive statement featuring sacks from Strahan, Osi Umenyiora, and Fred Robbins, each one followed by a fake basketball jump shot that must have been unsightly even to former Jet exhibitionist Mark Gastineau, the Giants killed all suspense in the first drive of the third quarter and went on to win, 19–3.

GIANTS

1-10-G31 Barber runs for 9
2-1-G40   Barber runs for 5
1-10-G45 Manning passes incomplete
2-10-G45 Manning passes to Brandon Jacobs for 9
3-1-R46   Jacobs runs for 2
1-10-R44 Barber runs for 7
2-3-R37   Barber runs for 2
3-1-R35   Jacobs runs for 4
1-10-R31 Manning passes to Plaxico Burress for 5
2-5-R26   Jacobs runs for 6
1-10-R20 Manning called for intentional grounding
2-20-R30 Manning passes to Burress for 4
3-16-R26 (shotgun) Manning passes to Amani
     Toomer for 21
1-G-R5   Barber runs for 3
2-G-R2   Manning passes to Burress for 2 and the
     touchdown; Jay Feely's extra point is good
          Giants 16, Redskins 3

Afterward, Coughlin wasn't able to laugh off all of the "insurrection in the locker room" stories (a couple of months later, they would resurface as "mutiny" stories), though laughter would have been a good option. "There wasn't anything that had to be quieted down," he said in a Commander Queeg–like reply to a leading question. "You take one statement [Shockey's] and run with it, which you all did—and enjoyed it—for two weeks. There wasn't any problem in the locker room." *And enjoyed it* was the part of his speech soaked in strychnine.

Newly acquired free agent LaVar Arrington, who figured to be the Washington game's central character, put in a mellow performance, making one tackle, batting down one pass, being just a serviceable cog in the combined defense. Once he was the Redskins' second overall pick in the draft, from Penn State. In March 2006, Arrington left the team after six seasons by mutual delight, weak-kneed but rich. In the New York tabloids, LaVar was known as "the $49 million man," a reference to what Ernie had agreed to pay him over seven years. It didn't take even a month of mediocre Sundays for this headline to appear: "LaVar Arrington. Why Did We Bring Him Here?" "You're supposed to act like those things don't bother you," LaVar said, "but they do."

Before his grudge match with Washington, Arrington mischievously hinted that he had pinched his old playbook, seven hundred pages thick, and brought it with him to New York. Redskins cornerback Shawn Springs and, more surprisingly, linebacker coach Dale Lindsey countered that LaVar had never seemed to grasp what was in that book anyway. "They literally insulted my intelligence," Arrington said huffily. "I had heard that expression my whole life." After the Giants' victory, LaVar could have razzed them both if he wanted to, but decided against it. "On the field," he said, "I did do a little trash-talking, but in a good spirit, because I know so many of them. Trash-talking used to be a big part of my game, even at Penn State."

Days after Washington was beaten, LaVar was sitting in the players' lounge with the television muted. He was kind of muted himself. "You know, I was always the star," he said, fiddling with his dreadlocks. That was certainly true. From the peewee leagues on, Arrington stood out above everyone else. As a senior running back and linebacker at North Hills High School in Pittsburgh, he was *Parade* magazine's trumpeted selection as the best prep player in the nation. At Penn State, Arrington won the Chuck Bednarik Award for being—if its namesake means anything—the most wanton defensive player in all of college football. LaVar also took home the Dick Butkus trophy as the premier linebacker. The NFL drafted him ahead of the likes of Jamal Lewis, Brian Urlacher, Bubba Franks, Plaxico Burress, Shaun Alexander, Thomas Jones, and Chad Pennington. Quickly LaVar staffed three Pro Bowls.

"But, you know," he said, drawing the words out carefully, "I've never lived up to the hype. Go back to draft day, 2000. The second pick overall. I've never lived up to what I was supposed to be. How could I? You know, since I was a little boy, I've never been allowed just to make a tackle. It's not enough for LaVar Arrington just to make a tackle. It has to be an extraordinary tackle. It has to be a tackle that takes *everyone's* breath away. He has to leap over the line in a single bound. He has to knock the quarterback unconscious, or something of the sort. So, he tries to do it that way, and you know what happens? He misses the sound tackle he might have made because he has to do it in the most dramatic fashion. And a game is lost. That's been my life in football."

For the first time in his life, LaVar was attempting to play within himself, within a system, and the coaches were generally satisfied. He heard no major complaints during film critiques. "He was poised and professional today," Coughlin said after the Redskins game. "He wanted to play well. He was physical and involved." But the media weren't happy. LaVar's performances looked dull to them. Here was another guy who seemed like he didn't care all that much.

"I would never ask anyone to take exactly what I say and run with it," Arrington said. "I mean it. I would never say, 'Write this about me or I'll never talk to you again,' because that's not fair. That's not life. They have to include their take, their part. I understand. I get it. But can't I have a little part, too? There's a picture being painted here, and it's supposed to be a picture of me. Can't I hold the brush for just a second? Please let me put a little paint on the damn canvas, so that this stroke here, that stroke there, are *my* strokes. They may not completely coincide with what's being written or what's being said, but there'll at least be touches of what I consider to be the truth. Most often, isn't the story already written by the time they come to you? Let's be straight here. Don't they just need a quote or two to fit into the second paragraph and the fifth? But I go on talking to them, and I'll tell you why. Because I figure that even if the publisher and the editor say this is the story they want, at the end of the day maybe I can raise the individual reporter's consciousness level just a little. Just one brushstroke. For what it's worth, that means something to me. I'll still get ripped, but I'll have had a small impact."

If LaVar were Dorian Gray, what would the picture in his attic look like?

"Like a veteran in his seventh year," he said, "who's finally learning how to play football and may not be allowed to do it much longer."

Sometimes, he said, looking around the New York locker room, he felt homesick for the Nittany Lions. "As always, there I was, trying to stand out; and there Joe Paterno was, trying to keep anything from standing out." The plainest white-and-blue uniforms. Bare legs. No names on the jerseys. If he could, Joe probably would take the numbers off as well. "Yeah, I bet he would," Arrington said. "I'll tell you, though, I learned so many lessons from that man. Of course I didn't know I was learning them at the time. How to win, how to lose, how to draw, how to love, how to hate. Do things the Penn State way, they told you, and your life will be a lot smoother. You want to hear something hysterical? I'm just starting to do things the Penn State way."

A few other players, including Manning, came into the room then and turned on the TV. So Arrington got up and, slapping his flip-flops against the floor on the downbeat, moseyed back to his locker. "No, I've never lived up to the hype," he finished as he had started. "Maybe that's why I can relate to Eli. He hasn't lived up to his hype yet, either. God, who could?"

Back in the front office, Accorsi said, "I want to show you something. My heart skipped a beat when I saw this." Ernie led the way to a couple of musty file cabinets tucked into an alcove around the corner from the draft room. "They're Wellington Mara's," he said. They were full of old college football magazines. Like *Football Quarterly,* autumn 1949, 25 cents. Charlie Justice of North Carolina was on the cover in a leather helmet. *Football Annual,* 1948, Chuck Bednarik snapping the ball between his legs for Penn. "This is Wellington's," Ernie said. "This is how he scouted in the old days. Look at the names he has underlined, only the right ones. Ernie Stautner, Ed Songin, Art Spinney. Almost every underlined name is someone who wasn't the biggest college star but ended up a solid player in the league."

There was a time when NFL teams didn't have so many resources, so many scouts. Oh, hell, let's just take Jim Brown.

10

RONNIE

I'M EXHAUSTED, I'M HURTING, I've got ice bags all over me, I love this game," said the old Giants tight end Mark Bavaro a few years ago, speaking pretty much for everyone.

Early Monday morning, even after night games, the players drag themselves back to the stadium and into the training room like casualties of war in a *M*A*S*H* episode. The relatively uninjured lift weights. The others line up for their various treatments or to schedule MRIs. They appear even huger up close, and yet more human. Many of them are the size of British telephone booths with heads like microwave ovens or nineteen-inch color television sets. To explain this race of superpeople whose program weights are underestimated at 302, 303, 306, 308, 310, 315, 317, 318, 319, 327, and 335 pounds, "strength" coaches point to modern training apparatuses like the Nautilus machines already clanking and humming before 7:00 A.M. But not even someone with the imagination of Jules Verne could stand beside an NFL offensive lineman and believe this is a product of normal exercise and natural nutrition.

In an area adjacent to the Giants' locker room, stainless-steel heat tubs were boiling and blue-padded examination tables were bustling. Win or lose, pro football players never sleep too long or too well on Sunday nights. "No, no, they can't," said Ronnie Barnes, the Giants' head trainer. "Adrenaline doesn't just stop flowing on a dime, you know. It's amazing, but no matter how early in the morning we arrive here on Mondays, there are always players waiting for us."

"Us" included assistant Johnny Johnson, a Giants trainer for more than half a century, who back in the 1950s taped the ankles of old number 42, the Mississippi quarterback Charlie Conerly. Upon hearing that, another Ole Miss quarterback, Eli Manning, politely asked Johnson if, just one time, he wouldn't mind taping Eli's ankles the same way. "I considered that to be a real good sign," said the old trainer with the world's most creased and kindest face.

"Johnny will be ninety this year," Barnes said. "He still loves it. He still cares. I think if his wife had not died he would have retired, but I'm glad he's still here. He's our continuity. That's a word I've always associated with the Giants. It's kind of typical of this organization to care about continuity."

Pro football players start to recover from the games the second they emerge out of the steam cloud of the locker room into the damp catacombs of the stadium where their families are standing in wait wearing their Sunday best. The youngest children are so innocent of injuries and losses that their fathers just have to smile again, to laugh, and even to sing. "I don't think that's phony, either," Barnes said. "It's a way for them to kind of put all of the bad stuff out of their mind, temporarily. But when they walk into this building the next morning, the pain comes back, and the memories, too. The penalties they were called for, the passes they could have caught, the runs that didn't go quite like they'd hoped they would. Mental well-being is a very big concern of this job. Plain, simple encouragement. On a regular basis, we have to pick them up and get them going again. We do it in a lot of different ways. If they want to talk about the game and talk about themselves, we do that. If they want to talk about absolutely anything other than football, we can do that, too. We do that frequently."

Many NFL teams, as Ernie had said, tried employing psychologists or psychiatrists for a while. But most of the shrinks turned out to be creeps. "They're outsiders; they're not insiders," Barnes said, "and they don't work very well in this setting. The players have a sense that they're snooping. Reading minds, collecting information, and not necessarily for the players' benefit, either. For management. You have to develop a trust with these guys to treat them. If you have their confidence, you can help them in a good many ways. Ernie sometimes asks me about conversations I have with the players, but he knows I'm only going to tell him so much. What he's really asking is: what kind of person do I think this player is? Of course, the cover doesn't always show you what's inside, what a player is struggling with. It may be two brothers in the penitentiary, or a mother who's recovering from a crack addiction. These are human beings, and though they're not adolescents, they're still learning how to be adults. From the cradle until here, they've been taken care of. Someone made sure they got to class. Now they have a real job. They're employees. And sometimes their supervisors don't say very kind things. The 'renewal contract' is the one that teaches the players this is a business, and they actually express that. 'I know it's a business, but . . .' What happened to that game they used to play?"

They are, as anyone can see, the most tattooed body of men this side of D block or the merchant marine. Written across one muscular back, in perfect block letters, was the philosophy "Everything happens for a reason." These elaborate etchings (Shockey's right arm might have been co-designed by John James Audubon and George M. Cohan) don't necessarily say anything about class or culture. When Dartmouth graduate Reggie Williams was serving both as a linebacker and as a city councilman in Cincinnati, he sported a musical tattoo on one bulging forearm. "It's a crescendo," Williams told me once. "Don't you have to have a certain rhythm in your life?"

Giants players often confide in Barnes, even about their contracts. They ask him how they're doing, too. He isn't always sure what to say. But they probably already know that answer. "I'm a medical guy," Barnes said, "so for me to tell Ernie 'I don't think this guy is going to be very good' wouldn't be appropriate. I wouldn't do it. Maybe the hardest part of this whole job is how much you know. You know what the coach thinks about a guy, what the general manager thinks about him, what the other players think about him. And then you have the one-to-one relationship with him. All these things are spinning around in the back of your head when a player is looking you in the eye and asking you, 'How do you think I'm doing?' 'What do you think my chances of coming back here next year are?' 'Do you think I'll get a contract extension?'

"I've stopped saying to myself, 'You shouldn't tie yourself emotionally to every single player,' because you really have no choice. They all get injured and you can't help but feel something. When they do have to leave, whether they retire, get cut, or leave by injury, every one of these guys takes a little piece of you with him and takes something away from you forever."

Barnes was born in Rocky Mount, North Carolina, and grew up loving all of the games that he was too slight to play. Because his father was a Baptist minister, Ronnie didn't see much professional football. Sundays were spent in church. By kickoff time, one o'clock, his father was just hitting his sermonic stride. Reverend Barnes could talk. Not so much a fire-and-brimstoner, he was more of a teacher. "His congregation appreciated that," Ronnie said.

Nineteen sixties integration, something North Carolina called "Freedom of Choice," delivered Barnes and ten or eleven other black children all the way across town into the midst of some twelve hundred white classmates at Charles L. Coon (swear to God) Junior High School. Barnes tried out for the basketball team but ended up the equipment manager, a first-aider, an adhesive taper, and a medic, one with a valuable sense of when to call the real doctor. Finishing high school in 1970, he majored in sports medicine at East Carolina University and pursued anatomy, physiology, kinesiology, and all of the body sciences to a master's degree at Michigan State. Ronnie studied compassion, however, under Wellington Mara.

A football owner who wouldn't ride in a limousine, Mara died on October 25, 2005, at eighty-nine, but remained a presence on the team. He was the conscience of the New York Giants. Everyone in the front office was still striving to meet his standard. At every turn, they asked themselves, "What would Wellington say? What would he do?" Barnes, maybe more than any of the others, had the answer. "He knew right from wrong," Ronnie said, "and he insisted on doing right."

Most of Mara's senior adult life, he was in relatively good health. But he had an octogenarian's typical list of maladies and took blood-thinning medication. "Coumadin," Barnes said. "Mr. Mara didn't like going to doctors, so I sort of became his physician. He'd drop down here to have his blood pressure checked or to have me look at something." Ronnie was the one who found the inflammation in Mara's lymph node. He was the first person to feel a stab of dread.

"I was scared," Barnes said. "He was planning to see a general surgeon, but I talked him into going to Memorial Sloan-Kettering. It's the best New York has to offer and probably the world. After his surgery, I spent the night with Mr. Mara in his hospital room. There was a couch there. That summer while we were in training camp, he recuperated at home. For the first two or three weeks back from camp, I didn't go to practice. He'd come down here. There were some skin issues, and I was helping him with those, and then we did some rehabilitation. He was convinced that if he could just get his arm back up he'd be all right. He was a hell of a competitor."

But he was growing weaker by the visit. "At first he started to hold on to the walls," Ronnie said, "then he would hold on to me, and finally on a Saturday morning I got a call saying, 'Dad doesn't want to come in today for rehab; he can't get out of bed.' 'He's got to go to the hospital,' I said. They called me back to tell me, 'He doesn't want to go; he wants to stay here.' But they put me on the phone with him, and I talked him into it. That's when I started staying with him every night on the couch."

For many days, Barnes left his players to the care of the assistants, concentrating on Wellington. At one point, Ronnie felt derelict enough in his duties to call Coach Coughlin and apologize for running out on the team. " 'I've abandoned you,' I said, getting a little emotional. There was a pause on the line. Tom told me in a low, cracking voice, 'You're doing God's work.'" The cover doesn't always show you what's inside. "My first year," Coughlin said, "there was one guy in the locker room every Sunday. He stood up against the wall, never said a word. He was just there. The players saw him. Wellington.

"I get hired, we get off to a pretty good start, but then we begin losing ball games. Little notes of encouragement start coming from Wellington. He'd stick his head in my office and say, 'I agreed with what you did there, we're thinking the same way,' little things like that. As much as this business puts you on an island and makes you feel like you're all alone, you were never alone if you worked for Wellington Mara."

Ronnie said, "In the hospital Mr. Mara and I talked about everything, about his family and how much he loved them, everything but football. One night he lost his rosary in the bedding. Just couldn't find it. We had this handoff routine we had silently worked on. If he got up in the middle of the night to go to the bathroom, he'd hold out his hand with the rosary and I'd take it. As soon as he was back in bed and had his pillows situated, he'd reach out again and I'd wind the beads around his fingers, and off he'd go to sleep." Cardinal Edward Egan replaced the lost rosary, and Mara graciously pretended that the substitute was just as good as the starter. There were bunches of rosaries tangled up in a drawer. "But we were both so glad when a nurse found the real one," said Barnes, the Southern Baptist.

New York was having a nice season, but Mara seldom asked about the Giants. "He had so much faith in John Mara," Barnes said. "He wouldn't say, 'I trust John to run the team. He always used both names, 'John Mara,' in what I took to be a sign of respect. 'Ask John Mara.' 'John Mara can handle it.' Mostly we talked about everything but the Giants.

"He asked about the night baseball games that he would start to watch on TV but in the middle of which he would inevitably fall asleep. 'How did the Yankees do, Ronnie?'" For some reason Mara became seriously wrapped up in the fortunes of the Cleveland Indians. In a panic, Barnes called Accorsi to ask, "Quick, what do I need to know about the Cleveland Indians?" They were hot. Ernie filled him in on the broadest details, and every day after that Accorsi sent Barnes the updated standings and statistics by BlackBerry, as well as the scuttlebutt surrounding the pennant race. Ronnie said, "My job was to straighten out the bed, elevate his legs, take his temperature and blood pressure, guard his rosary, and keep him abreast of the Cleveland Indians."

Eventually they talked about things much deeper than baseball. Barnes said, "There was an evening . . . you know, you lose your dignity when you're in the hospital. You're wearing hospital gowns, nurses are coming in and out. There was a particular moment when he said to me, 'Ronnie, I'm terribly embarrassed,' and I said, 'Mr. Mara, I'm here so you won't be embarrassed.' These are tough things for me to talk about because I lived them, but as much as I'm avoiding telling you some of the details, I remember every detail. I never thought that I could . . . I don't have children, never had children, and I've been told that once you've had children, the slightest noise in the night wakes you up. Now I understand. I wasn't sitting vigil with my eyes wide open. I had made my little bed and fallen asleep. Yet in the smallest voice he'd call out 'Ronnie?' and I'd be awake. Every hour almost on the hour he'd open his eyes and talk for a few minutes, and I wasn't tired the next day, either.

"Two or three days before Wellington died, in the middle of the night, he asked me for some water. So I got some cold water with ice. He drank the whole glass. I said, 'Would you like another?' 'Yes, I'd like another.' And then another. So having held on to this cold glass for so long—it was freezing—he began to shake. I went and got a bath towel, ran some hot water over it, and wrapped it around his hands to warm him. He looked straight at me. I think he was afraid. You know, Mr. Mara never said as much to you in spoken words as he did with just his eyes."

On their thirtieth day together in the hospital, Mara woke up and said, "Ronnie, I need you to tell me about my case." "I tried to think of something compassionate to say," Barnes said. "I didn't want to say, 'Mr. Mara, you're dying.' But it came out pretty straight. 'There's an awful lot of fluid around your lungs,' I told him, 'and it's apparent that the cancer has spread. Mr. Mara, the situation is quite grave. And I think at this point, given your great faith, you should put your hands in the hands of the Lord, and he'll take care of the rest. He'll lead you home.' Where that came from, I don't know. Probably somewhere in my Baptist background, maybe from my father. He said, 'Ronnie, I want to go home.' This was four o'clock in the morning. 'I'll have you home,' I whispered, 'before sundown tomorrow.' A few days later, he died at home."

Forty-eight hours after the funeral, granddaughter Kate Mara led the forty grandchildren, eleven sons and daughters, and 78,630 Giant Stadium spectators in a rendition of "The Star-Spangled Banner" that should have thrown a chill into the Washington Redskins because it was apparent in every note that this wasn't a normal Sunday. Coming off a three-point loss to Dallas and a one-point victory over Denver, the Giants beat the Redskins, 36–0, in what amounted to a perfect game. In the locker room afterward, Eli presented the ball to John Mara.

"You can't know anything about the New York Giants," Barnes said, sitting behind his desk, "unless you know something about Wellington Mara." On a bookshelf behind the trainer sat a framed photograph of the two of them. "He gave it to me two Christmases ago, but I didn't read the inscription then. I don't know why. I just didn't notice it until after he was gone. I remember the day exactly. I had this X-ray of someone's swollen knee or shoulder or ankle and I was trying to show it to the coaches. Well, you know coaches. They don't want to see it, because if they see it, they'll have to consider it. As soon as you start to hold up an X-ray to the light, coaches scatter. 'I don't want to look at that,' they say. They absolutely don't want to see it."

Back in his own office, still holding the X-ray, Barnes thought of Wellington Mara. "I imagined him storming in here and saying, 'Ronnie, I don't want you to play so-and-so until he's a hundred percent healthy, and I want you to call his wife right this minute. And I want you to call his mom and dad, too. No, never mind, I'll call his parents.'" Barnes looked away from the X-ray and up at the picture on his shelf, reading the inscription for the first time: "With appreciation and affection. Your patient, Well."

Then Ronnie called Ernie and told him that the player in question was definitely out of Sunday's game.

11

THE CAP

ATLANTA, THE GIANTS' next stop, represented a statistical haunted house. In their four games to date, the Falcons had allowed only one touchdown. On the offensive side, their 234.3-yard rushing average was on pace to break a seventy-year-old NFL record. Of course, the main hobgoblin was scrambling quarterback Michael Vick, who, sure enough, weaved twenty-two yards through the middle of the Giants' line to score the only touchdown in a 7–3 first half. On Atlanta's opening play of the third quarter, compact running back Warrick Dunn went ninety yards for a touchdown, farther than any Falcon had ever gone from scrimmage, causing Shaun O'Hara to say for the Giants, "So there we were, in our old, familiar back-to-the-wall position."

After a false start penalty on first down at the sixteen-yard line, that was about right.

GIANTS
1-15-G11 Eli Manning passes incomplete
2-15-G11 Tiki Barber runs for 29 yards

"Here's where the momentum changed," Barber said later, and Luke Petitgout, his destroyer escort, concurred. Luke said, "It's funny to look back on a running play that doesn't even get you out of your own territory, a play that leads to a punt, but that was the play that changed the whole fabric of the game." Falcons cornerback DeAngelo

Hall said, "Even earlier, it seemed to me that they were outhitting us. But we were leading, so I tried to tell myself, 'You must be mistaken.' But I didn't believe myself. I'm a terrible liar. Then Tiki ripped off that long run to make a first down. From that moment on, I had a bad feeling."

1-10-G40 Manning passes incomplete

2-10-G40 Barber runs for 16

1-10-F44 Brandon Jacobs runs for −1

2-11-F45 Manning passes incomplete

3-11-F45 (shotgun) Manning passes to Tim Carter for 15

1-10-F30 Barber runs for three

2-7-F27   Defensive pass interference

1-2-F2   Jacobs runs for 2 and a touchdown; Jay Feely's
     kick is good

Atlanta 14, New York 10

Following a three-and-out Falcons series, an effective punt backed New York up once again.

G I A N T S

1-10-G9   Manning passes to Barber for 16

1-10-G25 Barber runs for 9

2-1-G34   Jacobs runs for 5

1-10-G39 Manning passes to Jeremy Shockey for 19

1-10-F42 Jacobs runs for 8

2-2-F34   offsetting penalties

2-2-F34   Jacobs runs for 3

1-10-F31 (shotgun) Manning passes incomplete

2-10-F31 (shotgun) Manning passes to Shockey for 16

1-10-F15 Barber runs for 15 and an apparent touchdown,
     but the play is challenged and reversed; Barber stepped
     out at the 2

1-G-F2 Manning passes to Shockey for 2 and the
    touchdown; Feely's kick is good
New York 17, Atlanta 14

"This is just wrong, man," Jacobs muttered to Barber on the sideline. Brandon was probably the only one in the park mindful that, as much of a workhorse as Tiki had been for the Giants, he had yet to score a touchdown in 2006. "You shouldn't think that way," Barber told him. "I don't."

After a good Feely field goal and a bad Atlanta punt, New York was on the move again.

GIANTS

1-10-G45 Barber runs for 0
2-10-G45 Manning throws to Jim Finn for 6
3-4-F49   (shotgun) Manning passes to Shockey for 10
1-10-F39 Barber runs for 17
1-10-F22 Barber runs for 2
2-8-F20   Jacobs runs for 12
1-G-F8   Barber runs for 0
2-G-F8   Barber runs for 4
3-G-F4   Manning passes to Shockey for 4 and the
    touchdown; Feely's kick is good
New York 27, Atlanta 14

That was the final score. Barber carried twenty-six times for 185 yards, but the most telling numbers in the game, certainly the most satisfying ones to Tom Coughlin, were seven and four. The first was how many times Vick was sacked. The second was how many times he was pillaged, and subsequently fumbled. "Guys like Coughlin," Ernie said, "don't like to trick you as much as they like to punch you in the mouth. They want to beat the hell out of you. This game spoke to the fibers of what he believes. Smash-mouth. Physical. Vick took a tremendous beating, and we ran the ball down their throat with two backs, one of them

[Jacobs] weighing 260 pounds." Brandon accounted for fifty-three inside yards.

"What we do best," Barber said, something he had been saying for most of his career, "is run the ball. You may like two deep passes and a touchdown, but I like grind-it-out, NFC East–style football. First we wore them down, and then we wore them out. For me, this means more than coming back against Philadelphia. That was partly due to the Eagles' mistakes. This time we came back because of our own will. To my way of thinking, this was a lot, lot more satisfying."

"I hate to date myself," Michael Strahan said, "but the way Tiki hides behind an offensive lineman and then all of a sudden breaks out from the back of him into the clear reminds me of Emmitt Smith. That's what Smith did for the Cowboys throughout the nineties." Proving a victory can make a GM slightly light-headed, Accorsi looked at Barber in the locker room and thought he saw Jim Brown. "Maybe that was the last time we watched a running back get better, better, and better," Ernie said, "coming down the home stretch of his career." Brown scored three touchdowns in the Pro Bowl before he retired in costume on the London set of *The Dirty Dozen*. Ernie said, "Tiki has never played stronger, I don't think, than he's playing right now, and he's about to walk away."

At halftime, Coughlin came to Barber with a plea. "We need a boost," Tom said. "We're flat as hell." Maybe that's a key to Tiki because he seemed to grow taller after being consulted. In fact, he appreciated the compliment so much that he passed it on. To several waves of questioners, Barber said, "Don't forget to give the coaching staff some credit. Atlanta has a good defense, but we had a better plan. I'd say, if you boil it down to one thing today, everything went according to the coaches' plan."

Linebacker Brandon Short and defensive end Osi Umenyiora had two sacks apiece on Vick. "You have to be disciplined against him," Short said. "I'm talking about rush lanes and assignments, classroom stuff. You have to stick to your own job and resist the temptation to help somebody else do theirs. It's only human nature to want to make the play yourself. Everybody wants to do that. But you can't, not against guys like Vick. If he has success up the middle, the defensive men containing the outside have to stick to containing the outside. Otherwise, against a team this quick, you're lost. Except for two plays, we were a damned disciplined defense today."

Eli completed the fewest passes he had all year, seventeen; Vick completed the most, fourteen. The fact that Shockey, aching foot and all, caught six of Manning's throws for fifty-five yards and two touch-downs brought a new slogan to the Giants' locker room: "The renegade is back!" Jeremy felt good but was trying hard not to make any news. "My mother heard Troy Aikman say on television that I cry too much when I don't get the ball," he said. "Well, who doesn't want the ball?" One of the reporters asked Shockey, "What did you do to get open on that last touchdown?" He replied unhelpfully, "I got open," whispering aside, "I don't have to give all of my secrets away, do I?"

This was the bye week for the Indianapolis Colts and, on a busman's holiday, Peyton Manning journeyed to the Georgia Dome to observe Eli. "He came to see me last year," Peyton said in the vestibule, "so I owed him one."

What did Peyton notice?

"Ball control," he said. "How long did the Giants hold the ball there for that one stretch?"

Twenty-one of the first twenty-six minutes of the second half.

"There you go," Peyton said. "That's pretty impressive."

"It was Tiki," Eli said. "As soon as Tiki gets rolling, the play-action stuff starts to work. He was the one who was impressive. The game plan was impressive, too." The Giants were 3 and 2.

"Nice going, Field Marshal," Accorsi said to Coughlin, who looked at him quizzically. "Tom had a real good day," Ernie said. "George Young used to call all head coaches 'U-boat commanders,' because they're such natural generals, and they want to have complete control.

"'Where are your people from?' I asked Coughlin once. He says, 'My father is from County Kerry.' 'So, are you a hundred percent Irish?' 'No, my mother was German.' 'That explains a lot.' Traveling in Ireland last summer, I brought back a rock from County Kerry and presented it to Tom. I said, 'Keep this rock for the season, for luck.' I hope one of us doesn't kill the other with it."

Back in the office, it was time again for reviewing the salary cap situation, a never-ending concern that has to be revisited every few weeks. One of the worksheets read: "Possible roster cuts and corresponding cap savings—Tiki Barber, $4,000,000; Luke Petitgout, $3,210,000; Michael Strahan, $2,271,710; Amani Toomer, $1,750,000; Carlos Emmons, $1,000,000; Fred Robbins, $996,664; Tim Carter, $915,000; R. W. McQuarters, $900,000; Jeff Feagles, $820,000; Bob Whitfield, $753,332; Jason Bell, $610,000; Jim Finn, $560,000; Tim Hasselback, $501,666; Ryan Kuehl, $435,000; Chad Morton, $425,000; Jamaar Taylor, $410,000; Sam Madison, $400,000; Will Demps, $365,000; Ryan Grant, $285,000; LaVar Arrington $100,000."

Other sheets bore titles like "Candidates for Contract Extensions" and "Which Players Should We Allocate to NFL Europe in 2007?"

"In every other sport," Ernie said, "you want the developing players to have somewhere to play during the off-season. In baseball, they're sent to winter leagues in places like Venezuela and Puerto Rico. There are a million lower basketball leagues where a young kid can get off the end of the bench. But in football we generally prefer that they stay with us and work out with the coaches, so that we can develop them ourselves. Europe makes sense for some—it gives a guy a chance to play, a quarterback in particular. While Jared Lorenzen, the hefty lefty, our two-hundred-ninety-seven-pound backup quarterback, would seem a perfect guy to send to Europe, we don't dare send Jared over there because of all the sauerbraten. He'd come back weighing three hundred and fifty pounds. Lorenzen's not going to go over there and eat egg whites, you know." Such were the heavy decisions a GM had to make.

Because this was Accorsi's final season, he had resolved not to trade any draft choices in 2006, to preserve the full allotment of picks for his successor (who, incidentally, he hoped would be player personnel director Jerry Reese). "I'm trying to stay away from any decisions that influence the future more than the present," Ernie said, "because it just isn't fair. For example, Strahan is signed for two more years after this one. 'But,' his agent, Tony Agnew, asked me, 'what about the future?' I told him, 'I don't feel I have the right to make that decision. I'm not going to obligate my successor to do something that maybe he won't want to do.'"

Scott Pioli of the Patriots, considered by some a candidate for Accorsi's job, came back at Ernie several times during the last college draft. "Pioli kept asking me, 'Look, we have some extra choices. I'll give you some choices this year for some choices next year.' I said, 'Scott, I'm surprised you want me to put holes in next year's draft for you.' He didn't laugh at first."

There were a number of GM decisions Ernie purposely wanted to leave dangling. "Like, our field goal kicker, Jay Feely," he said. "I love the guy. He's a great guy. His contract is up after this year. He'll be a free agent then. My recommendation? I wouldn't extend him right now. I know a kicker is hard to find, but sooner or later, and probably sooner, Jay's going to have to win a game. He missed the winning kick three times in Seattle last year, and we lost in overtime. I mean, that really changed our season. We still won the division, but if we had gone to the play-offs as the number one seed—which we would have—there might have been a better aura around us, not to mention an easier path through the play-offs. I'm still feeling a little raw about that. Let's see how Jay does. Let's find out if he has recovered from Seattle."

Looking down the cold list, Accorsi's eyes stopped at receiver Tim Carter, who was probably a lame duck, too. Accorsi had always been Carter's sponsor, and Ernie wouldn't be there in 2007 to protect him anymore. "The coaches call Tim a heartbreaker," he said, "because on one side he has so much talent and on the other he's had so many injuries. You know football coaches—not just here, all football coaches. They blame the players for the injuries. And it's absolutely true that some players won't play hurt. But look at this guy's injuries: broken hip, broken collarbone, torn Achilles tendon, most of them occurring while he was doing something courageous. Kurt Warner, who quarterbacked that aerial circus in St. Louis, told me Carter was the fastest receiver he ever threw a ball to. It's not just Tim's brilliance, either, that makes me stand up for him. It's his makeup. When Carter became a free agent, he could have just walked away. He knew most of the organization was down on him. But he told me, 'You drafted me in the second round, I owe you for that. I want to prove myself *here.*' I tell the coaches, 'Do you want to know what heartbreak is? I'll tell you what heartbreak is. Heartbreak is Sunday night when you leave the stadium and go home and watch that kid catching touchdown passes all across your TV screen.' They might learn about that heartbreak next year."

There is one salary cap fact that everyone in the NFL grasps. As Accorsi said, "To be over it invites a million-dollar-a-day fine." "At the beginning of the cap," former Packers GM Ron Wolf said, "we weren't sure what the league was going to do if you were over. Take money from you? Strip you of players? And if it was players, would they go by alphabetical order or what? Nobody seemed to know. So, just to be on the safe side, in Green Bay we always made sure that we had a lot of players whose names began with letters that came before *F* [for Favre]." "When I became the Giants' GM," Ernie said, "the first thing I was handed was the cap. It was a mess. We were eleven million over, and I had like two weeks to get it down. There are tricks to it, of course. If I sign Strahan and give him a ten-million-dollar signing clause for a five-year contract, I can prorate that at two million a year. But if I trade him, I get hit with the whole ten. So that's the penalty that baseball doesn't have."

Coughlin left Jacksonville in what NFL teams call "cap hell." It wasn't his job, but Tom controlled the football operation, so he basically brought the players in who caused the cap trouble. The GM didn't say no. He has to say no. "Go ask Kevin Abrams for a simple explanation of the cap," Ernie said, "and then come back here and explain it to me."

Abrams said, "I only knew George Young a little bit, but he probably fell under the category of those who grew up in one NFL system, and when a new one came along in 1993, they just didn't want to embrace it. He may have re-signed a few too many of our players to deals that weren't commensurate with what they were going to be able to do for us. And when you have a cap, all of a sudden some of those wrong decisions can end up biting you in the ass. There was always a cash consequence to it, but now there's a functionality consequence as well. So we got in a little trouble with that.

"If you're over the cap, the league will call you in and say, 'You've got until midnight.' I've never been through this, never been in that situation. Of course, you go out of your way not to be in that situation. But the theory is, if you're over the cap, they'll give you X amount of time to get your ducks in a row. Then on the last day they'll say, 'If you can't get under it by midnight, we're just going to start lopping players off your options.' The players will become free agents, and you can try to re-sign them, but so can everyone else. I presume they'd start at your highest-paid guys, not the lowest, because that's going to make the biggest difference. This year the cap is a hundred and two million for your fifty-three-man roster and your practice squad and whatever injuries you might incur during training camp. Next year it's a hundred and nine million. And it's a firm cap, though not as firm as hockey's, which is absolutely firm. Ours can be considered over a number of years. The most simplistic way to say it would be that if you spend a hundred and five million this year, then that three-million overage is going to count against your cap next year and the years going forward, so whatever you spend over this year, it means you're going to have a cap deficit in future years, depending on how many years down the road you decide to allocate money that you're spending now. Sooner or later, you'll have less to spend than the rest of the league. Of course everyone's kiting to some extent. It's like credit card spending. But you don't want to push too much of the money off into the future, because if it doesn't get you this year, it's going to get you eventually.

"As for the million a day, it depends on what you've done that's in violation of the rules. For something very minor, it could be a five-thousand-dollar slap on the wrist. If it's something really egregious, they could take draft picks away and fine you even more than the million. But once you get into it, the cap isn't really all that complicated, though I have to admit we've had a number of young people in the office who have thrown up their hands and said, 'Let me out of here.' I've always wanted to have a second person who could read contracts and proofread and double-check my interpretation of the cap rules. So whenever anyone expresses the slightest interest, I get them all the guidebooks and maybe even schedule them for a labor seminar so they can listen to all the issues and get into things like insurance and arbitration and grievances and all that. But, invariably, the next thing I know, all of the books and charts are back on my desk. 'I don't want to talk about it anymore,' they say. I guess it is a little dull, but it's a part of the game.

"Take a team like Washington. They had a big off-season this year. I think they gave five players ten-million-dollar signing bonuses, and they already had a lot of players on their books for significant amounts of money. They're under the hundred-and-two-million salary cap, but I've got to believe they spent closer to a hundred thirty-five million this year. Because they've done that, they're going to have years coming up where the spending limit is a hundred nine million or a hundred sixteen, and a good bit of their money won't be there. If you think you're close to winning, or—for whatever reason—your sense of urgency is a little greater one year than it is another, you can do a lot of tricks with the money. But it's going to catch up to you eventually. It's going to happen. You'll end up in cap hell."

"Any questions?" Ernie said.

Though he was always more comfortable with a stopwatch in his hand than a calculator, Accorsi eased his way into the money part during those prehistoric days in Baltimore and Cleveland. "What I did, first of all," he said, "was know this: as long as you say no, you're safe. Number two, and I started this—a lot of others copied it—get a ladder in your mind. I put the players on rungs in my head, and if I had you tenth or eleventh, that's how you were going to be paid. The biggest problem I ever had with the ladder was in Cleveland, when both Kevin Mack and Earnest Byner were gaining a thousand yards apiece. I didn't want them coming up for renewals the same year and turning into an entry like Don Drysdale and Sandy Koufax. So I staggered them with two-year contracts. One jumped ahead one year, the other jumped ahead the next. 'Look, Mack is making more than you now,' I'd tell Earnest, 'but you're going to be making more than Mack soon.' It was the only way I could think to do it, and for some reason they let me. Maybe it was just a simpler time. Mack was actually better, but just a little. I loved both of those kids. That was a tough balancing act, but I got through it. The ladder kept me alive."

To review, the two things to remember: the fine of $1 million a day, and as long as you say no, you're safe.

12

PARCELLS

HAD CELL PHONES BEEN as omnipresent in January 1996 as they are today, Tom Coughlin's predecessor, Jim Fassel, never would have been the head coach of the New York Giants. Bill Parcells, whose eight-year run between 1983 and 1990 delivered two Super Bowl championships to the Giants, would have been brought back from New England for a second go-round in New York if only the Maras and the Tisches had been able to reach George Young in time. They missed him by approximately two minutes.

"There was no question that Dan Reeves was out," Ernie said. " 'I think I should go,' he told everybody in a meeting, and none of us disagreed. 'But you're going to pay me, right?'

"Bob Tisch said, 'You're quitting. We're not firing you.'

" 'Well, I think I still should get paid.'

"After they went back and forth like that for a while, Reeves said, 'Pam and I need to go home and pray over this.' "

Rumblings were coming from New England that Parcells was of a mind to return to New York. Of course, Parcells was a man who changed his mind rather often. Accorsi said, "Bill was telling everybody, including Will McDonough of the *Boston Globe*—they were close friends—that by some technicality in his contract he was free to leave the Patriots and return to the Giants if he wanted to. I happened to know the option was [New England owner] Bob Kraft's, not his. The Giants would have had to pay a very steep and severe compensation, two number ones and more, whatever it was. They started to look into it but hadn't yet figured out what the compensation would be. They were still trying to decide whether to offer him the job. He had already told the Maras he wanted it."

Did Wellington have an especially warm feeling for Parcells?

"He didn't feel warm about him," Ernie said, "but he wanted him back."

On hiring a general manager or a head coach, both halves of the ownership—Mara and Tisch—had to vote unanimously, 2–0. "George had to get both owners to agree," Ernie said. "At first, Joel Goldberg, who was the psychologist, talked Bob Tisch out of Parcells. And Young was trying to sell Fassel to Wellington. Jim had been an assistant here and George sort of liked him, though we had drawn up a list of potential Reeves replacements the year before—Lindy Infante, Joe Bugel—and Fassel wasn't even on it. George had decided Fassel was the man who could help him prove you could win with Dave Brown as quarterback, a hopeless cause if there ever was one."

Young had developed an undisguised dislike of Parcells, which was odd because, as Accorsi said, "they saw the game the same way, and everybody respected Bill as a coach. One day George quietly calls me into his office, asks Janice to get his moneyman on the line, and shuts the door. George's accountant was a former quarterback of his at City College High School in Baltimore. 'Bob,' Young says on the phone, 'do I have enough money to retire?' Well, I almost fall off the chair. George had his First Holy Communion money in an envelope, okay? He was making a million dollars a year for about six years. So he hangs up and says, 'Look, I'm going down to Wellington right now and tell him that if they hire Parcells, I quit. I'm sure you'll be my replacement.' I thought to myself, 'Yeah, I'll have the title of GM, but if Parcells is the head coach, will I really have the job?'" Maybe that's how Young felt as well.

Before George could issue his ultimatum, Wellington informed him that Tisch had put the kibosh on Parcells. "George said to Wellington, 'In that case, Fassel is really the only guy out there.' He wanted permission to offer the job to Jim right away. Reluctantly, Well said, 'Okay, go ahead.' Fassel was waiting nearby, at the Sheraton Meadowlands. As

John Mara says, 'That's the only time in George's life, including when he was twelve years old, that he ran a four-point-three forty.' But he isn't gone even two minutes when Bob Tisch calls to say he has changed his mind. 'If you want to hire Parcells,' he says, 'go ahead.' So John quickly calls our switchboard up front. 'Did George Young leave the building yet?' 'Yes, he just ran out.' They phone the hotel as quickly as they can, trying to cut him off. But they can't find him.

"Eventually they call Fassel's room, asking for George, and he comes on the line. Either John or Wellington, I can't remember which one—both of them, essentially—asks George, 'Have you offered the job to Fassel yet?' George says, 'Yes, I have.' 'Has he accepted it?' 'Yes.' 'Okay.' The Maras being the Maras, once the offer had been extended on their behalf, they weren't about to take it back."

By the way, this wouldn't be the last time it was whispered around the Giants' front office that Parcells was interested in returning to New York.

That 3-and-3 start for which Accorsi had only hoped remarkably became 4 and 2 when the Giants beat Parcells and his Cowboys, 36–22, on a Monday night in Dallas. "I'm ashamed to put out a team that plays like that," Parcells said immediately afterward. "They outplayed us. They out-everythinged us. They outcoached us. I apologize to all of the people who came out to watch that." In one of the papers, his monologue was punched up slightly to read more dramatically at the finish, "I apologize to the people of America." In either case, he was sorry.

Not three minutes into the game, Eli Manning threw a fifty-yard touchdown pass to Plaxico Burress, but the second Giant score and the events that followed were more lasting.

"Watch me this week," I heard LaVar Arrington whisper to Ernie in the lunch line a few days earlier. "This is the week I'm going to make you glad you brought me here."

With four minutes to go in the first quarter, Jeff Feagles punted the Cowboys all the way back to their own one-yard line, where on second down Arrington found a crack in the Dallas line and flashed through it to tackle thirty-four-year-old quarterback Drew Bledsoe for LaVar's first sack of the season and the only safety of his pro career. One series later, at about midfield, Bledsoe handed the football to running back Julius Jones, who took a step and a half, slid to a stop, and flipped the ball back to Drew. The flea-flicker fooled the Giants so thoroughly that Bledsoe had his choice of two open receivers, Terrell Owens on one side or Terry Glenn on the other. But as Bledsoe released the pass, Arrington's right arm got in the way, deflecting it incomplete. LaVar was having the game he promised.

Then, halfway through the second quarter, on the first down of a ten-play, eighty-yard Dallas drive, Arrington was clipped by a phantom blocker nowhere near the ball. The play was a simple dive off-tackle by Jones for three yards. "I thought somebody hit me from behind," LaVar said. "I was fuming. But then I looked around and nobody was there. I reached for my left leg. I said, 'Okay, if it's your knee again, you're finished.'" But it wasn't his knee, it was his Achilles tendon, which had ruptured. He went off the field on a cart and home that night on crutches. Arrington's season was over, obviously; his Giants career, too, it turned out; maybe his whole football life.

With New York leading, 12–7, the most fateful series of Bledsoe's fourteen NFL seasons closed the first half. Thanks to a Barber fumble, once commonplace but now a rare event, Dallas was at the Giants' fifteen-yard line and poised to take the lead. Tiki was knocked completely unconscious. When he awoke, he was able to remember both his own name and the exact reason why he was retiring. Hall of Fame Cowboys receiver Michael Irvin had a less polite word for it on ESPN. Pointing to the timing of Barber's declaration, with most of a season yet to go, Irvin said, "To me, that's not retiring. That's quitting."

C O W B O Y S

1-10-G14 (shotgun) Jones runs for 5
2-5-G9   Jones runs for 4
3-1-G5   Marion Barber runs for 1

1-G-G4   Barber runs for 0

2-G-G4   Bledsoe's pass intended for Glenn is intercepted
by Sam Madison

The play was called for the right side; Bledsoe threw to the left, ane-mically. "Too much improvising," Parcells grumped. "Too many mis-takes." He switched in the third quarter (in fact, forever) to a backup quarterback covered in cobwebs, Tony Romo of Eastern Illinois Univer-sity, who in four years as a Cowboys employee had thrown exactly two passes. The third one of his pro career was deflected by Michael Strahan and intercepted by Antonio Pierce at the Dallas twenty, brought ahead to the fourteen.

GIANTS

1-10-C14 Barber runs for 1

2-9-C13   Manning passes incomplete

3-9-C13   (shotgun) Manning passes to Jeremy Shockey
for 13 and the touchdown; Jay Feely's kick is good

New York 19, Dallas 7

Romo's second interception was caught by Fred Robbins. The third one, thrown from the Giants' eleven-yard line, Kevin Dockery returned ninety-six yards for a touchdown. But in the weeks ahead, Romo would blossom into George Clooney, and he would have his revenge against the Giants. Parcells, who looked historically spent on the sideline that Monday night, would pep up for a while.

"What's that, our third win on the road?" Coughlin asked rhetori-cally in the locker room. The coach appreciated Barber's 114 yards but seemed even more pleased with the contribution of Strahan. "Michael was very spry, very active," Tom said. "He pretty much stopped the run on his own in the first half." Ernie said, "That's the thing about Stray. He's famous for rushing the passer, but of all the great sack men in the history of the league, he may be the best one against the run."

"Two weeks ago, we were a bad team," Strahan said. "We were done, we were hopeless, nobody gave us a shot. But now we've beaten the Redskins at home and the Eagles and Cowboys on the road. Who's the class of the NFC East?"

Amani Toomer, who caught three of the twelve passes Manning completed, answered in a much softer voice. "We are," he said, "when healthy." It was a smart comment from maybe the smartest man on the team, who noticed that Arrington wasn't the only player who had to be helped off. Osi Umenyiora, Sam Madison, and Justin Tuck were injured, too. It was just the overture.

On the road, with no tunnel to skulk in, Accorsi watched from the second row of the press box, sitting alongside John Mara, as both of them tried not to slam their fists on the table too often. Ernie saw the games as a general manager would, flashing back to the first time he scouted a player or to the day he drafted him. When Jim Finn, for instance, made a good block that helped Barber, or ran for a short gain himself, Accorsi was almost the only one in the stadium who noticed Jim.

"Finn's just one of those team guys," Ernie said. "He still plays the position that they've basically eliminated in this league: fullback. Burton Catholic High School and Penn. It's funny, I saw him play against Fordham his senior year. Freezing cold day. I took the Saturday off—I'd been traveling so much. 'Oh, hell,' I thought, 'I'll go see Penn-Fordham. It's nearby. You can't not see a college football game on a Saturday.' Finn played tailback that day, but he looked like a fullback to me. He ended up a cap casualty in Indianapolis and now he's seven years in the league. Not a devastating blocker, but a good clutch player. If he's unaccounted for, he'll catch the ball and get as much as he can, every inch of that. Just a great guy to have on a team."

With five tackles, corner Corey Webster had an unusually strong game against the Cowboys. "Second-year guy, LSU," Ernie said. "Was on his way to being a first-round pick when he hurt his foot and played through it. After his stock dropped a little, I considered him the steal of the second round. But he hasn't developed as quickly as we thought. He hasn't gotten there yet. He still may. The talent is there."

Running back Brandon Jacobs: "If we would just spread the field with this big guy [six-four, 264]," Accorsi said, "we could ride him forever. In my opinion, he could be a truly great player. He's got a chance. Brandon's an absolute throwback to the days of Marion Motley in Cleveland. Maybe Rick Casares in Chicago is a better example. Jacobs is big and strong, but he's not a fullback. He's a halfback. I like a two-back offense, you know. I hate the single back even more than I do the I formation. I love the old split formations. The symmetry of them."

Safety Gibril Wilson: "Until he got hurt, he was the best blitzing safety in the league. A little safety—Gibril probably doesn't weigh two hundred pounds—is going to pay a price. Fifth-rounder three years ago. He told Ronnie Barnes, 'Mr. Accorsi never talks to me.' Ronnie said, 'Ernie probably isn't exactly certain who you are in the clubhouse. But he sure as hell knows who you are when you have your uniform on.' So I went around to say hello a couple of days ago. We bet a buck on the Tennessee game. He's a Volunteer. Gibril and Eli played against each other for four years, so now they're rookies together here, and in the very first team drill, Wilson makes a diving interception. 'That's one, Manning,' he whispers to Eli when they're together later on the sideline. Eli laughs. Great kid, Gibril. All football player. Only the injuries have kept him from coming into his own."

Kick returner Chad Morton: "He hasn't done much this year. Hasn't been as explosive. But I like him. He's a competitor. I just wish he'd start making a few big plays."

Safety James Butler: "Great nose for the ball. Great ball skills. Smart as hell. But it was touch and go this off-season, because he suffered a kidney injury and it was questionable whether he should play anymore. That scared everybody a little bit. But it's regenerated. I think he's okay. He's easing back in."

Safety Will Demps: "We used to have Brent Alexander here, who couldn't run anymore at the end but was still smart. We retired him for Demps, but Will has not had a good year. The first season coming off a knee is often shaky. But players develop. You have to have patience for that. I'm an impatient man who's patient with athletes."

Linebacker Gerris Wilkinson: "He's got some talent. They haven't discovered it yet."

Linebacker Carlos Emmons: "At the end of the trail. Very proud, very regal, athlete. He's been hurt a lot, but he's an NFL professional and really helps just being on your team, even if he's not contributing that much."

Linebacker Chase Blackburn: "Great young man, special teams. Suffered a dangerous injury last year, neck. He's just one of those terrific kids. Probably underestimated his whole life. Good special-teamer. Can run a little bit."

Linebacker Antonio Pierce: "Well, I don't even know how to describe him. He's almost as good a leader as I've ever been around in football. He's not Unitas, but he's just as understated. We don't get Arrington without Pierce. We don't get Pierce without Jessie Armstead, the jilted lover. It's the legacy of this organization. Armstead leaves here after the oh-one season, mad. But he calls Pierce when Antonio's a free agent, and tells him, 'If you have a chance to sign with the Giants, do it.' Antonio was in an airport at the time, on his way to Minnesota. Brandon Short called Arrington, too, even though that meant Short might be LaVar's backup. That's the legacy of this organization."

Center Shaun O'Hara: "He's just one of those guys you're always going to remember in your career. Hurt a lot. Plays hurt. A lunch-pail guy. Tough as anybody. Brunswick guy. Rutgers. Loves it here. I hope his agent lets him stay."

Cornerback Frank Walker: "He's not just in the doghouse here. He's got a suite of doghouses here. Not with me. I think he's a delightful character. But he can't stay out of trouble with the coaching staff. They're constantly wanting me to get rid of him, but I won't do it. He's a corner who can run, and they're not easy to find. I talked to him before the season. I said, 'Frank, can you *please* keep your mouth shut and stay out of trouble with the coaches?' Because he just rubs them the wrong way. I saved him about three times. 'Frank's reverting,' Coughlin will say. But then I check it out and the players still love him. He's a character. He's a wacko. He's a great kid."

To someone not in the racket, it sounds like one long list of great, injured kids.

"I have faults and weaknesses," Accorsi said, "probably more than most. But relating to young athletes is not one of my problems. I don't listen to the same music they listen to. I don't enjoy the same movies. We don't share the same hobbies. But I have a good relationship with these kids. I like them. I admire them. Even at sixty-five, a GM has to remember being young. Conspirators will come along, and I don't like conspirators any more than Tom does. But I find a lot more good teammates than conspirators. That's Jerry West's measurement, about as good a single barometer as a GM can have. 'Is he a good teammate?' West has always asked."

Whether in the tunnel or the press box, that's what Accorsi looked for when he watched the games: good teammates.

13

OFF THE STREET

AT SOME BIG MOMENT, maybe in a championship game, a player with an unfamiliar name will make a tackle or an interception and be identified on television as a loan officer at Wachovia Bank who, just a day or two before, was picked up off the street. "Off the street" is a phrase that directors of pro personnel, like the Giants' Dave Gettleman, use to describe replacement parts that come and go almost daily, all season long, through a revolving door that never stops spinning. But it's a misleadingly romantic label. Virtually all of these dreamers were on NFL rosters at one time. Without exception they are former football majors at some renowned cradle of learning still nursing an old college ambition on a loading dock or in a convenience store.

With Tom Coughlin looking on despairingly, his assistant coaches conducted the tryouts in the bubble by the practice field. Gettleman, who rounded up these unusual suspects, stood off to the side with his arms folded, looking exactly like both the prep coach and the small-college offensive lineman he once was. "If you were ever a high school football coach," George Young used to say, "more than a little part of you stays a high school football coach." Even twenty-five years removed from the sideline at Spackenkill High School in Poughkeepsie, New York, Gettleman still wore a figurative whistle around his muscular neck. He said, "I had this one kid"—they all had this one kid—"at Spackenkill, which was a small school of about six hundred and fifty ninth, tenth, and eleventh graders. Later, at a bigger school, Kingston High, I coached all kinds of kids with Division One potential, and a few of them won scholarships—full boats—to colleges large and small. But only this one kid at Spackenkill, a running back named Barry Lewis. Six foot two. About two hundred thirty, two hundred thirty-five pounds. Wonderful family. His father's name was Eli. Blue-collar guy. Black guy. Real quality guy. He worked on the docks."

After Barry's sophomore season, Gettleman visited the Lewis home and laid it out for the family. "Barry has legitimate ability," he told them. "If he applies himself, he has a real shot at a free education." Turning to Barry, he said, "But you can't just *be* in school, you have to *do* school." And to everyone's surprise, Gettleman said, "he did do school. Not great, but much, much better. Good enough." Two years later, Syracuse University came calling.

As Gettleman said, "The assistant coach recruiting our area showed up in my office looking about as harried as anyone I've ever seen, frustrated about something, maybe just exhausted. I guess their dance card was virtually filled. Probably he had just lost a much better recruit somewhere else. But he was ready to bring Barry to the Syracuse campus. Then, if the other black kids gave him a thumbs-up, he'd have his scholarship. I said, 'Terrific, wait right here.' So I went to get Barry out of class. It was an art class, I remember. He was at a potter's wheel. 'C'mon, c'mon, c'mon,' I said, 'wash your hands.' On the walk back to my office, he was very quiet. Barry was a naturally quiet kid anyway. 'Are you okay?' I said. 'I'm okay.' So I introduced the two of them, and the coach asked a couple of friendly questions, but Barry wouldn't answer him. Not even a grunt. The coach said something else. Barry just looked at him. This went on for about five minutes before I said, 'Coach, let me call a time-out here.' Barry and I went into the hallway. 'Please don't be afraid, Barry,' I said. 'You can do this. He's just a guy who happens to be a football coach at Syracuse. He already likes you. He already knows you can play. All he wants to do is converse with you. Are you ready now?' 'Okay, I'm ready.' But, back in the office, he froze up again. It was the saddest thing I have ever seen in my life. Do you know who that coach was? Nick Saban. I ended up getting Barry into North Carolina A and T on

Thirteen-year-old Ernie Accorsi's immense love for sports crystallized one day in a football game played on this unassuming little field in Hershey, Pennsylvania.
Courtesy of Ernie Accorsi

Ernie's first football job was under legendary Joe Paterno (left) at Penn State. His most vital function, at least as far as Paterno was concerned, was to keep a bowl in the coaches' office filled with red licorice, but he managed to bootleg a number of life and football lessons from Joe and assistant coach George Welsh. *© Jerry Pinkus*

Ernie left Penn State to join the Baltimore Colts. "As I was pulling away from Penn State, Paterno gave me a pep talk: 'You're swimming with the real sharks now, Ernie. If you try to play their game, you'll be eaten alive. Just be the way you are.' "
Courtesy of Ernie Accorsi

After a stint in the league office, Ernie returned to the Colts and in 1982 became General Manager, inheriting Coach Frank Kush (left), who was known as the toughest guy in the league. The Colts owned the top pick in the 1983 draft, but top pick John Elway publicly swore he'd never play for Baltimore. *Courtesy of Ernie Accorsi*

Ernie with Val Pinchbeck, Lamar Hunt, and George Halas. *Courtesy of Ernie Accorsi*

Ernie and Johnny Unitas (left) were so close that when Unitas' career ended in Baltimore, the great QB presented his last Colts jersey to Accorsi, not to the NFL Hall of Fame. *Courtesy of Ernie Accorsi*

Trainer Ronnie Barnes with beloved Giants owner Wellington Mara (right). Barnes sat a thirty-day vigil at Mara's bedside as the owner fought his final battles with cancer. At one point, Ronnie felt derelict enough in his duties to apologize to Coach Coughlin, who told him in a low, cracking voice, "You're doing God's work." *Courtesy of Ronnie Barnes*

Below left: When Ernie took over as Giants GM, he soon installed Kerry Collins as quarterback. Many considered Collins— whose personal life had been turbulent— damaged goods. But Accorsi followed his gut, saying, "I've always believed that if a kid was ever a good kid, he can be a good kid again." *© Jerry Pinkus*

Below right: Coming off a 4-12 2003 season, Ernie bet it all on Eli Manning. "I realized that I could turn out to be wrong on this kid. . . . I knew we might not know for sure until years after I leave. But I could live with it. We had a quarterback." *© Jerry Pinkus*

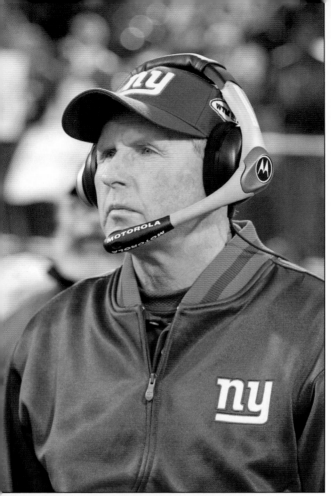

With the new quarterback came a new coach, disciplinarian Tom Coughlin. In time, Ernie would fret that his coach and QB weren't as closely bonded as he expected them to be.
© *Jerry Pinkus*

Eli Manning presents the game ball to John Mara after the Giants' October 30, 2005, victory over the Redskins, their first game after Wellington's death.
© *Jerry Pinkus*

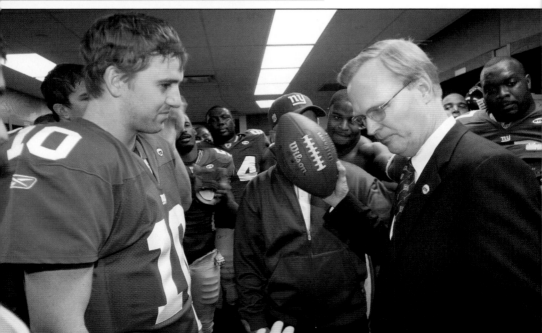

Above left: Coming into the 2006 season, veteran defensive end and team leader Michael Strahan was among the players who "declared" for the Super Bowl. When Strahan was lost to an injury in November, the team was devastated. © *Evan Pinkus*

Above right: Running back Tiki Barber's 2006 season proved spectacular, making him only the third player in NFL history to achieve four 2,000 total yard seasons. Determined to leave the game healthy, Tiki chose to retire at season's end. © *Jerry Pinkus*

After a devastating early loss to the Seahawks, fiery tight end Jeremy Shockey became the star of the postgame show, declaring, "We got outplayed *and outcoached.*" A big believer in Shockey, Accorsi had been ambivalent years before when he first watched him play, noticing that Shockey loved the spotlight. "But what a player." © *Jerry Pinkus*

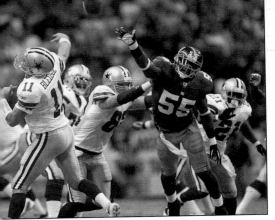

Newly signed linebacker LaVar Arrington, a three-time Pro Bowler who'd never lived up to his potential, was finally learning to play within himself as part of a system, but minutes after knocking down this Drew Bledsoe pass, a ruptured Achilles' tendon ended his season. © *Jerry Pinkus*

Six-foot-five wide receiver Plaxico Burress occasionally earned the ire of fans who questioned his desire, but his rebel reputation and jailyard stare hide a hardworking, dedicated teammate. Plax wears the number 17—an unusual number for a wide receiver—to commemorate the date of his signing with the Giants. © *Jerry Pinkus*

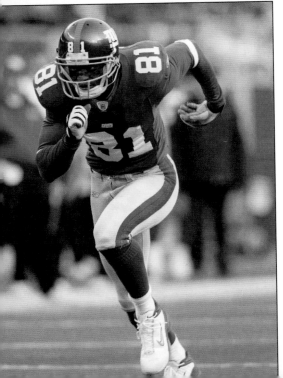

Amani Toomer, the stateliest presence on the team and the Giants' all-time career yardage leader (8,157—nearly 3,000 yards more than Frank Gifford), was lost to knee surgery halfway through the season. © *Jerry Pinkus*

The Giants' "walking miracle," six-foot-three, 305-pound utility man Rich Seubert. He suffered three horrible leg fractures six games into the 2003 season that left him out the rest of that season and the next. Seubert doesn't know why the Giants stuck with him: "I'm pretty sure the coaches didn't really have much to say about it . . . it was Accorsi and the Maras who kept me." © *Jerry Pinkus*

Despite a solid season, rookie Mathias Kiwanuka earned derision from fans when, leery of a "roughing the passer" call, he failed to bring down Titans QB Vince Young on a sack. Still, Coughlin assured, "Mathias is going to be a great football player." © *Jerry Pinkus*

When, one week, ailing punter Jeff Feagles was listed as "doubtful," Accorsi called on 45-year-old kicker Sean Landeta to stand by. Just for showing up, Landeta got paid $47,000, "the minimum for a player who's been in the league 403 years."
© *Jerry Pinkus*

The Giants' manager of personnel, Jerry Reese, Ernie's longtime protégé, at the press conference where he was introduced as Ernie's successor. Accorsi had been loud and unambiguous in recommending that Reese replace him, but the situation was delicate. © *Jerry Pinkus*

financial aid, but he hopped on a bus and came home after three days. I can't even tell you exactly how he died, just that he died very young. 'Barry's dead.' That's all you heard. He had legitimate ability, that kid. I look at all of these kids coming in here to work out for us, and I think to myself, 'Damn.'"

Gettleman was silent for a moment, sitting in his office. But when he switched on his computer to check the day's transactions, he smiled. "Look at this," he said. "Curry Burns is back with the Texans." Burns was a safety who played his college ball at the University of Louisville. "Houston drafted him originally," Dave said. "I think he went to New England from there, then to us, then to Washington, something like that. I know he hooked on with a number of practice squads. He has quite a few stickers on his suitcase. And now he's back where he started, full circle. Good old Curry Burns. He's off the street."

These searches in the bubble for a replacement or two always took Accorsi back to a three-week episode in 1987 when 90 percent of the NFL players had to be replaced. "Just about a year ago," Ernie said, "somebody came up and told me, 'There's a guy I met in Chicago who wanted to be remembered to you.' 'Who's that?' 'A quarterback. He said he played for you.' 'Not very many guys played quarterback—wait a minute, where? Cleveland? It wasn't Jeff Christensen, was it?' 'That's it!' 'Tell him to go to hell the next time you see him! He cost us home field advantage, and that ended up costing us the championship game!'"

Two weeks into the 1987 season, the players union struck for free agency and the owners decided to play on with Hessians, including a prisoner or two, a prison guard or two, and one gentleman under indictment for murder. On the first Sunday of replacement football, four punts were blocked for touchdowns, one kickoff was mistaken for a punt, and a fellow named Anthony Allen caught 255 yards' worth of passes for the Washington Redskins. With a straight face, the Associated Press referred to one of the starting quarterbacks as "an insurance salesman with a history of shoulder trouble."

Some NFL teams, like the Giants, had no heart for this pantomime.

"The Giants were coming off a Super Bowl year," Ernie said, "and George Young was adamant that he'd rather lose all of the replacement games than risk alienating one of the real players. As you might expect then, the Giants did lose them all." Other teams, like the 49ers and Browns, saw an opportunity. From chaos, there is profit. That first week at Giants Stadium, in the middle of the least-watched Monday night game in history, San Francisco coach Bill Walsh slyly inserted a running quarterback and suddenly switched to a wishbone offense. On the opposite sideline, head coach Bill Parcells performed a double take worthy of Casey Stengel and then exploded into laughter. The 49ers won, 41–21.

"I brought Christensen in to quarterback for the Browns," Accorsi said. "He was a guy in his thirties from Eastern Illinois, and he was no bum [originally drafted 137th by Cincinnati in 1983]. He shouldn't have had any trouble outclassing all of these school bus drivers, and he did make it look fairly easy the first week. We went to New England and in front of about fourteen thousand people beat the Patriots, twenty to ten. Larry Mason [*the* Larry Mason, from Troy State] ran for a hundred and forty yards. Our next game was at home against the Houston Oilers, who hadn't beaten us in something like ten straight games. But Christensen threw about a hundred interceptions, and we lost, fifteen to ten. As it turned out, that changed the world. That's how Elway got to be at home against us in the AFC Championship Game—you know, Byner's fumble. Then our third replacement game was in Cincinnati, where we almost never won, and the rumors were flying that this thing might be settled in the eleventh hour. Before we left, I got a phone call from Gary Danielson—he was the veteran quarterback behind Bernie Kosar—and Gary wanted to meet at Art Modell's house. He brought along Ozzie Newsome, the tight end, and Brian Brennan, the receiver, and Ricky Bolden, the left tackle. 'We're all older guys,' Gary said. 'I'm thirty-nine, okay? Let Bernie and the younger guys stay out to avoid recriminations. But if a handful of veterans at just the right positions crosses the picket line, we should be able to steal this game. The guys staying out have heard the plan and they're all for it.' "

"What Ernie didn't know," Danielson said, "was that Modell had called me first. Art put me up to coming back. 'We need a quarterback,' he said, 'and I can't ask Bernie to cross the line.' I said I'd do it, but I had to have somebody to throw it to. Okay, I thought—Brennan. You could talk Brenn into anything." Against the Bengals replacements, Danielson looked like a youthful Y. A. Tittle. "It was like watching Notre Dame taking on Hillsdale Junior College," Ernie said. "They were having so much fun. Brennan showed them this move, and then he gave them that move, and he didn't have to make a third move, because there wasn't anybody anywhere near him. I mean, some truck driver was thirty yards down the field. We were leading, thirty-four to nothing, it was pitch-and-catch, and Danielson had completed like twenty passes in a row, when suddenly it dawned on me that all of these records were going to count." Accorsi began to panic on behalf of Dante Lavelli and Paul Warfield, not to mention Otto Graham.

As a matter of fact, at Buffalo the week before, Gary Hogeboom of the Indianapolis Colts threw five touchdown passes to tie a twenty-two-year-old franchise mark that was presumed to be the property of Johnny Unitas but, as Ernie well knew, actually belonged to a dentist who used to back Unitas up, Gary Cuozzo. "I rushed into the coach's booth," Accorsi said. "I'd never done anything like this in my life. 'Tell Schottenheimer,' I shouted, 'to get Brennan the hell out of the game!' There were still seven minutes to go, and Brian needed only about two more catches and twenty more yards to extinguish Lavelli and Warfield.

"'We have a sacred trust!' I told the coaches, who had no idea what I was yelling about. But Brennan came out. He was pissing and moaning on the sidelines, waving his fist at the press box." "You had to know Brenn," Danielson said. "In The Drive game, he ran a great pattern and caught like a fifty-yard touchdown pass [forty-eight] to give us a twenty-to-thirteen lead with five minutes to go in the fourth quarter. After The Drive, and the overtime, and the terrible loss, all Brenn said was, 'Shit, now nobody's going to remember my touchdown.'"

In the locker room after the 34–0 replacement victory, Marty told Ernie, "I think you should know, I threw you under the bus with Brennan. After all, I have to go on coaching this guy. He says he's going to kill you." "You son of a bitch!" Brennan called out, flying across the room. "I said, 'Brian, Brian, Brian, calm down! I love you to death, you're having a very good career, but I'm not going to let you wipe Warfield and Lavelli out of the record books.'" "You love *me* to death?" Brennan said. "You love Webster Slaughter [the Browns' other receiver] more!"

"Yeah, but he's a better player than you are," Ernie said.

"He's a pain in the ass!"

"You're right, and you are, too. The thing is, he's good enough that I'll put up with him being a pain in the ass, and you're not. You're just not good enough to be a pain in the ass, Brian. Stop being a pain in the ass." Not that day, but soon, they were pals again. "Brian has never completely forgiven me for taking him out of that game," Accorsi said, "but he can almost laugh about it now."

"Ernie may be the only general manager," Michael Strahan said, "who has ever talked to a player that way. Or, for that matter, who talks to players at all. I knew George Young, but my relationship with George really wasn't much. It was kind of like he's the GM, I'm the player. He did his talking to my agent. With Ernie it has always been personal. He'll tell you what's wrong with you, but he'll compliment you, too, which you have to know is rare. Because, when contract time comes around, they're going to try not to pay you. But Ernie violates the GM code. 'Michael,' he'll say, 'you're the best. I've never seen a defensive end do that.' Just among players, I'll bet he leaves with as many real friends as anybody in the NFL."

Such as Sean Landeta.

Because Giants punter Jeff Feagles looked doubtful one week with an arthritic knee, Landeta, a former member of the Baltimore Stars (USFL), Philadelphia Stars (USFL), New York Giants, Los Angeles Rams, St. Louis Rams, Tampa Bay Buccaneers, Green Bay Packers, Philadelphia Eagles, Rams redux, Eagles redux, and Giants redux, was brought

back for a single game and technically a twenty-fifth year in professional
football. Ernie said, "First of all, we had to get both houses of Congress
along with the Armed Services Committee to force Tom to sign on. It
was a numbers thing, as usual. He was worried he might have to dress
two punters and lose a precious forty-sixth player. I said, 'Tom, if we
don't have a punter, the game is forfeited, okay?' Landeta was the obvious choice. He was nearby, on Long Island, and I know where Sean's
heart is—with this franchise. And I know he has ice water in his veins.
He's a Smoky Burgess. Fat or old, just roll ole Smoky out there and he'll
hit you a line drive double into the gap."

As it turned out, Feagles was able to go after all, and Landeta didn't
even dress. All the same, Sean's paycheck just for standing by was
$47,000. "It's the minimum," Ernie said, "for a man who's been in the
league four hundred and three years. For forty-seven grand, Sean got in
his car and drove sixteen miles. But don't forget, he had to cross over
two bridges, paying his own tolls both ways—seven bucks for the George
Washington Bridge alone. And do you want to know something else?
He'd have done it for forty-seven dollars. He'd have done it for forty-
seven cents."

Landeta said, "If the old rules were still in place, the pre-cap rules,
with no minimum salaries, I'd be able to play into my fifties [he was
forty-five] because I'd play for less than anybody. I'd be so cheap that I'd
be the most unpopular guy among the other punters in the whole history of punting. But I'd perform. Since I was nine, I've just enjoyed
doing this. I don't know how to explain it to you. I've loved all of the
things that sports are about. Being part of a team, especially. Working
toward a goal. Achieving that goal. To make your living, your life, at a
game: it's a little boy's dream, isn't it? I'll bet there are a hundred million guys out there who know exactly what I'm talking about."

He marked the starting point at age nine because that's how old
Landeta was in 1970 when Jim O'Brien of the Baltimore Colts kicked a
thirty-two-yard field goal with five seconds left to beat the Dallas Cowboys in Super Bowl V. "Growing up in Baltimore," Landeta said, "I was

like every kid in town, a Colts fanatic. All of us ran outside the moment that game ended, and with our heels made that little dent in the ground—remember?—to tee the ball up and kick it. Every one of us was Jim O'Brien. We didn't have goal posts, so we kicked the ball over a volleyball net and pretended it was to win the Super Bowl."

Fast-forward to 1978. "I had been punting and placekicking on sandlots for eight years, just for the fun of it," Landeta said. He wasn't even on the team at Loch Raven High School. "One morning, I came to school early to have my senior picture taken, and ran into the coach in the hall. 'I hear you can kick,' he said. 'Why don't you come out to the field this afternoon?' That was my only year of high school football. I punted and kicked field goals, both."

Just lately, the serendipity of that brush in the hall had been tumbling end over end in his mind. "What if I hadn't been there at that exact moment? What if the light that morning had been red instead of green? What if the photographer had taken one more shot? On top of which, the coach didn't have to ask me. He hadn't been looking for me. He just happened to see me." *Here comes the snap, and the boot . . .*

A kicking career at little Towson University (formerly Towson State Teachers College) led first to three seasons in the USFL and then to New York. In an NFC Divisional Play-off game against Chicago in 1985, Landeta dropped back to punt for the Giants, and a gust of Soldier Field wind blew the ball right out of his hands. On what was officially called a five-yard punt return, the Bears scored the only touchdown they would need that day. But just one autumn later, New York won the Super Bowl and Landeta joined Lawrence Taylor, Harry Carson, Leonard Marshall, Jim Burt, Joe Morris, Brad Benson, and Mark Bavaro at the Pro Bowl. Four years further on, Sean helped the Giants do it again. He really was Jim O'Brien.

"These days," he said, "I go out four or five times a week to a high school field or to a public park and punt footballs. Occasionally I have the luxury of a college or a high school snapper, but most of the time

I'm by myself. Coaches like to talk about a punter's soft hands, about the techniques of catching the ball, and holding it out there, and punting it. But the truth is, I've never thought about any of those things. I've never thought about rushing linemen, either. It's two seconds. You go out, you get set up, you catch the ball, you kick it. To me, it's the most natural thing in the world."

If he wanted to, Landeta could take a bag of twenty footballs out to the park. But, like a golfer on a practice putting green, he prefers to work with only three. "That way," he said, "I can go back and forth, get a little running in, think about what I'm doing, and just get ready." To Feagles, punting and golf have always seemed similar. "I think of the end zone as a green-side hazard," Jeff said. "I don't want to hit it in the water. I want to drop it on the flag. The way I look at it, the pin is tucked right next to the five-yard line." Landeta said, "I'm not much of a golfer, but I agree that a lot of the basics are the same. Make good contact. Don't try to kill it. Swing smooth. Hit the ball solid."

Considering all he had accomplished and how many memories were already in the bag, what was keeping Landeta standing by? "The possibility of doing it just one more time," he said simply. When will he finally let himself come to a stop? "I guess when there's only one team left that says it will keep me in mind," he said. "That might be next season, but I hope not. By my calculations, I have to have at least three or four GMs tell me that they'll consider me a candidate if their guy goes down or if he doesn't perform. Then it makes sense to stay ready. Only one 'maybe' out of thirty-two teams just isn't worth all of the work. Of course, if a day arrives when I don't feel like going to the park, that'll end it, too. And, obviously, my kicking won't be good enough for this level forever."

Saying goodbye to Ernie in his office, Sean headed back to his car for the drive home to Long Island. He had parked near the bubble, where big men just a little bit out of shape with surprisingly quick feet and astonishingly intent eyes were panting their lungs out and, in a few cases, trying not to faint. "It isn't the money," Landeta said. "Who doesn't like money? And everybody wants a job. But if a rule came in tomorrow that said all of the players in the NFL had to play for a fraction of their current salaries, all of them would still be out there."

Not all of them.

"Okay, ninety-five percent of them," he said. "You can see it, can't you? In their eyes?"

14

REESE

NEW YORK'S DIRECTOR of player personnel, Jerry Reese, was a former high school quarterback and small-college defensive back from the river town, the prison town, of Tiptonville, Tennessee. Reese seemed too small at five foot nine, not to mention too polite and well spoken, to be the fearsome blocker and tackler still whistled about at the University of Tennessee–Martin, where he is in the Hall of Fame. "You know what, I was probably an overachiever," Reese said with a grimace. (Overachieving is not much of a virtue in the scouting trade.) "I had a good coach who made me a better player, that's all. Lacking size and speed, I had to be really, really aggressive, and I guess I was." It was said that Reese *insisted* his high school team win the Tennessee state championship, and just when that perfect season was drifting away, Jerry personally retrieved it by running back a kickoff for a touchdown.

"I come from a single-parent family," Reese said. "My biological father died when I was seven, and I was twelve when my mother married my stepfather. He worked at the park, not as a ranger or anything like that, just mowing lawns, cleaning up. Tiptonville is a poor, rural town, but it's not a bad place to come from." Jerry's real father, J. C. Hillsman, died in an industrial accident at a mill that produced oil from cottonseeds. The seven children that Hillsman had with Jerry's mother weren't his only children in town. "We don't consider them half brothers and half sisters," Reese told John Branch of the *New York Times*. "They're brothers and sisters."

The consistent male influence in Jerry's young life was his great-grandfather, an equally hard and soft man who wasn't anything like his job: shooting, gutting, and skinning hogs in a backwoods slaughter-house. Just to be with him, Jerry was willing to tie a kerchief over his nose and assist in that putrid and dismal work. Reese also chopped cotton and cut grass. "One summer," he said, enjoying the memory, "a local farmer hired me as a flagman for the crop dusters. I'd march off eighteen rows and then signal for the drop." Eighteen rows and wave for the spray. Eighteen rows, all day long. "If I ever write a book," he said, "that's what I'm going to call it. *Eighteen Rows*." Every child of Ozella Garland—Miss Ozella, as she was still known in Tiptonville—had at least a shot at college, an unusual opportunity in Lake County, and they all took some advantage. Jerry earned a bachelor of science degree in health and education and a master's in education administration. "When your mother works for twenty years at the H.A.S. factory," he said, "standing at a machine all day, making denim, and then she takes a job as a corrections officer in the prison, you're pretty much obligated to succeed at something."

Football was a natural choice. That last year at Tennessee-Martin, Jerry was the Most Valuable Player in the Gulf South Conference, and when he stayed on as a graduate assistant at $400 a week, he fell in with one Jeremiah Davis. "At that time Jeremiah was an assistant coach at Tennessee-Martin," Reese said, "who thought enough of me to let me sleep on his couch. And he wouldn't let me pay him. Jeremiah and I were playing chess late one night when he looked up from the board to say, 'I'm going to work for you one day.' Just like that. I thought he was stalling because I was winning the game. I said, 'Come on, Jeremiah, make your move.' 'Listen to me,' he said, 'I'm serious. I'm going to work for you one day.' I didn't think anything else about it."

Davis, a scout's scout with the Giants now, joined the team as a summer intern twenty years ago. When the internship ended, Jeremiah wouldn't leave. Accorsi said, "George Young told him, 'You did a great job, Jeremiah, and we'd like to consider you for the future, but there's no position here now.' 'That's okay,' he said, 'you don't have to pay me. I can live with my mother. But I'm staying.' 'You don't understand . . .' 'I'm not leaving.' George went to the Maras and said, 'You've got to let me hire this guy.' On top of being stubborn and loyal, Jeremiah was good. He was just a special scout."

Michael Strahan said, "Jeremiah was the one who worked me out at school [Texas Southern] over and over. He was the only one, really, who kept coming back around until I hit the number. He put me on this training exerciser where you had to slam all these pads within a certain amount of time to prove your quickness. Jeremiah worked me like a dog. I kid him now that he tortured me more than anybody. 'And you're the only scout,' I tell him, 'who didn't at least have the decency to take me out afterward to get me something to eat.'"

To Davis, scouting wasn't a matter of arithmetic. "I didn't really care about the score Stray made," Jeremiah said. "I just had to get him to that number in case somebody else cared. It's never a number that you see in a player. It's something else." "It's a conviction," Ernie said. "All you can ask for in scouting is a conviction. After you have that, then you just need the balls. Guys like Jeremiah champion their causes. That's why they want to be in the draft room in April, so they can fight for their guys. I love the scouts. I don't think you could be a GM in this league if you had never done any scouting at all, if you didn't understand what it feels like to believe in a player. There's this peaceful—actually, exhilarating; *peaceful* is the wrong word—moment when you have a guy pegged. You've got him. You've watched him all day, or all season, and now you're ready to sit down and write your report. Some people will still protect themselves in the gray areas, but not guys like Jeremiah. Not guys like Reese."

"Years later," Jerry said, "when Jeremiah was with the Giants, he called me up. 'Jerry, we need a scout in the Southeast, are you interested?' I was, like, 'Are you kidding me? No way! I'm out of graduate school now. I'm the assistant head coach at UT-Martin. I'm making thirty-five thousand dollars a year—I can be the next head coach. I'm not going anywhere.' But he kept bugging me. My wife and I started talking about it, praying about it. Our daughter was only two—our son wasn't born yet. I already had a nice deal. I didn't want to mess that up. Then again, the NFL was the biggest game in the world. Gwen, also a UT-Martin graduate, finally said, 'Let's give it a shot,' and all of a sudden I'm a scout for the New York Giants."

The first thing you have to know about the scouting life, maybe the only thing, is that you will be on the road some 185 to 200 days a year. Get up in the morning, drive to the school, watch the videotape, talk with the contact people—trainer, strength coach, head coach, position coach—watch practice, take notes, get back in the car, drive three hours to the next economy motel, type up your report, go to bed, get up and do it again, and again, from Cracker Barrel to Cracker Barrel, on an endless highway.

"It's not digging a ditch," Reese said, "but it's hard work." It's hardest on the heart. "I'd go out for fourteen or sixteen days at a time, and when I'd get back, little JR wouldn't know me. He was just starting to walk. I'd reach out for him and he'd pull away. That kind of stuff can kill you."

Reese had very good eyes for the task. "I think some guys just have an innate ability to see it," he said. "If you work at it, I guess you could develop it. But I believe, even as a young scout, I had a pretty good fix on it. I could see things. Then you have to be able to express it, put it on paper, without writing a novel. You know, get to the point. What can he do? What can't he do? Can this guy contribute to our football team? Can he make it? Why will he make it? Why won't he make it? It's neither a science nor a crap shoot. It's an understanding. I don't know, I just had a feel for it, and a love for it."

Accorsi noticed. In fact, he saw a general manager in the making. Talking Reese into leaving the frontier and coming into the front office was the tricky part. Even New Jersey real estate prices scared Jerry and

Gwen. But Ernie made the sale. Then twice he jumped Reese over more experienced men, first to assist Dave Gettleman with pro personnel, then to handle the college personnel himself. "The best three years of my career was in the pro department," Jerry said. "When you're on the road scouting, you kind of forget who's actually playing in the NFL, who's good enough to contribute, I mean. 'Wow, this guy's really helping? I didn't think he was even close to good enough when I saw him a few years ago.' You stop thinking all of the time about the stars. You learn how a medium-level player, even a low-level player, can chip in something valuable. When you think about it, there really aren't that many great, great football players. Most are developmental projects. Picking out the top guys and the bottom guys isn't all that difficult. It's seeing those guys in the middle who can play a little—that's where you make your money. Maybe he's fast and nothing else. Maybe he's just big. But then, maybe he has something—the makings of something—that you just can't quite put your finger on. But you like it."

The few black executives in the National Football League in 2006 were mostly former stars like the tight end Ozzie Newsome, the quarterback James Harris, and the receiver Gene Washington. "Here was a guy," Ernie said, "who wasn't even a player in the league, who started off at the very bottom, like most of us, and worked his way up the same way, step by step." Accorsi was loud and unambiguous in recommending to John Mara and Steve and Jonathan Tisch that Reese replace him, but Ernie had to be careful not to push too hard. It was a situation of some delicacy.

Chris Mara, the Giants' vice president of player evaluation, wanted the GM job desperately, and he was eminently qualified. Since 1979, Chris had worked in player personnel for his father's team. When Wellington's second son didn't rise to the position of head of player personnel—"We can't have any fireproof heads of player personnel," George Young snorted—Chris went off on his own for a while to run a scouting service and eventually to be the president and general manager of the New Jersey Gladiators of the Arena Football League. They finished first in the Eastern Division of the National Conference. To be near his father for Wellington's last years, Chris returned to the Giants' front office in 2003. He had the skills absolutely to be an NFL GM, if only he had a different last name.

Chris' daughter, Kate, was a film actress with mounting credits (*Random Hearts, Brokeback Mountain, We Are Marshall, Shooter*) in increasingly juicier parts. She was both a Mara and a Rooney—Chris and the former Kathleen Rooney represent something of a Giants-Steelers merger—which is a little like being by the Triple Crown–winning sire Secretariat out of the Triple Crown–winning dam Genuine Risk. They could have called Kate or any of her three siblings "Six Crowns." But she was putting her dad in obvious danger of going straight from being Somebody's Son to being Somebody's Father, and the urgency of his campaign to be the next GM was a watercooler topic all season long in the New York front office. Outsiders like former Redskins GM Charley Casserly would be interviewed pro forma. That's standard. Scott Pioli of New England would make a small news item out of declining to be interviewed. But neither of them ever had a chance. There were only two serious candidates to replace Accorsi.

A few days after Halloween, on a windy Sunday in Giants Stadium, New York beat Tampa Bay, 17–3, in a punter's game. "It's been my experience," punter Jeff Feagles said, "that if there are a lot of reporters standing around my locker after a game, it isn't good news for me." And Feagles was more experienced than almost anybody else in the business. The Tampa game was the 295th without a break for this balding, forty-year-old island in the middle of a sea of twenty-two- and twenty-three-year-old men. Jim Marshall's fallen record of 282 games continued to be slightly more impressive, because Marshall had been a position player—a defensive end for Minnesota (who sometimes picked up the ball and ran the wrong way). Still, a punter has to stay employable for an awfully long while to head the NFL's all-time list for durability, sixty games in front of Brett Favre.

Actually, Feagles tried to retire during the last off-season, returning with his wife, Michelle, to their hometown, Phoenix, Arizona. But Ernie told Jeff, "You can't retire until I retire," refusing to submit his papers. And then an even funnier thing happened. The Feagles' four sons, ages six to sixteen, voiced a preference for Jersey over the Valley of the Sun, and Jeff came back to the Giants. Like Jim Bowie and Davy Crockett, Feagles and Accorsi were in it together until the end, trying not to strike out swinging at the Alamo.

"Usually when there are this many people around my locker," Feagles repeated after the Bucs game, "the smart money is on a blocked punt, although a high snap is well within the realm of possibility, too, or maybe it's just a good old-fashioned dropped ball. Whatever it is, you can be pretty sure it's a screw-up of some kind."

But no, this time the attention was on two coffin-corner kicks that qualified as the plays of the game in a forty- to fifty-mile-per-hour windstorm. "And we knew it would be this way when we went to sleep last night," center Shaun O'Hara said. "That's what you get when you play in the swampy Meadowlands. I thought to myself before I went to bed, 'Sunday might be a Jeff Feagles day.'"

On practice days, whenever the elements became uncomfortable enough for the team to seek shelter inside the bubble, Feagles always stayed outdoors to experiment with the wind currents in Giants Stadium. "It's a great place for punting in swirls," he said, "if you know the prevailing tendencies; in other words, if it's your home. The visiting punters look at the flags flapping atop the stadium. I've learned to ignore them. The twisting winds at field level are the important calculations. You have to time the gusts and adjust your drop. Today was a two-step drop, instead of a regular two-and-a-half-stepper. It's fun to see the ball hit at the five and back up like a sand wedge. It's fun to get up in the morning and know you're going to have a chance to make a real contribution today. Hell, I've always loved the Giants Stadium winds."

The Buccaneers were less enraptured. Antonio Pierce said, "On the field, they kept talking about how cold they were, how they had gone from a hundred-and-five-degree heat to this. 'Welcome to New York,' I said. 'Why don't you see a show while you're in town?' "

The battle of the Barber twins, Tiki and Ronde, was scored a draw. Neither stood out. Tiki won the game, while Ronde wrapped up their lifetime series, three victories to two. Twice in the course of the day's events they collided—Ronde is a defensive back—but only one rhubarb resulted. "He was mad that I hit him so low the first time," Ronde said. "So, nailing him again, I said, 'Is that high enough for you, Tiki?' 'Yeah, man,' he said. 'Thanks. That's perfect.' "

Ronde had less conversation and success trying not to be pancaked by Brandon Jacobs on the goal line ("I don't know who that number twenty-seven is," said Tampa coach Jon Gruden, "but he made a difference"). In an even less felicitous match-up, Ronde was hopelessly alley-ooped by Eli Manning and Plaxico Burress. "When you're five-nine-and-a-half," Ronde said specifically, "you might be able to cover a six-five guy in the end zone, but not if he can catch a ball one-handed—and left-handed—without even looking at it."

Two Giants series were sufficient to win, an extended one in the first quarter and a shorter one in the second that followed a fumble by Tampa's rookie quarterback Bruce Gradkowski.

GIANTS

1-10-G47 Barber runs for 4
2-6-B49   Manning passes to Burress for 13
1-10-B36 Barber runs for 4
2-6-B32   Manning passes to Jim Finn for 8
1-10-B24 Barber runs for 1
2-9-B23   Manning passes to Visanthe Shiancoe for 13
1-G-B10   Barber runs for 3
2-G-B7   Manning passes to Burress for 7 and the
          touchdown; Jay Feely's kick is good.

New York 7, Tampa Bay 0

GIANTS
1-10-B28 Manning passes to Burress for 25 yards

"In the locker room before the game," Plaxico said, "Eli told me, 'This might be a day when catching the ball is enough. Forget about getting yards after it. Just go down. No turnovers is the deal today.' And we had none."

1-G-B3   Barber runs for 2

"Evidently it's not my job to score touchdowns anymore," said Tiki, still without any for the year.

2-G-B1   Jacobs runs for 1 and the touchdown; Feely's kick is good
New York 14, Tampa Bay 0

Two field goals came later, one for the Buccaneers in the first half, one for the Giants in the second. As Kate Mara would say, when the punter plays the lead, the movie is usually a short subject.

Starting off the season with five straight losses, the Bucs had put together a pair of victories on their way to New York, including a stirring last-second one over Philadelphia. But now they were depressed again. The winners weren't overly ecstatic, either. They were professional. "The object is to win," Tom Coughlin said prosaically. About the growing roster of injuries—linebacker Brandon Short strained a quad muscle—Strahan said to the cameras, "The guys who came in all looked like starters to me." But, off to the side, he conceded, "There are reasons the starters are the starters and the backups are the backups."

Used to seeing more joy in a winning locker room, O'Hara delivered the day's punch line: "Hey, you can't go home with the prom queen every night."

15

GOODBYE, TOOMS

FOR AN ILLUSTRATION OF expectations in New York, consider how loudly the Giants were booed at home in the course of winning their fifth consecutive game. The level of the opponent—a second straight 2-and-5 team, the Houston Texans—had something to do with that.

And the Texans were ahead in the fourth quarter, 10–7, as Eli Manning started a drive on his own thirty-three-yard line with an incompletion. Not because they were so pressed for time, just to stir the tempo in the hope of reinvigorating their logy quarterback, the Giants switched to a no-huddle offense.

GIANTS

1-10-G33 Manning passes incomplete

2-10-G33 (no huddle, shotgun) Manning throws to Tiki Barber for 13

1-10-G46 (no huddle, shotgun) Barber runs for 12

1-10-T42 (no huddle, shotgun) Manning passes to Michael Jennings for 5

2-5-T37 (no huddle, shotgun) Manning passes to Jeremy Shockey for 14

1-10-T23 Offside, Houston

1-5-T18 (no huddle, shotgun) Manning passes incomplete

2-5-T18 (no huddle) Barber runs for −1

3-6-T19 (no huddle) Barber runs for 7

1-10-T12 (shotgun) Manning passes to Amani Toomer
    for 10
1-G-T2   Brandon Jacobs runs for −1
2-G-T3   Manning passes to Shockey for 3 and the
    touchdown; Jay Feely's kick is good
                New York 14, Houston 10

Houston had only one turn left, but it was looking like that would be enough.

T E X A N S
1-10-T30 David Carr passes to Wali Lundy for 2
2-8-T30   Carr passes incomplete

At this point rookie Mathias Kiwanuka, in at right defensive end for injured Osi Umenyiora, drew the first roughing-the-passer penalty of his professional career. "Talk about the difference between college and the pros," he said. "In college after making a play like that, you're getting head slaps and high fives on the sidelines. In the pros, you can expect a big fine, I'm told." Three games hence, this minor event filed away in the back of Kiwanuka's consciousness would lead to a major catastrophe.

1-10-T47 Lundy runs for 8
2-2-G45   Lundy runs for 3
1-10-G42 Lundy runs for 4
2-6-G38   Carr passes to Jameel Cook for 3; Cook fumbles
    to Corey Webster; the Giants survive the game, but
    not intact

Joining the burgeoning list of the infirm and ill, Plaxico Burress (back) and Kareem McKenzie (migraines) did not play. With no notice, grizzled pro Bob Whitfield, thirty-five years old and in his fifteenth (and final) NFL season, started at right offensive tackle for McKenzie. "I hear you're starting," Ernie said to him in the locker room. "Yeah, I got the memo," Whitfield said. Later, he confessed, "I was trying to find my game face. It wasn't in my bag. It's been so long since I needed it, I couldn't remember where I left it."

In the second quarter, wrestling with right tackle Zach Wiegert, Michael Strahan took an awkward step and had to leave the field with what at first was called a midfoot sprain. Adrian Awasom, just two weeks removed from the Giants' practice squad, replaced him. "I'm not talking about the foot," Strahan said afterward, filling the locker room with a sense of foreboding. "You lose Strahan," Antonio Pierce fairly whispered, "and you lose the face of the Giants' defense. Tiki, offense. Michael, defense. They're the Giants." Barber, by the way, finally broke through—on a sixteen-yard dash—to score his first touchdown of the season.

In Strahan's rookie year of 1993, he missed ten full games with a strained Lisfranc ligament in a foot. Jacques Lisfranc, a field surgeon for Napoleon, might be surprised to know how many men were still catching their feet in the stirrups while being thrown from horses on the Russian front. Strahan's Lisfranc suspicions would be confirmed in a few days, and that wouldn't be the worst news for the team.

At the same time, there was some silliness afoot. During the game, both Carr and top draft choice Mario Williams threw the Giants' basketball jump shots back in their faces. Wasn't that inevitable?

"There was almost a fistfight over it," said Williams, a six foot six, 293-pound defensive end from North Carolina State, whom the Texans preferred to Southern Cal running back Reggie Bush and Texas quarterback Vince Young in the last draft. But Chris Snee, Tom Coughlin's son-in-law, argued for leaving Mario alone, saying with undisguised admiration, "He's bigger than I thought he was before I actually saw him." Shaun O'Hara, a skilled hand at satire, especially for a center, said, "This is *our* basketball court. Nobody shoots jump shots on *our* court."

Chicago was next up in Giants Stadium, but no longer were the Bears undefeated. As New York was edging Houston, the Bears weren't just losing to 1-and-6 Miami in Chicago, they were basically being exposed, 31–13. Mike Singletary, William "the Refrigerator" Perry, Jim McMahon, and Walter Payton hadn't been reincarnated after all. As a result, quarterback Rex Grossman was under siege at home. His four interceptions and two fumbles in a slender victory over Arizona had been aggravated by three interceptions and a fumble against the Dolphins. Grossman's ratings were barely registering on the scale of quarterbacks, and, next to Rex, Manning appeared confident. "Eli's got confidence," Whitfield said sagely, "but he doesn't yet have what I call savvy confidence. It's how you walk and talk. The quarterback is a leader by default, but Eli still has to work on walking and talking."

Because Burress was out and Amani Toomer was reduced to just two short catches by a throbbing ankle and a nagging knee, Shockey served as Manning's primary target against Houston. Jeremy caught eight passes for sixty-six yards and a touchdown, and on a call in the end zone close enough to be challenged, Shock had a second touchdown slammed out of him by kamikaze safety Glenn Earl. Jeremy ran back to the huddle to tell Eli, "I have to make that catch, man."

Three days after the game, Toomer learned that his left knee wasn't merely sore. He had partially torn the anterior cruciate ligament and needed immediate surgery. Amani's season was over. "Man," Barber said, "where is the sniper hiding?" Toomer, the stateliest Giant, was the team's all-time career yardage leader (8,157) by nearly three thousand yards over Frank Gifford. Amani needed just two touchdown passes to overtake Kyle Rote (forty-eight) at the head of that list, too. Nobody— not Rote, not Homer Jones, not Del Shofner, not Earnest Gray—could touch him for hundred-yard games (twenty-two). "This is bad," Tiki said. "Unassuming. Quiet. Great. Whenever we needed a big play, Amani was there to make it. He isn't a player who came into the NFL guaranteed a great career, either. He's a guy who had to fight for it. That's why it's always meant so much to him."

On September 9, 1995, Accorsi scouted Toomer of the University of Michigan in a game against Memphis at Ann Arbor:

STRONG POINTS—EXCELLENT HANDS . . . ELUSIVE, CLEVER . . . WIGGLES ON THE QUICK SCREEN . . . MAKES PEOPLE MISS . . . BREAKS TACKLES, TOO . . . TALL AND RANGY . . . EXCELLENT SIZE, 6-3, 194 . . . WILL CATCH IN A CROWD . . . TAKE A HIT AND HOLD ONTO THE BALL . . . QUICK AND EXPLOSIVE OFF THE LINE OF SCRIMMAGE . . . BIG PLAY RECEIVER.

WEAK POINTS—THE ONLY QUESTION I HAVE ON HIM IS DURABILITY, AND THE FACT THAT THERE IS NO CONFIRMED SPEED. HE LOOKS FAST ENOUGH FOR HIS SIZE.

SUMMATION—BIG, RANGY RECEIVER WITH ENOUGH SPEED AND MORE THAN ENOUGH EXPLOSION . . . CAN RUN AFTER CATCH WITH THE ABILITY BOTH TO ELUDE AND BREAK TACKLES . . . HAS COURAGE TO CATCH IN A CROWD AND MAKES BIG PLAYS . . . EXCELLENT HANDS.

QUICKNESS 68, AGILITY 68, BALANCE 70, STRENGTH 68, EXPLOSIVENESS 70, COMPETITIVENESS 70, DURABILITY 66, QUICK FEET 68, HANDS 70, INITIAL QUICKNESS 70, RELEASE 70, SEPARATION 70, PATTERNS 68, FIND OPEN AREA 68, RECEIVE SHORT 70, RECEIVE LONG 70, ADJUST TO BALL 70, REACT TO CROWD 70, RUN ABILITY 70, BLOCK 66.

FINAL RATING—70. FINAL DESCRIPTION—THIS GUY'S A DIFFERENCE MAKER.

"That day," Ernie said, "he went up for a badly thrown ball, caught it and got hammered, broke two ribs, but came down with the catch. When I got back to the office, I told George Young, 'I probably shouldn't write a report on just one play, but I saw all I needed to see on that play. Hands, courage, got open, took a hit.' Toomer didn't have numbers, but nobody has numbers at Michigan." Just the fact that he went to

Michigan demonstrated that Amani was his own man. His father, Donald, played for Woody Hayes at Ohio State. Hayes once said that if his car ran out of gas in Michigan, he'd push it across the state line before he'd buy anything from those bastards.

The Giants selected Amani in the second round of the 1996 draft, using the thirty-fourth pick overall. That first season, they assigned him tight end Mark Bavaro's old jersey number, 89, and set him to work fielding punts. Amani returned two of them for touchdowns but missed the last nine games of the season when the other anterior cruciate ligament, the right one, blew. He returned from reconstructive surgery to become the definitive New York Giants receiver. In a princess-and-the-pea moment, Toomer switched to number 81, explaining that the 9 on the right side of his back felt a tad heavy; it was interfering with his equilibrium. Playing as many as 127 games without a pause, Toomer turned out to be a standard for durability and dependability as well. "He's been everything for us," Barber said. "He's Toom."

Soaking in a hot tub in the training room, Toomer said, "Sometimes I feel like I've been doing this eighty-five years. Other times it feels like I've just begun. I was watching a Monday night game recently, or maybe it was a later game after ours—I can't remember—but it was just another football game. And something dawned on me that I never even thought about before. The TV cameras can look inside our helmets! They can see inside our eyes! I thought, 'Man, I don't want to show them that much.' I always thought I was hiding out there. But that camera takes away your protection. I've been making a conscious effort to control my body language on the field, to develop a poker face at the bench, so as not to give away everything that's inside me. It's too personal. It's embarrassing. I'm going to work on that while I'm rehabbing. I hope to come back a complete mystery to the announcers in the booth."

Professional athletes who shrink from cameras or attention are fairly rare in the New York area, where a player without his own column or radio show is an object of pity. "It takes a certain kind of person to play well here," Toomer said. "It has nothing to do with whether he's from a rural area or a cosmopolitan area; it's inside him. Can he shoot for the stars? Can he stand daily pressure? You can't lay back here and just have a nice career. I had a rough start, but I just knew I'd make it, and I was sure I'd end up being a longtime Giant. Every now and then they'd draft a guy who looked like he was going to be my replacement, but those guys always tried too hard. In the pass-catching business, if you have to try too hard, something's wrong. When it's feeling good on the field, there's this amazing comfort level. You're primed at the line of scrimmage. You actually kind of hum, like you're a race car at the starting grid—five thousand RPM and shaking, shaking, shaking, and then all of a sudden, whoosh! You really get to know yourself on a football field. I know I've got some Giants records, but I'm not ready to look at them yet. I'm not ready to stop."

Not surprisingly, Manning took Toomer's loss the hardest. "He's the most consistent great player on our team," said Eli, deciding not to go into who was the least consistent. "You always know what you're going to get out of Amani. He does the right thing on every play. If the quarterback doesn't trust his possession receiver, if you have the slightest doubt that he'll get open, it makes you just a split second late, and that's when you commit your biggest errors." Toomer was the one who told him, way back when Eli arrived, "New York is for the strong-willed." Like a game plan, Manning had made a study of New York sports, immersing himself in the Knicks and Nets and even the Devils and Rangers. "I had never been to a hockey game until I got here," Eli said. "Those are good fun, too." A New York athlete can't ever get down, either on himself or on the team. "Because if he does," Manning said, "the media are going to go for the kill shot. They'll say, 'He's not strong enough to be here.'"

But a quarterback who loses his Raymond Berry can't help but feel a little down, at least momentarily. In the weeks to come, the *New York Times* would plot a steady decline in Manning's passing rating, especially on third-down plays, from the last short pass to Toomer that allowed the Giants to run out the clock against Houston.

Only for about a half a day did the players allow themselves to talk about the many injuries. After that, the dear departed were spoken of no more. "You can't talk about injuries in the NFL," said Brandon Short, another Penn State linebacker. "It's not just that it's an insult to the backup players, it's a built-in alibi for everyone on the team. It's a self-fulfilling prophecy. You just can't talk about it. You just can't think about it. You just have to keep on playing."

The first half of the season was over and the Giants stood 6–2. New Orleans, that team starting out in the opposite direction, was also 6–2. Their new quarterback, Drew Brees, was no longer being described as damaged goods from San Diego. Their rookie coach, Sean Payton—once a replacement quarterback in the strike year of 1987—was about to become the toast of the league.

"He was an assistant coach for us," Ernie said, "who never even got an interview. I blew it."

16

TIME-OUT, GIANTS

THE FIRST DOMINO FELL, the season began to be lost, on a time-out called by New York with 1:30 left in the opening half of a Sunday night game versus the Chicago Bears. Not one player, not one coach, not one reporter, not one fan—even in retrospect—would cite this as a significant event, let alone a seminal one, but Accorsi did, the moment it happened. "He didn't second-guess you, Tom," I told Coughlin many weeks later. "He first-guessed you. He first-guessed the hell out of you."

"Ernie picks his spots," Coughlin said.

Unable to decide between a drizzle and a downpour, the night was wet and cold, especially in Accorsi's Giants Stadium tunnel, which leaks. "Do you know who that is?" Ernie said, trying to dodge the heaviest drips. He nodded toward a Bears bystander, number 4, who in the pregame hour was also working hard to stay moderately dry. "Brad Maynard," Ernie said contemptuously. "He's a punter from Ball State. We had him here with us in the Super Bowl year, 2000. Every time we exchanged punts with the Ravens, they gained about six yards on us." When the other Bears players had joined Maynard in the tunnel, they put their fists together, and Thomas Jones, a running back, hollered, "We're the best team in the NFL! We've got to show them that right now!" Someone with a more modulated voice in the center of the scrum said, "Take it to the house on two, baby," and they all screamed, "Take it to the house!" and stampeded under the goalpost onto the field. Number 23 brought up the rear.

"That's the rookie Devin Hester," Ernie said, "a University of Miami guy. Wait till you see him. He was a little weird at the workout, but he's got a lot of ability. His father played at Florida State with Deion Sanders, who was coaching Hester in the workout. 'What's Deion doing here?' I asked the kid. 'Oh, he's my mentor, he's my guru.' But that wasn't really what worried me. Hester kept saying, 'I'm a defensive back, I'm not a receiver.' Well, they tried him at both positions, and he looked like a hell of a receiver to me. Great hands. But he didn't want to play there. He wanted to be Deion Sanders. And anyone could see he didn't have the instincts or the experience for that. The Bears are listing him as a cornerback, but they're using him as a kick returner. He sure has the instincts for that."

Taking the opening kickoff, the Giants wasted a nine-play drive with a missed field goal of thirty-three yards in a tricky wind. But on Chicago's third snap of the game, quarterback Rex Grossman made the exact mistake for which he was becoming infamous. "The book on Grossman," Accorsi said, "is that if you put pressure on him in his own territory, he's going to give you the game. He shows a lot more talent on your side of the field than he does on his, kind of like the hitter who can kill you when the count is three and one but has no chance at oh and two. Let Grossman get into a comfort zone, though, and he can play."

On third and nine at his own twenty-five, Rex threw a pass to the right side that was easily intercepted by Mathias Kiwanuka and returned to the one-yard line, from where Brandon Jacobs forced his way into the end zone. With neither quarterback shining in the rain, an exchange of turnovers—an interception of Eli Manning, a Jones fumble—brought about a swap of field goals. After the Giants struck for another three points, their scoring "drives" amounted to one yard, three yards, and nine yards.

Eli was not just struggling but foundering, especially since the two-minute mark of the first quarter, when left tackle Luke Petitgout limped out of the game. Still, the Giants had a 13–3 lead and it was raining hard.

BEARS

1-10-B26 Grossman passes to Mark Bradley for 6
Two-minute warning
2-4-B32   Grossman passes to Jones for 8
1-10-B40 Grossman passes incomplete
2-10-B40 (shotgun) False start, Chicago
2-15-B35 (shotgun) Another false start, Chicago
2-20-B30 (shotgun) Grossman passes to Jones for –2
3-22-B28 . . .

That's when the Giants called time-out with a minute and a half to go until halftime, to save some clock for themselves.

"No, no, no, *no!*" Accorsi cried out, turning into Rumpelstiltskin, startling the spectators in the seats above. "Don't be too smart! Don't be too smart!" This was a Paterno-ism. "The Bears are ready to settle for thirteen to three at the half! It's raining! Let them settle for thirteen to three at the half!"

Then came the second domino.

3-22-B28 Jones runs for 26 yards

"Third and twenty-two," linebacker Antonio Pierce said later, disgustedly. "It was a give-up play. Everybody in the league runs a draw or a screen in that situation. It was just a simple draw play." But the Giants, especially safety Will Demps, couldn't stop it; or didn't, anyway.

1-10-G46 Illegal shift, Chicago
1-15-B49 Grossman passes incomplete
2-15-B49 Grossman passes to Muhsin Muhammad
   for 22 yards
1-10-G29 Grossman passes to Mark Bradley for 29 yards
   and the touchdown; Robbie Gould's kick is good
               New York 13, Chicago 10

With the thirty-five seconds they had preserved, the Giants ran their own give-up play, a Barber plunge, and went off to the locker room looking like the trailing team. Both of Chicago's long passes at the end victimized corner Sam Madison, who tried bravely to come back from his hamstring strain but plainly had no legs. The latest injury, maybe the worst of all, walked right past Accorsi on a bare left foot. Petitgout, the left tackle, the quarterback's main protector, was limping to the locker room on a broken fibula. He was finished for the night and for the season. In fact, he was finished with the Giants forever. After every snap from center the rest of the year, Manning would move almost imperceptibly to his right before he did anything else.

"It's broken; he's out," Accorsi said, returning from the X-ray room to his tunnel just before the teams poured through for the second half. "Tiki is saying sprained, but his right thumb is broken, too. Tiki just doesn't have the time to have a broken thumb right now, God bless him. He only has a half a year left to go. Me too."

Chicago took the third-quarter kick and drove to the Giants' two-yard line before fumbling. But New York couldn't move an inch and Jeff Feagles had barely enough end zone space to launch a punt.

B E A R S

1-10-G43 Jones runs for 2

2-8-G41 Grossman passes to Jones for 4 (plus
  roughing the passer on William Joseph)

1-10-G22 Illegal contact, R. W. McQuarters

1-10-G17 Jones runs for 7

2-3-G10 Jones runs for 10 and an apparent touchdown,
  nullified by John Gilmore's hold

2-7-G14 Jones runs for 4

3-3-G10 Grossman passes to Muhammad for 10
  and the touchdown; Gould's kick is good

Chicago 17, New York 13

Old Bob Whitfield, the first-round draft choice from yesteryear (for Atlanta), who hadn't been as nimble since breaking his own leg in 2003, moved into Petitgout's position and was outclassed horribly by defensive end Alex Brown. One of Brown's two sacks caused a Manning fumble that left the Bears just twenty-one yards from another touchdown and a 24–13 lead. In his comfort zone, Rex Grossman certainly could play. Then a forty-six-yard sprint by Barber set up an eight-yard run by Jacobs for Brandon's second touchdown. The Bears led only 24–20, with 11:49 left in the game, when the last domino fell.

GIANTS

1-10-G21 Barber runs for 5 (personal foul, Chicago)
1-10-G41 Manning passes to Plaxico Burress for 10
1-10-B49 Barber runs for 8
2-2-B41   Manning passes to David Tyree for 12
1-10-B29 Manning sacked by Brown
2-24-B43 (shotgun) Barber runs for 9
3-15-B34 Manning passes incomplete

"Do you believe we called a pass play there?" Ernie asked. "Now we can't even try a field goal."

Wanna bet?

4-15-B34 . . .

"Oh, no," Accorsi whispered as Jay Feely came out to attempt a fifty-two-yarder. "Oh, God," Ernie said, "no!" Hester dropped back into the end zone. "Now we have all of our fat guys on the field," the GM said in a normal and resigned voice. "Watch Hester run it back all the way for a touchdown." And he did. As Deion's protégé crossed the goal line, he leaped into the air and fired an imaginary jump shot at the Giants.

Afterward, Whitfield was the most distraught. "I was watching to see the ball sail through the uprights," he confessed, "rather than running down there and covering the kick. Counting that play and the two sacks, I feel like I lost this game single-handedly." In days to come, in a poignant moment during a players-only meeting, Whitfield would rise to tell his teammates that he hadn't expected to have to come in and play such an important role. He beseeched the backups to the backups to try to be readier than he was when the call came.

In the locker room after the Chicago game, center Shaun O'Hara said of Hester's 108-yard run, "The last thing you think of is that it's going to be short and they're going to return it for a touchdown. Even if you had a crystal ball, you might not see that one."

The final score was 38–20. After that night, for any observer not too emotionally involved, the only unknown about the 2006 Giants was whether they would keep playing or quit. Maybe never in the NFL's history had there been so few good teams at the top and so few bad teams at the bottom and so many average teams in the middle. Where New York might fit at anything like full strength no longer mattered. Like the Super Bowl, full strength was out of the question now. The season, as a season, was over.

Walking into a pro football front office on a Monday morning, you wouldn't have to have seen or heard about Sunday's game to know the score. You don't have to pass a second desk to realize how good or bad it was. After a victory, any kind of victory, the workers are dancing in the aisles. After a loss, any kind of loss, the women and men darting here and there with a pen or a sheaf of paper aren't just depressed, they're despondent. The morning after the Bears game was worst of all.

"This is a scrambling day," Ernie said darkly. "We're waiting for the official word on Petitgout. We already got some bad news on Justin Tuck, who didn't play last night. His separation is worse. Ronnie Barnes is flying with him to Charlotte tomorrow for an operation, so Justin's lost. He has no family to go with him, and Ronnie doesn't want him to have to go alone. We need a left tackle, and of course Tom is looking for [the great 1950s pass blocker] Roosevelt Brown. You can imagine what's out there at this point in November with all of the injuries. There's nothing. Is there a tackle out there? Is there anyone even on a practice squad? It's hard to pry people from practice squads. The player has to notify his club, and the club immediately makes a counteroffer, or tries to arrange room for him on the roster, especially if it's a team not going to the play-offs. I doubt Petitgout will be back, but I'm not going to be in a hurry to put him on injured reserve. John Fox almost committed suicide in Carolina after he put running back Stephen Davis on IR and ended up going all of the way to the Super Bowl. By then, Davis was a hundred percent healthy and ineligible to play. If only to show our team I'm not quitting on them, I'm going to hold out that same hope for Luke."

Immediately after the game, Petitgout had said, "I'll be fine . . . a couple of weeks. Guys have played with this before."

"He would say that, wouldn't he?" Accorsi said, chuckling. "God, these guys are great. Luke's dreaming, of course, but I love dreamers."

At the moment, Ernie was not in love with his head coach. "I did a lot of bitching in the tunnel last night," he said, "and, frankly, when I think about that game, twenty-four hours later, I'm *more* angry. When Tom was hired, I asked him, 'Is there a bunker mentality among head coaches?' and he answered, 'I'm going to count on you to be blatantly frank with me and give me your slant so that I can always have a fresh point of view.' They all say that, but they don't really want to hear anything but what they want to hear. I'm going to write it out for him today in a memo. 'This is what I think.' I'm going to put it on paper, not for the record, just because I don't have time today to wage a running debate. Tom can look at it if he wants. He can throw it away if he wants. But here's my view.

"What we did last night, it violated everything I *ever* learned about football. It violated every principle Paterno taught me. Joe had two things that he screamed, I'm telling you, twenty times a day—I'm not exaggerating. One is field position, field position, field position. Number two, don't try to be too smart. Be sound. You're not going to outsmart anybody. It's going to blow up in your face, especially if you're trying to outsmart someone. If you're sound, you're going to win.

"I look at players' eyes in the tunnel. I learn a lot in that tunnel. It's thirteen to three—the Bears don't think they're going to win the game because they have to beat us by intercepting the ball or causing some other turnover or, somehow, unleashing Hester. What do we do? We give them the opportunity. Why do we want the ball back for thirty-five seconds to begin with? It's raining. We could fumble the kick, we could commit a holding penalty. We could give them life. Our quarterback is having a terrible night. What was to be gained? Had there been a single sign that we could take the ball and march it down the field in thirty-five seconds? After that, it's third and twenty-three. Chicago's giving up the ghost, right? Get in the locker room, Tom, with our thirteen-to-three lead! And when the Bears ran into the locker room, they were a different team. On the road in the NFL, it isn't long before you don't think you can win. 'We're not going to win this game, okay?' And they were getting awfully close to that. But no, we were too smart.

"Now we've come back to twenty-four to twenty and we're first and ten on their twenty-nine. We've got control of the situation. We're running the ball and they can't stop us. We ran for a hundred and fifty yards—no one has stopped us from running the ball all year in those conditions—and why we're not using Jacobs, I have no idea. He was unopposed on both touchdowns. We're wearing them down. The weather is bad. Maybe we won't be able to hold them later, maybe we'll screw up on defense later—six starters are out, after all—but we're going to go ahead in the game for the moment at least, if we just play smart. But instead, for some unknown reason, against *that* pass rush, with Eli having a bad night, we try to throw. Now it's second and twenty-four. We've changed the game. We get to third and fifteen, and Hufnagel says, 'Oh, I think I'll try this pass play to Plax. That's part of my philosophy.'

"Finally, rather than hand the ball to Feagles and trust the best plus-punter in the league to spin the ball inside the twenty and give Grossman a chance to give away the game in bad weather, we try a fifty-two-yard field goal in the same direction a thirty-three-yarder had already been missed. Our big, slow field-goal protection guys then get to watch Devin Hester dance a hundred and eight yards untouched. He would have scored in a two-hand touch football game.

"We could have won a thirteen-to-ten game. That's our kind of game."

The rush of words seemed to be over. A little chagrined, Ernie smiled. But he was just taking a breath.

"Tom said, 'I told Eli today that you don't score points by running the ball, you score points by passing it.' That kills any chance of me sleeping tonight. Tom had this long talk with Eli in which he basically told him, 'You're the reason we lost and you're going to have to play much better or we won't win.' Do you think Bill Cowher ever said that to Ben Roethlisberger? Pittsburgh never asks Roethlisberger to win a game by himself. They ask him not to lose by himself. 'I told Eli,' Tom said, 'You know why I made that stupid decision on the field goal, Eli?' Now listen to this. 'Because you weren't playing well and I didn't know how we'd get down there again.' Now I have to go to Manning sometime today and try to reassure him that it's not all his fault."

Ernie had one other thing on his mind.

"Do you know what all this takes me back to?" he said. "Alabama beat Penn State in the Sugar Bowl, fourteen to seven, to win the national championship in 1978. That was the goal line stand game. In the pregame, Penn State kicker Matt Bahr was booting one sixty-yard field goal after another. He'd never been in a dome in his life. He was laughing. 'How easy is this?' But every time they were in range for a long field goal, about seven times, Paterno kept calling for a third-down drop-back pass, and Bear Bryant, who never, ever blitzed, blitzed the hell out of them and knocked them back out of range every time. Following the game, Jim Tarman says, 'Why don't you come up to Joe's suite?' 'Thanks anyway, Jim,' I said. 'C'mon, Joe wants you up there.' Just a few people, Paterno's wife and brother, a couple of others, were in the room. Joe was staring out the window at the Mississippi River. I was almost afraid to go up to him, he looked so wounded. He turned to me and said, 'I did a bad job, Ernie. Maybe I can't do this at this level.' What? 'Maybe I'm not good enough to coach against a guy like Bryant'—whom he never beat, by the way. Back home, Joe told Sue, 'I think I'm going to quit.' In kind of a play on the advice Joe gave me, she told him to go back to New York, rent a car, drive to the old streets of Brooklyn, and walk around for three days.

"'Think of what you wanted when you were a kid,' she said, 'and then come home.' Walking the old streets, Joe said, 'What am I doing? When I was a kid, I would have killed for the job I have now. I had a bad game, and it was my fault. It was no one else's fault but mine. But I'm not quitting.' Paterno told me he has gone back there subsequently a few more times. And I do it, too, in Hershey. It clears your head. I've packed up a lot of my stuff already. Maybe in the next couple of days I should drop off a few of these boxes in Hershey."

Other than for a left tackle, Ernie had one great wish on this Monday morning.

"To hear some other head football coach," he said, "any other head football coach, say, 'I had a bad game, and it was my fault. It was nobody else's fault but mine.'"

17

"IT'S A FABULOUS GAME"

BOXES OF MEMORIES WERE disappearing from Accorsi's office and reappearing at his town house in Hershey. As Ernie was hauling a couple of heavy files up some steps at home, the contents shifted and he tumbled back down headfirst into a wall. Neither Chuck Wepner nor Carmen Basilio ever sported a shinier black eye. "My head was out to here," Ernie said a few days later. "It was like a baseball. So I called Ronnie Barnes right away. It was a Wednesday night, when the doctors regularly come to Giants Stadium for their midweek update of the players' conditions. One of the specialists asked me what day it was, what was the score of last week's game—hadn't I suffered enough?— what was my mother's maiden name. Then came the really scary questions: 'Do you have any feeling in your fingers and toes?' 'Yeah.' 'Are you sure?' *'Yeah!'*" Nobody could understand why he didn't have a broken neck or at least a fractured skull, but he didn't. What a year the Giants were having. Even the general manager was lining up for a CAT scan.

Two of the boxes he gave to me to deliver to Ron Wolf. The best gauge of whether Ernie would miss this work was probably Wolf, the former Green Bay Packers GM, who was a little older than Accorsi and retired on a similar schedule after about thirty-five seasons. For many years, they were each other's closest friend in the GM trade. "Wolf is from New Freedom, Pennsylvania," Ernie said. "When I first met him, he was traveling the East, scouting for the Raiders. He was their only scout. We'd see each other five or six times a year, and have a meal at this little luncheonette by the bus station." Now Wolf lived with his wife on a finger of water near Annapolis, Maryland, mostly ignoring the NFL. These days, Wolf said, he was less likely to watch a live football game than an old black-and-white tape from what he considered a much happier era. "I liked sports a lot better," he said, "in the days before ESPN."

It was Ernie's and Ron's shared habit to search out vintage and obscure pro and college films and pass them back and forth. "Wolf's a lot like I am," Accorsi said. "We speak the same language." Yeah, quarterbacks.

Ron was the assembler of the original Tampa Bay Buccaneers, the unchallenged worst team in the history of the league, loser of its first twenty-six games. After one of those losses, head coach John McKay was asked a question about his team's execution and replied, "I'm in favor of it." But, blessedly, Wolf was better remembered for his days in Green Bay. Between those jobs, he served the New York Jets as a player personnel man, and at one point was far and away the leading admirer of a Southern Mississippi quarterback named Brett Favre. The summer before Favre's senior year, an automobile accident took something out of him: thirty inches of intestine. "He was raw and took the darnedest chances, but I liked him," Wolf said. "He didn't play as well as a senior as he did as a junior, not too surprisingly." But he held himself like a great player, and Wolf believed he was.

Unfortunately, the Jets' best draft choice that year was a sixth pick in the second round. Favre went fifth in that round to Atlanta, where he sat on a shelf. Well, he didn't just sit on the shelf. He also went out on the town and had a hell of a good time.

After securing the Green Bay job, Wolf stood before the board of directors of the publicly owned Packers and heard himself tell them there was an obtainable player who was so gifted that he would make the citizens forget anybody else who had ever worn a Green Bay uniform. There was a gasp in the room, even before Wolf named the player, a third-stringer for the Falcons. "That's the fun of what I used to do and Ernie still does," Wolf said, "but I think it's less fun than it used to be. I don't miss it. I don't think he will, either."

And yet, in the middle of lunch on the Annapolis waterfront, not responding to a question, germane to nothing at all, Wolf suddenly looked up and said softly, "It's a fabulous game." No, he didn't miss it.

Back in the front office, an old man and a young man represented two other good measuring sticks for Accorsi. Harry Hulmes, the 1960s Colts GM who spoke kindly even of agents, was still standing up for decency, as now Ernie played the part of George Young. "Harry is probably the purest human being I've ever been around," Ernie said. "There's no guile. There's no con. He has empathy for absolutely everyone, and now I'm the one trying to talk him out of it."

Hulmes: "Oh, what a great punt!"

Accorsi: "No, Harry, that's not a great punt. That punt just pinned us down on the ten-yard line. It's a bad punt for *us,* Harry. Okay?"

Later—

Hulmes: "My God, that's one of the greatest runs I've ever seen!"

Accorsi: "Harry. That's the other team. It's a bad run. Bad. Very bad."

Ernie said, "With Wellington gone, Harry's my connection to the past, just like Matt's my connection to the future."

Matt Harriss was a kid in his twenties, the Giants' youngest front office worker, who already knew what he wanted. "Going on the road trips, just being part of the Giants, is wonderful," he said. "Ernie has taken me under his wing since the day I came over from the league office this year. I arrived in April. My last day with the league was a Wednesday, my first with the Giants was a Thursday. It was the day we signed LaVar Arrington. About three hours later, Ernie and I were just kind of getting to know each other, and Kevin Abrams walks out of his office. Ernie yells down the hallway, 'Hey, Kevin, what have you done today?' 'What do you mean?' 'Kid's been here three hours and has already signed us a linebacker. What the hell have you done?' I felt comfortable right off the bat. The more I'm around Ernie, the more sure I am that this is what I someday want to be. The losses are terrible, I know, but they don't make me want to be a GM any less."

"Matt gets my batteries charging, too," Accorsi said. "He takes me back to Upton Bell and those days. Showing him little things reminds me of them at the same time."

"He'll sit with me and watch a tape," Harriss said, "and just talk about what he sees, and suddenly I can see it, too. 'Look at this,' he'll say. 'Look at that.' The best things, though, are just little pieces of history or advice that he passes along. He called me in to show me the Pittsburgh Steelers' Christmas card. You open it up and it's just the team with signatures. Nowhere does it say 'world champions.' 'That's Rooney class,' Ernie said. He told me a story from the 1970s, when the Steelers were champions a lot. Walking into the office, Mr. Rooney heard a receptionist answering the telephone, 'World Champion Steelers.' He waited until she hung up the phone, and then told her in a kind way, 'You don't have to say that. They know.' Ernie loved that. I do, too."

"Ron is a reminder to me that it's okay to retire now, I'm ready," Accorsi said. "Harry is a reminder that it was never just the winning and the losing. Matt reminds me that this has always been a good thing to be. I've been lucky."

The game in Jacksonville, a 26–10 loss, was a reminder that Eli was still fogged in (nineteen of forty-one), and when Antonio Pierce expressed his solution, "We just need to get our guys back," was he speaking of this year or next?

18

TITANIC, HINDENBURG,

JOE PISARCIK . . .

WARMING UP AT LP Field in Nashville, home of rookie quarterback Vince Young and the 3-and-7 Titans, Jeremy Shockey had his first look at the skeleton inside the ring finger of his left hand. It was neither an inspiring sight nor a favorable omen. "It's a little frightening, to tell you the truth," Shockey said after catching a ball wrong, "to see the bones coming out of your hand like that. But the doctors pushed them right back in, sewed me up tight, numbed me up good, and I was ready to go. Hell, I was going to play, even if they cut it off."

And on Eli Manning's first completion of the game, Jeremy caught a seven-yard pass for a first down and laughed. The short stuff was key to the Giants' strategy. Narrowing Manning's responsibilities seemed to be the order of the day, until the end. "We knew exactly how they were going to play," Coughlin said. "We had a great game plan." It worked so well at the start, and for such a long time, that the entire New York team finally seemed to relax. "The Titans were asleep the whole game," Tom said. "Sound asleep. Willing to let us do whatever we wanted to do, until . . ."

That first Giants scoring drive of fifty-two yards was built on Tiki Barber and Brandon Jacobs runs plus Manning's twenty-yard pass to Plaxico Burress, who then scored the touchdown on just a three-yard Eli throw across the middle. New York's second good drive of seventy-six yards included quick completions to Burress, Shockey, and Barber, along with two blasts by Jacobs, for fourteen yards on a third down and for ten on the touchdown. Two more short Manning passes to Barber and David Tyree figured in the third success, capped by Jacobs' second touchdown on a four-yard run. The score was 21–0 at halftime, 21–0 throughout the third quarter, and 21–0 at 5:25 in the fourth. But there was a New York series that started in the third and ended in the fourth that was worth reviewing later.

GIANTS

1-10-G11 Manning passes incomplete
2-10-G11 Offensive holding, Kareem McKenzie
2-16-G5   Manning passes to Jacobs for 9
3-7-G14   (Shotgun) Jacobs runs for 10
1-10-G24 Barber runs for 9
2-1-G33   Barber runs for 6
1-10-G39 Manning passes to Burress for 11
1-10-50   Barber runs for 3
2-7-T47   Manning passes to Barber for 9
1-10-T38 Offensive holding, David Diehl
1-20-T48 (shotgun) Manning passes to Shockey for 7
2-13-T41 Jacobs runs for 5
3-8-T36   (shotgun) Manning passes to Jacobs for 5
4-3-T36   (shotgun) Manning passes incomplete;
    14 plays, 53 yards, no points, no field goal
    attempt, no coffin-corner punt

Over three seasons, the Titans were 1 and 21 in games they were losing after three quarters by so much as one point, let alone three touchdowns. "Tennessee went three and out then," said Accorsi, who was sitting in the press box next to John Mara. "So, on first down at our twenty-nine, Eli hands off to Tiki and he carries for six yards. It's second and four at the thirty-five. There are twelve minutes and some seconds to go, and Tennessee is basically on the brink of *no más*. We got a quarterback who's been shaky, but nonetheless, we're in complete control, and we're not playing the Bears either. What do we do? We empty the backfield and go into the shotgun. They know we're going to pass. You can't hand off to air. We throw a takeoff to Plaxico, who's covered by their best corner—their only corner—who intercepts the ball, and the game turns. 'Everything's changed now,' I whispered to John. Later I said to Tom, 'Why, Tom? I just would like to know why.' First of all, every time you run the ball, it's forty-five, fifty seconds off the clock. Let the time run out. The Titans wanted no more of number twenty-seven [Jacobs]. Just grind them down and send that big bastard straight at 'em."

The corner who made the interception and returned the ball twenty-six yards to the Giants' forty-six was Adam Bernard Jones, known as "Pacman" since childhood for the video game and its industrial efficiency he emulated while gobbling up rivers of milk. Pacman had changed drinks since, and when it came to legal scrapes involving gunfire and strip clubs, Jones was single-handedly holding his own against the entire fifty-three-man roster of pro football's Hole-in-the-Wall Gang, the Cincinnati Bengals. Incidently, a suspension for Pacman was on the way.

Significantly, the field position that accompanied Pacman's interception could only be put down to carelessness, in the worst sense of the word—apparent lack of caring—by Burress. Plaxico blatantly quit on his pass route—"I thought the ball was over both of our heads"—and made a quarter-hearted attempt at tackling Jones. "I guess I should have jumped on his back," Burress said, "and taken a penalty."

TITANS
1-10-G48 (shotgun) Young passes incomplete
2-10-G48 (shotgun) Young passes to Bobby Wade for 25
1-10-G21 (shotgun) Young runs for 2 (unnecessary
    roughness, Tennessee's LenDale White)

2-23-G34 (shotgun) Young passes to Travis Henry for 5

3-18-G29 (no huddle, shotgun) Young passes to Wade
for 9

4-9-G20   (no huddle, shotgun) Young scrambles for 7
(unnecessary roughness by New York's Frank Walker)

1-G-G6   (shotgun) Henry runs for −1

2-G-G7   (shotgun) Young passes to Bo Scaife for 3

3-G-G4   Young passes to Scaife for 4 and the touchdown;
Rob Bironas' kick is good

New York 21, Tennessee 7

Walker, the Giants defensive back with his own "suite of doghouses," started at left corner because Corey Webster had a swollen toe. Frank's hit on Young at the sideline probably would have qualified as assault even if the target hadn't been a quarterback. "When he crosses the line of scrimmage," Walker said, "he's just a regular football player to me. If I let him lean forward, he gets the first down."

Soon, Tennessee had the ball again, still behind by two touchdowns with about seven minutes to go. Without Plax's help this time, Pacman again flipped the field position by returning a thirty-nine-yard Jeff Feagles punt twenty-three yards to the New York thirty-six.

TITANS

1-10-G36 (shotgun) Young passes to Wade for 9

2-1-G27 (shotgun) Young passes to Wade for 11

1-10-G16 Henry runs for 9

2-1-G7   (shotgun) Young passes to Scaife for 5

1-G-G2   Henry runs for 1

2-G-G1   Young scrambles for 1 and the touchdown;
Bironas' kick is good

New York 21, Tennessee 14 (4:24 remaining)

Manning converted one third-down play with his own freelance run, but on third and nine at the Giants' thirty-three, Eli passed to Barber for only four, and Feagles punted again (3:07 remaining).

TITANS

1-10-T24 (shotgun) Young scrambles for 24 yards (offsetting penalties, no play)

1-10-T24 (shotgun) Young passes incomplete

2-10-T24 (shotgun) Young passes incomplete

3-10-T24 Young passes incomplete

4-10-T24 (shotgun) Apparently sacked, Young slips the grasp of Mathias Kiwanuka and scrambles for 19 (2:44)

1-10-T43 (shotgun) Young passes to Roydell Williams for 20

Two-minute warning

1-10-G37 (shotgun) Young scrambles for 16

1-10-G21 (shotgun) Young passes to Drew Bennett for 7

2-3-G14   (shotgun) Young passes to Brandon Jones for 14 and the touchdown; Bironas' kick is good

Tennessee 21, New York 21 (:44 remaining)

On second and one at his own twenty-eight, thirty-two seconds from overtime, Manning dropped back in the shotgun and aimed a deep pass at Tyree that again settled in the soft fingers and palms of Pacman Jones. Three plays later, Bironas kicked a forty-nine-yard field goal to complete either a sensational comeback or a hideous collapse, depending on how you looked at it. The city of New York looked at it only one way. The *Titanic,* the *Hindenburg,* and Joe Pisarcik were all back in the headlines.

"We're going to be sick about this one," Coughlin said in the locker room, "for, for, forever."

Of the final pass, Eli said, "If you miss, you have to miss high and away, not short. Throw it away. Get to overtime at least. I thought I had a chance to reach Tyree. There just wasn't enough on it." At one point

Manning was sixteen for twenty-one for 132 yards and a touchdown. But he ended up eighteen for twenty-eight for 143 yards and two interceptions. Much later, sitting by himself, Eli said, "If the media wants to put all of the blame on me, that's fine. I can handle it. I can take it. It doesn't bother me. The important thing is to continue trying to earn the respect of the players, to get to the point where they trust you. That's what really matters. That's what I'm striving for. The really important thing is to stay together in the meantime, while we're all learning, even through terrible, terrible losses. I know I sound pretty vague and stupid to the media, but I'm trying to be careful, measuring my words. They keep asking the same question a hundred different ways, trying to get me into fights with my teammates, hoping I'll throw somebody under the bus. Then they can slam me for that, too. 'Hell, don't feel sorry for yourself,' Dad called to say, 'I dealt with losing for fifteen years. Three losses in a row used to be a winning streak for the Saints!' That didn't make me feel all that much better, but it did make me laugh. 'Keep fighting,' he said."

"Eli was very, very affected by that last interception," Coughlin said many weeks later. "That was heartbreaking." But the Kiwanuka play was the one that reverberated not just through the Giants' clubhouse but throughout the league. "That's the one the media really killed me on, too," Coughlin said, looking back, "for my reaction on the sideline, you know, running back and forth. But think of this: I'm being told on the earphones by the defensive coordinator, 'We've got him! He's down! The game's over!' Only I look up and the son of a bitch is running out of bounds right in front of me! If we had him and he's down, what happened? What happened? What happened? The ball's almost to midfield. 'Kiwanuka let him go! He just let him go!'"

"I had my head down, buried in Young's chest," Kiwanuka said. The rookie imagined he could feel the throwing motion of the quarterback's arm across his body. Remembering the roughing penalty of a few weeks earlier, he let go. ("Thank God, thank God!" Young said. "He let me loose!") "I worried it might be a fifteen-yard penalty," Kiwanuka said, "if I didn't let him go. I didn't know he still had the football in his hand. As a pass rusher, you work all game long to get to the quarterback . . ."

Coughlin couldn't help but think of Steve McNair, the former Titan scrambler, who made so many Sundays so uncomfortable back when the coach was working in Jacksonville. "I had to play all those games against McNair," Tom said, "and now this guy does this. The game isn't in balance with these guys [running quarterbacks], and they tell you these guys can't survive in the NFL. Young runs for seventy yards against us. He's a runner! But we hit him on the sidelines and it's unnecessary roughness. Because he's a quarterback. A six-foot-five, two-hundred-thirty-five-pound quarterback. The league has got to do something about this, but they refuse to recognize that a few of these guys aren't your regular quarterbacks. They're just not the same."

In that cause, Coughlin found an unexpected ally in fellow Syracuse alum Keith Bulluck, a linebacker on the Tennessee side. Bulluck said, "We won, so I'm happy. But I think the NFL has a silly attitude about running quarterbacks. 'Whatever you do, don't hurt the quarterback, even if he's steamrolling your ass, about twenty yards at a clip.' It worked to our benefit today, but I still don't get it." Receiver Scaife, Young's old Longhorn teammate, said, "Vince did this same thing to Oklahoma State my senior year at Texas. We were down thirty-five to nothing, scored just before the half, then came back to win it. So I've seen it before. Nothing new to me. The whole NFL better get ready. It's going to be seeing this a lot."

If Tom looked a bit panicked on the sideline, he contended that he was panicking on behalf of Kiwanuka. "Mathias plays very, very hard," Coughlin said. "He's going to be a great football player, I think. But a play like that one can define a veteran, let alone a rookie. That's Jim Marshall of the Vikings running the wrong way. The next day, every team in the league made a point of calling every defensive player together and showing them that play. A new message went out. 'Don't throw the quarterbacks down on the ground, but grab them, hold them, squeeze them until the whistle blows.' The moment it happened, honestly, my first thought was that it could end up being this poor kid's identity."

Immediately following the loss so stunning that it literally rang in the losers' ears, Coughlin asked someone to go get John Mara. "You know John," Tom said. "He's a guy who always sticks his hand out to you after a loss. I'm still not used to that. He came in and sat down. 'John,' I said, 'I'm sorry, I'm sorry, I'm sorry.' I said, 'There's no explanation. I can't tell you what happened.'"

"Wow!" was all Titans head coach Jeff Fisher could say, over and over. "Did that really happen?" Young promised, "This is just a sneak peek into what's coming for me and for our team." But Fisher couldn't stop shaking his head. "I expected the Giants to grind the ball out," he said. "For whatever reason, they decided to go no back and throw the ball down the field. We were fortunate."

"I never thought they would go on to win the game," said Antonio Pierce in a daze, "until they went on to win the game."

"Let's face it," Brandon Jacobs said, "that's a team we should beat the shit out of. We pissed it away. They suck."

"Chill out, Brandon," Gibril Wilson said. "If they suck, what does that say about us?"

That made three New York losses in a row (one more to come). In 1994, Lawrence Taylor's first season of retirement, the Giants lost seven consecutive games to stand 3 and 7 with six to play, and their Hall of Fame linebacker returned to the locker room to deliver a pep talk. It wasn't Knute Rockne but it was memorable. At the height of his oratory, during what may have been a world record for profanity, Taylor shouted, "Even your bitches are ashamed of you!"

And the Giants won their last six.

19

K BALLS

TEAMS ON BAD STREAKS are often said to find entirely new ways to lose, but the way New York found next had such a trivial nature and such a terrible consequence that it probably *was* unprecedented. It had to do with two old-time employees in an officious mood (who were fired by Accorsi the following day) and with the football itself. Jay Feely, the Giants' placekicker, began to explain.

"Five or six years ago," he said, "my first year in the NFL, K balls came in, just for kicking. The reason for that, honestly, was because guys were working up the balls. They'd put them in an oven, they'd put them in a sauna, they'd do all kinds of stuff prior to the games to get the balls in the best kicking shape so they would fly as far as possible. The catalyst for the new rule, I've always heard, was a game between Green Bay and Minnesota, when Mitch Berger apparently kicked every ball through the end zone. At the same time, Gary Anderson made all of the Vikings' field goals with a little too much room to spare. Mike Holmgren, the Green Bay coach, was not too happy about it, and he was a member of the competition committee. Now, that's the story I heard. This was the genesis of the K balls coming in."

Reaching into his locker, Feely pulled out an average-looking football. "Here's a ball from last week's game," he said. It was stamped below the laces with a capital K.

"They all come from the same factory, but you can get a ball where the seams stick up more than others, and some are nubbier than others. They add that nubbiness to the balls when they're making them. I don't know if it's little stones or what, just some kind of a pebbling process. Now, the quarterbacks like the nubbier balls, because that gives them a little more grip. But a kickoff guy prefers them real smooth without a lot of pebbles, so they'll go farther. If the ball boys on the sideline know a good kicking ball from a bad one, they can make sure you get the decent ball to kick off. All of the balls are brand-new, but some of them will go at least ten yards deeper."

A designated ball preparer from each team—not a kicker, though—may rub the footballs down for thirty minutes before the game. No longer than that. But one is sure to be smoother than another. "Then the referee will take the balls and make his little mark," Feely said. "Some of them have a stamp, some write their initials. He also puts a little drawing on the nose, in ink, like the pennant on this one. See? So when the ball is tossed into the game, he can tell at a glance that it's one of the ones he's checked. It's a legal ball."

The men in charge of the balls on the sideline strut around like officials and sometimes forget that they aren't officials. Feely said, "The guys here don't want to be too proactively on the side of the kicker, for some reason. They won't go above and beyond a certain point. I'm not sure why." On the road, he'd never experienced any difficulty exchanging one K ball for another. But at a particular juncture in the Cowboys game at Giants Stadium—an important juncture—Feely asked if he could have a different K ball and was refused.

"When you have a bad ball in your hands," he said, "you can feel it right away. 'C'mon, give me the other ball,' I said. 'No.' I couldn't believe it. 'You've got the right ball, go ahead and kick off,' one of them said. 'You get the ball *I* choose,' the other one told me."

Shouting to his right and left, Feely alerted the other special-team players, "This isn't going to go very far! It's a bad ball! It's going to be short!" "Here's where your adrenaline is up," Feely said, "and you have a real chance of kicking the ball into the end zone and starting them off on their twenty. But I knew, even if I hit it as good as I could, this was not going to be a great kick." It wasn't. Why didn't Feely say something after the game? "In the NFL, kickers get made fun of all the time," he said. "We're these idiosyncratic little people who sort of play football. Everything is fodder for how ridiculous we are. I didn't even want to mention it to anybody."

Ernie said, "Feely's a great guy, the player rep, and he wasn't going to blow the whistle on the ball boys—I say 'boys,' they're seventy years old. One's a truck driver. But the good Lord gave me a big nose for a reason. Something just looked wrong about that last kickoff. So I called Jay into a side room. A few equipment men were there, too. 'I smell a cover-up here,' I said. 'What's going on?' Feely's really sheepish. After some prodding, he finally says, 'Well, the guys in charge of the balls wouldn't give me the K ball I wanted.' 'What?'

" 'They've been with the Giants since Yankee Stadium,' one of the equipment guys says. 'What?' 'We tried to fire them a few times, but they used to go straight to Wellington.' 'What?' And then I find out that the game officials had been begging us to replace these guys for years. 'They're so obstinate,' one of the referees says, 'we can hardly get the ball into the game on time. They act like it's their private domain.' Now, I ask you. Is there anything else that can go wrong?"

Had he told Coughlin?

"Yeah, he went ballistic."

Dallas came to New York in the midst of its own kicking rumpus. Six days earlier, Bill Parcells had dumped high-priced free agent Mike Vanderjagt in favor of old Martin Gramatica, who immediately missed a forty-four-yarder against the Giants but wasn't finished for the day. New York took possession at the thirty-four.

GIANTS

1-10-G34 Tiki Barber runs for 6
2-4-G40 Eli Manning passes to Barber for 6
1-10-G46 Barber runs for 7
2-3-C47 Manning passes to Jeremy Shockey for 5
1-10-C42 Barber runs for 1

2-9-C41   Manning scrambles for 7

3-2-C34   Brandon Jacobs runs for 11

1-10-C23   Barber runs for 5

2-5-C18   Barber runs for 1

3-4-C17   (shotgun) Manning passes to Shockey for 17 and
           the touchdown; Feely's kick is good

New York 7, Dallas 0

Three plays into the second Cowboy series, quarterback Tony Romo looked for wide receiver Terry Glenn but found defensive end Mathias Kiwanuka instead. Kiwanuka returned the intercepted ball twelve yards from his own twenty-eight to the forty before, inexplicably, untouched by anyone, he dropped the ball. He just dropped it. "He's got the ball! He's got the ball!" Coughlin reenacted the play several weeks later in his office. "In plus territory! He loses the ball! He drops it without getting hit! That's two colossal game-changing plays two weeks in a row! Those things can define a player, I'm telling you!"

DALLAS

1-10-G40   Romo passes to Terrell Owens for 10

1-10-G30   Julius Jones runs for 3

2-7-G27   Romo passes incomplete

3-7-G27   Defensive pass interference, Antonio Pierce

1-G-G1   Marion Barber runs for 1 and the touchdown;
           Gramatica's kick is good

New York 7, Dallas 7

Gramatica and Feely matched field goals for a couple of quarters until the score was 13–13, but there are good field goals and there are bad field goals, and the Giants' field goals were rancid. Third and goal at the five after one long drive, third and goal at the four after another, they reaped just six points. Fourth and one at the Cowboys' twenty-four got them nothing.

With under ten minutes to go in the game, Dallas took possession and maintained it for six minutes and eleven seconds.

DALLAS

1-10-C34 Romo passes to Owens for 11

1-10-C45 Jones runs for −3

2-13-C42 Romo scrambles for 10

1-10-G48 (shotgun) Romo passes to Owens for 11

1-10-G37 Romo passes to Owens for 6

2-4-G31   Romo passes incomplete

3-4-G31   (shotgun) Romo passes to Patrick Crayton for 11

1-10-G20 Jones runs for 3

2-7-G17   Jones runs for 2

3-5-G15   Romo passes to Glenn for 10 (personal foul,
   Jason Bell)

1-G-G2   Barber runs for 0

2-G-G2   (shotgun) Romo passes incomplete (false start,
   Owens)

2-G-G7   Barber runs for 7 and the touchdown;
   Gramatica's kick is good

Dallas 20, New York 13

Now about four minutes remained. Stood up for measurement next to another young quarterback whom the Giants fans were thinking they might prefer, Manning had outperformed Romo to that point. Eli had two touchdown passes to Tony's none. Romo had two interceptions to Manning's none. And now Eli had the ball. In a sixty-three-yard Giant offensive, Manning's arm would feature in fifty-nine of them, as he threw six passes and completed them all.

GIANTS

1-10-G37 (shotgun) Manning passes to Plaxico Burress for 8

2-2-G45   (shotgun) Barber runs for 4

1-10-G49 (shotgun) Manning passes to Barber for 2

2-8-C49   (shotgun) Manning passes to Burress for 9

1-10-C40 (shotgun) Manning passes to Barber for 28

1-10-C12 Manning passes to Barber for 7

2-3-C5   Manning passes to Burress for 5 and the
touchdown; Feely's kick is good

Dallas 20, New York 20

Feely's shallow kick with the wrong K ball only gave the Cowboys nice field position. It didn't complete the twenty-six-yard pass from Romo to tight end Jason Witten that really won the game. Slipping left, Romo saw Witten break off his route into a vacuum between Pierce and Will Demps. "It was nobody's fault," Pierce said. "It was just a great play." It was a splendid read and throw. Then, reconfirming Parcells' genius, Gramatica kicked a forty-six-yard field goal to win the game.

One of the reasons Romo could so easily sprint to the left side was that Michael Strahan was still in street clothes. He had spent the week sitting at his locker chewing on peanut butter sandwiches and reporters. "Two and a half hours before the game," Coughlin said, "we worked Michael out. But he couldn't go." Accorsi, the sentimentalist, thought Stray might be worth dressing just for the "Willis Reed effect." Tom looked at Ernie like he was Kiwanuka.

Parcells, whose nickname for Romo was Pancho Villa ("Sometimes he shoots at the first thing he sees"), took a soft look around Giants Stadium before he departed, saying, "Most of the great memories I have are centered at this place."

Hours even before Strahan's workout, maybe six hours before the game, Parcells sat with a former Giants colleague in a car in the parking lot. They didn't want to draw any attention to themselves. Old friends, they just wanted to talk. What Bill supposedly said became the lead item on the front office grapevine: "I'm available to be the Giants' GM if they get stuck. Keep me alive with John Mara, will you?"

That phrase blew around the front office like a prairie fire "if they get stuck." Weeks later, Parcells complained about the rumors flying that he was interested in replacing Accorsi. Bill asked John Mara to issue a press release denying that they had ever talked about the GM job. Mara had no trouble doing that.

But the reaction in the front office was hilarity. "The rumors started with the same guy who's upset that they're out there," everyone said. "Bill's the one who blew up all those trial balloons. He's the one who set them all loose. Now he wants us to pop them for him." Some men take so many different positions that it must be hard to remember them all.

Pat Hanlon said, "When Bill asked me if he and his grandson could watch some Giants games from the press box, I told him, 'Sure, Bill. I'll always have a space for you.'" Though not for a fact, Pat probably was the first one who knew Parcells wouldn't be returning for another season in Dallas.

Leaving the field after losing to the Cowboys, Manning and Burress had a significant exchange. The inconsistency of Plaxico's effort had been a topic since the Tennessee game, but Manning voiced no complaints.

"That last catch for the tying touchdown against the Cowboys," Burress said some days later, "was one of those catches I was telling you about, that I don't really understand. I reached back behind me with both arms, pulled my hands back over my head, and the ball was in them. Now we're walking off the field after another bad loss, the fourth in a row, and Eli looks over at me and says, 'Great catch, Plax.' He's heading to the locker room to face the music again, and he says that to me. I can't tell you how that made me feel."

"After the Jacksonville game, after the Tennessee game," Accorsi said, "Tom screamed at the players at the top of his lungs. *How could you do this? How could you do that? You did this wrong! You did that wrong! Where did the penalties come from?* 'Well, since you've been here, Tom, we've been leading the world in penalties, that's where they came from.' He couldn't see what a shattered state they were already in. But after the Cowboys game, Coughlin was great. First off, he said, 'Everybody close it up here.'

He pulled them all in. 'I just want you to know, we did some things I didn't like. But you played your hearts out and I'm proud of you. We didn't win and I know how much it hurts—and it should hurt. But this is a team full of winners. There's not one loser in here. We're still in this thing.'"

Incidentally, when Romo was promoted to starting quarterback, he continued in his previous job as the holder for extra points and field goals. In what probably qualifies as irony, the Cowboys' season would end in a 21–20 loss at Seattle, just one yard from a first down, just two yards from the goal line, on a nineteen-yard field goal attempt that neither Gramatica nor Vanderjagt could have missed. But a shiny K ball slipped through Romo's fingers. Those things can define a player, I'm telling you.

20

"NUMBER SIXTY-NINE
IS REPORTING . . ."

EVERY FOOTBALL TEAM has what Accorsi calls "a walking miracle." The Giants' version was a six-foot-three, 305-pound utility man named Rich Seubert. "He suffered the all-time broken leg six games into the 2003 season," Ernie said, "three horrible fractures, the worst Ronnie Barnes had ever seen. Go take a look at that leg. [The right one, he meant. Its scooped-out wound was covered over by a graft of nonmatching skin, as shiny pink as the neck of an auto racer who has been on fire.] Rich missed the rest of that season and the next. We just hung with him. You talk about patience. But you don't give up on a character like that."

"Fractured tibia, fractured fibula, shattered ankle—they didn't just break, they exploded," said Seubert, an undrafted free agent who from Western Illinois University walked onto the National Football League in 2001 to become New York's starting left guard the following season. "I don't know why Ernie stuck with me. I was in the hospital for three weeks, then on the injured reserve list for half a year, then on the physically-unable-to-perform list for a full year. With a skin graft, you know, you really can't do anything until it takes, and mine didn't take right away. I just lay in bed, losing weight. I went into the hospital weighing three hundred and came out maybe two-seventy. There wasn't much meat on me." Pro teams don't usually stick with a player that long just on the *chance* that he might be able to rehab himself enough to make some kind of lesser contribution than he was making before he was so badly hurt. "I'm pretty sure the coaches didn't really have much to say about it," Seubert said. "Put it this way, if they'd had something to say about it, I guess I would have been gone. I don't mean this bitterly. That's just the way it is in pro ball. It was Accorsi and the Maras who kept me. They could have just cut their ties and said good luck. But they gave me a chance to play again. Do you think I'm not going to play hard for this team?"

Seubert had to adjust everything, especially his own dreams. "I never thought I was going to be a Hall of Famer or anything like that," he said, "but I was having a good year, my second year starting, and then everything suddenly came to an end. I always figured football was like riding a bike—I've played football my whole life. It was the only thing I was ever really good at growing up, and I loved being good at it. I just loved the game of football. But it's not like riding a bike. I had to learn it all over again from scratch. Waiting for that first game back, and that first serious hit, I wondered how I was going to respond. You really don't know how you're going to feel. I had been lucky with injuries before."

Well, he broke a femur in high school. "But other than that," Rich said, "I was injury-free. I never missed games, never missed practices. I liked the hard work of football, I enjoyed it. But I can't say I always enjoyed the rehab. Different things kept going wrong. I had to have the screws taken out, and my toe was stuck up in the air, so they went and cut the tendons for that, so I could push down at least. I got into bad moods from time to time, sort of 'to hell with it' moods. But I always snapped out of them and I just kept grinding away. A lot of the guys on this team helped keep me going. Like Jeremy Shockey. We've been training camp roomies since I've been back. Players talk about their college teams as though they were their families. They're too embarrassed to talk about a pro team that way. But the truth is, a pro team is even more of a family, I think. I know for sure that an NFL team has no chance to succeed unless you want to play for the guys you're sitting in the room with. You don't have to like absolutely every guy. Just don't hold any hard feelings towards the ones you don't like. And play your heart out for the ones you love."

For the first twelve games of the season, Seubert's most visible role had been as an eligible receiver in short-yardage situations, whose entry into the game for some reason had to be announced over the stadium loudspeaker by the referee. "Number sixty-nine is reporting as an eligible receiver." Sometimes, when the official was slow switching off his microphone button, seventy-eight thousand people could hear Rich say, "Sixty-nine reporting, right. Thank you, sir." He was there to block, of course. Though technically Seubert was a third tight end, he lined up in the backfield like William "the Refrigerator" Perry.

Only once in Seubert's pro career, back in 2002, did he ever actually go out for a pass. It was the last down of the wild card play-off game. The Giants were losing in San Francisco, 39–38, and about to attempt what would have been the winning field goal when the snap was botched and Seubert took off downfield. With the ball in the air, he was interfered with blatantly by 49ers defender Chike Okeafor (the league's head of officials said so the next day) but nothing was called.

In the thirteenth game of 2006, against the Carolina Panthers at Bank of America Stadium in Charlotte, because of a chain reaction of in-game injuries, Seubert played center ("for the first time in a real game since sixth grade," he said), guard, and tight end, "and I stunk at all of them," he lied afterward.

Before the game, it had seemed that the Giants were finally going up against a team more damaged than they were. Panthers quarterback Jake Delhomme's right thumb looked like he had hit it with a hammer while hanging a picture. For the first time in four years, thirty-four-year-old Heisman Trophy–winning quarterback Chris Weinke was getting the start.

During those clipboard seasons, Weinke threw exactly thirteen passes, but before this day was done, he would heave sixty-one more. The last time Weinke was their regular quarterback, 2001, the Panthers won 1 game and lost 15.

Star linemen Mike Rucker and Julius Peppers aside, it seemed that
an army of total strangers had taken over the Panthers' defense. "Who *is*
that guy?" Plaxico Burress asked Eli Manning, nodding in the direction of number 27, the safety on Plax's side. That was Dion Byrum, an
undrafted rookie just signed off the Tampa Bay practice squad, a
refreshingly honest man. Referring later to the Giants' first touchdown,
a twenty-eight-yard pass from Manning to Burress, Byrum said, "I was
caught completely out of position. I was trying to get the call from my
safety on what coverage we were supposed to be in. But by the time I
could get his attention, the Giants had snapped the ball, and Plaxico
being six-five with that long stride of his, he already had me by those
eight or nine yards."

That made the score 10–0 early in the second quarter, but then
Weinke struck consecutively for twenty-one yards (Steve Smith) and
thirty-six (Drew Carter) to make it 10–7; that is, to make it a game. During the next series, center Shaun O'Hara turned an ankle and Seubert
brushed off his sixth-grade memories and picked up the ball. "The
shotgun snaps were what really scared me," he said. " 'Can't you just stay
under center for a while?' I asked Eli, but he smiled and said, 'You'll be
fine, Rich. Anywhere between my knees and my chin will be cool.' That
gave me confidence." (There's the Eli the public has never seen.)

Sometimes the center has a defensive player right on his nose.
Other times, there's absolutely nobody. "Yeah, I like it when there's
absolutely nobody," Seubert said. "But there's a beauty to the center
position, like every position. You've got two guys next to you and one of
them is usually working with you. And, unlike me, Chris Snee and David
Diehl knew what the hell they were doing."

With a thirty-seven-yard field goal, Carolina tied the game, 10–10,
but the Giants had the last word of the first half. Manning was having a
nice game.

G I A N T S

1-10-G21 Manning passes to Sinorice Moss for 7

2-3-G28   Tiki Barber runs for 18

Two-minute warning

1-10-G46 Offside, Panthers

1-5-P49   (shotgun) Manning scrambles for 9

1-10-P40 (shotgun) Barber runs for 5

2-5-P35   (shotgun) Manning passes incomplete

3-5-P35   (shotgun) Manning passes to Shockey
for 25 yards

1-G-P10   (shotgun) Manning passes to Visanthe
Shiancoe for 9

2-G-P1   Brandon Jacobs runs for −1

3-G-P2   Manning passes to Shockey for 2 and
the touchdown; Feely's kick is good

New York 17, Carolina 10

When Reggie McKenzie sprained his neck in the third quarter, Diehl had to move to right tackle for the first time all season, Seubert shifted to left guard, and O'Hara returned injured to the center position. ("Hurt enough to be questionable a week later," Ernie said, "that's how much guts O'Hara's got. High-ankle sprain. Do you know how much that hurts? But there are some guys you just can't keep off the field.") Among all of the Giants' offensive linemen, only Snee hadn't missed time or switched positions.

Throwing, throwing, and throwing some more, Weinke accumulated 423 yards passing but was intercepted three times, twice by Gibril Wilson. The second brought about another New York touchdown.

G I A N T S

1-10-P14 Jacobs runs for 6

2-4-P8   Manning passes to Barber for 6

1-G-P2   Manning passes incomplete
2-G-P2   Jacobs runs for −1
3-G-P3   Manning passes to David Tyree for 3 and the
    touchdown; Feely's kick is good
New York 27, Carolina 10

So the proverbial month of Sundays was over, 27–13. The Giants' four-game losing streak was ended. Barber had run for 112 yards and quietly slipped over the ten thousand mark in yards rushing for his ten-year career. "Despite the perception," Tiki said, "we actually have been having a pretty good time trying to practice our way out of this mess."

The Giants improved to 2 and 11 in games Michael Strahan had missed with injury, this being his fifth DNP of the season. "I never even heard of that stat until this year," Strahan said. "But somebody better do something about it next year. Like Ernie, I'm not going to be around forever." Eli completed seventeen of thirty-three passes for 172 yards, three touchdowns, and no interceptions. "It wasn't the prettiest second half in the world," he said, "but we didn't make any really big mistakes." On top of being thirty-four for sixty-one, Weinke set an unofficial but still imposing record when six different potential Panther receivers dropped balls that were right in their hands. You had to hand it to the Panthers. Dion Byrum, the honest safety, was credited with making seven tackles.

"You forget how good it feels just to win a game," O'Hara said. "It feels so good to win."

Coughlin said, "I give our players credit. They're a closer team than you know."

"It's not just a relief for Tom," Antonio Pierce said. "It's a relief for all of us. If anything bad happens to the head man, it runs down to us."

The snapshot of the game that fit in the family album was taken when Seubert was in at center and momentarily had the wind knocked out of him. As Seubert was being tended to in the middle of the field, off to one side of it, Grey Ruegamer was practicing a few snaps. In the NFL, one center usually hunkers down and stays put for a decade, if not a generation. Here were the Giants with their sixth-grade center on the ground and a second understudy in the wings trying to learn his lines during a time-out. In what was almost an exquisite injustice, Ruegamer also took one turn as the hippopotamus in the backfield ("Number sixty-five is reporting as an eligible receiver")—his only appearance in that capacity all season—and son of a bitch if Manning didn't try to throw the ball to him in the end zone. But a blitzer bumped Eli's arm at the last instant and the pass fell just slightly short. "Rich and Grey are good friends," O'Hara said, "but I'm not sure Rich would have ever forgiven him." "A better athlete would have caught the ball," Seubert said with a wink in his voice.

A couple of days later, Rich was sitting alone, panting, recovering from a wrestling match with one of the exercise machines. "This second life of yours," I asked him, "is it worth it?"

"Oh, a hundred percent worth it," he said. "I'd be back in Wisconsin probably doing something with my wife and child, and I'd be happy enough. I'm a happy guy. I'm a lucky guy. Maybe I'd be hunting, come to think of it. Shit, I could be hunting. But I wouldn't have this feeling of last Sunday inside me now. I couldn't sleep Sunday night. Of course I never sleep Sunday nights. None of us do, I don't think. You lie down and think about all of the plays you were involved in, the bad plays more than the good ones. I played three different positions Sunday, and I guess I'm proud of that. But who cares? Somebody gets hurt, I've got to play. If they come back and somebody else gets hurt, I've got to play. That's my job now. When you have one position—I'd love to be the left guard again—you get used to it, it becomes kind of your own. I don't like it on the other side of the line. Different stance. Different footwork. It's not as natural. I'm not as comfortable. But it's still football. As I said, I'm a guy who loves football."

Obviously Accorsi was thrilled to win the Panthers game, but there was a small catch, the old one. Carolina was one of the other National

Conference teams still alive for the wild card spot in the play-offs. "After you're in this league awhile," Ernie said, "everywhere you go, there's somebody you care about on the other side of the field." In Charlotte, it was the Panthers head coach, John Fox, the former Giants defensive coordinator who predicted that 41–0 shutout of the Vikings.

"Foxy's a great coach," Ernie said, "a pain in the ass, but a great coach. You have to love him, and I do. I certainly don't enjoy watching him lose a game he needed. That year the Panthers went to the Super Bowl [after the 2003 season] and just barely lost to the Patriots, I called him up after the conference championship game. They beat the Eagles to get to the Super Bowl. I knew he wouldn't be home; it was a road game. But I left him a message, or tried to. I started to congratulate him and just broke down. I couldn't finish. He called me back the next day to say, 'That's the greatest message I've ever received from anyone.' 'In golf terms,' I said, 'I withdrew. Did not finish.' 'I know,' Foxy said. 'That's what made it great.' "

21

STILL WATCHING FOOTBALL

GAMES ON TV

BILL WALSH, THE Hall of Fame coach and GM from San Francisco, spent the 2006 season fighting leukemia, the disease that took his forty-six-year-old son, Steve, in 2002. "My attitude is positive but not evangelistic," Walsh said on the telephone. "I've had a number of blood transfusions; they're exhausting. I have a bad stomach all the time. But otherwise I'm functioning pretty normally. I'm pragmatically doing everything the doctor recommends, working my way through it. Thank God for Stanford. Not only are they giving me the best treatment, they have a lot of volleyball and basketball games going on every day, and I'm enjoying watching these young people play. For a while there, I thought I was dead. I put all of my stuff in order. But I'm not dead. I'm still watching football games on TV. I'll accept my fate as it unfolds. I've always felt that way. I have no regrets."

The late-season emergence of Jeff Garcia in Philadelphia, who took over for injured quarterback Donovan McNabb in the eleventh week, delighted Walsh. "Do you remember that day we were talking about Jeff in my office?" he said. Of course I did.

During the 1990s Walsh left the football business for a few years to take a shot at television commentating for NBC. He worked the Notre Dame games mostly. But Bill was never at home in the broadcast booth. I ran into him when he was with the NBC Olympic party on a cruise ship in Barcelona harbor. "I know what you're doing here," he said. "What am I doing here?" As the century ran out, Walsh was more than glad to reclaim the GM chair in San Francisco.

During those years when Bill was out of football, he fell in love with this undersized and underpublicized quarterback, Garcia, at Walsh's alma mater, San Jose State. Though famous for schooling Joe Montana, Steve Young, Dan Fouts, and Ken Anderson, truth be told, Walsh derived an even greater satisfaction molding competent quarterbacks out of much lesser clay: Sam Wyche, Guy Benjamin, Virgil Carter. Carter was a brainy runt with petite hands who broke in with the Chicago Bears. Go check out the passing numbers Walsh pulled out of him in Cincinnati. With the 49ers, Steve DeBerg set an NFL record for completions the year before Bill traded him away to get his shadow off the new starter, Montana.

Though the San Francisco papers were still touting Jim Druckenmiller, Walsh told me in 2000, "Have a look at Garcia at practice today."

"The only thing I ever learn at practice," I said, "is not to go to practice."

Ignoring that, Bill said, "When I was out of the league, I tried to sell Garcia to one NFL team after another. Most of them didn't even answer my letter. So he went off to Canada instead, and played nicely. I'm not saying he's the quarterback of the future, but he's got instincts."

After five good years in San Francisco—a couple of them very good—Garcia wandered away to Cleveland and Detroit. Removed from the Walsh system, he looked less than ordinary. But when the Eagles came to Giants Stadium for Game 14, Garcia was the talk of the league. Philadelphia was on a two-game winning streak with the backup, and he would run that string to six.

Thanks to a thirty-eight-yard Chad Morton punt return, New York had a short path to the game's first touchdown.

GIANTS

1-10-E21 Eli Manning passes to Tiki Barber for 5
2-5-E16   Offside, Eagles
1-10-E11 Barber runs for 11 and the touchdown;

Jay Feely's kick is good
New York 7, Philadelphia 0

But Garcia asserted himself then—twice. The second time he was aided by a Manning interception.

EAGLES

1-10-E20 Garcia passes to Donté Stallworth for 5
2-5-E25   Brian Westbrook runs for 9
1-10-E34 Correll Buckhalter runs for 4
2-6-E38   Garcia passes incomplete
3-6-E38   False start, offense
3-11-E33 Garcia passes to Westbrook for 11
1-10-E44 Westbrook runs for 6
2-4-50   Garcia passes to Reggie Brown for 20
1-10-G30 Buckhalter runs for 7
2-3-G23   Garcia passes to Westbrook for 14
1-G-G9   Buckhalter runs for 3
2-G-G6   Garcia scrambles for 4
3-G-G2   Buckhalter runs for 2 and the touchdown;
   David Akers' kick is good
Philadelphia 7, New York 7

EAGLES

1-10-G41 Garcia passes to Westbrook for 8
2-2-G33   Buckhalter runs for 11
1-10-G22 Offside, defense
1-5-G17   (shotgun) Garcia passes to L. J. Smith for 9
1-G-G8   Westbrook runs for 6
2-G-G2   Westbrook runs for 1
3-G-G1   Buckholder runs for 0
4-G-G1   Westbrook runs for 1 and the touchdown;

Akers' kick is good
Philadelphia 14, New York 7

In the fourth quarter, the Giants were still within seven points, 29–22, when Eli's second interception was returned nineteen yards by Trent Cole for the clinching touchdown. The final score was 36–22, and Garcia wasn't finished with the Giants. They would see each other one more time.

New York was the loser of five of six, all without Michael Strahan. Now, of the fourteen games Strahan had missed since 2004, New York had lost a dozen. Someone with a sense of timing dug out a rookie photograph of Stray and pinned it up on the locker room bulletin board. This was intended to give the players a laugh, but that wasn't the effect. "It doesn't look a thing like me," Michael said. "Players keep saying, 'That's not you, that can't be you.' 'Yeah, it is.' But even I looked at it and saw a totally different person, a child." It turned into an object lesson for the whole team, and not a cheerful one. "Time is flying by," Strahan said.

One of the players observed, "As old as you look, Stray, maybe you should apply to replace Accorsi as GM."

"You know what," Strahan said, "just knowing the little bit I know about what it takes to do it, I don't want to even think if I could. Because I know I would never want to. Negotiating with a man about his financials, his livelihood, all of the little details that are mind-boggling to me anyway? No thanks. I'd be an honest GM, though. I wouldn't BS the players. A player would rather hear he's not good enough and what he has to work on than all the BS. Nobody has to tell the players what's happening to us now. We just have to keep going. That's the challenge from here on in, and everybody knows it. Keep going."

The most interesting thing that happened around the Philly game occurred on the floor of the New York Stock Exchange two days later when Steven Mara and another trader had a contretemps that reportedly involved at least one mimed jump shot and a couple of curse words. The Giants players were actually impressed. Somebody out there was fighting for them.

22

DOUBLE SAFETY DELAYED BLITZ

IF A HOME GAME started to go really sour, Accorsi might abandon his tunnel and begin moving around the stadium in search of a luckier vantage point. The television networks had monitors set up in back rooms. Maybe he'd stare at those for a while, or go to the TV set in the players' lounge of the locker room, or climb up to his office, switch on the game, turn down the sound, and continue packing his boxes. When John Mara stuck his head into Ernie's office a couple of days before the Saints game, Mara was startled by how barren it already looked. "Oh, man," John said. "You really *are* leaving."

The crate Accorsi was filling, with one eye on the television screen, would have made a perfect time capsule of the NFL over the last almost forty years. Included were two poems written by the tender and tough Giant Kyle Rote ("Where laden clouds nudge into winds, / Beneath an azure sky— / To soften sunlight's dancing on / A mountain stream nearby"); a letter from Weeb Ewbank, the winning coach for the Baltimore Colts and the New York Jets in the two most important pro football games ever played ("Dear Ernie, I'm sending you a hat I found in my basement. It's at least old and brown. Remember the string of victories we had in Baltimore because I kept wearing that same brown suit? That suit plus Art Donovan, Gino Marchetti, Raymond Berry, Jim Parker, Lenny Moore, John Unitas, Alan Ameche, Jim Mutscheller, and several other great guys did the job"); a note from Olivia Manning ("Thank you for the beautiful flowers—so pretty, so bright—and the kind words on my mother's passing. I must say that Eli's calm nature was probably inherited from his grandmother. That and some other good traits as well. She loved following Eli and the New York Giants—and probably still is"); a "Kosar the Viking" campaign button; a cigar still in its cellophane wrapper.

"Mr. Rooney gave me that," Ernie said. "I'd never smoke it, of course. I consider it a holy relic, a piece of bone from St. Francis of Assissi. If I unwrapped it now, it would crumble."

As part of the ceremony of leaving, Accorsi had made a pilgrimage to the Pittsburgh Public Theater to see an actor named Tom Atkins portray Rooney in a one-man play called *The Chief*. It was co-written by Rob Zellers and Gene Collier, a former *Post-Gazette* sportswriter.

"Atkins had him down cold," Accorsi said. "He walked like him, talked like him. Even smoked like him. Collier told me afterward that they had to get permission from a hundred fire wardens just to let him light the cigar onstage for one second. 'Oh, is this bothering anyone?' he says to the audience. 'I'll put it out.'" The playbill went into the capsule.

"Look," Ernie said, handing over a 1987 note from Jim Kensil in the league office. Next to Pete Rozelle, Kensil was the best executive the NFL ever had, another old sportswriter. "After all of my years in this business, with the league and the Jets," Kensil wrote, "you might think I'd do a book. But I'm not going to. I have no axes to grind, no kisses to tell. Sure, I've met and had to work with a few people I didn't like, but I'm certain there are many who feel the same about me. It's a wash. Anyway, pleasant memories need not be recorded publicly. Better to savor them privately with friends like you. If I did write a book, here's some of the things I'd say: 'Mike Ditka is my all-time favorite player, there's never been another coach as impressive as Lombardi, Pat Summerall makes for awfully easy listening, I miss the late Dave Brady of the *Washington Post*, my favorite movie is Red River. (Are you surprised?) George Halas's feistiness, Well Mara's dignity, Dan Rooney's patience and Jim Finks' candor are qualities I wish I had . . .'"

"You know what that is, don't you?" Accorsi said. "That's Jimmy Cannon in the old *Journal-American*. 'Nobody asked me, but . . .'"

"'. . . I never saw an ugly woman in a polka dot dress,'" I finished an old Cannon line, and we laughed, despite what was happening on the muted television.

"When this season is over," Ernie said, "I'm going to sit down and do the same thing Kensil did. 'Nobody asked me, but . . .'"

Reams of yellowed old sports columns fell into the box. "When I broke into sportswriting," Ernie said, "there were lyricists like Red Smith. If you enjoyed a big game, you couldn't wait to pick Red up in the morning and see what he thought of it and how he wrote about it. The best columnists in those days almost put sports to music. It was wonderful to read. There isn't as much emphasis on lyricism today. It's all reporting. The rumors seem to count for more than the writing now.

"After the Colts beat the Raiders in the AFC championship game, January of 1971—I was still the PR guy in Baltimore—Smith came up to me in the press box and said, 'Young man, could you help me get a cab back to the hotel? I'm with Jimmy Cannon.' I said, 'Mr. Smith, I would be happy to take you back myself.' As I drove, I listened as they recapped the game. They got to talking about Unitas [who was near the end]. 'Jimmy,' Red said, 'it used be like watching Bob Feller.' 'Now,' Cannon said, 'it's Eddie Lopat.'"

One of those color-coded play charts was a must for the capsule— "Denny's menus," Accorsi liked to call them. While he ragged the coaches for needing their chart, he didn't blame them for hiding behind it when plays were being called. On that subject, Ernie was the man who knew too much. "In the last game of the seventy-seven season," he said conspiratorially, "the Colts had to beat New England at home to win the division, and we just did, 30–24. A lip-reader named Bobby Colbert, who had been the head coach at the Gallaudet School for the deaf in Washington, 'saw' the Patriots' defensive coordinator say 'double safety delayed blitz.' It was third and eighteen, and we were on our own twelve.

"The word was flashed in to Bert Jones, who checked off to a pass down the middle for tight end Raymond Chester. He went eighty-eight yards for the winning touchdown. There have been binocular-wearing lip-readers in the league ever since. I'm not kidding."

Though no binoculars were handy, a slip of paper with X's and O's on it fell into the collection neatly.

"Back when the PR guys used to advance the road games," Accorsi said, "I was in Foxboro at practice on a Thursday. The cabbie who brought me all the way out there from Boston said, 'While I'm here, I think I'll buy a ticket.' I'm pretty sure that's the only ticket I ever sold advancing a football game. Following practice, I was introduced to the Pats' head coach, John Mazur. 'How long have you been here?' he asked. 'The whole practice,' I said. 'You spying son of a bitch!' he said, being a typical paranoid coach. Now I'm mad. I called our coach, Don McCafferty, as I normally would, to check on injury reports and to tell him the weather and read him anything interesting out of the Boston newspapers. 'You know, Mac,' I said, 'Mazur jumped down my throat at practice, so I might as well tell you what I saw there. In a full-house back-field, they put a receiver in at fullback and then motioned him out.' 'What day did you see this?' McCafferty asked. 'Today, Thursday.' 'You stupid son of a bitch,' he said. 'Don't you know that Wednesday is every-body's offensive day, and Thursday is everybody's defensive day? That's *our* offense you saw. The receiver at fullback motioning out is Ray Perkins.' "

In his desk Ernie found faded copies of the twenty-three ballots the owners needed to elect Rozelle commissioner in 1960. On the third go-round, a San Francisco attorney named Marshall Leahy missed being anointed by one vote. Baltimore favored interim commissioner Austin Gunsel, Chicago passed, Cleveland wanted Leahy, the Cardinals Leahy, the Lions Leahy, the Packers Leahy, the Rams Leahy, the Giants Leahy, the Eagles Gunsel, the Steelers Leahy, the 49ers Leahy, the Redskins Gunsel. "Ten years later," Accorsi said, "Tex Schramm [of the Cowboys] was presiding over a secret owners' meeting at the Hilton in Baltimore. Don Klosterman asked me to get a document out of his office desk and bring it to the hotel. I knocked on the door of the NFL suite. It was pretty easy to find. Smoke and noise were pouring out of it. A guy opened the door, took one look at me, and slammed the door in my face. That was Marshall Leahy."

A Pro Bowl program from Ernie's days with the league office surely fit. "Val Pinchbeck and I were running the two teams in New Orleans," Ernie said. "This is 1976, when no one cared about the Pro Bowl and the players wouldn't play. Val and I were walking along Bourbon Street one night when we heard shots—coming at us. Bullets were ricocheting off everything around us. We dived into an ice cream parlor on the floor, and Pinch was on top of me. He was heavier then. I ran the NFC team. Jim Hart of the Cardinals was one quarterback, but Fran Tarkenton didn't show and Archie Manning and Roman Gabriel were hurt. So I called Mike Boryla. He had taken over for Gabriel and won five straight games for the Eagles. My coach was Chuck Knox; Val's was John Madden. When Boryla arrives at practice, Knox comes up to me and says, 'Ernie, this guy can't play. I'm not playing him. So don't expect to see him. How did you come up with him?' I said, 'Coach, there was no one else.' In the fourth quarter, we're down by ten or so and Hart gets hurt. In comes Boryla. He throws two long touchdown passes and is named the MVP. I walk into the locker room and there's Chuck hugging Boryla and telling him how great he was."

Ernie took a little replica of Brooklyn's Ebbets Field off his bookshelf and tossed it in the box. "My greatest regret in sports," he said, "is I never saw Ebbets Field." Then he threw in a lot of books and photographs, one with Pinchbeck, Lamar Hunt, and George Halas. Halas, with one foot balanced on the running board of a Hupmobile in Canton, Ohio, was the man who started the National Football League in 1920.

"Because of Brian Piccolo," Accorsi said, "Papa Bear and I had a connection. I asked Halas once about playing right field for the Yankees just before Babe Ruth. He said, 'Ernie, I was lousy. I lasted one year. Couldn't hit. There were two other right fielders between me and Ruth. They were getting rid of me, anyway.'"

Accorsi decided to leave behind the old-fashioned Boy Scout hat, the kind Baden-Powell used to wear, a gift from a local troop and an unending source of laughter in the Giants' front office. But he packed the caps that said NYPD and NYFD, remnants of 9/11. "On the fourth anniversary, some of our players wanted to wear them on the sidelines," Ernie said. "You know the NFL and dress codes. 'Go ahead,' I told them. 'Sometimes it's better to ask for forgiveness than permission.' The league called me Monday morning to say, 'Don't do it again.' Unbelievable."

An old 8 mm film taken in 1958 joined the stack. "My dad and I," Ernie said, "took a post-Christmas trip to the Breakers Hotel in Palm Beach to play in the national father-and-son golf tournament. We bought tickets to the Orange Bowl at a department store in Miami. Oklahoma versus Syracuse. The worst seats in the house, or maybe the best, as it turned out. I had gotten the movie camera for Christmas and, on the opening play of the game, from the absolute perfect angle, a back for Oklahoma ran sixty-five yards for a touchdown straight to my lens. Do you know who it was? Prentice Gautt, the first black to play in the Orange Bowl. It's a little faded, but it's there."

It's all a little faded, but it's there.

Meanwhile, there wasn't really any game against New Orleans. After an early Eli Manning to Jeremy Shockey touchdown strike, the Giants were never again on the Saints side of the field. The final score was 30–7. "There was obviously some frustration," Tom Coughlin said, "and some despair." "I stood in the locker room and watched Tom afterward," Ernie said, "collecting himself to talk to the players, deciding what he was going to say. I have to admit, my heart went out to him." "After a bad loss," Bill Walsh said for all football coaches, "you're drained physically, mentally and emotionally. There's nothing left of you. You kneel down for the prayer and you can't get up, and somehow you make it back to the coaches' room and just break down, sobbing."

"Tom was good again, though," Ernie said. "He knows the difference between getting the hell kicked out of you by a healthier team playing a lot better than you are, and quitting. They still didn't quit." Now the Giants had just six days to find out if they could go the distance.

The next morning, Christmas morning, Coughlin took the play calling away from John Hufnagel and handed it over to quarterback coach Kevin Gilbride. Hufnagel offered to stay and help, but a day later he decided to go. "There's no offensive coordinator," Coughlin said. "If there would be one, it would be me." Soon, Gilbride would have the title as well as the Denny's menu.

When Tom made the decision on Hufnagel, he called Ernie. Dialing Accorsi's cell number on Christmas, the coach didn't realize that Ernie was right next door. "A second later, when I walked into Tom's office," Ernie said, "he did the all-time quadruple take and almost fell over. I tried to reassure him. I certainly agreed with the decision."

"I just hope the change gives us a spark," Coughlin said. "We've got to win a game."

"Yeah, do me a favor," Ernie said. "Just win a game, will you?"

23

REAL LIFE IN

THE SPORTS WORLD

DECEMBER 28, TWO DAYS before the last game on New York's regular schedule, was the forty-eighth anniversary of the sudden-death championship game between the Baltimore Colts and the New York Giants in Yankee Stadium. On that date every year, from the early 1970s until Johnny Unitas died in 2002, Accorsi always telephoned Unitas to remind him of what day it was. This time Ernie was the one being reminded, via an e-mail message. The Giants GM e-mailed back: "I thought of John this morning. Talked to him a little bit. Asked him to help Eli Saturday night. I miss calling him."

If the 7–8 Giants lost to the Redskins, Tom Coughlin was certain to be fired. This wasn't written down anywhere, but everyone in the front office knew it. (Everybody in town knew it.) The game was in Washington, two days before New Year's, and the only question was whether Coughlin would be fired on Sunday afternoon or Monday morning. The leading candidate to replace him was Charlie Weis, despite a multi-million-dollar buyout clause Notre Dame had built into Charlie's contract as an NFL moat. The second name on the list was Bobby Petrino of the University of Louisville, who, as the industry used to say of Sid Gillman, knew how to complete a pass.

Neither Weis nor Petrino nor anyone else had been contacted or sounded out or so much as whispered to. The Maras don't operate that way. If Coughlin was to be dismissed, Tom would have to be told first. So, by definition in a Mara organization, no potential replacement *could* have been called before then. Ernie offered to check out the landscape quietly, but John Mara declined, ghost-walking around the office all week with an anguished expression. He had to be the last of the NFL owners who worried about the assistant coaches' children maybe having to change schools. Win in Washington and the Giants were guaranteed to make the play-offs by the thickness of a membrane; lose and they were all but mathematically eliminated.

The Redskins were 5–10, but they were better than that. They employed too many $30 million players not to be a little better than that. Iconic head coach Joe Gibbs had returned from Canton and Gasoline Alley in 2004, for the money probably, which wasn't like him. It was more like Bill Parcells, who had to replenish his coffers following an expensive divorce. But Gibbs seemed almost as detached as Parcells on the sideline, and the Redskins looked nothing like their former selves. In the earlier game at Giants Stadium, a 19–3 New York victory, the *Washington Post* noticed that the Skins ran the ball just twenty times, including only six carries in the second half. Every third-down play with five yards or fewer to go was a pass play. Even at third and one on the Giants' twenty-four-yard line with a minute left in the third quarter, quarterback Mark Brunell tried a short pass to Chris Cooley. After the fourth-down field goal was missed, the score stayed 16–3.

That's not Joe Gibbs, John Riggins, Joe Bugel, the Hogs, or the Redskins.

"I don't know what's going on over there," Coughlin said. "They've got a cast of characters on that coaching staff, all different kinds of people, all different kinds of money. It looks to me like they've got a defensive coordinator who thinks he's the head coach. And an offensive coordinator who's got to be a little sensitive about making two million dollars a year. [Coughlin was making $3.3 million.] All kinds of staff, all kinds of people. Joe's in another role. He's not calling the plays. He's kind of stepping back, watching things. But they're not easy to beat,

I can tell you, especially in Washington. They play hard. Gibbs' teams always play hard."

Speaking of not calling the plays . . .

"I know, I know, Ernie is always getting on me about that," Coughlin said. "I've been the play caller; I've not been the play caller. It's not harder; it's not easier. It just—it's like this." He cupped his hands to his forehead and looked out at the narrow world as though through the turret slit of a Sherman tank. "You're in a conclave anyway," he said, "but when you're calling the plays, you're deep in a tunnel. You can't see anything else. You can't do anything else. You can't be involved in special teams or in what your defense is doing that week. It can be done. It's been done. I did it. But, I guess I've learned, you shouldn't try to be all things to all people."

Marty Schottenheimer told Accorsi that Coughlin had been a difficult man to coach against when Tom was in Jacksonville and Marty in Kansas City. "Sometimes you just match up well against certain teams," Coughlin said with a shrug. "We had great success against them." He went on to say, "I hated taking the play calling away from Hufnagel. I have a tremendous respect for John. He's the greatest worker you've ever seen. Unbelievable. I don't think the guy sleeps. I don't know. I really don't. I don't think he sleeps."

When the word came that Hufnagel had been forced to hand over the offense to Kevin Gilbride, the first thought was that at least in part it must have been Accorsi's doing. "No, it was entirely mine," Coughlin said. "We couldn't even cross midfield against New Orleans. We had to change something."

The night before the Redskins game, Roy Posner made Accorsi go to dinner with him in Washington. "Usually, the night before a game," Ernie said, "I never leave the room. I'm a room service guy when the kickoff is approaching. But on the road lately, Roy had been dragging me out. 'Come on, you're having dinner with me tonight.'" Once, and for a long time, Posner was the chief financial officer of the Loews Corporation. In retirement he had become an unofficial moneyman for

both partners, Tisch and Mara. Roy was seventy-three, ate steak at every
meal, and smoked like the old Camel sign in Times Square, more than
Paul Henreid and Bette Davis combined. "Roy, I don't know whether I
should leave my suite," Accorsi told him. "It's possible that this is the last
suite I'll ever stay in. I'm not going to be staying in suites on my own
nickel." But they went to dinner with Kevin Abrams and a couple of
others, and Ernie enjoyed it. " 'Kevin, you don't know me very well,' Posner said when Abrams passed the spinach. 'I have never eaten, nor will I
ever eat, a green vegetable.' " The Giants players were fond of Posner, a
grandfatherly figure with snowy hair. They weren't exactly sure who Roy
was, but he was a familiar presence on the New York sidelines, from
where he watched the game that Saturday night.

Bill Walsh, who sat down to view it on television from northern California, said, "To be honest with you, I expected the Giants to be packing
up their cars and getting ready to drive away. But no, they played their
hearts out." So did the Redskins, who took the opening kickoff and went
fifty-five yards before Ladell Betts fumbled. Giants tackle Fred Robbins
scooped up the ball and brought it back sixty-seven yards to set up a field
goal. Yet, fielding a second kickoff, Washington didn't look at all discouraged, Betts especially.

R E D S K I N S

1-10-R20 Betts runs for 9

2-1-R29   Mike Sellers runs for 2

1-10-R31 Jason Campbell passes incomplete

2-10-R31 Betts runs for 21 yards

1-10-G48 End around to Antwaan Randle El, who passes to
    Santana Moss for 48 and the touchdown; Shaun Suisham's
    conversion is good

Washington 7, New York 3

Pressed up against their own end zone, the Giants needed a thirty-two-yard run by Tiki Barber just to move out of the shadow. In what could have been his swan song, Tiki was warming up for something glorious.

GIANTS

1-10-R42 Eli Manning passes to Barber for 7

2-3-R35   Manning passes to David Tyree for 5

1-10-R30 Barber runs for 1

2-9-R29   Manning passes incomplete

3-9-R29   (shotgun) Manning passes to Plaxico Burress
   for 14

1-10-R15 Manning passes incomplete

2-10-R15 Barber runs for 15 and the touchdown;
   Jay Feely's kick is good

New York 10, Washington 7

In the next Giants series, Barber slipped off-tackle for fifty-five yards and a second touchdown. The score was 27–7, New York, when Washington started to make its fight with extended marches in the back of the third quarter and the front of the fourth.

REDSKINS

1-10-R31 Betts runs for 17

1-10-R48 Campbell passes to Moss for 3

2-7-G49   Betts runs for 4

3-3-G45   (shotgun) Campbell passes to Cooley for 16

1-10-G29 Betts runs for 4

2-6-G25   Face mask penalty, Redskins

2-21-G40 Campbell to Cooley for 12

3-9-G28   (shotgun) Campbell scrambles for 15

1-10-G13 Betts runs for 2

2-8-G11   Campbell sacked for –3

3-11-G14 Campbell passes to Betts for seven

4-4-G7   Campbell passes to Betts for 7 and the
touchdown; Suisham's kick is good

New York 27, Washington 14

R E D S K I N S

1-10-R34 Betts runs for 1

2-9-R35   False start, offense

2-14-R30 Campbell passes to Randle El for 24

1-10-G46 Illegal shift, offense

1-15-R49 Campbell passes to Randle El for 13

2-2-G38   Betts runs for 1

3-1-G37   Sellers runs for 2

1-10-G35 Campbell passes to Moss for 17

1-10-G18 Campbell passes to Moss for 13

1-G-G5   Betts runs for 4

2-G-G1   T. J. Duckett runs for 1 and the touchdown;
Suisham's kick is good

New York 27, Washington 21

Then came another Tiki tour de force.

G I A N T S

1-10-G25 Barber runs for 10

1-10-G35 Barber runs for 3

2-7-G38   Barber runs for 2

3-5-G40   Defensive holding, Washington

1-10-G45 Barber runs for 5

2-5-50   Barber runs for 50 and the touchdown;
Feely's kick is good

New York 34, Washington 21

All but 7 of Barber's 234—count 'em, 234—rushing yards were in the book, but if Tiki was about done, the Redskins were not.

REDSKINS

1-10-R32 Betts runs for 4

2-6-R36   (no huddle, shotgun) Campbell passes to
Randle El for 16

1-10-G48 (no huddle) Campbell passes incomplete

2-10-G48 (shotgun) Campbell passes to Moss for 10

1-10-G38 (shotgun) Campbell passes to Betts for 34

1-G-G4   Duckett runs for –5

2-G-G9   Campbell passes to Cooley for 8

3-G-G1   Campbell passes to Sellers for 1 and the
touchdown; Suisham's kick is good

New York 34, Washington 28

Second-year quarterback Jason Campbell was having a breakthrough game. "I was never impressed by him at Auburn," Accorsi whispered, though. "His problem is just about the worst one a quarterback can have, accuracy." When Campbell was momentarily knocked out of the game in the second quarter and the veteran Brunell replaced him for a play, Ernie actually shuddered. Coming back, Campbell demonstrated character. All the same, the Giants' GM was glad to see him. With 2:18 left, seventy-eight yards from a victory, Campbell threw four straight inaccurate balls and New York was in the play-offs.

"At least that's something," Accorsi said softly in the locker room.

It's everything.

"Our defense is so bad," he said, "so hurt or so bad, however you want to put it, we can't stop anybody. Every time we had the game won, they came right back down the field. You know, I don't like the Redskins any more than I do the Eagles or the Cowboys—or any of their fans, either. But I'll say this. Saturday night. December thirtieth. A five-and-ten record. No play-off possibility. And the stadium is not only packed, but at twenty-seven to seven nobody's leaving. And on that drive that got them to twenty-seven to fourteen, the people are going absolutely crazy. You've got to give it to them. They have a passion that's unbelievable."

So did at least two others in the building: Barber ("playing his last game, as far as he knew," Accorsi said, "playing for his life. I don't think I've ever seen a performance quite like that") and John Mara. If you think of owners only as money guys who aren't really competitors, you should have seen Mara standing off by himself in a corner of the underground, balling both fists. John was overjoyed. "We're off the Schneider," he said. For the first time since 1990, the Giants had qualified for the play-offs in back-to-back seasons. "I've never thought of myself as a money guy," he said when that term was suggested. "Competition. That's what my whole life has been about. I live and die every weekend. This has been true for me since I was a child."

He was nine in 1963, when a Y. A. Tittle–to–Frank Gifford touchdown pass wasn't quite enough to beat the Chicago Bears and win the NFL championship in frigid Wrigley Field. "We went from 1964 then," Mara said, "to 1981 before we were in the play-offs again. That comprised the balance of my childhood, my teenage years, and my young adulthood. For the most part, we had pretty lousy teams, too. I took that very personal. This notion of my father being such a revered figure, which he certainly was for most of his life, forgets that there was a down period, when he was subject to so much criticism. That was difficult to take, for his family and for him personally. I'm a very competitive person by nature. Yes, we want to be a well-run business. We want to make money and everything. But that's not why we do this. It never has been. My grandfather was walking down the street with the politician Al Smith—this is one of the stories I grew up on, from the days when the Giants lost money for years and years—and Smith said, 'Why don't you give it up. It's never going to amount to anything.' 'Well, you know,' Tim Mara said, 'I would. But my boys would kill me.'"

To be in the play-offs a second straight year may not sound like very much to others.

"In the interview room after the game," Coughlin said, "some guy tried to get in my craw. Did you see that? He said, 'You act like you're vindicated.' I said, 'How do you expect me to act? I'm supposed to act some other way to please you?' We'd just won a game, a hard-hitting, honest-to-God, real football game, to make the play-offs, and this guy says, 'Well, they're just a five-eleven team.' If these people would only watch the games, which they don't, they might understand what happened. That's the problem. Do you think winning there is easy? No. Winning a game to go to the play-offs, winning a game that changes everything—that is not easy. And if you want to know the truth, being asked day after day whether you're going to be back next year—it gets to you after a while. You get scarred up a little. It's tough. Your kids are waiting for you when you get home, saying, 'Dad, Dad, don't just stand there and take it! Fight back!' I've always tried not to read the papers or watch the TV too much. The only thing I allow myself to do, I listen to ESPN radio at five in the morning so I can get the scores. Well, this idiot, Jason Smith, is on, saying, 'How can the Giants bring Coughlin back? There's a mutiny in the locker room!' What mutiny in the locker room? Where does all this stuff come from? Then you win a big game, and somebody says, 'Well, what did you really win, anyway?' "

The players could have fired him that night. "I know," Michael Strahan said. "We all knew." George Welsh said, "But guys like Tiki Barber have too much pride ever to go in the tank, for any reason."

"That's it," Strahan said. "Being out of the lineup all these weeks, I've learned that you can't lead from the sideline or in the meeting rooms. Everybody knows what happened to us this season. We won five in a row and then started dropping like flies. Not just losing our best players, losing our most vocal players. You can't be a leader in street clothes at the bench. You have to be on that field. Toomer, Luke, even LaVar—LaVar was new, but he was verbal. Osi's a young guy, but he's verbal. He goes down, I go down." A snowball goes rolling down the hill.

"Losing four games in a row," Strahan said, "the guys who were left could have said, 'Man, what's the use?' This season, there were valid reasons for the Giants not to be good. But telling yourself that is just another kind of quitting. And the bottom line for this whole year, I think, is: nobody quit. I don't care what anybody says, I think Washington was a hell of a win."

"No matter how you cut it," Walsh said, "it was a kind of compliment to Coughlin." Getting out of the way for Tiki, Manning attempted twenty-six passes, completing twelve, for 101 yards. Walsh, the quarter-back specialist, didn't like to say what he thought on balance. "Eli has looked passive to me this year," Bill said, "almost fearful."

After the game, Accorsi, Mara, and Roy Posner, standing beside the Giant buses, were squirted by five flying lemons. "Roy was smoking," Ernie said, "as we were waiting to go to the train station at New Carroll-ton. 'As nice a compliment as it is to have fruit thrown at you,' John said, 'I think we better get on the bus.' 'You need six more lemons to make eleven!' I shouted at the fans. 'Which is exactly how many games you lost this year!'" Arriving at the train station, Roy and Ernie became sepa-rated for a moment. "And I heard Ronnie Barnes call out, 'Get the defibrillator, Roy's gone down!' He was surrounded by a huddle of team physicians and players. "Fight, Roy," center Shaun O'Hara exhorted him, "you've got to fight!" And the first report was hopeful. Posner could tell the doctors exactly how many yards Tiki had gained. Roy seemed to be back, he appeared to be okay. As he went off to the hospital in an ambulance, the Giants boarded their chartered train to go home.

In 1948, when Ernie was six, his father and mother took him on a train ride from Harrisburg, Pennsylvania, to Phoenix, Arizona. It was his first grand adventure. They had a compartment. The second, six years later, was a trip to New York City to stay at the Taft Hotel, to sail on the Circle Line around the five boroughs past the Polo Grounds and Yankee Stadium, then to go to the Roxy Theater and see a live entertainment followed by the movie *Three Coins in the Fountain*. On every train ride

Accorsi had taken since, these memories seemed to be spinning in the wheels.

"I was sitting there in the dark," Ernie said, "thinking about the season and looking out the window at the lights and homes and towns passing by when the message came that Roy was dead. He had gone back into cardiac arrest." Ernie didn't wake Mara or any of the others. He just kept looking out the window. At 2:35 A.M., he sent a note on his Black-Berry:

> You know Roy Posner, I think. Heavyset, white-haired retired Tisch moneyman who as a hobby takes all of the trips with us. Sweet, gentle man. Great guy. Drags me to dinner sometimes on the road. On the way to New Carrollton to get the train, everyone was hustling from the buses up the escalators to the platform, and Roy went down. We thought he just fell at first, but he had a heart attack. Six doctors and Ronnie were right there. They were able to revive him. He regained consciousness. Roy was aware of things, even how many yards Tiki had gained—234. They took Roy to the hospital, but he went back into cardiac arrest. He passed away a few minutes ago. Real life in the sports world.

24

"THERE'S A CHAMPIONSHIP

IN THIS ROOM"

IN THE DAYS LEADING up to the play-off game in Philadelphia, Ernie told Coughlin, "Tom, if we lose, I'd like to address the team on Monday." "I don't want to think about that," Coughlin said. "Tom, Dwight David Eisenhower was a five-star general. He had a backup plan at Normandy. You can have a backup plan too, okay?" "Well, what is it you want to say to them?" "Tom, I'm not asking you, I'm telling you. What do you think I'm going to do? Rip your development of Visanthe Shiancoe?"

On the second play of the wildcard game, four-thirty on a Sunday, Eli Manning and Plaxico Burress collaborated for twenty-nine yards and the Giants seemed to be picking up right where they'd left off in September. On third and one at Philadelphia's thirty-four, Manning was replaced by the hefty lefty, 297-pound quarterback Jared Lorenzen. To the Eagles and everyone else at Lincoln Financial Field, this telegraphed a quarterback sneak. But those who had been attending New York's practices all week became momentarily excited. A lot of interesting Lorenzen variations had been installed for the game. "Lorenzen had a good preseason," Ernie said. "He scares me—he's got a rocket arm, very slow release. He's the best quarterback sneaker in the history of the National Football League. He moves the pile."

A sneak it was. Eli returned, and on his first two plays back he completed fifteen- and seventeen-yard passes to Tiki Barber and Burress, the latter for a touchdown.

The game could have been won by New York in the next two series, when the Giants started first at the Philadelphia forty-nine and then at their own forty-eight. False starts by David Diehl and Kareem McKenzie helped scuttle the initial opportunity, but Manning's inconsistent arm was the main reason New York never got close enough even to try field goals. Along with a rain cloud, those squandered chances hung over the team the rest of the game.

Archie Manning had traveled to Philadelphia to see Eli play. From behind the press box in a cafeteria, Archie sat at a table with a cowboy hat tilted over his eyes, hearing the crowd reactions and the public address announcements before the delayed picture flashed on a screen in front of him. "It took Eli a while to take charge at Ole Miss, too, you know," Archie said. "It wasn't until he was a senior that it was really his team."

By now the common, almost universal description of Eli was "a deer in the headlights."

"I know," Archie said, "but it's not fair. He's a quiet kid. He's always been a quiet kid. But it's not from fear. I don't see any fear. And I know him pretty well."

Brett Favre could throw four interceptions and still appear completely convinced that he was the best player on the field that day, and not only that day, any day, any field. Johnny Unitas, my ass. Even if Favre couldn't have been more wrong, he was sure of himself and showed it. The Tennessee rookie Vince Young was already acting a little like that. Every move he made seemed to shout, "Who's the man?" Even in Eli's most brilliant moments, the tantalizing ones that showed absolutely it was in him to do this, he never looked anything like the two of them.

"In this department," his father said, "I expect him to take a giant step forward in the off-season. He's a guy who identifies the problems and works to correct them. If you can practice being more assertive, Eli will practice it this spring and summer. I won't talk to him about it— well, I might talk to him about it, but I'm not going to work with him on it. But Peyton will, I bet you. Eli will never be a screamer, but he's got a lot more fire in him than most people know. Of course he wants to be more consistent. He wants to be more of a leader. Next year, I'm serious, might be his senior year."

Matching Tiki Barber with Brian Westbrook step for step (the two five-foot-nine backs would split 278 rushing yards almost down the middle), Philadelphia tied the game at the start of the second quarter and took a 17–10 lead at halftime. The score was 20–10 in the fourth when, after a Manning incompletion at Philadelphia's six-yard line, the Giants settled for a short field goal. Their next and last drive of the game and the season took four seconds shy of ten minutes and, counting two false starts and a hold, covered a full one hundred yards.

GIANTS

1-10-G20 Barber runs for 13

1-10-G33 Barber runs for 5

2-5-G38   Defensive holding

1-10-G46 Manning passes to Jim Finn for 3

2-7-G49   Barber runs for 3

3-4-E48   (shotgun) Manning passes to Tim Carter for 14

1-10-E34 Barber runs for 3

2-7-E31   Manning passes to Barber for 6

3-1-E25   Barber runs for 2

1-10-E23 False start, David Diehl

1-15-E28 False start, Chris Snee

1-20-E33 Manning passes to Barber for 19, nullified by offensive holding on Snee

1-30-E43 (shotgun) Manning passes incomplete

2-30-E43 (shotgun) Manning passes to Burress for 18

3-12-E25 (shotgun) Manning passes to Burress for 14

1-10-E11 Manning passes to Burress for 11 and the touchdown; Jay Feely's kick is good

New York 20, Philadelphia 20

With about five minutes left in the game, Reno Mahe returned the kickoff to the Eagles' thirty-four, where Westbrook lifted the team onto his square shoulders and carried it home.

EAGLES

1-10-E34 Westbrook runs for 11

1-10-E45 Jeff Garcia passes to Matt Schobel for 6

2-4-G49　Westbrook runs for 5

1-10-G44 Garcia passes to Reggie Brown for 7

2-3-G37　Westbrook runs for 5

Two-minute warning

1-10-G32 Westbrook runs for 13

1-10-G19 Westbrook runs for −1

2-11-G20 Westbrook runs for 0

3-11-G20 Garcia keeps for 0

4-11-G20 David Akers kicks a 38-yard field goal as time
　　runs out

Philadelphia 23, Giants 20

The second that the game and the season ended, Marty Schotten-heimer left this message on Accorsi's phone: "Ernie. Marty. I know you're very, very disappointed. I share your disappointment. I also know this: you're a champion. You and I spent a lot of years together, the best years of my coaching experience, and I'm ever grateful for that. But I want you to know I'm thinking about you. When you look back on it, it's been a great career. I love you. You're one of the all-time best. I cherish you as a friend. Thanks, Ernie. Bye."

Schottenheimer was now the head coach in San Diego, the NFL's top seed in the play-offs. Over the last three seasons, his Chargers had posted the league's third-best won-lost record, behind only Indianapolis and New England. But in contrast to his coach-GM relationship with Accorsi, Marty and Chargers general manager A. J. Smith not only weren't warm friends, they worked in an icebox; they didn't even speak.

Schottenheimer said, "A couple of years ago, six or eight times over the period of a year, I went to him and said, 'What's the problem here? Let's talk about this.' But all he ever said to me was, 'I don't want to talk about it.' 'What do you mean? That's childish.' If the coach and the GM aren't on the same page, you have a dysfunctional organization. When Ernie and I hit an impasse in a draft, it was Ernie's call. I was fine with that. The problem here is, they don't even ask me. When they traded [backup quarterback] Cleo Lemon, I found out about it reading the newspaper the next day. Ernie and A.J. are totally different people. Ernie did not ever care who got the credit. I can leave the rest unsaid. It speaks volumes. I say no more."

After the Giants' last loss, most of the attention in the New York locker room fell on Barber. "It's fitting that it ends for me in Philadelphia," Tiki said, "because this is one of the hardest places I've ever played. Give Brian Westbrook credit today. When they needed a big play, he made it for them. He reminds me of myself when I was younger. After the game, [Eagles safety] Brian Dawkins came up to me and said, 'You're a warrior,' and that means a lot to me, coming from him. Because that's his mentality when he plays the game. It made me feel good."

Barber had generous words for teammates and opponents alike, even for Coughlin. "If it wasn't for the guys around me picking me up and keeping me going," Tiki said, "I don't know what would have happened. And that includes the coaches. Tom Coughlin was instrumental in that. I can remember a Philly game when I had three fumbles. It could have killed my confidence. But he kept pushing me upward. Coach Coughlin has done great things in his three years here."

In weeks past, Barber had complained about the way Coughlin was apportioning the ball. In days to come, he would condemn Coughlin for overworking his players, practicing too much in pads. Like a lot of politicians, Tiki had trouble keeping his stories straight. Hell of a player, though.

In conclusion, Barber said, "I told Eli Manning—and Eli's already well aware of this—'Use your voice next year. It doesn't have to be loud and screaming or demeaning. But use your voice. Tell people what you feel and what you need. Be honest about it. They might dislike you for a moment, but if you're honest, they can never fault you.' Eli has to find a comfort level still, but he's well on his way to finding it. I'm excited about what he'll be for this organization for years to come."

Moving from locker to locker, Accorsi touched every player and had a few words for some. He advised Brandon Jacobs, "Don't let anyone tell you that you don't have the stuff to be a great running back, because you do. Don't let them make you a short-yardage back, either." "I just want to be here," Jacobs replied. "That," Ernie said, "I can't do much about."

Accorsi told Plaxico Burress, "You're the best free agent signing of my career." ("You know, it's interesting," Ernie said. "Ever since Plax gave up on that play against Pacman Jones in the Tennessee game, he's been unbelievable. His body language. The big plays. No drops. I think that changed him.")

Ernie shook David Tyree's hand, saying, "You're the best special-teams guy I've ever been around." "You've got the talent," he told Sinorice Moss. Accorsi said to Tim Carter, "You didn't have a great year, Timmy, but don't let them beat you down. Trust your ability. You've certainly got the ability."

Throwing his arms around the punter Jeff Feagles, placekicker Jay Feely, and long snapper Ryan Kuehl, Accorsi said, "You are the three guys who allow a GM to sleep at night." A little sheepishly Feagles informed him, "I'm breaking our retirement pact, Ernie. I'm going to go for a twentieth season." "Well," Ernie said with a laugh, "you're on your own now, Jeff."

Center Shaun O'Hara had yet to be re-signed—Shaun's representative was historically fascinated by free agency. "You should think about staying, though," Ernie told the center. "You fit here." O'Hara was the one bent over the fallen Roy Posner at the Washington train station, urging, "Fight, Roy. Don't give up, Roy." "What a man O'Hara is," Ernie said.

To Rich Seubert, the walking miracle, Accorsi said, "You're one of the toughest guys I've ever been around." "Fuck Philadelphia," Seubert said.

"If I make up an all-time list," Ernie told Jeremy Shockey, "you're on it." "Do you like fishing?" Shockey asked. "No, but I'll go fishing with you as long as you're not the one driving the boat."

"Boy, am I glad we brought you back," Ernie said to Brandon Short. ("We drafted Short, lost him, then brought him back. He played his heart out this year. We knew his knee was shaky when he came. Then he got that ankle. But he played hard all the way through it. He's classic Penn State. Everything about him is Penn State.")

"Thanks again for not giving me up," Osi Umenyiora told Accorsi, who wouldn't even discuss Osi when San Diego sought him in the Manning deal.

Jim Finn put out his hand. ("Finn gets every molecule out of his body," Ernie said. "Whatever's there, he gets. Every time you throw him the ball, he's not going to get any more than he's supposed to get, but he gets every inch of that. If there's eight yards there, he'll get all eight and be fighting for the ninth.")

Ernie's message to Manning was whispered. "I'd do it all over again, Eli," he said, "and you're going to win a championship." "Ernie wants me to be the best decision he ever made," Manning said later, "That's what I want to be, too."

"I'm making my rounds," Accorsi said, "and all of a sudden I look over my shoulder and Carter's standing behind me. 'Yeah, Timmy.' 'Mr. Accorsi,' he said, 'I didn't know you were retiring.' Someone in the background yelled, 'Where the fuck have you been?'" "Thanks for believing in me," Carter said. "You're the only one who did. Thanks for picking me." Two months later, Carter would be traded to Cleveland for running back Reuben Droughns.

Monday morning, when the Giants players mustered in the big meeting room, Accorsi thought of asking the coaching staff to leave. But tight ends coach Mike Pope beat him to the punch, saying for all of them, "I ain't missing this."

"Good morning, men," Coughlin said.

"Good morning, Coach," the players responded.

"Good morning, men!" he sang louder.

"Good morning, Coach!" they sang back.

Tiki was right; Tom did treat them like schoolchildren.

"The last time I heard anything like that," Ernie said, "was in Sister Veronica's second-grade class at St. Joan of Arc elementary school in Hershey. Before I started to talk, I looked hard around the room, into every player's face. Their eyes were unbelievably attentive."

This is what he said: "I wanted to say goodbye to you before I left. You are my thirty-fifth and last team. I've been with two Super Bowl teams, one that won the championship. Twelve play-off teams. Six teams that went to the conference championship game. Nine divisional champions. Some of those teams that went farther than you did, I didn't really like that much. Some I loved. But there was no team that I liked more than this one. I know some of you better than others. You younger guys, who haven't been around as long, I don't know quite as well, obviously. But I had something to do with acquiring every player in this room except Michael Strahan, and I made sure Michael never left.

"Tiki, I have been with six NFL Hall of Fame players: Johnny Unitas, Ted Hendricks, John Mackey, Franco Harris, Jack Ham, and Ozzie Newsome. You will be the seventh and Michael will be the eighth. Tiki, you have been the most remarkable back I have not only ever been with but that I have ever seen. You have defied every rule of reason in this game, every actuary law in the game of football. You have gotten better and faster as you have gotten older at a position that has the lowest career expectancy in the National Football League. It's been an honor to watch every play of your great career.

"This team has endured more than any team I've ever been with. If I were an objective observer and had been told last August, 'Here is a team that is supposed to be a contender. It's going to be given the most difficult start of a schedule perhaps in history. It's going to lose two All-Pro defensive ends, one of them a Hall of Famer, plus its number one backup, an All-Pro linebacker, both starting corners, the left tackle, and the greatest receiver in the history of the franchise. What do you think its record is going to be?' I would have said four and twelve, or five and eleven. You have endured an incredible amount of criticism from *all* quarters ["That," Ernie said later, "was directed at the coaches"], and yet you made the play-offs and played your hearts out to the last second of the last game. You're good kids. Stay together. Trust each other and be good teammates to one another. I believe there is a championship in this room. I won't be here with you, but I will be cheering for you. Thank you for giving me a lot of great moments."

He saluted them and walked out to a standing ovation.

25

COUNTDOWN

AS THE DAYS DWINDLED down, Accorsi took an inventory one morning. Precisely forty-two remained in his general-managing career. Naturally, that made him think of Jackie Robinson. When forty-one days were left, he remembered Whitey Ford had drawn that unfamiliar number first, before 16. Gale Sayers and Hopalong Cassady both wore 40, Roy Campanella 39. It became a game in Ernie's head, a countdown for an old sports fan getting ready to leave the field.

"Why couldn't he have started at eighty?" said Jeremy Shockey, meaning his own jersey numeral.

"That would be the old Baltimore Colt defensive back Andy Nelson," I told him.

"Really?" he said in a subdued voice.

"No, it would be you, Jeremy," I said, "and Andy Nelson."

Franco Harris and Billy Packer, 34; Bob Turley with the Orioles, Bill Dickey as a coach, 33; Elston Howard, 32; Brian Piccolo at Wake Forest, 31; Bobby Shantz and Eddie Lopat, 30; Bobby Richardson, first number, 29; Jimmy Orr, 28; Clyde "Smackover" Scott, 27; Lydell Mitchell, 26; Hank Bauer, first number, 25; Lenny Moore, Willie Mays, Matt Guokas, 24.

When John Mara announced that Tom Coughlin was returning, and a year would be tacked onto the year he had left, Mara said, "I think there is substantial support for him in that locker room. That's the feedback I have received, and that's what I've observed with my own eyes. There's this notion out there that he's lost the locker room, that there's a mutiny going on down there. That is definitely not the case."

The reporters were so disappointed that one of them, noting that Accorsi hadn't as yet been replaced, plaintively inquired if the new general manager could still fire the coach. "No, Tom Coughlin is our coach for 2007," Mara said, "and hopefully for many years after that. That's the final decision."

"How does it feel," Pat Hanlon asked Mara in the front office that afternoon, "to be even less popular than George Bush?"

It did no good to tell the fans that coaches of consecutive play-off teams in the NFL were almost never fired, especially by a Mara. For many fans, this was a decision beyond explanation. "I'm certainly sensitive to what the fans think," John said. "I have received a lot of mail. But at the end of the day, you can't make decisions on what the fans say, but what your eyes tell you and what your experience in the game tells you."

Shockey, of "outcoached" fame, said, "Everyone on this team, no matter what anyone from the outside says, understands that nothing is more important to Coach Coughlin than winning, and that's what you want from your coach. He deserves to be the head coach of the Giants. I'm glad he's coming back, and I've told many people over the last few days that I hoped he'd be coming back."

"I had some of my best conversations with Tom this season," Michael Strahan said. "We're getting there."

Those like Tiki Barber who contended that Coughlin was too much of a disciplinarian were contradicted by, if nothing else, the cold statistics. With eighteen personal fouls, the Giants led the league in lack of discipline.

For a moment, just a moment, Coughlin was giddy enough to be out of the guillotine's shadow that he started to bring up the subject of a raise. But, hearing distant thunder, he took it back as fast as he could before the stonemasonry came down on top of him. Even the patience of a Mara has limits. "We did not consider an extension for more than one year," John said pointedly.

Tom and Ernie still had a few rounds to go, too. "Pro football is a game that can feed on and profit from antagonistic attitudes," Ernie said. "It's not *My Fair Lady.*" When Coughlin neglected to mention to Accorsi that he was firing defensive coordinator Tim Lewis, Ernie couldn't resist lumping Tom with Robert Irsay. "That's the last time I had to get news of that sort on the television," he told the coach. Tom apologized profusely but just wished Ernie would take back the word *classless.* "It was a classless act," Accorsi said, "but you're not classless, Tom. Your class is your saving grace, as a matter of fact."

"I just would like a pat on the back now and then," the coach said.

"You shouldn't need it," said the departing GM.

"We weren't two and fourteen, you know."

"That makes me wonder if you aren't satisfied with eight and eight."

But just a few weeks later, when Coughlin brought spice to the league meetings with a quotable illustration of how unpopular he was with the New York media ("Hitler and then me, in that order," he said), Accorsi called him from retirement to say, "Leave Hitler out of it, will you please?" "I usually say, 'Genghis Khan,'" Tom told him. "Leave him out of it, too," Ernie said. The point is, Accorsi was calling because he was still on Coughlin's side. He was for him. And, of course, Ernie was going to back John Mara in the end, whatever he did, both his decision and his reasoning. If you ask me whether it was lucky for Tom that Ernie wasn't staying, I can't say for sure. But I have an opinion.

Recalling the day of the Coughlin job interview and what Ernie had said afterward ("If we can't win with this guy, I'm taking up tennis"), Mara told me, "For a going-away present, I thought of giving Ernie a tennis racket."

Bobby Thomson, 23; Allie Reynolds and Don Mueller, 22; Bob Kuzava, Tiki Barber, and Roberto Clemente, 21; Frank Robinson, 20; Johnny

Unitas, Bernie Kosar, and Alvin Dark, 19; Don Larsen, 18; Vic Raschi, 17; Frank Capitani and Whitey Ford, second number, 16; Thurman Munson, 15; Bill (Moose) Skowron and Otto Graham, 14; Wilt Chamberlain, 13; Gil McDougald and Roger Staubach, 12; Johnny Sain and George Welsh, 11; Phil Rizzuto and Eli Manning, 10.

An e-mail to Tom Webb, an old Accorsi friend, in Baltimore: "Tomorrow—Hank Bauer, the Splendid Splinter, Maurice Richard, Gordie Howe, Bobby Hull, Joe Grabowski (remember him?), Gino Cimoli, Hank Sauer, Johnny Callison (with the Chisox), and Joe Adcock. In other words, nine days left."

Five days after Coughlin was retained, Accorsi sent this e-mail to me: "Jerry Reese just came into my office and told me they gave him the general manager's job five minutes ago. I'm so happy I could cry. In fact, when he came in to hug me, we both cried. What a wonderful day."

Many of the writers, like Vinny DiTrani of the *Bergen Record,* wrote variations of "The Giants must think the team is on the right track. Last week they decided to retain Tom Coughlin as head coach. Today they will introduce Jerry Reese as their new vice president and general manager." But Shaun Powell, a black columnist at *Newsday,* had a different take.

"In the NFL," Powell wrote, "bold is a white executive hiring a scout who happens to be black, then grooming him as a trusted apprentice, then recommending him over the team president's brother to take over as general manager . . . Accorsi knows just about everyone in football and could have gone the usual route by tapping into the old boy network . . . The lack of black head coaches and GMs has less to do with racism and more to do with indifference. Accorsi took the road rarely traveled and convinced a young assistant coach at tiny Tennessee-Martin that the big city was worth a try. Reese started as a scout, then was an assistant in pro personnel, then took over the Giants' college scouting operation four years ago. Pretty soon, Accorsi found the man to lead the

Giants. Accorsi saw potential where others didn't bother to look. But that's what the good talent scouts do."

Yogi Berra and Willie Marshall, 8.

The Reese announcement was made on January 16, the day after the Martin Luther King Jr. holiday. Mara had put off the news twenty-four hours to avoid exploiting the coincidence. Jerry wasn't being hired for his blackness.

At his press conference, Reese said, "I live to put my eyes on the players. I'll never stop being an evaluator. That's what I am. That's what I know. But it's really my time to carry the torch and I don't take it lightly. I have to be successful on a lot of levels, to keep the dream alive."

Doug Williams, the first black quarterback to win the Super Bowl, was one of the first to telephone Reese. Harry Carson, the Giants' Hall of Fame linebacker, attended the press conference. Chris Mara didn't.

"I'm ecstatic," Carson said. "I feel like a little kid. I'm glad for Jerry, and I'm proud of my organization, my old team, for making this statement. It's a huge statement throughout the league."

When Reese came back up the winding staircase to the front office, I said to him, "The GM."

"Ernie won't tell you," he whispered, "but we both cried."

On each end of a small town in Tennessee, road signs were going up: "Welcome to Tiptonville, Home of Jerry Reese, General Manager of the New York Giants."

Peyton Manning finally won his Super Bowl, 29–17 over Rex Grossman and the Chicago Bears. The TV announcers emphasized Grossman's shortcomings, making him sound like an utter neophyte who could barely transact an exchange from center. "Did they notice it was raining?" Bill Walsh asked. Bill still tended to stand up for young quarterbacks.

Eli watched most of the tournament with Archie, Olivia, and the rest of the family upstairs in a private box, and was later introduced with them by Peyton to the audience of *Saturday Night Live.* "Maybe," Walsh said, "it's time for Eli to stop being Peyton's little brother and to start being the quarterback of the New York Giants."

After fourteen victories and just two losses, Marty Schottenheimer's top-seeded San Diego Chargers were ousted in their only play-off game when once again, as the sportswriters say, New England quarterback Tom Brady "found a way to win." The way he found this time was, on fourth and desperation, to throw the ball to the Chargers and rely on them to fumble it back. Safety Marlon McCree had only to bat that ball down, but he obliged. "Brady's Steady Hand Points the Way Again," blared the banner headline in the *New York Times.* Though nobody wanted to notice, the Patriots' estimable quarterback had been in full interception mode for some time, and would throw another one at the end against Indianapolis.

"Sometimes," said Schottenheimer, who was now 5 and 13 in NFL play-offs, "the football gods step in and say, 'Not today.' " Like Coughlin, Marty was offered a second year to go with the season that remained on his contract (in Schottenheimer's case, a $4.5 million per year contract). But club president Dean Spanos and GM A. J. Smith, Marty's nemesis, attached a $1 million buyout clause, which Schottenheimer rejected. "I'm very comfortable fulfilling the contract I signed several years ago," he said coldly. After both of his coordinators departed, Schottenheimer, fourteen wins and all, was fired. Four and a half million dollars will pay a lot of greens fees.

"Talk about a killer loss, that San Diego–New England deal was about as bad as it gets," said Coughlin, who knew of such things. "Brady tried to throw interception after interception down the stretch. You don't think of Bill Belichick's teams getting fifteen-yard penalties and having twelve men on the field, either. This game can turn around on you pretty quickly."

To Coughlin I said, "When Ernie and I visited Charlie Weis at Notre

Dame, I told him, 'I like you, Charlie. You remind me of me. You're the hero of all your stories.'"

"Did he get it?" Tom asked. "Did he laugh?"

"He thinks he can fix Eli."

"Maybe Charlie should fix Notre Dame," Coughlin said, "because Eli doesn't need fixing. He just needs the maturity that comes with time."

"The blind-side tackle, Luke Petitgout, goes down. Eli's Raymond Berry, Amani Toomer, goes down. And everyone wants to know, 'What's the matter with Manning? He doesn't look as happy as he used to.'"

"Yeah," Coughlin said, laughing, "and he's drifting to the right on every play."

It's a hard job, quarterbacking in the NFL. "It's so much the hardest job in sports," Don Shula said, "nothing else is even second."

Joe Namath, an expert on quarterbacking in New York, said, "Eli's biggest problem may just be the way he looks. Maybe if he changed his mannerisms or facial expressions just a little bit."

The image of an NFL quarterback now is Peyton at the scrimmage line, gesticulating like an auctioneer. "I think Peyton's theatrics are just a little exaggerated," Walsh said. "He doesn't have to do all of those things at the line before every play." Coughlin respectfully disagreed. "Even with Eli," Tom said, "Ernie would often say to me, 'Why is it so slow at the line? What's all this pointing about?' But an unbelievable chess game is going on. The kid has a thousand things to do. He's got to make the mike [middle linebacker] call. Who's the mike? That's the starting point for all your protection. Then the defense shifts and he's got to make another mike call, and the clock's running down on him. So now they bring a safety up and he's got to rename the mike again. Okay, so how do you want to designate that guy over there, number ninety-three, an end the last time with his hand on the ground, who's now standing up? What is he, a linebacker? Is he a defensive lineman? Where do you want to send your people? And who's the mike now? Okay, fifty-seven is the mike. Good. But, wait a minute. Another safety has moved to the side. You've got to change the call again. Five, four, three, two . . . it ain't easy."

Making himself the mike, Coughlin said, "Here's what's going to happen with Eli. This is what I really believe is going to prevail. Eli will look back on this year and realize that next season, the first person that will be condemned to death is me. And the second person they're going to come for is Eli. It's going to toughen his ass up. I really believe that. I think you're going to see a different guy next year, one with just a little more seriousness about the consequences that go with this job. We both might look back on 2006 as the season that made us. That's what I think."

"We played a tough schedule," Eli said, "and we lost a lot of tough games in almost the absolute toughest ways. We just weren't finding ways to win at the end. But it's not like we were playing hopeless football. We were making awful mistakes, but we weren't beaten. We weren't beaten down, anyway. Out on that practice field, it was high energy, full speed, every day. After the worst losses, after Tennessee, after the Cowboys, I never stopped seeing hope on the practice field. We were still having not just good but great practices. Players weren't down and out. They weren't just jogging around. They were running, laughing. Enjoying being on the field again. We hadn't quit. Not one guy. Couldn't the media see that? Maybe they are just so pissed off that Coughlin has restricted them to one corner of the practice field that they don't look at the football. They never seemed to see us. You don't have to know the players to see the enthusiasm. For as bad as a loss was, for all the rough things that were being written and said, not only didn't anybody quit. It was even better than that. Nobody stopped enjoying being a football player. I think we gained a lot of respect for each other this year, and something deeper, too. But it starts with mutual respect."

Schottenheimer said, "The quarterback question is, and always has been, just this: When all hell breaks loose and nothing is going right, where does your guy stand? That's what you've got to know. Is he even there? I like Eli, but he's now in a crucible. Now we're going to find out. The classic example of the quarterback in the crucible was Ryan Leaf. I'm not comparing Eli to Leaf, believe me. On his worst day, Eli is worlds better than Leaf. But Ryan is the classic example of the guy in the crucible. I went to watch him work out. I studied all of the tape, I talked to his parents, the whole bit. The guy could make every throw a quarterback needed to make. He was the whole package, he could do it all. But when he got into that crucible, the flame was turned up, and up, and up, and he completely melted. That's what happens at that position."

Truth be known, Schottenheimer fought in San Diego to keep quarterback Drew Brees, rather than let him go to New Orleans. "But I wasn't winning any fights then," Marty said. Brees led the Saints to the final four. Schottenheimer said, "We drafted Eli in San Diego because he was the value in the draft, but I coached Philip Rivers in the Senior Bowl and I liked him, too. So did Ernie."

"I know," I said. "One of the signature things about Accorsi is that he believes what he believes, and he never second-guesses himself. Without even pausing to take a breath, he'll say, 'I love Philip Rivers. Wonderful kid. He had a lot of success this year. I hope he has a lot more. Eli's better.'"

"That's Ernie," Schottenheimer said. "I happen to think Philip Rivers is going to be a very, very fine, winning NFL quarterback. But I'm not betting against Manning because I don't root against, and I don't bet against, Accorsi."

When Ben Roethlisberger won a Super Bowl with the Pittsburgh Steelers, people said Ernie should have picked Roethlisberger instead of Eli. But after Ben took his helmetless, not to say mindless, fall from a motorcycle and began threatening the league lead in boneheaded plays and interceptions, that talk quietly dissipated. Then, people said, Ernie should have kept Rivers instead of Eli, although Rivers never got off the bench for two years behind Brees, when Manning was winning a division title. "Rivers is one of the nicest guys I've ever been around," Ernie said, "but I didn't consider him for three seconds. I saw him against Wake Forest, and with *their* defensive backs, it took forever for the ball to get there. I mean, I hope Philip has a great career because there's no better kid on the face of this earth. But there was no doubt in my mind about the three then, and there's no doubt in my mind now."

Tony Romo, nailed to the Dallas bench for four years, was another budding quarterback the New York fans began to think the Giants should have gone for. "I got the guy I wanted," Accorsi said with a comfortable laugh. "In all of my retirement interviews, everyone asks, 'What was your best deal?' 'Manning,' I say, just to drive them crazy. But, the funny thing is, it's true."

Mickey Mantle and Bobby Sollinger, 7; Stan (the Man) Musial, Al Kaline, and Willie "Puddin' Head" Jones, 6; Joe DiMaggio and Brooks Robinson, 5; Carl Braun and Lou Gehrig, 4; Babe Ruth and Jimmy Lynam, 3; Derek Jeter, Frank Crosetti, and Granny Hamner, 2.

"At Baltimore in 1978," Accorsi said, "we drafted this skinny punter from Richmond, Bruce Allen, in the twelfth round. Of course, David Lee was going to be our punter again, for about the hundredth straight year. Dick Szymanski was the GM then, I was his assistant, handling all of the low picks. I guess Bruce weighed about one-sixty. 'We're going to have a blocked punt drill now,' Ted Marchibroda tells Allen at practice. 'Don't let it bother you.' Well, we block fifteen straight punts on the poor kid, and whatever confidence he had was shattered forever. He couldn't kick the ball at all after that. He lasted about seven days."

Ernie was telling this story by way of explaining the final official transaction that had just come across his desk, forwarded by John Mara. It was from the Tampa Bay Buccaneers:

CONSENT FORM

Club Requesting Consent: Tampa Bay Buccaneers Employer Club: New York Giants Employee's Name: Ernie Accorsi Employee's Current Position: General Manager (motto: "God doesn't want me to be happy.") Position to be Interviewed for: TBA

We are looking for a talent evaluator (especially punters), friend, storyteller, NFL historian, Major League Baseball historian, negotiator, advisor, medical translator, scout translator, head coach's confidant, golfer, writer, PR advisor and, most importantly, we want someone who is loyal to his organization.

Signed: Bruce Allen, General Manager, Tampa Bay Buccaneers

Permission is granted:

Permission is denied: X

("Sorry," Mara wrote under the X, "but we do not have anybody here with these qualifications.")

Eddie Joost, 1.

Borrowing his exit line from DiMaggio, Accorsi said, "I want to thank the good Lord for making me a New York Giant," and left. Watching his mentor go, young Matt Harriss was interrupted in his reverie by capologist Kevin Abrams, who said, "Get yourself a plane ticket, Matt. You're going to the Senior Bowl." Harriss threw his arms in the air.

Ernie headed to baseball's spring training. ("I had a great day with Joe Torre Saturday," he reported via e-mail. "When Carl Pavano got hit with a liner, Joe said, 'Oh, shit.' They're just like us.")

Come late summer, when the Giants would be reassembling for the 2007 season, Ernie expected to be "zigzagging all over the country," looking for Rickey's grave in Ohio and Mantle's tin barn in Oklahoma. "I want to go to Fort Wayne, Indiana, to the arena where the Pistons used to play. It's still standing. I want to go see the Quonset hut where Bradley played its games during those great Missouri Valley Conference years. I want to go to the Eisenhower and Truman libraries, to Davenport, to Moline, to Quad Cities, to Yellowstone Park and Mount Rushmore and Squaw Valley, to see if that arena is still there where the first

Miracle on Ice took place. I've been to Chavez Ravine before, but I've never seen a ballgame there. Then I'm going to go to Vancouver and take that Canadian railroad back to Montreal—it's a three-day trip through the Canadian Rockies. I'm going to get a compartment."

"Ernie is the last of his breed," said Pat Hanlon, who may be the last of his breed, too, a PR guy who speaks his mind. "Ernie represents the Pete Rozelle era. Smaller organizations. Less specialization. Nobody else is ever going to start as the PR director of the Colts and end up the general manager of the New York Giants. That's never going to happen again. A lot of the fans are playing fantasy football and acting just like GMs, but are any of them true believers? Will any of them end up the real thing?"

Like Red Smith rattling off a pitching line, John Mara, sitting in his office, ticked off the necessary qualities of a GM: "High degree of intelligence. Ethics. Courage. Trust. Respect. The ability to work as part of a team. Someone who is willing to make bold moves that more cautious people are afraid to make. Someone who will communicate with everybody in the office. When I was writing out this list," he said, "I realized I was describing Ernie Accorsi. I think of Ernie as an executive as much as a judge of talent, and I see an executive ability in Jerry Reese, too. But, as the GM job continues to evolve in that direction, some element of the scout will always be important to me. If the GM is going to be the last authority on player decisions, before we commit millions of dollars on a signing bonus, I want to know he's seen the player with his own eyes and is capable of making his own judgment."

On the walls surrounding Mara's desk were black-and-white photographs of Tim Mara and Art Rooney at the racetrack, homburg hats, binoculars, and cigars. "If you could name three people to have dinner with someday," John said, "two of them would be my grandfather and Mr. Rooney." Who can't name the third?

Walking me to the front office door, John asked, "Do you think Ernie will ever come back?"

"To work?" I said. "No."

"I guess that's right. He always described Sundays as agony, and I certainly understand that. But do you think he'll ever come back just to see the games?"

"Oh, yeah," I said. "I'm sure he will."

It's a fabulous game.

EPILOGUE

BY ERNIE ACCORSI

Nobody asked me, but . . .

- Baseball is the best game.
- Professional football is the best-*run* game.
- Unlike in football, basketball, and hockey, the baseball umpires don't determine the outcome of close games. The players do.
- That said, no professional sport has been managed as successfully as the National Football League.
- In primitive times, the NFL was more than blessed to have a blood-and-guts commissioner, Bert Bell.
- But looking back at the league's success, the indispensible person was very simply Pete Rozelle.
- I'm encouraged by the start new commissioner Roger Goodell has made.
- Rozelle's right-hand man, Jim Kensil, is the most underrated, most forgotten sports executive in the history of this country. Bill Granholm and Seymour Siwoff are close behind.
- The most thankless position is supervisor of officials. Art McNally and Jerry Seaman were the best.
- The two greatest-run sporting events in America are the Masters golf tournament and the Atlantic Coast Conference basketball tournament.
- The greatest pro football teams I ever saw were the 1975–79 Pittsburgh Steelers.

- In my lifetime, the second-greatest team was the 1962 Green Bay Packers.
- The Cleveland Browns teams of the first half of the 1950s were great, but twice they lost to what I consider to be the most underrated team of the modern era, Bobby Layne's Detroit Lions.
- Not too many coaches have ever outsmarted the competition, but I think Bill Walsh did.
- Just as I think Bill Belichick does now.
- Chuck Noll, Vince Lombardi, and Paul Brown had superior intellects. Brown virtually invented the modern NFL.
- Tommy Henrich and Hank Bauer were the first players I idolized, but neither of them as much as Mickey Mantle. When Mantle limped, I limped, too.
- I still follow the Hershey Bears hockey team every day.
- My most heartbreaking losses weren't the 1986 and '87 AFC championship games between the Browns and Denver. Worse was a Little League play-off loss to the Harrisburg Suburban Americans.
- The first football team I ever fell in love with was the Hershey High School Trojans of 1952–53. They played two ties, 0–0 and 6–6, against their bitter rivals, the Milton Hershey Spartans, who had a single-wing tailback named John Elway.
- When Peter Gammons was inducted into the writers and broadcasters wing of the Baseball Hall of Fame, he said something that put my childhood in perspective: "My role models were already in place by the time I was fourteen years old." Me, too. My mom and dad, Tony DeAngelis, Flash Petrucci, uncles Ovidio and Tom, aunts Nardina, Margaret, and Lena. I was surrounded by character.
- Jim Brown was the greatest running back I ever saw.
- Gale Sayers was the greatest halfback. I haven't seen anyone yet like him; I have Lenny Moore a close second.

- In my opinion, we—the Giants, that is—never competed in the 2000 Super Bowl against Baltimore. I would love to criticize our offensive game plan, but I don't know that we had one.
- The best assistant coaches I was ever around were John Sandusky, Bobby Boyd, George Welsh, Jerry Sandusky, Lindy Infante, John Fox, Sean Payton, and Marty Schottenheimer before he became our head coach in Cleveland.
- It was obvious being around Jack Ramsay at St. Joe's and Joe Paterno of Penn State that I was around greatness. You didn't need to define it to know it.
- Being around Paterno turned on the electricity in my soul. I was lazy when I arrived there. I didn't know I was, but I was.
- One of the greatest joys of going to Wake Forest was befriending Pat Williams, ex-NBA GM, quite simply the most remarkable man I have ever known. Pat and his wife have nineteen children of all races and creeds. I have often told him, "Pat, you're going to heaven on the first ballot, but the good Lord is sending a private plane for your wife."
- The New York media are not only the best, they have as much integrity as any I've known.
- When I was a sportswriter with the *Philadelphia Inquirer,* I was lucky to be near George Kiseda, the all-around greatest newspaperman.
- Some of my favorite people in sports today are Tim Duncan, Joe Torre, Brian Cashman, Omar Minaya, Jim Leyland, Mark Shapiro, Terry Ryan, Albert Pujols, Derek Jeter, Joe Mauer, and Ryan Howard.
- Unitas and Paterno were the two toughest men, mentally and physically, I have ever been around.
- The best spaghetti sauce and pizza in the world come from Fenicci's in Hershey, formerly the DeAngelis Grill.
- The most breathtaking places I have ever seen are the birthplaces of my parents, in Paris, France, and Pitigiliano, Italy. And the shores of Omaha Beach.

- I saw every shot of Jack Nicklaus' record-tying 64 on Saturday at the 1965 Masters.
- I saw Secretariat in the homestretch at Pimlico.
- I saw Brown score five touchdowns, Unitas throw for 397 yards, and Raymond Berry catch twelve of John's passes, all in the same game.
- I saw Jimmy Walker of Providence score fifty points to win the Holiday Festival at Madison Square Garden.
- I saw the University of Pennsylvania tie Notre Dame 7–7 before eighty thousand in Franklin Field.
- I saw Mantle hit a home run over the hedge in dead center field in Baltimore. In fact, I saw him hit eleven homers. Not bad for living in Hershey.
- The first time I saw the Phillies in the brilliant cherry-red pin-stripes, playing the regal Dodgers in their gray away uniforms in 1950, it was over for me. Then, on a rainy Sunday in '51, I saw the great DiMaggio in his final season and the template was cut.
- It was important to my father that I see Jackie Robinson play.
- I saw live 140 of the 191 players in the Pro Football Hall of Fame, and I watched thirteen of the twenty-one inducted head coaches do their work.
- Of the twenty modern-day quarterbacks in the Hall, I saw nineteen.
- If Bert Jones hadn't hurt his shoulder, I believe he would have been there, too.
- Dammit, I never saw Sid Luckman play.
- I saw Yankee Stadium, Augusta National, Michie Stadium, Cameron Indoor, Wrigley Field, Roland Garros, Lambeau Field, Fenway Park, Saratoga Race Course, Pebble Beach Golf Course, Wembley Stadium, the Pit at the University of New Mexico, Camden Yards, Lamade Little League Stadium in Williamsport, Pennsylvania, the Old Course at St. Andrews, the Rose Bowl, the Boston Marathon course, and the Daytona Speedway.
- I also saw the Polo Grounds, Crosley Field, Forbes Field, Griffith Stadium, what's left of Braves Field, and old Comiskey Park.

- I saw the definition of leadership: Unitas getting on the team bus.
- I saw Henry Aaron hit his 399th and 400th homers in the same game.
- I saw Mays and Musial and Williams and Berra.
- With apologies to Jim Murray, I see them yet.

Will you tolerate an afterword now? The loves of my life, the most important people on earth for me, are my children and granddaughter. My oldest son, Michael, who graduated from the University of Pittsburgh, received his master's at Virginia while he was a graduate assistant coach under George Welsh and then became a coach at the University of Maryland. He got into high school coaching at Bishop McNamara High School in Maryland because he loved teaching young kids, and he is now teaching history at Archbishop Mitty High School in San Jose, California.

My daughter, Sherlyn, graduated from Penn State University and lives in Cherry Hill, New Jersey, with her husband, Jim, who is a career Air Force man, and my precious granddaughter, Alexandra. Sherlyn is a wife, a mother, and a sales executive.

My youngest child, Patrick, is currently living in Manhattan and giving me such an added joy of having a weekly dining partner. He is a sales executive with the Oxo Company in New York. Patrick graduated from the University of Maryland after attending the University of Kentucky first. I have always felt he is a Wildcat first, then a Terrapin.

The joy of my children at this point of my life is that they have now become more my advisors and someone for me to lean on. Life comes full circle.

—Ernie Accorsi

INDEX

LIBRARY
LEWIS-CLARK STATE COLLEGE
LEWISTON, IDAHO

D0949946

WITHDRAWN

WITH DRAWN

A HISTORY OF MODERN BURMA

Burma has lived under military rule for nearly half a century. The results of its 1990 elections were never recognized by the ruling junta and Aung San Suu Kyi, leader of Burma's pro-democracy movement, was denied her victory. She has been under house-arrest ever since. Now increasingly an economic satellite and political dependent of the People's Republic of China, Burma is at a crossroads. Will it become another North Korea, will it succumb to China's political embrace or will the people prevail? Michael Charney's book – the first general history of modern Burma in over five decades – traces the highs and lows of Burma's history from its colonial past to the devastation of Cyclone Nargis in 2008. By exploring key themes such as the political division between lowland and highland Burma, monastic opposition to state control, the chronic failure to foster economic prosperity, and the ways in which the military has exerted its control over the country, the author explains the forces that have made the country what it is today.

MICHAEL W. CHARNEY is Senior Lecturer in the Department of History, School of Oriental and African Studies, University of London. His previous publications include *Powerful Learning: Buddhist Literati and the Throne in Burma's Last Dynasty, 1752–1885* (2006) and *Southeast Asian Warfare, 1300–1900* (2004).

A HISTORY OF MODERN BURMA

MICHAEL W. CHARNEY

School of Oriental and African Studies, University of London

CAMBRIDGE
UNIVERSITY PRESS

CAMBRIDGE UNIVERSITY PRESS
Cambridge, New York, Melbourne, Madrid, Cape Town, Singapore, São Paulo, Delhi

Cambridge University Press
The Edinburgh Building, Cambridge, CB2 8RU, UK

Published in the United States of America by Cambridge University Press, New York

www.cambridge.org
Information on this title: www.cambridge.org/9780521617581

© Cambridge University Press 2009

This publication is in copyright. Subject to statutory exception
and to the provisions of relevant collective licensing agreements,
no reproduction of any part may take place without
the written permission of Cambridge University Press.

First published 2009

Printed in the United Kingdom at the University Press, Cambridge

A catalogue record for this publication is available from the British Library

Library of Congress Cataloguing in Publication data
Charney, Michael W.
A history of modern Burma / Michael W. Charney.
p.   cm.
Includes bibliographical references and index.
ISBN 978-0-521-85211-1 (hardback) – ISBN 978-0-521-61758-1 (paperback)
1. Burma – Politics and government – 1948–   I. Title.
DS530.4.C45   2008
959.105 – dc22   2008037150

ISBN 978-0-521-85211-1 hardback
ISBN 978-0-521-61758-1 paperback

Cambridge University Press has no responsibility for the persistence or
accuracy of URLs for external or third-party internet websites referred to
in this publication, and does not guarantee that any content on such
websites is, or will remain, accurate or appropriate.

Contents

Figures

Maps

Chronology

1943	Ba Maw regime granted independence by the Japanese
1944	The Anti-Fascist People's Freedom League established
1945	Burmese rebellion against Japanese; Japan defeated; end of World War II; British Military Administration; First Executive Council
1946	Labour forms government in Britain
1947	Second Executive Council; Panglong Conference; national elections; Aung San assassinated
1948	Burma becomes independent; U Nu is first Prime Minister
1949	Civil War breaks out; Guomindang in Shan State
1954	Burma rejects membership in South East Asia Treaty Organization; Sixth Great Buddhist Council held
1956	Second national elections since independence; U Ba Swe becomes Prime Minister
1958	AFPFL "split"
1958–1960	Caretaker Government
1960	Nu returns as Prime Minister
1961	Buddhism made the state religion
1962	Military coup; Revolutionary Council established under Ne Win
1963	Eradication of the private press begins; management of economy changes from Brigadier Aung Gyi to Brigadier Tin Pe
1964	Monastic riots; nationalization of private businesses
1965	Renewed monastic disturbances
1966–1967	Key civilian political leaders released from detention
1968	Internal Unity Advisory Board established
1969	Nu establishes the Parliamentary Democracy Party
1970	The United National Liberation Front established
1971	First BSPP Congress
1972	UNLF invasion
1973	Nu expelled from Thailand
1974	Burma's second Constitution; nominal civilian rule under BSPP; labour strikes; U Thant riots
1976	Military Coup plot foiled; World Bank Aid Consortium for Burma established
1977	Purge of BSPP leadership
1978	General election
1981	Ne Win formally steps down as President of the Union

1983	North Korean agents kill South Korean cabinet members visiting Rangoon
1987	Sale of land or businesses to foreigners banned; UN gives Burma Least Developed Country status; demonetization decree causes widespread hardship
1988	Popular revolution; Ne Win resigns from BSPP; fall of BSPP government; the State Law and Order Restoration Council seizes power under General Saw Maung; National League for Democracy established
1989	Communist Party of Burma dissolves
1990	National elections; National League for Democracy victory; results ignored by SLORC
1991	Aung San Suu Kyi awarded the Sakharov Prize for Human Rights and the Nobel Peace Prize
1992	Convening Commission for the National Convention established; Than Shwe replaces Saw Maung as SLORC Chairman
1993	Union Solidarity and Development Association established
1993–1995	Ceasefire negotiations with ethnic rebels
1997	SLORC replaced by the State Peace and Development Council; US sanctions declared by Clinton administration
2000	Improvement in Myanmar–Indian relations; state exerts control over Internet access
2002	Ne Win family arrested; Myanmar Consortium on HIV/AIDS established
2003	Dipeyin incident
2004	Purge of Khin Nyunt and associates
2005	Capital begins to shift from Rangoon to Naypyidaw Myodaw
2007	Monk-led demonstrations in Rangoon (Yangon) and other cities, suppressed by the Burmese security forces
2008	Constitutional referendum; Cyclone Nargis

Abbreviations

ABPO	All-Burma Peasants' Organization
ABSDF	All Burma Students' Democratic Front
AFPFL	Anti-Fascist People's Freedom League
APCLGB	Abstract of the Proceedings of the Council of the Lieutenant-Governor of Burma
ASEAN	Association of Southeast Asian Nations
BBAQB	*Burma British Association Quarterly Bulletin*
BBC	British Broadcasting Corporation
BBCN	BBC News
BBCSWB	BBC Summary of World Broadcasts
BCP	Burma Communist Party (the White Flags)
BDA	Burma Defence Army
BEDC	Burma Economic Development Corporation
BIA	Burma Independence Army
BNA	Burma National Army
BSC	Buddha Sasana Council
BSSO	Buddha Sasana Sangha Organisation
BSPP	Burma Socialist Program Party
BWB	*Burma Weekly Bulletin*
BWPP	Burma Workers' and Peasants' Party
CASB	Civil Affairs Service (Burma)
CCEI	Committee to Combat Economic Insurgency
CIA	Central Intelligence Agency
CPB	Communist Party of Burma (the Red Flags)
CSB	Civil Supplies Board
DSI	Defence Services' Institute
DVB	Democratic Voice of Burma News
FEER	*Far Eastern Economic Review*
FT	*Financial Times*
GCBA	General Council of Burmese/Buddhist Associations

GEACPS	Greater East Asia Co-Prosperity Sphere
GMD	Guomindang
GMR	*Guardian* magazine (Rangoon)
GNP	Gross National Product
GNR	*Guardian* newspaper (Rangoon)
GUK	*Guardian* (United Kingdom)
IBMND	Intelligence Bureau of the Ministry of National Defence
ICS	Indian Civil Service
IHT	*International Herald Tribune*
ISI	Import Substitution Industrialization
IUAB	Internal Unity Advisory Board
JMA	Japanese Military Administration
JVC	joint venture corporation(s)
KIO	Kachin Independence Organization
KKY	Ka Kwe Ye
KNDO	Karen National Defence Organization
KNLA	Karen National Liberation Army
KNU	Karen National Union
LAD	*The Legislative Assembly Debates*
LDP	League for Democracy and Peace
LORC	Law and Order Restoration Council(s)
MIS	Military Intelligence Service
MNDO	Mon National Defence Organization
MP	Member of Parliament
MPT	Myanmar Post and Telecommunications
MTA	Mong Tai Army
NAB	*News Agency Burma*
NBW	*New Burma Weekly*
NDF	National Democratic Front
NGO	Non-Governmental Organization
NLD	National League for Democracy
NSA	National Solidarity Association(s)
NUF	National United Front
NUP	National Unity Party
NYT	*New York Times*
PBLC	*Proceedings*, Burma Legislative Council
PDC	Parliament, House of Commons, *Debates*
PDP	Parliamentary Democracy Party
PRC	People's Republic of China
PVO	People's Volunteer Organization

PWG	*People's Workers' Gazette*
RASU	Rangoon Arts and Sciences University
RDT	Rangoon Development Trust
RHS	Rangoon Home Service
RIT	Rangoon Institute of Technology
RU	Rangoon University
RUSU	Rangoon University Students Union
SAC	Security and Administrative Committee
SLORC	State Law and Order Restoration Council
SPDC	State Peace and Development Council
SUA	Shan United Army
UN	United Nations
UNICEF	United Nations Children's Fund
UNLF	United National Liberation Front
US	United States
USAID	United States Agency for International Development
USDA	Union Solidarity and Development Association
VOA	Voice of America
VOM	Voice of Myanmar
VOPB	Voice of the People of Burma
YMBA	Young Men's Buddhist Association

Introduction

This book examines approximately 122 years of Burmese history, from the annexation of Upper Burma by the British at the beginning of January 1886 until the devastation of Cyclone Nargis in 2008. The main reason for writing this book has been to provide the story of modern Burma as the country moved from the era of high colonialism, through the Japanese occupation and the Cold War, to the present. Although it is sometimes claimed that there is a paucity of research on the country, a view no doubt strengthened by very real limitations placed by the current government on access to government archives and even to everyday Burmese people, in reality both Burmese and foreign scholars have persevered. The body of specialized work on the country is huge, diverse, and valuable. Perhaps because of the enormity of the task of bringing this research together, few general histories of modern Burma have emerged since the works of John F. Cady and D. G. E. Hall half a century ago. Thus there is a need for a general history encompassing the colonial and postcolonial periods. Despite government censorship and political suppression, international interest in the country, awakened mainly by the events of 1988, 1990, and 2007 and fed by the work of indefatigable political activists, NGOs, foreign governments, and Burmese political organizations inside and outside the country, has not diminished. This book has been written to provide a general view of the country's experiences, often relating events as they unfolded, for both the nonspecialist audience and for undergraduates who might find the specialized literature too inaccessible to develop what in popular parlance is referred to as "the big picture."

The present history is divided into chapters according to the major phases of the modern Burmese experience. While colonial rule in Burma did not begin in 1886, this year marked the beginning of what is generally understood as "colonial Burma," when the major institutions of colonial rule were in place. Stepping back any further would necessitate a lengthy diversion into the politics, economy, and society of the Konbaung Dynasty, Burma's last, and its competition with the areas of Burma under British rule that would eventually be welded together into British Burma. This would have expanded the volume to an unwieldy size, and in any case this period has already been more than satisfactorily covered by other histories, some of them very recent. Instead, the first two chapters of the present history focus on the 1886–1937 period, when Burma was a part of British India, a colonial possession within a colonial possession and when Burmese were not only under the British, but also at the bottom of a social hierarchy headed by Europeans and a range of Asian immigrant minorities. During this period, liberation meant not only separation from London but also separation from India. The division of this period into two chapters is intended to address the unique position of Rangoon (present-day Yangon) in the colony both as a foreign city on Burmese soil and in terms of its central position in the narrative of Burmese anti-colonialism and early nationalism. By contrast with the wealth, large colonial buildings, and feisty "big city" politicians of Rangoon, rural Burma was another world, closer to fields, the monastic order, and to Burmese Buddhist traditions. The third chapter, covering the period from 1937 to 1947, was perhaps the most volatile and certainly one with the most serious ramifications for the future political history of the country. Although not completely independent, Burmese were subject to two different kinds of limited self-rule, one British and one Japanese, that attempted to mask very real foreign control. This period might also justifiably be called the "era of Aung San," for it saw this student leader rise to head an army and then a nation, before he fell to an assassin's bullet shortly before Burma achieved true independence. His death, as much as his life, would remain the focal point of Burmese understandings of the birth of their nation.

The four decades between 1948 and 1988 have been divided into four chapters according to the different regimes that held sway over the country. The main reason for doing so is not to provide an essentially political history, but in recognition of the fact that a succession of different social, economic, and cultural policies accompanied political change, often influenced to a degree by the changing international context or the direction in the tide of a civil war that figured prominently in the concerns of most Burmese. Chapter 4 examines the first democratic period, from 1948 until 1958, which saw a regime fight desperately to preserve itself from powerful political and ethnic insurgencies, in the face of the threat of a spillover of the Cold War across its borders, plagued as well by political infighting and the challenges of erecting a socialist system in the country.

The consequences, explored in Chapter 5, were the establishment of a military caretaker regime (1958–1960), its more Western-oriented economic policies, and its succession by a new democratic government that compromised on such issues as the separation of church and state and rejected the economic reforms only recently introduced. From 1962 until 1988 Ne Win dominated Burma, in two essentially separate but not easily delineated periods. Chapter 6 examines the first, the military government of the Revolutionary Council, which sought to build a new Burma from scratch eschewing democratic principles and civil liberties in favor of fostering tight national unity. One of Ne Win's underlings, Tin Pe, helped pave the way to economic disaster as he sponsored a Marxist reworking of the economy. A new ideology, intended to give the Revolutionary Council "revolutionary" credentials, provided justification for political, intellectual, and social suppression. This period established the foundations for the Burma Socialist Program Party (BSPP) government years, discussed in Chapter 7, when new constitutional arrangements gave an apparently civilian face to what remained essentially a one-man dictatorship. Nonetheless, Burma's economic problems increased and by the end of the BSPP years, Burma had become one of the least developed of third world nations.

The period from 1988 to the present is divided into two chapters. Revolutionary Council and BSPP rule led to a popular revolution in 1988 and national elections in 1990, this volatile two-year period being the subject of Chapter 8. Dire economic performance, political and intellectual suppression, and outright atrocities against Burmese students and others led to mass protests and violent confrontations with Burmese soldiers and police. Under the weight of domestic opposition and a crumbling economy, Ne Win had run out of ideas and his regime folded. The popular revolution brought to the fore of Burmese politics new leaders, especially Aung San Suu Kyi, and even returned some from a previous era, like U Nu. This revolution was not just about "bread and butter" issues, but also about the desire for genuine recognition of the principles of Burmese nationalism voiced since the days of anti-colonialism, especially for a return of representative, elected government and the return of civil liberties. In a bid to prevent the erosion of their power, the military, influenced or controlled by Ne Win behind the scenes, seized power to buy time to erode popular opposition. Although Aung San Suu Kyi's political party, the National League for Democracy (NLD), won an overwhelming electoral victory in 1990, the regime stepped back from its promises and refused to transfer power. Chapter 9 examines the two decades that followed. In what might best be referred to as the "politics of delay," the military regime, referring to itself at first as the State Law and Order Restoration Council (SLORC) and then the State Peace and Development Council (SPDC) spent these years attempting to intimidate, remove, and otherwise erode popular support for the NLD. It has simultaneously engaged in a circular series of face changes and constitutional steps apparently designed to prolong its hold on power rather than to make meaningful progress. When and how this period will end remains unpredictable, although the "Saffron Revolution," in which monks led mass protests against the regime in September 2007, has made it clear that popular hopes for freedom and democracy have not diminished since the Burmese took to the streets in 1988.

While this book is structured according to periods of Burmese history, certain themes transcending these phases dominate its coverage. These include the struggle between civilian politicians bent on representative, democratic rule and those favoring authoritarian rule over the country, whether in the form of British colonialists or indigenous military officers; the political division of the country between essentially lowland Burma and highland Burma, both during the colonial period and the civil war; monastic opposition to state supervision and control; the attempts by Burma's political leaders, both civilian and military, to separate domestic politics from foreign influence, and the chronic failure to foster economic prosperity. These themes will be brought together in the Conclusion, which will focus on the "rhythm" of modern Burmese history.

CHAPTER I

Burma under colonial rule

A century and a quarter ago, the British annexed the last vestiges of the kingdom of Burma, what had once been mainland Southeast Asia's greatest empire. Burma was carved up by the British in three Anglo-Burmese wars (1824–1826, 1852–1853, and 1885) and for much of the nineteenth century there were two competing Burmas, a shrinking independent state in the north and an expanding colonial entity in the south. While a desperate Burmese court raced to introduce administrative reforms and to modernize with the latest Western technologies, court politics and a poorly developed economy ensured its ultimate defeat.

Colonial rule created much of the "Burma" seen by the outside world today. The extension of the Great Trigonometrical Survey of India into Burma in the late nineteenth century defined Burma's political geography and recorded its topography. Western writers associated in one way or another with the colonial state produced representations of Burmese culture, how Burmese thought, and how they behaved, that have shaped contemporary understandings. It could be suggested that perhaps more foreigners over the years have read George Orwell's *Burmese Days* than any other single publication about the country. D. A. Ahuja who ran a photographic studio in Rangoon in the first quarter of the twentieth century produced by far the most popular series of postcards of Burma, amounting to over 800 "scenes" of Burmese pagodas, architecture, and people. Mailed out to locations throughout the British Empire, the English-speaking world was provided with snapshots of what "typical" Shan, Burman, Kachin, Mon, Karen, and other peoples looked like and how they dressed.

The foreign imagining of Burma had little to do with how Burmese viewed their own country – that is, how Burma was viewed from the inside. For the most part, indigenous chronicles and literature, the local monastery or spirit shrine, the general continuity of precolonial material culture, and a range of other survivors of the British annexation continued to shape daily life and perspectives on the vast rural landscape well into the twentieth century. The most serious challenges to the continuity of precolonial social and cultural life would occur in the colonial capital at Rangoon, as we shall see in the following chapter. Nonetheless, important changes did occur for rural Burmese with the arrival of colonial rule and these involved mainly administrative and economic transformations.

Colonial rule disrupted traditional reciprocal relationships between the landed gentry and the peasants. The basic unit of administration and realm of social life throughout rural Burma was the village. While the precolonial state had exercised tighter administrative control over the country than any of its predecessors, it had touched upon village life only lightly and indirectly. The village headman acted not only as an agent of the state or of the revenue-grantee, but also as a representative or protector of the village community. When harvests were bad, he could work through a chain of patron–client ties to soften the revenue demands for that year. The village headman was responsible for supplying the necessities for village festivals and a range of other communal needs. In return, villagers provided a pool of labor for working his land or for supporting him at times of conflict, whether in cases of contributing men to local contingents required by the throne for war or for more personal conflicts with other powerful men in the local landscape.[1]

Economic change connected to the political reconfiguration of Burma from the mid nineteenth century encouraged the initial breakdown of the rural society. The piecemeal annexation of Burma by the British and the economic reforms in Upper Burma together changed the face of rural society in Burma. The eventual emergence of a large rice-exporting economy in Lower Burma after the mid-1850s led to a 600 percent increase in acreage under cultivation in Lower Burma between 1860 and the end of the 1920s, with most of this growth occurring between 1870 and 1910. Moreover, cultivation was intense, leading to a twenty-three-fold increase in the volume of rice cultivated over the course of the same period. The growth of the rice export economy in the south encouraged a massive migration of cultivators from the north into the delta, attracted by growing prosperity. Because of Lower Burma's sparse settlement, there was a yet unexploited rice frontier in the south that could be opened up for rice cultivation by northern settlers. Over the course of the next few decades tens of thousands of villagers packed up their possessions and with their draft animals in tow resettled in the delta.[2]

SUBMISSION TO THE COLONIAL STATE

For those Burmese who moved south between the 1850s and 1880s and for Burmese who came under British rule after 1885, life under colonial rule meant the loss of the headman as an important mediating buffer between themselves and the state. An even more unfortunate development was the colonial Village Act. Under its terms, all Burmese, except for Buddhist monks, had to *shikho* (a salutation reserved for important elders, monks, and the Buddha) British officers, as a demonstration of their recognition of submission to British mastery. Villagers were required to erect thorn walls around their villages and serve rounds as nightwatchmen. Villagers were also required to provide inter-village transport, as well as food and firewood, on the appearance of colonial military or civil officers. More importantly, the village headman was now an appointee of the government and was transformed into an agent who relied solely on the state for his status, income, and property rights and now owed his responsibilities to the colonial state alone. Villagers were required to attend upon the village headman upon the beat of his gong and to perform whatever service he demanded or be punished with twenty-four hours in stocks. With the end of the protective buffer of the village headman, the rural population also became more vulnerable in times of poor harvests and revenue demands were now marked by their regularity and uniformity rather than their flexibility in response to local and temporary conditions. Moreover, villagers suspected of theft could be imprisoned for a year without trial.[3]

The colonial authorities expected that they would receive the same obedience from the Burmese as the indigenous court had enjoyed and urged them to retain their "natural traits" of obedience to authority. When Lord Curzon, Viceroy of India, visited Mandalay in 1901, he held an audience for chiefs from the southern Shan states, the chief notables of Upper Burma, and other "native gentlemen of Burma." He did so in the West Throne-room of the former royal palace, seemingly presenting himself in the same position of authority as the old indigenous rulers of the kingdom. After speaking to the Shan chiefs, the first time a Viceroy of India had done so, he turned to the Burman attendees and explained to them (in English, which was then translated into Burmese) that

the British . . . do not . . . wish that the people should lose the characteristics and traditions . . . of their own race . . . The Burmans were celebrated in former times for their sense of respect – respect for parents, respect for elders, respect for teachers, respect for those in authority. No society can exist in a healthy state without reverence. It is the becoming tribute paid by an inferior to a superior . . . The most loyal subject of the King-Emperor in Burma, the Burman whom I would most like to honour, is not the cleverest mimic of a European, but the man who is truest to all that is most simple, most dutiful, and of best repute in the instincts and the customs of an ancient and attractive people.[4]

Colonial authority was backed by the broad intrusion of foreign institutions and practices that regulated or interfered with rural life to a degree greater than any indigenous, central institution had attempted in the precolonial past. The degree to which paper now governed life was astounding. Relationships with local administrators, the resolution of gripes with one's neighbors, the establishment of land titles, the payment of taxes, and a range of other activities now required the completion of a myriad of forms, visits to township or district law courts, and submission to information-gathering by government clerks and investigators on a regular basis and everywhere, customary arrangements gave way to legal ones. Births and deaths now had to be officially registered locally.

The colonial state, through a series of censuses taken in 1872, 1881, and every tenth year thereafter until 1931 demanded information on every aspect of people's lives, from their occupation to their religion, and about every member of the household. The collection of census data was problematic. In many spheres of Burmese life, identities and identifications that were fluid, syncretic, multiple, or even undefined were common. Whether in terms of religion, ethnicity, or culture, it was not unusual for an individual or a group to change their self-identifications in different contexts. "Karens," or rather, "Kayins," for example, might be freely used by writers and others; these terms were vague and masked significant diversity. Colonial administrators and writers differed in their approach as they brought an understanding developed in the West that national, racial, and other identifications had to be essentialized so that they could be incorporated into classificatory schemes for people, following the same approach adopted for the classification of animals and plants. Thus, as one scholar notes, and despite the substantial cultural, linguistic, and religious differences among Karen groups, a Karen identification based on the practices of only one group, that of the Christianized Sgaw Karen, was applied to the Karen in general, in large part because this community had more records than others and because they had been the main subject of missionary reports.[5] These generalizations would remain current in scholarship well into the twentieth century, with Karens often being referred to as Christians, and many would be surprised when, in the 1990s, Buddhist Karen rebelled against their Baptist leadership.

In keeping with European practices, the colonial census required Burmese to give single, unqualified answers as to their affiliation with a prescribed set of exclusive ethnic categories. Although the Burmese language had generally become the main medium of daily intercourse throughout the Irrawaddy Valley, many who, to foreigners, appeared to be Burmese, dressed like Burmese, and spoke Burmese, would not, in fact, have considered themselves to be Burmese. Likewise, precolonial Burman migration into the Lower Delta was especially intense in the last half of the eighteenth century and there was significant intermarriage between different ethnic groups, so that individuals who could claim ancestry from among the Mon, the Burmans, the Karens, and numerous other ethnic groups were very common in the delta. Given these two situations, one in which non-Burmese might be confused as being Burmese and another in which an individual could claim multiple ethnic origins, problems necessarily ensued when census-takers sometimes asked headmen or others to inform them about the ethnic identity of people in the area or required that interviewees tell them exactly which particular ethnic group they belonged to. Census data collected on religion, ethnicity, language, and a range of other identifications thus presented an artificially rigid, and largely incorrect, picture of rural society and its components.[6]

Especially resented by rural Burmese was the required submission to the colonial medical establishment, particularly when it came to epidemic diseases such as smallpox. The practice of inoculation was common in rural Burma from the late eighteenth century and by the colonial period had emerged as the method of choice in preventing smallpox. Colonial medical authorities, largely dismissing indigenous medicine as quackery, preferred to impose on Burmese society a visually very similar but fundamentally different procedure: vaccination. The actual differences between inoculation and vaccination are largely irrelevant to the present discussion, as regardless of vaccination's eventually demonstrated advantages, the indigenous population preferred to be treated by indigenous inoculators by accepted means rather than submit to foreigners applying an equally foreign method. In the 1920s, the colonial medical establishment, stymied by the continued popularity of inoculators, turned to legislation as a means of enforcing vaccination. In the absence of significant efforts to persuade them on an intellectual basis of the advantages of vaccination, the Burmese were faced with fines and imprisonment by colonial authorities that preferred to force submission. Not surprisingly, when rural Burmese set up organizations to fight colonial courts and agents, as well as moneylenders, in the 1920s, these organizations also interfered with the work of colonial vaccinators.[7]

Although colonial rule alienated some segments of the population and introduced – by some accounts – over-intrusive regulation, it also presented economic opportunity. The main concern of colonial authorities was how to produce enough revenue to pay for the costs of administration. Ultimately this meant developing a large rural class of cultivator-owners. This was achieved with some degree of success in the early twentieth century. Participation in the rice-exporting economy provided cash incomes that could be used to pay land taxes and purchase the necessities of life, and even then many of the otherwise most costly requirements, such as building materials for homes, and fish and vegetables to supplement a diet of rice, were readily acquired from the local environment at little or no cost. Cash also provided opportunities to purchase a few luxuries, either products of indigenous cottage industries or even Western goods. On the other hand, the rigidity of the colonial taxation system, which rarely afforded relief during bad harvests, and dependence upon a single crop in the context of fluctuating world markets meant that a cultivator's economic situation could change dramatically from one year to the next. Moreover, the costs of opening up land and maintaining cultivation of a surplus for export, beyond personal subsistence, were high. To meet these demands, Burmese cultivators (see Fig. 1.1) increasingly found themselves turning to moneylenders.

LAND ALIENATION

From the 1890s on, rural agricultural land was gradually alienated to moneylenders. This problem is sometimes attributed to the nefarious practices of the Indian Chettyars. The Chettyars were a moneylending caste indigenous to Chettinad in the Madras Presidency. Although their business dealings in the colonial period extended throughout much of Southeast Asia as well as in Sri Lanka, their main area of interest was Burma. Their presence was uneven, however; in some districts they maintained a small presence, while in a few others, such as Hanthawaddy and Tharrawaddy, they were the overwhelming source of loans for Burmese agriculturalists. The Chettyars operated through widely cast family networks that could channel capital easily between India and Burma. These networks were geared toward taking reasonable risks in moneylending and hence loaned out money at low rates of interest to cultivators who appeared capable of paying the money back. The goal was to use the profits from moneylending

Figure 1.1 Burmese village scene today

in Burma to build up further capital for financial reinvestment or to pur-chase land in India, and if land was acquired in Burma it was mainly to avoid or prevent the complete loss of return on a bad loan. The Chettyars were not the only foreign moneylenders, for other Indians and Chinese were also involved, though not to anything like the same extent as the Chettyars. In terms of land alienation, however, the most significant cul-prits prior to the Great Depression were Burmese moneylenders. They more commonly made risky loans and charged higher rates of interest. Although their main purpose was also not to foreclose, they frequently acquired land in default of repayment of a loan because the loans made had been so risky in the first place.[8]

The colonial authorities were slow to respond, but from 1900 to 1930 two solutions were put forward to resolve the problem of land alienation. The first sought to curb the practice through legislation on the grounds that the Burmese were incapable of exercising self-control in the economic arena. The second – which advocated cooperation rather than compulsion – recommended educating the Burmese in the ways and means of combating land alienation. In the end, regardless of these efforts, and largely as a consequence of the Great Depression, more and more land was handed over to the moneylenders, even though the the latter would have preferred the repayment of their loans.[9]

In the early 1920s, village associations emerged in response to a diverse range of interests. The conventional view is that these organizations were prompted by encouragement from the General Council of Burmese Associations (GCBA) to promote rural-based nationalist agitation. Many organized or joined other rural associations, however, to resolve serious rural economic or legal problems, especially colonial tax demands and exploitation by moneylenders. In an effort to empower the rural population, the village associations also sought to appropriate for themselves the authority claimed by colonial law courts and local government officers. In some villages, associations formed their own "courts" and encouraged the population to resort to them rather than to colonial judicial authorities. Such village courts, headed by indigenous "judges," handled the full range of peasant disputes, assigned penalties, and ordered the payment of damages.

The village associations also opposed the local agents of the colonial regime, the village headman and his close relations, as well as moneylenders. Although monks also cooperated with these associations in social sanctions and were frequently portrayed as the instigators of this activity, it was sometimes the case that local associations merely made use of the moral authority of the monk to legitimize their actions. In one case, an eighty-year-old monk was made the chair of a village association meeting at which a social boycott of an offending villager was decided. Although the monk "seemed to be deaf, inactive and not much interested in what the meeting resolved," he was put on trial for the offense.[10]

From the beginning, village associations encouraged the general population to boycott foreign goods and to revert to traditional, indigenous ways. They urged Burmese not to buy imported British textiles but to rely instead on homespun, and home-products exhibitions were set up at conferences to encourage home industry. Burmese cheroots were to be smoked instead of Virginia cigarettes, the population was discouraged from using Burma Oil Company candles to light Buddhist shrines, no one was to wear coats, boots, or shoes exceeding the value of twenty rupees, and the hair was to be worn long as in precolonial times. In keeping with Buddhist scriptures, the eating of meat, the drinking of alcohol, and the taking of opium were all proscribed. The village associations were able to enforce the boycott of colonial taxation and the purchase of foreign goods by applying social pressure. Villagers who collaborated with the government or the moneylenders, for example, faced social ostracism, the stoning of their homes, denial of help in planting, being banned from employment, the maiming of their cattle, destruction of their crops, and even death. Further, although both Burmese and Chettyar moneylenders were targeted, Chettyars were especially despised for being foreign.[11]

Rather than deal with the economic roots of the problem, the colonial regime focussed its criticism on the village associations. In a speech in October 1924, Governor Sir Spencer Harcourt Butler accused an unnamed central organization of encouraging village associations to resist colonial decrees, thereby undermining governmental authority. The village associations, he argued, prevented free speech and actions and thus he promised the government would use all available powers to suppress them. Citing examples of intimidation, including two murders, the government accused the organizers of attempting to establish "a kind of reign of terror." It then strengthened the police force and declared a number of important Burmese associations to be unlawful. Another tool utilized by the colonial state was the Anti-Boycott Act under the terms of which the village headman only needed to persuade one of the villagers to make a complaint in order to bring charges against the president or committee members of a particular village association. Additional instructions in reference to the Act provided for the public acknowledgement by offenders of the wrongs they had committed against the colonial regime and the propagation of the confessions of their guilt in order to avoid prosecution.[12]

THE *HSAYA* SAN REBELLION

Although the *hsaya* San rebellion that broke out in late 1930 is often seen as the first armed rebellion in rural Burma in the twentieth century, it had numerous predecessors, including a 1910 rebellion of petty cultivators at Sagaing, Shwebo, and Lower Chindwin Districts, the Mayoka uprising of 1913, and a miscarried rebellion in Tharrawaddy in early 1928.[13]

Hsaya (teacher) San, a one-time traditional medical practitioner, had been born into a rural family in independent Burma in 1879 and had published books urging the Burmese not to accept expensive Western medicine and to rely instead on Burmese traditional medicine, which was cheaper and more reliable. He traveled around rural Burma where he observed the poverty of Burmese cultivators in the colonial economy and joined the GCBA sometime after its foundation in 1920. At its annual conference in 1925 at Paungde, the congress of the GCBA turned to San as a literate peasant with a clear dislike of British rule to investigate the problems of Burma's rural population. San thus became the head of the enquiry commission whose purpose was to examine peasant complaints about the collection of taxes. From 1927 to 1928, San and the commission toured districts where clashes had reportedly occurred between peasants and government forces. The completed report related ill treatment of Burmese cultivators and disrespect for Buddhism. The report recommended that the capitation tax and the Thathameda tax be resisted and that forest laws which prevented peasants from collecting bamboo and timber should be opposed by nonviolent means. When the annual conference of the Soe Thein branch of the GCBA (which had by then divided into different organizations, many retaining the GCBA label) met in 1929, however, San was dismayed that no proposal was made to take action on his report. He made a motion in favor of organizing "People's Volunteers" to defy the colonial government, but was opposed by monks who argued that this amounted to sedition. This prompted yet another division in the organization and, on the grounds that the association was too weakened to be effective, San resigned, and planned an armed uprising.[14]

There is considerable controversy regarding the nature of the *hsaya* San rebellion and the timing of its outbreak. The controversy can be divided into two different, but intimately connected, issues. The first issue is the timing of the rebellion and the debate focusses on whether or not it was sparked by the Depression and the parlous economic circumstances of peasants unable to pay colonial taxes or, alternatively, whether the rebellion was a millenarian revolt and thus a response to the displacement by colonial rule of the traditional, precolonial moral order; or that it represented a transition into a new stage of rural anti-colonial politics, supported by new political networking.[15] These propositions are not mutually exclusive, for the underlying motives of or methods deployed by the rebellion's leader, San, and the reasons for his success in mobilizing large numbers of rural cultivators to rebel may have been very different. Moreover, a new discussion is emerging over the sources for understanding this rebellion. Conventional dependence upon colonial records frequently means that the participants in the rebellion, mostly illiterate peasants, have no voice. Some of the key documents regarding the rebellion, for example, have been shown to be dubious.[16]

Although some scholars have argued that the rebellion represented a millenarian revolt or the fruition of one man's political maneuvering through the village associations that dominated rural politics in the 1920s, it is difficult to deny that the outbreak was intimately connected with the effects of the World Depression that gradually hit Burma over the course of 1930. During that year, the price of rice paddy per 100 baskets dropped from

145 rupees in April to 94 rupees in December. Paddy sellers, frightened of fluctuating prices, disposed of their rice paddy stocks at lowered rates. Cultivators in Tharrawaddy District petitioned the government not to reduce taxes but rather to postpone their collection until May. On 22 December, the acting governor, Sir J. A. Maung Gyi, told Tharrawaddy residents that no delay could be granted because of the government's difficult financial position. The rebellion broke out later the same day.[17]

San's personal motivations or beliefs also seem irrelevant in explaining why so many Burmese responded to the call to revolt. Regardless of whether San was a manipulative politician or a sincere believer in Burmese traditional politics, for example, he mobilized peasants using a vocabulary and symbols that would be meaningful to rural Burmese. Reportedly, in early January 1930 San began organizing "galon" *athins*, secret societies, in rural villages in Upper Burma and on 18 January he went to Tharrawaddy to recruit a *galon* army. The *galon* was a mythical bird that kills *nagas* (snakes) and San characterized foreigners, especially the British, as *nagas*. The *galon* emblem would be tattooed on members of his army and they would be required to take an oath to the *galon athin*. At the end of November, San is reported to have claimed *minlaung* (a king to be) status with the title of Thapannakate Galuna Raja, while his wife became the chief queen and the *galon* army became the royal army. On 5 December, the foundation stone was laid at Alan Taung for the construction of his royal capital, naming it Buddha Raja. San now prepared for the forthcoming war with the British. Village blacksmiths made small arms and cannon, as well as swords and spears, which were stored in the royal armory; uniforms and war flags with the emblem of the *galon* defeating a *naga* were made for the army, and amulets and charms that would provide invulnerability (including immunity from bullets) were distributed.[18]

The rebellion began with an attack on government officials in Tharrawaddy district but soon spread to the other districts. William Louis Barretto, the Deputy Commissioner for Pyapon, was responsible for suppressing the rebellion once it reached Pyapon. A well-known Burmaphile who had written a play, in Burmese, on the Cooperative Movement, he was not inclined to inflict unnecessary casualties. When confronted with a rebel group, he ordered his men to first fire above their heads rather than to shoot to kill. Seeing that the guns had been discharged and yet no one was hurt, the rebels believed that they were immune to bullets; they then charged and many were killed. As a result of this incident, the Riots Manual was thoroughly revised. Despite their assumed immunity, the fighting went poorly for San's army after the British called in reinforcements from India and San's forces began to suffer from dysentery and fever during the 1931 rainy season. At the same time, bandits took advantage of the situation, also calling themselves *galon*, and under the pretence of being rebels, stole from the Burmese.[19]

San, disguised as a monk named U Nyana, had meanwhile abandoned his capital and had arrived in the Northern Shan State in early March 1931 to mobilize Shan peasants into another army. After organizing this army, he chose the site for his new royal capital and appointed new generals. By this time, however, the rebellion was dying out. San's soldiers were poorly armed to face British machine guns and government officials dispatched Buddhist monks to rural areas to urge peace and persuade peasants that the struggle was futile. In early August, San was captured and, over the course of the following year, colonial soldiers and police gradually suppressed the rebellion. However, their methods created long-term resentment among the Burmese, especially those in rural areas. In order to make an example of the rebels and warn others, photographs of their decapitated heads were posted at the main police stations throughout the country. As the police had mistreated villagers during the rebellion, local dislike of the British government and especially of the police lingered at least into the late 1930s.[20]

San's trial before a special tribunal arranged at Tharrawaddy provided a martyr for Burmese nationalism. Despite the efforts of his defense counsel, Dr. Ba Maw, to portray the rebellion as a riot, which was a lesser offense, San was sentenced to death and hanged in the Tharrawaddy jail on 28 November 1931. The main political impact of the *hsaya* San rebellion was that it helped to further encourage the nationalist movement and this process was aided substantially by the Burmese press, for various newspapers, including *The Sun* and *The New Light of Burma*, had published the news about the fighting between the *galons* and the British, sometimes exaggerated and biassed in favor of the rebels. The colonial government reacted with censorship and the imposition of substantial fines. San's trial also reaffirmed the nationalist credentials of Ba Maw who would eventually become the Prime Minister of Burma.[21]

CONCLUSION

The political and economic transformation of rural Burmese society began in the mid-nineteenth century well before the British arrived. Some might say that the problems associated with that transformation would also have occurred under indigenous rule, given late precolonial reforms, the emerging world market, and political centralization. Nevertheless, the economic opportunities that accompanied colonization had their downside.

First, of course, was the blight of foreign rule as well as the decision to rely on Indians and ethnic minorities in the administration and defense of the colony more than on the Burmans. The feelings of alienation and disenfranchisement in their own country that led to the rise of village associations in the 1920s and the mishandling of a rural situation that spawned the *hsaya* San rebellion were likewise poor choices for which the colonial administration was at fault. On the other hand, British rule also brought to rural Burma new economic opportunities, better transportation infrastructure, and some of the benefits of Western medicine, whether or not the Burmese appreciated the way in which the latter was introduced. The rural Burmese experience, both positive and negative, would connect with the urban experience, especially in the colonial center at Rangoon, to provide the context for the push for separation from India and limited self-rule from 1937, as well as the cooperation of some Burmese nationalists with the Japanese Imperial Army in 1942, as will be discussed in the next two chapters.

CHAPTER 2

The colonial center

Rangoon was not colonial Burma's only urban center, nor the only center for British settlement, administration, or commercial operations. Different centers had been important at earlier stages of colonial rule, such as Akyab and Moulmein, while Mandalay played a role in the north – though to a lesser degree – akin to that of Rangoon in the south. However, Rangoon was the most significant center for the colony as a whole as well as the colonial capital.

More importantly, Rangoon was a foreign city erected on Burmese soil. It was here, to the exclusion of anywhere else save for a few hill stations, that Burmese life was thoroughly pushed to one side. In its imposing architecture, its physical arrangement, its landscaped gardens, its focus on the harbor and maritime trade, the ethnic division of its population, and in many other ways, Rangoon was a mimeograph of dozens of port cities scattered throughout colonial South and Southeast Asia. A person only had to squint to be confused as to whether he or she was standing in Singapore, Penang, Calcutta, or elsewhere.

Colonial Rangoon became not so much a melting pot as a pressure cooker, where Burmese witnessed both the positive and, mostly, the negative consequences, direct and indirect, of the growing colonial economy and foreign rule. Rangoon clarified the social distinctions between the ruler and the ruled: the perception of all foreigners, European and Asian alike, as being economic exploiters; the sense of political disenfranchisement, and moral indignation regarding prostitution and other vices. In this context, Rangoon saw the emergence of new generations of Burmese leaders who pushed the colonial regime for political concessions and greater respect for Burmese traditional institutions and culture.

THE BIG CITY

Prior to the British acquisition of Rangoon in 1852 (they had briefly occupied the town from 1824 to 1826), Rangoon had experienced nearly a hundred years of indigenous rule since its establishment by King Alaungh-paya (r. 1752–1760) in 1755. European travel accounts during this long period typically begin with the arrival of a European mission at Rangoon, at the time known as Yangon, and the governor of Hanthawaddy, who ruled the town, was the first major Burmese official encountered by European visitors. Despite its importance to European visitors and its economic importance as Burma's preeminent maritime port, however, its scale and grandeur were far from those of the royal capital. The town had always been, by Burmese and European standards alike, a run-down port area, dominated by palm-leaf huts and timber shacks. Roads within the town were mere muddy tracks that were so formidable to pedestrian travel that planks had to be thrown over and around them to allow residents to walk without drowning in a mixture of mud, filth, and animal excrement. For many years after its colonial makeover in the 1850s, Rangoon remained a small town, quickly overtaking Akyab as the key exit point for rice exports, and, from 1862, became the administrative center for all of British Burma. The new Rangoon was completely different from its predecessor, for the British laid out their capital on a square grid pattern that replaced the haphazard layout of the old city.

Rangoon's modest proportions were rapidly transformed by new waves of merchants and laborers. Immigration took place on such a scale that it made Rangoon the world's leading port of entry for immigrants, topping even New York City.[1] One consequence of rapid population growth and a strong colonial economy was the rise of new buildings. During the building boom of the late 1880s and 1890s, wooden houses quickly gave way to masonry buildings in the downtown area (reinforced concrete structures were not introduced in Rangoon until 1911). The annexation of Upper Burma gradually brought more wealth into the colonial capital, but it also brought an expansion in the administration and thus new commercial and government buildings were constructed. Rangoon opened its new, grand town hall in November 1886, the Dufferin Hospital was opened in 1887, a new Secretariat building was constructed between 1890 and 1905, a new Government House was built between 1892 and 1895, and the Diamond Jubilee Hall was completed in December 1898. Rangoon as it would appear for the remainder of the colonial period was beginning to take its final form. While the colonial government and merchant areas of the capital were turning to masonry, colonial land policy was a deterrent to such a transformation in outlying areas of the town. The short-term leases granted to urban residents prevented any substantial investment in housing and thus residential areas remained flimsy, wooden structures. The town's

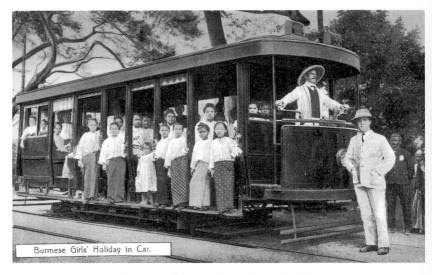

Burmese Girls' Holiday in Car.

Figure 2.1 Burmese girls enjoy trolley ride

water supply was not extended to many of these areas, making sanitation a serious challenge.[2]

As Rangoon underwent its steady transformation from colonial outpost to modern metropolis, it adopted what at the time was state-of-the-art transportation technology. Until the 1880s, land transportation in Rangoon was limited to horse-drawn vehicles. In 1884 J. W. Darwood laid the lines for steam tramways in the city and built a depot where Bogyoke Aung San Market now stands, fifteen locomotives being put into service to carry passengers along the central business district. At the end of the nineteenth century, however, the streets were still lit by oil lamps and the tramlines had fallen into serious disrepair. From 1900 onward the Rangoon Municipality sought to reverse this situation by electrifying everything from transportation (see Fig. 2.1) to lighting. A power station was built at Ahlone on the Rangoon River in 1906, the steam trams were replaced with electric trams between 1906 and 1908, and electric street-lighting was extended around the city between 1907 and 1911.[3] It was very much a "city of light" that contrasted sharply with rural Burma, where such conveniences would remain unavailable, in many areas even to this day. Such disparities helped lend weight to emerging impressions that whatever prosperity the colonial order offered was not for the benefit of the Burmese.

Developments in urban transportation were mainly limited to the center of Rangoon, preventing the population from moving outwards and encouraging overcrowding. The introduction of the private automobile, which first appeared in Burma in 1905, followed by the motor bus in 1913, made an expansion of urban settlement possible. Alongside automobiles, horse-drawn vehicles continued in operation but became more of a nuisance because of the excessive use of powerful double-toned gongs, which became common by 1907. By 1915, Rangoon had 8 buses, 139 motorcycles, 28 taxicabs, and 426 private cars and lorries, operating on 183 miles of road. By 1936, trolley buses (electric buses running on tires rather than rails) began to replace Rangoon's electric trams, marking the last major transportation initiative in the municipality before the Japanese occupation.[4]

The expanding limits of settlement in Rangoon and the need to develop better roads for the growing number of motor vehicles went beyond the capabilities of the Reclamation Advisory Committee. Further, overpopulation in central Rangoon naturally raised the costs of housing. Two other factors propelled these costs to the extreme. First, in order to clear land for development, many poorer residents of Rangoon were evicted from their homes over the course of the first two decades of the twentieth century if they refused to accept the terms of the new ninety-nine-year leases.[5] Lacking resources to purchase new property many became renters. But land speculation accompanied development, driving up property prices and thus rents, and bringing misery to Rangoon renters. This was especially a problem during the land boom of 1903–1904, when many of Rangoon's largest government and commercial buildings were erected, such as the Chief Court buildings (see Fig. 2.2) and Messrs. Rowe & Company. Second, most could not afford motor transport, especially when buses were withdrawn from service in 1915.[6]

In 1920 the Municipal Government placed the Government Estate, the powers to develop this estate, and the authority to acquire land for development into the hands of the newly created Rangoon Development Trust (RDT). Over the course of the next two decades, the RDT would reclaim land to the east and west of the city center and build roads that encouraged the development of suburbs. The RDT's stated purpose was to eradicate swampy and unsanitary settlements and provide housing to Rangoon's poorer occupants. Its activities also included opening up new markets, such as Scott Market (today, the Bogyoke Aung San Market) in 1926. Nevertheless, the RDT's activities also remapped European settlement in the municipality, relocating the Agri-Horticultural Gardens and the Rangoon Turf Club. Several RDT projects substantially benefited Rangoon's wealthier

Chief Court · Burma.

Figure 2.2 The Chief Court Buildings under construction

inhabitants, as in the cases of the suburbs of Windermere Park and Golden Valley, two enclaves of Europeans and rich Chinese and Indian merchants. Burmese resentment at the loss of Burmese land to wealthy "foreigners" was spelled out in words and illustrated in cartoons in the vernacular press.[7]

IMMIGRANTS

According to the Census of August 1872, over two-thirds of Rangoon's population was Burmese. The Burmese proportion of Rangoon's population steadily shrank, however, and by 1937, of Rangoon's 400,000 residents, only 127,000 were Burmese. Thousands among the Burmese residents were more or less permanent immigrants from Upper Burma, while several thousand others were itinerant boatmen or seasonal laborers such as mill-hands. The "floating" population as a whole probably numbered as many as 20,000, as the reports of headmen, who did not include this population on their rolls, produced a total population for Rangoon of 77,777 in 1872, compared to a return of 98,745 by the official census for that year, which included everyone.[8]

The diverse origins of the immigration that consumed Rangoon produced a social and cultural milieu comparable to other British colonial port towns such as Singapore and Penang. Most of Rangoon's immigrants came from Southeastern India and Southeastern China, particularly the Hokkien and Guangdong. Straits Chinese and Europeans provided smaller, though important, increments to population growth. Chinese settlers entered Burma both from Yunnan in the northeast and through Rangoon and other ports in the south. The former often moved back and forth across the border in conjunction with the caravan trade, while the latter became more or less permanent residents, whether they intended to remain or not. The most significant Chinese population in Burma was to be found in Rangoon, numbering about 24,000 people in 1921. Indian immigrants included Chittagonians from Bengal, Ooriyas from Ganjam, Bihar, and Orissa, Tamils from the southern Madras Presidency, Telugus from the Coromandel Coast, and other groups, whether Hindu or Muslim, considered together by colonial authorities under the general heading of "Hindustani," mainly from the United Provinces of northern India. Although the Indian population was widely distributed geographically, mainly in Lower Burma, its concentration was in Rangoon, where it made up the majority of Rangoon's population (55 percent in 1921). Indeed, before World War II, the majority of Rangoon's population came from South Asia (the modern independent countries of Bangladesh, India, and Pakistan, with smaller contributions from Nepal and Sri Lanka).[9]

Being considered by the colonial administration as too backward for equal treatment with the Indians, as well as too lazy to compete with them for manual labor, and too inept to compete commercially with the Chinese, Burmese easily associated their complaints against colonial rule with the Asian immigrant communities. J. S. Furnivall, who would later develop the idea of plural society, found when he arrived in Rangoon in 1908 a city focussed on profit only and uninterested in the welfare of Burma generally. As he observed in one letter:

the only link between all these individuals of different nationalities has been the lust of acquisition, immediate and personal profit has been the aim of almost every one of them, a crowd of greedy folk recognizing no duty to the country where they have been striving to make their fortunes, no common principle to which they owe allegiance but the single principle of making money. There has not even been the check of complying with the traditions of the country; those of the Burmans are of no account, and the impersonal rule of an official hierarchy has no effectual tradition save that of leaving things alone . . . and the Burman who would talk with the European in the Rangoon streets must speak in Hindustani.[10]

Burmese feelings of exclusion were bolstered by immigrant dominance in commerce, industry, and administration. Hindustani, for example, emerged as the lingua franca of the colonial capital and Europeans in government (and often even commercial) service were required to pass exams in this language and not Burmese. As colonial Burma was administered as part of British India until 1937 and many of those British companies that dominated commercial life in Rangoon had already emerged within the Indian context, Indians found it easier than Burmese to dominate middle and lower echelon commercial and government positions. Brahmin Hindus, for example, monopolized the cash departments of British companies in the city. Other immigrant groups were able to bring skills learned at home to monopolize particular occupational niches. Thus, Ooriyas living in Rangoon worked mainly on the docks or on the railways; Tamils who did not venture into the countryside to become field laborers worked the Rangoon rice mills or became government or commercial clerks; Chittagonians worked on the river boats, including the big river steamers of the Irrawaddy Flotilla Company, and Telugus provided muscle for factories, mills, and transport.[11] Among Chinese immigrants, people from Guangdong Province dominated the construction industry and the Hokkien dialect group from Fujian Province dominated gold selling and other trades. Above everyone sat the European population of the city.

The Burmese who attempted to make a life for themselves in Rangoon were the outsiders in a very real sense. As former British residents remembered, Rangoon was unique in the social segregation of different ethnic communities. The critical mass of foreign settlement meant that it was possible in Rangoon, to a degree not found elsewhere in the colony, to recreate "home" in miniature, where one did not have to – or perhaps should not – interact intimately with members of other communities. The two most prominent Chinese dialect groups were the Guangdong and the Hokkien, for example, and they lived in two symmetrical blocks of the town opposite each other along Dalhousie Street (today Mahabandula Street).

There were many immigrant success stories that helped to make Burmese economic disenfranchisement clear by comparison. One of the most famous Chinese success stories was the family of Chan Mah Phee. In 1861 Chan Mah Phee, a Hokkien, left Xiamen (Amoy) in Southeastern China to take up small trading in the Straits Settlements. After two years he resettled in Burma where he spent a decade trading in piece goods in independent Burma. In 1883, he established the firm Taik Leong in Rangoon, trading in oil, rice, and tobacco. As his business expanded, he bought city land, built houses and shops on it, and then rented them out, becoming the largest landowner among the Chinese community in Burma. In the late 1890s he also became the most important Chinese rice dealer in Burma. Part of

Chan Mah Phee's success can be attributed to the fact that although he did not speak English, he had married a Burmese farmer's daughter and undertook patronage of the Shwedagon Pagoda, aiding him in building up local connections that transcended the Chinese community. His son, Chan Chor Khine (born in 1886), maintained and expanded his empire while maintaining a balance between colonial Rangoon high society and his Chinese roots. The younger Chan initially received an English education at St. Paul's Institution in Rangoon, where his interest in sports was fostered and would provide the background for his position on the Rangoon Turf Club Committee and his personal collection of prize-winning racehorses. Upon the completion of his education in Rangoon, Chan's father sent him for a second education in China. After his return, Chan joined his father's company and became sole manager upon the latter's retirement. At the same time, he served as Honorary Magistrate, Councilor on the board of the Corporation of Rangoon, and member of the Burma Legislative Council. Chan's well-endowed estate, "the Brightlands," located opposite Dalhousie Park and the Royal Lakes, as well as his membership of the Orient Club, reflected his wealth and place among the general colonial elite. Nevertheless, he made certain to keep a conspicuous place at the top of Chinese society in Rangoon, serving as a trustee or president of many of the city's Chinese associations and providing patronage, such as his gift of ten acres for the construction of the Chinese High School.[12]

The promise of new opportunities and higher incomes, and the potential for a new beginning, certainly played a role in attracting immigrants to the colony. These expectations were buoyed by the well-known immigrant success stories mentioned above. However, once in Burma, particularly in Rangoon, poorer immigrants found a rougher side to life in the Big City. Many immigrant Asians in Rangoon lived and worked in such miserable conditions that they soon found the notion that life was any better in Rangoon surprising. The accommodation available was poor, a discomfort made obligatory by the low wages and debt burden of contract laborers. Often they amounted to barracks with no ventilation, poor drainage, and insufficient provision of latrines.[13]

Ethnic tensions in Rangoon would make themselves strongly felt with the impact of the Great Depression in 1930, when Rangoon experienced several major communal riots. On 5 May 1930, a severe earthquake rocked Rangoon, causing severe damage made worse by the slow colonial response, and news was received of Gandhi's arrest in India. The combination of these two events created excitement that resulted in a stoppage of dock work on 6 May, strikers demanding a pay increase. Between 14 and 22 May, two thousand Burmans were brought in to replace Indian dockworkers. The two groups came to blows on 26 May and the fighting spread into the town, leading to four days of communal rioting, bringing Rangoon to a stop. The complaint was rooted in economics, as in Rangoon Burmese were being denied dock labor in favor of imported South Indian coolies, who were preferred by the British because they were cheaper. In January 1931, Rangoon experienced another riot, this time between Burmans and Chinese, resulting in twelve deaths.[14]

RANGOON VICE

Until the last few decades of the nineteenth century, Rangoon could still be viewed as a kind of frontier town, boomtown, or at least a colonial outpost. Crime, opium, gambling, and a range of other vices were part of everyday life. As Rangoon's European population and that of Westernized Burmese, Chinese, and Indians grew, late Victorian values gradually began to influence colonial legislation. Opium had been targeted in the 1890s, after controversy over its medicinal value in the middle of the decade. Opium dens, filled with "torn mats . . . [and] grimy pillows soaked in perspiration" thrived in Rangoon into the 1930s.[15] The early twentieth century also saw a rapid increase in the use of another drug, cocaine, which colonial lawmakers argued was much worse than opium. Arguing that cocaine caused permanent problems such as loss of memory and mental control and often resulted in insanity, the Lieutenant-Governor's Council decided to bring cocaine under control in the same way as other intoxicating agents, according to the Excise Act of 1896.[16]

Another important feature of daily life in central Rangoon also became a major concern of the government. Much of the life in Rangoon after work and evening meals revolved around sex, particularly paid sex, and Rangoon saw the growth of a lively commercial sex industry; its red-light district was reportedly the largest in British India. Numerous brothels emerged around the town, becoming sites of remunerative liaisons typically between European, Indian, Chinese, and Burmese men, on the one hand, and Burmese women, on the other. Chinese, British, German, Russian, and Japanese sex workers also arrived in Rangoon to service male clientele with particular ethnic tastes and the means to indulge them.[17]

The overwhelming majority of Asian immigrants were male. In 1911, for example, among Chinese residents in Rangoon, the ratio was about one female to every five males, although by 1931 the gap had shrunk to about one in two. The disparity among Indian immigrants remained higher in

Rangoon, mainly because of the kinds of labor in which they were engaged and the fact that most of them were temporary immigrants, who sought to return to India when it became economically feasible.[18]

While many more prosperous immigrant males married Burmese women, most immigrants remained too poor to afford a family or had a family at home to support. In such circumstances, many immigrant males often turned to prostitutes. While this pattern was shared by all immigrant communities in Rangoon, a more conspicuous clientele were the British and Indian soldiers garrisoned in the town. In 1901, the Rangoon Municipal Council considered ways to resolve the problem of people loitering around the military cantonment to solicit for prostitution. This was not a problem found in Rangoon alone, for it was seen wherever military stations were found in the colony, such as at Mandalay and Thayetmyo. Nevertheless, visiting prostitutes was or became a regular activity for many Burmese males traveling to the "big city" in search of work or schooling.[19]

Prostitution in colonial Burma was legal, but frowned upon by colonial authorities and it became a recurring issue. Under the Rangoon Police Act of 1899, law enforcement was only permitted to keep prostitutes off the main streets and to act elsewhere if they had become a public annoyance. From 1901, the government adopted a segregation policy, giving powers to local government to identify prostitution-free areas where no brothels would be allowed, and thus force prostitutes to remote areas of the town. Brothels were restricted to a particular area of town and subject to closure elsewhere upon complaint. From 1914, the whole of Rangoon fell under notification, so the Commissioner of Police was authorized to close brothels at his own discretion, a power rarely exercised. An amendment in 1902 limited prostitution within central Rangoon to two areas, 33rd and 34th Streets between Fraser and Montgomery Streets and 27th, 28th, and 29th Streets between Dalhousie and Montgomery Streets.[20]

There was considerable hypocrisy in the colonial concern for isolating brothels, a reflection of earlier imported Victorian-era puritanical values. It was not uncommon for colonial officers and businessmen to keep Burmese concubines, much like Flory in George Orwell's *Burmese Days*. One man who did so was John Cowen, who had been brought to Rangoon by the local Bishop to stamp out prostitution as a sinful practice. Nonetheless, Cowen launched a vigorous propaganda campaign that targeted the civilian side of the trade, the government's complicity in making prostitution available to the troops by sanctioning prostitution areas near the barracks, and even concubinage, of which he himself was a practitioner! There were also very real health concerns regarding the spread of venereal disease, endemic but not limited to the sex trade. In one school, all Burmese boys over the age of fifteen were believed to have contracted one or another venereal disease.[21]

Rarely was the negative impact on the lives of the women drawn into the trade reflected upon until the 1920s. In 1921, with the argument that brothels were a source of venereal disease, that women kept in the brothels lived in virtual slavery, and that the operation of brothels encouraged the continual trafficking of poor Burmese girls from rural areas into the city for the purpose of prostitution, members of the Legislative Council introduced the Burma Suppression of Brothels Bill. The resulting Act made the closure of brothels not discretionary but mandatory, making it a crime for a man to live off of the earnings of a prostitute, to manage a brothel, or to traffic women and girls for immoral purposes. The Act, however, specifically limited itself to brothels and refused to penalize prostitutes themselves, for at the very least they were independent women. In 1925, the provincial government also targeted the sources of prostitutes. Attempts were made to end the trafficking of girls under fourteen years of age from impoverished families in Tavoy into Rangoon to work as servants, sometimes under work agreements, but in several cases sold outright. Such girls frequently ran away from abuse and were believed to have entered illicit Rangoon brothels. Gambling, alcohol, and drinking establishments also emerged as targets for social reform. In the first decade of the twentieth century, billiard-saloons and ring-throwing establishments provided public entertainment but also opportunities, it was claimed, for drinking and gambling, and in addition to being on the increase, a number had opened near schools and colleges in the city. Rangoon lawmakers also banned the employment of women as barmaids in liquor bars, because of the "evils which have been found to attend the employment of barmaids in Rangoon," although this was lifted sometime afterwards under pressure from angry liquor bar proprietors.[22]

THE BURMESE

Although a minority in Rangoon, the Burmese population still dominated the outer wards and had a noticeable presence in the city center. It was largely Burmese who carted in agricultural produce and other resources that were not ferried in on barges or by rail, helping to sustain the urban population and supplying the factories and commercial firms. Rangoon represented a new order of things in which the Burmese occupied the lowest rung of a colonial hierarchy that sought not to give, but to take. The best railway carriages were designated "Europeans only." Regulations stipulated that headmasters and superintendents of Anglo-Vernacular Government High Schools had to be British. Burmese names on tax revenue receipts and summonses bore inferior prefixes such as "Nga" and "Mi."[23]

Especially conspicuous in Rangoon was a small but growing group of Western-educated Burmese who were joining the lower and middle echelons of the colonial administration and Rangoon-based commercial enterprises. Rangoon's concentration of so much wealth and people in a single city encouraged a new consumerism and exposure to new, Western-oriented intellectual currents. Books and newspapers drawn from every corner of the British Empire flooded news stands and bookshops, while Western cigarettes and Virginia pipe tobaccos, the latest Western clothing fashions, and a rich medley of international foods all added to the flavor of life in central Rangoon, merely noticed by Burmese laborers, but embraced by their upwardly mobile, elite compatriots.[24]

A good example of the emerging Westernized Burmese middle class was U Kyaw Min, a prominent member of the Orient Club, the Pegu Club, and the Rangoon Golf Club. Born at Akyab in 1899 into a family of Cambridge-educated lawyers, Kyaw Min was educated in St. Anne's convent at Akyab and St. Xavier's College, Calcutta before joining Trinity Hall in Cambridge in 1918. There he became President of the Cambridge University Billiards Club and co-founded the "Crocodiles Club" which he served as treasurer and then as president; received College honours for hockey, was a first-string track runner for the college, and undertook radio communications as a hobby, before receiving his B.A. in 1921 and his law degree in 1922. He took the ICS competitive examinations in August 1922 and passed on his first attempt, becoming Headquarters Assistant, the only Burman in the ICS at the time to have qualified by competitive examination. His rise up the administrative ladder was rapid, from a subdivisional officer in 1924 to Deputy Commissioner in 1931, and to Deputy Secretary of the Education Department in 1936. After limited self-rule was inaugurated in 1937 he became Secretary of the Forest Department. Tellingly, when the Japanese invaded Burma in 1942, he chose not to remain in Burma but to retreat with the Government of Burma to Simla in India, where he spent the entire war. He served the returned Government of Burma as a commissioner from 1945 to 1947.[25] Cooperative, capable, sporting, and Western-educated, he represented the kind of Burmese that colonial authorities sought to foster.

Among those members of the Burmese middle class who participated in government service, either in Rangoon or on tour in one of the rural districts, feelings of social isolation were probably common. Until the mid-1930s, Burmese officers had mimicked the dress of their European counterparts, complete with trousers and coat. This was partly to prevent the Burmese official from being confused with other Burmese and thus of inferior social status. Learning English was perceived as the key to professional and social advancement, so much so that some "attached so much importance to acquiring the correct English accent that they had succeeded in learning very little else." Even so, throughout Burma there had always been a bar to Burmese participation in the social life of colonial officialdom. European and Burmese officers had separate clubs. While Europeans belonged to Gymkhana Clubs in different government stations, Burmese joined Burmese officer clubs, and if there were none of the latter, they joined the Rotary Club, the oldest club in Burma. Although Europeans might sponsor a Burmese, if he had effectively adopted European manners, for membership in the Gymkhana Club, social interaction with other club members was often minimal. Club activities were beyond the normal experiences of Burmese and some had not yet become skilled in playing bridge, tennis, golf, or polo. As one Burmese officer remembered, "It was an artificial life as there was very little in common between me and the non-Burmese members of the Club." Constitutional change would encourage changes in the ways in which Burmese officers perceived their place in colonial society. In the mid-1930s, as Burma headed toward home rule, younger Burmese officers had begun to abandon European dress and instead wear *longyis* and *gaungbaungs* (a turban-like headdress). While some did so for nationalist reasons, others did so for comfort after deciding that it was no longer necessary to prove social equality with British officers.[26]

While the colonial government grappled with prostitution, city planning, and increasing state revenues, this emerging class of educated Burmese was more concerned about the degradation of their culture and the decline of Buddhism under British rule. As an ethnic minority in the country's largest and most important city, there was an increasing awareness among them of their own vulnerability to becoming lost in the multicultural urban milieu, especially under foreign rulers uninterested in involvement in such matters. As the Burmese language was no longer the medium of commerce and administration, it became more closely linked to ethnic identity, just as Buddhism, no longer the state religion, had also become a mark of being Burmese. Growing self-awareness contributed to and was strengthened by the emergence of a vernacular press.[27]

The sense of alienation and second-rate status in Rangoon and other important towns intersected with this clarification or production of ethnic

identity to contribute to Burmese Buddhist communalism and the realization that if they were to be preserved under colonial rule, the Burmese
had to act to save themselves. From the late nineteenth and early twentieth
centuries onward, Buddhist lay organizations began to emerge everywhere,
often founded and led by Burmese who had been educated in Western or
Anglo-Vernacular Schools and who were able to mobilize Western organizational techniques and media (such as the new vernacular newspapers)
to promote traditional culture and Buddhism. Many such organizations
soon reorganized into a larger body, the Young Men's Buddhist Association
(YMBA), which was founded in 1906.[28] The YMBA's chief concern was
the decline of Burmese civilization. As one of its founders complained in
1908:

> On all sides we see the ceaseless, ebbless tide of foreign civilization and learning
> steadily creeping over the land, and it seems to me that unless we prepare ourselves
> to meet it, to overcome it, and to apply it to our own needs, our national character,
> our institutions, our very existence as a distinct nationality will be swept away,
> submerged, irretrievably lost.[29]

Direct confrontation with the government took place as a result of the
"shoe question." In 1916, a young lawyer, U Thein Maung, found a sign
at the Shwe Sandaw Pagoda in Prome that read "No one permitted to wear
shoes in this Pagoda but Englishmen and Asiatic Europeans." He replaced
the sign with another that banned footwear for everyone and refused to
take it down a few months later. The local deputy commissioner demanded that Thein Maung provide scriptural evidence regarding footwear
removal. The *Thathanabaing*, a government appointee, refused to intercede
and Thein Maung brought the matter before the YMBA. The YMBA
passed two resolutions. First, it would protest the use by foreign companies
of the Buddha and pagodas in their trade or brand marks. Second, it would
protest the wearing of footwear in religious precincts and order members to
put up signs to this effect at all religious places. As the pagodas throughout
Burma began to put up signs, tensions grew. One angry monk even took
a knife and cut the face of an offending European who had walked upon
the sacred ground of the Mahamuni Shrine in Mandalay with his shoes
on. In May 1918, the YMBA also demanded the removal of the British
war cemetery and cantonment on Shwedagon Hill in Rangoon. After the
government raised questions about whether the YMBA had the right to
engage in political activity, for the shoe question had now become a political
issue, older members of the YMBA including many government servants
were pressured to leave the association. Younger, more radical members

would soon form a new political organization to continue the struggle over the shoe question and to push for Burmese home rule.[30]

ANTI-COLONIALISM AND NATIONALISM

Some scholars have argued that pacification was never complete and that Burmese resistance to British rule continued until the latter left. Nevertheless, modern nationalism was indeed new and unfamiliar to the bulk of Burma's general population. So too were the organizational techniques of Western politics. It would take several decades for a handful of Burmese thinkers and political activists to develop popular acceptance of and participation in both. Modern Burmese nationalism slowly emerged over the first few decades of the twentieth century. The defeat of a European power by an Asian one in the Russo-Japanese War of 1904–05 was one source of encouragement. In 1908, a Japanese movie exhibition brought gas-lit projectors and a film of the actual fighting in that war to Rangoon. The film, shown in darkened areas on the streets, was the first movie ever shown in Burma.[31]

An especially important figure in the early stages of Burmese nationalism was the Buddhist monk, U Ottama (1879–1939). Ottama was an Arakanese monk who had gone to India to teach Pali and Buddhism at the National College and was eventually drawn into the Indian National Congress, which spearheaded Indian anti-colonial efforts. Ottama thus gained familiarity with modern political campaigning. He soon left India and traveled to various countries, including China, Korea, Vietnam, the United States, Britain, and Japan, observing their contemporary condition relative to Burma, before returning to Burma in 1918. Ottama had been particularly struck by the example of modernization in Japan, another Asian country. Both in his writings and in speeches (re-circulated in the vernacular press) during his tours of the colony, Ottama informed Burmese of Japan's ongoing industrialization and urged them to follow Japan's example of self-development.[32]

Ottama was imprisoned in 1921 for denouncing imperialism in a speech, but immediately resumed his anti-government activities within weeks of his release from prison in August 1924. In Mandalay, police stopped a procession organized by Ottama leading to violence that left several dead and many wounded. Ottama ran into trouble again in early October when he was charged with sedition for two speeches he made in Rangoon and imprisoned for three years with hard labor. His sentence was viewed as too harsh for a monk and led to a demonstration in Fytche Square in downtown

Rangoon by a crowd led by outraged monks. After three warnings to disperse were ignored, aside from booing, Rangoon City Mounted Police were then ordered to charge the crowd. In the ensuing violence, in which the monks resisted the police, a number of monks were injured. When popular demands were made for an inquiry into police behavior, the colonial government refused, arguing that no inquiry was needed because no one had been hurt in the incident. In reality, the wounded had not gone to hospital for fear of arrest. The Rangoon authorities then banned all public meetings in Rangoon for a month. After the Fytche Square Incident, Governor Sir Spencer Harcourt Butler received a telegraph from an assembly of monks at Moulmein calling Ottama's arrest unlawful, for it interfered with the Buddhist religion. The monks offered to take Ottama's place in prison and demanded the repeal of the section of the Penal Code by which Ottama was convicted. The Governor responded that it did not amount to interference with religion, as none of Burma's residents were above the law, and he argued that it was against Buddhist tenets to spread hatred for the established government. Monks in Rangoon took more direct action. After confronting non-European police officers on patrol and threatening to kill them if they did not resign, gangs of monks knifed four Europeans in a series of attacks. As for Ottama, he was imprisoned again and would remain there until his death behind bars in 1939.[33]

The delay by colonial authorities in responding to indigenous desires for participation in the administration of the colony helped to sustain Ottama's early activism and popularity. The Secretary of State for India, Lord Montagu, was partly to blame for Burmese disappointment. He had made a declaration on 21 August 1917 in the House of Commons that included the possibility of Indian self-government. As Burma was a province of India, some Burmese believed that self-rule was on its way for their country as well. Subsequent Burmese demands for reform may have come as a surprise to British authorities, for colonial authorities such as the former Lieutenant-Governor of Burma (1910–1915), Harvey Adamson, believed that the Burmese were unprepared educationally or politically for self-rule; Adamson argued at the time that the Burmese intelligentsia were fifty years behind that of India. The joint report drawn up by Lords Montagu and Chelmsford (thus known as the Montagu–Chelmsford reforms), which led to the Government of India Act, 1919, excluded Burma, declaring that its political development would be left aside as a separate issue to be dealt with at some point in the future.[34]

Burmese advocates of Home Rule continued to press for the same concessions for Burma as were granted to India in the Montagu–Chelmsford scheme. Lieutenant-Governor Sir Reginald Craddock disliked the proposed reforms and suggested a modified scheme in May 1919 that called for indirect election to the Legislative Council for rural areas and direct election for special constituencies and towns. The Executive would consist of four boards and heading each board would be a non-official member of the Legislative Council who would not be responsible to the legislature. As Craddock further elaborated in April 1920, he was also against Burma's separation from India. It was probable that Burma would ultimately separate from India, after further political development. In the meantime, if that view was taken and reasonable recognition was given of Burma's differences with the Indian Provinces, Burma would benefit from its continued membership in the Government of India's "family of provinces." Indians who lived in Burma, he argued, had no reason to fear ultimate separation, for there were no measures in preparation to restrict any of their privileges as British subjects in Burma. Nevertheless, Indians, he continued, should remember their obligations regarding living in Burma and not disturb the "calm atmosphere" of Burma with essentially Indian problems.[35]

In early 1920, Burma was shaken by a large number of unrelated labor strikes. In this volatile context, the University Act Bill was submitted for discussion in the Legislative Council. Many Burmese viewed the proposed Act, and the requirement that classes be taught in English, as a means of preventing them from overcoming the claims of the Montagu–Chelmsford reform scheme. Although rural Burmese had contributed to the University Endowment Fund by collections at festivals held all over Burma, they had little hope of sending their children to the university. Burmese political associations asked that passage of the bill be suspended until the Reformed Legislative Council was put in place, but the Lieutenant-Governor refused. Instead, he opted to enlarge the Legislative Council with the inclusion of prominent Burmans who were associated with opposition to the bill. Although the latter fought in the Legislative Council for additional concessions, the bill was made law anyway.[36]

Rangoon College students went on strike on 5 December 1920. The students were going to "smash" the University Act because, they argued, it was nothing more than a government instrument to "keep the nation in chains." Burma, they claimed, needed a "national college" where the kind of education that was suited to the "sons of the soil" could be given. In part their complaints were over issues of powers and representation. Students had not been asked for their views on the Act and now they demanded that the university council and senate should represent all classes of people and views and that students should have representation as well. Moreover, the

Chancellor's power should be less arbitrary and he should not be able to appoint professors directly. The demands also related to university requirements and costs. The university, for example, was to be residential, making the cost prohibitive to poor Burmese. More importantly, the fact that instruction would be in English not only disadvantaged Burmese and Indian students but also lengthened the term and thus the cost of study because it meant a preliminary year course in English had to be undertaken.[37]

As the student boycott movement spread throughout the colony and soon involved virtually all government schools, it became the vanguard of political unrest directed at colonial rule. Strikers organized ninety national schools all over Burma and a national college in Rangoon.[38] Ultimately, the strike helped to foster greater political awareness and solidarity among Burmese across the colony, a development that pushed the British to grant the colony greater political concessions than it had formerly been willing to make.

The political awakening that was occurring among Burmese was soon channeled into electoral politics. In 1921, the Secretary of State for India finally recommended to Parliament the extension of the Act of 1919 to Burma. Under diarchy, certain non-critical areas of government would be "transferred" to two Burmese ministers chosen by the Legislative Council, while all other areas of importance to the Indian Government would be "reserved" and remain under the control of the Governor (who would replace the lieutenant-governorship on the establishment of diarchy in 1923). A committee under Sir A. F. Whyte visited Burma in 1922 to examine the degree of self-rule that would be appropriate to Burma and how to determine "reserved" and "transferred" subjects. The Committee's proposed Draft Rules were accepted with minor modification by Parliament and were put into force with the arrival of Harcourt Butler as Governor on 2 January 1923. The irony, as pointed out by one scholar, was that although the British had originally intended to give Burma less than was given to India, the terms of the extension of this Act to Burma in 1923 proved to be more liberal than those that had been granted to India. First, women were given complete equality with men because of their allegedly high social status in Burma. Second, the franchise was much wider than in India because of the greater diffusion in Burma of elementary education. Under the "diarchy" system, the executive authority was vested in the Executive Council, called the Governor-in-Council. This consisted of two members in control of transferred subjects, including Agriculture, Education, Excise and Forests, Local Self-Government, and Public Health, and two members in control of reserved subjects, including Finance, General and Judicial Administration,

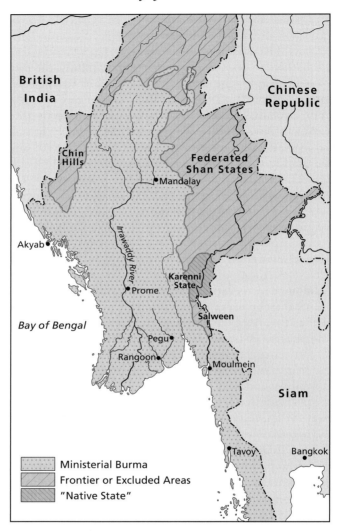

Map 1 Colonial Burma

Police, and Revenue. The former were designated Ministers and were chosen from and responsible to the Legislative Council, while the latter were responsible to the Governor and not to the Legislative Council.[39]

Diarchy was not for everyone. The colonial authorities had other plans for the ethnic minorities in the hill areas. There, according to colonial authorities, "racial" and local administrative peculiarity meant that integrating them with the rest of Burma would be a bad idea. There was probably also some truth to claims that the authorities were responding to local desires, for these areas had always enjoyed substantial autonomy from precolonial central control and this autonomy, including the local authority of the Shan *sawbwas*, had been preserved thus far under colonial rule. Under diarchy, local autonomy might easily be eroded by a Burman majority that would presumably dominate the forthcoming Legislative Assembly, despite significant and automatic representation of several ethnic groups in that body (the so-called "reserved seats"). In 1922, the Kachin Hills, the Chin Hills, and the Shan states were thus placed under a new civil service called the Burma Frontier Service. The Shan states were divided into two newly created administrative units, the Northern Shan State and the Southern Shan State, and these two halves were joined together in another new administrative unit called the Federated Shan States, headed by an advisory council, and administered through a commissioner appointed by the Governor of Burma. This arrangement would isolate the Shans and others from further constitutional reforms granted to what became ministerial Burma until the end of the colonial period. Even during the Japanese occupation period, the Shan states and the other frontier areas would remain separate from the lowland Burmese administration.[40] In the longer term, it set the stage for the continuity of divisions that have fueled an ongoing civil war.

Ethnic minorities in the hill areas were not the only ones who feared Burmese domination. There were of course the substantial Chinese and Indian communities, both of which Burmese nationalists increasingly characterized as foreign and unwanted in the country. A smaller, though very important group concentrated in Rangoon were the Anglo-Burmans, often the children of unions between European men and Burmese women, but sometimes vice versa. They sat uneasily between two worlds, one Burmese-speaking and indigenous and the other English-speaking and foreign. Many Burmese nationalists viewed them as part of the colonial elite, benefiting from advantages in commerce and administration that stemmed from their connexion with the British colonial establishment, their Western education, or both. After independence, many would lose their businesses with the introduction of Burmanization programs. Many Anglo-Burmans had indeed become successful in the colonial period, but, like many of their Westernized Burmese compatriots, they also served as an intellectual bridge between the West and Burma. Still, fear of being overwhelmed or cast out by majority Burmese rule would lead them to seek special recognition and legal protection when Burma headed for self-rule in the years ahead.[41]

Aside from the university strike and the introduction of diarchy, the most important political development in colonial Burma in the 1920s was the emergence and then fissure of the General Council of Burmese Associations (GCBA). In September 1920, the aforementioned YMBA split into two groups. The younger, more radical, and larger group established a new organization, the GCBA, which supported the university boycott. Two men soon came to dominate the GCBA, the great orator, Tharrawaddy U Pu, who served as president and the forty-three-year-old U Chit Hlaing (1879–1952), the son of a teak merchant educated in London with a degree in law, who served as secretary. The GCBA experienced its own division in 1922 over the issue of how to react to the diarchy reforms. While the main GCBA leadership opposed cooperation with the government and sought immediate dominion status for Burma, twenty-one prominent members who disagreed with this policy and sought to fight for concessions within the forthcoming Burma Legislative Council left the GCBA and formed the Nationalist Party. The GCBA, however, clung to non-cooperation. This proved a disaster for the GCBA in the long run. First, staying out of the Council meant that the GCBA was steadily deprived of supporters from among the more anxious urban politicians who sought to legitimate their nationalist credentials, in the eyes of the government, through open election. Second, by virtually abandoning the Council and the urban electorate to opposing parties, the GCBA found that it increasingly depended upon rural and small town branches of the party. When GCBA politicians preached Home Rule to villagers, they quickly learned that the latter misunderstood the call to mean the abolition of taxes and the restoration of the monarchy. Party leaders thus often found themselves outside their element.[42]

In 1925, the GCBA finally resolved to fight for Home Rule both within and without the Council. It would also encourage Burmese to resist and thus make rule through the Legislative Council impossible. The party now sought to purge the GCBA of title and place-hunters, promote the election of Home Rule candidates who would obstruct the work of the Council if their demands were not met, to organize Burmese labor, to improve industry and agriculture, and, hopefully, to affiliate with the British Labor Party, who had the means to guarantee that Parliament would hear about Burmese grievances.[43]

BURMESE WOMEN

Although, as mentioned, Burmese women were accorded higher status under diarchy than their counterparts in India, the position of women in colonial Burmese society was by no means equal to that of men. While they could vote under the new system, they could not yet hold office and hot debates broke out in the Legislative Council as to whether they should be accorded this right as well. On this issue, the extension of further constitutional rights was favored more by Rangoon-based representatives, both Burmese and non-Burmese alike, than by representatives elected by constituencies outside Rangoon. The main reason for this divide was that the image of women and their proper place in Burmese society differed between the cosmopolitan, foreign-oriented world of Rangoon and the tradition-entrenched world of the village whose grip even included important towns like Mandalay.

Western observers had early on remarked on what they saw as the independence of Burmese women.[44] Positioned as the mirror image of Burmese men, whom the colonial discourse tended to portray as lazy and backward, women were portrayed as hardworking and industrious. Indeed, as the country's small traders they were highly visible to Europeans in the urban centers, who rarely stepped outside the confines of town even to notice Burmese men at work in the fields, though of course women were hard at work here too. Colonial photography and literature eventually emphasized the "exotic" Burmese beauty and replaced images of women pounding unhusked rice with studio shots of brightly clad women posing with parasols and long cheroots. Orwell in *Burmese Days* and other writings contributed as well to a notion of the sexual accessibility of Burmese women, which was strengthened by Rangoon's growing reputation as the main center for prostitution in British India. Even so, Europeans and Western-educated Asians in Rangoon never questioned the intellectual independence of the Burmese woman.

In the later 1920s, Western-educated Burmese politicians argued forcefully that Burmese women should have full political equality with men.[45] Burmese politicians from rural constituencies, however, fought to counter such views. In traditional Burmese Buddhist society, they argued, Burmese women were not equal to men. As U Kyaw Dun (representative of Mandalay Rural) argued before the Burma Legislative Council in 1927,

The faults of women mentioned by the Buddha are too numerous . . . Women have seven [sic] inherent faults, namely, untruthfulness, artfulness, indiscretion, vanity, uncleanliness and cruelty. The wise and the virtuous have never placed women on the same footing as men. Placing women in the same position as men amounts to damnation of women to hell. According to the time honoured Buddhist custom, a woman has to walk behind a man in travelling. She has to sleep and eat after her husband. All these prove woman's inferiority . . . Western customs have been introduced into our country. I beg you not to adopt them wholesale. Our customs are quite different from those of the Western countries . . . [46]

Kyaw Dun's argument was not unrepresentative of the prevailing views of Burmese men who eschewed "Western" influences. Their continuity with the precolonial past is indicated in part by the late-1870s writings of U Po Hlaing, in then independent Upper Burma, who made the same general observations about the proper role of Burmese women in Burmese Buddhist society.[47] These views, including the importance of preventing Western notions from influencing Burmese society, would persist beyond independence and six decades later would echo among the many arguments set forth by a military government attempting to prevent a Western-educated Burmese woman, Aung San Suu Kyi, from gaining leadership over the country.

SEPARATION FROM INDIA

The Government of India Act of 1919 had stipulated that after ten years a Statutory Commission would be appointed for examining progress made in education and representative institutions and on the working of the government system. Sir John Simon was appointed as the Chairman in 1928. The Simon Commission, which visited Burma in 1928–1929 as part of its mandate to examine representative institutions in India, including Burma, recommended abolishing the diarchy system and increasing provincial autonomy as much as possible. The first Indian Round Table Conference held in London in 1930–1931 supported Burma's separation from India. A special Burma Round Table Conference was held in London in 1931–1932 where nearly all of the Burmese participants confirmed that they favored separation in principle, but disagreed on certain details.[48]

The 1932 Burma Legislative Council elections largely focussed on the question of separation. Some Burmese politicians favored separation, while others formed a noisy anti-separationist alliance. The latter argued that Burma's connection with India should continue until India had achieved full dominion status; otherwise Burma would be relegated, as a crown colony, to a status inferior to that of India, should the latter become a dominion. The anti-separationists won a majority of the seats and the new Legislative Council adopted a resolution opposing either separation from or federation with India. Parliament decided that since the Burmese could not settle the separation issue, the British government would decide for them, resulting in the India Act, 1935 (reenacted separately for Burma as the Government of Burma Act, 1935), which included a new constitution for Burma. Burma was now to be a unitary state separate from India.[49]

The Government of Burma Act of 1935, not put into force until 1937, established a new structure of government, in which the Governor remained the head of the executive with the assistance of a ten-member Council of Ministers. The Governor also chose these ministers, including the Chief Minister, who was called the Prime Minister. The Legislature was expanded to two houses. The Senate consisted of thirty-six members, half elected by members of the House of Representatives and the other half nominated by the Governor. The House consisted of 132 members elected by different geographical, ethnic, organizational, and commercial constituencies. The qualifications for franchise were reduced. Now, the payment of any municipal tax qualified a member of a municipality to vote, while the rural vote was limited to the payment of tax or the possession of land revenue of not less than five rupees. Any laws passed by the legislature were subject to veto, first by the Governor, and, second, by the Secretary of State.[50]

A NEW GENERATION

A new, more cosmopolitan generation of Burmese leaders was emerging from Rangoon University (RU) in the early Depression years. Some were conservative and Western looking. They bought English pipes, then in fashion among their peers, at department stores such as Rowe & Co. in downtown Rangoon, and pinned their hopes for future success on winning positions in the Indian Civil Service. Other students and graduates looked at the colonial government and the West in a different, more critical way. In 1930, students and recent graduates of RU formed the Dobama Asiayone (We Burmans Association). They protested against British rule and called for the creation of a national organization to put forth demands for Burmese rights. They made their rejection of subservient status to the colonizers known by abandoning the use of Maung or Ko before their names and replacing it with Thakin, or "Master," indicating that they were the masters in their own country. This was highly symbolic; as in the case of "sahib" in India, "thakin" was the term that Burmese were expected to use in addressing the British. They also wrote and sang the Dobama song as their anthem (which would later become the national anthem of independent Burma) and replaced the peacock of the Burmese royal household with a tricolor flag representing the Burmese nation as their banner. Some British observers and conservative Burmese condemned the Thakins as hotheaded young men, but they emerged as popular leaders among the Burmese in general. The Thakins organized cultivators, laborers, education circles, and itinerant libraries, as well as a parliamentary political group, the Ko Min Ko Chin Party. However, the Thakins lacked any coherent ideology, loosely borrowing ideas from the Irish Sinn Fein, Hitler, Mussolini, Lenin, and Kemal Ataturk.[51]

As many of Burma's future leaders spent the early and mid-1930s together in RU, their experiences there in student organizations and their development of strategies to deal with the Principal, the hard-working but stubborn D. J. Sloss, were an important influence in shaping how Burmese leaders would deal with British diplomats after the war and with parliamentary democracy and state building from 1948. As U Nu, Burma's future prime minister and an RU alumnus, later admitted, at this time everything British school authorities did was perceived as imperialist in intent, and RUSU leaders took it upon themselves to protest Sloss's efforts to develop the university into a world-class institution. When Sloss rejected their attempts to reverse a decision he had made for preliminary examinations, on the grounds that he refused to be intimidated by RUSU, Nu and his friends used their connexions to editors at Burmese newspapers to plant stories that Sloss had actually rejected Burmese political parties and Burmese political leadership in general. Although Sloss demanded a retraction, the newspapers refused. The RUSU leaders then began to make speeches to mass meetings in and outside of Rangoon (see Fig. 2.3), calling for Sloss's resignation. The Governing Board of the University soon caved in and canceled the preliminary examinations.[52]

The students rose to national prominence as nationalist leaders as a result of the university strike at RU in 1936. Among the organizers and leaders of the strike were many of the main national leaders of post-war Burma. The main force behind the strike was the RUSU. Nu was elected to the post of President of RUSU in August 1935. He stood out partly because he was a few years older than the other students, for he was a graduate of the university, who had returned for a law degree. One of the powers behind the scene in the election was U Kyaw Nyein, Nu's future political rival, who chose not to stand for election and among the other candidates elected for the nine posts on the RUSU executive committee was Ko Aung San, the future father of Burmese independence. Aung San was selected by the committee to serve as editor for RUSU's magazine, the *Oway*. Among others involved in the magazine was the future Communist leader, Thakin Than Tun, who provided material for publication.[53]

Figure 2.3 Colonial architecture in Rangoon today

RUSU became involved in several disputes between students and the university in late 1935. The most important occurred as a result of the publication in *Oway* in late February of an article written under a pseudonym by one of Aung San's friends. The article, entitled "Hell Hound at Large," was a satirical treatment of the sexual advances of an unnamed Burmese member of the university administrative staff to female students. As the article described the administrator: "A pimping knave with avuncular pretensions to some cheap wiggling wenches from a well-known hostel . . . His only distinguishing marks were buboes and ulcers due to errant whoring." Although Sloss was said to be aware of the author's identity, Aung San refused to confirm it.[54]

With Nu already expelled and an order to expel Aung San from the university imminent, the other seven members of the RUSU Executive Committee made two resolutions. First, they would refuse to sit for the University examinations. Second, they would hold a general meeting of the student body in Union Hall on 26 February 1936 to inform them of the first resolution. At the meeting, the students determined to undertake strike action at the Shwedagon Pagoda in downtown Rangoon. There, the strikers would remain for the next two months. To provide for supreme authority over the student strikers, a Boycotter's Council was created, consisting of the nine members of the RUSU Executive Council and two representatives each from the twelve university hostels. Due to its large size, a smaller inner council was created, with Nu as President, U Raschid as Vice-President, and Aung San as Secretary. Rangoon's general population supported the strikers materially and in spirit. They were also supported by the Burmese press – and were criticized by the two English newspapers in town.[55]

On the day of the examinations, Raschid was sent with 600 strikers to picket the university entrances. Although some students did sit for the exams, these were very few in number, leading to a postponement of the examinations. The inner council now determined on making formal demands and publicizing them to the Burmese public. The demands included the reinstatement of expelled students, changes in the University Act to allow the RUSU to seat two representatives on the University Council, the holding of examinations a month after the end of the strike, and a greater role for students in the management of campus hostels. The University finally conceded on most of these demands and the strike was officially called off on 10 May 1936. Ultimately, Professor Pe Maung Tin replaced Sloss as the principal of the university, becoming the first Burmese to head the institution.[56]

The RUSU strike brought to the fore of Burmese politics a new generation of Burmese leaders. Aung San, Nu, Than Tun, and others were able to use Western institutions and political tactics against the British, as were more established politicians such as Ba Maw. What set the RUSU protestors apart was their solidarity, their ability to mobilize themselves and others without the complications of overdeveloped egos. While the Burmese politicians of the 1920s often sought to promote themselves at the expense of national solidarity, the student leaders acted more as comrades than as political competitors. This new attitude and willingness to suppress individual rivalries for the national cause would contribute heavily to the forging of alliances that carried Burma to independence a decade later.

CONCLUSION

Colonial Rangoon's place as the center of colonial life and politics naturally made it the site for some of the most important confrontations between the Burmese and the British. The position of the Burmese as a minority in the city contributed to the mounting tension. It was thus in Rangoon that the impact of British rule and the economic domination of Western commerce and Asian immigrant minorities was clearest, or at least in the case of the latter this image was most easily manufactured, and most despised. These perceptions would be carried into the countryside, often by the vernacular press, but more frequently by Rangoon-based Burmese politicians.

At the same time, colonial Rangoon was included in a circuit of colonial ports that connected Burma with intellectual and material flows emanating from Europe, and particularly from Britain. New consumer items, the latest fashions, new political ideas, and news from around the globe contributed to the emergence of a new Burmese self-awareness that no longer merely drew upon Burma's precolonial past, but also on the international present. Westernization became equated with modernization and advancement. Burmese attraction to industrializing Japan, for example, was not due to the continuity of Japanese traditional culture, but the fact that an Asian people could develop a state and economy that was equal to those of the Europeans. This did not mean that the "colonial" Burmese were not informed to a strong degree by the precolonial past. Instead, recognition of the importance of the latter was cultivated in new lay associations built upon Western organizational models.

Rangoon thus made an important transition in the colonial period, from a foreign control center, to the center of Burmese nationalist activity. In the years that lay ahead, Rangoon would maintain its place as the center of the Burmese state for well over half a century. Nevertheless, its "foreignness" would remain an important issue throughout the post-independence period.

CHAPTER 3

Self-government without independence,
1937–1947

Historians usually view the late 1930s and the Japanese occupation period (1942–1945) separately. Certainly, in the context of the greater Asia-Pacific region, Burma can be viewed as an example of a colony that was shaken and redirected by Japanese wartime occupation. From the perspective of Burmese efforts to achieve independence from Britain, however, late 1930s parliamentarianism and "independence" under the Japanese between 1942 and 1945 were part of a single period in which unique circumstances allowed the Burmese to gain fluctuating degrees of independence and experiment with different models of government and political control. Thus examining the 1937–1947 years as a single period makes good sense, at least in terms of Burma's political history.

During this period, the Burmese experienced different political arrangements under the British and the Japanese that allowed for limited self-rule, but never complete independence. The main reason was that the controlling power, whether Britain or Japan, was reluctant either to lose control of the Burmese economy and Burma's resources or to compromise broader regional security (in Britain's case, the security of India; in Japan's, its strategic position in wartime Southeast Asia). At no point prior to 1947 was Burma a unified whole, the Scheduled Areas (later renamed the Frontier Areas) remaining separate from parliamentary (lowland) Burma under both the British and the Japanese.

Given the entrenched British interests in Burma, it would be difficult to imagine the constitutional situation being any better during these years had World War II not broken out. At the same time, while the Japanese occupation did not create the nationalist forces that would drive Burma to independence in 1948, it did help to clear the political field of conservative and moderate politicians who might have provided more competition to Aung San and other leftwing politicians. The Japanese occupation and its collapse also ruined the reputation of Ba Maw, arguably pre-war Burma's foremost political leader. Ultimately, the assassination of Aung San thrust into the forefront of national politics the unlikely figure of Nu, both charismatic and erratic. Another impact of the war was that Burma was laid waste by both sides as the colony became a battleground. The ruination of the colonial economy would hamper Burma's post-war economic recovery in the decades ahead. This was indeed a decade of important and unpredictable change.

THE BA MAW, PU, AND SAW GOVERNMENTS

Separation from India occurred with a perhaps unexpected ease. Upon the commencement of separation, Burmese members simply vacated their seats in the Indian Legislative Assembly. It also had little impact on the colonial administrators in Burma itself. Since Burma was no longer part of India, ICS officers posted to Burma had the choice to retire, to transfer to India, or to join the new Burma Civil Service, and the vast majority chose the third option, mainly because they were familiar with Burma and did not want to be burdened with adjusting to a new linguistic and cultural environment. Indians and other minorities living in Burma were concerned about their status and security in a Burmese-ruled state. These concerns grew when Burmese politicians turned their attention to taking control over the Rangoon Corporation. In 1937, the thirty-three councilors managing the Corporation consisted of two Chinese, three Anglo-Indians, nine Indians, eight Europeans, and eleven Burmese. Now, Burmese politicians pushed through a bill in the House of Representatives to increase Burmese representation on the Council to 50 percent.[1] As separation turned to nationalization, Asian immigrant communities in Rangoon grew concerned about how far the new Burmese government would go.

In reality, the new Burmese government was saddled with too many other problems, including its own instability, to present an important threat to anyone. U Ba Pe's United Party had won the most seats in the 1936 election and Ba Pe was thus asked to form a government. Over the course of the next two months, however, Ba Pe proved either unable or unwilling to negotiate with other parties and proposed only members of the United Party for cabinet positions. Ba Maw, who had campaigned to wreck the Constitution, dropped this course of action and joined a coalition of seven parties, leading by March to his selection as Prime Minister of the prospective government, although at Ba Maw's request this title was changed to that of Premier. Ba Maw's government, however, never proved to be very stable and in 1938 found itself increasingly mired in strike actions by labour, especially by oilfield workers. Rioting broke out in July between Burmese and Indians as the result of the publication of a pamphlet, deriding Gotama Buddha, authored by a Burmese Muslim. In December, the arrest of two university students led the RUSU to launch a protest demonstration at the Government Secretariat. After police brutally broke up the student demonstration, the death of one student was taken up as a cause by the Burmese press and student strikes now broke out throughout the country. In February 1939, police fired on demonstrators in Mandalay, killing seventeen, including many Buddhist monks. The Ba Maw coalition government could no longer maintain its position and by the end of the month, U Pu became the new premier.[2]

In September 1939, World War II broke out in Europe when Germany invaded Poland. This event changed London's attitude to the Burmese government as Britain now sought solidarity in the empire for the fight against fascism. Governor Sir Archibald Cochrane requested that Pu solicit a formal declaration of war from the Burmese legislature, but Pu refused, on the grounds that it would split his party. On 18 November 1939, the Thakins, the All-Burma Students' Organization, and the Sinyetha Party of Dr. Ba Maw created the Burma Freedom Bloc Organization under the secretaryship of Aung San, to push the British to set a definite date for Burmese independence in exchange for Burmese participation on the Allied side in the war. Winston Churchill, who had replaced Neville Chamberlain as British Prime Minister shortly after the outbreak of war, however, rejected the demand. Churchill, an unashamed imperialist, would resist any move toward independence in the colonies, as he would again in Burma after the war. The Freedom Bloc organization thus launched an anti-war campaign on the grounds that the war was an imperialist war and was unrelated to the issue of Burmese independence. In its first few months, the activities of the Freedom Bloc consisted of mass meetings and anti-war demonstrations in Rangoon. The government responded by suspending civil liberties in the colony, and arrested and imprisoned leaders and members of the Freedom Bloc, forcing the Thakins and others underground.[3]

In these conditions and as a result of its own problems with the British Government, the Pu Government fell in September 1940. U Saw, the head of the Myochit Party, now became Premier. Political rivals viewed Saw as a man with fascist tendencies, especially since he had a small private army, known as the Galon Tat, which sometimes came to blows in the districts with the Thakins' own volunteer organization. Saw, like other Burmese nationalists, hoped that cooperation with the British during the war would bring complete independence and flew to London in October 1941 to gain political concessions. In a meeting with Churchill, Saw promised

Burma's loyalty in the war, but demanded the application of the third clause of the Atlantic Charter, the right of self-determination of nations, to Burma. On this basis, Saw demanded a British promise of the grant of dominion status to Burma at the end of the war. However, Burma was not promised dominion status, Churchill merely repeating the vague promise of discussions on self-government at some point after the conclusion of hostilities. Saw then turned his hopes to convincing US President Franklin D. Roosevelt to put pressure on Churchill to give in, but without success. Disappointed, Saw flew from Washington DC to Hawaii, where he would continue on to Burma. By coincidence, his plane landed in Honolulu on the night of 7 December 1941. He thus witnessed the confusion and devastation just wreaked on the US naval base there, including the crippled Pacific Fleet, many of whose surviving or destroyed vessels were still burning, and the significant casualties. The effect must have been alarming. Blocked from returning to Burma by the western route, Saw now flew east. Landing in Lisbon, he went to the Japanese embassy and reportedly offered Japan Burma's cooperation in the war. In early January 1942, as he flew on to Palestine, the British, who had become aware of the meeting, intercepted his plane in mid-air and forced it down. Saw was then sent to Uganda where he was interned in a detention camp for the duration of the war. His Myochit Party could not survive without him and disappeared from Burma's mainstream nationalist struggle. His place as Premier was given to Sir Paw Tun, who held it briefly until the government was forced to flee to India a few months later.[4]

THE THIRTY COMRADES

Although Burma had separated from India and now had limited self-government, these gains remained unsatisfactory for many Burmese nationalists. The British Governor still controlled major areas of the government and a colonial elite dominated by Europeans, Eurasians, and Asian minorities controlled the economic wealth of the country and dominated the capital, in which the Burmese population remained a minority in 1937. Burma was not yet fully extricated from a colonial empire in which "things British" remained the measure of civilization and modernization. Another model of modernization, one that was Asian and hostile to European colonialism, was Japan. British accounts of the Second World War frequently suggest surprise at the rapid pace of the Japanese conquest of Burma in 1942 and a disbelief that the Burmese would cooperate with the Japanese invader. Since the Japanese victory against the Russians in 1905, however,

Japan had been admired by nationalists throughout Southeast Asia as an Asian country that could not only adopt the best that Europe had to offer, but also use Western weaponry with success against the Europeans. Burmese intellectuals attempted to draw the attention of literate Burmese to Japan's success in everything from business to medicine. One such effort came in 1937, when Maung Khin Maung published his Burmese-language account and photographs of the machinery and factories of Nagoya, Japan, in *The Sun*.[5]

Finding little hope for his vision of complete Burmese independence in continued association with the British and, indeed, pursued by the police at home, Aung San sought support, not from the anti-Communist Japanese government, but from the Chinese Communists. On 8 August 1940, Aung San and a comrade thus slipped out of Burma on a steamer to Amoy, China. There is disagreement over whether Ba Maw and other nationalists at home had meanwhile made arrangements with the Japanese to "find" Aung San at Amoy or whether Aung San changed tactics once he was arrested by the Japanese there. In either case, Aung San now fully accepted Japanese patronage.[6]

One can easily imagine the excitement with which Aung San prepared for the liberation of Burma, a dream repeatedly stymied by the colonial authorities. In November 1940, he flew to Tokyo where he spent the next few months at the War Office with Colonel Keiji Suzuki (Bo Mogyo) outlining plans for the campaign. He would return to Burma four times between February and June 1941 to see whether the Freedom Bloc would ally with Japan and, if so, to recruit Burmese for military training by the Japanese. Aung San found among the Thakins twenty-nine recruits, soon to be known, along with Aung San as the Thirty Comrades. He secreted them out of Burma in groups during each of the four trips for Japanese training in warfare and administration. The twenty-nine members of the Thirty Comrades (one, Thakin Than Tin, had died during training on Formosa [Taiwan]) were organized into the Burma Independence Army (BIA) in Bangkok in December, in preparation for the Japanese invasion of Burma (Japan declared war on Britain on 8 December). The BIA followed the Japanese invasion route, first into Tenasserim, and then from Tavoy and Moulmein to Rangoon in March 1942 and its numbers eventually grew to 50,000 – almost as many as the Japanese invasion force of 60,000 men.[7]

Britain's neglect of Burma in the interests of India proved a decisive factor. One of the main reasons for the quick British defeat was the failure to develop a Burmese army that had an incentive to defend their own land. Separation from India had required breaking down the Indian Army of which some Burmese units were a part. Upon separation, for example, the Indian Army lost four battalions of the Burma Rifles, three units of the Indian Territorial Force, and five units of the Auxiliary Force. The British government promised, however, that Indian troops would "not normally be employed in Burma," aside from a few minor units that would remain until Burma could raise comparable units of its own. This had left the issue open as to whether the Indian Army would in future be available for the defense of Burma, which remained under consideration. To augment local forces for Burma's defense, the governor, who was still responsible for matters of defense, began to recruit soldiers for a "frontier force" from non-Burman ethnic minorities, such as the Chins, Kachins, and Karens, although this was opposed by some missionary elements in the colony.[8] Such efforts did not come to fruition by the time of the invasion and the Indian Army viewed Burma as expendable.

When a BIA unit under the command of Ne Win entered Rangoon, they found it largely deserted. The Japanese had made a devastating air attack on Rangoon on 23 December 1941, prompting a mass exodus of 75 percent of the municipality's population. While Burmese were left to fend for themselves and fled to the villages, British authorities appointed "Evacuation Officers of the Indian Evacuees" to aid the Indian population that began to "walk" to India along the Rangoon–Prome Road (some 180 miles long) and then across the Arakan Mountains. The hardships of the evacuation led to the deaths of thousands from exposure and exhaustion. British Advanced Army Headquarters, as well as administrative units and all troops not assigned to demolition, withdrew from Rangoon on 7 March 1942. As Burma was to be sacrificed to the Japanese for the better defense of India, British demolition teams were put to the task of destroying much of Rangoon's economic and transportation infrastructure. The BIA and the Japanese took Rangoon the following day. One Burmese town after another was similarly sacrificed as the British continued to retreat toward the Indian frontier. The Japanese took Prome after the British withdrawal on 2 April, and then repulsed the Chinese Fifth Army that had only recently taken up the defense of Toungoo. Mandalay, Maymyo, and many other towns fell soon after, followed by the Arakan region, until the Japanese reached the difficult, mountainous terrain to the northwest. Topography more than British military prowess halted the Japanese advance. Burma was now a land laid waste by both sides in the war. More destruction would follow.[9]

Those Allied troops captured in Burma and elsewhere were soon put to work on building a railway to supply the Japanese Army in Burma overland from Thailand. As was typical of most European colonies, the transportation infrastructure was oriented toward taking raw materials and agricultural produce to the main port to be shipped back home (and conversely to bring imports in from the colonial metropole), rather than to encouraging overland trade with neighboring colonies, one of the colonial legacies that would hamper development in the post-war years. The Japanese trans-Burma railway was thus a major feat, built across rugged terrain, in a very short period. It would run from October 1943 until very nearly the end of the war, carrying a maximum of 500 tons per day.[10] Nevertheless, this line, popularly remembered as the "death railway," caused the deaths of thousands of prisoners of war, who were worked, starved, and beaten to death in their struggle to build it, and whose graves can still be found on both sides of the Burmese-Thai border.

"SELF-RULE" UNDER THE JAPANESE

The Japanese were never really interested in Burma for itself. The real prizes of Southeast Asia were Indonesia for its oil and the Malay Peninsula for its tin and rubber. In fact the Japanese would create a lot of misery in the country when they tried to get Burma to produce something useful for the war effort, such as cotton, because rice could be had nearly everywhere else. Burma's main place in Japanese wartime planning was first as a springboard into India and second, as the western wall of a "fortress Asia" when Japanese fortunes declined (incidentally, very early in the war). Hence the Japanese Army was given considerable latitude in handling Burma and the Japanese Military Administration (JMA) could afford to make political concessions there, as well as in the Philippines, that it was unwilling to give in other areas of Southeast Asia until 1945 when the end of the war approached.

The Japanese had given permission for the BIA to organize the administration of liberated villages, towns, and districts and when Thakins under Thakin Tun Oke reached Rangoon, they organized the Bama Baho government. This made economic concessions to the Japanese and promised to pay 3,000 rupees for every Japanese killed in Burma during the war. The Thakins, however, began pushing for more independence than the Japanese were willing to concede. Moreover, the Thakins' small experience in administration made them poor rulers and they proved unable to keep law and order. The Japanese Commander-in-Chief in Burma, General Shojiro Iida, thus abolished the Bama Baho government on 5 June 1942 (he would disband the BIA the following month), turning to Burma's older, more experienced leaders instead. One day earlier, Iida had called a meeting at Maymyo of important Burmese leaders who remained in the country. He promised that in return for Burmese cooperation in the war and participation in the Greater East Asia Co-Prosperity Sphere, they could set up a Central Government under Japanese military control and later would be given independence. Ba Maw agreed and set up an interim government. A preparatory committee was then established, chaired by Ba Maw, to prepare for the creation of a Central Government. The interim government would last from 5 June to 1 August. This was replaced, from August 1942 until August 1943, by the Burmese Executive Administration, again under Ba Maw, who served as Chief Administrator as well as Executive for Internal Affairs. Soon after, the name of the committee was changed to the Provisional Government of Burma and Ba Maw was named as Prime Minister. Under the Burma Executive Administration, the whole administration, including the Chief Administrator, were under the authority of the Japanese Commander-in-Chief. Beneath him was a shadow hierarchy of Japanese officers attached to the central office of each department as well as to Burmese district officers. Burmese administrative autonomy was a myth.[11]

The Burmese Executive Administration launched countrywide campaigns in support of Japan. These claimed that the "Japanese and the Burmans were brothers, being Asiatics, that they were also of the same race and same religion, and that, therefore, they must move together with Nippon as the mighty leader." A totalitarian order would have to be established in order to win the war. Political parties were then abolished and a new unitary party was established, the Dobama Sinyetha Party, later renamed the Maha Bama Sinyetha Party. Three thousand men of the BIA, which had been disbanded in July, were remobilized under the title of the Burma Defence Army (BDA) under the command of Aung San. This army underwent instruction from Japanese officers, whom many found to be too overbearing. There were also complaints that they were underpaid.[12]

The Burmese who had welcomed the Japanese into the colony waited anxiously for independence. Movement in this direction began in early 1943. In January, the Japanese Prime Minister, General Tojo, announced before the Imperial Diet that he intended to grant Burma independence within one year. In March, Ba Maw headed a delegation, including Aung San, which flew to Tokyo to discuss the issue. The Japanese Army agreed to speed up the transition to independence in order to use Burma as an example to stimulate rebellion in India. Later in March, General Iida appointed a Supreme Court in Burma and in April he set up the twenty-two-member

Burma Independence Preparatory Committee under Ba Maw, to draft a new constitution. This body soon operated as Burma's Constituent Assembly.[13]

On 1 August, the new Constitution was finally promulgated, creating the office of *Adipati* ("dictator"), a cabinet of ministers, and a thirty-member privy council to serve as a consultative body. After Ba Maw was chosen as *Adipati*, he declared Burmese independence, formally ending the JMA. As the capital of the now independent "Bama" state, the Rangoon Municipality was eloquently renamed "Rangoon Naypyidaw." Colonel Ne Win was appointed as the commander of the new Burma National Army (BNA) that replaced the BDA, while Aung San, the Minister of Defense, devoted himself to developing the BNA into a genuine fighting force. A significant number of Burmese were then sent to the Imperial Military College in Japan.[14] Despite the formal declaration of independence, the Burmese government remained under close Japanese "guidance."

THE "OTHER" BURMA

The development of independence out of liberation required a definition of what Burma was and what it was not. The Japanese had to act both pragmatically and politically. Thailand was a wartime Japanese ally and was rewarded with various territorial concessions, including Western Laos and Western Cambodia, which were transferred from French Indochina to Thai control. Thai nationalists, borrowing from the examples of Fascist ethno-centered views of history being played out in Europe, also sought to reconnect the Thai with other branches of the "Tai race" who made up the main population of the Shan states. Ultimately, the Japanese transferred ownership of Kengtung and Mongpan States to the Thai Government.[15]

The Japanese-sponsored redefinition of Burma reinforced the rough division between ministerial Burma and the "Scheduled Areas" inherited from the pre-1942 period. The Japanese recognized the political autonomy of the Shan *sawbwas* in the states and these states were thus left out of the newly "independent" Burma under Ba Maw. Likewise, Ba Maw's Burma did not include the Karenni States, which had always enjoyed the status of a "native state" under the British. Although the Japanese could afford no major ethnic rebellions within a major war front area, which Burma constituted, ethnic tensions were perhaps unavoidable. In 1940, two years before the invasion, Burmans made up only about 12 percent of the Burma Army, while the Kachins and Chins each made up about 23 percent of the troops, and the Karens nearly 30 percent.[16]

By contrast, the BIA was largely recruited from urban areas in Lower Burma and it generally did not recruit from either the Asian immigrant minorities, such as the Chinese and Indians, or the hill tribes. Almost by default, the BIA became an armed Burman ethno-nationalist force and, as a result of colonial favor to the Karens and the legacy of colonial generalizations of the Karen on the basis of the Christian Sgaw Karen, the BIA closely associated the Karens in general with the British, whom they had just removed from Burma with Japanese help. When the BIA began to disarm Karens in Myaungmya, fighting broke out, Burmans and Karens burning scores of villages on each side. In order to restore stability behind their lines, the Japanese Army moved in to stop the violence that now swept through the delta. The Myaungmya violence was not the only reason many Karen favored the Allies in the war; many Karen from the colonial army who had remained behind in Burma, particularly in the hill areas, after the British withdrew, were already hostile to both the BIA and the Japanese and would become key to the organization of Karen attacks on the Japanese later in the war. The Kachins also lent their support to the anti-Japanese cause by joining the US Office of Strategic Services' Detachment 101 in the north. Operating from mountain outposts, they were mainly involved in destroying the transportation infrastructure and gathering intelligence, but in the process reportedly killed over 5,000 Japanese soldiers.[17]

The emergence of the BIA and its successors, the BDA and the BNA, under the Burmese together with support for the Allies among the ethnic minorities, on the one hand, and the constitutional division of Burma, under the Japanese, into a Burman state and ethnic hill areas, on the other hand, fostered an ethnic dimension to the war that would contribute both to the prolonged duration of negotiations for independence once the British returned in 1945, and the civil war early after independence. As one scholar observes, among some of Burma's hill minorities, the heritage of World War II was the rise of their own ethno-nationalism and expectations that they would be rewarded, after the Allied victory, for their wartime service. Among some Karen leaders, these expectations included the establishment of an independent Karen state.[18]

THE SOCIAL AND ECONOMIC IMPACT OF OCCUPATION

Under Japanese rule, civil liberties were severely curtailed and promised freedoms for which the Thakins had agreed to aid the Japanese were denied. The Burmese were particularly upset over the way in which Japanese soldiers would publicly slap them across the face for petty offenses. The

Japanese secret police (*Kenpeitai*) scoured the country for opponents to the Ba Maw Government and, as the war dragged on and the Allies began their advance into Burma, the Japanese adopted stricter security measures. Among these were restrictions on the movements of Burmese who were now required to carry passes issued by local headmen when traveling outside their own towns and villages. The Ba Maw Government re-imposed the system of communal responsibility under which families and sometimes the whole village were held responsible for the misbehavior of a single individual. From April 1943, the Japanese also required local Burmese officials to recruit *heiho* (auxiliary troops) to help provide local security, but most were sent to Rangoon to serve as laborers for the Japanese Army. Although formally a volunteer force, difficulties in recruitment led to coercion. Many Burmese naturally deserted whenever the opportunity presented itself.[19]

The Japanese were also concerned that the disappearance of the export market would create political problems when Burmese farmers were left with too much excess paddy on their hands or problems for the Japanese if Burmese farmers reduced their production to meet self-sufficiency alone. Without the export market, much of the 1941–1942 crop went unutilized and the same was true for the 1942–1943 crop. In June 1943, Agriculture Minister Than Tun announced the Purchase of Paddy Scheme under which the state would purchase the whole of the surplus of the paddy crop from the 1942–1943 season from thirteen districts, thus reducing agriculturalists' hardships, restoring the desire to cultivate crops for the 1943–1944 season, and encouraging the circulation of funds to support the economy. Little preparation was made for the scheme and only 160 officials, given only one day's training, were mobilized to carry out the program. By the end of 1943, the Ba Maw Government had given out in loans only a quarter of the funds needed to finance the paddy crop and cultivation declined. In early 1944, Rangoon Radio broadcast a one-act play in Burmese in which a mother taught her daughters to cook grass as well as explaining the nutritional value of grass and that it could be eaten in difficult times such as the present. As agriculture continued to collapse, Nu, the Foreign Minister, complained that it was difficult to find food even to give to the monks.[20]

THE ANTI-FASCIST PEOPLE'S FREEDOM LEAGUE

Although Tojo decorated both Ba Maw and Aung San in Tokyo in mid-1944, Aung San had already gone far in preparations for turning against the Japanese. The war minister had begun to send representatives in secret across the front to make contact with the Allies in India from December 1943. The Allies eventually promised to train Burmese troops to work as a fifth column and promised to include arms for the Burmese in future air drops. Force 136 entered Burma to establish resistance bases in Karen areas. By August 1944, the Anti-Fascist People's Freedom League (AFPFL, also known as the Anti-Fascist Organization to the Allies, as well as the Burma Patriotic Front in India) was formed to prepare for the Allied invasion. In preparation for the uprising to meet it, Aung San ordered the officers and men of the BNA to cease shaving their heads, as the Japanese had required, and wear their hair long like other Burmese men so they could merge easily with the general population when the time for revolt came.[21]

The war on the northwestern front quickly turned against the Japanese in late 1944 and early 1945 and Aung San prepared to make his move. On 24 March 1945, Aung San made a pledge at the Shwedagon Pagoda to begin the BNA's campaign against the Allies, while a Japanese military band provided the rhythm for the BNA units that marched out in the direction of the front. Once out of Rangoon, these units dispersed to pre-designated base areas in six zones throughout Central and Lower Burma and on the prearranged day, 27 March, they began their attack on Japanese forces. Before the end of May, Aung San's forces had fought 1,000 engagements and claimed, with considerable exaggeration, to have killed as many as 20,000 Japanese soldiers. Lt.-General William Slim's Fourteenth Army finally captured Rangoon on 3 May and talks began with Aung San two weeks later. Slim was impressed with Aung San and took him to be a genuine nationalist and an honest man. Aung San liked Slim as well and promised him that he would continue to support the Allies militarily and delay talk of independence until the Japanese defeat.[22]

As they had been cut off from communications with Japan during the Allied advance, Japanese soldiers in Burma, as in many other areas of Asia, fought on for weeks after the surrender of Japan. On 16 August, the Allies began airdropping leaflets across Burma informing Japanese soldiers that the war was indeed over. Still, Japanese soldiers fought on (and Allied planes were greeted with anti-aircraft fire from the ground), in the belief that this was simply enemy propaganda. Finally, on 24 October, the Japanese commander of the Burma area, General Kimura, formally surrendered his sword to Lt.-General Sir Montagu Stopford (Twelfth Army) at Rangoon University.[23]

THE BRITISH MILITARY ADMINISTRATION

The war had devastated Burma. As one observer commented after it had ended, "I believe there was a higher degree of destruction in [Burma] than in any other area in the East."[24] Two major campaigns had been fought across the entirety of the country, first by the Japanese to push the British out and then by the Allies, joined later by the AFPFL, to drive the Japanese out. In early March 1942, the British set fire to oil refineries in the vicinity of Rangoon and later burned Prome, they scuttled 95 percent of the five hundred steamer fleet of the Irrawaddy Flotilla Company, destroyed bridges, and engaged in a range of other efforts to "deny all to the enemy." While Japanese and later Allied planes would pound remaining installations and towns into rubble, after occupying the country, the Japanese engaged in no major wartime reconstruction, beyond the needs of the Japanese Army. Alongside the Japanese Army, Japanese companies were brought in to help in the procurement of supplies. Some of these, especially those in front-line areas, relied on harsh measures to achieve this. As a result of commandeering, the number of cattle in Burma dropped by two-thirds, severely hurting agricultural output. Japanese currency used to buy commodities quickly became inflated. Clothing became scarce and expensive. Things worsened as Japanese forces, cut off from supplies from abroad due to Allied submarines and aircraft, took all available resources.[25]

In the last months of the war, underground movements also began destroying bridges, communications, and harbors in order to pin the Japanese Army down. In Rangoon, the port and the railway station had been put out of commission. Half of the public and commercial buildings and one-third of homes had been ruined. Of those buildings that remained, they were empty shells after all their windows, doors, furniture, and electrical and sanitary fittings had been removed. It was estimated that 80 percent of the city had to be rebuilt. Myingyan, Meiktila, Prome, and Myitkyina had been completely flattened. Of Burma's 1,200 passenger railcars only 12 remained, 200 of its 250 locomotives had been destroyed, only two-thirds of its freight wagons survived, and as late as December 1945, only 800 out of 2,000 miles of railway track had been reopened. Bridges throughout the country had been destroyed and roads were in serious disrepair. Oil production and mining operations had completely stopped. Burma's rice acreage had also been cut in half, from thirteen million acres to a little over six million acres. Disease and starvation plagued the country.[26]

The immediate task of reconstruction fell to the British Military Administration (BMA), whose tenure ran from 6 May until 16 October 1945.

Although the British occupation had brought with them Indian notes stamped with a Burmese inscription as well as pre-war Burmese notes, they were not yet in general circulation and Burmese had continued to use the Japanese notes because they were the only widely distributed form of currency. In late May, as Burma quickly fell under re-occupation, the British Army issued Proclamation No. 6, which declared Japanese currency invalid without any offer of compensation or exchange. This declaration wiped out overnight whatever Burmese had saved over the past three and a half years, impoverishing all indigenous classes except for those who had fled to India (who had lost much themselves in the 1942 exodus). Riots broke out, shops closed, and crafty town-dwellers drove trucks full of Japanese notes into the countryside to buy goods from peasants who had not yet learned about the proclamation. For Burmese families, the cost of living index had risen to 679 by November (based on the figure of 100 for 1941).[27]

Impoverished civilians poured into Rangoon, which had become nearly deserted over the course of the war, for shelter. They found little left. Timber housing in the city had all gone up in flames. Besides their destroyed homes, the military had occupied all of the best surviving buildings, including the schools and the RU Campus. British troops are remembered to have been "greater vandals than the Japanese." They scoured buildings for flooring and stairs that could be used for firewood and broke up surviving bungalows for this purpose as well. Even the famous Minto Mansions Hotel, which had remained in fair condition, was demolished for masonry to exchange a dirt floor for a solid foundation in a depot one unit occupied. The BMA appears to have given low priority to finding shelter for the Burmese. Thus, thousands were forced to erect mat huts in every available space, especially pavements, which made better flooring than muddy soil. The Royal Lakes now became hidden by shanty towns and the main streets of Rangoon were lined with huts: "Rangoon was a veritable metropolis of matting and thatch."[28]

The BMA established the Civil Affairs Service (Burma) or CASB which set up a system of government projects. A consortium of pre-war British and Indian commercial firms, working as agents of the government and employing their skilled workers to rebuild industries in the areas of civil supplies, transport, timber, and rice, ran each project. The projects were designed so that the industries so revived could eventually be transferred to the ownership of the commercial firms involved. The Civil Supplies Board (CSB), for example, was established on 27 August 1945 and was given "dictatorial powers," being responsible only to the CSB and then to the governor on his return. The CSB had powers to search for goods, make compulsory purchases, and control the transport of commodities. Further, it nominated certain commercial firms as its agents and "liquidated" any competition. As boats and steamers came back into service, they were run for the government by the Irrawaddy Flotilla Company, at government expense, with the agreement that when water transport had returned to normal the company had the right to take over ownership of the craft "at a value." The projects continued to be run by the CASB until 1 April 1946, when responsibility was transferred to the governor.[29]

Although other projects were agreed in principle with companies, they were not wholly put into operation immediately because commercial firms refused to rebuild their installations until Britain agreed to compensation for wartime damage. They also refused to invest new capital in Burma until the government had established a clear policy on these lines. The projects would also be severely criticized by Burmese leaders. Burmese were not informed of the "policy, organization, and the actual working of these government projects." The CASB operated with a kind of secrecy, according to Burmese critics, and they were not told how the commercial firms were benefiting from their participation in the projects, whether or not (and if so, how much) the CASB was profiting from the sale of Burmese rice in India, or what the ultimate policy of the government would be regarding the projects and the commercial firms. The information gap left much room for the Burmese to suspect the intentions of the British government and many Burmese understandably interpreted these projects to be British support for a return of British and Indian commercial domination.[30]

THE EXECUTIVE COUNCIL

In October 1945, the BMA was ended and the government in exile (in Simla) was reinstated under Governor Sir Reginald Dorman-Smith. While Dorman-Smith would be personally blamed for the faults of the returned colonial administration, the evidence indicates that he often disagreed with the policies he was ordered to pursue and his suggestions to government on making concessions were just as frequently rejected.

The British plan was for the governor to rule with emergency powers until the pre-war Burmese government could be reestablished and this government, elected under the 1937 Constitution, would determine Burma's future. Dorman-Smith announced on 17 October 1945, the day after he arrived in Burma, that he would create a fifteen-member Executive Council as an advisory body and a fifty-member Legislative Council. He invited the AFPFL to join. A week later, the League's Supreme Council adopted a resolution that it would cooperate if the governor filled eleven of the fifteen seats with League nominees, leaving four seats for him to select. The eleven League-nominated members would have to be allowed to work as a team, decide the allocation of portfolios among themselves, and to resign as a group if the League decided by a 75 percent vote that they should do so, or if at any point they felt they were not accomplishing their objectives within the Executive Council. The League also resolved that the Executive Council would have to prepare for a general election based on universal suffrage for a constituent assembly rather than for a legislature, and also act as a "popular Government and undertake other tasks" that were not specified. Aung San later repeated these demands to the governor, further requiring that a League member should control the Home Affairs portfolio. By 28 October, talks with Dorman-Smith broke down and he approached other politicians in order to appoint an Executive Council, now reduced to eleven members, without the League for the time being. He then filled the Executive Council with pro-British Burmese with no popular appeal, as well as a British general and a British civilian official by mid-November.[31]

Dorman-Smith proposed to London in March 1946 to increase the powers of the Executive Council and the Legislature prior to the planned elections, but these measures were refused. Dorman-Smith also proposed including Aung San in the Executive Council, but London denied permission for this move as well, citing outstanding murder charges against the AFPFL leader. In response, Dorman-Smith sent a strong protest to London, arguing that "rigid adherence" to these rulings might provoke an "open rebellion."[32]

Since the British continued to prove reluctant to grant independence, Aung San now began a constitutional struggle, demanding the creation of an interim representative government with full powers over the affairs of the colony. Aung San also called for Burmese non-cooperation in matters of the payment of rent and taxes, and the sale of rice to official government purchasing agents. In June, Dorman-Smith was recalled to London to report to the government on the situation in Burma. He did so in early August, and resigned afterwards. The AFPFL interpreted the recall as an indication of British weakness. Emboldened, the League now promised to support all public service personnel in their demands against the government; it would force the latter to restore press freedom and civil liberties, and ordered all League branches to fly only the party flag and celebrate "national" days it identified.[33]

The new governor, Major General Sir Hubert Rance, the former head of the CASB, faced a seemingly hopeless situation when he arrived in Rangoon at the end of August 1946. He was tasked with ending the strikes, bringing the AFPFL to heel, and establishing the conditions necessary to continue with reconstruction. Yet more obstacles were already in the works. Burmese nationalists were already remobilizing their paramilitary forces, including Aung San's People's Volunteer Organization (PVO) and Saw's Myochit Party's paramilitary wing. More strikes were also being organized. On 1 September, at a time when "dacoity" was everywhere, police officers went on strike in Rangoon and in several rural districts. Despite the tensions now boiling over, Rance held firm and announced what the British government was prepared to allow. There would be no "epoch making changes." The powers of the Executive Council would not be increased, the country would be prepared for dominion status rather than outright independence, and the government would seek the participation of both the Myochit Party and the League. His government's three main objectives included reconstruction and rehabilitation, the creation of the conditions necessary to hold elections in the spring of 1947, and the restoration of law and order.[34]

Despite the unyielding rhetoric, perhaps intended to please politicians at home, Rance in actuality abandoned non-cooperation and adopted a more conciliatory approach than had Dorman-Smith. On 21 September 1946, Rance met with Burmese leaders to discuss the membership of the reformed Executive Council. To ensure that there would be no colonial backpedaling, Aung San increased the pressure. During the negotiations, the strikes continued and were joined by employees of the Postal Department and the Central Government Press, while Aung San simultaneously called for a general strike to take place on 23 September. The governor caved in completely and announced that a new Executive Council had been formed, giving the AFPFL a majority of six members in the nine-member Executive Council, under his own chairmanship. League members only accepted the concessions on the understanding that the Council would operate as a normal Council of Ministers and that the governor's veto would be used as sparingly as possible. Most of the strikes ended within a week.[35]

THE LONDON AGREEMENT

Burmese politicians remained frustrated by the White Paper issued by the Conservative government on 17 May 1945, which offered a three-stage independence plan. First, for a three-year interim period, until or before 9 December 1948, Burma would be governed under the rules of the emergency administration set up in 1942. However, there would also be an executive council including Burmese and perhaps a colonial legislature. By the close of this period, an election would be held for a government like that granted under the Government of Burma Act, 1935. The Burmese would then write a new constitution and negotiate with Britain regarding what the latter would continue to control, such as the Scheduled Areas (the Frontier Areas), after final independence. At a yet undetermined time (suggested by some as being about mid-1953), Burma would gain independence within the British Commonwealth with limitations that had been determined in the second stage.[36]

The Executive Council complained of the "leisurely and protracted" pace of preparations for independence outlined in the White Paper and the more "energetic" program regarding the creation of an interim government and a constituent assembly to replace it in India. There was also some unhappiness that the White Paper did not limit the term for the governor's discretionary powers. Nor was there any provision for a Burmese-led interim government to rule the country until the promulgation of a constitution. Instead of the White Paper's program, the Executive Council, following the resolutions made by the AFPFL Working Committee in early November 1946, demanded

(1) the immediate establishment of an interim national government with the governor serving as constitutional head;
(2) a British promise by 31 January 1947 to grant independence in one year;
(3) a firm statement by the British that the Burmese had the right to decide whether or not Burma would join the Commonwealth;
(4) use of the scheduled forthcoming elections for a colonial legislature for the election of a constituent assembly instead;
(5) an inquiry into how to fit the Frontier Areas into independent Burma;
(6) that all British financial projects be restructured or ended prior to 31 January 1947,

and promised that if the British did not concede on all of these points, all of the League members of the Executive Council would resign.[37]

Changing political fortunes in Britain favored the successful outcome of AFPFL demands. By December 1946, a Labour government had replaced the Conservatives in Britain and Clement Attlee was now Prime Minister. On 20 December, Attlee announced that Britain would review its policy regarding Burma. Britain did not want people in the Commonwealth against their will, he explained, and Burmese nationals should frame their own constitution after the election of a constituent assembly, "on the analogy of what has already been done in India." Furthermore, in the meantime, the British Government would not interfere in the way in which the Burmese members of the Executive Council handled everyday administration. In January 1947, a Burmese delegation led by Aung San went to Britain for negotiations with the government and determined on reaching a settlement. Stopping in New Delhi in the first week of January on his way to London, Aung San took time to study how the interim government was working in India, in order to prepare for one in Burma. Aung San warned from the outset of the negotiations that he had to reach a settlement by the end of January or he would go back to Burma and there would be a political deadlock. He also added to previous AFPFL demands that the Executive Council have free access to the Frontier Areas to persuade the people there to join Burma. The British and the Burmese delegations eventually arrived at an agreement, the London or Anglo-Burmese Agreement, on 27 January. The Agreement promised independence to Burma and that she could decide whether or not to join the Commonwealth but did not mention when independence would be granted.[38]

While the Burmese delegation had achieved most of its objectives, not all Burmese were satisfied. At home, some Burmese claimed the delegation had achieved nothing, while others said, figuratively, that it had achieved 75 percent of its goals. There was dissent among the delegation. At 11:15 P.M. on 26 January 1947, after the parties had agreed on all the major points, Saw and U Ba Sein, having given no indication of opposition previously, suddenly announced that they did not wish to sign the agreement. When Attlee and Aung San both pressed the pair for an explanation, they simply said that the agreement "did not go far enough." Saw eventually relented and gave a quick, ill-thought-out response that he wanted elections for the legislature, even though the agreement had gone far beyond this. When Aung San suggested their immediate resignations, the British side said the matter could be resolved when the Burmese delegation returned to Burma. A British critic of Saw and Ba Sein conjectured that their move had something to do with their frequent meetings with former governor Reginald Dorman-Smith and an effort by right-wing British politicians to sabotage Burmese reconstruction. In early February, both Saw and Ba Sein resigned from the Executive Council.[39]

Elections for the Constituent Assembly were held on 9 April 1947. The AFPFL won a landslide victory, taking 248 of 255 seats, while the Burma Communist Party took the remaining seven. U Saw's Myochit Party, Ba Maw's Maha Bama (Sinyetha) Party, and Thakin Ba Sein's Dobama Asi-ayone had boycotted the election, as they could expect only a small share of the vote. The Assembly finally met on 9 June. Soon after, Nu was elected President of the body, Aung San's resolution outlining the seven main points on which to draw up the Constitution was passed, and the Assembly created a fifteen-member select committee to draft the Constitution.[40]

THE FRONTIER AREAS

According to the British White Paper of May 1945, the Scheduled Areas of which the Shan states were a part were renamed the Frontier Areas and remained, as before, outside of "ministerial" Burma and thus outside the authority of the Executive Council and directly under that of the governor. A separate Frontier Areas administration was then set up in 1946 under the Director of Frontier Areas. The first Frontier Areas' Conference, also being the first such meeting between Burmese and "Frontier Areas" leaders, was held at Panglong from 27 March to 2 April 1946. Shan leaders of the thirty-four federated Shan states, presided over by the *Sawbwa* of Tong Peng, met to discuss their goals regarding trade, culture, and welfare. The conference had also invited Karen, Kachin, and Chin representatives, several Burmese leaders, including Saw and Thakin Nu, and the governor (who did not attend due to illness) to discuss future relations between the Frontier Areas in general and the Shan states in particular with ministerial Burma. The Director of Frontier Areas announced the creation of Regional Councils to advise British residents and State Councils to advise the *sawbwas*. Saw also gave a speech urging the representatives of the Frontier Areas' peoples to agree as soon as possible to unity with ministerial Burma regarding economy and defense, promising autonomy in all other matters. The second Frontier Areas' Conference (usually remembered as *the* Panglong Conference), mentioned in the London Agreement, was held at Panglong from 9 to 12 February 1947. The conference was to determine Frontier Area representation in the Executive Council and the forthcoming Constituent Assembly. The Chins and Kachins wanted separate, autonomous states, under a central government that handled defence and foreign policy. The Shans, already having the Shan States Federation, wanted to negotiate their relationship with the future central government.[41]

Under the agreement reached and put into operation at the end of March 1947, during the interim period, the Frontier Areas would be brought within the authority of the Executive Council on matters of "common interest," in such cases as defence and external affairs, "but without prejudice to full internal autonomy." The Agreement also preserved the existing

Frontier Areas' internal administrative autonomy. The Agreement did not change the status of financial assistance to the Chin and Kachin Hills and the financial autonomy of the Shan States Federation. The Executive Council would now include a member representing the "frontier peoples" and this member would be appointed by the governor on the recommendation of the Supreme Council of the United Hills Peoples. Since there were three ethnic groups or "races" to be represented, after the councilor was selected, the two "races" which he did not belong to would be represented by two councilors who would assist him and act on the principle of joint responsibility and would be able to attend the Executive Council meetings when their areas were under discussion. The first appointees included a Shan *sawbwa* as councilor, along with a Chin and a Kachin deputy councilor. The Agreement guaranteed the citizens of the Frontier Areas "the rights and privileges which are regarded as fundamental in democratic countries." The Panglong Agreement also created the Frontier Areas Enquiry Commission, planned for in the London Agreement. The commission visited the Frontier Areas and conducted numerous interviews and on this basis submitted a unanimous report that asserted that representatives "of all states, districts and local areas" wished to be associated with the forthcoming Constituent Assembly. It also recommended increasing the size of the Assembly by the creation of an additional forty-five seats, all reserved for the Frontier Areas.[42]

While the Shans, Chins, and Kachins occupied ethnically identifiable and distinct zones in the Frontier Areas, the situation of the Karens was more problematic. Relatively small pockets did exist that could be identified as Karen, the largest being the Salween District, but these were scattered in the hill districts of the Frontier Areas. A failed plan to establish a semi-autonomous Karen state in August 1947, for example, suggested that it should include the Salween District, the Karenni States, and the Toungoo Karen Hills. Such a state would lack geographic connectivity and be unworkable as an administrative unit, in addition to lacking, it was argued at the time, an economically stable basis for survival. Further, most Karens lived in the Burmese lowlands, intermixed with other ethnic groups, especially the Burmans. Erecting an integrated Karen homeland was thus more problematic than for the Shans, the Kachins, or the Chins. The biggest challenge, however, was the bifurcation of Karen leadership between those who favored integration with Burma and those who preferred to establish an independent state. This made a united Karen front impossible. Although Karen leaders were not included in the delegation that negotiated the London Agreement, pro-union Karens supported it, since that Agreement proposed to double the number of seats reserved for the plains Karens from twelve in the old colonial legislature to twenty-four in the forthcoming Constituent Assembly. A boycott of the Panglong negotiations by some Karen leaders meant that only a small body of Hill Karens attended the conference and even they did not participate in the proceedings. Consultations were then begun between the various Karen groups to determine what their position was relative to the Panglong Agreement.[43]

The Karen National Union (KNU) was formed in 1947 out of the remnants of the Karen Central Organization, founded in 1945, which in turn had succeeded the Karen National Association founded in 1881. The KNU's purpose was to represent those Karens who saw no future for themselves in a united and independent Burma. They were not alone, for the Mons also sought independence from the forthcoming Union of Burma and began writing to different governments for help at about the same time. The KNU announced that it would not take part in the April elections because the Karens had been allotted insufficient seats in the forthcoming Constituent Assembly. Instead, they pressured Saw Ba U Gyi, a member of the Executive Council, to resign and sent a deputation to the Frontier Areas Commission of Inquiry to lodge a complaint. After the KNU pulled its candidates from the election, the AFPFL nominated twenty-four members of the Karen Youth League to run for election. Thus, pro-union Karens swept the polls for the reserved Karen seats. Further, the two Karen seats in the Executive Council both went to pro-union Karen leaders.[44]

The anxieties of anti-union Karens would become feverish by October. Karen separatists sent to Governor Rance a letter they wanted him to forward to Prime Minister Attlee that claimed that they had arms and would not surrender. Rance refused to send this officially to the government, but did forward it on an informal basis. Although the AFPFL was aware of the situation, it downplayed its significance, choosing instead a policy of placating the Karens by putting them into important positions of authority. In Karen areas, administrative offices were given to Karens. The League had also determined to replace the commander of the Burma Army, General Thomas Latter, with Smith Dun, a Karen and a graduate of Sandhurst Military Academy, when the British Military Mission withdrew in the forthcoming months. The Karens remained concerned, however, since future Burmese leaders might entertain a different policy. Despite the League's awareness of the crisis emerging regarding the Karens, it delayed on recovering weapons from the Karens.[45]

THE ASSASSINATION OF AUNG SAN

As a result of both the London Agreement and the prospective Anglo-Burmese Treaty, some parties formed an opposition bloc. This included Saw and his Myochit Party, Ba Sein and his Dobama Party, and Ba Maw's Sinyetha Party. Their opposition was not mainly ideological, but grew out of personal jealousy of Aung San. Of these leaders, Saw would emerge as the most notorious. Saw had become a sad figure since his pre-occupation days when he had been Prime Minister. He had spent the war in a detention camp and after his return to Burma a jeep pulled up alongside his car and a revolver was fired at him at close range. A window had deflected the bullet, but shattered glass hit Saw in the face and lodged in one eye, for which reason he wore dark glasses in public. Saw struggled to find his place in the new Burma and was frustrated by the popularity of the AFPFL that made a serious political comeback difficult. He deeply distrusted Aung San, whom he saw as nothing more than a Japanese collaborator, and strongly felt that Rance made a serious mistake in giving Aung San leadership rather than himself.[46]

Claims later emerged that Saw had attempted to assassinate Aung San in February 1947 and had given six months of weapons training to members of his Myochit Party for a second attempt in the future. Conservative elements in Britain also disliked Aung San. Winston Churchill continued to deride Aung San, even after his death, as a "traitor rebel leader," the organizer of a "Quisling army," and a man guilty of "great cruelties" against loyal Burmese during the war. Only when the British Army advanced into Burma did Aung San, "whose hands were dyed with British blood and loyal Burmese blood," conveniently switch to the Allied side.[47]

At 10:00 A.M. on the morning of Saturday, 19 July 1947, the Governor's Executive Council held a meeting to discuss national security regarding the theft of 200 Bren guns from the Ordnance Depot a week earlier. The session, presided over by the Council Deputy Chairman, the thirty-three-year-old Aung San, was held in the Council Chamber of the Secretariat Building. As usual, Aung San, who had exchanged his military uniform for a silk jacket and a Bangkok *longyi*, seated himself at the center of the large u-shaped table, whose mouth faced the entrance. On the north side of the table sat Thakin Mya, Mahn Ba Khaing, Deedok U Ba Choe, A. Razak, and U Ba Win (Aung San's elder brother). On the south side sat Sao Sam Htun (the *Sawbwa* of Mong Pawn), U Ba Gyan (Member for Rehabilitation and Public Works), U Aung Zan Wei, and Pyawbwe U Mya. Shortly before 10:30 A.M., five men dressed in the jungle-green uniforms of the

Twelfth Army pulled up to the Secretariat Building in a jeep bearing a false license plate. Police waved them in without much thought. In Rangoon and elsewhere in Burma, old military uniforms were worn regularly by many, even within the Secretariat, and PVO members and the militia of other organizations could be seen everywhere, many armed. The men got out at the entrance to the Shan State Ministry and went up to the first floor, while their jeep waited with the engine running. As they did so, the Deputy Secretary of the Ministry of Transport and Communications, U Ohn Maung, entered the chamber to submit a report to the Council. At about 10:37 A.M., the men, led by one Hmon Gyi, approached the Council Chamber. With their three Bren guns and one Sten gun in hand, they knocked down a guard at the door, pushed it open, and entered the room, shouting "Don't run away!" As Aung San rose to face the men, they opened fire, dropping him to the floor. They sprayed gunfire first across the middle of the table, killing Ohn Maung, and then across the table's northern half, killing three of the ministers, and mortally wounding a fourth (Ba Choe died later the same day), seated on this end. As the gunmen then swung their guns toward the southern side of the table, the ministers on this end fell to the floor in a split second, saving their lives, with the exception of the *Sawbwa* of Mong Pawn who was wounded in the face (and died on the operating table the following day). After three more rounds of firing, the assassins fled the area, mortally wounding Razak's personal bodyguard on the stairs as he rushed up to see what had happened. Seven of the ten men in the room were dead or dying. As the survivors ran out, they left behind a miserable scene that would alter the course of Burma's history forever: the smell of carbide, blood-stained floors, spent cartridge cases, and the bodies of the father of Burmese independence and some of his closest associates. Although another pair of assassins had also been sent out to kill Nu, they were unable to find him that morning.[48]

Colonial officials at first believed that the assassinations had been the work of the Communists. On 19 July, however, government forces raided Saw's house and arrested both him and four men who were ultimately accused of having carried out the attack. U Ba Nyun, a witness for the prosecution in the trial that followed, explained that the jeep had returned immediately to Saw's house, where the license plate was replaced and the jeep's genuine number was now painted once again on its side. The men then changed their clothes and began drinking alcohol in celebration. Saw was even reported to have drunk alcohol from the barrel of the gun that had killed Aung San. The guns and license plate were then dumped into Inya Lake near where Saw lived, and the discarded uniforms burned.

Police action against Saw had been quick, because he had been under secret surveillance by the police on another matter for some time and the departure and return of the jeep had been noted. Eight hundred others would eventually be arrested in the investigation as well. A British police officer (Burma was still a colony) was put in charge of the investigation. The police found that the jeep was still covered in wet paint, divers recovered the guns and ammunition from the lake, and remnants of burned uniforms were found in the kitchen fireplace. A bevy of witnesses came forward to provide evidence of Saw's complicity in the conspiracy.[49]

Ironically, the existence of an orgy of evidence that too clearly identified Saw as the killer has led to speculation that the assassination was carried out by the British government, another political rival to Aung San, or both. Some, such as the BCP leader (and Aung San's brother-in-law) Than Tun, accused the British of ordering the assassination through counter-revolutionary allies. A British Labour MP even told Parliament that members of the British Conservative opposition bore more "moral guilt of the assassination" than the gunmen for having encouraged Saw to carry out "treachery and sabotage." As rumours of British involvement grew, the Government of Burma made a public declaration that neither the British Government nor Rance were in any way connected with the killings. Saw's defense attorney argued that he was being framed, for how could someone of his intelligence entertain the murderers at his home shortly after the crime took place? Saw himself testified that the man who had turned King's evidence, Ba Nyun, and other followers had suggested at one point that AFPFL members should be "wiped out," but that he himself, despite having had numerous political rivals over the course of his career, had never considered killing any of them. After hearing the case, a tribunal convicted Saw of the murder. After appeals failed, Saw was hanged.[50]

Steps toward independence moved very quickly after Aung San's assassination. The draft constitution was put before the Constituent Assembly on 31 July and was unanimously approved on 24 September. The following day, this body also unanimously elected Sao Shwe Taik, the *Sawbwa* of Yawnghwe, and Nu as Provisional President and Prime Minister, respectively. Meanwhile, the formalities of severance from Britain continued to proceed. The Constituent Assembly also voted unanimously not to participate in the British Commonwealth, despite Rance's encouragement to join it. The Anglo-Burmese Treaty setting out the terms of Burma's relationship with Britain was finally signed on 18 October 1947. The Burma Independence Act was then put before the Parliament and was approved against strong Conservative opposition. Independence was finally declared on 4 January 1948.[51]

CONCLUSION

The Burmese had several tastes of independence during the 1937–1947 period. From 1937 to 1942, the Burmese had limited self-rule without formal independence; under the Japanese, from 1942 to 1945, they had formal independence and less self-rule, while during the 1945–1947 period, although formal independence was taken away, they nearly had de facto control of the colony, made clear by the general strike. These years included many potential watersheds, or lost opportunities. One wonders if, had the British granted dominion status to Burma, as Saw demanded in 1941, or if the war had not broken out at all, a conservative nationalist leadership would have led independent Burma. On the other hand, the Japanese invasion ensured that whatever concessions were made, it was Aung San and his comrades who were assured supreme nationalist credentials. When the British returned, whatever they were willing to offer was irrelevant as Burma's course to independence had already been established by the actions of the AFPFL in early 1945.

More importantly, the 1937–1947 period served as a long trial run for independence. All of Burma's major political leaders for the next four decades emerged on the national scene during these years, held commanding positions in the state or army, and gained the kind of administrative experience necessary for the challenges ahead. The period also saw the end of the careers of the leading members of Burma's pre-independence national leadership: Aung San, who was assassinated; Saw, who was hanged; and Ba Maw, who was politically dead due to his close collaboration with the Japanese. With the charismatic center of Burma's leadership gone, their lieutenants would lead Burma headlong into one of the world's longest civil wars.

CHAPTER 4

The democratic experiment, 1948–1958

Aung San's assassination in 1947 cast a long shadow over independent Burma. Nu was handed the task of leading Burma in an experiment with democracy that ended badly. This was partly due to the fact that Nu lacked much of the single-minded focus, political skills, and organizational ability of his predecessor. Perhaps more blame could be directed at the myriad political, ethnic, and institutional forces set loose. It could be said that by comparison to the 1945–1947 period, when the Burmese had unity, but not independence, that under Nu, Burma had independence, but not unity. The Burmese had achieved independence without a revolution, which prevented the emergence of internal solidarity or the squeezing out of rival groups and ideologies that occurred, for example, with the Vietminh in the face of French military efforts to reestablish their control in the First Indochina War. Whereas the Vietminh were provided with the opportunity to cultivate the political solidarity originally developed to oppose the Japanese and Vichy French, after World War II, in Burma the old political rivalries reemerged very quickly, especially as the British left.

To make matters worse, guns and other weaponry were everywhere, whether abandoned by the British in 1942 or by the Japanese in 1945, or supplied to the men of the BIA. Around the country were PVO soldiers, consisting mainly of men demobilized from the BIA and then remobilized but kept in a virtual limbo to give Aung San potential muscle in his negotiations with the British. With Aung San gone, the PVOs were directionless, although mostly left-leaning, and looking for a cause. Communists, rightists, Karens, Mons, and a number of other groups, several of whom had begun revolt under the British and now determined to continue against the Nu regime, thus had the means available to make war on the young government.[1]

THE INSURGENTS

It is impossible to understand the Nu years, or indeed any period of post-independence Burma without considering the ongoing civil war. Among the Nu government's most serious challengers were the Communists. Aung San had helped organize the Burmese Communist Party prior to the outbreak of World War II. The Communists overtly split into two factions in 1945, but the leadership had already begun to divide with the beginning of the Japanese occupation. While Aung San and Than Tun collaborated with the Japanese and accepted positions in the various Ba Maw regimes, the more radical and doctrinaire Thakin Soe spent the war years moving around rural Burma, building up an organization and spreading propaganda geared toward revolution against either the Japanese or the British when the war was over. In mid-1945, Than Tun was able to oust Soe from the party leadership, creating a split between the more moderate and larger Burma Communist Party (BCP) "White Flags" under Than Tun and the smaller and more radical Communist Party of Burma (CPB), also known as the "Red Flags," led by Soe. Both groups were popular among the peasantry, for they had both advocated alleviating rural problems, but differed over cooperation with the AFPFL in negotiating independence from Britain. The gap widened when the British declared the CPB illegal, marking the beginning of its insurgency.[2]

Prior to independence, Nu's impression of BCP leaders was that they were nationalists and not directed by the Soviet Union. Nevertheless, Nu was confident that they would never get strong support from the general population because of the latter's religiosity. In November 1947, AFPFL willingness to negotiate with the BCP for reconciliation died and Nu canceled planned talks between the two. Nu had considered inviting the BCP back into the League after they disarmed, although he was wary that they might attempt to seize power from within the AFPFL. The BCP, it was asserted, talked about unity with the League, on the one hand, but had actively tried to undermine the credibility of the AFPFL by supporting student strikes and looting of rice, on the other. When the AFPFL announced on 17 November that it could no longer consider the re-inclusion of the BCP, its leader Than Tun accused the League's leadership of being rightwing and of seeking every opportunity to prevent reconciliation. In May 1948, the Nu government botched an attempt to arrest its leadership, marking the beginning of the BCP insurgency.[3]

After the failure of negotiations with the BCP, Nu announced his plan to create the Marxist League, fusing together the Socialist Party and the

PVO, the two strongest constituent parts of the AFPFL, with moderate Communists in order to stabilize the government and draw support away from the BCP. In order to accomplish the political fusion, the PVO would cease as an independent organization and its members would have to disarm and become civilians. Negotiations with the PVO faltered, however, and although the Marxist League plan was floated as one part of the Leftist Unity Programme in 1948, it was dropped from the program in order to win over moderate Communists. Political infighting followed and even this plan failed by July 1949, when the majority of the PVOs rebelled. As with the Communists, their loyalties were represented by the government in colors, with those who rebelled becoming known as the "White Band" PVOs and the more moderate and loyal faction, the "Yellow Band" PVOs. The sheer numbers and dispersement of the White Band PVOs (they could be found in most local areas) and their military experience, for they were all ex-soldiers, made them a potentially greater threat to the government than the Communists, with whom many now joined or cooperated.[4]

Thus far, rebellions against the Nu government were mainly limited to local ones, such as in Arakan, inherited from the pre-independence period, or ideological ones, such as the Communist and PVO rebellions. Within six months, major ethnic rebellions broke out as well. The armed wing of the KNU, known as the Karen National Defence Organization (KNDO), became one of the most important and most durable armed ethnic forces facing the Burmese state. Initially, the Karen, Kachin, and Chin units had remained loyal when desertions to the BCP began in mid-1948. In November, however, the KNU, along with two Mon separatist groups demanded the grant of independence to a Karen–Mon State, consisting of much of Lower and Southeastern Burma. From December, when the government refused the request, numerous Karen soldiers and police officers joined an unofficial KNU rebellion, followed by the Third Battalion Karen Rifles and then the First Kachin Rifles.[5] The rebellion became official in January.

Karen Christians dominated the KNU leadership, but much of the rank and file consisted of Karen Buddhists. Ethnic affinities, shared traditions of relative autonomy from central control, and the memory of harsh treatment at the hands of the BIA in the early months of the Japanese occupation were thus far more important than religion in mobilizing Karens against the Nu government. Moreover, not all Karens supported the Karen rebellion, for there were many others fighting on the side of the Rangoon regime. The Karens, sometimes in cooperation with BCP (with whom they took Mandalay) and White Band PVO units, launched a lightning sweep

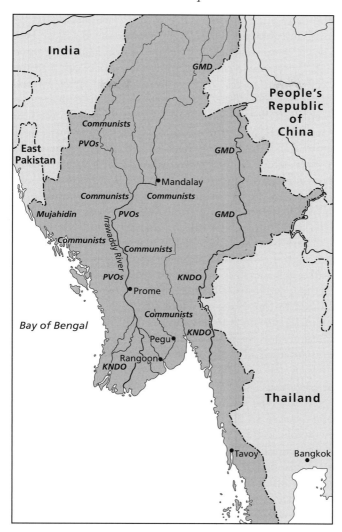

Map 2 Civil war in the early 1950s

through the Lower Burma delta region and very nearly took Rangoon.[6]
Although the KNU was soon forced back away from the capital, their near
success in toppling the Nu regime made certain that suppressing domestic
rebels would remain a chief priority, whether in words or in fact, of every
government after independence.

After the early years of the civil war, however, the insurgents faced a number of disadvantages in their fight against the Burmese government. In many ways, these weaknesses paralleled those facing the opponents of the Communist regime in the Russian Civil War between 1918 and 1921. In that war, the "White forces" had two fundamental flaws. First, they consisted of a myriad of tsarists, ethnic groups, and foreign interventionists who were only very weakly united in their opposition to the Communist regime. Unlike the Communists, they lacked a common ideology that would help to bind their forces together and mobilize the general population on their behalf. Second, they were unable to wrest control of the transportation infrastructure, which allowed Leon Trotsky, as overall Commander of the Red Army, to move his forces from one front to another with great speed. Trotsky was thus able to hit them quickly at their weakest points, exploit their geographical dispersement, and eliminate them one at a time. These flaws were essentially true of Burma's ethnic insurgents as well, although the BCP did have the potential (never realized) to compete for national leadership. This is not to say that the insurgents did not attempt to organize. In 1956, they created the Democratic National United Front followed by the National Democratic United Front in May 1959. The latter included the Karenni Progressive Party, the All-Burma Chin National League, and the Mon State Party, as well as the BCP.[7] Yet another united front emerged in 1960, when the National Liberation Alliance was formed.

In each case, the insurgent alliances proved temporary, due to differences in goals and the same kinds of personal conflicts that plagued the Nu regime. Unable to effect external unity, the insurgent groups were frequently unable, as the Communists had demonstrated even before independence, to maintain internal unity. In mid-1958, for example, several of the insurgent groups agreed to return to the legal fold. In late July, members of the People's Comrade Party (the former PVO) began to surrender, as did the Mon National Defence Organization (MNDO). Nevertheless much of this represented merely a fragmentation within these organizations, as one faction would make the arrangement and follow through with it, but others continued to resist in the name of the organization or joined other, ongoing insurgencies. The MNDO, for example, split between those who wanted autonomy within a federal system and those who would be happy with nothing less than a completely independent Mon state centered on Moulmein. Thus, while Nu's promise of autonomy was an incentive for many in the MNDO to surrender, it had little appeal for others, some of whom formed the insurgent New Mon State Party.[8]

In response to early rebel gains, Ne Win, who replaced Smith Dun as commander of the Armed Forces in 1949, began a dramatic expansion and improvement of the army. Burma was under martial law during 1948–1950, viewed as the worst years of the civil war for the government. By 1951, the Burmese Armed Forces were still insufficient in number to end armed opposition to the government. According to a CIA report, the Burmese Armed Forces were "small, inadequately trained, and poorly equipped." It was mainly an infantry force, consisting of about 43,000 regular and auxiliary troops. Although the Navy had been able to effect control over the delta and main waterways, it was small and composed only of coastal and river craft. The Air Force was also small and only capable of limited tactical reconnaissance and ground support. The armed forces controlled the central valley, where they were concentrated, while insurgents were scattered on the edge of the central valley, which meant that any attempt to concentrate Burmese forces against one or another rebel group would mean dangerous vulnerability somewhere else.[9]

In response to the challenge, Ne Win oversaw an expansion of the Army, focussed on improving its weaponry and the efficiency of its command and administration, and mobilized new resources for the war effort. Colonel (later Brigadier) Aung Gyi and Lt.-Colonel Ba Shin, for example, launched the Women's Auxiliary Corps as a means of mobilizing women for the war effort. They were to serve first in the Armed Forces secretarial branches and would later be "fully militarized." The nucleus of the corps was formed in April 1953 with forty-five women (soon expanded to over eighty). In the next five years, the experiment was considered a success and each of the branches of the Armed Forces began recruiting and training its own female wing.[10]

Slowly, the Army was able to return much of lowland Burma to central control and increasingly to isolate the insurgents to pockets around the northern and eastern rim of the country. The impact of the intersection of the insurgencies, the Cold War, and the growth of the Army on regional autonomy was significant. As in the colonial period, the Shan states had remained under the authority of local Shan *sawbwas* who exercised considerable political authority and maintained their own police forces. The fact that, in 1949 and 1950, parts of the Shan states had been overrun both by the Guomindang as it moved back and forth across the border with Yunnan and by the KNDO in its struggle with government troops forced the Army to assert its control over the area to avoid compromising its own strategic situation. In 1952, martial law was again declared, the *sawbwas'* governments were brought under Army administration, their police forces were integrated into those of the state, and the *sawbwas* agreed that after the termination of the military government (which occurred in 1954), their authority would be replaced by democratic government. Despite these developments, and the effecting of some centralizing reforms, the *sawbwas* remained in place, albeit with more circumspect authority. Their vulnerability at the hands of the Army, however, encouraged their establishment of the Social Democratic Party in 1955, to protect their position from further erosion. Nonetheless, in 1958–1959, they and the Karenni (Kayah) *sawbwas* handed their formal power over to the government, although they would continue to exert substantial, informal influence in their former domains.[11]

As the 1950s progressed and Nu became more confident that the rebellions were on the wane, he took a harder line on negotiations with the rebels. In a March 1957 speech on government policy before the Chamber of Deputies, Nu separated himself from the opposition, which favored a negotiated peace with the rebels. Nu believed that the rebels and their offers of peace could not be trusted; peace could not be had by negotiation, as the rebels, currently relying on outdated arms, would only remain above ground until a new opportunity for rebellion arose. If the government did make peace with them, the government would be betraying those, such as the armed forces, who were laying down their lives to save the union. Nu predicted that after such a peace, when the rebels went underground again, as he expected, those now supporting the government would refuse to help again, turning down the request with an "I told you so," and the country would be doomed. Instead, Nu proclaimed, if the rebels were sincere about peace, they would have to lay down their arms and subject themselves to legal prosecution. Their act of surrender would be considered as a mitigating circumstance, for those sentenced to death, the state would not actually execute them, and others would not have to serve full prison terms. Only after this and their abandonment of the "cult of the gun" would their political organizations be legalized.[12]

THE COLD WAR

The Nu government also had to respond to the pressures from both the Communist and non-Communist blocs to draw Burma into the Cold War, an agenda that was not shared by most of the insurgent groups, with the exception of the Communists. Nu's solution was neutrality in international affairs. Very early on, Nu had joined Jawaharlal Nehru and Sukarno in their opposition to alignment in the Cold War on the grounds that participation by young states in Africa and Asia would distract them from the more important challenges of developing their economies and ensuring political stability and the promotion of social welfare. Moreover, the Cold War powers were seen as possibly replacing old-style European colonialism with neocolonialism.

Nu also had concerns specifically related to Burma's ongoing domestic insurgencies, in that Cold War alignment would invite external intervention and possible connection with domestic insurgents. Burma had already faced the likelihood of the intersection of the Cold War and its own civil war in 1949, after Guomindang (GMD) remnants from China's own civil war fled into the Shan State, which they used as a base for several attempts to reinvade Yunnan. Repulsed by the People's Liberation Army, the GMD settled in for a longer stay in Burma, supplied by Taiwan and the CIA. Nu's concerns that a prolonged GMD presence in northeastern Burma would invite PRC intervention, a fear shared by the Burmese Army, were realized when the PRC began making threats about resolving the problem if Burma could not (and briefly invaded under the pretext of a boundary dispute). Nu successfully waged a diplomatic offensive in the UN that led to a nominal withdrawal of GMD forces, although many of its officers and soldiers would remain for decades, playing a significant role in the opium trade. Through shrewd political maneuvering, Nu was able to maintain an effectively neutral position between the PRC and the US into the mid-1950s, frequently supporting the PRC internationally, although criticizing in the UN Communist aggression, such as the North Korean invasion of South Korea that sparked the Korean War. The last incident reminded Nu of how precarious was his bifurcation of Burma's problems into internal and external spheres. When the government supported UN action in Korea in 1951, for example, the pro-Communist Socialists in the AFPFL who opposed the move were removed from the AFPFL and they organized the opposition Burma Workers' and Peasants' Party (BWPP).[13]

Despite US and Taiwanese promises to the contrary, GMD forces were never fully withdrawn and the responsibility for suppressing them fell back on the Army. The Army was generally successful in defeating the GMD in the field, but the difficult terrain of the Shan State that made insurgencies generally difficult to put down also worked in the GMD's favor. With each GMD defeat, the Nu government had been able to convince the UN to put pressure on Taiwan and more troops would be withdrawn, such withdrawals occurring in 1953, 1954, and 1961 but the GMD core continued to revitalize itself with local Shan and Wa recruits. Even as late as 1961 it still numbered up to three thousand men. The GMD was also slowly undergoing two transitions. First, it was changing shape from a foreign army to a local insurgent force, on the one hand, and a drug operation, on the other. The GMD had initially become involved in opium smuggling, soon bringing 90 percent of Burma's opium exports under their control, in order to finance themselves as US and Taiwanese support became irregular. After the 1961 defeat, the GMD withdrew first to Laos and then into Northwestern Thailand, along the Burmese border, where they recommenced their involvement in opium trafficking.[14]

Nu's policy of neutrality had successfully warded off serious attempts by the US to mobilize Burma against the Communists. It had also reduced the potential for PRC intervention to suppress the GMD. Nevertheless, the US continued to prepare for the time when, it hoped, Nu would change his mind. The revised US Cold War strategy in Burma was laid out in the National Security Council's statement of policy on US "Objectives and Courses of Action with Respect to Southeast Asia," adopted in January 1954. The US would make clear to the Nu government that it was interested in resolving the GMD issue and would be prepared to provide logistical support to accomplish this task. The US would act quickly on a recent agreement to supply arms and supplies to the Burmese Army, would be ready to recommence economic and technical assistance if asked to do so, and would urge Nu's cooperation with anti-Communist countries. As long as the Burmese government remained non-communist, the US should step lightly to prevent alienation of that government. In the meantime, the US would raise Burmese awareness of the PRC threat and the need for military defense, including "coordinated military action with other Southeast Asian countries." The US should also take steps to prepare alternative anti-Communist forces in case the Nu government was unable to stem the Communist advance. The US should develop cooperation among indigenous anti-Communist groups in the country, prepare for the organization among "suitable" ethnic groups of guerrilla forces, and activate the latter if local Communists made a large-scale attempt to seize power. If the PRC made an overt assault on Burma, the US would support a Burmese appeal to the UN, take military action against the PRC "as part of a UN collective action or in conjunction with France and the United Kingdom and any other friendly governments," and employ GMD forces in China proper, Korea, or Southeast Asia. If all or a substantial part of Burma were to fall to Communism, the US would support reliable anti-Communist resistance. When the Eisenhower Administration attempted to attract Burma into its new collective security arrangement in the region, the South East Asia Treaty Organization (SEATO), in 1954, Nu resisted.[15]

Burma had a number of reasons not to join SEATO. It had only recently gained the upper hand against domestic Communist rebels; it was still weak militarily and economically and first had to "set its own house in order." Even if Burma joined such a grouping, it would be unable to make a military contribution. It was not in the position to provoke the PRC, with which it had a 1,000-mile common border. It also remained unclear if there was strictly PRC aggression yet and it was still too difficult to differentiate between covert subversion and manifest invasion when assessing the nature of the PRC threat.[16] Nu extended an uncompromising view of extreme neutralism to the Non-Aligned Movement as well, for although he was willing to promote the principles of the Bandung Conference (1955), he was unwilling to join another bloc of states, even one built on the principle of non-alignment. To Nu, this would still represent a form of alignment.

BURMESE SOCIALISM

As one scholar points out, there is a myth that pervades historiography on the Nu period. In attempting to emphasize the catastrophic economic consequences of prolonged military rule, the Nu period is characterized as a time of prosperity. In reality, Nu's Burma was from the start an economic nightmare, though how much of this was due to the legacy of World War II destruction, the devastation of the early years of the civil war, or a combination of both is unclear.[17] Regardless of the government's unfortunate economic starting position, Nu and many of his associates viewed unbridled capitalism as a serious obstacle to reinvigorating the economy. Before independence, the Burmese experience with capitalism was inseparably intertwined with that of colonial rule, which had introduced it. For the average Burmese, at the root of colonial exploitation was the ruthlessness of foreign capital, the cruelties of the world capitalist order, and the greedy intentions of agents of foreign companies. Moreover, those non-European elites in the cities, whether Chinese, Indian, or Eurasian, owed their greater prosperity vis-à-vis the Burmese to capitalism. Burmese nationalism since the 1920s had been directed toward gaining self-rule and then independence, not so much to gain democratic freedoms, of which the average villager understood very little, but to alleviate the burdens of colonial economic exploitation.

Aung San had laid out the principles for the economy of independent Burma in May 1947 at the Sorrento Villa Conference, promising that capitalism would never again dominate Burma. Aung San understood, however, that there could be no sweeping, overnight economic revolution and that, in reality, private property could never be abolished. He instead called for the careful construction of a socialist state. At first, the state would merely control the country's sources of natural power, its communications and transportation infrastructure, its teak forests, and its mineral wealth. When Burma was ready for state socialism, the state or people's cooperatives would assume control of all means of production, while allowing private ownership. The Sorrento Villa Conference thus established the economic basis of a truly independent Burma, one that would inform national planning until 1988.[18]

Along these lines, foreign businesses became the first target of the Nu government when it took power in 1948. Nu had argued, more vocally in mid-1947 than ever before, that during the colonial period, a small class of foreign capitalists had dominated the Burmese economy. Foreign businesses in Burma were not surprised when the government began nationalizing their concerns because AFPFL statements over the course of 1947 had foreshadowed this, although foreign businessmen had held on to the hope that London would negotiate with Rangoon on behalf of their interests. The Burmese government would only concede non-interference with British commercial concerns in the country during the interim period between the signing of the treaty and January 1948, when independence was formally declared. Winston Churchill, the leader of the Conservative opposition in the British Parliament, strongly voiced his concern regarding the fate of British businesses. Nevertheless, Labour MPs who wanted to distance themselves from colonialism as quickly as possible overrode his opposition.[19]

The Nu government quickly took steps to control the flight of capital from the country, particularly to India. This first took the form of strict control on the export of precious stones, government control of Sterling Area currency and security transactions, and limits on single normal business remittances to £100. The government also prohibited the transfer of savings-bank accounts out of the country and limited money-order remittances to forty rupees per person per day. Unlike the case in many other newly independent countries that utilized nationalization, Nu did not seek simply a turnover of business elites. He did not want to see the emergence of a new Burmese business class to usurp this position, but rather the creation of state socialism, which he saw as the only way of preventing the same kind of social inequalities Burma had suffered in the colonial period. Later, however, the Nu government wanted Burmese businesspeople to set up effective businesses as a means of putting the country's commerce into Burmese hands. However, by 1955, it complained

Figure 4.1 Nu-era state propaganda promises a better life for rural cultivators

that Burmese businessmen were trying to make a quick profit by selling their import or export licenses to foreigners and the latter in turn hoarded the goods and profiteered.[20]

By 1950, Nu had developed the Pyidawtha, or "pleasant country," scheme for government-directed economic development and the creation of a welfare state (see Fig. 4.1).[21] The first eight-year plan, whose goal was to increase the country's level of production by 88 percent, was begun in 1952. State investment increased steadily in the first few years and, by the end of 1954–1955, investment had reached 31 percent of the total planned. In terms of real growth Burma's GDP was 30 percent greater at this time than it had been from 1950 to 1951 and thus the government expected to reach its target on time. Despite the grand hopes of the economic development plans, Burma failed to escape from its colonial-era dependence on its main export crop, rice. Thus, the prosperity of the domestic economy was pinned to fluctuations in the world market. When the Korean War broke out in 1950, Burmese rice exports grew, but then fell from 1953 with the collapse of rice prices when that war ended, reducing export earnings. This would later lead the Caretaker Government (1958–1960) to emphasize the diversification of crops so that Burma would not remain so dependent upon rice exports. Dependence on artificial sources of income thus grew as Burmese rice exports slumped. A peace treaty was signed with Japan in November 1954, for example, which included a reparation agreement. Japan agreed to repay Burma 200 million dollars in goods and services over a ten-year period. Another 50 million dollars was allotted for joint enterprises over the course of the same period. In December 1955, Nikita Khrushchev arrived in Rangoon for a one-week visit during which he promised Russian aid for Burmese economic development, including industrial plants and major irrigation works. In exchange, the Burmese would supply the Soviet Union with rice.[22]

By 1957, the Nu government's economic and social initiatives had led to severe problems threatening the stability of the country. Nu had realized that he had made a serious error in emphasizing economic reform and social welfare from 1951 without first having resolved the ongoing civil war. As he explained:

our greatest blunder . . . [was] our diversion to economic and social welfare activities as soon as the law and order situation improved slightly, instead of concentrating all our energies on the complete restoration of law and order in the country.[23]

A major financial crisis also resulted from inflation, the failure of the rice crop due to drought, rising costs of living, and falling foreign exchange reserves.[24]

A DIFFICULT DEMOCRACY

Although the first fourteen years of Burmese independence hold the romantic appeal of being Burma's only democratic period, the "Nu years" were difficult for the country. Independence under the Japanese during the war had proved to be a poor training ground for the real independence from 1948. Operating under the observation and manipulation of Japanese military authorities, the kind of bureaucratic and political infighting that would dominate Burmese politics in the years ahead was generally absent. After the war, the solidarity forged by opposition to the return of British rule and the presence of the charismatic Aung San had already begun to fall apart in 1947, the assassination of Aung San and his cabinet serving as the main catalyst. It was already apparent to many even before the British flag was finally lowered that this solidarity had begun to disintegrate and that a new kind of politics would ensue. As early as November 1947, Nu had planned to serve as Prime Minister for only the first six months following his assumption of office. He would then step down, in July 1948, in favor of his deputy prime minister and would then devote himself to strengthening the AFPFL as president of the organization. For Nu, this was necessary because it had become clear that some members of the League had turned away from the "correct path" and had begun to engage in wrongdoing by asking for privileges as a reward for their sacrifice during the independence struggle, competing for personal power and influence, and misusing power.[25] The overwhelming challenges faced by the new government in holding the country together forced Nu to abandon these plans to surrender power to a successor early on. Alongside the outbreak and continuance of the civil war, the corruption and political infighting would emerge as a significant challenge to the Nu administration, leading to its downfall, twice, in 1958 and again in 1962.

The first post-independence national elections held in 1951 were compromised by party politics within the AFPFL and the ongoing civil war. The League had originally been dominated by the Communists and other leftwing groups but after the war had expanded to include a heterogeneous assembly of parties and groups, many of which reflected the interests of the middle class. As mentioned, Communists leaders were expelled or shunned, most of the PVOs had joined the former with the outbreak of the Civil War, and in December 1950, leftwing Socialists who had abandoned the moderate Socialist Party that now controlled the AFPFL to form the BWPP were expelled from the League. This meant, as one scholar has pointed out, that as the original leadership of the AFPFL was overturned and their Marxist ideology was abandoned, the League lost "its initial unifying set of beliefs."[26] In this confusing ideological landscape, the AFPFL relied mainly upon its association with the late Aung San and Nu's personal charisma, the fact that many of its serious rivals were now in arms against the government, and that elections could only be held in government-controlled and thus AFPFL-dominated areas to garner a 1951 electoral victory that amounted to less than 60 percent of the vote cast in an election in which less than 20 percent of qualified voters cast a ballot.[27]

In the April 1956 elections for the House of Deputies, the AFPFL ran on its record and on the continuation of state policies. Its chief opponent was the National United Front (NUF), which ran mainly on the pledge that it would immediately begin peace negotiations with the rebels. The AFPFL won the elections, in part because Nu asked Ne Win for the Army's support in order to keep likely opposition voters away from the polls in some cases and to throw Army votes to weak League candidates in others. The following month, Nu temporarily relinquished the prime ministership for a one-year period during which, in his continuing capacity as President of the AFPFL, he would reorganize the League. Meanwhile, Ba Swe took Nu's place at the helm of state. Ba Swe intended to make the restoration of law and order the first priority of his government. Since reason and liberal amnesty offers had all failed to stop the violence, the government would intensify its efforts to bring matters to a close by increasing the effectiveness of the police, expanding the Army, and intensifying the activities of paramilitary brigades. The government would also take on the nation's moral decay by educating people in administration and politics in the "evils of corruption," by taking severe measures against those guilty of immorality, and by cleaning up the administrative and political system.[28]

Nu resumed the prime ministership in June 1957. A few months earlier, U Win Maung had been unanimously nominated as the President of the Union, a position second only to that of the Prime Minister. Win Maung's selection was due to the AFPFL principle at the time that given Burma's multi-ethnic makeup, the presidency should be rotated among the different ethnic groups. Burma's first president had been a Shan and the outgoing president, Dr. Ba U, was a Burman. Thus, the presidency would now go to a Karen, Win Maung, followed, it was predicted, by an Arakanese, a Chin, a Kayah, and a Mon.[29]

THE PRESS AND PROPAGANDA

Nu's estimation of the importance of print propaganda is hard to gauge. Since the 1930s, he himself had used print literature to spread political ideas. Not only did he write his own plays to convey political messages during the colonial period; he had also helped encourage the influx of foreign ideologies into Burma through the Nagani (Red Dragon) Book Club, which he co-established with Than Tun in Rangoon in 1937. On the other hand, while Nu had suggested in 1947 that the US launch a propaganda counteroffensive against anti-US stories appearing in the Burmese press, he intimated to the US chargé d'affaires that mass propaganda would not really work because most Burmese did not read the papers. Instead, Nu advised that the best way to win over the Burmese masses was to provide solid US assistance in the form of infant and maternal welfare.[30]

Whether or not Nu was misunderstood, when he became Prime Minister, Nu took the press seriously and reacted very harshly to negative coverage of his government's performance. This reaction, perhaps even overreaction, indicated that Nu indeed saw the press as a very powerful propaganda tool. The Soviet Union and later the PRC saw it too. Since publishing houses in these countries were state-owned, they could afford to pump thousands of books into Burma at cheap prices, most of these books having a strong ideological slant. The PRC developed an especially effective approach, having Chinese books translated into Burmese in China, printing them in Burmese script, and then exporting them to Burma. After complaints from the Burmese press, both from political and financial considerations, the Nu government banned the importation of Burmese language books that had been printed abroad.[31]

The first major problem with the domestic press occurred in Rangoon in March 1948, when AFPFL supporters protested against criticism of the AFPFL by certain newspapers. The protest turned violent, leading to damage to the presses of *The Economic Daily*, *The Forum*, and *Oway*. Nu, while stressing the problem of demonstrators taking the law into their own hands and promising legal action against them, agreed with the demonstrators that the press criticism of the AFPFL was "unrestrained and unwarranted." The press was voicing the hostility of the "great land owners" and the "great capitalists." As he admonished, the "workers and peasants should not . . . allow themselves to be tricked by newspapers into losing sight of their real enemies and of being diverted." Nevertheless, Nu explained that instead of violence, he would pursue the "correct course" of beginning legal proceedings against the newspapers. The government tackled the press vigorously during the year that Ba Swe officially served as Prime Minister, although Nu, as AFPFL president, remained influential from behind the scenes. In May 1956, U Pe Thein, the chief editor of the Mandalay daily *Ludu* was arrested for an editorial he had written criticizing Nu's policies, while U Hla, the publisher, was sentenced to nine months' "rigorous" imprisonment. Hla's crime was that his newspaper had mistakenly claimed that a certain monk had died in a riot several years earlier.[32] On 17 August, in his capacity as AFPFL president, Nu told students at the School of Journalism that while democracy needed a free press, journalists needed to remember that the newspaper is a public utility and advised them that when they decided what or what not to write about, "the general test to be applied is whether what you propose to write is in the interests of the people of the country . . . if it is not, you should refrain from writing it."[33]

Nu also mobilized his skills as a playwright to produce favorable propaganda that warned the Burmese about foreign intervention and political manipulation of internal political groups. The best example is the play *The People Win Through* (*Ludu Aung Than*). Written in cooperation with a number of well-known Burmese literati and U Thant, *The People Win Through* is the story of a young Burmese who joins the Communists in the ongoing civil war and soon becomes disenchanted with the rebels. The story emphasizes not so much the evils of Communism but the problems caused when external forces, from any quarter, attempt to interfere in Burma's internal problems. This became one of the most heavily circulated publications of the Nu period, leading to both radio performances and a cartoon strip, and was included in the national school curriculum as required reading. Hollywood and the US Embassy eventually became involved, transforming the play into a specifically anti-Communist story, and produced a Burmese language movie that was by the mid-1950s shown everywhere in Burma, not only in city theaters, but in makeshift cinemas in warehouses and in roadside stalls. Soon after, an English translation of the play was published in New York for an American audience, strengthening yet again the play's anti-Communist message. In this way, Burmese propaganda against the intersection of foreign interests and domestic rebellions was manipulated by Cold War politics into propaganda that served the interests of the West.[34]

BUDDHISM AND THE STATE

While Nu is remembered for having encouraged a strong relationship between Buddhism and the state, prior to 1949 there were few indications in his official speeches, policies, or appointments that he would soon move in this direction, although admittedly in his personal life he was a devoted Buddhist. It has thus been suggested that perhaps the shedding of the Communists and other far left leaders from the AFPFL in the early independence period gave Nu the freedom to explore more traditional means of encouraging national unity, while others have entertained the notion that Nehru may have recommended to Nu that now that leftist unity had failed, he should pursue "Buddhist Unity."[35]

Whatever the reasons for the timing, three main factors encouraged Nu's adoption of this approach. First, throughout his rule and after, Nu was particularly keen to produce meritorious works out of genuine personal religiosity. Second, monks had formed a powerful lobby since the end of World War II. Some monastic leaders pushed in 1947 for the designation of Buddhism as the state religion on the grounds that over 80 percent of Burma's population was Buddhist. The All-Burma Buddhist Association and the All-Burma Pongyi Association had been particularly vocal in their opposition to provisions in the 1947 Constitution that allowed freedom of religion. Third, Nu believed that promoting Buddhism was one way to fight the attraction of Communism among segments of the general population. Nu's Buddhist program began with the passage of the Vinasaya Act of 1949, which required all monks to be registered and established ecclesiastical tribunals to judge cases of monastic misbehavior. The Pali University and Dhammacariya Act of 1950 set up a Pali University that would train monks in the Dhamma and produce Buddhist missionary monks. The same year, the Buddha Sasana Council Act provided the means to enforce the government's policies regarding Buddhism. With Nu's encouragement, Buddhist laymen, many of them wealthy, served on the Council. As a result of large private donations and generous state funding, the Rangoon headquarters of the Buddha Sasana Council (BSC) expanded rapidly to include Buddhist universities and an advanced institute, the Maha Pasana Guha, a large man-made cave, and the World Peace Pagoda. The Pali Education Board Act of 1952 created a body to oversee government-sponsored Pali examinations.[36]

The BSC represented a state-backed body for the promotion of Buddhism. The BSC Executive Committee passed on to the government resolutions it had made on 19 September 1954. These included the resumption of Buddhist religious instruction in state schools and the formation of an Inquiry Committee to study the matter of providing non-Buddhist religious instruction in the schools as well. Nu afterwards announced that both requests were acceptable and took steps to initiate both. Nu began having Buddhism taught in state schools, but also tried to allow the teaching of the Bible and the Koran as well. However, monks tried to block this. Thereupon, Nu, arguing that if the Bible and the Koran could not be taught, then the Buddhist scriptures could not be taught either, suspended the teaching of Buddhism in state schools. Monks and laymen protested. In order to get dissenting monks to withdraw their complaints, Nu broadcast a speech on 25 September in which he called upon the monks to view religion and politics separately. Nonetheless, as would also the military later on, Nu used Buddhism as a means of expelling the Communist-oriented BWPP from the AFPFL and challenging the appeal of the Communist insurgents, on the basis of their adoption of atheistic Marxist-Leninist doctrine.[37]

Arrangements for the Sixth Great Buddhist Council to commemorate the 2,500th anniversary of Gotama Buddha's Enlightenment began in 1951 but were not completed until 1954. The Great Council lasted for two years, from May 1954 until May 1956. At some point toward the close of the proceedings the suggestion was made – rekindling an old dream of Burmese monks – that Buddhism should become the state religion. Nu resolved to work toward the realization of this goal. In March 1956, Nu outlined his three reasons for doing so: to make another deed of merit equal to that of the convening of the Council; the realization that other monks and laymen would share this desire; and that if this was delayed, it would be taken up by fanatical politicians, monks, and laymen. If the issue did fall into the hands of fanatics, Nu argued, then this would not be good for Buddhism as it would bring discrimination against non-Buddhists, and it would work against liberty, equality, and justice. If Nu sponsored the project, however, he would be able to confront the fanatics without being accused of betraying the religion.

The proclamation of Buddhism as the state religion was delayed for a considerable period. Opinion was still strongly influenced by Aung San, who, in 1946, had called for a clear division between politics and religion in an independent Burma. One scholar has even suggested that the influence of Aung San's style of nationalism was so complete that the earlier tradition of Buddhist nationalism promoted by Ottama and San was nearly forgotten until Nu attempted to take the AFPFL back in this direction. As for the Army, which would soon emerge as preeminent on the political scene, it still espoused a kind of secularism that went hand in hand with its perception that this was part of the proper orientation of a modern military force. The Army also had important practical reasons for avoiding the promotion of Buddhism. Chief amongst these was the ongoing civil war, in which many of the opponents the Army sought to pacify were non-Buddhists.[38]

THE AFPFL SPLIT

The AFPFL was about fourteen years old when it finally imploded in 1958. The causes of the split were both institutional and personal. On the one hand, this odd political umbrella for diverse and constantly bickering parties had lasted so long mainly because of the popularity and aura of its late founding father, Aung San. Further, the departure of the CPB in 1946 and the expulsion of the BCP in 1948 – and their subsequent armed insurrections against the government – removed its most extreme wings and encouraged support for a more moderate leadership that appealed broadly to Burmese (especially Burman) nationalists for a number of years. However, as the regime wore on and military successes seemed to have reduced the insurgent threat, internal disagreements over domestic and foreign policy became more severe. These differences were further complicated by personal rivalries among AFPFL leaders that transcended policy issues. Such a rivalry emerged slowly between Kyaw Nyein and Nu. As personal rivalry broadened to include other major party leaders, the AFPFL split in April 1958 into two competing halves: the "Clean" faction led by Nu and Thakin Tin, the latter viewed as an "uneducated" socialist, because he favored developing agriculture as the main goal of the government; and the "Stable" faction led by Kyaw Nyein and Ba Swe, both viewed as "educated" socialists because they favored industrialization.[39]

To shore up support for the Clean AFPFL, Nu released and pardoned numerous political prisoners, including one hundred students detained since the government ban on the organization of student unions in 1956. Nu also softened his opposition to autonomous states and legalized formerly illegal parties, such as the Communists. The Army was worried that the government was falling under Communist influence while Nu worried that the Army supported the Stable AFPFL. Nu then dissolved parliament, announced new elections, and passed the Budget by presidential decree. The Clean faction then pushed for the expulsion of members of the Stable faction from the police and civil government, and then from the Army, to hurt their chances in winning the next election. By mid-September, the political crisis that had been caused by the split had gone beyond Nu's ability to cope. Murders of Clean and Stable AFPFL members were reported to the police. In the middle of the crisis, Nu left on a tour of Upper Burma and only returned on 22 September. In the meantime, the Army had surrounded the capital and prevented many, but not all, of the Union Military Police Units loyal to Nu from entering it. Even so, in the Clean AFPFL strongholds in the Tharrawaddy, Insein, and Prome districts there were over 10,000 militiamen who were ready to come to Nu's aid should he need it. Reportedly, the Army wanted no confrontation between itself and the Nu government, for this would only create an opportunity for the Communists to re-assert themselves. The Army decided to act upon Nu's return and so brought the chief strategic points in Rangoon and Insein under its control, secured the armories of the city police and Union Military Police, and sealed off all road connexions. On 23 September, Colonel Maung Maung visited Nu to warn him that, if Clean AFPFL forces attacked the Army, the Army would defend itself. Maung Maung visited Nu again the following day, this time with Colonel Aung Gyi, and complained of how Nu had manipulated the Constitution for his own ends and that the situation was a powder-keg, although they would try to prevent violence if they could. Ultimately, Nu agreed to resign and hand over power to a "caretaker" government, under the leadership of Ne Win, that would manage the country for a six-month period.[40]

CONCLUSION

Even before independence, the AFPFL had suffered an irreparable blow with the assassination of Aung San, although the full impact would not be realized for years. Without strong central leadership, something the erratic Nu could not offer, there was little to hold an umbrella organization together. The AFPFL was hydra-headed and as it shed its original leadership and shifted toward the political center, it lost its vision. But the AFPFL was not the only problem. The Nu government was under constant pressure to build a socialist economy while fighting an ongoing and very serious civil war, on the one hand, and maintaining an equally challenging neutral position in the Cold War, on the other. Political fragmentation, economic slowdown (after the end of the Korean War), and a careful international balancing act, all played out in the context of a country divided into republican and rebel areas, prevented the Nu government from developing effective state institutions. Nu had no choice but to surrender control to the military, temporarily, in 1958. While his regime was overstretched, underdeveloped, and riddled from within, over the course of the 1950s, the military became larger, better equipped, and better managed.

CHAPTER 5

Dress rehearsals, 1958–1962

The period from 1958 to 1960 is often viewed more or less correctly as a dress rehearsal for the military takeover in 1962. In actuality, there were two. Nu had plans to take Burma in a new direction in the 1960s, including relinquishing his leadership. Preparations for this new Burma were built around Buddhist nationalism, and were less elitist, and economically more socialist than anything seen in the 1950s. Just as the military took Burma along a "revolutionary" course, Nu's vision of the future promised nothing less. There is another reason for considering the period from 1958 to 1962 as one entity. Although the military surrendered its direct involvement in the civil administration, it did not surrender its physical control of territory under the republic's control, probably to avoid the kind of tense situation with regard to the militias that had existed in 1958. The military waited until 1962 to put an end to the Nu regime, but it had the capacity to do this at any time it wished. In the meantime, Burmese watched to see if Nu's Burma between 1960 and 1962 could live up to the heightened economic prosperity and efficiency of the military caretaker government from 1958 to 1960.

THE INTRODUCTION OF THE CARETAKER GOVERNMENT

Nu announced the end of his five-month-old Clean AFPFL government in a brief broadcast on the evening of 24 September 1958. If general elections were held as scheduled in November, he argued, these would be neither free nor fair. Nu then explained that he had invited General Ne Win to make it possible to hold truly free elections within six months (April 1959) and Ne Win had accepted. He now appealed to the entire population to "give their support to General Ne Win in the same way as they have given their support to me." Nu had also written two letters that he postdated to 26 September 1958, the date of the proposed transfer of power. In the first, Nu undertook to resign the prime ministership and promised that the

Chamber of Deputies would elect Ne Win as the new Prime Minister. The second letter was Ne Win's letter of acceptance. Both letters stressed that the Army should not become involved in politics beyond the performance of their new administrative duties, that internal peace should be restored, and that Burma should continue to follow a strictly neutral foreign policy. Burmese soldiers then entered government buildings and police stations, mounted two-inch guns at the airport, and set up roadblocks throughout the city to check automobiles for hidden firearms.[1]

Students protested against the changeover, as did different political groups who had had problems with the military in the past or sympathies with the insurgents who were currently fighting the Army. It took some weeks for Burmese to understand fully that this was not a military coup. Two weeks after the transfer, the NUF was still convinced that members of the Stable AFPFL had joined with the military to seize power. Nu publicly countered claims that he had been forced to surrender power at gunpoint, explaining that he had only done so to prevent internal political disintegration, foreign intervention, and bloodshed.[2]

TRAINING AND MORALITY

One of the targets of the caretaker regime was bureaucratic inefficiency and corruption. Part of their solution was to build up a new spirit of personal and institutional responsibility to the state and to the people. The caretaker regime ran training and reorientation classes for government officials, reeducating 9,000 in the first nine months. The government was also to abandon some administrative practices inherited from the colonial period. In April 1957, the Home Ministry had ordered that all government correspondence, except foreign correspondence, was to be in Burmese, but civil servants continued to rely upon English anyway. However, the Caretaker Government now enforced the order. In November 1958, it created a Screening Committee to investigate the promotions, demotions, dismissals, and transfers of government officials made by the Nu-Tin government during its five months in office. In December, the Council of Ministers formed an Executive Branch Punishment Committee, consisting of heads of departments, to guide ministries in rooting out inefficiency and negligence among civil servants, with the exception of the judicial services. Civilian politicians were also investigated and three months later, 371 civilian politicians had been arrested, including 58 from the Clean AFPFL, 4 from the Stable AFPFL, and 309 from other parties.[3]

The Caretaker Government created social and discussion groups for people of different ages known as the "National Solidarity Associations" (NSAs). The NSAs were organized throughout the country at the ward, village, town, and district levels to make the population aware of their civic responsibilities and mobilize them in carrying them out. Through the NSAs, the Army believed it was creating a new forum for communication between the general population and the government. The NSAs would achieve this in two ways: by allowing democracy to flourish (by helping the authorities to fight and apprehend economic and political insurgents, as well as other criminals, in order to eliminate lawlessness) and by the creation of peaceful conditions necessary for the masses to pursue happiness and economic prosperity. In order to accomplish these goals, the associations were empowered both to aid the government in maintaining public morality and suppressing crime, and to educate the masses concerning their rights and responsibilities in a democracy. Further, the NSA Constitution required collective efforts to counter attempts to "undermine the development of democratic institutions, the maintenance of stable social conditions and the development of trade and progress." The NSA Constitution also stipulated that there would be no central unit or headquarters to control association activities. However, it also arranged for annual conferences of the associations at which a nine-member executive committee served for a one-year term; this council mainly handled applications for membership and discussion of proposals for association activities. NSA members were supposedly drawn from "among prominent non-political citizens" in order to provide the population "with possible alternative leadership to local politicians who formerly were dominant."[4]

The smooth functioning of the associations required the separation of association activities from those of politics. The association was not to become a political organization in any way. Members were allowed to engage in politics and belong to political parties, but, according to the NSA Constitution, they were not allowed to discuss politics, promote political parties, allow the introduction of an "aura of politics" within the association itself, or take sides in any political conflict. The NSAs, armed with crossbows and bamboo spears, were said to act as "the people's sentinels," always watching out for criminals and insurgents. They helped make the courts operate more efficiently, organized supplies of firewood, helped solve sanitation problems, and engaged in a number of other tasks. Simultaneously with the emergence of the NSAs, the Army overhauled the leadership of Burmese labour unions, banning politicians from union leadership. All union leaders were now required to "come from the ranks."[5]

THE SWEAT CAMPAIGNS

The Corporation of Rangoon was declared incompetent on 29 November 1958, leading to the compulsory retirement of all thirty-five of its elected councilors. The former Municipal Commissioner blamed the dismal state of the Corporation on a lack of civic pride among the public and the incompetence of both the councilors and the corporation civil staff. In place of the elected leadership, a highly decorated brigade commander, Colonel Tun Sein, was now appointed simultaneously as Corporation Commissioner of the Rangoon Municipal Corporation and Mayor of Rangoon. The 38-year-old, 240-pound, graduate of the University of Rangoon and the Military Academy, was the son of a schoolmaster and an inspectress of schools, and was known then and a few years later (when he was reassigned to Kengtung) as an efficient administrator who liked to keep things clean and tidy. Like other military men assigned to civil posts during the Caretaker period, he cut through the kind of red tape that had hamstrung the Nu government. Daw Khin Ma Gyi, who opened up the Khant Khant Gyi Photo Studio in Rangoon on the corner of 35th and Mahabandula Streets in 1952, relates how she had erected a huge (and illegal) sign that took up the entire corner; she paid the yearly fines levied by the municipality rather than remove the sign because it was cheaper than paying for legal advertising. When Tun Sein took charge of Rangoon, he explained that there would be no more fines and ordered her to take down the sign immediately; she quickly complied with the order.[6]

Tun Sein's present task was to restore Rangoon to the splendid, smoothly functioning city it had been (or was remembered to have been) prior to World War II. While much had been rebuilt since the devastating Allied air attacks of that war, Rangoon was unprepared for the volume of refugees who would seek shelter there during that conflict and after the outbreak of civil war in Burma from 1948. New homes were not built privately or by the cash-strapped Nu government. Instead, hundreds of thousands lived in fire-prone ramshackle huts scattered about the capital where overcrowding and overburdened sanitation systems led to disease. When Nu promised in 1957 to deport the squatters to new settlements in four months, he retracted his statements in the face of squatter protests. With greater determination and perhaps greater intimidation, the Caretaker Government moved squatters, vagrants, beggars, and lepers out of Rangoon. To house them, army engineers conducted surveys for the creation of three satellite towns on the outskirts of Rangoon, named Okkalapa North, Okkalapa South, and Thaketa. Over 150 miles of new roads soon followed, as did streetlights and piped tap water for each town block. Every squatter family was registered and given a lot in one of the satellite towns and a deadline for evacuation from Rangoon. Within six months, 170,000 people were shipped out, with their belongings, on army trucks. Supplies of lumber, roofing, and bamboo were also shipped in for sale at cost for use in building new homes. Reflecting the lowered population level and perhaps the removal of the threat to public health associated with the former slums, the total number of deaths in Rangoon dropped from 7,603 (1957–1958) to 5,328 (1958–1959).[7]

Simultaneously with resettlement, Tun Sein launched "sweat" campaigns to instill civic pride and an awareness of public responsibilities in keeping Rangoon clean, both physically and morally. The streets and pavements of Rangoon were covered with garbage mainly because of corruption – out of every three trips a garbage truck driver was required to make, he might make only one and sell the remaining gasoline on the black market. The campaigns also were meant to raise respect for the law as all of the measures represented a strict reading of the Corporation of Rangoon's municipal by-laws. They provided 3,000 garbage cans and organized the systematic disposal of their contents. On 7 December 1958, Tun Sein began "Operation Clean-up" to remove dirt and litter from Rangoon's streets with a "mass assault" by over 5,000 members of the government, the armed forces, and the public in four separate areas. A week later, a second "assault" included over 9,000 soldiers, government servants, and members of the public who cleaned another four sections of the city. Thereafter, 2,000 government servants would sweep the streets and clean the pavements every Sunday. Similar "sweat" campaigns were conducted all over the country, in small towns and villages.[8]

Unauthorized stalls were removed from the pavements and from parking spaces. Tun Sein also targeted the problems of water supply and sewerage. To keep people from defecating and urinating in drains, existing latrines were now put under proper maintenance and additional temporary bamboo latrines were erected until underground toilets could be built. Tun Sein contracted with the US International Co-operation Administration to purchase US$700,000 worth of equipment to improve Rangoon's supply of water and its sewerage system. Streets were widened and potholes were filled. Another public blight was the red coating that resulted from spat betel juice. Burmese chew the betel nut, wrapped in a banana leaf, as a mild stimulant, which results in red, bitter saliva. Under the Caretaker Government, betel-chewing became taboo in Rangoon, where the municipality prohibited shopkeepers from selling "pan" which was the "betel leaf concoction," in order to keep the pavements free of ugly red blotches that looked disturbingly like blood. Noise pollution in the form of the unrestrained use of radio sets was also brought under control and owners were forced to take out licenses for them. Seventeen revised bus lines helped to relieve the problem of urban congestion in Rangoon.[9]

The clean-up campaign also targeted crows, flies, mice, and other stray animals, even moving stray cattle out of the downtown area. Stray dogs were a particular problem on Rangoon's streets, being a nuisance to both pedestrians and motorists. On Buddhist grounds, the Nu government had refused to allow the extermination of the animals and developed an impractical plan of capturing them, dividing them by gender, and then resettling them on same-sex islands. Under Tun Sein's administration, soldiers toured the streets of Rangoon by night, laying pieces of poisoned meat by the stray dogs they came across. Within six months 50,000 dogs and 10,000 crows were exterminated in this manner.[10]

Tun Sein emphasized civic responsibility as well. In early December 1958, he told 1,500 teachers from 250 Rangoon schools to foster greater discipline among their students. He also pressured bus-drivers and conductors to adopt good manners and polite language. The Army began giving "practical lessons" in citizenship and enforced tight moral discipline. It suppressed vendors of pornographic literature. It now had every household member above twelve years old in Rangoon photographed for national registration. Both soldiers and police were ordered to hunt down street toughs and gangs who were despoiling public buildings. Among them were two gangs of juvenile delinquents, called the "Eagles" and the "Road Devils," who had been heavily influenced by Western comic books and Hollywood movies. They had begun to assault other young people leading the Rangoon Police Commissioner to order their arrest in February 1959. Crime rates quickly plummeted.[11]

Aung Gyi was put in charge of the Committee to Combat Economic Insurgency (CCEI). The Caretaker Government targeted "economic insurgents" in order to limit profiteering, secure fair prices and thus stabilize the cost of living. The anti-hoarding campaign focussed on Rangoon and involved the cooperation of the Army, the police, and the Bureau of Special Investigation. It began in late November 1958 with the sealing up of 300 shops and warehouses in Rangoon in order to check stocks for hoarding. In official press releases, the fight against economic insurgents was lauded for putting a number of Indian and Chinese traders out of business. The Civil Supplies Department also issued orders against the hoarding of canned fish. The next day, shops and warehouses in Chinatown in Rangoon were sealed up to check for hoarding. The investigators then hit Mogul Street to look for smuggled gold and over the course of the following three days they sealed and then investigated safe deposit boxes in Rangoon banks. As fines alone had proven not to work for preventing hoarding, the penalty was raised to three years in prison. In expectation of the courts being over-burdened by a tremendous increase in cases against economic insurgents, the government posted magistrates at police stations so that they could quickly pass judgments as cases emerged.[12]

Aung Gyi also sought to reduce the cost of living. In order to lower the prices of consumer goods, the Army sold beef and distributed firewood. Restrictions were introduced on the retailing of essential commodities. Fish, firewood and other domestic requirements and essential commodi-ties such as textiles were now sold at controlled prices. By mid-December 1958, the government's price control program began limiting importers and wholesalers to 5 percent profit each and retailers to a profit of 10 percent. Nylon was declared an essential consumer item and made a government monopoly. The Civil Supplies Department, cooperatives, joint venture cor-porations (JVCs), and the Defence Services' Institute (DSI) opened more retail shops. Although the military issued regular statements about their success in lowering the cost of living, this was claimed to be propaganda by the civilian opposition. U Ba Nyein of the NUF claimed in Parliament in August, that in reality many essential items, such as fish, poultry, and fuel, were almost unavailable. If someone wanted any of the few items available, they had to stand in line for hours from early dawn.[13]

THE RETURN TO CIVILIAN RULE

Ba Swe, leader of the Stable AFPFL, announced on 1 January 1959 that he had no objection to adding another six months to the six months already given to the Caretaker Government and in mid-February he tabled a motion to this effect. The Clean AFPFL, with the support of the NUF, then pressured the Caretaker Government to stick to its promise to hold new elections by April. In a shrewd political move, Ne Win and his cabinet resigned in February while simultaneously explaining that it would be impossible to hold fair and free elections in April without putting the anti-insurgency campaign in jeopardy. In order for the Caretaker Government to accomplish its mission, Ne Win demanded that Section 116 of the Union Constitution be amended to remove the six-months limitation on the term of office of non-parliamentary members. The Caretaker Government also released copies of a Communist Party directive regarding its plans to infiltrate the Clean AFPFL. Ne Win was afterwards re-confirmed as prime minister and the Constitution was amended to allow him to remain in this capacity until 1960.[14]

There were strong indications that the caretaker regime would end with an electoral victory by the Stable AFPFL. By February 1959, the Stable AFPFL had gained a majority in the Parliament due to desertions of MPs from the Clean AFPFL. The two AFPFL parties both took stands against the measures adopted by the Caretaker Government, Nu also complaining that the Army was bullying the people. Stable AFPFL President Ba Swe promised that all difficult measures imposed on the people by the Caretaker Government would be removed and that army officers occupying civil administrative posts would resume their military duties. The Stable AFPFL, however, was unable to compete with Nu's appeal among the Buddhist majority, his promise to make Buddhism the state religion, the active aid lent by monastic organizations to his campaign, and his use of the color of monastic robes as his party's campaign color. Further, to the Army's dismay, Nu promised autonomous states to the Arakanese and the Mons. Thus, in the February 1960 elections, Nu's Clean AFPFL won a landslide victory, including all nine Rangoon constituencies. Stable AFPFL morale was particularly hurt as party leaders Ba Swe and Kyaw Nyein both lost their seats.[15]

As Ne Win had promised, he relinquished control and the Nu government commenced on a sounder economic and perhaps political footing than it had enjoyed at any time in the 1950s. Nu immediately sought to cultivate the image of national unity and democratic stability. The All-Burma Conference of the Clean AFPFL now renamed the party the Pyidaungsu Party (the Union Party), while Nu promised that the Party would be completely reorganized around a popular democratic principle. The Party would be rooted in the masses, all leaders in the Party would have to rise from the bottom, and all Party decisions would be made after discussion and consultation with the masses. In doing so, its component organizations were also dissolved and incorporated directly into the new party, with the exception of the All-Burma Peasants' Organization (ABPO) and a few others that would remain separate. In June, the new Pyidaungsu government adopted a two-cabinet system of government, with one cabinet for the Union and the other for the States. To correct problems of inner-party disputes within the Pyidaungsu Party, Nu initiated the practice of "eating together," whereby each Party leader invited colleagues to dinner.[16]

Nu, apparently attempting to compete with the successful administration under Ne Win, also sought to demonstrate that the new government would be more efficient than it had been prior to 1958. In August

1961, the government temporarily suspended the ten-year-old Democratization of Local Administration Scheme on the grounds that three obstacles had emerged over the course of its implementation: "Deficiencies of the legislation, deficiencies of the public servants, deficiencies of the people." To rectify these problems, an advisory committee was set up under Dr. Ba U to hold consultations and report to the government. The New Pyidawtha Scheme, launched in October, reformed local administration. Until then decision-making regarding agriculture, communications, rural economy, education, health and social services had been slowed by bureaucratic red tape, such as financial sanctioning procedures and correspondence, as orders would have to be elicited from central departments. The new scheme would transfer authority to new decision-making bodies organized in rural districts that would be empowered to take "rapid action." The New Pyidawtha Scheme was viewed as a transitional measure, necessary before the democratization of local administration would be recommenced.[17]

By early 1962, however, it was apparent that Nu's return to power promised to rekindle a number of developments inimical to the interests of the military, among others. Nu's Pyidaungsu Party began to split into factions, for example, just as the AFPFL had prior to 1958, which was taken as a sign that democratic institutions would be no more successful in maintaining national political solidarity than they had been prior to caretaker rule. The civil war was on the verge of re-escalation. Worse, from the perspective of field commanders, there were signs that hard-fought victories over ethnic insurgents would be sacrificed to autonomy concessions. In June 1961, at the Conference of States held at Taunggyi, the Shan capital, federalism received a majority of the votes from delegates thus outvoting the official Karen, Chin, and Kachin leaders. While the Burmese press launched a media campaign against the Conference's decision, the Stable AFPFL proclaimed that federalism would threaten national unity. Nu held a press conference at which he said that if the demand was made in a democratic manner, it would be considered. For the Army, Nu's subsequent agreement to formally discuss with Shan leaders the replacement of Burma's unitary with a federal constitution was taken as a sign of unforgivable weakness.[18]

BUDDHISM

When Nu returned to power he was even more vigorous in promoting Buddhism through the means of the state than ever before. There was now even broader popular appeal for this effort than there had been before 1958. Ironically, this was partly the result of military efforts during the Caretaker period. In an effort to whip up popular support for the struggle against the Communist rebels, the military's Psychological Warfare Department began an anti-Communist propaganda effort in 1959 that focussed on the alleged Communist campaign against Buddhism. The centerpiece of this effort was a pamphlet entitled "Buddhism in Danger" that outlined the nature of the Communists' anti-Buddhist program. In response, 800,000 lay Buddhists and monks attended hundreds of mass meetings to mobilize active popular support for the war against the Communists. Although the military was essentially attempting to influence public opinion against the Communists it also fostered greater popular interest in encouraging state promotion of Buddhism. Thus, it also ensured Nu's victory in the 1960 elections.[19]

At the All-Burma Clean AFPFL Conference at the World Peace Pagoda in Rangoon from 31 August to 2 September 1958, Nu promised that if the Clean AFPFL came to power he would implement his 1954 undertaking to make Buddhism the state religion. Nu's efforts eventually led to charges, made by the Stable AFPFL in November and December 1959, that he was exploiting religion "as a stepping stone" and that his plan violated the Constitution. Nevertheless, once returned to power in 1960, Nu recommended his campaign for an officially Buddhist Burma, arguing that if this was not done it might create animosity in Burma against other religions. In March, the United Sanghas Association and the Annual Meeting of the All-Burma Presiding Monks' Association both urged Nu to keep his promise. Under their unrelenting pressure, Nu formed two committees, a Commission of Monks and a Commission of Laymen to solicit from both monks and laymen their views on the prospective establishment of Buddhism as the official religion. After their reports were submitted in 1961, Nu conferred with his Cabinet and then decided to submit the Constitution Amendment Bill to Parliament.[20]

Non-Buddhist opposition was quick to emerge. Kachin protestors stoned one of the committees. On 11 February 1961, the National Religious Minorities Alliance, representing three million non-Buddhist Shans, Chins, Kachins, Karens, Burmans and others held a special meeting on the subject and adopted the position that making Buddhism the state religion would make non-Buddhists second-class citizens. Shortly after, Nu also promised a meeting of Christian bishops that the move would not alter the freedom of religion for non-Buddhists in any way. On 1 August, the Union of Burma National Muslim Affairs Committee wrote to Nu asking him to act as Defender of the Faiths rather than making Buddhism the state religion.[21]

The push to introduce the amendment was intensified as monastic problems grew. In February 1961, young Buddhist monks complained that the Religious Affairs Department was not doing enough to rectify cheating in the religious Patama-byan examination. As the department delayed in deciding who should pass and who should fail, the monks demanded that cheats be identified publicly. On 16 February, monks surrounded the Secretariat building, not letting any high-ranking government servants in or out, for twenty-six hours, immobilizing the government ministries. Nu, on vacation, had to rush back to Rangoon, where he brought the crisis to an end by promising a government inquiry into the matter. Nu feared violent opposition to the constitutional amendment when he introduced it to the Chamber of Deputies in mid-August. That morning, he took the precaution of placing soldiers with fixed bayonets at strategic points in Rangoon and encircling the Old Secretariat building (which housed the Chamber of Deputies) with armored cars, riot cars, and Bren machine-gun carriers. Those members of the public who had applied to the government for permission to demonstrate were denied permission and only allowed to hold private meetings. Nu attempted to placate the opposition by promising that the proposed amendment would avoid any provision that would infringe on the rights of non-Buddhists to practice their religion or that would create classes of Buddhists and non-Buddhists. Non-Buddhist students responded to these developments by marching to Aung San's tomb and calling to him, complaining that Nu was destroying his vision of a united and secular Burma.[22]

Nu urged Burmese monks and lay people to differentiate between restrained and unrestrained monks. Restrained monks, Nu claimed, followed the twelve principles included in the Dhamma Vinaya Order that had been promulgated by the Sixth Great Buddhist Council, including avoiding commerce, prescribing medicines, attending puppet shows and so on. Unrestrained monks were those who did not observe these rules and should be identified and expelled from the monkhood. Nu understood non-Buddhist objections to making Buddhism the state religion. They were afraid, he observed, that it would encourage fanaticism among Buddhists and lead to the end of freedom to practice other faiths and even encroach upon their social and economic rights. However, Nu believed that existing laws could help to protect against these developments and, if not, new protective laws could be promulgated. He also admitted that laws would not be enough and that Buddhist monks and laymen would have to adopt "the right view" and exercise restraint, including avoiding certain kinds of speech, acts, and thoughts. The State Religion Act was promulgated by a vote of 324 to 28 in the Joint Session of the two Houses of Parliament. In adopting Buddhism as the state religion, the government was now responsible for matters relating to maintaining, preserving, and printing the Pali Canon, holding a yearly consultation with leading monks, aiding in the restoration of damaged pagodas, constructing special hospitals throughout the country for monks, the protection of the religion, the promotion of the study and practice of Buddhism, and a minimum state provision of half a percent of the state's annual budget for religious activities.[23]

In the following months, Burma witnessed an upsurge in religious violence. Hindu Tamil demonstrators protested against the screening of an Indian film whose theme centered on a Muslim king who fell in love with a Hindu girl. The government, in response to Muslim protests, had previously banned a film that depicted a Hindu king falling in love with a Muslim girl. The demonstration soon descended into rock throwing and eventually shots were fired, leaving one of the protestors dead. The government then ordered an investigation into why the earlier film had been banned and the new film not. At the end of October 1961, militant monks, complaining of the high number of mosques in North Okkalapa, outside Rangoon, stormed and seized control of a partially finished mosque, promising to leave only if the government sealed up the mosque. The government, arguing that it would not be intimidated, brought in the police. After other monks smashed the streetlighting, the monks inside the mosque set fire to it and other mosques in the area. As rioters began to sack stores and homes, police opened fire, killing five. To resolve the protests, the government agreed to the advice of presiding monks to take the charred mosques under its control. In response to the violence, the Ministry of Religious Affairs issued a call for the building of sand pagodas all over the country "to ward off dangers and bring peace." This call was answered on 9 December, when Burmese throughout the country simultaneously built 60,000 nine-cubit-high pagodas.[24]

Nu also faced a hostile press. Nu's poor relationship with the press in the 1950s was still a recent memory and the caretaker regime had brought the newspeople no relief. Ne Win had personally shunned publicity and only held one press conference, telling reporters to write whatever they wanted. Subsequently, newsmen and newspaper owners frequently found themselves in trouble with the law, either on charges of contempt or sedition, for writing or publishing articles critical of the government, and several newspaper presses were confiscated. The resumption of civilian rule under Nu initially saw a continuity of government suppression of the press rather than the revocation of harsh government controls. Nu asked newsmen to exercise restraint in reporting the news in order to prevent "untoward incidents" and later argued that "irresponsible and wild speaking, writing, and acting as one's thoughts incline is not democracy." Arrests and restrictions on press freedom led to demands for the restoration of civil liberties guaranteed by the Constitution. This was followed by the publication of two protest articles in all major newspapers in late November. Nu responded by finally agreeing to end laws that restrained the press and similar laws that violated personal freedoms in the country, a promise he carried out in February 1962.[25]

THE ECONOMY UNDER THE RETURNED NU GOVERNMENT

The Nu government was unhappy with many of the Caretaker Government's policies. It thus undertook a number of steps to reverse them. First, it suspended the reorganization of the Highways Department. It then reinstated 165 of the more than 2,000 firms that had been deregistered under the caretaker regime. Nu did compromise with the Army over the commercial ventures of the DSI. The Burmese military had initially established the DSI in 1951 to supply consumer goods at inexpensive prices to military personnel. Over the years, its economic activities expanded and became a model of the kind of efficiency that civil branches of the Nu government lacked. It minimized red tape, supposedly had no private profit motive, and employed significant numbers of foreign experts and, by 1958, had become the largest economic enterprise in the country. Nu, however, did not want an "Army-controlled economy." The Burma Economic Development Corporation (BEDC), which was run along the same lines as the DSI, but not under Army control, assumed control of nineteen of the DSI's commercial ventures. Cutting off this avenue of funding meant the Army would have to rely on government funding alone, thus making it more dependent upon civil government.[26]

The government had created the first JVCs from 1956 to 1957 because Burmese nationals proved unable to wrest control of Burma's foreign trade from foreigners. Afterwards, imports increased dramatically. By 1961, the JVC share of imports was still only 8 percent, cooperatives 4 percent, other government agencies and boards (mainly the Civil Supplies Management Board) 55 percent, and private importers 33 percent, 87 percent of whom were Burmese. However, prices rose rather than dropped. Burmese private traders began to make significant earnings by selling import licenses to foreigners at a profit reaching as much as 200 percent of the value of the license. Since the foreigners had to absorb these additional costs, prices were guaranteed not to fall. Further, limited supply of goods and an uncontrolled black market also worked to raise prices further. From October 1961, the government began to reform the system of commodity distribution through the JVCs, Consumers' Cooperatives, and the Parahita shops. Shops and retailers began to be shut down. The government also announced plans, in response to corruption and bureaucratic inefficiency in state agencies and among importers, to put the private import trade into the hands of the JVCs. This move promised to stop Burmese businessmen from selling licenses to Indians, Chinese, and Europeans. Finally, the government extended Burmanization to industry and to bazaar and market stalls.[27]

CONCLUSION

The AFPFL never recovered from the "split" (discussed in Chapter 4) and while Nu sought solutions in a Buddhist revival, the military continued to be held in high regard for its genuinely praiseworthy performance in the period 1958 to 1960. By 1962, the AFPFL was all but dead, Nu even choosing to abandon association with the party name. The AFPFL, to many, had almost become a dirty word. Some, such as the army leadership, had come to associate the AFPFL specifically and democracy, generally, with political infighting and national disorder. As Nu increasingly relied on a cult of personality and the promotion of Buddhist nationalism, in the context of his perceived attempts to sacrifice national unity, the Army wondered if it could now, as it had just a few years before, do a better job at managing the country.

CHAPTER 6

The Revolutionary Council

There is a tendency to treat the Revolutionary Council period, from 1962, and the Burma Socialist Program Party (BSPP) years that followed it, as one entity. This has been partly for reasons of simplicity. The point at which the Revolutionary Council ended and the BSPP Government began is hazy, due to the myriad political steps that were involved in the process, including the opening up of the BSPP for mass membership in 1971 and the promulgation of a new constitution in 1974. The most important change, however, occurred in 1972 when the Revolutionary Council was transformed into a civilian body and a new administrative system was established. Another reason for the presumed continuity was that the main leaders of the Revolutionary Council remained the ruling cohort of the BSPP government. In an arguable sense, then, the establishment of the BSPP government meant no real change in the political leadership of the country. Finally, it is convenient to consider 1962 as the beginning of a single period of military rule as it adds weight to understandable assertions of the overlong tenure of military men at the helm of state and their responsibility for the country's economic woes since the Nu years.

Nevertheless, there are equally sound reasons for considering the Revolutionary Council era separately. One is that it was a period when the final fate of the country remained unclear, when policies remained unfixed in one direction or another, and in which it was not yet clear to anyone, including Ne Win and his friends, if they would continue to hold on to power (in which case the Revolutionary Council would have been viewed merely as a second caretaker regime). A political compromise with Nu and other democratic leaders was still a possibility, though admittedly a distant one. By contrast, Burma under the BSPP government would be without the possibility of alternative paths, so much so that it took a popular revolution to end it.

THE COUP

In a radio broadcast delivered at 8:50 A.M. on 2 March 1962, General Ne Win, Commander-in-Chief of the Armed Forces, informed Burmese throughout the country that he had launched a military coup. Earlier, at dawn, tanks entered Rangoon while soldiers entered the home of every government minister, woke them, and, lined up with leveled rifles, read out Ne Win's instructions that they were now under protective custody. Nu and five government ministers were placed in custody, as were forty others, mostly prominent Shans. The airport was then closed and troops took control of the law courts, the Telegraph Office, and police stations throughout the city. At 1:15 P.M., another radio broadcast announced the creation of a military government headed by the Revolutionary Council under Ne Win's chairmanship. The Council included among others brigadiers Aung Gyi, Tin Pe, San Yu, and Sein Win. The Council dissolved Parliament the following day. As those MPs who represented states also constituted state councils, the state councils, including the Shan, Kachin, Karen, and Kayah, as well as the Chin Affairs Council, were all dissolved and new state supreme councils were created to administer the states.[1]

The Revolutionary Council quickly made it clear that the main reason for the coup was disapproval of ongoing negotiations between the Nu government and Shan State leaders. Shan leaders had demanded that Burma adopt a federal rather than a unitary government or they would secede from the union. As Aung Gyi explained at a news conference on 7 March, the question of federalism was very delicate. The States already had autonomy, but if they were allowed to secede, division in a small country like Burma would cause the same problems as were then being experienced in Laos and Vietnam. In this situation, the Shan *sawbwas*, who wanted a return to feudalism, were pushing matters to a point beyond the control of either the Shan leaders or the Burmese government. Aung Gyi asserted that the states could not even support themselves financially and depended upon Burma proper to subsidize them. Money from taxpayers in the Shan State, for example, had not been used to improve the condition of the people by building schools, farms, or a health system, but rather had been used by the *sawbwas* to build luxury homes and buy automobiles. The Council, he claimed, was also not like other coups because, rather than ban political parties, it sought instead to encourage "healthy politics." Finally, Aung Gyi made an indirect critique of the failures of the Nu regime by stressing three new developments. First, the Council intended to abandon government economic "prestige" projects such as the construction of the Taungup

Road to Arakan, the Parliament Building, and a National Theatre, and focus instead on agriculture, by building water pipes and fertilizer and insecticide plants in order to allow dry areas of the country to grow an extra crop in the dry season, and small industry. Second, the Council believed in freedom of religion and it did not plan to emphasize one religion at the expense of another. Third, the Council supported freedom of the press.[2]

After declaring its adherence to socialism, the Revolutionary Council provided an outline of its guiding principles in *The Burmese Way to Socialism*, signed by the members of the Council on 30 April 1962. Social problems, such as "anxieties over food, security, clothing, and shelter," could not be resolved without removing economic systems that allow the exploitation of man by man. This could only be achieved by establishing a just socialist economy. The new socialist economy would be based on the principle of popular participation and ownership and economic planning for the good of the people. Burma's new society would provide for peace and prosperity by being morally better and more economically secure than the one that preceded it. Self-interest and self-seeking would be removed as motives for participation in society and in the economy. The state, cooperatives, and collective unions would own all means of production. The new system would narrow gaps in income. The new society would foster unity among all the nationalities.[3]

According to the Revolutionary Council, since parliamentary democracy, which was suitable in other countries, had failed in Burma because of abuse, the military government would produce the right kind of democracy for Burma. The new society, however, would not appear overnight. Instead, it would have to undergo a transitional period, in which the Council would rely on organizations based on peasants and industrial workers to build up a suitable political infrastructure. After political organizing, the people would be given democratic education and training to ensure "conscious participation" in the system. The people would also have to be educated to take pride in doing hard work. Simultaneously, the Council would undertake efforts to foster genuine personal morality taught by every religion, while eradicating "bogus acts of charity and social work," for vainglorious and hypocritical religiosity.[4]

From the beginning, the Revolutionary Council favored the eventual establishment of a single-party state that would prevent the kind of political infighting that had weakened the Nu government (twice). It was initially uncertain of how to achieve this goal. Its first strategy was to convince the leading political parties, the AFPFL, the Pyidaungsu Party, and the NUF to merge. While all three agreed in principle with the goal of establishing socialism in the "Burmese way," they disagreed on the means to achieve it. The Council thus adopted the second course of action, to develop the nucleus of an entirely new state party that would eventually develop a civilian mass base.[5]

With the adoption by the Revolutionary Council of a party constitution on 4 July 1962, the Burmese Way to Socialism Party (the BWSP, later known as the BSPP) was formally established. The justification for the creation of the BWSP/BSPP was that the Council was revolutionary in essence, but due to a historical accident, wore "the outward garb" of a military junta. The Council, it was claimed, did not like this situation, arguing that instead the natural leader of the new Burma should be a revolutionary political party. The BSPP was initially a cadre party organized on the principle of centralism, with membership drawn mainly from the armed forces. However, the cadre party was only a transitional stage as it was always intended that the BSPP would grow into a national or state party. As explained in the party constitution, the Council promised that as the BSPP grew into a mass party, it would be reorganized on the principle of democratic centralism, a new party constitution would be written, and party leadership would be popularly elected. For now, the Council, which the party constitution deemed the supreme authority in the party during the cadre phase, would begin to set up the organizational structure of the BSPP. Two of the three major party committees, the Central Organizing Committee and the Disciplinary Committee, were formed in July 1963 (a Socialist Economic Planning Committee would be added in 1967).[6]

The Revolutionary Council approached the dissolution of political parties slowly, indicating that it had not yet decided what to do with them. A year later, this decision had been made. In early August 1963, the Council made sweeping arrests of important civilian politicians and other public figures on charges that they were turning back emissaries and blocking letters sent by insurgents asking for peace talks. In October, when the government arrested more League leaders for allegedly working against the Council and its socialist program, it stressed that it had not taken the last step of dissolving the political parties. In March 1964, Ne Win informed representatives of the Pyidaungsu Party, the AFPFL, and the Burma Workers Unity Party (formerly the National United Front) that the existence of all political parties would be terminated, due to the use by some political organizations of obstructionist tactics. All property of the parties would be confiscated, anyone continuing to work for political parties would be imprisoned for five years, and the only organizations that would be allowed would be religious ones. In July, the Council terminated preexisting local administrative systems and rules and established Security and Administrative Committees (SACs) in local areas, occupied by local military commanders.[7]

CENSORSHIP

In its first year of control from 1962, the Revolutionary Council stepped lightly in dealing with the public media. Even before the coup had been announced on radio, representatives of the Burma Journalists Association had been promised that the new government would "honor the freedom of the press." Shortly after, Aung Gyi had also promised that the government would observe freedom of the press, including criticism of the government, so long as it did not support the cause of the insurgents. The Council first applied soft pressure in an attempt to woo the press over to its side. In its first few months, the Council actually stopped pending legal action by the government against certain newspapers, as in the case of the withdrawal of legal action against the *Red Star* newspaper, for a story it had run in 1958, on 2 April.[8]

The Minister for Information, Colonel Saw Myint, also arranged a short-term course in journalism for 700 correspondents from around the country from 31 August to 5 September 1962 in Rangoon. The lectures given here were far from the poor quality, "diktat" style addresses made by military officers and civilian drones to half-asleep audiences in later decades. Rather, respected and leading editors and journalists spoke on various substantial matters regarding historical, technical, legal, and terminological aspects of journalism and publishing. From all appearances, the course indicated that the Council felt that by improving the professionalism of the press corps and, of course, by effecting positive bonds between the government and the press, the press would treat the new government more kindly than it had the Nu government.[9]

The regime's concern with the press was not just political but stemmed also from a nationalist and puritanical view of Burmese culture that viewed Western influence, both colonial and postcolonial, as damaging to the national spirit. Within a few months of the coup, for example, the Revolutionary Council had clamped down on the nation's moral decay. It banned beauty contests for hurting moral standards among both men and women and doing nothing to support the responsibilities of women in the new socialist economy that the state was creating. Ne Win informed the directors of the Rangoon Turf Club that horse racing in Burma would be banned within a year, which would put 10,000 people connected with racing out of work. "Houses of ill repute," such as dance halls, as well as "superfluous" activities, such as ballet schools, were all banned.[10] While the symptoms of Western influence could be treated, however, its future eradication depended upon the control of the press.

The Council's initial observance of press freedom soon began to break down. It attempted to bring the press firmly under state control in six ways. First, it set up its own periodicals and newspapers, such as the *Loktha Pyithu Nezin* (first issue, 1 October 1963), and its English-language version the *Working People's Daily* (first issue, 12 January 1964), which were to serve as "a beacon of light to the working people" and follow a neutralist foreign policy.[11]

Second, the Revolutionary Council isolated Burmese private newspapers from foreign news sources and vice versa. The government described the foreign press as consisting of "capitalo-rightist newspapers, journals, and magazines." Since "anti-socialist forces guided it" coverage of Burma from abroad was consistently biassed. Thus, on 26 July 1963, the Council inaugurated the News Agency Burma (NAB, the planned creation of which had been announced on 6 June) which assumed control of the distribution of news from private wire services operating in the country after signing agreements with Tass, Agence France Presse, United Press International, Associated Press, and Reuters. The main purpose, according to the Council, was to censor biasses that would favor either of the two power-blocs in the Cold War, in keeping with Burma's strict neutrality in foreign policy. Less emphasis was placed by the government on perhaps its most important function, the dissemination abroad of domestic news, over which it now exerted a monopoly. In July 1963, BEDC subsidiary Ava House assumed a monopoly over imports of foreign books and periodicals.[12]

Third, the Council gradually eliminated the private press, beginning in the second week of March 1963. This mainly took the form of arresting editors and publishers on seemingly minor complaints, followed by the closure or nationalization of one press after another, beginning with *The Nation*. In December 1966, most of the remaining private newspapers were banned explicitly, except for all Chinese and Indian-language newspapers, which were in effect banned due to the cancellation of their annual re-registrations. On 14 March 1969, thirteen presses owned by Burmese were nationalized, while twenty-nine foreign-owned presses were put under closer scrutiny. By the end of December, the government had nationalized both the *Hanthawaddy* and *Myanma Alin* dailies.[13]

The fourth response to journalistic criticism moved from the practical to the ideological. Even prior to February 1963, the Revolutionary Council viewed press criticism as a problem involving pseudo-journalists who had infiltrated the press corps. On 22 September 1962, for example, the Directorate of Information began to consider how it could identify bogus journalists and weed them out from the press corps. It then initiated a plan to issue identity cards to bona fide journalists as determined by the Information Department. The Printers and Publishers Registration Act of 1962 specifically targeted "bogus" journalists. The Act removed the one-time, life registration of journalists and publishers and now required them to re-register within ninety days and thereafter on an annual basis. They would have to do so with a new, single state authority, the Central Registration Committee. This law also affected foreign diplomatic missions and consular offices that also wanted to distribute any publication within Burma. The Press Registration Board and the Press Scrutiny Board were formed to enforce the Act.[14]

The Revolutionary Council, however, eventually decided that biased journalists were a product of Western imperialism and the press corps was hopelessly riddled with anti-socialist elements. A new breed of journalists would have to be trained in the socialist spirit. At first, aspiring journalists were sent to East Germany for training, but were later trained locally. The School of Journalism was opened in December 1967. In addition to teaching the technical aspects of journalism and newspaper and radio news administration, the curriculum included study of the philosophy of the Burmese Way to Socialism. Special attention was paid to three principles of socialist newspapers:

(1) earning the trust of workers by avoiding sensationalism, promoting patriotism, mobilizing workers to contribute to socialist construction, and only publishing news that benefited the country and the workers;

(2) acting as a bridge between workers and the government by circulating information about government programs, informing the people of the benefits of these programs if they were successful, and presenting the suggestions of the people to the government; and

(3) only making use of the freedom of the press to serve workers. The socialist journalists also had to be wary of saboteurs and opponents of socialism.[15]

Fifth, the Revolutionary Council developed elaborate bureaucratic control mechanisms to guide Burma's new press over the long term. In July 1964, the Council created the Policy Direction Board for Newspapers, Journals, and Publications to direct the modus operandi of the media. In

September, a new Printers and Publishers Registration Board informed 200 printers and publishers that they should not print anything that contradicted the government's policy of strict neutrality in foreign affairs. The Council dissolved the redundant Policy Direction Board the following year.[16]

Sixth and finally, the Revolutionary Council organized journalists into a self-administering body guided by the Burmese Way to Socialism philosophy. This effort began on 3 December 1966, when the Information Ministry announced the creation of a preparatory committee to establish a writers and journalists' federation that would consist of two unions representing both. The purpose would be to mobilize both groups for the good of socialist construction. A week later, the National Literary Association dissolved and its members were told to join the new Writers and Journalists' Association.[17]

As with the press, the Council moved to reduce the autonomy of the cinema. The Council's concerns about the cinema were sometimes political, but were mainly directed, like Singapore's moves against "yellow" culture, at taking leadership in the shaping of a new national culture and eradicating unwanted foreign influences. Films and other visual media were especially important in a multi-lingual country like Burma with significant levels of illiteracy. Among the first moves to bring the cinema under state control was a July 1962 order that local film producers and importers of foreign films cease producing or importing films that adversely affected the national unity, character, or morale of the population. This was followed by a ban on showing films depicting nats (spirits), ghosts, or witchcraft. A more comprehensive law was the Union of Burma Cinematograph Law of 1962. The law expanded the supervisory and control powers of the Information Minister over every aspect of the cinema industry in Burma. The new law established a ten- to twelve-member Film Censor Board, under the Ministry of Information, to replace the Board of Censors. Under the new board, all films, domestic and imported, for private or public exhibition, even films brought in by foreign diplomatic missions, were now subject to state censorship. The law was intended to protect both the domestic film industry and the country's moral fiber, by preventing the exhibition of films detrimental to national culture and foreign films containing propaganda material. Any part of a domestic film censored by the board would be destroyed, while parts of foreign films censored would be impounded and returned only when the film was to leave the country. On the grounds that domestic producers were hurt by competition with foreign films, the dubbing or subtitling in Burmese of any foreign film was also banned. The law also required films imported by foreign diplomatic missions for private or public use to be submitted to the board for censoring. The Committee would also determine the nature and themes of foreign films that could be imported.[18]

In October 1965, the Revolutionary Council explained that the film industry had a major role to play in the social revolution and had been given instructions on how it should behave, but this advice was thus far not heeded. The guiding principles for movie makers should be: plots should be up to date and correspond to contemporary life; costumes should be appropriate to the character being depicted; raw materials should not be wasted (because they had to be imported and thus paid for with foreign exchange); titles should be appropriate to the theme of the film and not antagonize members of different ethnic groups; and Western music in films should preferably be replaced with indigenous music, or at least be selected with greater care. Films should be original, but also not incompatible with the Council's policies and should not portray the Armed Forces irresponsibly. Out of 171 film scripts submitted to the Censor Board in 1964, 97 were banned. In November 1966, the Film Council of Burma restricted actors to involvement in only three films at any one time and limited them to clothing and hair styles that "conformed to the national tradition and culture." Finally, between December 1968 and July 1969, all cinemas and motion picture companies in the country were nationalized and those cinemas with foreign names were given new, Burmese ones.[19]

REINING IN STUDENTS AND MONKS

Among the first targets for government restraint were university students, who had been the vanguard of the anti-colonial movement in the 1930s and had supplied the country with some of its most dynamic political leaders on all sides of the ideological spectrum in the 1950s. This trend persisted in the decades that followed, leading to continual government efforts to rein the students in, including closing the universities from time to time and even breaking them up altogether into smaller more geographically isolated units, as is the case today. The event that is viewed as the beginning of this process took place in July 1962, about five months after the coup.

Ne Win believed that foreign ideologies were interfering with Burmese domestic politics because of the inclusion of politics in education. Thus, the Revolutionary Council dissolved the university councils of both Rangoon and Mandalay universities and assumed their authority in May 1962. Under military supervision, moral reintegration would resolve alleged problems between the students and their teachers. A curfew of 8:00 P.M. was then imposed on university students, campus hostels being closed. After three days of breaking through the locked doors, the RUSU took leadership as it had in the 1930s. While the RUSU led students on a one-hour protest, government security forces raided the Rangoon University campus and took control of the student union. In the ensuing riot, one hundred students were killed. The following morning, the Army blew up the RUSU building on campus. The university was then closed indefinitely, but reopened four months later.[20]

The destruction of the RUSU building dealt a significant blow to Ne Win's chances of developing popular support. It was more than a student union. It was the site of the beginning of Burma's nationalist struggle and was closely associated with the martyred Aung San, the father of Burmese independence. The destruction was also clearly a sign that the military regime now in place, whether it admitted it or not, saw itself as rooted in a tradition other than the Burmese nationalist struggle cherished by most Burmese. It is unclear how early Ne Win realized the gravity of this act, but he eventually did. In the face of widespread Burmese opposition in the streets in 1988, one of the key episodes he referred to in his departure speech was the destruction of the RUSU building. And as on many other occasions in covering up different errors he had made, he attempted to shift blame on to subordinates. On that occasion, after denying personal responsibility, he claimed that there had been confusion in the relaying of orders. There appears to have been little truth in his claims.[21] As the students would demonstrate again in the mid-1970s and late 1980s, the destruction of RUSU was not the end to student political activism.

Although many members of the Revolutionary Council were devout Buddhists, the Burmese military had a long tradition of favoring the separation of politics and religion. It could be argued that the Council's efforts to separate them were inconsistent with the traditional role of the ruler as chief patron and protector of the monastic order. On the other hand, it was consistent with the obligation of the ruler to prevent monastic corruption, which included monks becoming involved in mundane matters such as politics. As one scholar observes, the professional soldiers who now ruled Burma preferred the more conservative monastic sects, such as the Shwegyin Sangha, as opposed to the more politicized Thudhamma Sangha that Nu had favored and who had also pushed for making Buddhism the state religion, for "[t]he ascetic qualities of the fundamentalists complemented the austerity and discipline of the military ideologues."[22]

The Revolutionary Council thus expressed its belief in freedom of religion and promised not to privilege one religion over another. This was demonstrated in 1962 by its abrogation of the closures of government offices on Buddhist Sabbath days, as required by the State Religion Proclamation Act of 1961, and by revoking the ban on slaughtering cattle. While both measures could be ascribed to efficiency and economy, in the latter case because the extra meat would help lower the price of foodstuffs in the market, they were just as clearly strikes against the Nu policy of making Buddhism the state religion. The ban on the sale of alcohol on Buddhist Sabbath days, for example, was also lifted. Other early measures taken by the Council included the freezing of state funds intended for the construction of state nat shrines in Mandalay and Rangoon, the suspension of the printing and distribution by the government of Buddhist texts, drastic reductions in the broadcast of Buddhist sermons on state radio, and the abolition of the Buddha Sasana Council.[23]

Removing religion from the state, however, did not mean ending state interference with religion, particularly when religious issues threatened public order. When monastic complaints about the Revolutionary Council's policies surfaced, the Council gradually found that involvement in religious matters was impossible to avoid in the long term. It is true that the Mandalay monk, U Kethaya, a vocal anti-Communist, had turned his criticism on the Council's socialist policies. Voicing his complaints to audiences as large as ten thousand, he predicted that Ne Win would soon be assassinated just as Aung San had been, goaded the Council to arrest him, and claimed that when he was arrested he would become a martyr to the Buddhist cause. In this case, the Council avoided direct confrontation. It is probably the case that it did not want to move too quickly against Buddhist opposition to its policies before it had time to solidify its control. The Council may also have been at a loss regarding how to deal with monastic opposition at all. Ne Win's response was to grant the *sangha* a limited period of time in which it would be allowed to purge itself of false monks, warning monks generally not to involve themselves in political affairs. In April 1964, Ne Win proposed the creation of a unitary monastic organisation, the Buddha Sasana Sangha Organisation (BSSO). Registration was ordered but, in the face of serious monastic opposition, the Council reversed itself within a month and made an exception for purely religious organizations.[24]

The Revolutionary Council persisted in attempts to interfere with monastic affairs in reaction to, or through, it was alleged, the actions of

Shin Ottama, a monk who had recently converted from Hinduism. Ottama had an advertisement relating to religion, "Warning for the Purification of the Sangha," published in the Mandalay periodical *Bahosi*, criticizing other monks for being "unproductive, religiously ignorant, and full of political intrigues" and calling upon the Council to purify the monastic order. He became the focus of an equally severe smear campaign directed by monastic associations in Mandalay who accused him of being a Hindu pretending to be a Buddhist whose actions would spark violence between the Hindu and Buddhist communities. In mid-August 1964, young monks from these associations caused disturbances, destroyed the *Bahosi* office and damaged the house of its chief editor. A week later, a meeting of monks in Rangoon condemned the monastic violence in Mandalay and asked newspapers and printing presses not to publish anything that would create misunderstandings between the monastic order and the government. Monks had also grown unhappy after the government demonetized 50- and 100-*kyat* notes, costing the monastic order a significant loss of accumulated donations, and a meeting of monks thus also demanded that the government compensate fully the pagoda trust funds and Sangha common funds for the donated and now demonetized currency. On 27 August, the government repeated its commitment to freedom of religion, but denounced both those who tried to portray the Council as being Communist and those who, it asserted, tried every means available to engage in anti-government activities. Over the course of the next three days, Ottama as well as the chief editor and publisher of *Bahosi* were taken into protective custody to testify before the Shin Ottama Enquiry Commission. In December, a Vinicchaya (Ecclesiastical) court excommunicated Ottama for profaning the Religion.[25]

The Revolutionary Council subsequently told the heads of monastic sects to hold sectional meetings to discuss how to carry out their responsibility for maintaining the purity of the monastic order, and then convene an Inter-denominational Sangha Convention to coordinate their discussions into a unanimous decision, which would then be enforced by the monastic order. Ne Win, who was concerned that the monastic order was being used against him, moved against monastic autonomy. On 18 January 1965, the Council repealed the Vinicchaya Tribunal Act, the Pali University and Dhammacariya Act, and the Pali Education Board Act of 1952. The Ministry of Religious Affairs claimed that the repeals had been made because the acts had failed to achieve their intended goals. The state then took control over cases handled by the ecclesiastical courts as well as the administration of Pali examinations. The Revolutionary Council also attempted to nationalize the *sangha* by assuming control and authority over monastic examinations and the selection of the monastic hierarchy. Ne Win now ordered the creation of the BSSO as quickly as possible, prompting the 17 March All-Sangha, All-Sect Convention at Hmawbi, attended by over two thousand monks, to draft the BSSO's constitution. The Hmawbi Convention had two goals. First, it would allow Ne Win to eradicate the potential involvement of the monastic order in political affairs. Second and more symbolically, it allowed him to realize the traditional responsibility of a Burmese ruler to purify the monastic order when necessary. While the BSSO Constitution would establish a single hierarchy controlling the monkhood, what angered monks most was the requirement that all monks would now have to carry BSSO identity cards. The Council would claim that 80 percent of the monks had supported the draft, but monastic critics argued that this referred only to the percentage of the speakers, who were a very small group.[26]

The Revolutionary Council's BSSO plans resulted in an uprising, mainly among monks at Mandalay, characterized by the torching of army trucks and government buildings. On 25 March, the day after the congregation closed, thirty monks attacked and damaged the BSPP unit office at Taungbyin, referring to it as "The Taungbyin Communist Training School," and injured members of staff. Within a few days, monks put up posters for a rally to begin another attack on the Taungbyin office. The violence only receded in late April, when the government arrested ninety-two monks throughout the country on charges of economic insurgency, lawlessness, and engaging in political activities. Within a year, over 900 other monks would be arrested as well, mainly for encouraging monks to engage in anti-government political activity. The government did back down a little. Despite the existence of the BSSO, many monks did not heed intrusive parts of the BSSO constitution, but enforced self-regulation of monastic discipline to stave off state intervention. For its part, the Revolutionary Council did not enforce many parts of the BSSO Constitution after the monks abandoned destructive, public opposition. The Council even repealed the order requiring monastic registration with the government. The following year, the last foreign Baptist missionaries and foreign Catholic priests and nuns left Burma, as the government either refused to renew their stay permits or explicitly ordered them out of the country.[27]

The Revolutionary Council's confrontations with the monastic order were primarily rooted in two state policies. The Council had first attempted to reduce the place of religion in the state and then sought to bring the

monastic order under the state's control. This approach reflected the measured steps that the Council took in approaching many other political and
social institutions. The Council was not to be a caretaker regime to resolve
a short-term emergency, but instead a more commanding force in rede-
veloping Burma with a view toward fundamental, long-term change. By
all appearances, monastic opposition had forced the Council to back away
from its intended program for the monastic order. In actuality, the monastic order won only a temporary reprieve, for the Council only delayed
a monastic policy that would be recommenced once other aspects of
state and society were reformed. This was to be an unavoidable collision because an independent monastic order had shown itself to be a threat
to the state, especially one, like the Council, possessed of a totalitarian
orientation.[28]

FROM AUNG GYI TO TIN PE

While the 1962 coup, the declaration of a new state ideology, the elimination of freedom of the press, moves against monastic autonomy, and the
extension of other forms of social control all represented fundamental and
massive changes in the country, the most serious internal disagreements and
problems faced by the Revolutionary Council were over economic policy,
even with the upsurge in the insurgencies after the decline of armed opposition in the late 1950s and early 1960s. Initially, the main force in guiding
the Council's economic reforms was Aung Gyi, who had served under
Ne Win during the campaign against the Japanese in 1945 and remained
a close collaborator thereafter. Aung Gyi was also the economic hero of
the Caretaker Government, as he had salvaged the quickly disintegrating
economy after 1958 and the economic revival continued to bear fruit even
after the return of Nu in 1960. Aung Gyi headed a powerful clique within
the Council, known as the Paungde group, which favored industrialization
and a moderate approach to nationalization. With the establishment of the
Council, he was given the post of Minister of Industries and dominated
the Council's economic policies into early 1963. Aung Gyi had supported
the continuity of a private sector in industry and limited private import
and export trade. Through the BEDC, he had also established semi-official
trading companies.[29]

Under Aung Gyi's guidance, the Revolutionary Council's initial industrial policy was to follow a course of Import Substitution Industrialization
(ISI) while simultaneously attracting foreign investment. Too much foreign
exchange was being wasted on imports of foreign goods. To reverse this,

Aung Gyi advised that traders shift to industry and begin with small industries that would produce domestically items that were otherwise imported. The caretaker regime had initiated ISI, but the Council gave it greater emphasis. Aung Gyi also advised foreigners in the private import trade (they were allowed to remain in the import trade until September 1962) to invest their capital instead in heavy industries. Agriculture would now be mechanized as well along with the construction of water pumps, pipes, and fertilizer plants, and the production of insecticides.[30]

By the end of 1962, the Revolutionary Council had determined on a more thorough restructuring of the economy to parallel its political and social reforms. The major force behind this change was the grumbling and determined Tin Pe, the "Red Brigadier." Tin Pe had been a battalion commander under Ne Win when the BNA turned on the Japanese in 1945 and, on one occasion, Ne Win placed his command in Tin Pe's charge when he had to leave the front. After the war, Tin Pe steadily rose up the ranks to brigadier. During the caretaker period, he was one of the select few army officers Ne Win assigned to ministerial posts, being appointed as Minister for Mines, Labour, Public Works, and National Housing. Although Tin Pe and Aung Gyi had collaborated frequently in the past, as in the Caretaker Government's campaign against the black market, they disagreed strongly on economic policy. By contrast to Aung Gyi's moderate approach to nationalization, Tin Pe led a faction of Communist-oriented officers strongly influenced by the Marxist economist and former Communist U Ba Nyein. This faction was aided by the influx of Marxist theoreticians who had joined the government when members of the National United Front proved to be among the few political groups that responded positively to Ne Win's call for cooperation.[31] While Aung Gyi controlled overall economic policy, he had grown discontented over the role played by Tin Pe. He would publicly characterize Tin Pe and his associates of this period a quarter of a century later, as "people who did not even know the shape of rice and who pointed to the rice they ate when asked about rice products."[32]

Brigadier Tin Pe, in his capacity as Minister for Co-operatives and Supply, Acting Minister for Finance and Revenue, and Minister for Agriculture and Forests, had spent 1962 and early 1963 pushing for his own agricultural program. In June 1962, Tin Pe cited the cooperative movement as a critical part of the Burma Way to Socialism Program, calling it a virtual battlefield and saying that all necessary measures should be undertaken to ensure its success. To improve the agricultural situation, he oversaw changes in the ways in which agricultural loans were handled. In the past, these loans had been made out on the repayment record of the cultivator for previous loans received. This was now forgotten and the new system of granting agricultural loans was based on the crops to be cultivated. District Commissioners and officers of the SACs and, from June, the State Agricultural Bank disbursed the loans. Tin Pe also arranged paddy transplantation competitions among cultivators to boost agricultural production. Cultivators were encouraged to rotate their crops to improve the fertility of the soil and to provide them with high-quality seeds. Land reclamation was another major project directed toward increasing agricultural productivity. In late August, the Burmese government signed an agreement with the US Agency for International Development (USAID) for a US$ 3.4 million loan to begin a program of land reclamation in the Irrawaddy and Pegu Divisions. Two days later, on the recommendation of Tin Pe, the Revolutionary Council signed an agreement with the Soviet Union for the construction of an irrigation dam in the Myingyan district. Under this arrangement, Burma would repay the Soviet Union over a period of twenty years for the employment of the foreign (Russian) engineers, the machinery, and other construction costs related to the dam itself and the twenty-six-mile canal that would feed the reservoir.[33]

More radical steps than those thus far taken were partly justified when the BSPP's ideology was formally laid out in a published declaration entitled *The System of Correlation of Man and His Environment*, on 17 January 1963. This ideology amounted to a mixture of Marxism, historical dialecticism, and Buddhism. Man's needs were both material and spiritual (intellectual and cultural) and he participated in society to fulfill these needs. Man was responsible for cultivating the growth of society's spiritual life and the latter affected the growth of material life and thus the production of material needs. As man was both an egocentric and an altruistic social animal, social and economic systems, which always undergo change, eventually produced people who exploited others. Another aspect of man is that he constantly strives to seek freedom from oppression. He should reject those social and economic systems that permit exploitation of man by man and oppose the classes and strata that perpetuate such systems. The only reliable classes were those who contributed to the material needs of society, such as the peasants and the industrial workers, and those, such as the intelligentsia, who contributed to its spiritual needs. As these productive forces attempted to change the economic and social system, those whose greed was satisfied by the existing system oppressed the material and spiritual producers. This oppression was responsible for class antagonisms. To abolish these class antagonisms, the conditions that created them must first be abolished.

Only then could a socialist society without exploitation be established. As everything was in a constant state of change, greed would linger, a condition that had to be eradicated by the production of physical and spiritual happiness. Further, the conditions and needs of society would change as well. Hence, party members had to understand that the ideology and programs of the party were merely "relative truths," rather than final and without need of amendment or alteration.[34]

As Tin Pe's influence grew, Aung Gyi was pushed out of the way. In February 1963, Aung Gyi resigned from the Revolutionary Council and from his various other posts. In his resignation letter, Aung Gyi maintained his belief in socialism, as he had for twenty years, but explained that he differed in opinion "in some tasks" with his colleagues. Aung Gyi's closest associates were also removed from the Council, the Army, and other government services. In early June 1965, Aung Gyi was arrested.[35]

After Aung Gyi's initial departure, the Revolutionary Council set about launching a quick Marxist transformation of the Burmese economy. The new economy policy adopted many of the measures that had been opposed by Aung Gyi. Whether or how far Ne Win agreed or was pushed to adopt this redirection in the Council's economic reform program is unclear, although three months later there were suggestions that Ne Win was unable to control either Tin Pe or the commerce minister who were determined to turn Burma into a communist state. Tin Pe gradually expanded his already extensive portfolio by becoming chairman of the Finance Committee of the Revolutionary Council in late November 1964.[36]

Under Tin Pe's guidance, Burma saw sweeping nationalization in all areas of the Burmese economy (all twenty-four private banks in Burma had already been nationalized in 1962). The distribution of domestic rice purchases and the import and export trade were totally nationalized, as were all private businesses, regardless of size, including general stores, department stores, brokerages, wholesale shops, and warehouses. In early March 1965, Ne Win promised to launch an "agrarian revolution" that would bring the tenancy system to an immediate end and, a month later, the Council issued "The Tenancy Law Amending Law" freeing tenant-cultivators from paying land-rents to landlords. A new sweep of nationalization hit the factories and mills in December 1968, including textile factories, sawmills, chemical works, and food industries.[37]

In 1965, the Revolutionary Council invited candid opinions from the public on its performance, but was unprepared for the volume or degree of criticism that was subsequently voiced. Popular discontent had grown mainly over the worsening economy and shortages of consumer goods.

Figure 6.1 Present-day Burmese deliver unhusked rice to mill by boat

The Council's first response was to seize more control over the economy. It promulgated "The Law Empowering Actions in Furtherance of the Construction of the Socialist Economic System of 1965," giving the government more power to build a socialist economy in which the state owned all means of production and distribution. On the same day, the government dissolved the People's Stores Corporation, which had controlled commerce after wholesale and retail businesses were nationalized and which was the main object of public complaints. In its place, it formed a nine-member council called the Trade Council under the chairmanship of the Minister for Trade. The Trade Council would decentralize domestic commerce and, it was hoped, lead to better communication between government suppliers and local consumers. Its explicit purpose was to meet the consumer demands of workers, which were currently being met by a swelling black market. At the close of 1965, Ne Win admitted to a BSPP seminar that the economy was a "mess" and that everyone would be starving if Burma were not essentially an agricultural country.[38]

At the heart of the problem was that from 1964, Burma lost its position as the world's biggest exporter of rice (see Fig. 6.1) as its exportable rice surplus steadily declined. That year, the government had lowered the price of rice to help reduce the cost of living, but two years later, Ne Win voiced concern that the agricultural loans made to farmers might not be paid back. The

Revolutionary Council tried everything to boost agricultural productivity, offering farmers goods not available to anyone else, soft and then hard pressure, and confiscation of pounders and husking blocks necessary for polishing rice, but farmers would not stop hoarding rice and burying it underground where much was lost to decay. From the late 1960s, the government advised farmers to adopt modern cultivation techniques. It sought to reduce dependence on expensive, foreign chemical fertilizer by building a fertilizer plant, and by 1969, it had turned to the mechanization of agriculture as "the key to successful socialization of [the] farm." Tractors were now sold on credit to village cooperatives and training was provided in how to operate and maintain the tractors. Nevertheless, the rice surplus continued to shrink.[39]

THE INSURGENCIES

In April 1963, the Revolutionary Council offered amnesty to insurgents who would lay down their arms, and rewards for the capture of leaders of rebel forces were canceled in June. To prevent sabotaging of the peace talks, the government began arresting the central leadership of the AFPFL in early August and its provincial party secretaries in October. Dissatisfied with the terms offered, however, most rebel groups abandoned the talks by the end of the year. The Council responded to the failure of the talks by blaming the National Democratic United Front's strategy of erecting a parallel government in areas under Communist and ethnic insurgent control. It even claimed that Burma was on the verge of a national divide akin to the divisions between North and South Korea and Vietnam.[40]

While the Revolutionary Council returned to an offensive strategy, the Communist insurgents were in the midst of a crisis. The souring relationship between the Soviet Union and the PRC influenced the inner workings of the party through cadres who were separately associated with either Moscow or Beijing. While the split that led to the emergence of the BCP and the CPB had been serious, the forthcoming conflict within the BCP threatened to become much worse.

The PRC had been hesitant to become involved with the two Communist insurgencies in Nu's time. Nu had been careful to develop a very amicable relationship with Burma's gargantuan and seemingly erratic neighbor. After the Bandung Conference in 1955, the PRC, anxious to promote itself as a neutralist force in world affairs, formally renounced any connexions with the Burmese communists. Things changed, however, after the 1962 coup that put the Revolutionary Council into power. The PRC encouraged both the BCP and the CPB to engage in the 1963 amnesty negotiations. Even the volatile CPB leader Soe, who had gone into hiding in Arakan, agreed to do so, but by August he was unhappy with the terms offered, broke off talks and went back underground. The BCP soon followed. The Council reacted harshly, arresting four senior Communists and 400 above-ground leftist politicians. The Council's growing relationship with the Soviet Bloc, especially after Aung Gyi was booted out, further alienated the PRC. The growing rift between Burma and the PRC soon led the latter to label the Ne Win government as reactionary and to engage in active but covert support for the Communist insurgencies. Things picked up steam from 1966 with the beginning of the Cultural Revolution in the PRC and the attack by PRC thinkers on Khrushchev's revisionism of Communist doctrine. For its part, the Council was concerned about signs that the Cultural Revolution was being exported to Burma through the local Chinese community. This concern, along with the decision by some Chinese students in Burma to wear Maoist badges to school, sparked riots in Rangoon that, while essentially rooted in anxieties caused by food shortages, nonetheless mobilized an anti-PRC vocabulary. This was followed by an intense media barrage and mass demonstrations before the Burmese embassy in the PRC.[41]

The BCP had decided in 1964 upon the strategy of concentrating their strength in the Pegu Hills (Pegu Yoma) where they would develop a base area from which to launch offensives against the Burmese Army. While some Party leaders began to voice concern over the wisdom of the new strategy, Than Tun allied himself with a clique of "Beijing returnees" in the Party. They borrowed from the model of the Cultural Revolution's "Red Guards" and established their own Red Guard units drawn from younger members of the Party. Over the course of 1966–1967, the Red Guards increasingly replaced established members of the Party, sometimes accompanied by executions. In December 1967, Than Tun pushed through the Politburo a decision to formally purge the Party of revisionism and rebuild the BCP on the basis of uncorrupted Marxist-Leninist-Maoist thought. The label "revisionist" was cast around liberally and a major purge commenced. This included mass trials of the "Moscow returnees," intellectuals who had joined the BCP after the 1962 coup, and the original leadership of the BCP. At least fifty-seven BCP leaders were executed, including Bo Yan Aung, one of the Thirty Comrades. The "new" BCP also attempted a local pilot scheme of desecrating Buddhist temples and assassinating monks to determine how successful a general campaign against Buddhism in Burma would be. While the BCP was tearing itself up from within and alienating the local population, the Burmese Army launched a new offensive. Than Tun first turned on the Beijing returnees and, after more executions, fled as the Burmese Army overran BCP positions. On 24 September 1968, Than Tun was assassinated by one of his own bodyguards (possibly a government agent). Remnants of the Party regrouped near the Chinese border, rebuilt its strength with mainly Shan and Wa recruits, and allied with the PRC-backed Kachin Independence Army (KIA). In later years, the BCP would reject this period as a freakish occurrence, something that should have never happened.[42]

The Army's successes against the BCP afforded little time for rejoicing, because elsewhere, along the Thai border, another insurgent force was emerging. The 1950s insurgencies had continued to hold much of highland Burma after the 1962 coup, when they were joined by yet more rebel groups, particularly among the Shan. The rapid increase in the number of insurgent groups simultaneously increased the need for unity while making attempts to unify more difficult. Numerous attempts at bringing rebel groups together, such as the United Nationality Front in 1965, the National United Front in 1967, and the National Liberation Council at the end of 1967 all failed, as would 1972's Revolutionary Nationality Liberation Alliance.[43]

Shan insurgents were also finding it difficult to oppose the government in the face of challenges at home from armed groups interested in controlling the opium trade, whose epicenter was in the Golden Triangle. The Golden Triangle is a mountainous area, distant from major political centers, that overlaps the borders of Laos, Thailand, and Burma. The possibility of living off of funds secured by controlling opium trafficking, the area's isolation, the ability to move out of reach across the border in the face of one or another government offensive, and the apparent willingness of local army or police commanders inside the Thai, Lao, or Burmese borders to be bought off, made the zone an ideal home for rebel groups on the mend.[44]

The GMD was one of the first groups to take advantage of the trade, although from the early 1960s, they operated from bases in the Thai area of the Triangle. In 1972, a Chinese general, commanding an organ of the Government of Taiwan called the Intelligence Bureau of the Ministry of National Defence (IBMND), established himself in the Thai section of the Golden Triangle. Here, he set up a base, the Mainland Operation Department, brought the "Chinese irregular forces," as the old GMD remnants were now called, under his command, and occasionally deployed across the border into Burmese territory. The GMD found Thailand a safe home for years, as they served as a vehemently anti-Communist force along its northwestern frontier at a time when Thailand was anxious about the perceived threat posed by Communist insurgents at home, the BCP across the border in Burma, and the Khmer Rouge in Cambodia.[45]

In 1963, the Revolutionary Council encouraged the establishment of independent local militia units, known as the Ka Kwe Ye (KKY), in the Shan State to fight ethnic insurgents. The KKY units were given a free hand to support themselves and administer areas under their control as they wished, so long as they fought insurgents opposed to the Council. Several years later, the Council allowed any rebel group to become KKY under the same terms. Some of the KKY leaders were chameleon-like in their political outlook and easily shifted allegiances with changing circumstances. The main reason was that their primary interest was in enriching themselves through opium smuggling to Thailand and their militias amounted to mainly private armies used to control the trade. Two KKY leaders, Khun Sa and Lo Hsing-han, for example, followed a comparable path as rebel leaders, state prisoners, and agents of the Burmese government (in fomenting problems among the rebels on the government's behalf); eventually they led lives of luxury in Rangoon under government protection.[46]

In response to international pressure at a time when Ne Win was attempting to change the face of his regime, the BSPP government promulgated a narcotics law in 1974 that made drug addiction a notifiable disease and the production, possession, or smuggling of narcotics illegal. Those guilty of these offenses, or even of having contacts with international drug rings, would be sentenced to death. Only about 19,000 acres under poppy cultivation in the Shan State were exempted for a period of five years, for the purposes of the Burma pharmaceutical industry. The following year, Burma cooperated with the US in an effort to halt the illicit trade in opium and was allowed to purchase eighteen helicopters, followed by a further seven as well as four transport planes, for this purpose. Despite promises otherwise, the helicopters and planes were deployed against bona fide ethnic insurgents as well.[47]

THE RETURN OF NU

The flagging strength of the rebels seemingly provided the Revolutionary Council with space to resolve questions about Burma's political future. Before it could move confidently forward, the Council first determined to secure the visible if not sincere support of parliamentary leaders held in detention since 1962 and 1963, including Nu, Ba Swe, and Kyaw Nyein. Between October 1966 and August 1967, they were all released on the condition that they sign a pledge to remain out of politics and not remobilize their political parties. They were soon included in a thirty-three-member Internal Unity Advisory Board (IUAB) established by Ne Win in December 1968 to help promote national unity and prepare for the writing of a constitution. The IUAB recommended the reestablishment of a parliamentary democracy. Nu's personal recommendations were treated separately from those of the other members of the IUAB, who advised the creation of either a socialist state or a democratic socialist system. Nu favored a multiphase plan, which would lead to the restoration of freedoms of association, speech, and expression. First, Nu would be given the power necessary to establish an interim government with the guidance of the IUAB and this peaceful transfer of power would remove the stigma of the seizure of power by the current government. Second, the old parliament would be reconvened, which would enact legislation legitimizing Ne Win's election as President of the Union. Nu would then resign and Ne Win would form a government drawn from both the armed forces and from different political parties. Ne Win would also convene a representative National Convention to draw up a new constitution. Ne Win, however, rejected Nu's suggestions on the grounds that they lacked a "specific goal." Nu thus abandoned any hope of reforming the Ne Win government.[48]

Since his initial release, Nu had been touring the country giving talks on Buddhism throughout Burma. When he continued to do so after he joined the IUAB, he aroused concerns among the Revolutionary Council leadership that he was rebuilding his popular base. It was probably for this reason that Ne Win gave permission for Nu to go abroad on a Buddhist pilgrimage to India, where there would be some distance between himself and the general Burmese population. In August 1969, Nu announced the formation of the Parliamentary Democracy Party (PDP) under his leadership, based in Bangkok, with himself as chairman. Its goals were to replace Ne Win peacefully or, if this failed, to begin an insurrection. Nu began his campaign against Ne Win with a world tour, including the United Kingdom, the United States, and Japan, to secure international support for the new party. Nu believed he had (and probably did have) the support of much of the monastic order, underground student groups, most rural Burmans, and some sections of the Burmese civil service and military. Popular recognition of Nu as Burma's preeminent lay Buddhist leader was indicated in part by the mass appeal of his lectures on Buddhism prior to his departure from the country.[49]

Nu turned from politicking to plans to topple the Revolutionary Council by force. In 1970, he and a number of prominent men, including former Prime Minister Bo Let Ya and *The Nation* editor Edward Law Yone, who had been prominent in the 1950s and supported his PDP, joined forces in Bangkok. As Nu's record as Prime Minister meant that he was almost as mistrusted by ethnic minority leaders as Ne Win, these men did the hard work of negotiating an alliance with four of the five major ethnic insurgencies who combined as the United National Liberation Front (UNLF). While the Kachins, who fought for complete independence from any Burmese government, refused to join, the Chin National Democratic Party, the KNU, New Mon State Party, and Shan State Army did. The deal worked out for the pact involved the creation, after their success in felling the Revolutionary Council, of a federal system of states and a joint military high command. On paper, at least, the front was a force to be reckoned with. Its combined strength in regular and irregular troops numbered 50,000 and the territory under its control, not counting isolated towns and cities occupied by the Burmese Army, amounted to over half of Burma's total area. Meanwhile, Ne Win would still have to face the seven-thousand-man-strong BCP, which was not included in the Front, and further territory under their control. In April 1970, the UNLF held its annual conference at which it decided it had the military muscle now to begin a full guerrilla campaign, dominated mainly by attacks on infrastructure for which it had trained men in demolition, against the Burmese Army. The UNLF predicted, given reports of Ne Win's chronic poor health, that by the end of the year either Ne Win would be dead or they would have captured Rangoon, but neither materialized.[50]

The Revolutionary Council took the propaganda offensive rather than the defensive. All of the details and activities of the front published in the West were repeated in state-controlled newspapers and magazines. At the same time, the Ministry of Defense challenged the various claims made by the front, which it called the "unholy alliance." The touted strength of the UNLF was attributed to its leaders simply adding zeros to the numbers of troops it actually had. At the same time, it was asserted, the forces of UNLF allies were rapidly disintegrating in the face of army offensives. With some justification, the Council also observed that the UNLF lacked a "systematic political or military organization" and that strong rivalries within the front threatened to pull it apart. The front, in short, was a paper tiger. To counter claims of Nu's mass support, the Council staged its own mass demonstrations against the UNLF.[51]

At first the UNLF campaign consisted of leaflet dropping and, according to the Burmese government, a series of bomb attacks in Moulmein and Pegu, and related attempts in Rangoon. They were even accused of having plotted to dig a tunnel and plant bombs under the Martyrs' Mausoleum, which they planned to detonate when Ne Win and other Revolutionary Council members came to speak on Martyrs' Day on 19 July 1970. If the bomb plots were genuine, they were foiled. In 1972, the UNLF sent in 500 well-armed commandos, bringing with them gold coins minted by the UNLF to pay for supplies and recruits within Burma. In a few weeks, most of these commandos had been killed, captured, or had fled back inside the Thai border. As mentioned above, by the end of 1970, the UNLF claimed a total fighting force of 50,000 men, including both regular and irregular troops. On the one hand, this was hardly sizeable enough to guarantee victory against a Burmese Army of 150,000 men. On the other hand, it was significant enough for Ne Win to be concerned, for, had a popular uprising greeted the rebel army, as the UNLF hoped, this force would have swelled considerably, but this too never materialized. Nu began to downplay his role in the UNLF and then finally ended his relationship with the anti-Ne Win coalition and, after a state visit by Ne Win to Thailand in June 1973, Thailand asked him to leave the country. Nu then headed for exile elsewhere.[52] The UNLF did not outlive the Revolutionary Council. As we shall see, it would not be Nu's last attempt to make a political comeback, but it proved to be his "last best hope."

CONCLUSION

It is sometimes asserted that the Caretaker Government was a dress rehearsal for the Revolutionary Council period. The military may have stood back to watch the restored civilian government fail to match the record of the 1958–1960 period. The military may also have found that controlling the government helped to provide the kind of national unity necessary to fight the civil war effectively. Certainly, the military found it necessary to remove from Nu the means by which he, by all appearances, would sacrifice the territorial gains made by the military since 1949. Nevertheless, the Council went far beyond these interests. It exerted control over all aspects of the state and society within its grasp and transformed the government and society in fundamental ways. With the disappearance of civilian rule came the demise of freedom of expression and an eradication of foreign influences in the country. Moreover, the Council contradicted the economic approach it had followed in the Caretaker period under Aung Gyi. Although Aung Gyi remained at the helm of the government's economic policies for a brief period, the shift of control to Tin Pe marked the beginning of an economic nightmare that destroyed any real possibility for the Council's popularity.

While Ne Win was once rejected out of hand as a dictator by scholars and domestic opponents alike, it seems likely that during his first decade at the helm of the state at least, he and his colleagues believed that what they were doing was in the country's best interests. The Revolutionary Council produced its own ideology, mixing Marxism together with Buddhism, mobilizing leftist intellectuals and left-leaning military officers to attempt to reshape Burma along lines that, they felt, the Nu regime should have done, but never did. It may have been genuine interest in the welfare of the country among at least some members of the Council that helped speed along the transition to at least nominal civilian rule based on at least nominal civilian consensus. If such a motive was there, it would gradually erode in the years of BSPP rule ahead.

CHAPTER 7

The BSPP years

By the mid-1960s, Ne Win had found that the replacement of civilian rule by the Revolutionary Council, more thorough and penetrating than the earlier caretaker regime, had drawn both himself and the Army into a quagmire of problems. The military was unable to both fight a civil war and manage the state with equal success and its performance in the first area was steadily weakening. Moreover, the Army had become popular in the 1950s as defenders of the Union and for the administrative successes of the caretaker regime. Now that the military was permanently in charge of the government, they were held responsible for the country's economic performance, its social ills, its ethnic problems, and a range of other issues. In other words, without a civilian government, there was no one else to blame.

The general thus began to look for ways to mobilize the civilian population in administration, or rather to give the government a civilian face, without sacrificing real power, for otherwise it would probably invite a return to the political factionalism and state fragmentation witnessed in the latter years of the Nu regime. Moreover, the stated goals of the 1962 coup, while intended to legitimate the takeover, bound Ne Win to a particular direction of reform that substantially reduced alternative options. Further constraints would emerge from increasing economic woes, for which the Council was largely responsible, and reorganization among the rebels.

DEVELOPING A CIVILIAN MASS BASE

The Revolutionary Council began to act on its initial plans to make a transition from military to civilian rule, as Ne Win spelled out in his March 1966 speech to a mass peasants' seminar in which he expressed his concern about the possible emergence of a personality cult. A workers' seminar drafted a constitution for a workers' council and the aforementioned peasants' seminar did the same for a peasants' council. The next stage would involve the creation of a people's party on the basis of the "Burmese Way to Socialism."[1]

The considerable length of time it took for the BSPP to make the transition from a small cadre organization to a mass party – about nine years – indicates, as one scholar observes, "the military's perception of the need to have an effective, totally subservient means to mobilize the population for the leadership's perceived ends."[2] In the late 1960s, the Revolutionary Council sped up the development of the political organs on which a future, civilian single-party state would depend. These included the creation of people's workers' councils and people's peasants' councils at the village, township, district and central levels. In November 1969, Brigadier San Yu (Chief of Staff of the Army) told BSPP cadres that the party would be transformed into a mass party and, one year later, the party drafted the People's Party Organizational Plan. Finally, at the First BSPP Congress held in 1971, the BSPP formally opened up for mass membership, promising a true "People's Party."[3]

At the First BSPP Congress, San Yu, now the General Secretary of the party's Central Organization Committee, also announced that a new constitution, replacing the Constitution of 1947, would be drafted and Burma would be returned to civilian rule. Although the Revolutionary Council would still exercise civilian powers until the new constitution had been written, the Council would now reorganize itself, and the BSPP would be put in charge of the country, with a Prime Minister and a cabinet, until a socialist constitution could be drawn up. San Yu was made chairman of the ninety-seven-member New State Constitution Drafting Commission. To grant the new constitution the veneer of legitimacy, the writing process was emphasized as being more democratic than had been the case for the old constitution. Although an elected body had approved the old constitution, for example, lawyers had done the actual writing. By contrast, the new constitution would go through a series of drafts (there were ultimately three), with popular input. The Commission split into fifteen field teams who circulated around the country holding mass meetings, attended in total by 105,000 people, and asking for opinions, of which it received a total of nearly 5,000. After the BSPP Central Committee drew up the first draft, in March 1972, on the basis of the BSPP guidelines and suggestions gathered by the field teams, the draft was explained to the general population in more meetings, attended, it was claimed, by a total of seven million people, and gathered almost 50,000 more suggestions. After the BSPP Central Committee drew up a second draft one year after the first, the process was repeated, with the new constitution explained to eight million people and more suggestions were collected. The third and final version of the constitution was then drawn up.[4]

Ne Win had explained initially that the right conditions had to be set before the constitution could be promulgated. These included the transition of the Revolutionary Council from a military to a civilian body and the establishment of a new administrative system, both of which were achieved in 1972. Ne Win and twenty other senior officers in the government accordingly resigned from the Army and officially became civilians.[5]

At the Second Congress of the BSPP held in October 1973, with Prime Minister Ne Win as Chairman of the Executive Committee and San Yu as General Secretary of the BSPP, an election was held for its central and executive committees. The BSPP also approved a final draft of the new constitution. According to this constitution, Burma would become a one-party socialist democratic republic entitled the Socialist Republic of the Union of Burma. In December, a countrywide referendum on the new constitution was held in which a majority voted in favor of the new government. The new constitution established a unicameral People's Assembly (*Pyithu Hluttaw*), whose members were elected for four-year terms. This body would elect the State Council from among its own members. The members of the State Council would then elect from among themselves a Chairman, who would also automatically become the President of the state, and a Vice Chairman of the State Council. The highest organ of public administration was now the Council of Ministers, whose members would be elected by the Assembly from a list submitted by the State Council.[6]

The second step in the transition to civilian rule took years of preparatory work. In June 1969, a seven-man committee was formed to eliminate "bureaucratism." In theory, the SACs that had been set up in 1962 to replace commissioners, deputy commissioners, sub-divisional officers, and township officers, also became more representative in the new administrative system. Between 1962 and 1972, they had mainly consisted of members of the military and police forces. In the new administrative system, the SACs, at the central, divisional, township, and village levels (wards were now dropped as a unit of administration), would now consist of representatives drawn from the BSPP membership, the people's peasants' councils, and the people's workers' councils.[7] The people, the Revolutionary Council promised, would now "have to participate daily in the work of legislation, administration and judicial process by making decisions, making arrangements, supervising, inspecting, taking necessary action and making necessary changes."[8]

The year 1974 opened with the preparations for a new government system, albeit with no major change in the leadership. In January, elections were held for seats in the 450-member Assembly, although only candidates from the BSPP, the sole officially permitted party, were allowed to run. Officially, military rule ended on the night of 2 March, when Ne Win, in his capacity as Chairman of the Revolutionary Council, handed power over to the Assembly. Upon its inauguration, the Assembly elected the highest authority in the new government, the twenty-eight-member State Council, which in turn named Ne Win as President.[9]

THE POST-TIN PE ECONOMY

In August 1967, Ne Win rehabilitated Aung Gyi, releasing him from custody and asking him to return to the government. The fact that he did so while Tin Pe happened to be out of the country raised speculation that Tin Pe's influence on Revolutionary Council economic policy was quickly coming to an end. In November 1968, as Ne Win prepared to make major changes in Burma's national policy, Tin Pe made final efforts to escalate nationalization before his influence with Ne Win was terminated. Finally, in November 1970, Tin Pe was forced to retire.[10]

Ne Win and the Revolutionary Council had taken significant steps toward changing the face of the regime from a military junta to a one-party socialist state. However, they left unresolved the fundamental economic problems created by twelve years of military rule. The negative impact of Tin Pe's management of the economy not only lingered, but actually grew as the Revolutionary Council found it difficult to reverse the downward slide. In September 1972, Ne Win warned of a possible rice shortage by December. This message led to panic buying and hoarding by Burmese consumers. As prices for rice and cooking oil skyrocketed, the Burmese government launched a campaign against "economic insurgents," such as hoarders and profiteers, who were out to destroy the socialist economy, taking 530 dealers into custody within a week.[11]

In order to encourage increased rice paddy cultivation and its domestic availability, in May 1973 the government both partially decontrolled the rice trade and suspended the export of rice. Anything grown beyond a set quota, to be delivered to the government, could be directed to the free market. As the government purchase price was 25 percent below that available on the free market, farmers hoarded their crop and minimized their delivery to the government. This helped to keep rice prices high in the general economy, doubling the price of rice. With insufficient rice stocks, the government had to reduce the monthly rice ration, forcing workers and others to purchase more rice at substantially higher prices from private traders and encouraging an increase in the price of other basic commodities. By April 1974, the government recognized that the majority of workers were both demoralized and angry as a result of rising prices for rice and other essential commodities.[12]

As rice prices increased to as high as five times the official retail price, the Burmese government faced major labour unrest. This began in early May 1974, when a workers' strike broke out at the state-owned Railway Corporation's central workshop near Mandalay. Strikes soon spread to other state-owned facilities throughout central and Upper Burma, eventually followed by general demonstrations demanding that the government do something about the rising price of rice and other commodities. Some of the demonstrations turned violent and were harshly put down by the Army.[13]

The government attempted to stabilize the situation through various measures until the end of June 1974. It lifted strict controls on the sale, milling, and transportation of rice. It made emergency issues of rice and fish to office and factory workers. A new distribution scheme provided government workers with a monthly ration of rice twice that usually allowed to civilians. In early July, Ne Win attempted to save the government's face by blaming two elements: free traders who speculated on the price of rice and caused the food shortage, and the former Nu government, from which, he claimed, the Revolutionary Council in 1962 had inherited inequalities and unjust practices in different factories and mills. The continuity of labor problems was due to (1) the need to hastily build factories and mills and get them operating in the years that followed, (2) the impossibility of the government being aware of all the numerous problems that continued to exist, (3) the preoccupation of the government in the past two years with the writing of a constitution, and (4) subversive agents, guided by "outside influence," in the factories and mills who coerced otherwise patient and loyal workers into labor action. Government efforts to relieve these problems were delayed in August, when the worst floods in sixty years hit Burma accompanied by an outbreak of cholera.[14]

Retired UN Secretary General U Thant had become a symbol of the old pre-1962 period by the time he died of cancer in New York on 26 November 1974. The return of his body to Rangoon provided a catalyst for the release of frustrations with all the economic problems the Burmese faced. At a public ceremony attended by 50,000 mourners, students seized his body and held it in the RU Convocation Hall. On 8 December, draping the body in the United Nations flag, a procession of students and monks carried it to be entombed in a rough mausoleum they had built close to the site of the student union building (demolished in 1962). After U Thant's body had been seized, the government temporarily closed educational institutions and cut off international communications with the country. On 11 December, 1,000 soldiers and police raided the university campus, forcibly repossessed the body, and carried it to the cantonment gardens where it was re-interred in the mausoleum built by his family. Students, youths, and even Buddhist monks rioted in protest throughout Rangoon, attacking troops and police. Reports claimed that they damaged police stations and markets, destroyed the government's Road Transport Corporation building as well as the Housing Board building, set fire to automobiles, and damaged a train at a local railway station, leading to at least 4,000 arrests. Police had also opened fire on rioters killing nine and wounding seventy-four others. Martial law was declared on the same day over the Rangoon Division, and special tribunals were established to try rioters. After the U Thant riots, the government closed Mandalay and Rangoon universities for five months.[15]

Student protests also forced the government to take further steps to save the economy. On 6 June 1975, after seizing a hall where BSPP members were supposed to meet, students in the Institute of Economics called for a strike and an examinations boycott. They then marched on various campuses, including the Rangoon Institute of Technology (RIT) and RU, and the State Textile Mill, where they gathered more supporters, demanding the release of those students and workers who were still in detention after the December 1974 riots. The following day, 500 of the protestors marched from RU to Sule Pagoda Road and into central Rangoon (see Fig. 7.1), by which time their numbers had grown to 3,000, and burned effigies of Ne Win and San Yu at the Independence Monument. Their demands now included an end to military rule, an end to rising prices and unemployment, and the right to organize a student union. More demonstrations occurred in the capital and demonstrators made camp at the Shwedagon Pagoda. The government responded by deploying tanks and troops, making arrests, and banning further demonstrations. It also established price controls to halt soaring prices for rice and other basic foodstuffs in order to improve production by improving living conditions, easing commodity flow "among producers, traders and consumers," and establishing proper benefits for both traders and producers. As a result of the strong student role

Figure 7.1 Sule Pagoda in Central Rangoon

in the June unrest, the government closed the universities again in June 1975. Shortly after reopening the following January, however, 5,000 RU students held demonstrations demanding political reform. In late March, the government responded by closing all universities and colleges yet again. Martial law over Rangoon, which had commenced in December 1974, was not lifted until September 1976.[16]

Monastic involvement in the riots had raised again the potential threat to the BSPP public order of monastic involvement in mundane affairs. The U Thant riots did not spark an immediate attempt to resolve this situation, perhaps because of the monastic resistance shown on other occasions when the Revolutionary Council and the BSPP had attempted to bring the order under state control. Nonetheless, several years later, in late 1979, Ne Win again attempted to "purify" the order. From December of that year until January 1980, the BSPP held another All-Sangha All-Sect Convention, for the first time since 1965, which succeeded in the monastic acceptance of national registration, an accomplishment that had eluded the 1965 Convention. Consistent with traditional Buddhist rulership, the conclusion of the Convention was accompanied by a general amnesty and the release of 14,000 prisoners, including Ne Win's political opponents. An invitation was also made for the return of those of his opponents who had fled abroad, such as Nu, who would be forgiven if they promised to remain out of politics. Nu was impressed with Ne Win's meritorious behavior, and accepted the offer. The 1979–1980 Convention's success was probably due to the fact that this time, the government depended for leadership in the proceedings not upon the smaller Shwegyin sect, but the giant Thudhamma sect, that included most monks. The religious purification also led to the disbanding of small, heretical sects and the defrocking of individual monks. From June, ecclesiastical courts were set up to try hundreds of monks, including forty senior monks, for violating the monastic code, some on the charge of having sexual intercourse with women.[17]

COMPETITION FOR LEADERSHIP

Another possible reason for Ne Win's softer approach was personal insecurity about his own position in the BSPP government as potential threats within the Army and the BSPP began to emerge. In July 1976, the Burmese government announced that it had uncovered a coup plot leading to the arrest of three army captains and eleven other officers. The conspirators, who planned to assassinate Ne Win, San Yu, and intelligence chief General Tin Oo, sought to liberalize the government. The government claimed the main goal of the plot was to "destroy the socialist economic system." As the trial progressed, however, extensive state press coverage revealed resentment in the ranks concerning corruption within the BSPP, including special purchases of cars by BSPP leaders at about 10 percent of their market value. Stories also began to circulate that BSPP leaders were building up private fortunes and squandering party funds to the point of exhaustion. Ne Win's subsequent call for party leaders to live more economically austere lives appeared to substantiate these beliefs.[18]

Deteriorating political, social, and economic conditions led to the calling of the Third BSPP Congress in February 1977, eight months earlier than scheduled. The Congress saw severe criticism over the failure of Prime Minister Sein Win and Deputy Prime Minister (and minister of National Planning and Finance) U Lwin to adhere to national economic plan guidelines and policies. The Congress also elected a new central committee. Sixteen senior leaders, including Sein Win and Lwin, were left out of the elections in order to allow an infusion of new blood. In a surprising development that suggested that Ne Win was also blamed for the poor economy, San Yu received more votes than Ne Win. The central committee pushed the vote aside and soldiers surrounded party headquarters and seized documents that supposedly linked central committee members with the Soviet KGB. The following purge saw 113 central committee members, the "Gang of 113," forced out of the Party. At the end of March, both Sein Win and Lwin resigned from the government, while U Maung Maung Kha, formerly in charge of the army engineering corps and the defense services industries, became the new Prime Minister.[19]

Another BSPP Congress was then called in November 1977, at which San Yu claimed that corruption and malpractice was hurting the BSPP. Responsibility was attributed to a faction that had formed and acquired positions on leading committees. To resolve this problem, the BSPP was to revise its constitution. In the general election in January 1978, Ne Win was approved to rule for four more years and in March, the People's Assembly re-elected President Ne Win to his second four-year term. At the BSPP Congress held in August 1981, Ne Win finally announced that he would retire as President of the Republic, which he formally did on 9 November. San Yu was unanimously elected by the Assembly to take his place as Chairman of the Council of State and thus, automatically, President of the Republic.[20]

Although Ne Win stepped down as President, he remained in control of the BSPP and thus in firm control of the country, until the collapse of the Party in 1988. With Ne Win's formal departure from the presidency, the government attempted to demonstrate its legitimacy by targeting old problems, especially government corruption and the status of Asian immigrant minorities. From May to June 1983, Ne Win personally led the latest purge of government leadership. Initially, Tin Oo was ousted and confined to his house, accused of building up a private power base outside the official military hierarchy. Ne Win had also complained about Tin Oo's conspicuous spending habits, which had included an expensive wedding and honeymoon abroad for his son and a similarly expensive medical trip to London for his wife. Further, his well-known protégé, Bo Ni, who had been Home and Religious Affairs Minister, was also on trial for misusing private funds after he reportedly used a medical trip to London to purchase luxury goods and smuggle them illegally through Burmese Customs. The following month scores of military men and officials were sacked. While most evaded prison sentences, Tin Oo was sentenced to two life terms and found guilty of misappropriating state funds to finance his property holdings, and Bo Ni was also given a life sentence with hard labour.[21]

The purge of Tin Oo and the resulting disarray in Burma's security and intelligence services was soon blamed for a major intelligence failure of international dimensions. In October 1983, a bomb killed four South

Korean cabinet ministers and fifteen others at a ceremony at the Martyrs' Mausoleum in Rangoon. While the bomb was eventually traced to North Korean agents, just as South Korea's leadership had immediately suspected, other theories held that the bomb was probably planted by the BCP or by dissidents in the Burmese Army in retaliation for the recent purge. Once the North Korean connection was proven, the Burmese government severed diplomatic links with North Korea, ordering North Korean diplomats and their families to leave the country within forty-eight hours, this being the first time that Burma had ever taken such a measure.[22]

In 1981, Ne Win announced BSPP plans to promulgate a new citizenship law within a year. The new law was to include three citizenship classes, including indigenous people, "mixed people" (descendants of intermarriage between Chinese and Indian immigrants and Burmese), and naturalized citizens. Ne Win located the emergence of Burma's foreigner problem in the period between 1824 (the beginning of the First Anglo-Burmese War) and 1948, the period of colonial rule, when the Burmese and indigenous institutions were no longer in control of who could and could not live in the country, nor did the colonial regime restrain the inflow of immigrants. First the British came and they were followed by a multitude of other foreigners, mostly for economic reasons. Thus, when Burma achieved independence in 1948, it found itself with a heterogeneous population of nationals, foreigners, and the descendants of mixed marriages of both, whom Ne Win labeled "thwe hnaw" or mixed blood. In order to determine who were to be citizens in the new republic and who would remain foreigners, the Nu regime passed the Union Citizen Act (4 January 1948), which defined "genuine" citizens and their rights, and the Union Citizenship Election Act (9 May 1948), which gave foreign-born individuals in the country the option of applying for citizenship. One problem was that after the 1948 citizenship laws, many foreigners remained but did not know how to properly apply for citizenship, or indeed, were unclear of what their actual national identity was. These people were categorized as "resident citizens" under the 1948 law, as differentiated from genuine citizens. A second problem was that under Nu, many foreigners who came to Burma after 1948 were improperly given citizenship certificates. Ne Win, using the example of Indians and Chinese in Burma, argued that resident citizens and those post-1948 immigrants who had acquired citizenship certificates should be allowed to remain and work, but should be excluded from involvement in determining the country's future. Some of the Indians and Chinese who left Burma moved to various countries and maintained transnational networks of family members in Burma and abroad for the purposes of black-marketeering. Such people, Ne Win argued, could not be trusted in national organizations and could not be given full citizenship.[23]

The new Burma Citizenship Law established three categories of citizenship. "Genuine citizens" included only "pure blood" nationals. "Resident citizens" included those foreign immigrants who had come to Burma and properly applied for citizenship under the 1948 laws. "Naturalized citizens" included those pre-1948 foreign immigrants who had not applied for citizenship under the 1948 laws, because they either did not know about them or did not understand them, and were found after application and scrutiny by the state to meet the requirements for citizenship. Immigrants who knew about the laws and refused to apply for citizenship, or who did not know or understand the laws and did not qualify after scrutiny, would be denied citizenship. Ne Win also explained that while there were three categories of citizen now, in the future there would only be one, as the third generation descendant of a resident or naturalized citizen would become a "genuine" citizen.[24]

THE CONTINUING CIVIL WAR

After so many failures at unifying themselves into a broad alliance, in 1976, thirteen insurgent groups succeeded in doing so with the establishment of the National Democratic Front (NDF) under the command of KNU General Saw Bo Mya. The NDF based itself at Manerplaw ("Field of Victory"), established as the KNU capital in 1974, on the Thai border. Bo Mya was a pro-Western commander who had rapidly emerged as leader of the KNU. In the 1960s, the KNU was wracked by military reverses, failed negotiations with Rangoon, and two major schisms, the last in 1966, only to be disappointed in the early 1970s by the failure of the UNLF. Bo Mya's predecessor, Mahn Ba Zan, had attempted to graft a leftist ideology onto the KNU and formed an alliance with the BCP. During this period, the KNU's military wing, the KNDO, was renamed the Karen National Liberation Army (KNLA). Under Bo Mya, the KNU would become an anti-Communist force, despite a military alliance with the BCP in the mid-1980s.[25]

Aside from the KNU and four other relatively minor insurgencies, the NDF included the Arakan Liberation Party, the Kachin Independence Organization (KIO), the Karenni Progressive Party, the Kayan New Land Party, the Lahu National Unity Party, the Union Pa-O National Organization, the Palaung State Liberation Organization, and the Shan State Progressive Party. Although the NDF intended to raise an army of

100,000 men, its initial combined strength amounted to only 10,000 fighters. The main weakness was the absence of outside support. Members of the NDF would not cooperate much militarily, but the alliance did cause the various ethnic insurgent groups to abandon their earlier demands for separate sovereign states and accept the establishment of a federal union as a common goal. The NDF frequently lost soldiers to the better-funded BCP. Nonetheless, the NDF rivaled the BCP in numbers of soldiers and territorial control and, unlike previous attempts at non-Communist alliances, the NDF endured.[26]

Despite greater cooperation with other insurgent forces, however, KNU fortunes would rapidly decline from the mid-1980s. The BSPP government launched a massive counter-insurgency campaign in 1984 eventually leading to the capture of the KNU base at Palu in 1986. More importantly, the KNU was cut off from its main source of revenue. Unlike some of its opium-enriched competitors, the KNU depended upon a 10 percent tax it levied on goods passing through transit points it controlled along the Thai border. From 1984, Thailand's improving relationship with Rangoon led it to seal off this trade.[27]

The notorious Khun Sa (Chapter 6) returned to the Triangle after the creation of the NDF to rebuild the Shan United Army (SUA), which gradually grew to 5,000 soldiers. Although he claimed to be fighting for Shan independence, the fact that the Burmese Army was strangely reluctant to attack his bases did not help his reputation. Khun Sa appears to have mainly been intent on rebuilding his opium empire. Establishing control over territory on both sides of the Thai–Burmese border, he ran between ten and twelve heroin refineries. In 1981, the Thai government and the US Drug Enforcement Agency each put out rewards for his capture, dead or alive. The Thai Army began an offensive in 1982 that drove his forces out of their main base at Ban Hin Taek in northwestern Thailand and out of another stronghold at Doi Sanchu, also in Thailand, in August 1983. By 1985, the indefatigable Khun Sa had rebuilt his forces yet again and expanded his army further when he forced the Thailand Revolutionary Council to merge its forces with his own SUA, creating the Mong Tai Army (MTA).[28]

THE CRACKING OF THE ECONOMY

In the mid- to late-1970s, it appeared that international help might resolve Burma's economic woes. In 1976, the World Bank set up an aid consortium, including Britain, the US, Japan, Germany, France, Australia, and

Canada for consultation and the establishment of a common policy regarding aid to Burma. In 1977, San Yu reported to the BSPP Congress that isolationist policies had hurt Burma's social and economic progress and would cease. While it had been hoped that Burma's gross national product would increase by 4 percent, it had only grown by 2.6 percent; productivity among state and cooperative sectors of the economy had been projected to increase at 2 percent per year, but had only achieved a 1.2 percent rate of increase. In order to exploit its natural resources, and establish joint enterprises with other countries, without sacrificing the socialist economic system, Burma would need significant capital investment, foreign technical assistance and equipment. Although Japan and West Germany were the largest of foreign aid donors, the PRC also emerged as a major source of loans to the country from 1979.[29]

The Burmese economy began to crack again by the mid-1980s. Between 1981 and 1986, the national debt doubled to US$ 2.8 billion. By 1986, the net debt burden was 650 percent of foreign exchange earnings, with a debt–service ratio of almost 60 percent of foreign-exchange earnings. During the same period, the World Bank estimated that the value of Burma's export declined by half, having dropped by 15 percent in 1985 alone, while rice ceased to be the major export item, being displaced by teak and hardwood. As a result, Burma's creditworthiness began to slip in international eyes. In early November 1985, the Burmese government attempted to fight the black market by withdrawing, without prior notice, high denomination notes for the second time. The 100-*kyat* note, Burma's principal unit of currency, ceased to be legal tender and would be replaced by a new 75-*kyat* denomination note.[30]

Ne Win announced that steps would be taken to liberalize the rice trade in 1987. Although some parts of private trade were being opened, foreign investment was still blocked. In March, the BSPP government passed a law which limited the sale of land or buildings to or from foreigners and forbade such transfers by gift or mortgage as well, violation of this law being subject to up to five years in prison and confiscation by the government of the property concerned. In September, the government lifted the ban on citizens buying or selling domestically rice paddy, maize, mung beans, butter beans, and a range of other crops. It also announced that peasants cultivating these crops would pay their taxes with a share of the crops rather than by paying cash.[31]

The government's rice procurement program, which supplied much of Burma's urban populace, was severely damaged because government prices could not compete with those on the black market. Shortages of spare parts and petrol also created transport problems that made it difficult to distribute the rice that had been procured. This would be followed on 5 September 1987 with the demonetization of 25-, 35-, and 75-*kyat* notes as well. The following day, students protested the measure, leading to the closure of universities for a month. In August, Ne Win admitted to the BSPP Central Committee that there had been mistakes in the regime's economic policies and announced that it would now experiment, through a short-term program, with allowing the private trade in rice to resume. Like the cultivators, private businessmen would also pay their taxes in the form of crops or commodities rather than cash. The government also gave cooperative societies and private entrepreneurs (Burmese citizens only) permission to begin exporting rice.[32]

The Burmese economy hit rock bottom by late 1987. In November of that year, the UN granted Burma Least Developed Country status, shared by forty other poor countries, which in theory made the country eligible for special technical and development assistance, as well as low or zero interest loans. This new status, however, came too late to save the BSPP government, as revelations made in early 1988 would indicate. In mid-March 1988, the Deputy Prime Minister and Minister for Planning and Finance, U Tun Tin, told a People's Assembly budget session that the GDP growth rate for 1987–1988 was almost half the expected target of 5 percent. He also announced, for the first time, that Burma had a foreign debt of US$4 billion. In the new budget, the GDP growth rate target would only be 2.3 percent.[33]

The deteriorating economic situation raised concerns about unrest. At the end of March, General Saw Maung explained that an unstable world economy had adversely affected Burma and to adapt to this situation, the government had begun to undertake economic reforms. A month later, San Yu observed that Burma's industrial sector suffered from many problems. First, factories were not operating at capacity because they lacked raw materials, oil, and spare parts. As a result, there was a decline in available consumer products. The yearly decline in oil production also meant that the economy could not meet the needs of the production and transport sectors. The government also attempted to speed up the delivery of goods to port for export, by ending the government's monopoly on the transport of private goods. "Unrestricted" private transport would be allowed, with the exception of government department and cooperatives' goods, which would have to continue to rely on government-controlled transport. After a few months, however, Rangoon authorities warned private traders not to escalate prices of basic commodities. The purpose of freeing up trade, they argued, had been to bring prices down "while enabling private traders to enjoy justifiable profits." However, commodity prices were now spiraling out of control as a result of the "greed" of the private sector and amounted to the exploitation of Burmese consumers. The basic problem was that as the *kyat* had become unreliable, rice became the new currency and so was hoarded.[34]

CONCLUSION

Whatever the underlying motives for the transition from Revolutionary Council to BSPP rule, the latter's failure was not so much political as economic. The legacy of Tin Pe's misdirection of the economy, the problems of supplying consumer demands, demonetization, and corruption at the top all contributed to the general malaise and popular dissatisfaction with the regime's performance. Despite the promises of the Revolutionary Council period, the BSPP government had not eliminated greed or economic exploitation, but instead, as in many of the Communist states that collapsed in the 1980s, saw the emergence of a privileged class of military and associated families who thrived. Many of these families would move to prevent democratization in the years after the collapse of the BSPP government in 1988.

CHAPTER 8

Toward democracy, 1988–1990

Although, as we have seen, Burma underwent several major watersheds in its modern historical development, the most crucial and perhaps most surprising, given the scale, the suddenness, and the importance of its impact, is the popular revolution of 1988. While Burmese were clearly unhappy with the BSPP government, the state had successfully managed its international image, convincing the world not that it was a good government, but rather that domestic opposition was largely a problem of ethnic polarization (the ethnic insurgencies) and foreign intervention (the Communists).

Regardless of how much resignation the general population displayed until this point, the BSPP government would fall as a result of the release of popular pent-up frustrations before the year was finished. As one Burmese leader from the period later recalled:

As the years rolled by, we had started to equate lethargy and lack of change with stability; speeches and motions with no progress; excuses with reason; and manipulated statistics with real facts. Our people are not that simple; they saw, they felt, and they knew, but they can be patient, and they can wait. When all the waiting they could do was done, the storm broke.[1]

THE STUDENT DEMONSTRATIONS

The collapse of BSPP rule had surprisingly small beginnings. Indeed, its spark was regarded at the time as almost insignificant. On 12 March, four months after universities and colleges reopened, several RIT students became involved in a brawl with local people at the Sanda Win teashop. The incident began with an argument over a song request and a local hitting one of the students over the head with a stool. Although arrests were made, the offending parties were released the following day, the main culprit being the son of a local party official. In the days that followed, more clashes between locals and outraged RIT students occurred until riot police fired on the students, wounding many, several of whom died when police forbade doctors to operate. RIT students soon demanded a report on the killings and compensation for the families of those killed. On 15 March, soldiers and police raided the RIT campus. The police were unusually swift and brutal, beating students with batons and arresting them en masse, state radio later claiming that the students were completely at fault for the raid. The following day, as student protestors who had collected at Rangoon University passed the White Bridge on Prome Road, demanding an end to one-party rule, they were stopped by a barbed wire barricade and soldiers armed with clubs and automatic weapons. In the ensuing one-hour carnage, reputedly orchestrated by General Sein Lwin, as many as one hundred (some say 200) students were beaten to death. Female students dragged off by the soldiers were gang-raped. Recognizing that the violence had gotten out of hand even by the standards of the military government, and in the tense atmosphere of an economy ruined by a quarter of a century of military rule, on 17 March, the government established a commission to investigate the initial student death, but refused to acknowledge the White Bridge incident.[2]

Reacting to the harsh response by the authorities, more protests erupted in the following few days, broken up by riot police. One of the most serious episodes occurred when forty-one students died of suffocation after being packed into a single prison van for two hours on the ten-mile journey to prison. The bodies were cremated the following day, it was claimed, because of their poor condition. The government knew about this incident, but, claiming that the police had been short of prison vans, it would delay admitting responsibility until mid-July, leading to the resignation of the Home Minister. In response to the March events, retired Aung Gyi wrote to Ne Win demanding an immediate inquiry. If the security forces had acted as rumored, he argued, then they were guilty of human rights violations and this would hurt Burma's international image.[3]

Little had been resolved by early June. The government blocked a student attempt to organize a peaceful memorial ceremony on 13 June for the students who had been killed in the March riots. On 16 June, the students of Rangoon Arts and Sciences University (RASU) gave the government one day to meet their demands to release 1,500 imprisoned students and allow freedom of association. When the government made no response, 5,000 students of the RIT and two medical schools boycotted their classes and began protests. The protests grew over the course of the following week, leading to a major confrontation with riot police on 21 June. This time, after the police killed several children, ordinary citizens lent aid to the students, killing some of the police at a Rangoon market. In other skirmishes that day elsewhere in the city, police fired indiscriminately into protesting crowds. The government was outraged and closed the universities and declared curfews over the city. Nevertheless, in the next few days, riots, met by mass arrests and more curfews, spread to Mandalay and Pegu.[4]

The seventy-year-old Aung Gyi, who had criticized the security forces' handling of student protestors in March, wrote a forty-one-page letter to Ne Win and San Yu criticizing the government's handling of the economy. He claimed that Burma had been transformed into a "beggar nation," because of Tin Pe's misunderstandings of socialism in the 1960s. He now urged Ne Win to undertake serious economic reforms such as those then underway in the Soviet Union and China. Aung Gyi was then arrested for leaking his letters criticizing Ne Win to the public.[5]

THE FALL OF NE WIN

The curfew over Rangoon was finally lifted on 30 June, followed by the lifting of curfews in Pegu, Prome, and Moulmein and a week later, the government began releasing hundreds of students detained for the March and June riots. Violence broke out again in the middle of July at Taunggyi and Prome. In view of the deteriorating domestic situation, an extraordinary congress of the BSPP was called for on 23 July and was attended by 1,062 BSPP delegates. There was wide speculation that as the Home Minister and the Rangoon police chief had resigned already, Ne Win would use the session to legitimate a prospective purge of the government. Instead, two major changes were proposed. First, U Aye Ko, the General Secretary of the BSPP, admitted that the BSPP government's approach to the economy had been wrong and said that it would now fully open up the economy.[6]

The key to improving the economic performance of the private, public, and cooperative sectors, he asserted, was in fostering conditions and making guarantees that would mobilize private entrepreneurs to increase investment and provide economic dynamism. The private sector should now be allowed to own land and farm machinery; participate in the fishing and timber industries; establish and operate all industries (apart from munitions) for the construction of homes, roads, and bridges, the operation of air and rail transport, the manufacture of automobiles and trucks, local and foreign trade, and the publication of periodicals. The private sector would not be allowed to operate in certain areas, such as cinemas and the music industry, but the changes now proposed amounted to a sweeping retraction of much of the economic legislation of the Revolutionary Council and BSPP periods.[7]

Second, Ne Win explained that the bloodshed of March and June indicated significant mistrust of the government. To decide whether this reflected a majority or a minority, he called for the congress to approve his proposal that a national referendum be held, as soon as possible but no later than the end of September, to decide whether Burma should maintain a single-party system or revert to a multi-party system. If the latter were voted for, the Constitution would have to be amended to accommodate a multi-party electoral system and the newly elected Parliament would have to write a new Constitution. To prevent chaos, Ne Win asked existing organizations to remain in place until that Parliament could establish new organizations. If the new Parliament no longer wanted the organizations it inherited from the BSPP government, these should, without hesitation, hand over their responsibilities.[8]

If the national referendum were to vote for a continuity of the single-party state, however, Ne Win would clarify his personal position. Accepting indirect responsibility for the March and June events and observing that he was now very old (seventy-seven), he asked the Congress to allow him to resign from his position as BSPP Chairman and from the BSPP altogether. This would require an amendment to the party regulations that denied any full member the right to resign from the Party. Ne Win further explained that he had tried in the past to resign and retire, but his colleagues had stopped him from doing so, thus trapping him in the "whirlpool of politics." This time, however, these colleagues, such as Vice-Chairman San Yu and BSPP General Secretary Sein Lwin, not only agreed, but also submitted their own resignation letters as well. The Congress refused Sein Lwin's resignation and while it accepted those of San Yu and Ne Win, it did not permit them to leave the Party. The Congress also decided not to hold a national referendum, on the grounds that the government should first concern itself with resolving the country's economic problems. Ne Win also denied responsibility for the dynamiting of the RU Student Union in 1962, claiming that there had been confusion in the relaying of orders.[9]

SEIN LWIN

At the Tenth Meeting of the BSPP Central Committee, Sein Lwin was named the new Chairman of the BSPP, and thus became President of Burma. The sixty-four-year-old was a known hardliner and was held to be responsible for the White Bridge incident and for brutally crushing the RU student demonstrations in July 1962. On 27 July 1988, Sein Lwin had claimed that it was not the "Burmese Road to Socialism" that had caused

Burma's economic crisis, but rather "bad officials." After his appointment, Sein Lwin immediately issued dismissal orders for Prime Minister U Maung Maung Kha and the Chairman of the Council of People's Attorneys U Myint Maung (now replaced by Dr. Maung Maung). Saw Maung was also promoted to Minister of Defense.[10]

Upset at Sein Lwin's promotion, students in the capital immediately began to make public speeches, put up anti-government posters, hold protest marches to the Shwedagon Pagoda, and hand out pamphlets referring to Sein Lwin as "The Butcher of Rangoon" and leaflets calling for a general strike in demand for a return to democracy and multi-party elections. This continued from 28 July until 3 August. At one demonstration at the Shwedagon alone, 500 students and monks participated. Rather than attempt dialogue, Sein Lwin took a hard line, responding in the same way that the military had to most civil disobedience since the 1962 coup. The government placed under detention Aung Gyi and ten other former army officers, officials, and businessmen associated with him, followed by the arrest of two of the surviving eleven members of the Thirty Comrades, as a precautionary measure. Two days later, martial law was declared over the Greater Rangoon area. Even so, the protests continued to grow in numbers and frequency, and spread from Rangoon to other major towns in Burma, including Mandalay and Moulmein.[11]

In his resignation speech in July, Ne Win had given a stern warning to protestors. He explained that

when the army shoots, it shoots to hit; it does not fire in the air to scare. Therefore, I warn those causing disturbances that they will not be spared if in the future the army is brought in to control disturbances.[12]

Although the Army fired only warning shots when confronted with 10,000 protestors on 4 August, further confrontations over the course of the following week led to bloodshed at Mandalay, Mergui, Pegu, and Thanpinit, but failed to deter other demonstrations, which by 9 August had broken out in most towns throughout the country.[13]

The government's response to the breakdown in public order was confused and desperate, as it vainly sought ways to stem the growth of the opposition. On 7 August it secured the agreement of the State Sangha Maha Nayaka Committee and Sangha Nayaka committees at the state, divisional, township, ward, and village levels not to allow monks to participate in the "disturbances." The following day, it retroactively raised the pay of the armed forces, pensioners, mill and factory workers, and other government employees. On 9 August, the Ministry of Education closed all primary, middle, and high schools as well as teacher training institutes, reportedly in order to protect the students from the demonstrators. That same day, the government announced a curfew from 8:00 P.M. until 4:00 A.M., and banned groups of five or more from marching, gathering, walking, making speeches, or chanting slogans. As deaths mounted, the State Sangha Maha Nayaka Committee called on the government to "uphold the 10 kingly virtues" and "to concede to the demands of the people" as far as permitted by law. Elements among the demonstrators took the law into their own hands, beheading three policemen, burning buses, and damaging government buildings. On 10 August, tanks and machine-gun carriers were brought in to form barricades to prevent demonstrators from moving through Rangoon. Demonstrators also erected their own barricades and those who had been able to steal guns from ransacked police stations now fired back on the soldiers. The next day, the Air Force began dropping leaflets warning that they would begin bombing if demonstrators did not remove the barricades. The following day, 12 August, Sein Lwin resigned as Chairman of the BSPP, Chairman of the State Council, and as President of Burma, bringing the demonstrations to a halt. By this time, the government claimed that one hundred people had been killed, although hospital staff estimated that 3,000 had died in Rangoon alone.[14]

THE MAUNG MAUNG GOVERNMENT

Ne Win's long-time friend and biographer, Dr. Maung Maung, replaced Sein Lwin, taking office on 19 August 1988. On the same day, the BSPP government began to make a flood of concessions to demonstrators, whether asked for or not, beginning with the declaration that the public, cooperatives, and private sectors were now allowed to publish newspapers, journals, and magazines. Those publications and presses that had been nationalized under the Revolutionary Council in the 1960s were now to be returned to their original owners. All sectors were also now allowed to become involved in public entertainment, to build cinemas, and to show commercial films.[15]

The opposition was generally unsatisfied with the choice of Maung Maung to head the government and his succession to office was rejected by tens of thousands of demonstrators. They associated him with Ne Win and felt he was no better. He had helped draft the 1974 Constitution that established one-party rule. They also claimed that in his role as Chief Justice, the senior legal officer of the BSPP government, he was responsible for illegalities and for the regime's poor record on human rights. There was also significant opposition to Maung Maung's creation of the Public Opinion Soliciting Commission on 19 August 1988. The Commission consisted entirely of government people. Its purpose was to determine authentic popular opinion on the condition of the country and interview members of state organizations and individual citizens, Maung Maung promising that no one would be punished for freely expressing opinions. The Commission's questionnaires asked for views on the direction government reform should take, including whether a one-party system should be continued, whether the judicial system should be maintained as it was, and whether student unions should be permitted. The Commission was then to submit a report to the People's Assembly in October.[16]

The government also took pains to approach the demonstrations in a new way. Regarding numerous demonstrations that took place on 23 August, government radio repeatedly stressed how demonstrators were acting peacefully and that security forces had not shot anyone. The following day, Maung Maung announced that the government had now lifted martial law in Rangoon and Prome. He explained that the Army did not like to confront civilians and that it meant no harm to genuine demonstrators. It only acted as necessary when troublemakers took advantage of the situation in order to loot and cause destruction and in these circumstances it was difficult for the Army to differentiate between them. Maung Maung further announced that the government had decided to call an extraordinary party congress on 12 September to discuss holding a national referendum on whether or not Burma should continue to have a one-party system. If the Congress decided to remain with a one-party system and not hold a national referendum on the matter, Maung Maung promised that he and the entire BSPP Central Executive Committee would immediately resign and end their membership in the Party. The next day, on 25 August, the Maung Maung government released Aung Gyi from prison.[17]

As the number of protesters grew from thousands to tens of thousands and then hundreds of thousands, a unifying force was needed. The most popular emerging figure was the charismatic Aung San Suu Kyi (born in 1945 in Rangoon). She had left Burma with her mother, when the latter was appointed Ambassador to India. Aung San Suu Kyi had lived abroad for most of her adult life. She had no direct claim to leadership, but as the daughter of Aung San, the widely recognized father of Burmese independence (and the Army), she had an aura of legitimacy. She had come to Burma earlier in 1988 to attend her sick mother. Aung San Suu Kyi first entered the fray when she wrote to the Council of State in August, while it was deciding on a new leader following Ne Win's resignation, proposing the establishment of a consultative committee whose members would be independents drawn from outside the ruling BSPP elite. They would oversee the establishment of a multi-party political system. The Council made no comment. By 25 August she was urging that there should be no problems between the Army and the people. Many of the protestors began to recognize her as the leader of the pro-Democracy movement after her speech before a mass audience at the Shwedagon Pagoda on the following day. Aung San Suu Kyi viewed the popular protests as a "second struggle for Burmese independence," for while the Burmese had secured independence from colonialism, they did not now enjoy a political system that fully observed human rights. It was now too late for the BSPP government to hold a referendum, for the popular desire for multi-party elections had already been demonstrated through the protests. By late August, she still foresaw no particular role for herself in a future government, as she was not attracted to a "life in politics," but, for the time being, because of her father's name, she was satisfied to serve merely as a "kind of unifying force."[18]

Demonstrators gave the Maung Maung government a 7 September deadline to resign, or they would launch national strikes and demonstrations. When that deadline arrived, the Maung Maung government instead announced that people in Rangoon could "no longer live in peace and security" and that some people participating in the rallies were only doing so to loot public property. As the demonstrations grew, the government curiously began to release over 10,000 criminals from prison in an apparent attempt to discredit the democracy demonstrators or to encourage the view of a breakdown in national order. It was widely believed that the government wanted an excuse to summon army intervention. Prior to the deadline, a group of students, monks, and others who had formed a vigilante committee and taken over an abandoned police station attempted to maintain order when looters, many recently released from prison, broke into a biscuit factory. Eight were killed, including the deputy abbot of a local monastery. Hundreds of people then stormed the factory and a battle involving axes, knives, and slingshots immediately ensued. Some of the looters who were captured were burned to death, hung from trees or lampposts, or decapitated. After teachers of the Hmawbi Military Academy and several battalions declared that they would not shoot demonstrators, the BSPP government made a special effort to coordinate between departments to withdraw 600 million *kyat* from the Union of Burma Bank to pay its soldiers, presumably to keep them loyal and dissuade them from abandoning their posts.[19]

Despite the protests, 968 out of 1080 (about 90 percent) BSPP delegates attended the emergency congress, which was held two days earlier
than originally scheduled, on 10 September. The delegates were to vote
for a national referendum to determine whether Burma should continue
as a one-party state or change to a multi-party state. At that congress,
75 percent of delegates voted against holding a national referendum and in
favor of holding a general election instead. The People's Assembly would
now hold a session on the following day to identify respected elders who
could form an electoral commission to supervise the holding of free and
fair multi-party elections with the help of local elders, monks, and students
to observe the polling booths. The Army would not be allowed to support any party in the elections the Congress held, following its tradition
of neutrality in politics. These elections would be for the parliamentary
level only. This parliament, when constituted, would form a government
that it saw fit to run the country and make the necessary changes to the
existing Constitution. Finally, in order to hold fair elections, the BSPP government would have to secure law and order, assure food supplies at low
prices for the people, and make certain that transportation was operating
smoothly. The following day, the Assembly also voted in favor of multi-
party general elections and stipulated that these elections would be held
within three months.[20] The five-member Multi-Party Democratic General
Election Commission was finally formed on 12 September.

Maung Maung had earlier publicly admitted the failings of the BSPP on
1 September 1988. The 1974 Constitution, he explained, was arranged so
that there was a diffusion of power from the central government down to the
level of wards and villages, so that no one could command absolute power.
However, since 1974, these remained only "printed passages on paper," and
this denial of power grew into frustration over the fourteen years of BSPP
rule. Maung Maung gave another speech following the 10 September vote
in which he praised the delegates for having put the interests of the people
above those of the BSPP.[21] He argued that the historical development of the
BSPP had made it incapable of handling new conditions. As he explained:
"the weakness of the party was that it was born as a ruling party and
grew up as one. In practice, it lacked the experience of making sacrifices,
taking risks, and working hard to overcome difficulties . . ."[22] The BSPP,
in short, had failed, just as the AFPFL had failed by 1958, and thus the
BSPP provoked the anti-government demonstrations that now challenged
the Party's and the government's survival. As Maung Maung continued,
"Changes come about once every 10 or 12 years. If they do not come about
peacefully, they come about in a violent and torrid way."[23]

Maung Maung was instructing BSPP delegates concerning the legitimacy of the reasons for popular unhappiness with the government and with the Party, but he was in no way supporting the forces that were taking shape to lead the people in their protests. He believed that the protestors represented anarchy:

They – whoever "they" might be – wanted to sweep everything aside, bring everything down, rush in on human waves shouting their war cries to the cheers and applause of outsiders, and establish their occupation.[24]

Thus, while viewing Ne Win's retirement as a "benevolent act," he also viewed the protestors as riddled with opportunists, destructive elements and their "slanderous statements," and foreign influence. These people did not value law and order, which was a violation of Burmese culture and, Maung Maung argued, did not represent genuine democracy. Even so, he warned the BSPP delegates not to "hold grudges" or to retaliate in any way, but rather to change according to the times and conditions at hand and exercise patience with the newly emerging parties.[25]

Nu had returned to Burma under amnesty in 1980, vowing that he would stay out of politics and spend the rest of his life devoted to Buddhism.[26] Nevertheless, in late August 1988, the 81-year-old Nu now re-emerged to make another bid for political leadership. Having entered and removed himself from national leadership so many times before, he now jumped back again into the fray at the head of a motley crew of former ministers and military men. On 9 September, Nu invited local and foreign journalists, foreign embassy staff, and representatives of unions to a press conference at which he announced the creation of a parallel government, and listed the twenty-six members of this new government, among whom many were members of the old government. Nu argued that the only legal constitution Burma had was the 1947 Constitution. According to this constitution, he was the legal prime minister of Burma. As Nu explained: "I have exercised my constitutional right . . . I have taken back the power which General Ne Win has robbed from me . . . sovereign power no longer rests with General Ne Win. It has come back into my hands, and I announce this fact with joy." He explained that although this amounted to high treason in the eyes of the BSPP government and that he had no interest in political office, it was something that had to be done. Nu issued a statement on 19 September repeating his claims as well as explaining that he had the power to dissolve Parliament. Other opposition leaders had already warned Nu that the establishment of his rival government was "a dangerous move."[27]

The future founders of the National League for Democracy (NLD), Aung San Suu Kyi, Tin U and Aung Gyi, also had initially rejected the proposed multi-party elections in mid-September. At a coordination meeting arranged by the Election Commission on 13 September, they and others were told that it would be neutral and the election would be fair; in exchange, those present would have to cooperate sincerely with the commission. After explaining the details of the election process, Aung Gyi, Aung San Suu Kyi, and Tin U argued that while they respected the members of the commission, the fact that the BSPP government had created it meant that it was not legitimate and could not be trusted. Further, if the elections were held in the current circumstances, the elections would not be fair for two reasons. First, the new political parties – without financial resources – would have to face a state-financed BSPP, entrenched for twenty-six years; and second, although the armed forces promised to remain neutral, the fact was that all armed forces personnel and a majority of other state employees were BSPP members, and there would be no possibility of the general population having faith in that guarantee. Instead, a neutral government would have to be established before multi-party elections could be held. Aung San Suu Kyi had stressed the previous day that the creation of such a neutral government could only be achieved if Ne Win were exiled first from the country.[28]

The BSPP Election Commission delayed but eventually relented on some of these demands. On 16 September, the State Council announced that since government servants should "be loyal to the state and only serve the people" and in keeping with the multi-party system that the government now promised to create, all state employees, including the military, could no longer be members of a political party including the BSPP. The BSPP government announced that if government employees took part in the demonstrations to encourage multi-party elections "in the belief that such a national movement would bring about the best system for the state," then the BSPP government would not criticize them for doing so. However, the government argued that now that the demand for holding multi-party elections had been agreed to, the political movement could no longer be viewed as a national movement, but instead as a party movement. In parliamentary democracies abroad, the government asserted, the code of conduct of government employees did not allow them to participate in party movements. Only by observing this apolitical code of conduct would the popular needs of peace, prosperity, food, clothing, shelter, and transport be met. Thus, government employees should abandon strike action and return to work with effect from 19 September and if they had not done so within one week, the government warned, public service rules and regulations would be invoked to take action against them.[29]

At this point, the Army grew more alarmed. It faced three major problems, none of which it would allow to progress any further. First, despite lip service to multi-party elections and the removal of the armed forces and government personnel from the BSPP, large numbers of demonstrators continued their protests while the Army was becoming less potent a force in stopping them. This was underscored on 16 September when 7,000 demonstrators surrounded the Defense Ministry Building and only pulled back on the urging of Aung Gyi. The following day protestors surrounded government buildings, including the City Hall and the Central Bank. When drunken soldiers on top of the Trade Ministry Building taunted another crowd and then fired into it, protestors stormed the building and nearly decapitated the offenders before Aung Gyi and Tin U persuaded them to disperse, but not before they had burned three motor vehicles.[30] After decades of total control, the Army was extremely concerned about the complete breakdown of government authority. Indeed, due to the strike, government machinery had simply evaporated in the capital and in many of Burma's main towns.

Second, foreign diplomats and others in the country grew confident that the BSPP government would give in and allow the formation of an interim government, which would suddenly remove the armed forces' authority as well; there was no guarantee what their authority would be under the BSPP government's interim or permanent successor. Third, the Army was most concerned about its internal disintegration. On the one hand, it faced popular former generals in Aung Gyi, Tin U and others. On the other hand, it was beginning to lose soldiers on a daily basis; individuals crossed the lines to join the demonstrators and whole units mutinied, as in the case of 200 Air Force personnel in Rangoon who ignored army orders and joined the demonstrations as well.[31] The disintegration of the armed forces appeared to go hand in hand with the collapse of the BSPP government.

On 18 September, Ne Win's close associate, Saw Maung, staged a coup (considered by some to have been a fake), toppling Maung Maung and the BSPP government. The new government authority consisted of military officers headed by Saw Maung. He immediately changed Maung Maung's request for government servants to return to work to an order; established a curfew that forbade anyone being on the streets; and explained that during non-curfew hours, walking in procession, chanting slogans, gathering in groups of five or more people, opening a strike center, blocking a road, and interfering with soldiers carrying out their orders were now crimes.

The Army then began breaking up the strike centers and shooting students who resisted.[32]

THE ESTABLISHMENT OF THE SLORC

After seizing power, Saw Maung and his officers initially called themselves the Organization for Building Law and Order in the State. This body immediately declared an end to state institutions, including the State Council, the Council of Ministers, and all councils down to the ward and village levels. All deputy ministers were also suspended from their duties. Saw Maung also announced on 18 September that the coup was unavoidable lest the country fall deeper into anarchy. He explained that the Military Council would restore law and order and rebuild the administrative machinery of the state. It was the responsibility of corporations, cooperatives, and "private concerns" to restore communications in order to deliver goods to the people and to "alleviate the food, clothing and shelter needs of the people." After these tasks were accomplished, Saw Maung assured the country, the multi-party elections would be held and the Military Council would not interfere in any way with the Election Commission. On 20 September, the Military Council announced the new cabinet and the responsibilities they would assume on the following day, at which meeting Council members elected Saw Maung as Burma's new prime minister.[33]

By 26 September the junta had established itself as the State Law and Order Restoration Council (SLORC). Regional and local Law and Order Restoration Councils (LORCs) were also established at the divisional, township, ward, and village levels. The township councils would have a military officer as chairman, the deputy head of the state and divisional general department, the deputy commander of the state and divisional people's police force, and the chairman's choice of secretary. At the ward and village tract level, the LORCs would consist of three local elders, one of whom would be selected by a higher ranking LORC as chairman, and a local council clerk with no history of involvement in political organizations.[34]

After the coup, Saw Maung laid out the SLORC's four immediate tasks:
1. law and order and peace and tranquility
2. secure and smooth transport
3. easing the food, clothing and shelter needs of the people and
4. holding democratic multi-party general elections.[35]

The immediate goal of the junta was to reestablish law and order. On 5 October 1988, Burmese troops killed twelve looters, raising the official death toll to 440 since 18 September. On 19 October, the SLORC announced that while subdued politicking was permitted, it would take strict action against political parties that caused misunderstandings between the military and the people. Suppression associated with the coup led to between 8,000 and 10,000 deaths. The Council then called for the punishment of government workers guilty of corruption, bribes, embezzlement, and self-aggrandizement as these acts were incurring the loss of state funds and hindering the development of the economy.[36]

The SLORC explained that martial law was necessary because unlawful acts had been perpetrated by elements among the protestors and the political parties had done nothing to stop them and even abetted them in some cases. Some members of political parties, it claimed, were even giving training in small arms and the use of hand grenades. The press would be allowed freedom so long as they also took responsibility and acted according to the rules and regulations of publishers. The Army, it claimed, was not guilty of intimidation. Rather, it was those "under internal and external influence," including some political parties, who were making the threats. It also claimed that the release of political prisoners was a moot issue as there had been no political arrests, only the arrest of criminals. The Universal Declaration on Human Rights would only be observed if people were responsible and did not abuse these rights as they did in the demonstrations. The SLORC also complimented those who submitted articles to newspapers contributing to the four tasks of the SLORC and asked the people to take a nationalistic stance and support this kind of writing. Above all, the SLORC urged, "Please do not antagonize, attack and oppose the SLORC."[37]

Saw Maung also announced that the interim government would proceed with Ne Win's earlier proposal of a multi-party political system. The SLORC enacted the Political Parties Registration Law on 27 September 1988, requiring all parties that wished to run for election to register with the Election Commission. By the 28 February deadline, 233 parties had registered. Not all of the new parties were legitimate, for some appear to have been merely fronts for the military. Others were formed simply to take advantage of rationing allotted by the government to political parties, including petrol and four telephones per party. On 3 November 1988, the junta, claiming that certain people had complained that their names had been put forward as patrons or executive committee members of newly registered parties without their consent, required parties to submit, along with their registration, letters of consent from those named as leaders of the party being registered. Two weeks later, SLORC

Figure 8.1 Military propaganda poster

propaganda (see Fig. 8.1) claimed that the majority of the people were unhappy with the "activities of some small groups of people" who were holding demonstrations and engaging in disturbances. Worried that these acts would give their local areas a bad name, they wanted to cooperate with the government by reporting on these activities and those involved in them, and publishing this information on television, radio, and in the newspapers.[38]

THE ALL BURMA STUDENTS' DEMOCRATIC FRONT

After the Saw Maung coup, thousands of students fled to the border areas and to Thailand. Some fled for safety while thousands of others fled to ethnic rebel camps to prepare to launch armed resistance against the government. Bo Mya, the leader of the KNU, promised students who had gone underground military camps, weapons, and training. By late September, Burmese students at a KNU guerrilla camp were being trained in how to use mortars. The BCP's Tenasserim Military Command also gave students an eleven-day course in the use of small arms. These students expected to begin a guerrilla campaign against the Saw Maung regime within three to four months. The goal would be to establish a democratic government in Burma. They had obtained weapons and supplies in Burma's border areas. Some among Burmese communities abroad also offered support. The Burmese students also wanted to be as independent as possible from the ethnic rebels. By 9 October 1988, there were 2,000 students and protestors training in one KNU camp (Thay Baw Bo) alone. A month later, fifty delegates from the estimated 10,000 Burmese students who had fled Rangoon agreed on the creation of the All Burma Students' Democratic Front (ABSDF), an umbrella organization to supervise the student war on Rangoon.[39]

The SLORC announced an amnesty program for those students who returned to government-held areas by a deadline of 18 November. The Council claimed that while it could legitimately view the students in the border areas as insurgents, it still chose to view them as simply "misguided youths." Reception committees and twenty-seven camps in border towns under government control (such as Bhamo, Buthidaung, Kale, and Tavoy) were opened on 14 October to receive the returning students. The SLORC claimed that these camps would provide returning students with the basic necessities, such as medicine, shelter, and food, and then send them back home to their parents as quickly as possible. The government claimed students taking refuge with the rebels had been prevented from listening to anything but British Broadcasting Corporation (BBC) and Voice of America (VOA) broadcasts and so were unaware of either the amnesty offer or the "true stand of the Defence Forces." Thus, it began air-dropping pamphlets indicating the locations of the twenty-seven camps. By 24 October, 380 students had taken advantage of the amnesty. The deadline for the returning students was later extended to 31 January 1989 and even when this day approached, the SLORC explained that the twenty-seven "reception centers" would remain open anyway. By 3 February, the SLORC claimed that 2,401 students had returned.[40]

THE ELECTIONS

Brigadier Khin Nyunt gave a press conference on 20 January 1989, which elaborated on the terms of holding an election as formerly enunciated by Saw Maung and others. Khin Nyunt explained that the right to organize freely and issue press releases would gradually be extended to the political parties. However, the holding of elections would depend on cooperation among the government, the people, and the political parties. The date would not be set until the parties had finished organizing, when the people were ready to cooperate, and when the country "is peaceful and tranquil without disturbances." Khin Nyunt did not make clear what was meant by cooperation or how it would be determined whether the parties were finished organizing. However, the third condition, that of restoring internal peace, was the most worrying requirement. Khin Nyunt explained that the restoration of peace could not be viewed in the context of one area, but as a nationwide situation. This seems to have meant not only the end of looting and demonstrations, but also the end of the ethnic and Communist insurgencies, which previous regimes had failed to bring about since 1948. Khin Nyunt's statement, then, could be interpreted to mean indefinite military rule over the long term. As Khin Nyunt confirmed, the SLORC was trying also to change from one economic and political system to another to provide stability to the next government and this task could not be completed in a hurry.[41]

However, BBC and VOA broadcasts had been airing reports and statements from various political parties that claimed that no elections would really be held, or, if held, would take at least two or three years. In this context, the Election Law Drafting Committee produced an election timetable in February 1989, which scheduled general elections for May 1990, some fourteen months later. The SLORC announced this schedule along with strong denials of reporting by VOA and the BBC, suggesting that the two developments were strongly linked. The exact date of the elections, 27 May, however, was not decided until a meeting of the SLORC and the Election Commission held on 6 November 1989. The draft Election Law barred government servants, members of the military and police, monks, ethnic rebels, foreigners, and anyone funded by foreign organizations from voting, the last indicating again the SLORC's fear of external intervention in Burma's domestic affairs.[42]

The underlying problem was that the SLORC viewed civilian party politics as necessarily chaotic and contributory to national disunity. Khin Nyunt asserted on 20 January 1989 that the government was hesitant to lift the restrictions on political campaigning and remove the curfew because of infighting among the numerous political parties that had emerged since September. If the political parties were given too much freedom too quickly, they would only attack each other, creating additional security problems for the country and for the SLORC. In the meantime, the SLORC made several efforts to develop support among government servants and keep them from supporting the political opposition. In February, the government raised the pay of civil servants and asked teachers not to participate in politics or be influenced by political parties.[43]

THE MAJOR POLITICAL PARTIES

The government began to take steps to officially dissolve, but unofficially to reshape, the BSPP. The big sign that such a change was imminent came on 10 September when the government granted permission to military and civil service members to resign from the Party. Although the government would not officially announce the end of the BSPP Party until 11 October 1988, the date when it began to repossess BSPP property, cars, and funds, its membership flowed from the now defunct BSPP into a new entity, the National Unity Party (NUP), which had been established two weeks earlier on 25 September. The switch fooled few Burmese and the NUP commanded little loyalty from the demonstrators.[44]

On 29 August 1988, Nu had organized the League for Democracy and Peace (LDP) and, in early September, he called for supporters to set up local branches in provincial towns. The LDP, although eventually inconsequential, was the first formal political coalition to emerge from the protests and the first independent political organization in the country in two and a half decades.[45] The major problem for the LDP was Nu, as the old man found it difficult to build alliances with anyone but monks and the politicians from the pre-1962 period. The LDP thus failed to make inroads among the younger generations of voters. Likewise, few took seriously Nu's attempt to form an alternative government, especially when he became embroiled in a futile attempt to force Ne Win to confess to his "wrongs." After Nu was arrested, the LDP lost its center of gravity and posed no real challenge to anyone.

Aung Gyi, Tin U, and Aung San Suu Kyi initially formed the National United Front for Democracy in late September 1988 but soon after changed the name to the National League for Democracy (NLD). Aung San Suu Kyi, the party's General Secretary, headed a group of intellectuals, who were soon joined by writers and lawyers. Party Vice Chairman Tin U had at one point been defense minister and commander-in-chief of the armed forces, during the time of the U Thant funeral crisis in 1975, but resigned from both posts afterwards and was later imprisoned in connection with the 1976 coup plot. In September 1988, Nu had appointed him Defense Minister as part of his alternative government. League Chairman Aung Gyi headed a faction of anti-leftists, including former regional commanders. Among the League's first acts was to call for Burmese to ignore the government's order to return to work.[46]

Unity among the NLD triumvirate soon broke down into rivalry for control of the party. Aung Gyi was immediately identifiable with the protests due to his much-publicized criticism of the BSPP government earlier in 1988. He was also considered to be one of the most capable potential leaders because of his successful economic reforms during the Caretaker period. Aung Gyi, however, was not happy to permit extreme leftist influences to take control over the League and also publicly downplayed the importance of Aung San Suu Kyi in the Democracy movement. In early December, he was removed as League Chairman and replaced by Tin U. Aung Gyi and twelve others then resigned from the League and formed the Union National Democracy Party. However, Aung Gyi later changed tactics and for months claimed that he remained Chairman of the only real NLD and that the Tin U–Aung San Suu Kyi organization was illegal.[47]

The NLD faced the most serious intervention by the SLORC. In January 1989, League campaigners, including Aung San Suu Kyi, were harassed during their campaign tours. During a ten-day tour of the Irrawaddy Delta, a number of incidents occurred, including one case in which soldiers fired guns above spectators. In Bassein, local SLORC officials closed markets and government buildings, cut off electricity and water in the area of town hosting the League office, prevented Aung San Suu Kyi from hiring transport, and arrested fourteen League organizers, with sixty more arrests following in February. The most serious confrontation between Aung San Suu Kyi and the military occurred on 5 April at Danubyu, fifty miles from Rangoon. While she was campaigning in the town, a Burmese captain and a squad of soldiers approached and ordered her to leave the streets. The captain ordered his men to aim and shoot her at the count of three if she did not vacate the area. Instead she walked toward them, reportedly causing the soldiers to shake nervously. Before the captain counted three, a superior officer rushed out of a teashop and countermanded the order.

Aung San Suu Kyi observed that the incident demonstrated that the fact that the captain could give such an order on his own initiative highlighted the Army's inability to manage the country.[48]

Toward the end of June 1989, the SLORC became increasingly vocal regarding its views of the NLD's admitted transgression of martial law and the ban on public assembly. It claimed that Aung San Suu Kyi was deliberately instigating disturbances. Both Aung San Suu Kyi and Tin U were placed under house arrest on 20 July for allegedly attempting to create conditions dangerous for the state and for attempting to get the Burmese to dislike the Army. Upon her own arrest, Aung San Suu Kyi began a hunger strike, not called off until the government assured her that League members would not have to undergo "inhuman interrogation." By that time, between 2,000 and 6,000 League members had been arrested. The SLORC then began a press campaign to associate Aung San Suu Kyi and the League with BCP agents, on the one hand, and with foreign rightist elements, on the other. In either case, it was implied, she threatened the nation by inviting foreign intervention in Burmese affairs.[49]

TOWARD THE ELECTION

The SLORC began to tighten its control from 17 July 1989 by extending the powers of military commanders to try those committing offenses. For general offenses a military commander could choose to submit the case to a law court or to a military tribunal, but in the case of an offense against Council orders, the case could only be tried by a military tribunal. Regardless of existing laws, for such an offense the military tribunal would have to pass one of three sentences: death, life imprisonment, or three years' hard labour, with or without an additional fine. Military tribunals were now allowed to exercise summary trials, waive unnecessary witnesses, indict an offender without witnesses, and change members of the tribunal during the trial. The army commander-in-chief could revise sentences, including increasing them, as he saw fit. On the same day, Rangoon military command delegated its judicial and executive powers to divisional commanders and military region commanders, dividing Rangoon up into military zones. Orders were also given that the names of all guests and strangers in the forty-one townships of Rangoon Division had to be submitted to the local LORCs.[50]

Other steps were taken by the SLORC to bring the elections under tighter control. In August 1989, the SLORC began a six-month campaign to issue citizenship identity cards to every Burmese aged eighteen and over, in order to assist "the holding of the election." In November, it also began scrutinizing the citizenship of political candidates. The issue of citizenship was then used by the NUP as a means of attacking the eligibility of Aung Gyi, on the grounds that he was of partial Chinese ancestry (this was true, however, of former leader Ne Win and future prime minister Khin Nyunt as well), and Aung San Suu Kyi, on the grounds that she was married to a foreigner, to run for election.[51]

The SLORC also took steps to downplay the negative image produced by the large number of former high-ranking officers taking leading roles in the opposition civilian parties. Another concern was probably lingering loyalties within the military to these officers. In October 1989, the SLORC made it a crime for ousted military men to refer to their former military ranks or to their being retired from the military. The new law covered those officers who had been removed from the military or had been convicted of a criminal offense (as many had under earlier regimes) and imposed a prison sentence of up to five years. The overt purpose of the law was to prevent those who had been disgraced from enjoying the normal respect Burmese society paid to members of the armed forces. From March 1990, the SLORC slowly began to lift martial law in various townships, although it remained in many areas until one week before election day and was not lifted in twenty-six townships until 26 May. The SLORC now began disrupting NLD campaigners and detaining NLD officials.[52]

The NLD swept the 16 June elections with over 7.9 million votes, winning 392 of the 447 seats contested. These results must have come as a shock to the SLORC, which was widely believed to have expected a victory for the NUP. The latter immediately claimed that the election was fraudulent. This charge, however, was poorly thought out, and quickly abandoned, for since the SLORC was responsible for the fairness of the election, complaints about the proceedings amounted to a negative critique of their management of the country. Further, although from 15 May the SLORC had banned all foreigners from remaining in Burma to prevent foreign intervention in the electoral process, it partially reversed the decision ten days later and allowed foreign journalists to cover the electoral process. These journalists could easily have countered the NUP charges. The NUP did file an official complaint, but the state-controlled media did not carry the story. Instead, Saw Maung claimed that the results demonstrated the SLORC's fairness.[53]

CONCLUSION

The popular revolution that toppled the BSPP regime in 1988 caught the latter by surprise nearly as much as the 1990 elections results caught the SLORC. While the BSPP government knew that it had problems and Ne Win began to admit these even in 1987, the SLORC leadership exhibited surprising arrogance in allowing the election to go forward. Fourteen years (1974–1988) of success in controlling the country through nominal civilian government had created a political culture wherein civilian politicians reflected and did not direct the military agenda. In retrospect, the SLORC would have had a much easier time in controlling the country after 1990 had they not held an election at all. Ultimately, they produced a martyr whose international prominence has made her virtually untouchable by the military, other than by prolonged house arrest.

On the other hand, the SLORC realized that once it had waded successfully through a sea of political rivals, the NLD had a certain degree of domestic support. This domestic support, however, was associated with the same kinds of opposition that fueled the numerous rural insurgencies in the ongoing civil war. Mass demonstrations, street violence, and calls for the fall of the BSPP government all contributed to the image that the demonstrators, like the ethnic insurgents, represented a threat, the responsibility for suppressing them belonging to the Army. Aung San Suu Kyi's personal connections to the West, general calls for Western-style democratic government, and complaints by the BSPP leadership that the domestic turmoil was being manipulated by Western journalists all added to perceptions that as with the civil war in earlier decades, external intervention was partly – perhaps mostly – at work. The SLORC's solution, to promise preparations for a democratic transition and the eventual holding of elections, was thus paired with efforts to destroy the opposition before things went too far.

The failure of the democratic opposition to prevent the entrenchment of military control, particularly in late 1988, meant that it has lost its best and perhaps only real opportunity to establish a civilian government while confusion in the country still reigned and the government remained bewildered and unable to act. During the year and a half that followed, the military developed a political agenda to retain complete authority for itself and to close off the options for political leadership.

CHAPTER 9

Perpetual delay, 1990 to the present

One of the hallmarks of the military regime has been delay, a process it began in 1988, even before the elections. This seems to have been partly because the new military leaders were at a loss regarding what to do. They knew they did not want to hand over power to the NLD or to any other genuinely popular government. They also knew the ins and outs of keeping a country under martial law, what military regimes are particularly good at, over the course of short periods of time. Something permanent had to be found to provide a state apparatus that could nominally run the country in their name. Another factor was that they remained under the influence of the powerful Ne Win, who remained behind the scenes and for whom, it could be argued, they were nominally in charge. If the SLORC can be viewed as another Ne Win governing entity, then the politics of delay had historical antecedents. Ne Win was equally confused about what to do with the country when he seized control in 1962, other than to provide a more elaborate version of the caretaker regime, albeit with the promise of a more representative regime, as the later BSPP government would be portrayed.

What made the post-1988 delay longer, perhaps, was that Ne Win had run out of ideas. The Revolutionary Council was not a success economically or in putting down the civil war. The BSPP government, as 1988 demonstrated, was a resolute failure on all fronts. What is certain about the post-1988 regime was that it lacked even the rich ideological element that the earlier Ne Win regimes had been able to cultivate. Burma's new leaders were a less creative lot than Ne Win, Aung Gyi, or Tin Pe. Indeed, most "creations" of the post-1988 regime have been rehashed from the Revolutionary Council and BSPP periods.

Another aspect of the post-1988 regime that sets it apart from earlier military regimes is the unabashedly conspicuous carving up of the country's commercial assets by the ruling families. Ne Win and his friends had been keen on preserving the image of austerity in public and more than one erstwhile subordinate was broken down on charges of corruption. Although

Ne Win profited as much as anyone else, he paid lip service to socialism and attempts to improve the lives of the average Burmese. In the years after 1988, however, this changed. The families of the military elite and their friends openly flaunted their wealth, drove expensive cars, loaded themselves with jewels, and took over ownership of new companies that replaced formerly state-run enterprises. As socialism gave way to consumerism, the families of the military elite visibly became Burma's nouveau riche, while the rest of the population continued the long slide into abject poverty

CHANGING NAMES

While the country and the world were transfixed on the forthcoming elections, there were many indications that the military regime was intent on more than reestablishing law and order. One of the most obvious signs was the sudden makeover that the SLORC gave to the naming of the country, its towns, and its population. On 19 October 1988 (with retroactive effect from 18 September), the Council enacted the Law on the Substitution of Terms. This law changed "Socialist Republic of the Union of Burma" to "Union of Burma," "Council of State" to "State Law and Order Restoration Council," "Chairman of the Council of State" or "State President" to "Chairman of the State Law and Order Restoration Council," and a range of other official terms and titles.[1]

The SLORC was also determined to change the way Burmese and foreigners referred to Burmese ethnic groups, cities, and rivers when writing in English. The Council had already begun to use "Myanma" in its own English correspondence and announcements, when it began to refer to the country as the "Union of Myanma." On 26 May 1989, the Council made this official when it held a press conference explaining that the use of Burma in English apparently corresponded to "Bama" which could only refer to the main ethnic group, Burman. The SLORC argued that this usage was incorrect as the word Burma as used in Union of Burma, really referred to all national groups within the country, such as the Kachin, Karen, Mon, and so on. To correct this error, the Council would now require the use of "Union of Myanma" to refer to the country in English. It had even toyed with the idea of changing it again to "Myanma Naingngan" (State of Myanma). On 18 June, the SLORC promulgated the Adaptation of Expressions Law, which was to change English names used for Burmese people and places so that references would conform to Burmese pronunciation. This law officially changed the English term for "Union of Burma" to "Union of Myanma," "Burman" to "Bamar," and "Burmese"

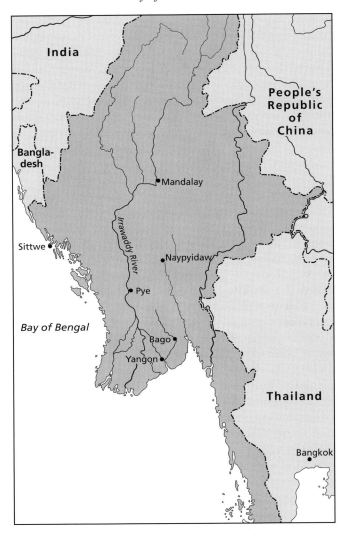

Map 3 Burma today

to "Myanma."[2] Eventually, the spelling of "Myanma" was also changed to "Myanmar."

The Adaptation of Expressions Law also provided for continued changes as the SLORC saw fit, including the change, when necessary, of English terms for "any state, division, townships zone, township, town, ward, village tract or village, or the name of any river, stream, forest, mountain or island." The SLORC also amended the national anthem, as the use of "Bamar" would now suggest that the anthem applied only to the Burmans, even though the anthem referred to all of Burma's "races." Hence, "Bamar" was now replaced with "Myanma."[3] This change was broadly expanded on the same day, when the SLORC issued Notification No 5/89 of the Government of the Union of Myanma Names in Accordance with Myanma Pronunciation, which indigenized place and ethnic names for use in the English language. What these efforts indicated was that the SLORC had a particular view of how the future of the country should be shaped. As events would soon demonstrate, this view was hostile to both foreign interference and democracy, which in the Council's eyes became inextricably linked.

DE-DEMOCRATIZATION

After the NLD victory in the 1990 elections, the Army did not lose composure and Saw Maung ordered it to respect the wishes of the voters. Instead, the SLORC reversed its announcements on the state of the country to legitimize continued military rule over the long term in order to prevent the League from taking power. On 29 April, when the SLORC was assumed to be confident of a victory for the NUP and themselves, Khin Nyunt, in his capacity as Secretary Number 1 of the SLORC, told township and ward-level LORCs in a broadcast speech that the Army had by this time achieved three of its four main tasks. The final task was holding the multi-party democratic elections the following month. At the end of May, however, as the early election results indicated a sweeping NLD victory, Saw Maung changed the SLORC's view of the election in the context of the continuity of its control of the state. The election had been, as SLORC claimed all along, only one task it had to complete before handing over power to a new government. Now, by contrast to what Khin Nyunt had said a month earlier, the tasks of restoring "law and order and regional peace and tranquility . . . facilitating transport" and communications, and meeting people's needs for food, clothes and shelter, all remained to be completed. Regardless of whom government servants had voted for, they were not to bring party politics into the workplace. The fact that Khin Nyunt gave essentially the same speech on 15 June indicated that Saw Maung's comments reflected an official posture regarding the elections and the longevity of the SLORC.[4] A new government would not be established for a considerable period of time.

Saw Maung began to work on de-democratizing the country from the end of June. In a hint at what was to come, Saw Maung warned that the SLORC would not tolerate a repeat of the pro-Democracy demonstrations in 1988 and mentioned the possibility of an "indefinite ban on public political gatherings." As the SLORC made clear that it would not respect its original promises regarding the due recognition of the results of the multi-party elections, popular anger was aroused. Among the most important incidents was the confrontation between army troops and monks at Mandalay on 8 August 1990. A group of 500 monks began moving through the town with their alms bowls, and over time were joined by other monks, students, and others. At one juncture, they began to shout slogans and were asked by soldiers to stop. In the commotion that followed, the Army claimed that the monks and students began to stone the soldiers and attempt to take their weapons from them. Although several were injured, no one was killed, and after the soldiers fired their guns into the air, the crowds dispersed. Other sources, however, indicated that the monks had numbered 5,000 and that the soldiers had fired into the crowd, killing at least four people. The government later blamed the NLD for the disturbances, citing a League directive calling for ceremonies on 8 August to mark the 1988 demonstrations, claiming that the League was attempting to "destroy the country."[5]

Saw Maung had also explained in late June 1990 that before the SLORC handed over power, the 1947 Constitution, which he argued was seriously flawed, would have to be rewritten. Khin Nyunt reaffirmed this two weeks later, when he explained that both the 1947 and the 1974 constitutions were unsuitable because of "changing times and conditions" and that a new constitution would have to be written from scratch. The purpose of the call for a new constitution was to delay or prevent a handover of power to the NLD. In late July, the SLORC announced that the NLD would not be handed state powers until after the SLORC, since it alone "has the right to legislative power," had overseen the drafting of a new constitution by the elected assembly, and its approval by the Burmese (which nearly twenty years later, it nominally did). Although the elected assembly would conduct the drafting, they would have to do so according to guidelines established by the army-appointed special convention.[6]

Another issue was the role of Aung San Suu Kyi. The NLD had insisted that Aung San Suu Kyi should play a leading role in negotiations with the SLORC concerning the Constitution, despite her house arrest. In July 1990, Khin Nyunt argued that he was concerned that this amounted to a personality cult and that this was not the time to insist on a particular individual being allowed to participate in the constitutional process. As he asked of the NLD rhetorically: "Which is more important: obtaining power and the release of Daw Aung San Suu Kyi, or the long-term interests of the country and the people?" Instead, Khin Nyunt demanded, the

Figure 9.1 Burmese democratic protest. Demonstrators hold posters of Aung San Suu Kyi

victorious parties should be striving for unity "in the spirit of patriotism and in the interests of the country" without "attachment to personalities." The SLORC then began to increase its association between Aung San Suu Kyi (see Fig. 9.1) and "foreign elements," in delaying its own pace of constitutional drafting.[7]

The regime created the Convening Commission for the National Convention on 2 October 1992. After establishing the Commission but before the National Convention could take place, the SLORC began to eradicate prospective NLD participation in the constitutional process. It would be difficult to produce a constitution amenable to the SLORC if the overwhelming majority of elected MPs were represented by the NLD. Thus, the SLORC, working through the Election Commission and citing violations of that body's rules and regulations, began nullifying the election of individual NLD MPs. The abolishment of other parties also ensued.[8]

While the National Convention was briefly opened in January 1993 with over 700 delegates, only an initial speech was made before the Convention was adjourned for another month.[9] In the meantime, having significantly weakened the NLD, the SLORC began a campaign that specifically targeted Aung San Suu Kyi. The SLORC asserted that the Nobel Peace Prize Committee had given the award to a "follower they [the West] had raised" and that it would "never accept the leadership of a person under foreign influence who will dance to the tune of a foreign power and who has always opposed the Defence Forces." Aung San Suu Kyi, the SLORC suggested, represented not Burmese, but foreign imperialist powers who "continue their habit of brutally bullying the weak and interfering shamelessly in the internal affairs of other countries." A patriotic Burmese, it argued, should not "be wasting one's time on the narrow personality cult and interests of an organization [the NLD]."[10] Khin Nyunt was even blunter. He argued that the original elections commission had erred when it gave Aung San Suu Kyi hope that she could stand for election, because this was against the law. He then quoted a fifteenth-century Burmese treatise that purportedly instructed readers "There is destruction when the leader is a female." Following this treatise, he argued, it was clear that "a female should never be a leader in Myanmar [if so] the country will be in ruin."[11]

FROM SAW MAUNG TO THAN SHWE

Saw Maung's fortunes began to wane by early 1992. The regime's image as a reforming council had not been secured either at home or abroad. In its early days, Saw Maung had stressed that the small number of the members of the SLORC and the multiple portfolios each held demonstrated that this was not a government meant to last in the long term. However, the expansion of the SLORC by three additional generals and four civilians in late January indicated to many that the SLORC would now remain more or less a permanent government. Saw Maung also began a purge of the government when the SLORC fired 15,000 civil servants. This was the final stage of asserting government control over dissident elements, as students, politicians, and monks had already been dealt with. Simultaneously, Aung San Suu Kyi was also becoming a permanent symbol of popular opposition to the government. To domestic support was added international recognition of her struggle in the form of the Sakharov Prize for Human Rights, awarded to her by the European Union, and, in December 1991, the Nobel Peace Prize. The latter was accepted in her name because the SLORC would refuse her readmission to the country if she left.[12]

Over the course of December 1991 to January 1992, there were signs that Saw Maung was having a nervous breakdown. In addition to the continual stress of running the country since 1988, balancing out competing cliques within the SLORC, and an inability to deal effectively with the continued defiance of the NLD, Saw Maung, a heavy drinker, was also suffering from diabetes. In mid-December, he was hospitalized for two days after he collapsed and was unconscious for a forty-minute period. In a golf tournament attended by other top generals, he reportedly burst out screaming "I am King Kyansittha!" and telling those around them to be careful lest he kill them with his pistol. In January, in a speech broadcast on Burmese television, Saw Maung continued referring to King Kyansittha, assured viewers that he did not practice Black Magic, and asserted that martial law in Burma meant "no law at all."[13]

Two of Saw Maung's most powerful subordinates, Than Shwe and Khin Nyunt, competed to succeed him. Khin Nyunt, head of the intelligence services, was a protégé of Ne Win. Than Shwe, a conservative general, disliked the brash Khin Nyunt and the younger officers who backed him. In March 1992, Than Shwe assumed Saw Maung's positions as defense chief and head of the Army and, in late April, he also replaced Saw Maung as Chairman of the SLORC and assumed the prime ministership. By the end of the year, maneuvering by Khin Nyunt led to four regional commanders, with whom he had difficulties, being "kicked upstairs," that is, reappointed to powerless positions in Rangoon, and replaced by officers connected with himself.[14] This balance of power would carry on beyond the tenure of the SLORC.

As head of the junta, Than Shwe began a number of new initiatives designed to shore up internal security. After exhaustive attempts to capture Karen headquarters, the regime declared a ceasefire. The effectiveness of the military's leadership was also improved through internal reorganization and a restructuring of the state. Several regional military commanders were integrated into the central administration, to keep them closely connected to the SLORC. The cabinet increased in size and specialization as ministries were split (Forestry was divorced from Agriculture and Trade from Planning and Finance).[15]

Teachers, whom the SLORC held responsible for the behavior of their students, were also brought under tighter control. The SLORC's view was that student unrest was the result of teachers having been weak in the guidance and organization of their students. Teachers were also unable to keep politicians, opportunists, and foreign elements from using campuses as base areas for unrest and had failed to cooperate with the government to prevent these "subversive" activities. Hence, teachers now needed to be reeducated to "uphold and implement" the perpetuation of national sovereignty, preservation of national unity, and prevention of national disintegration. The Central Institute of Public Services, a reeducation camp offering "refresher courses," was thus set up for thousands of teachers who now underwent a four-week course of physical exercise and lectures. The camp followed the model of the rural reeducation camps for the Red Guards in the PRC during the Cultural Revolution. Teachers would attend courses on the history of the armed forces and on the national liberation struggle, the emergence of the SLORC, its economic endeavors, and its laws and decrees, so that they would be able to "enlighten their students." Reeducation, and with it the creation of "genuine" students and "responsible" teachers, was to be completed before colleges and universities would reopen. The SLORC also hoped to lessen the potential for student demonstrations by initiating a distance education program.[16]

In an attempt to improve its international standing the SLORC tried on several occasions to soften its approach to the NLD. In April 1992, the regime announced that it would hold a national convention to establish the principles for a new constitution. With this effort in mind, in June and July they met with representatives of the NLD and other opposition parties as well as members of the pro-regime NUP. In September the SLORC lifted the curfew and martial law and released about a quarter of its political prisoners, some 534 people, including Nu and many NLD members. While Aung San Suu Kyi remained under house arrest, the SLORC now allowed her family to visit her. The SLORC also rejoined the Non-Aligned Movement in September, signed four articles of the Geneva Convention (1949) regarding the treatment of civilians and, in December, hosted a meeting of the Colombo Plan in Rangoon.[17]

THE STATE PEACE AND DEVELOPMENT COUNCIL

In November 1997, the SLORC was dissolved and replaced by the State Peace and Development Council (SPDC). Lack of transparency in the inner workings of the government since 1988 has made it difficult for foreign (and domestic) observers to determine the precise reasons for changes within the ruling Council. As a result, analysts necessarily rely on circumstantial evidence to identify the possible factors involved. Generally, these factors are both external and internal. Government changes often occur when there is a pressing need to shore up the government's image abroad. The SPDC, for example, had been set up to replace the SLORC at a time when the regime needed more respectability as it prepared for ASEAN membership in 1997. In this and other turnovers, charges of corruption are usually made to give the move legitimacy, although, given the widespread nature of official corruption, such claims are frequently dubious as main factors in dismissals.

Most foreign observers of Burma view the replacement of the SLORC with the SPDC as merely a cosmetic change. Scholars have followed suit, referring to the SLORC and the SPDC not separately, but as the same government, hence "SLORC/SPDC." While it is true that leadership remained the same, there are fundamental differences that mark the SLORC and the SPDC not as separate governments, but as distinguishable phases of military rule since 1988. The SLORC phase was characterized in part by the absence of Western sanctions, warfare with numerous ethnic insurgencies, problematic relationships with at least some of its Southeast Asian neighbors (especially Thailand), and a continuity of influence from the leaders of the Ne Win period. By contrast, the SPDC period has generally been characterized by severe Western sanctions, ceasefire agreements with most ethnic insurgents, membership in ASEAN, and the elimination of the Ne Win "old guard." The "spirit" of the government had also changed, for during the SLORC period, Burma's leadership were clearly desperate to find ways to deny the establishment of an NLD government, but during the SPDC period the government moved at a more leisurely pace with clear confidence that whatever would be done concerning the NLD, they need not be in any great hurry.

One scholar suggests that the change from the SLORC to the SPDC was partly effected to reduce tensions between the ruling junta and regional military commanders, who had accrued significant wealth and power in outlying commands or in ministerial positions in Rangoon. The SPDC removed some ministers from their posts, replaced them with regional commanders drawn from outside the capital, and in their place appointed junior commanders. Indeed, the chief internal factors in government purges are widely held to be personal political ambitions, disagreements over policy (whether to take seriously dialogue with the NLD), or business rivalries, as the ruling generals have amassed significant commercial portfolios. For any or all of these reasons, government change within the SPDC leadership has consistently favored a concentration of power in the hands of a slimming minority at the top, as purges afforded the most powerful men in the Council the opportunity to replace rivals with less powerful clients. The top four generals, Than Shwe, Maung Aye, Khin Nyunt, and Tin Oo, were reduced to three when Tin Oo was killed in a helicopter crash in 2000 and was not replaced. In 2001, in the biggest purge since 1997, seven generals and ministers were replaced, two on charges of corruption and five on the basis of enforced retirement.[18]

On 7 March 2002, the 92-year-old Ne Win's son-in-law and three grandsons were arrested in a restaurant in Rangoon's Chinatown, while Ne Win and his daughter were placed under house arrest. They were charged with plotting the overthrow of the government. Reportedly, the coup-plotters had planned to enlist support from elements of the Army, kidnap Than Shwe, Maung Aye, and Khin Nyunt, and, having brought them to Ne Win's house, force them to agree to a new government. In the wake of the arrests, four generals were dismissed. Other arrests followed, including Ne Win's personal astrologer. Two separate trials were held for the ringmasters and members of the military connected with the coup plot. In mid-September, eighty-three officers and soldiers were sentenced to fifteen years in prison and by the end of the month Ne Win's son-in-law and three grandsons were sentenced to death. Although they appealed the ruling, the Supreme Court upheld the convictions in late December 2002, Ne Win having died earlier in the month.[19] The Ne Win family lost yet another appeal in August 2003.

The arrests and dismissals may have been used as a means of pleasing ASEAN by removing corrupt senior officers, as those dismissed were initially intimately connected with the Ne Win family's business activities. The ruling triumvirate may also have used the opportunity to continue the replacement of more powerful commanders with younger, more reliable officers. In September 2002, the SPDC announced a flurry of promotions, including Maung Aye who became deputy senior general and Khin Nyunt who became general, and numerous other officers who were promoted to the rank of lieutenant-general.[20]

As potential challenges from within the military declined, rivalry between Khin Nyunt and Maung Aye intensified. This rivalry had serious ramifications for the country as each had come to represent different approaches to dealing with the NLD and the outside world. While the conservative Maung Aye took a hard line, the more flexible Khin Nyunt favored a more pragmatic approach, including international engagement and the paying of at least lip service to the inevitability of a return to democracy. In August 2003, in response to the new US sanctions, another changeover at the top, including the retirement of five ministers and two deputy ministers, appeared to indicate that Khin Nyunt and his approach had gained the upper hand. Than Shwe, who continued as head of state, transferred the office of prime minister to Khin Nyunt, Lieutenant-General Soe Win taking Khin Nyunt's place as SPDC Secretary Number 1. Shortly after, at the end of August, Prime Minister Khin Nyunt announced a seven-point plan. According to this plan, his "roadmap to Democracy," the SPDC would reconvene the National Convention (suspended since 1996), write a new constitution, and hold free elections.[21]

THE FALL OF KHIN NYUNT

The most serious purge since 1988 brought down Khin Nyunt in October 2004. Although clearly the result of Khin Nyunt's long political rivalry with Maung Aye, the purge was characterized as a move by the SPDC to eradicate corruption. As it announced at the time of his dismissal, Khin Nyunt had been allowed to retire "for his violation of Tatmadaw discipline, such as insubordination, for his involvement in the bribery and corrupt practices, and for failure to carry out the duties properly." Khin Nyunt was accused of illegally smuggling 30,000 luxury vehicles from Thailand and China into Burma, circumventing registration laws and thus import duties, which would otherwise have amounted to 400 percent of the price of the vehicle. Such corruption, the government charged, threatened army unity.[22]

Due to Khin Nyunt's extensive connexions and his control of the Military Intelligence Service (MIS), eradicating his base of support meant a massive overhaul of security forces. The purge began with a raid on the MIS Headquarters on 18 October, and the arrest of Khin Nyunt and his two sons the following day. Over the course of the following week, MIS units around the country were dissolved. In November, all of the agents of the SPDC's computer department were fired, relatives of MIS agents were removed from the civil service, the ambassadors to Singapore and Indonesia were dismissed, and Brigadier-Generals Thein Swe and Than Tun were given twenty-two-year prison sentences. Soe Win, who had been head of the Union Solidarity and Development Association (USDA), took Khin Nyunt's place as Prime Minister. Lieutenant-General Than Sein, Chairman of the Convention Convening Committee, then took Soe Win's place as Secretary Number 1.[23]

The SPDC moved quickly to offset criticism that these moves represented anything more than an anti-corruption campaign. It attempted to do so by declaring that no change had taken place in SPDC policies. Thein Sein declared that the roadmap to democracy would continue as it had under Khin Nyunt. In November 2004, the SPDC demonstrated that it was serious about reform by releasing nearly 4,000 prisoners it claimed had been wrongfully imprisoned as a result of Khin Nyunt's intelligence services. The purge continued into the middle of 2005, as individual trials and confessions yielded more information on the extent of corruption and Khin Nyunt's connexions. Beginning in January, hundreds of new arrests were made among border officials, while the Mayor of Mandalay and four ambassadors were all sacked. Khin Nyunt was not put on trial until 12 June and, the following day, was delivered a suspended sentence of forty-four years, his two sons also receiving suspended sentences.[24]

FOREIGN INVESTMENT AND THE BOYCOTTS

From the beginning, the SLORC badly needed foreign aid and investment to help pay off its external debt, which amounted to US$4–5 billion by 1990. The biggest foreign aid donor was Japan, which, in 1987, had furnished over half of Burma's foreign aid, equal to roughly 10 percent of its GNP. A major factor that had helped to push the SLORC in 1988 and early 1989 to keep its commitments on eventually holding elections was the suspension of aid after the Saw Maung coup by West Germany, the US, and Japan. These countries pinned the resumption of aid on the restoration of democracy and respect for human rights. Britain also froze aid to Burma in early November 1988.[25]

With the abrogation of the socialist economic system in October 1988, however, the SLORC now also had access to foreign investment. Among the SLORC's early acts was the liberalizing of trade, domestic and foreign, declaring that Burma would now have a market-oriented economy. The following day, Colonel Abel, the Minister of Trade, announced that laws were being planned that would open up to the private sector trade in

Figure 9.2 A symbol of the "new" Rangoon, the refurbished Strand Hotel

most commodities, with the exception of teak, petroleum, natural gas, and gems. To entice foreign investors, the SLORC would provide tax relief and exemptions and agreements with foreign companies would include guarantees that for the duration of the contract, the company would not be nationalized. At the end of November, the SLORC promulgated the Union of Burma Foreign Investment Law that established the Union of Burma Foreign Investment Commission with the authority to approve investment proposals that promoted the interests of the state, determine the financial credibility of an investor, the "economic justification of the business enterprise, and appropriateness of technology," issue foreign investment permits, and grant tax exemptions or relief. The law also set up basic regulations covering insurance, foreign currency and *kyat* bank accounts, guarantees against nationalization, and related matters. The justification of the law was that it would help the SLORC meet one of its avowed goals of "easing the people's needs for food, clothing, and shelter." It claimed the new foreign investment would provide employment opportunities and technical training and help develop and expand Burma's weak economic infrastructure.[26]

From early 1989, a figurative gold rush began when foreign companies raced for access to the new Burmese economy (see Fig. 9.2). Japan was the first, after it recognized the SLORC government in February. Others quickly followed. A cheap labor supply and cooperative government made Burma a profitable place for Western, South Korean, and Taiwanese clothing companies to make inexpensive clothing that could be sold abroad under designer labels. US soft drink makers found a new untapped market for their products, while Thai companies made logging and fishery deals.[27] Oil was another big area for investment.

Foreign investment handed the SLORC an economic lifeline while it eradicated the democratic opposition. But Burmese campaigners for democracy were not idle. Among the most vocal was the NLD leader Aung San Suu Kyi. In April 1989, Aung San Suu Kyi admonished foreign businessmen for doing business in Burma when the situation was so grave for the Burmese people and, in June 1989, called on foreign countries to boycott trade and aid with Burma until the government stopped reneging on its promises regarding the elections. While foreign governments underwent cycles of economic sanctions regarding aid to the SLORC, they were initially hesitant to restrict private investment in the country. A boycott of the products of Western companies doing business in Burma, however, eventually gained momentum in the mid-1990s and began to show clear signs of success. One major international company after another pulled out. In 1995, three foreign apparel manufacturers succumbed to the boycott campaign and agreed not to contract the manufacture of clothing in Burma any longer. In 1996, a soft drink company and two foreign brewing firms announced they were pulling out. Having successfully dented Western beverages sales and apparel manufacturing in Burma, activists next directed boycotts at the big oil companies. The intended impact of the boycotts, however, was offset by the willingness of companies within the Association of South East Asian Nations (ASEAN) to step in to buy the equity of fleeing Western companies.[28] Ultimately, the boycotts only changed the face of investment and reduced potential Western leverage in the country.

ASEAN, while paying lip service to a policy of constructive engagement, generally followed a hands-off approach to problems in Burma for fear that it would force the SLORC to be even more resistant to change. In July 1991, ASEAN foreign ministers even rejected urgings from the West to cooperate on pressuring Burma to undertake democratic and human rights reforms. Two main issues, treatment of the Rohingyas (Muslim Arakanese) in Arakan State and Burmese border incursions into Thailand, however, have plagued relations. In 1989, the SLORC began settling Burmese Buddhists in new towns it was building in the Rohingya-dominated areas of northern Arakan, while simultaneously doubling the number of Burmese troops in the area to over 20,000. In some areas, the new settlers displaced the Rohingyas and took over their lands and homes. Burma's relations with Bangladesh eroded further from December 1991, when the Army drove 145,000 Muslims out of Arakan in western Burma. In pursuit of fleeing Rohingyas, the Burmese Army also attacked Bangladeshi border posts. Under the old BSPP citizenship laws, the SLORC asserted that the Rohingyas were foreigners who did not have the right to live in Burma nor to own land or the property they held. Refugees complained that the Burmese had taken their identity papers and property and killed or raped resisters.[29]

For several years after 1989, the Thais were willing to overlook incursions by the Burmese army across the Thai border because of the substantial concessions given the Thais over teak reserves in Karen-held areas. This ended in March 1992 with a major Burmese incursion intended to end with an attack on Manerplaw from the rear. Thai aircraft now fired rockets, while Thai artillery bombarded the Burmese, and drove them back across the border.[30]

As the SLORC's actions regarding the Rohingyas and the KNU were potentially destabilizing factors in the region, ASEAN slowly began to change its approach. Malaysia officially protested the SLORC's treatment of Rohingyas on 10 March 1992. Singapore and Indonesia then called on Burma to resolve the situation peacefully. Malaysia then called for the Association to develop a unified front to persuade Burma against these activities using diplomacy. However, it announced that sanctions were not yet necessary at this stage.[31]

Burma's inclusion in ASEAN was partly responsible for the changeover from the SLORC to the SPDC. By January 1997, consensus had grown among ASEAN members that Burma (along with Laos and Cambodia) should be allowed into the Association later in that year. Although efforts by the US and the European Union to prevent Burma's inclusion were thwarted, the West found other ways to isolate the SPDC. In March, the European Union suspended preferential trade benefits to Burma. The Clinton administration, under pressure from anti-government groups, also declared in April that it would impose a formal ban on new US investment in the country on the grounds that the regime's human rights violations had increased. These were the first sanctions imposed by the US, which by then was Burma's fourth most important investor, since 1988. According to the 20 May presidential order, the government suppression in Burma represented a national emergency for the US, on the grounds that the

"Government of Burma has committed large-scale repression of the democratic opposition in Burma . . . and further . . . the actions and policies of the Government of Burma constitute an unusual and extraordinary threat to the national security and foreign policy of the United States."[32]

Following the renewed house arrest of Aung San Suu Kyi in May 2003, President George W. Bush signed into law the Freedom and Democracy Act, which imposed new sanctions on Burma, including a ban on important exports to the US, a ban on visas to SPDC officials, and the freezing of Burmese assets in US banks. Some analysts criticized these sanctions since Burmese exports to the US were dominated by textiles, and the sanctions would thus mainly hurt textile workers and not the SPDC. Over one hundred small factories closed as a result of the new sanctions, putting between 40,000 and 80,000 textile workers and others in the industry out of work. Since the textile industry mainly employed young women whose families had become dependent on their regular income, many of these women were forced into Rangoon's thriving sex and entertainment industry. In August 2006, Bush signed an extension of the Freedom and Democracy Act, citing the continued failure of the regime to engage in meaningful democratic reform and its continued detention of Aung San Suu Kyi.[33]

The results of Western sanctions imposed on the SPDC in order to provoke dialogue with the NLD and meaningful political change have been controversial. Whatever their short-term impact, the government was able to adjust to isolation from the West by turning to the East. This was possible because of its admission to ASEAN, which has historically frowned upon foreign intervention in the region and generally refuses to take a stand on domestic issues in member states; the cooperation of the People's Republic of China, which has been unsympathetic to Western challenges of its own human rights record; and the efforts of Russia and India to build links with Burma in the context of their individual geopolitical strategies.

Under the SPDC, Burma has been able to develop strong links with its two most powerful neighbors, India and China. In the PRC's case, this cooperation has been on the basis of resolving border problems and suppressing the production of drugs in Burma that would largely be destined for the PRC, and in the case of India, in fighting ethnic insurgents fighting New Delhi. International rivalry has also played a role as India sought to offset increasing Chinese influence in the country. India's relationship with Burma improved from about 2000. India represents an alternative source of military training and supply, Burma purchasing its ammunition and tanks. India also engaged with Burma in the construction of a joint high-way connecting India with Mandalay and a second highway connexion between Mandalay and the Thai border.[34]

The PRC established the strongest economic and military linkages with Burma from 1988, supplying most of its military hardware, including jet fighters and tanks. The People's Liberation Army began to provide special-ist training for Burma's army and air force, which soon became so depen-dent upon China for military supply that by the SPDC years Burma's military leadership began to look for other potential sources of supply. The PRC also granted to Burma low-interest loans and technical advi-sors to help build new airports, roads, and a deep-sea port at Mergui. In exchange for its support, the PRC has likely been given a free hand in intelligence gathering regarding the Indian Ocean, but the chief gains for China have been economic. By 2001, the PRC was Burma's third most important trading partner, while access to Burma's Indian Ocean ports now gives the PRC better access to markets in South Asia and the Middle East. More recently, in 2006, the SPDC has turned to the PRC for help in reforming its failing banking system, in recognition of the fact that the PRC has had ten years' experience in successful banking reform.[35]

Russia's relationship with Burma, which had been very strong before the collapse of the Soviet Union, grew stronger after 2000. This began with the government's purchase of Russian MIG fighters, to the great displeasure of the PRC. In February 2001, the Russian Atomic Energy Ministry announced that it would make a proposal to build a nuclear reactor in Burma for research purposes. The SPDC accepted the plan and dispatched over 200 technicians for nuclear training in Russia. There were also unconfirmed reports that the SPDC had given sanctuary in the coun-try to two Pakistani nuclear scientists. The avowed purpose of the reactor was initially to produce isotopes for medical research, but the scope of the nuclear program grew to include the provision of nuclear power, cru-cial for a country suffering under a severe energy crisis. An International Atomic Energy Commission inspection team sent to the country in late 2001, however, concluded that Burma's safety measures were not up to international standards and opposition to the program was voiced not only by the US, but by the PRC as well. A formal agreement was signed in May 2002, in which the scope of the program was expanded to include, in addition to a low-powered reactor, the construction of a nuclear study center, a nuclear waste site, and two nuclear laboratories. Fuel would be supplied by Russia.[36]

THE CEASEFIRES

Unlike earlier Ne Win-led regimes, the SLORC now faced a non-violent, internationally backed Democracy movement that threatened its survival from within. This was a more dangerous and immediate threat than the widespread, but divided, insurgencies it faced along its borders.

In order to shore up its strength, the SLORC sought to end the insurgencies. The BCP collapse in 1989 presented new political possibilities in the border areas. Various armed units in the BCP had mutinied against the Party leadership and transformed themselves into ethnic armies. The most important of these armies and one that soon outgrew in strength the forces of the KNU was the United Wa State Army. Like many of the other ex-BCP insurgent groups, it entered the 1990s with increasing interest in participating in the new business opportunities available in the border area and proved more than willing to consider cooling down the civil war. The Burmese government thus began a determined campaign between 1989 and 1990 to create ceasefire arrangements that permitted the insurgents to keep their weapons, and to control (and exploit economically) areas under their sway, political questions being laid aside until a new constitution had been written. Other ethnic groups were also offered ceasefires on the same terms, but these offers were coupled with military attacks in order to pressure these groups into acceptance. A new counter-insurgency strategy was invoked to isolate ethnic insurgents from their base of support, by forcibly relocating ethnic minority civilians to new camps located near Burmese Army camps. The KIO was the first non-BCP group to agree to a ceasefire in 1993, while most others agreed to ceasefires by 1995.[37]

Although the KNU refused to sign a ceasefire, it was removed as a major threat to the regime by other developments. A group of Buddhist Karen soldiers mutinied against the KNU's Christian leadership and formed the Democratic Karen Buddhist Army (DKBA) in December 1994. Although DKBA numbers were small, this proved to be a devastating blow to the KNU. The DKBA allied itself with the Burmese Army and provided it with intelligence on KNU defenses and the government, seeing an opportunity in the division among the Karens, moved quickly to exploit it. Unable to resist a government offensive of 15,000 men, the KNU torched Manerplaw as they withdrew on 26 January 1995, two days before the Burmese Army overran the Karen capital. Also ousted were the NDF and the Democratic Alliance of Burma that had been based there as well.[38]

The MTA situation was more complicated because of the chameleon-like nature of Khun Sa. After the fall of Manerplaw in January 1995, one of the few significant areas of Burma not in government hands (aside from territory under the control of the United Wa State Army and several Kokang rebel splinter groups) was controlled by Khun Sa's MTA, which consisted of GMD holdovers from the 1950s and local Shan recruits and now numbered some 15,000 well-armed troops. As Khun Sa was wanted in the US on charges relating to heroin trafficking, in 1994, the SLORC tried to use him as a bargaining chip. It offered to crush Khun Sa, who supplied most of the heroin sold in the US, if the US would lift its embargo on arms sales to Burma. The deal was not accepted. For the first time, Khun Sa launched a major offensive against Burma, attacking Tachilek. The MTA's position was made untenable, however, by both counter-attacks by the Burmese Army and by an anti-trafficking campaign by the Thai government, with the support of the US Drug Enforcement Agency which destroyed his supply network in March 1995. As with the KNU, the SLORC also encouraged an ethnic rift within the MTA. Unhappy with reported anti-Shan discrimination within the MTA, for example, one commander defected and raised a new, anti-MTA force. As his position became more vulnerable, Khun Sa even toyed with the idea of relinquishing his place as head of the MTA and having his realm turned into a drug-free zone under UN control. Ceasefire arrangements made by the SLORC with his narcotics rivals who could now operate openly within the country made a similar arrangement with the SLORC look very attractive. In January 1996, Khun Sa allowed his headquarters to be "taken" after he made a deal with the SLORC. He then took up residence in an exclusive Rangoon residential area.[39]

The turning tide of the civil war and the ceasefire arrangements of the mid-1990s, as well as the mobilization of certain groups such as the Buddhist Karens as pro-regime forces (in the Karen case as the Democratic Karen Buddhist Army) altered the SLORC/SPDC's approach to the ethnic insurgents. A new strategy re-divided Burma's twelve or more ethnic groups into 135 races, smaller groups that could be played off against each other more successfully. Further, by allowing significant local autonomy in exchange for the ceasefire agreements, the SLORC/SPDC had surrendered more government control over Burmese territory than any previous government since independence.[40]

Nevertheless, after the 2004 purge of Khin Nyunt and his supporters, Than Shwe and Maung Aye have taken Burma in a different direction from the more moderate engagement of the insurgents encouraged by Khin Nyunt. Ethnic minority insurgents were told that under ceasefire agreements they could keep their arms until a new constitution was in place.

After Khin Nyunt, the SPDC demanded that demobilization take place before the constitutional process reached fruition and some insurgents are considering recommencing their armed conflict with the Burmese state. The Army has also intensified its attacks on the KNU, which never signed a ceasefire agreement despite talks in 2004, and the Karenni, who broke theirs.[41] It remains to be seen how the latest twist in the ever-changing military approach to the ethnic minorities will be reflected in future national politics.

CONTROLLING THE POPULATION

The military regime eventually realized, as Ne Win had in the 1960s, that it could not control the country indefinitely by manufacturing consent. Added to this realization was the equally important challenge presented by international boycotts. As Burma's domestic situation intersected with international boycotts, the government sought a means of transferring power to a nominally civilian government, while simultaneously rejecting the 1990 election results. The solution found echoes in the spirit of the creation of the BSPP government in 1974 and the constitutional and organizational efforts that preceded it since the 1960s. This has been the creation and expansion of the now gargantuan USDA.

The USDA was originally established by the SLORC in 1993. Although it is always used for the domestic political purposes of the regime, it remains officially a non-governmental social organization. The reason for this seeming anomaly is that the SLORC prohibition on members of the armed forces and civil bureaucrats becoming members of political parties would have otherwise prevented the latter from joining the USDA. Guiding the organization is a Central Executive Committee made up of high-ranking government officials, including ministers, who are also frequently high-ranking generals as well. The organization has a regional structure, paralleling that of government territorial divisions. The USDA is a means of generating popular support for the regime through the sponsorship and organization of mass rallies and the participation of Association members in rural development projects in order to gain the general population's trust and support. By early 2002, there was a new push, marked by town rallies, to persuade the general population to accept USDA guiding principles, the same as those of the SPDC, in preparation for the expected transfer of power from the junta to the Association.[42]

The USDA has also been involved in violent confrontations with the political opposition. An attack by Association members on NLD supporters rallying during Aung San Suu Kyi's visit to Dipeyin on 30 May 2003 led to unwanted international attention at a time when the SPDC was attempting to improve its image. As a result, Than Shwe ordered the closing of the offices of the Association a month later, on 29 June, leading to rumors that the organization was going to be disbanded. Speculation at the time held that the regime used the pro-regime Association attack and the closure of its offices to demonstrate its even-handedness after having closed down NLD offices earlier.[43] The Association, however, was not disbanded and survived the crisis.

Under the leadership of its secretary and government minister, Aung Thaung, the scope of the USDA role in daily life has expanded rapidly to control all significant social activities in the regions. In addition to attempting to assert control over all non-government organizations in the country, the Association's Central Office directs members to recruit those expelled from the NLD (and persuade others to quit the League), to support them in public protests before the League's offices, and to produce and circulate anti-NLD leaflets. Association members are also to report on local NLD activities both to the Association's central organ and to military intelligence, although its performance of this function was far from effective.[44]

Today, the USDA appears poised to replace the military when it steps down from power after the implementation of the new constitution. It held 633 seats (58 percent of the total number) in the National Convention and the SPDC claims that the organization has 28 million members. Although critics claim that most members have been forced into the Association through intimidation and harassment, it nonetheless represents a large civilian body that will be useful, in a future government, in downplaying international complaints about military rule.[45] At such a time, recognition of the 1990 election results will be a moot point. The parallels between this model of transition to civilian rule and the change from the Revolutionary Council to the BSPP government are very strong indeed.

In order to prepare the USDA for future leadership in the country, in every sphere of national life, the SPDC runs training courses at the central, state, and divisional levels. At the USDA Central Training School in Rangoon, a small cadre of Association members study Burma Affairs and International Studies; Public Relations and Information Management Courses; a Diploma Course on Leadership; and a Basic Journalism Course. At the state and divisional levels, SPDC members receive training in national development, organizational skills, management, national culture and morality, efficiency, sports, music and art, among other subjects. Consensus is built up through annual general meetings at the state and divisional levels so that the Association will be able to implement their intended tasks.[46]

A NEW CAPITAL

Rangoon, the former capital, was always a problem for the SLORC/SPDC. As the center for government and the country's largest urban area since the nineteenth century, it was only natural that it should be the main location of governance. To do otherwise would have entailed substantial costs that the cash-strapped regime could not afford to cover. On the other hand, fears of the mob have always worried dictators. The most serious of the 1988 popular protests in Burma were in Rangoon. The military could take some comfort in the barbed wire and soldiers stationed around government buildings, the machine gun nest located on the crossover near the Traders Hotel, soldiers stationed on the ground floors of housing complexes near RU, and squads in dozens of other locations, but this was not a permanent solution to security.

Not all concerns regarding Rangoon were directly related to security. Rangoon was an aging city and investment in new buildings, save for some socialist architecture in the 1950s and a number of hotels built in the 1990s, did not keep pace with population growth or the new commercial or technological demands placed on the city. In a repeat of the Caretaker Government's resettlement of squatters in Rangoon between 1958 and 1959, for example, the SLORC began a massive resettlement program in the city from October 1988. On 23 October, the Rangoon Division LORC announced that "squatters" in the Rangoon city development area had been moved to the new towns, one of which was Hlaing Thaya across the river from Insein, Padamya, and Okpo. In January 1989, the SLORC announced, just as the Caretaker Government had almost thirty years earlier, that the government was cleaning up the cities so that they would now look like proper cities and to improve sanitation and avoid fire hazards. To do so, they had to "systematically" remove densely populated squatter areas. Soldiers then put the squatters into army trucks and removed them. The SLORC also emphatically denied that people within proper buildings were being removed as well. Resettlement accelerated in March and April 1990. Over half a million people were moved to new, hastily constructed towns, such as Dagon town, in outlying areas. The new towns were to have hospitals, electricity, water, schools, and markets. In many cases, however, people were simply dropped off into areas that still needed to be reclaimed from the jungle and lacked access to transport, with no local means of employment, and even without shelter. There was some speculation that the resettlement merely amounted to deportations to eradicate centers of opposition within the capital.[47]

Some towns, such as Dagon, were intended to house public servants so that they would own their own homes by the time they retired. However, the government also began to move the homeless and those living on government, factory, and religious lands out of Rangoon. The plan was to reconstruct Rangoon in blocks following a square pattern, fringed by new satellite towns, but the government failed to meet the end of March deadline for the completion of the project. The SLORC blamed government departments for lending only minimal aid to the project and not fulfilling their obligations regarding land allocation, the building of homes, and the movement of new settlers. The SLORC also announced, in mid-April, plans to construct a super-city to the south of Rangoon. The 1,600-square-kilometer city, to be completed by 2005, was to be a four-million-person metropolis, a new center for economic growth in the entire Indian Ocean area. Building the city would cost the government US$1 billion per year for fifteen years, and it would be constructed by a consortium of up to 200 Japanese companies. The city would include twenty-five zones according to function, linked by advanced telecommunications and transport, and an "emphasis on flow of information, rather than materials," as well as 4,000 man-made lakes, highways, and offices built to give it an "atmosphere of a resort."[48]

It was partly a combination of the dream of building a modern super-city, the demand for greater security, and profits from growing Chinese investment that eventually led to the realization of plans to create a new capital city. On 13 June 2005, the SPDC issued orders to key ministries to prepare for relocation to Pyinmana. It was not until November, however, that the government publicly announced that the capital would be shifted from Rangoon and specified a location about 26 kilometers from Pyinmana and 600 kilometers north of Rangoon. The new site was named Naypyidaw Myodaw in March 2006. It was in reality a military compound, occupying ten kilometers, which had been planned for years, although construction had really only been underway over the course of the preceding year.[49] Civil servants were given little warning before they were told to pack their belongings, pile into military trucks, and resettled in a site plagued by malaria and sparse accommodation.

The official reasons for the shift were never satisfactorily explained and popular imagination ran wild in attempting to fill the information gap. One rumor was that Than Shwe, deeply superstitious, made the decision for the move on the basis of the claim by an astrologer that Rangoon (see Fig. 9.3) would soon collapse. Two reasonable observations, however, are convincing. First, in terms of domestic security, the administrative chaos

Figure 9.3 Present-day Rangoon

produced by the demonstrations of 1988 has encouraged a shift of the government away from a major population center to a new, more easily managed site. The latter concern appears to have been confirmed by the SPDC Information and Propaganda Minister, who argued that the move was due to the better communication lines at Pyinmana, which is more centrally located than Rangoon. Second, in terms of international security, the regime appeared concerned about the vulnerability of Rangoon, close to the coast, to a seaborne invasion, if foreign powers were determined to intervene. Some foreign scholars have argued that the move represents a return to a long-term historical norm of having a capital based in Upper Burma, but this argument explains neither the timing nor the fact that the new capital has been located far outside the zone that hosts the major precolonial capitals of Amarapura, Sagaing, Ava, and Mandalay. This does not mean that Pyinmana is without historical precedent. During World War II, the town had been the headquarters for the BDA and Aung San had launched his independence movement from it.[50]

The shift of the capital also indicated that the military was centralizing authority over the country at a time when the drawing up of a new constitution was reaching its final stage. The National Convention, without the participation of the political opposition, met in May 2004, for the first time since 1996, and reconvened on 17 February 2005, in order to draw up the new constitution. However, the result of the Convention, announced in September 2007, was merely a set of guidelines for drafting a new constitution. Predictably and in keeping with the regime's policy of delay, the guidelines required six more steps on what is termed the "road map to democracy." Even then, the guidelines were arranged to establish military dominance in any new government, including control of all major ministries, substantial numbers of reserved seats for the military in legislative bodies, and legal "national security" constraints regarding respect for human rights. The guidelines also established limitations that would prevent Aung San Suu Kyi from holding political office. As a guarantee of meeting the goals of these guidelines, the government announced in December 2007 that the new constitution would be written by a 54-member constitution-drafting commission nominated by the SPDC. Although the completed constitution was subject to a national referendum, held in May 2008, like other steps in the constitution-drafting process, this proved to be a carefully orchestrated sham and merely another step in the long process of delay in the handing over of power to a popularly elected government.[51]

THE SLOW BOIL

As promises and continual preparations with no clear end in sight regarding the economy, the transfer of power, and other matters appeared to be no more than delaying tactics, frustrations among the Burmese population simmered for years. Perhaps just as important as the issue of democracy has been the failing economy. International sanctions and other efforts to isolate the regime have hurt the general Burmese population, pushing most further into poverty and sending many now unemployed female textile workers and others into prostitution.

By contrast, Burma's elite military families have shown incredible resourcefulness in maintaining and expanding their personal wealth. This was demonstrated most recently by the opulent wedding of Than Shwe's daughter, who, in a video leaked to the outside world, was shown sporting jewelry worth many millions of dollars.[52] Subordinate officers also benefited from patronage, extensively used by the junta to maintain officer corps solidarity, in the form of business loans, the purchase of land far below its real value, and opportunities to forge highly rewarding connexions with private businesspeople.[53] The growing disparity in wealth between the general population and military families became very difficult to ignore.

From late 2006, prices of daily necessities, such as cooking oil, began to increase by up to 40 percent, pushing family economies almost to a breaking point. Although life became almost unaffordable, Burmese tolerance of hardship, built up from experience of other long-term hardships that have plagued the country since the early 1960s, proved resilient. Quiet resentment of misrule changed to open protest, however, after 15 August 2007, when the government, apparently taking to the extreme International Monetary Fund advice to take the population off subsidized fuel, issued an overnight increase in fuel prices of between 100 and 500 percent. The sudden increase meant it was now impossible for the average Burmese to afford transport to work, especially as the bus lines immediately stopped running. Increased fuel prices meant that already inflated prices of other basic commodities began to increase further. The protests that broke out on 19 August and carried on into September highlighted the desperation to which the general population has been driven. From 22 August, the government began crushing local demonstrations and arresting protestors.[54]

While the regime remained confident of its ability to suppress the resistance of ordinary citizens, it faced a different kind of opponent in mid-September 2007. In what has become known as the "Saffron Revolution," after the garb of its leaders, monks (numbering some 400,000 in Burma), outraged at what the military has done to the country, began protests in northwestern Burma in support of general protests against the government's new economic policies. When the government physically beat protesting monks on 5 September at Pakokku, where monastic opposition began, monastic protests spread through the country. Ultimately, monasteries at Mandalay, the most important monastic center in the country, called on all monks to refuse donations from the families of the military elite, which effectively meant that they could not earn merit in Buddhist belief.[55] Soon, monks led peaceful protest marches in the capital (see Fig. 9.4). While monks are not supposed to engage in mundane politics according to the monastic code, they have become involved in politics at numerous historical junctures in the past. Indeed, some of the leading anti-colonial activists, including Shin Ottama and others, were monks, and monks participated to some degree in the popular revolution of 1988. At the same time, the fact that harming a monk earns one bad merit and thus rebirth as a lesser being in Buddhist thinking meant that the military was hesitant to stop the protests.[56]

Nevertheless, as the world watched through short video clips or viewed photographs sent out of the country by ordinary Burmese, the military was concerned that years of state media and regime apologists telling the country and the outside world that the Burmese were happy with military rule were being revealed as state propaganda. As the United States and the European Union talked of more sanctions, the military struck on 26 September, beating, shooting, and arresting monastic and other protestors. Early the following morning, several monasteries were raided; monks were forcibly (and illegally under Buddhist law) defrocked, beaten, and interrogated, many being killed in the process. Soldiers fired on street protests that ensued. The violence with which the regime suppressed peaceful monastic protests represents, it has been asserted, a historical watershed in the relationship between the Burmese state and the monastic order. The United Nations responded by forcing the government to accept two visits by a special envoy, Ibrahim Gambari, to evaluate the situation. Gambari would press the government to begin talks with detained NLD leader, Aung San Suu Kyi.[57]

The government tried once more to gain control by spinning a different account of events, outlawing cell phones, blocking email and internet access, and cutting communication posts. Nevertheless, footage already leaked out showed soldiers calmly walking up to a wounded Japanese cameraman and shooting him point-blank to death. Reports have since

Figure 9.4 Monks march in protest against the military junta

emerged that the Army burned bodies shortly after these events to hide evidence of the atrocities. The All-Burma Monks Alliance is currently pressuring the UN to ascertain how many monks were killed.[58]

The Burmese monastic order is under close government surveillance, while the chief monastic council, the Supreme Council of Abbots, has been dissolved by Than Shwe for refusing to defrock monks involved in the protests. Monks were also sent out of Rangoon back to their villages in an effort to prevent a re-congregation of this now potent, political force. This has not been completely successful, as indicated on 31 October by a monastic demonstration at Pakokku, where the monastic opposition had originally begun.[59]

CONCLUSION

Burma has now experienced an unbroken two-decade period of post-BSPP military rule. The SLORC/SPDC has managed to retain power by force rather than consent. Although the promulgation of a new constitution was a constant promise, it was made and broken repeatedly. Even when such a constitution was realized, it has proven not to be truly representative of the desires of most Burmese. At the same time, the NLD, once the focus of so many hopes and dreams among the general population, has only survived in emaciated form. For long, the regime appeared to have successfully stymied, with occasional slip-ups, Aung San Suu Kyi's attempts to reactivate the forces that spawned the 1988 popular revolution. Even so, recent events, especially the extension of monastic support to Burmese opposition to the government and popular unhappiness with the regime's dismal response to Cyclone Nargis (May 2008), indicate that these forces may actually be growing stronger than at any time before.

Bunkered in Naypyidaw, backed by diplomatic and material help from powerful neighbors such as China and India competing with each other for privileged access to Burma's natural resources, and having just crushed the most serious challenge to its rule in two decades, the country's military rulers proceeded with the constitutional referendum in two rounds in May 2008. This confidence was shattered by Cyclone Nargis that struck the Burmese coasts with winds of over 190 kilometers an hour on 2–3 May, sending a 6-meters-high wall of water across the delta. Nargis left behind an estimated 150,000 people dead and missing and another 2.5 million homeless and in desperate need of care. Hundreds of thousands of livestock were lost and much of the country's rice stocks were ruined. The regime delayed for three weeks in admitting most international aid, refusing visas to aid workers and storing in warehouses the few supplies it allowed to be flown in, while it proceeded with the constitutional referendum and informed the world that there was no crisis. An international stand-off ensued leading to the gathering of Western naval vessels, including a US aircraft carrier, off the coast and frantic efforts by the UN Secretary General to gain permission for the introduction of international rescue and care workers. When Western countries threatened to bring the generals up before the International Court at The Hague on charges of Crimes Against Humanity and as even China became concerned about the regime's neglect of the wellbeing of its own people, Than Shwe caved in. How far the millions of dollars in promised aid will go in rebuilding the lives of those living in the devastated areas and not into the bank accounts of the generals remains unclear, but Cyclone Nargis has, like the Saffron Revolution eight months earlier, drawn the world's attention to the plight of one of Asia's most oppressed populations.[60]

Conclusion

In its modern history, Burma has been shaped and reshaped over again by different governments in the context of significant pressures emanating from both within and without the country. Despite its diverse and challenging historical experience, one is often struck by how little Burma appears to have changed, especially in relation to its more politically dynamic and economically more prosperous neighbors in the region. The Burmese today are just as unhappy with their government as earlier generations; economic poverty continues to figure as prominently among Burmese concerns as it has at any time in the past. Basic civil liberties are denied today as they were almost a half-century ago. Continuity has characterized some of the basic themes of modern Burmese history that have transcended the phases of the Burmese experience outlined in this book and contribute to something that might be called the rhythm of Burmese history.

Among the most vexing issues that have plagued the country since the colonial period has been the relationship between the Burman-dominated lowlands and the ethnic minority-dominated highlands. What, after all, is Burma and who are the Burmese? Before colonial rule, the Burmese throne considered the highlands to be part of the royal kingdom, but not of the Burman "country." Under the last Burmese dynasty, highland states were ruled by autonomous, tributary chiefs (in the Shan case, *sawbwas*), separated from lowland centers under the control of direct appointees of the Burmese court. Political anxieties rather than ethnic ones dominated conflicts, although cultural, linguistic, and other differences among the diverse peoples that made up the kingdom were indeed recognized.

The highlands retained their autonomy when, over the course of the nineteenth century, the British first carved up and then welded back together the lowlands into direct-rule districts of British Burma. After the grant of diarchy, as the Scheduled Areas, they were constitutionally separated from parliamentary (lowland) Burma. This typical colonial strategy of "divide and rule" encompassed more than regional autonomy, for it also represented a more visible separation of ethnic groups. Despite the claims of the current regime, the British did not create Burma's "ethnic" minorities, but colonial rule did exacerbate them.[1] Colonial administrators and writers essentialized ethnic identifications, thus creating perceptions of cohesiveness and homogeneity within ethnic groups, and clarified what had been vague boundaries between them and other groups, especially in separating Burmans from non-Burmans, both in terms of ethnicity and geography.[2] The British also exacerbated problems between these groups and the Burmans by both favoring and "protecting" ethnic minorities from what the British portrayed, and ethnic minority leaders eventually accepted, as the threat of Burman domination, not just political, but cultural, linguistic and religious as well. Their separation from Rangoon's control continued under the Japanese, the war working also to put Burmans and the ethnic minorities on opposite sides, and after the war as the Frontier Areas.

Ethnic insurgencies that followed independence maintained de facto separation for decades. The 1962 coup sought to undermine attempts to negotiate constitutional recognition of ethnic (highland) autonomy, but by the late BSPP period, Burma's new citizenship laws made it clear that as members of the privileged "indigenous races," highland minorities were officially considered along with the Burmans as part of the same ethnic family, despite the fabricated differences, the government claimed, introduced by the British.[3] The official view has not eroded ethnic minorities' concerns about integration into a Burman-dominated state although it did make it easier for the SLORC/SPDC to go ahead with ceasefire arrangements with many insurgent groups that left the latter in control of their base areas. However, this has left open the question of federalism in the promised constitution. Even if significant political concessions are made in the direction of highland autonomy once the constitution is promulgated, it is likely that the lowland–highland, and thus Burman–minority, bifurcation of the country will remain an important determining factor in the trajectory of Burmese history in the twenty-first century.

Another continual theme of Burma's modern history has been poverty for the general Burmese population. While colonial economic development marginally improved the economic lot of many Burmese, true economic prosperity was enjoyed by very few, mainly among the colonial elite. Even then, the connexion of the Burmese economy to the world capitalist system and the failure to sufficiently diversify the economy left it vulnerable to the whims of Western markets and the World Depression. The major blow to Burma's economic growth came with the outbreak of World War II, in the form of British destruction of Burma's economic and transportation infrastructure in 1942, the separation of Burma from world markets thereafter, and fighting between the Allies and the Japanese, especially in the last months of the war. British efforts to reestablish the colonial economy after the war for the benefit of colonial interests did too little to help most Burmese. Burma after independence had to cope with the devastation and costs of a civil war that dragged on longer than any other conflict anywhere else in the world. What has also hurt post-independence regimes, aside from the more market-oriented reforms of the Caretaker period, were Burma's confused attempts to promote socialism, the chronic corruption that has continued despite regime facelifts, and, in more recent decades, the impact of Western sanctions.

Although the avowed purpose of establishing the socialist economy was to promote the welfare and economic prosperity of the nation, most of the post-independence regimes sacrificed the wellbeing of the country for the economic benefit of the ruling minority. One of the main underlying reasons for this is the association of wealth with political power, perhaps inherited from precolonial times, but certainly strengthened by the colonial period, in that there is an expectation that political power should bring with it personal wealth. Complaints during the colonial period that Burmese politicians were enriching themselves through their offices at the expense of the general population appear no less relevant when one views the control over the economy exerted by the families of prominent SPDC officers today. Whether this would be different under a democratic government is of course unclear, but the current regime has by no means contributed to changing this association, which would be a helpful step toward the fostering of general economic prosperity.

Another long-term theme of modern Burmese history is the struggle between civilian politicians bent on representative, democratic rule and civil liberties and authoritarian control, whether under British colonialists or indigenous military officers. Although colonial-era Burmese nationalists won their struggle against the British, the latter's absence after independence removed from the political scene a singular, visible opponent that could help maintain political solidarity. The AFPFL was an umbrella group of political parties that was held together by both their shared opposition to colonial rule and the personal charisma and political skills of Aung San. When Aung San was assassinated in 1947, it left Nu in charge. Although Nu is admirable for many reasons and his commitment to the country is unquestioned, his behavior was both too quixotic and often too erratic to hold the political coalition together. Moreover, the push for independence had temporarily pushed aside many political questions that now had to be resolved with too many and too diverse political forces in the field. Military officers viewed civilian politics of the time as inimical to the promotion of national unity and developed notions, strengthened by the caretaker regime's admittedly effective performance, that the military could do a better job at running the country. In other words, in the context of Burma's civil war, its economic woes, and the factious democratic politics, Burma could only be preserved and national unity found through authoritarian military rule. Divided democratic forces could do very little to oppose the 1962 coup.

One tool used by post-1962 regimes in attempts to legitimize their control was inherited from the colonial period. The British had successfully prolonged colonial rule in Burma in part by permitting minor constitutional concessions while retaining control of the real centers of power in the colonial administration. This put Burmese into visible positions within the administration, usually over areas of governance the British were not really interested in anyway, but did not lessen overall colonial authority. Ne Win was especially adept at using similar tactics to the degree that one might view the Revolutionary Council period and its BSPP successor as ideologically rich compared to the SLORC/SPDC. Despite Tin Pe's adventurous Marxist-oriented reforms, lip service to mass participation in governance, and the structures of a civilian, one-party state, Ne Win and the military remained in full control of the country. As one scholar has observed, those most committed to the principles of the Burmese Way to Socialism ideology were squeezed out of the BSPP government, senior leadership positions being determined by personal loyalty to Ne Win.[4] Ne Win had even tried in the late 1960s to bring cowed former Nu-era politicians into a committee to legitimize his proposals, but realizing that these offered no real democratic concessions, they turned to armed rebellion instead, indicating that the struggle between civilian politicians and the military was by no means resolved.

The SLORC/SPDC borrowed significantly from the Ne Win era, particularly the formation of the BSPP as a civilian mass base to seemingly legitimate the preservation of the military's interests. The USDA is perhaps the best example of this attempt. But there are important differences. By contrast with the ideology-rich Revolutionary Council and BSPP governments, the slow pace of reform after 1990 is partly due to the intellectual and ideological hollowness of the current regime. Beyond slogans and bullet points, couched in calls to resist foreign intervention, no systematic ideology has emerged to make government policies meaningful, even understandable to the general population (or even to themselves). Certainly, the end of the Cold War and the collapse of Communism in most of the world has reduced the availability of powerful ideologies that can be used as models for states, such as Burma, that are desperately in search of identities. The fact that the Communists disappeared so quickly from the civil war landscape, in 1989, deprived the military of one of its main justifications for continued control. In the place of ideology, the SLORC/SPDC has utilized what could be called "sustained delay," whereby military control remains always temporary, always on the eve of transfer of the state to civilian control, and continually vigilant about so-called technical problems in the drafting of the Constitution, requiring more committee meetings and more preliminary decision-making. If the country is always kept on the verge of the transfer of power, there is no compelling reason to legitimate present government policies to any significant degree. The democracy issue has thus been "lost in committee" and has been so for nearly two decades.

Another theme of modern Burmese history that the SLORC/SPDC has attempted to mobilize in its favor was sparked under colonial rule, that is, the fear of foreign domination. Anti-colonialism and early Burmese nationalism justifiably saw colonial rule as inimical to the interests of the Burmese population. Such sentiments were certainly strengthened during World War II when Burmese nationalists such as Aung San realized that Japanese "liberation" really meant continued foreign control. After the war, when the British returned to Burma, they made it clear if any doubts still lingered, through the activities of the CASB, that if Burma were to be developed in the interests of the Burmese, then foreign involvement meant commercial exploitation and, necessarily, domination by foreign minorities within the country. The outbreak of the Cold War, which roughly accompanied the grant of independence, deluged Burma with both Western and Communist propaganda but it also brought exposure to leaders in other newly independent countries, such as India and Indonesia, who argued that participation in the Cold War offered nothing for countries like Burma and, indeed, threatened the extension of a new kind of foreign domination, neocolonialism. Moreover, Nu believed that the US, through its support of the GMD, and the Soviet Union, through its perceived backing of the Communists, were exacerbating the civil war that broke out after independence. Indeed, the fundamental message of his play, *The People Win Through*, is that Burmese should not fall under the spell of foreign powers and invite external intervention in Burma's domestic problems. Nu's attempts to placate the PRC were likewise directed at preventing PRC intervention in the country rather than developing any sort of alliance.

Burma's post-1962 regimes maintained the official international neutrality promoted under Nu and although the Revolutionary Council and the BSPP governments associated closely with the Soviet Union and were indeed estranged from the PRC, no official alignment was considered. Whether this was intended to allow the government to use the Cold War to its advantage, by gaining aid from both sides, or to maintain the principle of isolating Burma from external intervention is unclear. In either case, the SLORC took the fears of external intervention to new levels, in a very public way, in 1988. Aung San Suu Kyi's close personal connexions with the West and her support within it have helped to make the appeal, among Burma's military rulers, of rejecting Western interference all the more powerful. This is also partly due to the continued presence of Aung San Suu Kyi and the fact that the denial of recognition of the 1990 election results continues to ride mainly upon foreign intervention. International sanctions strengthened the government's resolve to reshape the external threat to include the West in general.

One more major theme of Burmese history has been monastic participation in politics. According to the monastic code, monks are not supposed to involve themselves in mundane politics, but historically this involvement has been very real, both before colonialism and after. As we have seen, monks such as Ottama and the political monks of 1920s rural Burma played leading roles in Burmese anti-colonialism. Monastic organizations played a fundamental role in pushing for state recognition of Buddhism as the national religion and mobilized against the Communist insurgency during the Caretaker period and after. As under colonial rule, the monastic order fought vigorously Ne Win's attempts to exert control over the monastic order in order to silence monastic criticism of his rule, during both the Revolutionary Council and the BSPP governments. Many monks also took to the streets in 1988 to help bring down the BSPP regime and restore democracy to the country.

The basic problem facing the SPDC in relation to monks is that in Burmese society they are potentially very powerful. In the Burmese Buddhist system of belief, donations to monks are an important way to accrue merit in order to experience a better rebirth on the path to Enlightenment and should these donations be refused, then one faces the prospects of an inferior rebirth. On another level, Burmese monks have been, since precolonial days, the keepers of Burmese tradition and the core of Burmese intellectual life. When Burmese Buddhist boys, even those who grow up to be soldiers, become novices they are taught in the monasteries and learn to recognize the unquestionable authority monks have in determining what is and what is not proper Burmese Buddhist behavior. This is easily extended to politics and if monks disapprove of the regime's claims to represent the "real" Burma, it has an importance greater than any other voice of dissent.

When the monks refused donations from the families of the military elite and complained of the directions in which the country was headed, the government lost whatever gains, if any, it had made in attempting to foster domestic political legitimacy. This was guaranteed when soldiers and police arrested, defrocked, and beat monks in a desperate attempt to suppress what may prove to have been a mortal blow to the regime. Certainly, all indications are, at the time of writing, that monastic opposition has not been cowed. Monks will continue to play an important role in shaping the country's political future, especially since the monastic role in the demonstrations clearly showed that legitimacy rested with the opposition.

Notes

I BURMA UNDER COLONIAL RULE

1. James C. Scott, *The Moral Economy of the Peasant: Rebellion and Subsistence in Southeast Asia* (New Haven, CT: Yale University Press, 1976).

2. Ian Brown, *A Colonial Economy in Crisis: Burma's Rice Cultivators and the World Depression of the 1930s* (London: RoutledgeCurzon, 2005): 9, 11.

3. *Forward* 9.7 (15 November 1970): 18.

4. "Durbar at Mandalay," 28 November 1901, in *Lord Curzon in India* (London: MacMillan, 1906): 215; *Times*, 30 November 1901, 7.

5. Kazuto Ikeda, "The Myaungmya Incident during the Japanese Occupation in Burma: Karens and Shwe Tun Kya," in Kei Nemoto (ed.), *Reconsidering the Japanese Military Occupation in Burma (1942–45)* (Tokyo: Tokyo University of Foreign Studies, 2007): 60–61; Ito Toshikatsu, "Karens and the Kon-baung Polity in Myanmar," *Acta Asiatica* 92 (2007): 105.

6. The problems of the colonial census are tackled by the late Judith L. Richell in *Disease and Demography in Colonial Burma* (Copenhagen: NIAS Press, 2006).

7. Atsuko Naono, *The State of Vaccination*, forthcoming.

8. Michael Adas, *The Burma Delta: Economic Development and Social Change on an Asian Rice Frontier, 1852–1941* (Madison, WI: University of Wisconsin Press, 1974): 118–119; Cheng Siok-Hwa, *The Rice Industry of Burma*, 186–188.

9. "Land Alienation," *World of Books* 23 (November 1937): 448.

10. *Forward* 9.7 (15 November 1970): 18; *Times*, 24 May 1921, supplement, xiv; *Times*, 17 October 1924, 13; *Memorandum Submitted by the Government of Burma to the Indian Statutory Commission* (1930), 25–26; Maurice Collis, *Into Hidden Burma: An Autobiography* (London: Faber, 1953): 162; PBLC 4.5, 25 September 1925: 107, 116, 117, 120.

11. *Forward* 9.7 (15 November 1970): 18; Collis, *Into Hidden Burma*, 164; PBLC 4.5, 25 September 1925: 107, 113–114, 116–117; *Times*, 24 May 1921, supplement, xiv; *Times*, 20 September 1924, 9; 7 October 1924, 13; 17 October 1924, 13; 9 April 1928, 9.

12. *Times*, 20 September 1924, 9; 7 October 1924, 13; 17 October 1924, 13; PBLC 4.5, 25 September 1925: 107, 114; PDC, 5th Series, volume 213, 13 February 1928, 496.

13. *Times*, 9 November 1910, 5; 12 November 1910, 7; 3 December 1910, 7; PDC, 5th Series, volume 28, 11 July 1911, 181; APCLGB 6 April 1914, 346–347; 13 March 1913, 277; 13 March 1914, 311–313; *Memorandum Submitted by the Government of Burma to the Indian Statutory Commission* (1930), 26.

14. Khin Maung Nyunt, "Supannaka Galuna Raja," GMR 15.4 (April 1968): 11.

15. Brown, *A Colonial Economy in Crisis*, 101–108.

16. Maitrii V. Aung-Thwin, "British Counter-Insurgency Narratives and the Construction of a Twentieth Century Burmese Rebel," PhD dissertation, University of Michigan, 2001.

17. Kyaw Htun, "Of Such Stuff Are Heroes Made," GMR 14.4 (April 1967): 22; U Tin Maung, "A Short History of Newspapers," *Burma Digest* 1.14 (1 October 1946): 29.

18. Khin Maung Nyunt, "Supannaka Galuna Raja," 11–12.

19. U Htin Fatt, "Sidelights on Burma's Struggle for Freedom," GMR 16.5 (May 1969): 32; Khin Maung Nyunt, "Supannaka Galuna Raja," 12; Tin Maung, "A Short History of Newspapers," 29–30.

20. Khin Maung Nyunt, "Supannaka Galuna Raja," 12–13; Tin Maung, "A Short History of Newspapers," 30; Zeya Maung, "Saya Lun and the Galon Rebellion of Saya San," GMR 22.2 (March 1975): 21–22; Htin Fatt, "Sidelights on Burma's Struggle for Freedom," 32.

21. GMR 5.8 (August 1958): 42; Htin Fatt, "Sidelights on Burma's Struggle for Freedom," 33; Tin Maung, "A Short History of Newspapers," 30, 32.

2 THE COLONIAL CENTER

1. John L. Christian, "Burma Divorces India," *Current History* 46.1 (April 1937): 82.

2. B. R. Pearn, *History of Rangoon* (Rangoon: American Baptist Mission Press, 1939): 264–266, 283.

3. "The Rangoon Electric Tramway & Supply Company Limited," *BBAQB* 8 (April 1938): 42–44; Pearn, *History of Rangoon*, 266, 278.

4. "The Rangoon Electric Tramway & Supply Company Limited," 45; Pearn, *History of Rangoon*, 279; APCLGB, 9 March 1907, 118.

5. Pearn, *History of Rangoon*, 280; PDC, 4th Series, volume 179, 6 August 1907, 1819.

6. APCLGB 2 January 1920, 628–629.

7. Pearn, *History of Rangoon*, 280–281, 283, 284; U Tun Shein, *Yangon Yazawin Thamaing* (Yangon, Zwe-sape-yeibmyoun, 1962): 152.

8. *Census for 1872*, 17; appendix II, 4; BBAQB 7 (July 1937): 12.

9. GMR 19.6 (June 1972): 17; Richell, *Disease and Demography in Colonial Burma*, 266, 272.

10. J. S. Furnivall, "Burma Fifty Years Ago: Little Picture of Progress," GMR 5.10 (October 1958): 29–30.

11. Alister McCrae, *Scots in Burma: Golden Times in a Golden Land* (Edinburgh: Kiscadale, 1990): 70–71; GMR 19.6 (June 1972): 17.

12. *Who's Who in Burma: under the distinguished patronage of HE Sir Harcourt Butler* (Calcutta: Indo-Burma Publishing Agency, 1927): 54; H. A. Cartwright and O. Breakspear (eds.), *Twentieth Century Impressions of Burma: Its History, People, Commerce, Industries, and Resources* (London: Lloyd's Greater Britain Publishing Co., 1910): 309, 312.

13. GMR 19.6 (June 1972): 17, 19.

14. Ba Maw, *Breakthrough in Burma: Memoirs of a Revolution* (New Haven, CT: Yale University Press, 1968): 13; Pearn, *History of Rangoon*, 290–291.

15. U Nu, *U Nu Saturday's Son*, translated by U Law Yone (New Haven, CT: Yale University Press, 1975): 19.

16. APCLGB 8 December 1903, 3.

17. Emma Larkin, "The Self-Conscious Censor: Censorship Under the British, 1900–1939," *Journal of Burma Studies* 8 (2003): 71.

18. Richell, *Disease and Demography in Colonial Burma*, 266; GMR 19.6 (June 1972): 17.

19. APCLGB 19 December 1901, 3–4; Nu, *Saturday's Son*, 22.

20. APCLGB 19 December 1901, 3–4; 8 December 1903, 3; 29 February 1908, 132; 26 February 1921, 761–765; *Rangoon Municipality Handbook*, 459.

21. Larkin, "The Self-Conscious Censor," 71–72; George Orwell, *Burmese Days* (San Diego: Harcourt Brace, n.d.).

22. APCLGB 26 February 1921, 761–765; *Times*, 24 November 1925, 13; PDC, 4th Series, volume 113, 21 October 1902, 352.

23. *Forward* 9.7 (15 November 1970): 17.

24. Ibid., 18.

25. *Who's Who in Burma*, 154; *Who's Who in Burma, 1961* (Rangoon: People's Literature Committee, 1962): 104–105.

26. U Shwe Mra, "A Civil Servant in Thayetmyo 1935–36," GMR 13.4 (April 1966): 46–47.

27. *Forward* 9.7 (15 November 1970): 18.

28. Christian, "Burma Divorces India," 85; U Htin Fatt, "Burma's Constitutional Developments Before the Second World War," GMR 17.2 (February 1970): 40; *Forward* 9.7 (15 November 1970): 18.

29. *Forward* 9.7 (15 November 1970): 17.

30. Tun Shein, *Yangon Yazawin Thamaing*, 209; Khin Maung Nyunt, "The 'Shoe' Question," GMR 17.2 (February 1970): 26–27.

31. Michael Aung-Thwin, "The British 'Pacification' of Burma: Order Without Meaning," *Journal of Southeast Asian Studies* 16 (1985): 247; Christian, "Burma Divorces India," 85; Htin Fatt, "Burma's Constitutional Developments," 40; Tetkatho Minwaethan, "Burmese Movies in Retrospect," GMR 16.9 (September 1969): 45.

32. GMR 10.1 (January 1963): 29; *Forward* 9.7 (15 November 1970): 18; Htin Fatt, "Sidelights on Burma's Struggle for Freedom," 30–31; Mya Han, *Koloniket, Myanma Thamaing Abhidan* (Yangon: Universities Historical Research Center, 2000): 209–210.

33. Htin Fatt, "Sidelights on Burma's Struggle for Freedom," 31; George E. R. Grant Brown, *Burma as I Saw It, 1889–1917, With a Chapter on Recent Events* (New York: Frederick A. Stokes and Company, 1925): 171; Albert D. Moscotti, *British Policy and the Nationalist Movement in Burma, 1917–1937* (Honolulu, HI: University of Hawaii Press, 1937): 48; Donald Eugene Smith, *Religion and Politics in Burma* (Princeton, NJ: Princeton University Press, 1965): 121; *Times*, 19 August 1924, 10; 6 October 1924, 11; 9 October 1924, 13; 10 October 1924, 11; 11 October 1924, 9.

34. Harvey Adamson, "Burma," *The Asiatic Review* 16.46 (April 1920): 286; Christian, "Burma Divorces India," 84.

35. APCLGB 17 April 1920, 701–702; Spencer Harcourt Butler, "Burma and Its Problems," *Foreign Affairs* 10 (1932): 655; Htin Fatt, "Burma's Constitutional Developments," 41; Henti, "A Scheme of Reform for Burma," 21–22, 42–43.

36. *Forward* 9.8 (1 December 1970): 20; *Times*, 24 May 1921, supplement, xiv.

37. *Forward* 9.8 (1 December 1970): 21; U Lu Pe Win, *History of the 1920 University Boycott* (Rangoon: U Lu Pe Win, 1970): 243–244.

38. Maung Maung, "Mr. Justice Chan Htoon," GMR 2.2 (December 1954): 34; ibid., "Dr. Htin Aung, The Fourth Brother," GMR 5.8 (August 1958): 25; *Forward* 9.8 (1 December 1970): 21.

39. Robert H. Taylor, "British Policy Toward Burma (Myanmar) in the 1920's and 1930's: Separation and Responsible Self-Government," in *Essays in Commemoration of the Golden Jubilee of the Myanmar Historical Commission* (Yangon: UHRC, 2005): 149; Htin Fatt, "Burma's Constitutional Developments," 41; Christian, "Burma Divorces India," 84; *Times*, 2 January 1923, 9; 29 April 1924, 11.

40. Sai Kham Mong, "The Shan in Myanmar," in N. Ganesan and Kyaw Yin Hlaing (eds.), *Myanmar: State, Society and Ethnicity* (Singapore: Institute of Southeast Asian Studies, 2007): 259–260.

41. John F. Cady, *A History of Modern Burma* (Ithaca, NY: Cornell University Press, 1958): 295.

42. *Forward* 9.7 (15 November 1970): 17; *Memorandum Submitted by the Government of Burma to the Indian Statutory Commission* (1930), 25; Moscotti, *British Policy and the Nationalist Movement in Burma, 1917–1937*, 48; Cady, *History of Modern Burma*, 250; *Times*, 6 August 1925, 11; 22 August 1925, 9; 30 July 1925, 13.

43. Zeya Maung, "The Khway Tike of Mr. Maung Hmine," GMR 22.2 (February 1975): 15; *Times*, 30 July 1925, 13; 31 July 1925, 9.

44. Cheryll Baron, "Burma: Feminist Utopia?" *Prospect* 139 (October 2007).

45. PBLC, 9 August 1929, 282.

46. PBLC, 3 February 1927, 201.

47. Unpublished translation by L. E. Bagshawe of Yaw Mingyi U Po Hlaing, *Rajadhammasangaha*, 167–170.

48. Htin Fatt, "Burma's Constitutional Developments," 41; Christian, "Burma Divorces India," 84–85.

49. Christian, "Burma Divorces India," 85–86.

50. Htin Fatt, "Burma's Constitutional Developments," 42.
51. M. B. K., "U Ba Sein, Attorney-General," GMR 6.1 (January 1959): 41; Maung Maung, "Mr. Justice Chan Htoon," 35; Thakin Lay Maung, "A Short History of the Dhobama Asiayone (Thakin Party) and its Policy," *Burma Digest* 1.8 (1 July 1946): 31–32.
52. Nu, *Saturday's Son*, 61–63, 74, 77–78.
53. Maung Tha Hla, "The 1936 Rangoon University Strike [I]," *NBW* 1.4 (21 June 1958): 8; Maung Maung, "U Nyo Mya, Or Maung Thumana," GMR 5.10 (October 1958); 24.
54. Maung Tha Hla, "The 1936 Rangoon University Strike [I]," 9–10, 13.
55. Maung Tha Hla, "The 1936 Rangoon University Strike [II]," *NBW* 1.6 (5 July 1958): 12–14; Maung Maung, "U Nyo Mya," 24.
56. Maung Tha Hla, "The 1936 Rangoon University Strike [III]," *NBW* 1.9 (26 July 1958): 7, 11, 13, 14.

3 SELF-GOVERNMENT WITHOUT INDEPENDENCE, 1937–1947

1. [31 March 1937] *LAD* 3 (1937): 2417; BBAQB 7 (July 1937): 11–12; A. J. S. White, *The Burma of "AJ"* (London: BACSA, 1991): 211, 214–215.
2. BBAQB 6 (April 1937): 3–5; Htin Fatt, "Sidelights on Burma's Struggle for Freedom," 33; GMR 9.5 (May 1962): 13–14.
3. Ba Maw, *Breakthrough in Burma*, 35, 69, 87; Lay Maung, "A Short History of the Dhobama Asiayone," 33–34; GMR 9.5 (May 1962): 15; Htin Fatt, "Sidelights on Burma's Struggle for Freedom," 33.
4. *Time Magazine* 3 November 1941; 17 November 1941; Ba Maw, *Breakthrough in Burma*, 52, 61; PDC 443, 5 November 1947, 1849; *Times*, 2 November 1945, 3; 4 September 1946, 5.
5. Maung Khin Maung, "Nagoya Bya-bwe-gyi," *Sun Magazine* 21.1 (March 1937): 83–87.
6. Robert H. Taylor, *The State in Burma* (Honolulu, HI: The University of Hawaii Press, 1987): 232; Cady, *A History of Modern Burma*, 428–429; 14 August has also been given as the date for Aung San's departure for Amoy. See Thant Myint-U, *The River of Lost Footsteps: Histories of Burma* (New York: Farrar, Straus and Giroux, 2006): 228.
7. GMR 7.1 (January 1960): 13; 9.5 (May 1962): 16; 9.6 (June 1962): 14; 11.5 (May 1964): 36; Maung Maung, "General Ne Win," GMR 1.12 (October 1954): 57; Thant Myint-U, *The River of Lost Footsteps*, 229–230.
8. [19 March 1937] *LAD* 3 (1937): 2181; [30 March 1937] *LAD* 3 (1937): 2328; John F. Cady, *Contacts with Burma, 1935–1949: A Personal Account* (Athens, OH: Ohio University Center for International Studies, 1983): 25.
9. GMR 11.5 (May 1964): 36–38; Thant Myint-U, *The River of Lost Footsteps*, 230.
10. Kazuo Tamayama, *Railwaymen in the War: Tales by Japanese Railway Soldiers in Burma and Thailand 1941–1947* (Houndmills: Palgrave MacMillan, 2005): 12–13.

11. M. B. K. "U Ba Sein, Attorney-General," 43; GMR 11.5 (May 1964): 39–40; Maung Maung, "General Ne Win," 57; GMR 10.1 (January 1963): 30; *Burma Today* 1.5 (March 1944): 3; 1.11 (September 1944): 9; 1.12 (October 1944): 1.

12. *Burma Today* 1.12 (October 1944): 2; Maung Maung, "General Ne Win," 57; *Times*, 14 December 1943, 5.

13. GMR 10.1 (January 1963): 30; 11.6 (June 1964): 17; Ba U, "My Burma: Under the Japanese Occupation," GMR 5.1 (January 1958): 20.

14. Tun Shein, *Yangon Yazawin Thamaing*, 249, 254; GMR 10.1 (January 1963): 31; *Burma Today* 1.12 (October 1944): 2; Ba U, "My Burma," 20; Maung Maung, "General Ne Win," 57; GMR 11.6 (June 1964): 17.

15. David I. Steinberg, *Burma: A Socialist Nation of Southeast Asia* (Boulder, CO: Westview Press, 1982): 48.

16. Ibid., 60.

17. Taylor, *The State in Burma*, 233; Steinberg, *Burma: A Socialist Nation of Southeast Asia*, 48; Thant Myint-U, *The River of Lost Footsteps*, 231, 236; Ikeda, "The Myaungmya Incident during the Japanese Occupation in Burma: Karens and Shwe Tun Kya," 64–67.

18. Steinberg, *Burma: A Socialist Nation of Southeast Asia*, 48.

19. U Thaung, *A Journalist, a General and an Army in Burma* (Bangkok: White Lotus, 1995): 58; *Burma Today* 1.5 (March 1944): 3; 2.1 (November 1944): 2; GMR 11.9 (September 1964): 17; Takahiro Iwaki, "Heiho Mobilization and Local Administration in the Japanese Occupation Period: The Case of Pyapon District," in Kei Nemoto, *Reconsidering the Japanese Military Occupation in Burma (1942–45)*, 101–106.

20. *Burma Today* 1.4 (February 1944): 4, 12; 1.5 (March 1944): 4; 1.7 (May 1944): 1, 4, 10, 12; 1.8 (June 1944): 2; 1.9 (July 1944): 4.

21. GMR 11.11 (November 1964): 20; Clarence Hendershot, "Burma Compromise," *Far Eastern Survey* 16.12 (18 June 1947): 134; GMR 9.6 (June 1962): 16–17; *Times*, 31 May 1945, 5.

22. GMR 9.6 (June 1962): 18; 11.11 (November 1964): 20–21; Christopher Bayly and Tim Harper, *Forgotten Armies: The Fall of British Asia 1941–1945* (London: Allen Lane, 2004): 434.

23. *Times*, 16 August 1945, 3; 17 August 1945, 4; 29 August 1945, 4; 25 October 1945, 3.

24. PDC, 2 May 1947, 2357.

25. GMR 10.1 (January 1963): 30; 11.5 (May 1964): 37–38; 11.11 (November 1964): 18; *Burma Digest* 1.15 (15 October 1946): 10.

26. G. Appleton, "Burma Two Years After Liberation," *International Affairs* 23.4 (October 1947): 510–511; PDC 406, 12 December 1944, 1088; 421, 3 April 1946, 1536–1537; 2 May 1947, 2357, 2313; *Times*, 8 March 1946, 5.

27. Frank Gubb, "The Burmese People's Anti-Fascist Freedom League," *Burma Digest* 1.3 (March 1946): 19; Virginia Thompson, "The New Nation of Burma," *Far Eastern Survey* 17.7 (7 April 1948): 81; PDC 425, 8 July 1946, 19; *Times*, 22 May 1945, 4, 8.

28. Appleton, "Burma Two Years After Liberation," 514; Emile C. Foucar, *I lived in Burma* (London: DuFour, 1956): 187, 189.

29. Hendershot, "Burma Compromise," 133–134; Appleton, "Burma Two Years After Liberation," 512; Harold Roper, "Current Affairs in Burma," *Asiatic Review* 42.150 (April 1946): 115; Gubb, "The Burmese People's Anti-Fascist Freedom League," 18; U Set Kya, "Burma's Projects," *Burma Digest* 1.15 (15 October 1946): 7; *Times*, 15 May 1946, 3; Foucar, *I Lived in Burma*, 191–192; *Burma Today* 2.11 (October 1945): 7.

30. *Foreign Relations, 1946*, VIII, 2; Set Kya, "Burma's Projects," 6–7; Appleton, "Burma Two Years After Liberation," 514.

31. Sydney D. Bailey, "The Transfer of Power," GMR 1.12 (October 1954): 53; Hendershot, "Burma Compromise," 134; PDC 421, 5 April 1946, 1529–1530; *Times*, 24 October 1945, 4; 29 October 1945, 3.

32. *Foreign Affairs*, 1946, VIII, 3.

33. GMR 9.6 (June 1962): 18; Bailey, "The Transfer of Power," 53; Hendershot, "Burma Compromise," 134–135; *Times*, 3 June 1946, 4.

34. Hendershot, "Burma Compromise," 135–136; *Foreign Relations, 1946*, VIII, 4.

35. Thompson, "The New Nation of Burma," 81; Bailey, "The Transfer of Power," 53; Hendershot, "Burma Compromise," 136; GMR 9.6 (June 1962): 19; Cecil Hobbs, "Nationalism in British Colonial Burma," *Far Eastern Quarterly* 6.2 (February 1947): 119; *Times*, 2 January 1947, 5; 20 February 1947, 3.

36. Alice Thorner, "White Paper on Burma," *Far Eastern Survey* 14.11 (6 June 1945): 145.

37. Hendershot, "Burma Compromise," 136; *Times*, 2 January 1947, 5.

38. PDC 431, 20 December 1946, 2342; *Times*, 2 January 1947, 5; Bailey, "The Transfer of Power," 53; *Foreign Relations*, 1947, VI, 2; *Conclusions Reached in the Conversations Between His Majesty's Government and the Delegation from the Executive Council of the Governor of Burma* (London: HMSO, 1947): 2.

39. *Foreign Relations, 1947*, VI, 7–8, 13; Bailey, "The Transfer of Power," 53; *Times*, 20 February 1947, 3; PDC, 2 May 1947, 2335.

40. GMR 9.7 (July 1962): 13–14; Vum Ko Hau, "Nu–Attlee Treaty Was Signed," GMR 12 (October 1954): 49–50; *Times*, 9 April 1947, 5; 12 April 1947, 3.

41. *Times*, 28 March 1946, 3; 3 April 1946, 3; 10 February 1947, 4.

42. *Times*, 13 February 1947, 3; PDC, 2 May 1947, 2306–2307; Vum Ko Hau, "Nu–Attlee Treaty Was Signed," 49.

43. PDC 434, 3 March 1947, 18; PRDC, 2 May 1947, 2308; *Times*, 16 August 1947, 3.

44. *Foreign Relations, 1947*, VI, 46; PDC, 2 May 1947, 2308–2309; *Times*, 13 April 1947, 3; Taylor, *The State in Burma*, 243; Cady, *A History of Modern Burma*, 592.

45. *Foreign Relations, 1947*, VI, 44, 47.

46. Thompson, "The New Nation of Burma," 81; *Times*, 23 September 1946, 3; 12 April 1947, 3; *Foreign Relations*, 1947, VI, 3–4, 14.

47. *Times*, 31 October 1947, 3; PDC 443, 5 November 1947, 1848.

48. *Times*, 17 October 1947, 3; 18 October 1947, 3; Foucar, *I Lived in Burma*, 201; Vum Ko Hau, "The July Murders," GMR 1.9 (July 1954): 41; GMR 9.7 (July 1962): 14; GMR 24.10 (1 July 1986): 8–17; GMR 17 (August 1970): 32, 34; *Forward* 6.23 (15 July 1968): 7–8; *Time Magazine* 28 July 1947.

49. *Times*, 18 October 1947, 3; 31 October 1947, 3; Foucar, *I Lived in Burma*, 201–202; GMR 17 (August 1970): 32; *Foreign Relations, 1947*, VI, 38.

50. GMR 10.1 (January 1963): 31–32; *Times*, 26 July 1947, 3; 12 December 1947, 3; PDC 440, 867.

51. *Foreign Relations, 1947*, VI, 44; Vum Ko Hau, "Nu–Attlee Treaty Was Signed," 49–50; *Times*, 25 September 1947, 3; 18 October 1947, 3; Bailey, "The Transfer of Power," 53.

4 THE DEMOCRATIC EXPERIMENT, 1948–1958

1. Thant Myint-U, *The River of Lost Footsteps*, 259.

2. Taylor, *The State in Burma*, 238–239; Martin Smith, *Burma: Insurgency and the Politics of Ethnicity* (London: Zed Books, 1999): 61, 67–68.

3. *Foreign Relations, 1947*, VI, 47; *Times*, 19 November 1947, 3; Taylor, *The State in Burma*, 241; Klaus Fleischmann, *Documents on Communism in Burma 1945–1977* (Hamburg: Institut für Asienkunde, 1989): 69.

4. Thompson, "The New Nation of Burma," 81; *FEER* 5.8 (25 August 1948): 173; *Times*, 25 November 1947, 3; Cady, *A History of Modern Burma*, 584, 588–589.

5. Taylor, *The State in Burma*, 236, 243; Cady, *A History of Modern Burma*, 592.

6. Thaung, *A Journalist, a General and an Army in Burma*, 15.

7. *Times*, 25 April 1961, 13.

8. GMR 5.8 (August 1958): 7, 9; John Hail, "A Blow to the Heartland," *FEER* 108.20 (9 May 1980): 39.

9. *Foreign Relations, 1951*, VI, 281; *IHT*, 15 February 1950.

10. Ba Chan, "A Women's Auxiliary Corps," GMR 1.2 (December 1953): 28; GMR 5.7 (July 1958): 37.

11. Taylor, *The State in Burma*, 268–270; James Dalton, "Babes in the Wood," *FEER* 69.34 (20 August 1970): 31.

12. BWB 5.48 (7 March 1957): 389.

13. Thant Myint-U, *The River of Lost Footsteps*, 275; Daniel Wolfstone, "The Burmese Army Experiment," *FEER* 28.7 (18 February 1960): 352.

14. Brian Crozier, "What Now for the Kuomintang?" *Times*, 10 October 1973, 18.

15. *Foreign Relations, 1952–1954*, XII, 367–376.

16. Ibid., 471–472.

17. Thant Myint-U, *The River of Lost Footsteps*, 269–270.

18. *Times*, 21 May 1947, 3; GMR 9.7 (July 1962): 14.

19. Foucar, *I Lived in Burma*, 204; *Times*, 3 November 1947, 4; PDC 443, 5 November 1947, 1851.

20. *FEER* 6.13 (30 March 1949): 399; *Times*, 24 September 1947, 3; BWB 4.35 (1 December 1955): 276.

21. Thant Myint-U, *The River of Lost Footsteps*, 272–273.

22. U Kyaw Nyein, "Burma's Eight Year Plan," GMR 3.1 (November 1955): 41; *Times*, 5 February 1960, 11; GMR 10.2 (January 1963): 29; *BWB* 4.36 (8 December 1955): 282; 4.37 (15 December 1955): 295.

23. *BWB* 6.9 (13 June 1957): 64.

24. *NBW* 1.2 (7 June 1958): 2.

25. *Foreign Relations*, 1947, VI, 47; Nu, "Consolidation of the AFPFL," 25 May 1948 broadcast, in *Toward Peace & Democracy* (Rangoon: Ministry of Information, 1949): 98–101.

26. Taylor, *The State in Burma*, 245, 247.

27. Ibid., 245, 247.

28. Maung Maung, *The 1988 Uprising in Burma* (New Haven, CT: Yale University Southeast Asia Studies, 1999): 17; *FEER* 20.21 (24 May 1956): 643; *BWB* 5.14 (12 July 1956): 97, 99.

29. *BWB* 5.20 (21 March 1957): 402.

30. *Foreign Relations*, 1947, VI, 47; Smith, *Burma: Insurgency and the Politics of Ethnicity*, 55.

31. Thaung, *A Journalist, a General and an Army in Burma*, 24–25.

32. Nu, "Acts of Lawlessness," 12 March 1948 broadcast and "The Newspapers and the Law," in *Toward Peace & Democracy*, 46–49; GMR 3.8 (June 1956): 40.

33. *BWB* 5.20 (23 August 1956): 145.

34. Michael W. Charney, "Ludu Aung Than: Nu's Burma and the Cold War," in Christopher Goscha and Christian Ostermann (eds.), *Imperial Retreat and the Cold War in South and Southeast Asia (1945–1962)*, forthcoming.

35. E. Michael Mendelson, *Sangha and State in Burma: A Study of Monastic Sectarianism and Leadership* (Ithaca, NY: Cornell University Press, 1975): 263.

36. Smith, *Religion and Politics in Burma*, 117; James Joseph Dalton, "The 1,000-Year Struggle," *FEER* 67.10 (5 March 1970): 19; *Foreign Relations*, 1947, VI, 24, 26.

37. *BWB* 3.26 (29 September 1954): 200; 10.19 (7 September 1961): 148.

38. *BWB* 10.18 (31 August 1961): 137; Smith, *Religion and Politics in Burma*, 117–119, 121, 127.

39. GMR 5.6 (June 1958): 9; *Times*, 5 February 1960, 11.

40. U Sein Win, *The Split Story: An Account of Recent Political Upheaval in Burma* (Rangoon: The Guardian Press, 1959): 79–83; Wolfstone, "The Burmese Army Experiment," 356; Taylor, *The State in Burma*, 248; *NBW* 4.6 (7 February 1959): 190; GMR 5.8 (August 1958): 7, 10; 5.10 (October 1958): 10; 6.3 (March 1959): 6; 7.8 (August 1958): 10; *Times*, 5 February 1960, 11.

5 DRESS REHEARSALS, 1958–1962

1. *NBW* 2.7 (4 October 1958): 214; *Times*, 5 February 1960, 11; *Time Magazine* (6 October 1958).

2. *NBW* 2.8 (11 October 1958): 242.

3. Wolfstone, "The Burmese Army Experiment," 357; GMR 5.12 (December 1958): 10; *NBW* 3.6 (20 December 1958): 165; 4.1 (3 January 1959): 4; 4.7 (14 February 1959): 228.

4. *Times*, 5 February 1960, 11; GMR 6.10 (October 1959): 8; 7.7 (July 1960): 12; *BWB* 8.6 (4 June 1959): 49–50; 8.8 (18 June 1959): 67; 8.14 (30 July 1959): 119.

5. Wolfstone, "The Burmese Army Experiment," 357; GMR 6.5 (May 1959): 6; 6.10 (October 1959): 8; GNR, 21 August 1959; *BWB* 8.6 (4 June 1959): 49; 8.8 (18 June 1959): 67; 8.14 (30 July 1959): 119.

6. Keith Dahlberg, "Remembering the Coup," *Irrawaddy* (July–August 2002); *Myanmar Times* 4.70 (2–8 July 2001); *NBW* 3.4 (6 December 1958): 1001; GMR 6.1 (January 1959): 7; *Who's Who in Burma 1961*, 150.

7. GMR 6.1 (January 1959): 7; 6.5 (May 1959): 6; 6.10 (October 1959): 8; *NBW* 1.6 (20 December 1958): 166; *Times*, 5 February 1960, 11; Albert Ravenholt, "Burma Army Gives Rangoon New Face," *BWB* 8.14 (30 July 1959): 118.

8. Ravenholt, "Burma Army Gives Rangoon New Face," 118; GMR 6.1 (January 1959): 7, 9–11; *NBW* 1.6 (20 December 1958): 166; 4.1 (3 January 1959): 4–5.

9. GMR 6.1 (January 1959): 7, 10; *NBW* 1.6 (20 December 1958): 166; 4.1 (3 January 1959): 4.

10. *NBW* 4.1 (3 January 1959): 4; GMR 6.1 (January 1959): 7; 6.10 (October 1959): 8; Ravenholt, "Burma Army Gives Rangoon New Face," 119; Wolfstone, "The Burmese Army Experiment," 357.

11. GMR 6.1 (January 1959): 10; 6.10 (October 1959): 8; *NBW* 1.6 (20 December 1958): 166; 4.8 (21 February 1959): 263.

12. *Times*, 5 February 1960, 11; GMR 6.1 (January 1959): 7, 9, 10; *BWB* 8.8 (18 June 1959): 66; 8.14 (30 July 1959): 119; *NBW* 3.4 (6 December 1958): 100; 3.5 (13 December 1958): 134.

13. *NBW* 4.1 (3 January 1959): 5; GMR 6.1 (January 1959): 10–12; Wolfstone, "The Burmese Army Experiment," 357–358; *BWB* 8.8 (18 June 1959): 66; *Nation* 21 August 1959.

14. *NBW* 4.8 (21 February 1959): 262; 4.9 (28 February 1959): 294; GMR 6.12 (February 1959): 9; *Times*, 5 February 1960, 11.

15. *Times*, 5 February 1960, 11; *NBW* 4.8 (21 February 1959): 262; GMR 7.2 (February 1960): 15; 7.3 (March 1960): 12; Steinberg, *Burma: A Socialist Nation of Southeast Asia*, 71–72.

16. GMR 7.5 (May 1960): 18; 7.7 (July 1960): 11; 7.8 (August 1960): 10; 8.1 (January 1961): 11; *BWB* 8.50 (7 April 1960): 456; *Times*, 8 February 1960, 9.

17. *BWB* 10.18 (31 August 1961): 144; 10.19 (7 September 1961): 147.

18. Daniel Wolfstone, "The Phongyis and the Soldiers," *FEER* 33.7 (17 August 1961): 322; *FEER* 35.10 (8 March 1962): 539; Steinberg, *Burma: A Socialist Nation of Southeast Asia*, 72; GMR 8.8 (August 1961): 6.

19. Smith, *Religion and Politics in Burma*, 133, 135.

20. *BWB* 8.50 (7 April 1960): 456; 10.18 (31 August 1961): 138; GMR 7.1 (January 1960): 10–12; 7.5 (May 1960): 18–19; *Times*, 5 February 1960, 11.

21. GMR 8.5 (May 1961): 10; 8.10 (October 1961): 11; Wolfstone, "The Phongyis and the Soldiers," 323.

22. GMR 8.3 (March 1961): 6; 8.9 (September 1961): 6; *BWB* 10.18 (31 August 1961): 138.
23. Smith, *Religion and Politics in Burma*, 275; *BWB* 10.18 (31 August 1961): 139, 140, 144; 10.19 (7 September 1961): 149; GMR 8.12 (December 1961): 9.
24. Smith, *Religion and Politics in Burma*, 171, 278–279; GMR 8.12 (December 1961): 6; 9.2 (February 1962): 9.
25. *BWB* 10.14 (3 August 1961): 105; 10.20 (14 September 1961): 160; GMR 9.1 (January 1962): 6, 10; 5.10 (October 1958): 10; 5.12 (December 1958): 10; 7.2 (February 1960): 14; *NBW* 3.6 (20 December 1958): 161; *GNR*, 20 August 1959; *Time Magazine* (15 February 1960).
26. GMR 7.7 (July 1960): 11; 8.1 (January 1961): 11; 8.12 (December 1961): 10–11; Daniel Wolfstone, "Colonels in the Economy," *FEER* 33.7 (17 August 1961): 296; Taylor, *The State in Burma*, 257.
27. GMR 8.12 (December 1961): 11; 9.1 (January 1962): 9; *FEER* 35.10 (8 March 1962): 539; S. C. Banerji, "Nationalising Import Trade," *FEER* 35.10 (8 March 1962): 547–550; *Forward* 1.4 (22 September 1962): 14.

6 THE REVOLUTIONARY COUNCIL

1. James L. Dalton, "One Man's Tears," *FEER* 65.38 (18 September 1969): 733; *BWB* 10.42 (8 March 1962): 386–387, 391; *Times*, 3 March 1962, 8; 5 March 1962, 8.
2. *Times*, 3 March 1962, 8; *BWB* 10.46 (15 March 1962): 395, 398.
3. GMR 9.7 (July 1962): 29–31.
4. Ibid.
5. S. C. Banerji, "The Burmese Way," *FEER* 37.6 (9 August 1962): 248.
6. *Forward* 1.1 (7 August 1962): 6.
7. GMR 9.7 (July 1962): 8; 10.11 (November 1963): 6; 11.3 (March 1964): 8; *Times*, 10 August 1963, 5; 30 March 1964, 11; *Forward* 2.17 (7 April 1964): 2; 3.10 (1 January 1965): 29; James Dalton, "Babes in the Wood," *FEER* 69.34 (20 August 1970): 31.
8. Thaung, *A Journalist, a General and an Army in Burma*, 51; *BWB* 10.52 (12 April 1962): 427.
9. Smith, *Religion and Politics in Burma*, 295; *Forward* 1.4 (22 September 1962): 2.
10. *BWB* 10.47 (22 March 1962): 407; *Times*, 16 March 1962, 9; GMR 9.7 (July 1962): 6.
11. *Forward* 2.5 (7 October 1963): 7.
12. Smith, *Religion and Politics in Burma*, 294; *Forward* 1.16 (22 March 1963): 3; 1.22 (22 June 1963): 6; 2.1 (7 August 1963): 23; 2.11 (7 January 1964): 17; GMR 10.7 (July 1963): 9.
13. GMR 10.5 (May 1963): 9; 11.3 (March 1964): 8; *Times*, 10 August 1963, 5; Bertil Lintner, "Proud Past, Sad Present," *FEER* 127.12 (28 March 1985): 38–39; *Forward* 7.13 (15 February 1969): 6; 7.16 (1 April 1969): 3.

14. *Forward* 1.5 (7 October 1962): 22, 23; GMR 9.12 (December 1962): 9; Thaung, *A Journalist, a General and an Army in Burma*, 57.

15. Lintner, "Proud Past," 38–39; Maung Wun Tha, "Journalists Go to School," *Forward* 7.6 (1 November 1968): 13; *Forward* 6.10 (1 January 1968): 2; GMR 15.8 (August 1968): 4–5.

16. GMR 11.9 (September 1964): 6; 11.10 (October 1964): 6; 12.2 (February 1965): 6; 14.6 (June 1967): 6; *Forward* 3.8 (1 December 1964): 4.

17. *Forward* 5.9 (15 December 1966): 3; 5.10 (1 January 1967): 23–24.

18. *Forward* 1.9 (7 December 1962): 22; 2.11 (7 January 1964): 18; GMR 9.9 (September 1962): 9, 10; 9.12 (December 1962): 7; 11.3 (March 1964): 9.

19. GMR 13.1 (January 1966): 6; *Forward* 1.9 (7 December 1962): 22; 4.7 (15 November 1965): 2–3; 6.23 (15 July 1968): 4; 7.10 (1 January 1969): 2; 7.17 (15 April 1969): 9; 7.24 (1 August 1969): 7.

20. Christina Fink, *Living Silence: Burma Under Military Rule* (Bangkok: White Lotus, 2001): 31; *Times*, 12 May 1962, 6; 9 July 1962, 8.

21. RHS, 23, 25, 26 July 1988, BBCSWB.

22. Jon Wiant, "Tradition in the Service of Revolution: The Political Symbolism of the Taw-hlan-ye-khit," in F. K. Lehman (ed.), *Military Rule in Burma Since 1962: Kaleidoscope of Views* (Singapore: Maruzen Asia, 1991): 63.

23. Smith, *Religion and Politics in Burma*, 283–286; James Joseph Dalton, "The 1,000-Year Struggle," 19; *BWB* 10.46 (15 March 1962): 395, 398; GMR 9.7 (July 1962): 6.

24. Smith, *Religion and Politics in Burma*, 301–302; *Forward* 3.3 (15 September 1964): 2–3; Dalton, "The 1,000-Year Struggle," 19; John Ashdown, "Burma's Political Puzzle," *FEER* 44.12 (17 September 1964): 516.

25. *Asian Recorder* 10.38 (16–22 September 1964): 6039; GMR 11.10 (October 1964): 7; 12.2 (February 1965): 6; *Forward* 3.3 (15 September 1964): 3; P. H. M. Jones, "Burmese Deadlock," *FEER* 47.12 (25 March 1965): 561; Smith, *Religion and Politics in Burma*, 303–304; Dalton, "The 1,000-Year Struggle," 19–20.

26. *Forward* 3.3 (15 September 1964): 2; 3.12 (1 February 1965): 2; Smith, *Religion and Politics in Burma*, 305; Dalton, "The 1,000-Year Struggle," 45; Sterling Seagrave, "The Minorities Unite," *FEER* 70.45 (7 November 1970): 39; GMR 12.4 (April 1965): 4; Wiant, "Tradition in the Service of Revolution," 63.

27. Seagrave, "The Minorities Unite," 39; Dalton, "The 1,000-Year Struggle," 20; Jones, "Burmese Deadlock," 561; GMR 12.5 (May 1965): 6; *Forward* 3.19 (15 May 1965): 2; *Time Magazine* 3 June 1966.

28. Smith, *Religion and Politics in Burma*, 306.

29. *FEER* 57.5 (3 August 1967): 227; Maung Maung, *Burma and General Ne Win* (London: Asia Publishing House, 1969) 149; *Times*, 16 February 1963, 6.

30. S. C. Banerji, "Industrial Plans," *FEER* 36.4 (26 April 1962): 74; *Forward* 1.1 (7 August 1962): 3–4, 15–17; 1.2 (22 August 1962): 3–4; 1.3 (7 September 1962): 3; 1.5 (7 October 1962): 9, 11; GMR 9.10 (October 1962): 9.

31. Maung Maung, *Burma and General Ne Win*, 145, 149, 155, 166, 255, 260; John F. Cady, *The United States and Burma* (Cambridge, MA: Harvard University Press): 239; Jones, "Burmese Deadlock," 561.

32. RHS, 22 April 1990, BBCSWB.

33. *Forward* 1.1 (7 August 1962): 3–4; 1.2 (22 August 1962): 4; 1.3 (7 September 1962): 2; GMR 9.8 (August 1962): 8; 9.10 (October 1962): 10.

34. *The System of Correlation of Man and His Environment* (Rangoon: Union of Burma, 1963).

35. *Times*, 11 February 1963, 9; GMR 11.6 (June 1964): 8; *FEER* 48.11 (10 June 1965): 495; 57.5 (3 August 1967): 227; Jones, "Burmese Deadlock," 561; *Forward* 3.22 (1 July 1969): 22.

36. Jones, "Burmese Deadlock," 561; *Times*, 16 February 1963, 6; 16 March 1963, 9; Kennedy Library, National Security Files, Countries Series, India, "Krishna-machari Visit." *Foreign Relations* 1961–1963, XIX, 601; *Forward* 3.10 (1 January 1965): 27.

37. *FEER* 81.27 (9 July 1973): 18; Jones, "Burmese Deadlock," 561; *Forward* 3.18 (1 May 1965): 2; 7.10 (1 January 1969): 2; 10.14 (1 March 1972): 7; GMR 13.2 (February 1966): 4; *Times*, 16 February 1963, 6; 3 March 1965, 10.

38. GMR 12.11 (November 1965): 8; *FEER* 50.5 (4 November 1965): 194; *Time Magazine* 24 December 1966.

39. *Forward* 2.24 (1 August 1964): 22; 8.24 (1 August 1970): 2; 8.10 (1 January 1979): 2; *Times*, 3 March 1966, 11; *FEER* 81.27 (9 July 1973): 18; "A Political Alert," *FEER* 63.3 (16 January 1969): 106; Than Win Naing, "Spearheading Agricultural Mechanization," *Forward* 8.19 (15 May 1970): 15; Maung Yin New, "Of Growing More Rice," *Forward* 8.10 (1 January 1970): 19–21.

40. *Times*, 2 April 1963, 9; 28 June 1963, 11; 8 October 1963, 13; 25 November 1963, 8.

41. Robert A. Holmes, "Burmese Domestic Policy: The Politics of Burmaniza-tion," *Asian Survey* 7.3 (March 1967): 193–194, 196; Taylor, *The State in Burma*, 335; Frank N. Trager, "Burma: 1967 – A Better Ending Than a Beginning," *Asian Survey* 8.2 (February 1968): 112–113; *Times*, 28 June 1963, 11; 21 August 1963, 6; 8 October 1963, 13.

42. Smith, *Burma: Insurgency and the Politics of Ethnicity*, 231–234; VOPB, 15 June 1986, BBCSWB; Bertil Lintner, *The Rise and Fall of the Communist Party of Burma (CPB)* (Ithaca, NY: Cornell University Press Southeast Asia Program, 1990): 23; S. C. Banerji, "Buddha Awakes," *FEER* 69.35 (27 August 1970): 15; Silverstein, "Minority Problems Since 1962," 57; *FEER* 57.5 (3 August 1967): 227; *Financial Times*, 17 February 1987, 3; *Times*, 19 January 1968, 3; Frank N. Trager, "Burma: 1968 – A New Beginning?" *Asian Survey* 9.2 (February 1969): 106.

43. *FEER* 57.5 (3 August 1967): 227.

44. Neil Kelly, "Thais Put Price on Head of Drugs Chief," *Times*, 30 June 1981, 5.

45. Kelly, "Thais Put Price on Head of Drugs Chief," 5; Melinda Yu, "Warlords, Rebels, and Smugglers," *FEER* 105.35 (31 August 1979): 13; *FEER* 81.27 (9 July 1973): 19; Smith, *Burma: Insurgency and the Politics of Ethnicity*, 297.

46. Kelly, "Thais Put Price on Head of Drugs Chief," 5; Smith, *Burma: Insurgency and the Politics of Ethnicity*, 95–96, 221, 335.
47. *Times*, 23 February 1974, 6; Silverstein, "Minority Problems in Burma Since 1962," 58; Henry Kamm, "Burmese Fighting Rebels on Four Fronts," *Times*, 15 August 1980, 5.
48. *Times*, 28 October 1966, 14; *FEER* 57.5 (3 August 1967): 227; 63.3 (16 January 1969): 105; S. C. Banerji, "The Nu Burmese Way," *FEER* 64.26 (26 June 1969): 698; *FEER* 65.29 (17 July 1969): 151; Richard Harris, "U Nu Says Burmese Regime Must Go," *Times*, 30 August 1969, 4.
49. *FEER* 64.20 (15 May 1969): 374; *Times*, 28 April 1971, 9; Seagrave, "The Minorities Unite," 38.
50. *Times*, 28 April 1971, 9; Seagrave, "The Minorities Unite," 38–39.
51. *Forward* 9.7 (15 November 1970): 3.
52. Seagrave, "The Minorities Unite," 37; M. C. Tun, "Trouble at Home," *FEER* 78.46 (11 November 1972): 17; *FEER* 81.27 (9 July 1973): 18.

7 THE BSPP YEARS

1. *Times*, 3 March 1966, 11; *Forward* 8.12 (1 February 1970): 2; GMR 17.2 (February 1970): 12.
2. David I. Steinberg, *Burma: The State of Myanmar* (Washington, D.C.: Georgetown University Press, 2001): 100.
3. Maung Lu Law, "A Historic Decade," GMR 19.5 (May 1972): 42; GMR 17.2 (February 1970): 12; *Forward* 8.10 (1 January 1979): 2; 8.12 (1 February 1970): 2; 10.14 (1 March 1972): 6.
4. Richard Harris, "Burma on a Slow Road to Progress," *Times*, 30 April 1974, 16; *Times*, 30 June 1971, 8; M. C. Tun, "Change of Status," *FEER* 81.36 (10 September 1973): 24–25.
5. Jon A. Wiant, "Burma: Loosening Up on the Tiger's Tail," *Asian Survey* 13.2 (February 1973): 180; Harris, "Burma on a Slow Road to Progress," 16; John McBeth and M. C. Tun, "Goodbye to the Good Life," *FEER* 120.22 (2 June 1983): 15.
6. Harris, "Burma on a Slow Road to Progress," 16; *Times*, 24 October 1973, 6; 24 December 1973, 4; *Forward* 10.19 (15 May 1972): 7–10.
7. GMR 19.4 (April 1972): 4–5; *PWG* 26.9 (September 1973): 2.
8. *PWG* 26.9 (September 1973): 2.
9. *Times*, 24 October 1973, 6; 24 December 1973, 4; 4 March 1974, 7.
10. *FEER* 57.5 (3 August 1967): 227; 63.3 (16 January 1969): 105; Cady, *United States and Burma*, 265, 272.
11. *Forward* 11.11 (5 January 1971): 1; 11.12 (1 February 1973): 6; M. C. Tun, "Out of the Frying Pan," *FEER* 79.3 (22 January 1973).
12. S. C. Banerji, "Lack of Cooperation," *FEER* 83.6 (11 February 1974): 40; M. C. Tun, "Turning Against the Socialist Way," *FEER* 85.26 (1 July 1974): 30; M. C. Tun, "Feeding Unrest in Burma," *FEER* 85.31 (9 August 1974): 36; *Times*, 21 December 1974, 4.

13. Tun, "Turning Against the Socialist Way," 30; Denzil Peiris, "Socialism Without Commitment," *FEER* 85.36 (13 September 1974): 27–28; *Times*, 10 June 1974, 8.
14. *Times*, 1 July 1974, 5; *Forward* 12.11 (1 August 1974): 4–6; *FEER* 85.36 (13 September 1974): 47.
15. *Times*, 9 December 1974, 7; 12 December 1974, 6; 13 December 1974, 10; 4 January 1975, 4; 14 May 1975, 5.
16. M. C. Tun, "Five Fiery Days," *FEER* 88.26 (27 June 1975): 20; *Forward* 13.10 (1 July 1975): 3; *Times*, 25 March 1976, 8; 2 September 1976, 5.
17. *Times*, 2 December 1981, 8; Wiant, "Tradition in the Service of Revolution," 64.
18. *Times*, 21 July 1976, 6; Rodney Tasker, "The Power Game," *FEER* (7 July 1983): 31; M. C. Tun, "Purge Points to a Power Struggle," *FEER* 98.51 (23 December 1977): 24–25.
19. *Times*, 22 February 1977, 7; 28 February 1977, 6; 30 March 1977, 9; Tasker, "The Power Game," 31; Tun, "Purge Points to a Power Struggle," 24.
20. *Times*, 16 November 1977, 13; 18 January 1978, 7; 4 March 1978, 4; 10 November 1981, 7.
21. *Times*, 29 June 1983, 5; Neil Kelly, "London Spree Leads to Burma Purge," *Times*, 19 July 1983, 7; Neil Kelly, "Burmese Tipped to Succeed Ne Win is Jailed for Life," *Times*, 15 November 1983, 5.
22. *Times*, 10 October 1983, 1; 11 October 1983, 5; 12 October 1983, 15; Kelly, "Burmese Tipped to Succeed Ne Win is Jailed for Life," 5; Neil Kelly, "Burma Cuts Links With N. Korea," *Times*, 5 November 1983, 5.
23. *Times*, 3 December 1981, 9; RHS, 8 October 1982, BBCSWB.
24. RHS, 8 October 1982, BBCSWB.
25. Bertil Lintner, "Loss and Exile," FEER 158.9 (2 March 1995): 23; Smith, *Burma: Insurgency and the Politics of Ethnicity*, 280, 284, 298–299; *Times*, 13 February 1964, 13; 14 March 1964, 7.
26. *Nation* (Bangkok), 14 July 1986, BBCSWB; *Times*, 2 June 1976, 5; Paisal Sricharatchanya, "Choosing Losing Sides," *FEER* 134.50 (11 December 1986): 33; Smith, *Burma: Insurgency and the Politics of Ethnicity*, 280.
27. Martin Smith, "Karen War Strikes an Impasse," GUK, 18 June 1986; Neil Kelly, "Key Rebel Base Falls to Burma," *Times*, 9 May 1986.
28. Kelly, "Thais Put Price on Head of Drugs Chief," 5; Neil Kelly, "Drive Against Narcotics," *Times*, 13 August 1981, 5; Neil Kelly, "Thais Tame Warlord's Town," *Times*, 8 February 1982, 6; Neil Kelly, "Warlord's Heroin Base Seized," *Times*, 24 August 1983, 4; *Times*, 6 August 1984, 5; Smith, *Burma: Insurgency and the Politics of Ethnicity*, 315, 343.
29. *Times*, 13 September 1976, 15; 17 March 1977, 7; 21 October 1980, 5; *Forward* 26.3 (1 December 1987): 1; 25.11 (1 August 1987): 1.
30. *FEER* 131.1 (2 January 1986): 9; Paisal Sricharatchanya, "Isolation Patient," *FEER* 132.16 (17 April 1986): 114, 115, 118; *Times*, 7 November 1985, 8; Alan Hamilton, "When Money Turns into Confetti," *Times*, 19 November 1985, 36.

31. Anatol Lieven, "Economic Ills Fuel Riots," *Times*, 25 June 1988; Chit Tun, "Burma Property Curbs," *FT*, 19 March 1987, 4; RHS, 1 September 1987, BBCSWB.

32. RHS, 5 September 1987, 9 October 1987, 19 October 1987, 28 October 1987, 2 February 1988, BBCSWB; Kuala Lumpur Radio, 6 September 1987, BBC-SWB; Lieven, "Economic Ills Fuel Riots."

33. *Xinhua* (English), 14 March 1988, BBCSWB.

34. RHS, 27 March 1988, 20 April 1988, 24 May 1988, 3 July 1988, BBCSWB; Dennis Barker, "Top Gun Fuels Burma Riots," GUK, 12 August 1988, 2.

8 TOWARD DEMOCRACY, 1988–1990

1. Maung Maung, *The 1988 Uprising in Burma*, 1.

2. Bertil Lintner, *Outrage: Burma's Struggle for Democracy* (London: White Lotus, 1990): 1–7; RHS, 14, 15, 17 March 1988, BBCSWB; Chit Tun, "Burmese Shortages Spark Surge of Discontent," *FT*, 14 July 1988, 3.

3. *Times*, 20 July 1988; Chit Tun, "Burmese Minister Quits Over Police Van Deaths," *FT*, 21 July 1988, 4; RHS, 19 March 1988, BBCSWB; Chit Tun, "Burmese Shortages Spark Surge of Discontent," 3.

4. Lintner, *Outrage*, 75–77; Agence France-Presse, 16 June 1988, BBCSWB; *Xinhua* (English), 16 June and 18 June 1988, BBCSWB; Nick Cumming-Bruce, "Burma Puts City Under Martial Law," GUK, 23 July 1988; Chit Tun, "Burmese Shortages Spark Surge of Discontent," *FT*, 14 July 1988, 3; RHS, 20, 21 and 22 June 1988, BBCSWB; *FT*, 24 June 1988, 1.

5. Chit Tun, "Burmese Shortages Spark Surge of Discontent," 3; Anatol Lieven, "Economic Ills Fuel Riots," *Times*, 25 June 1988.

6. RHS, 7, 9, 13, 22, 23, 24 July 1988, BBCSWB; John Miller, "Ne Win Offers to Step Down," *Times*, 24 July 1988.

7. RHS, 24 July 1988, BBCSWB.

8. RHS, 23 July 1988, BBCSWB; Miller, "Ne Win Offers to Step Down."

9. RHS, 23, 25, 26 July 1988, BBCSWB.

10. RHS, 26 July 1988, BBCSWB; Barker, "Top Gun Fuels Burma Riots"; *Times*, 28 July 1988.

11. RHS, 1, 3 August 1988, BBCSWB; Neil Kelly and Anatol Lieven, "Martial Law Declared," *Times*, 4 August 1988; Nick Cumming-Bruce, "Burma's New Leader Imposes Martial Law," *GUK*, 4 August 1988.

12. RHS, 23, 25 July 1988, BBCSWB.

13. Neil Kelly, "Warning Shots Fired," *Times*, 5 August 1988; Various, 8 August 1988, BBCSWB; Neil Kelly, "Burma Rioters Killed," *Times*, 8 August 1988; Various, 9 August 1988, BBCSWB; RHS, 8, 9 August 1988, BBCSWB; Nicholas Cumming-Bruce, "At Least 36 Die," GUK, 10 August 1988.

14. Richard Gourlay, "Burmese Protestors Open Fire on Troops," *FT*, 11 August 1988; RHS, 7, 9, 10, 12, 13 August 1988, BBCSWB; Neil Kelly, "1,000 Die," *Times*, 12 August 1988; Richard Gourlay, "Troops Killed 3,000 in Rangoon Rioting," *FT*, 18 August 1988.

15. RHS, 19 August 1988, BBCSWB.

16. Neil Kelly, "Dr. Maung Maung Elected President of Burma," *Times*, 20 August 1988; Richard Gourlay, "Dismay Greets General Ne Win Surrogate," *FT*, 20 August 1988, 3; RHS, 19 August 1988, 22 August 1988, BBCSWB.

17. RHS, 23, 24 August 1988, BBCSWB; Richard Gourlay, "Burmese Reject Slow Change," *FT*, 26 August 1988, 16.

18. Roger Matthews, "The Monday Interview: An Inheritance by Election," *FT*, 24 October 1988; Nicholas Cumming-Bruce, "Burmese Hero's Daughter Puts Democracy Plan," *GUK*, 18 August 1988; Karan Thapar, "People's Heroine Spells Out Objectives," *Times*, 29 August 1988.

19. Nicholas Cumming-Bruce, "Burma Party Faces Strike Ultimatum," *GUK*, 6 September 1988; RHS, 7, 8 September 1988, BBCSWB; Neil Kelly, "Vigilantes Lynch Rangoon Looters; Savage Lawlessness Could Help Rangoon Regime," *Times*, 7 September 1988; Richard Gourlay, "Burma in Confusion as Neither Side Ready to Yield," *FT*, 8 September 1988, 3.

20. RHS, 10, 11 September 1988, BBCSWB.

21. RHS, 1, 10 September 1988, BBCSWB.

22. RHS, 10 September 1988, BBCSWB.

23. RHS, 10 September 1988, BBCSWB.

24. Maung Maung, *The 1988 Uprising in Burma*, 117.

25. RHS, 10 September 1988, BBCSWB.

26. *Times*, 30 July 1980, 7.

27. RHS, 17 November, 29 December 1989, BBCSWB; Martin Smith, "Move to Democracy in Burma 'Unstoppable'," *GUK*, 5 September 1988; the quote from Nu is take from Anatol Lieven, "Opposition in Burma Sets Up 'Government'," *Times*, 10 September 1988; Jon Swain, "Burmese Students Win Their Fight for a General Election," *Times*, 11 September 1988.

28. RHS, 13 September 1988, BBCSWB; Nick Cumming-Bruce, "Burma Opposition Rejects Regime Offer of Elections," *GUK*, 13 September 1988; Neil Kelly, "Opposition Unmoved by Burmese Election Offer," *Times*, 12 September 1988.

29. RHS, 16 September 1988, BBCSWB.

30. Lintner, *Outrage*, 128; *Times*, 18 September 1988.

31. *Times*, 10 September 1988; 18 September 1988.

32. Mya Maung, "The Burma Road From the Union of Burma to Myanmar," *Asian Survey* 30.6 (June 1990): 617; RHS, 18, 19 September 1988, BBCSWB.

33. RHS, 18, 19, 20, 21 September 1988, BBCSWB.

34. RHS, 26 September 1988, BBCSWB.

35. These four tasks are taken verbatim from Saw Maung's speech to the Institute for the Development of National Groups recorded in RHS, 1 March 1989, BBCSWB; see also Mya Maung, "The Burma Road From the Union of Burma to Myanmar," 618.

36. Sein Win, "Troops Shoot 12 in Rangoon," *Independent*, 5 October 1988; RHS, 19 October, 9, 11 November 1988, BBCSWB; Mya Maung, "The Burma Road From the Union of Burma to Myanmar," 617.

37. RHS, 11 November 1988, BBCSWB.

38. RHS, 27 September, 20 October 1988, 3, 14, 16 November, 7 December 1988, 18, 19 January 1989, 23 February 1989, BBCSWB; Neil Kelly, "Intelligence Chief Emerging as Burma's Leader," *Times*, 23 January 1989; Mya Maung, "The Burma Road From the Union of Burma to Myanmar," 617–618.

39. AFP, 3 October 1988, BBCSWB; RHS, 3 November 1988, BBCSWB; Neil Kelly, "Rebels Train Students for a Burma Offensive," *Times*, 1 October 1988; *Bangkok Post*, 10 October 1988; 6 November 1988.

40. RHS, 17, 24 October 1988, 3 February 1989, BBCSWB; Terry McCarthy, "Rangoon Pressed on Fate of Students," *Independent*, 7 January 1989.

41. RHS, 20 January 1989, BBCSWB.

42. RHS, 16, 17 February, 7 November 1989, BBCSWB; GUK, 2 March 1989.

43. RHS, 20 January, 9 February, 1 March 1989, BBCSWB.

44. RHS, 26 September, 11, 14 October 1988, BBCSWB; Donald M. Seekins, *Historical Dictionary of Burma (Myanmar)* (Oxford: The Scarecrow Press, 2006): 128, 326.

45. Bertil Lintner, *Burma in Revolt: Opium and Insurgency since 1948* (Boulder, CO: Westview Press, 1994): 283.

46. *Xinhua*, 27 September 1988 and RHS, 12, 28 September 1988, BBCSWB; Roger Matthews, "Opposition in Burma Set up Political Party," *FT*, 28 September 1988; *Times*, 10 September 1988.

47. RHS, 10 August, 16 December 1989, BBCSWB; Japan Broadcasting Corporation (NHK), 1 September 1988, BBCSWB; *Loktha Pyithu Nezin*, 16 March 1989, BBCSWB.

48. GUK, 25 January 1989; 2 March 1989; Terry McCarthy, "Burmese Dissident Cheats Death," *Independent*, 13 April 1989; Terry McCarthy, "Aung San Suu Kyi Appeals to Burmese Army," *Independent*, 19 April 1989.

49. Jon Swain, "General Jailed," *Times*, 24 December 1989; RHS, 21 July, 5, 18 August 1989, BBCSWB; *NYT*, 13 August 1989; *Independent*, 29 July 1989; Martin Smith, "Suu Kyi Ends Protest Fast," *GUK*, 15 August 1989.

50. RHS, 11 January, 18 July 1989, BBCSWB.

51. RHS, 18 August, 16 November 1989, BBCSWB; *FT*, 9 January 1990; Chit Tun, "Burma's Suu Kyi Wins Poll Ruling," *FT*, 16 January 1990; Terry McCarthy, "Rangoon Bars Opposition Leader," *Independent*, 30 January 1990.

52. Chit Tun, "Burma Outlaws Privileges for Ousted Military Men," *FT*, 11 October 1989; RHS, 26 May 1990, BBCSWB; *NYT*, 10 May 1990.

53. Khin Kyaw Han, "1990 Multi-Party Democracy General Elections"; Robin Pauley, "Burma's Army Leaders Seek to Keep Election Victor from Power," *FT*, 16 June 1990; *Independent*, 25 May 1990; AFP, 16 May 1990, BBCSWB; RHS, 30 May 1990, BBCSWB.

9 PERPETUAL DELAY, 1990 TO THE PRESENT

1. RHS, 19 October 1988, BBCSWB.

2. *Times*, 3 June 1989; RHS, 26 May, 18 June 1989, BBCSWB.

3. RHS, 18 June 1989, BBCSWB.
4. RHS, 29 April, 30 May, 18 June 1990, BBCSWB.
5. Roger Matthews, "Burma's Rulers Show Their Hand," *FT*, 21 June 1990; RHS, 8, 10 August 1990, BBCSWB; *NYT*, 9 August 1990.
6. Matthews, "Burma's Rulers Show Their Hand"; RHS, 13 July, 27 July 1990, BBCSWB; *Independent*, 28 July 1990.
7. RHS, 13 July 1990, 27 August 1990, BBCSWB.
8. David I. Steinberg, "Myanmar in 1992: Plus Ça Change . . . ?," *Asian Survey* 33.2 (1993): 178–179; VOM, 2, 6, 8, and 25 January, 2 and 13 February 1992, BBCSWB.
9. Steinberg, "Myanmar in 1992," 178–179.
10. VOM, 27 January 1992, BBCSWB.
11. VOM, 28 January 1992, BBCSWB.
12. Bertil Lintner and Rodney Tasker, "General Malaise," *FEER* 155.6 (13 February 1992): 15; Steinberg, "Myanmar in 1992," 176; Jon Swain, "General Jailed," *Times*, 24 December 1989; Abby Tan, "Lecturers Among Thousands Sacked," *Times*, 10 April 1992.
13. Lintner and Tasker, "General Malaise," 15.
14. RHS, 23 March 1992, BBCSWB; Steinberg, "Myanmar in 1992," 176; Bertil Lintner, "Army Divisions," FEER (23 April 1992): 16; Steinberg, "Myanmar in 1992," 176; Bertil Lintner, "Flanking Movement," FEER 155.41 (15 October 1992): 20.
15. Steinberg, "Myanmar in 1992," 176–177.
16. *VOM*, 27 January 1992, BBCSWB; Abby Tan, "Lecturers Among Thousands Sacked"; Steinberg, "Myanmar in 1992," 176–177.
17. Bertil Lintner, "The Secret Mover," FEER 155.18 (7 May 1992): 20; Steinberg, "Myanmar in 1992," 176–178.
18. Mary P. Callahan, *Making Enemies: War and State Building in Burma* (Singapore: Singapore University Press, 2004): 217; Mary P. Callahan, "Cracks in the Edifice? Military–Society Relations in Burma Since 1988," in Robert H. Taylor (ed.), *Burma: Political Economy Under Military Rule* (London: Hurst & Co., 2001): 39; GUK, 22 November 2001.
19. BBCN, 10 March 2002; 12 March 2002; 15 September 2002; GUK, 27 September 2002.
20. Larry Jagan, "Behind Burma's Non-Coup," BBCN, 18 March 2002; DVB, 22 September 2002.
21. Jonathan Head, "Burma Promises Free Elections," BBCN, 30 August 2003; Larry Jagan, "Cabinet Reshuffle in Burma," BBCN, 25 August 2003; BBCN, 15 August 2003.
22. DVB, 25 October 2004; Tony Cheng, "Burma Crackdown on Luxury Cars," BBCN, 11 November 2004.
23. *NYT*, 20 October 2004; BBCN, 22 October 2004; DVB, 21 October 2004; 23 October 2004; 24 October 2004; 26 October 2004; 5 November 2004; 8 November 2004; 11 November 2004.

24. BBCN, 18 November 2004; DVB, 23 October 2004; 9 February 2005; 10 February 2005; 11 February 2005; 12 July 2005; 22 July 2005.

25. Robin Pauley, "US Senate Takes Lead," *FT*, 25 May 1990, 6; Ian Rodger, "Japan Recognizes Burmese Regime," *FT*, 18 February 1989, 3; *Times*, 5 November 1988; Martin Smith, "Bonn Ties Burma Aid to Reform," GUK, 2 November 1988.

26. RHS, 31 October, 30 November 1988, BBCSWB.

27. Roger Matthews, "Burmese Regime to Start Opening Schools," *FT*, 10 May 1989, 4; Chit Tun, "US Companies in Burma Deals," *FT*, 27 September 1989, 7; Pauley, "US Senate Takes Lead," 6; Ian Rodger, "Japan Recognizes Burmese Regime," *FT*, 18 February 1989, 3; *NYT*, 2 April 1996; 26 April 1996; 11 July 1996; *IHT*, 16 July 1996.

28. Terry McCarthy, "Aung San Appeals to Burmese Army," *Independent*, 19 April 1989, 12; *Independent*, 2 June 1989; *NYT*, 2 April 1995; 26 April 1996; 11 July 1996; Michael Richardson, "Is it Possible to Pressure Burma?," *IHT*, 16 July 1996.

29. Michael Richardson, "ASEAN Weighs Moves Against Abuses in Burma," *IHT*, 31 March 1992; S. Kamaluddin, "The Arakan Exodus," *FEER* 155.12 (26 March 1992): 25.

30. Rodney Tasker, "Drive Against Karen Rebels," *FEER* 155.13 (2 April 1992): 11.

31. Richardson, "ASEAN Weighs Moves Against Abuses in Burma"; Michael Vatikiotis and Paul Handley, "Anxious Neighbors," *FEER* 155.12 (26 March 1992): 27–28.

32. Michael Richardson, "A Green Light for Burma to Join ASEAN's Ranks," *IHT*, 25 January 1997; Brian Knowlton, "Albright says Regime Continues Repression," *IHT*, 23 April 1997; Executive Order 13047 of May 20, 1997, *Federal Register* 62.99 (22 May 1997); *NYT*, 23 April 1997.

33. BBCN, 29 July 2003; Larry Jagan, "US Sanctions hit Burma Hard," BBCN, 3 October 2003; *Irrawaddy*, 2 August 1006.

34. Larry Jagan, "Indian and Burmese Forces Bond Afresh," BBCN, 7 December 2001.

35. BBCN, 11 December 2001; *Irrawaddy*, 4 August 2006.

36. BBCN, 10 February 2001; 11 December 2001; 21 January 2002; 16 May 2002; Larry Jagan, "Burma Announces Nuclear Plans," BBCN, 11 January 2002.

37. Josef Silverstein, "For Burma's Minorities, a Reckoning," *IHT*, 25 December 1993; Smith, *Burma: Insurgency and the Politics of Ethnicity*, 440.

38. *NYT*, 28 January 1995; *The Independent*, 30 January 1995; Bertil Lintner, "Loss and Exile," *FEER* 158.9 (2 March 1995): 23.

39. *NYT*, 15 July 1994; 5 March 1996; *The Independent*, 25 August 1995; Bertil Lintner, "The Noose Tightens," *FEER* 158.42 (19 October 1995): 30; Bertil Lintner, "Dangerous Play," *FEER* 158.10 (9 March 1995): 26; *NYT*, 5 March 1996; Smith, *Burma: Insurgency and the Politics of Ethnicity*, 440, 447. Additional helpful comments were provided by one of the anonymous referees.

40. Silverstein, "Minority Problems in Burma Since 1962," 51; Callahan, *Making Enemies*, 224–225.
41. Larry Jagan, "Burma's Military: Purges and Coups Prevent Progress Toward Democracy," in Trevor Wilson (ed.), *Myanmar's Long Road to National Reconciliation* (Singapore: ISEAS, 2006): 35.
42. DVB, 1 February 2002; 3 July 2003; Steinberg, *Burma: The State of Myanmar*, 110.
43. Steinberg, *Burma: The State of Myanmar*, 110; DVB, 3 July 2003.
44. DVB, 20 April 2005; 24 May 2005; 17 October 2005; 27 October 2005; 4 November 2005.
45. Aung Lwin Oo, "Report Spotlights USDA's Political Ambitions," *Irrawaddy*, 30 May 2006.
46. Myanmar State Television, 10 November 2005, BBCSWB.
47. *NYT*, 21 March 1990; Roger Matthews, "Burmese Announce Plans for a Super City," *FT*, 25 April 1990; RHS, 23 October 1988, 11 January 1989, 29 April 1990, BBCSWB.
48. RHS, 2 April 1990, BBCSWB; Matthews, "Burmese Announce Plans for a Super City"; Donald M. Seekins, *Burma and Japan Since 1940: From "Co-Prosperity" to "Quiet Dialogue"* (Copenhagen: NIAS, 2007): 117.
49. DVB, 15 June 2005; BBCN, 6 November 2005.
50. BBCN, 17 February 2005; 6 November 2005; 7 November 2005; DVB, 6 November 2005; 7 November 2005; Jan McGirk, "Burma's Rulers Take the Road to Mandalay," *The Independent*, 8 November 2005.
51. Seth Mydans, "Myanmar Constitution Guidelines Ensure Military Power," *NYT*, 4 September 2007; *Xinhua News Service* (English), 3 December 2007; Katerina Ossenova, "Myanmar Constitution to be drafted solely by government-appointed panel," *Jurist*, 3 December 2007.
52. Jonathan Head, "The Hardship that Sparked Burma's Unrest," *BBCN*, 2 October 2007.
53. Callahan, "Cracks in the Edifice?" 47.
54. Seth Mydans, "What Makes a Monk Mad," *NYT*, 30 September 2007; Seth Mydans, "Myanmar Monks' Protest Contained by Junta's Forces," *NYT*, 28 September 2007; "Myanmar Quashes Fuel Ration Cut Rumors," GUK, 1 January 2008; "Timeline – A Timeline Charting Myanmar's Fuel Protests," *Reuters*, 31 August 2007; Head, "The Hardship that Sparked Burma's Unrest."
55. Patrick Pranke, "Religion and Politics in Burma: The Use of Buddhist Symbolism in the Burmese Democracy Movement," Center for Asian Democracy Speaker Series, University of Louisville, 15 November 2007; Mydans, "What Makes a Monk Mad."
56. Michael W. Charney, "Burma: The History Behind the Protests," *New Statesman* (online), 26 September 2007.
57. Pranke, "Religion and Politics in Burma"; Mydans, "Myanmar Monks' Protest Contained by Junta's Forces"; Seth Mydans, "Myanmar Raids Monasteries Before Dawn," NYT, 27 September 2007.

58. Michael W. Charney, "Buddha's Irresistible Maroon Army," *Times*, 14 December 2007.
59. Pranke, "Religion and Politics in Burma"; Chris McGreal, "Spies, Suspicion and Empty Monasteries – Burma Today," GUK, 15 December 2007; Aung Hla Tun, "Myanmar Monks March Again, U.N. Envoy Due Back," *Reuters*, 31 October 2007; Personal communications from informants living in Burma who must remain anonymous.
60. Charney, "Burma: The History Behind the Protests"; "The Saffron Revolution," *The Economist*, 27 September 2007.

CONCLUSION

1. Tin Maung Maung Than, "The Essential Tension: Democratization and the Unitary State in Myanmar (Burma)," *South East Asia Research* 12.2 (July 2004): 188–189.
2. Despite the arbitrary nature of the division of highland Burma into "states" as opposed to lowland "divisions," they nonetheless contributed to the notion of these areas as "nation-states." Rachel M. Safman, "Minorities and State-building in Mainland Southeast Asia," in N. Ganesan and Kyaw Yin Hlaing (eds.), *Myanmar: State, Society and Ethnicity* (Singapore: ISEAS, 2007): 55.
3. Seekins, *Burma and Japan Since 1940: From "Co-Prosperity" to "Quiet Dialogue"* (Copenhagen: NIAS, 2007): 25.
4. Kyaw Yin Hlaing, "Reconsidering the Failure of the Burma Socialist Program Party Government to Eradicate Internal Economic Impediments," *South East Asia Research* 11.1 (March 2003): 5–58.

Readings

Although Burma is often referred to as being understudied, there is actually a substantial body of literature available for the interested reader. Good general works that cover the breadth of modern Burmese history are the old standard John F. Cady, *A History of Modern Burma* (Ithaca, NY: Cornell University Press, 1958) and the more recent Thant Myint-U, *The River of Lost Footsteps: Histories of Burma* (New York: Farrar, Straus and Giroux, 2006). The standard study of the Burmese state throughout most of the period examined in the present volume remains Robert H. Taylor, *The State in Burma* (Honolulu, HI: University of Hawaii Press, 1987). For the ethnic insurgencies, the two main works are Martin Smith, *Burma: Insurgency and the Politics of Ethnicity*, 2nd edition (London: Zed Books, 1999) and Bertil Lintner, *Burma in Revolt: Opium and Insurgency since 1948* (Boulder, CO: Westview Press, 1994). A good reference work complementing the aforementioned books is Donald M. Seekins, *Historical Dictionary of Burma (Myanmar)* (Oxford: The Scarecrow Press, 2006).

Works (including some fiction) more circumspect in their periodization are listed below according to the most appropriate chapter and topic. In a limited list such as this it is not possible to include anything but a small representative sample.

BURMA UNDER COLONIAL RULE

Adas, Michael, *The Burma Delta: Economic Development and Social Change on an Asian Rice Frontier, 1852–1941* (Madison, WI: University of Wisconsin Press, 1974).

Brown, Ian, *A Colonial Economy in Crisis: Burma's Rice Cultivators and the World Depression of the 1930s* (London: RoutledgeCurzon, 2005).

Cheng Siok-Hwa, *The Rice Industry of Burma, 1852–1940* (Kuala Lumpur: University of Malaya Press, 1968).

Ghosh, Parimal, *Brave Men of the Hills: Resistance and Rebellion in Burma, 1825–1932* (Honolulu, HI: University of Hawaii Press, 2000).

Richell, Judith L., *Disease and Demography in Colonial Burma* (Copenhagen: NIAS Press, 2006).

Scott, James C., *The Moral Economy of the Peasant: Rebellion and Subsistence in Southeast Asia* (New Haven, CT: Yale University Press, 1976).

THE COLONIAL CENTRE

Bhattacharya, [Chakraborti], Swapna, *India–Myanmar Relations, 1886–1948* (Kolkata: K P Bagchi & Co., 2007).

Christian, John LeRoy, *Modern Burma* (New York: Institute of Pacific Relations, 1942).

Furnivall, J. S., *Colonial Policy and Practice: A Comparative Study of Burma and Netherlands India* (Cambridge: Cambridge University Press, 1948).

Larkin, Emma, "The Self-Conscious Censor: Censorship Under the British, 1900–1939," *Journal of Burma Studies* 8 (2003): 64–101.

Orwell, George, *Burmese Days* (San Diego, CA: Harcourt Brace, n.d.).

Pearn, B. R., *History of Rangoon* (Rangoon: American Baptist Mission Press, 1939).

Pham, Julie, "Ghost Hunting in Colonial Burma: Nostalgia, Paternalism and the Thoughts of J. S. Furnivall," *South East Asia Research* 12.2 (July 2004): 237–268.

SELF-GOVERNMENT WITHOUT INDEPENDENCE, 1937–1947

Ba Maw, *Breakthrough in Burma: Memoirs of a Revolution* (New Haven, CT: Yale University Press, 1968).

Bayly, Christopher and Tim Harper, *Forgotten Armies: The Fall of British Asia 1941–1945* (London: Allen Lane, 2004).

Kratoska, Paul H. (ed.), *The Thailand–Burma Railway, 1942–1946*, 6 vols. (New York: Routledge, 2006).

McEnery, John H., *Epilogue in Burma 1945–1948* (Bangkok: White Lotus, 2000).

Nemoto, Kei (ed.), *Reconsidering the Japanese Military Occupation in Burma (1942–45)* (Tokyo: Tokyo University of Foreign Studies, Research Institute for Languages and Cultures of Asia and Africa, 2007).

Singh, Balwant, *Independence & Democracy in Burma, 1945–1952: The Turbulent Years* (Ann Arbor, MI: University of Michigan Centers for South and Southeast Asian Studies, 1993).

Tamayama, Kazuo, *Railwaymen in the War: Tales by Japanese Railway Soldiers in Burma and Thailand 1941–47* (Houndmills: Palgrave Macmillan, 2005).

Tarling, Nicholas, *A Sudden Rampage: The Japanese Occupation of Southeast Asia, 1941–1945* (London: Hurst & Co., 2001).

THE DEMOCRATIC EXPERIMENT, 1948–1958 & DRESS REHEARSALS, 1958–1962

Butwell, Richard, *U Nu of Burma* (Stanford, CA: Stanford University Press, 1968).

Callahan, Mary, *Making Enemies: War and State Building in Burma* (Singapore: Singapore University Press, 2004).

Mendelson, E. Michael, *Sangha and State in Burma: A Study of Monastic Sectarianism and Leadership* (Ithaca, NY: Cornell University Press, 1975).

U Nu, *U Nu Saturday's Son*, translated by U Law Yone (New Haven, CT: Yale University Press, 1975).

U Sein Win, *The Split Story: An Account of Recent Political Upheaval in Burma* (Rangoon: The Guardian Press, 1959).

Tinker, Hugh, *The Union of Burma* (London: Oxford University Press, 1957).

Walinsky, Louis, *Economic Development in Burma 1951–1960* (New York: Twentieth Century Fund, 1962).

THE REVOLUTIONARY COUNCIL

Cady, John F., *The United States and Burma* (Cambridge, MA: Harvard University Press, 1976).

Maung Maung, *Burma and General Ne Win* (London: Asia Publishing House, 1969).

Seekins, Donald M., *The Disorder of Order: The Army-State in Burma Since 1962* (Bangkok: White Lotus, 2002).

Smith, Donald Eugene, *Religion and Politics in Burma* (Princeton, NJ: Princeton University Press, 1965).

Steinberg, David I., *Burma's Road to Development: Growth and Ideology Under Military Rule* (Boulder, CO: Westview Press, 1981).

U Thaung, *A Journalist, a General and an Army in Burma* (Bangkok: White Lotus, 1995).

THE BSPP YEARS

Kyaw Yin Hlaing, "Reconsidering the Failure of the Burma Socialist Program Party Government to Eradicate Internal Economic Impediments," *South East Asia Research* 11.1 (March 2003): 5–58.

Lehman, F. K. (ed.), *Military Rule in Burma Since 1962* (Singapore: Maruzen Asia, 1981).

Smith, Charles B., *The Burmese Communist Party in the 1980s* (Singapore: Institute of Southeast Asian Studies, Regional Strategic Studies Programme, 1984).

Steinberg, David I., *Burma: A Socialist Nation of Southeast Asia* (Boulder, CO: Westview Press, 1982).

TOWARD DEMOCRACY, 1988–1990

Aung San Suu Kyi, *Freedom from Fear and Other Writings* (London: Penguin Books, 1991).

Lintner, Bertil, *Outrage: Burma's Struggle for Democracy* (Bangkok: White Lotus, 1990).

—, *The Rise and Fall of the Communist Party of Burma (CPB)* (Ithaca, NY: Cornell University Southeast Asia Program, 1990).

Maung Maung, *The 1988 Uprising in Burma* (New Haven, CT: Yale University Southeast Asia Studies, 1999).

PERPETUAL DELAY, 1990 TO THE PRESENT

Carey, Peter (ed.), *Burma: The Challenge of Change in a Divided Society*, foreword by Aung San Suu Kyi (Houndmills: Macmillan, 1997).

Fink, Christina, *Living Silence: Burma under Military Rule* (Bangkok: White Lotus, 2001).

Rotberg, Robert I. (ed.), *Burma: Prospects for a Democratic Future* (Washington, DC: Brookings Institution Press, 1998).

Seekins, Donald M., *Burma and Japan Since 1940: From 'Co-Prosperity' to 'Quiet Dialogue'* (Copenhagen: NIAS, 2007).

Selth, Andrew, *Burma's Armed Forces: Power Without Glory* (Norwalk, CT: East-Bridge, 2002).

Skidmore, Monique (ed.), *Burma: At the Turn of the 21st Century* (Honolulu, HI: University of Hawaii Press, 2005).

South, Ashley, *Mon Nationalism and Civil War in Burma: The Golden Sheldrake* (London: RoutledgeCurzon, 2003).

Steinberg, David I., *Burma: The State of Myanmar* (Washington, DC: Georgetown University Press, 2001).

Taylor, Robert H. (ed.), *Burma: Political Economy Under Military Rule* (London: Hurst & Co., 2001).

Tucker, Shelby, *Burma: The Curse of Independence* (London: Pluto Press, 2001).

Index